FODOR SHELL

NEW ENGLAND

Connecticut
Rhode Island
Massachusetts
Vermont
New Hampshire
Maine

FODOR

NEW

Editorial Consultants: MALCOLM McTEAR DAVIS, LEAVITT F. MORRIS, HARRY RYAN

Drawings: LASZLO

Cover: WALTER BROOKS

Maps: H. M. GOUSHA CO.

Research Director: ANN D. PARISH — Research Assistants: ELEANOR FERRIS, ADELA HORODECKI, LINDA HULL
Hotel Consultants: A. STUART POWELL, JR., FRANK C. BROMBER — Restaurant Consultants: EDWARD GREENE, VALERIE L. GREENE

SHELL *TRAVEL GUIDES U.S.A.*

ENGLAND

EUGENE FODOR

ROBERT C. FISHER BARNETT D. LASCHEVER

editors

CASKIE STINNETT

introduction

Contributors: EUGENIA BEDELL, SANDO BOLOGNA, BARNETT D. LASCHEVER, FLORENCE LEMKOWITZ, PHILIP WALLWORK

FODOR'S MODERN GUIDES, INC.

DAVID McKAY CO. INC. - NEW YORK

Library of Congress Catalog Card No. 66–18838

Travel Books Edited by Eugene Fodor

1936 ON THE CONTINENT

1937 IN EUROPE

EUROPE IN 1938

AUSTRIA, BELGIUM AND LUXEMBOURG

BRITAIN AND IRELAND, FRANCE

GERMANY, GREECE, HOLLAND

ISRAEL, ITALY, PORTUGAL

SCANDINAVIA, SPAIN

SWITZERLAND, YUGOSLAVIA

GUIDE TO EUROPE

MEN'S GUIDE TO EUROPE

WOMAN'S GUIDE TO EUROPE

GUIDE TO THE CARIBBEAN, BAHAMAS AND BERMUDA

HAWAII, GUIDE TO INDIA

JAPAN AND EAST ASIA

GUIDE TO MOROCCO

GUIDE TO SOUTH AMERICA

Manufactured in the U.S.A. by Arno Press, Inc., New York

CONTENTS

PRACTICAL INFORMATION

The *Practical Information* sections of this book include listings of *Hotels, Motels,* and *Restaurants* and detailed information on some or all of the following subjects: State Facts and Figures, How to Get Around, Seasonal Events, Tourist Information Services, Drinking Laws, National Parks, State Parks, Indians, Where to Go, What to Do with the Children, Hotels and Motels, Hotsprings and Resorts, Youth Hostels, Farm Vacations and Guest Ranches, Camping Out, Trailer Tips, Dining Out, Bars, Nightclubs, Coffee Houses and Outdoor Cafes, Casinos, Music, Stage and Revues, Tours, Special Interest Tours, Industrial Tours, Historic Sites, Museums and Galleries, Libraries, Gardens, Shopping, Summer Sports, Winter Sports, Recommended Reading, and Retirement Areas

EDITORS' FOREWORD

After 30 years of editing and publishing travel books on foreign countries, we have answered a new challenge: the compilation of a definitive series of guidebooks to the United States of America.

It was a momentous, but completely satisfying, job, the climax of a lifetime's experience. We had to take this immense country of magnificent variety apart and put it back together between the covers of eight regional volumes.

To this end we used the best talents the travel writing profession had to offer. Over 100 travel editors, free-lance writers, researchers, photographers, cartographers, and artists devoted themselves to the creation of a novel type of guidebook which we hope will open a new window on our land. But we did not stop there. Novelists, writers in other fields than travel, even a statesman, were called upon to express their views of America.

Unlike other guidebook editors, we started out with the basic editorial concept that the nation and the people are inseparable. If the land shaped the people, the people also shaped the land. Human geography, natural geography, and travel information, we contend, are the three basic and equal elements of any true portrayal of the country.

We guide our readers on many tried and tested tours of exploration in each state, taking in the stirring sights, vibrant cities, grandiose landscapes and the innumerable man-made wonders of our America. At the same time, sympathetic essays spell out the endless variety and individuality of the American people, wherever they live. Innumerable practical tips on all aspects of travel speed the vacationer on his way.

We are most grateful to the public-spirited *Shell Oil Company,* which offered to share the heavy burdens of such an ambitious and difficult project. They did so in an effort to make travel in this country more enjoyable, as well as to assist the U.S. Government in its "Discover America" program. In the true tradition of the American concept of editorial freedom, the company left all editorial responsibility where it belongs—with the editors.

Thus, all views expressed in these books are those of the editors and writers, and we assume full responsibility for them. The immensity of the project precludes perfection. Any errors, gaps, or other shortcomings are ours. Tell us about them—your contributions will be invaluable as we will strive to make each revision more accurate, more fun to read, and more useful to you.

WELL-BRED NEW ENGLAND

A Hallowed Past—A Brilliant Future

by

CASKIE STINNETT

(Travel Editor of Holiday Magazine, *Mr. Stinnett formerly held top editorial posts on such national magazines as* The Saturday Evening Post *and* Ladies Home Journal. *He also is the author of several novels.)*

When I think of New England I think of the late Rachel Carson, because no one more fittingly represented this place than this gentle woman. One afternoon, in the library of her home, she was speaking to me of the many hours she had spent observing microscopic marine life in the tidal pools of Maine's Penobscot Bay shoreline. When the weather grew nasty, as it does so often on that exposed shore, she said she would scoop up samples of water from the pools and carry them to her house, a few hundred yards away, where she kept a small laboratory. "Of course," she added hastily, "I always took the samples back and put them in the pool." When I said that this seemed unnecessarily cautious, that the balance of nature would hardly be upset by her failing to return a thimbleful of water to the Atlantic Ocean, she smiled shyly, and said that was only part of it. "If the marine life that is in my sample is going to survive," she said, "it must be returned to the sea at the same tide level from which I took it. This means that sometimes I have to come down to the sea in the middle of the night to pour the water back."

This, I think, is a New England woman. Not that all New Englanders share Miss Carson's reverence for life, but they share her respect for order, for a natural fitness of things, for a determination that when one has finished with something it be returned—either to a neighbor or to God—in good working condition. Years ago, in reading *One Man's Meat,* I remember E. B. White commenting on a Maine neighbor returning a borrowed book to him on a stormy night. The book was wrapped in brown paper and tied tightly with a string which, as Mr. White pointed out, is the way a book should be returned. There's a right way and a wrong way, and in New England the right way more often than not turns out to conserve, to retain value, to use sparingly. Perhaps what I'm saying is that New Englanders are frugal. All right, they're frugal.

It's a real temptation to say that New England frugality is traceable to the hardships of the Massachusetts Bay colonists as well as those of Rhode Island and New Hampshire. But this is a temptation that must be resisted. There were hardships all right, and the colonists had to make their own household products because there was no choice. The New England colonist grew grain, and his horses and oxen and sheep furnished food and transportation. He made his own meal, cheese, candles and soap. He grew his own wool and flax, and in the winter the wool was cleaned, carded, combed, spun, woven, and dyed. The dye came from hickory or butternut bark. The colonist made his own shoes, even tanning the leather. But I seriously doubt that all of this hardship and industry molded the regional character into what it is today. The Jamestown colonists in Virginia endured hardships but instead of becoming flinty, they relaxed and grew tobacco, which is hardly a life-sustaining plant.

Honoring Plain Talk

No, I believe that the New Englander draws his character from a more ancient source and one that pervades his nature more thoroughly. He comes primarily from Puritan stock, and Puritans were objecting people. They objected to the formalism of the Church of England and after they came to the New World they kept on objecting. Even today, in the town meetings of New England villages you are likely to hear more dissenting than assenting. The dissent comes easily to the man of New Hampshire or Vermont; he is plain-spoken and he knows that he has nothing to fear from his neighbor if he speaks his mind. It is the man who agrees too readily who is looked upon with distrust in New England.

It was this kind of free-spoken dissent that caused Roger Williams to be thrown out of the Puritan colony, which proves a variety of things including the fact that there were limits beyond which the Puritans did not care to be pushed. Williams held some unpopular beliefs, such as the peculiar notion that the Indians really owned the land in America, and when he persisted in this kind of talk, the Puritans pointed him in the direction of Rhode Island and told him to form his own colony. Williams did just that, and that was how Providence Plantation came about. I am citing this because the New England character of today draws as much from Providence Plantation as it does from the Puritans, as that unflinching old New Englander, Henry David Thoreau, demonstrated a hundred years ago.

So much for character. Don't let me give the impression that New Englanders are grumpy folk who find pleasure only in abstinence. I have spent many Christmases in a small village in Maine and they have convinced me that people outside of New England don't know how to get their money's worth out of Christmas. In fact, Christmas and New England go together: the natural conservationist there has resisted efforts to hang too much tinsel or to make it spurious. The air is crisp and cold, snow falls according to some high-level pre-arrangement, church bells ring, children sing, blazing logs light up hearths, and long-forgotten uncles show up bearing armfuls of gifts. Metro-Goldwyn-Mayer couldn't do it any better. There is a Dickensian feel to the whole season, and one that scatters all suspicion that a local community booster organization is the Hidden Persuader behind the event.

A strange sort of reason seems to prevail in New England, and this is appealing in an age of Pop Art, shoulder length hair for men, abstract theater, and the horrid smartness of our time. New Englanders possess a keen admiration for the dollar, and I can't see them taken in by something of transient and dubious value. Too often in normal business dealings they automatically tap the coin on the counter to see if it gives off a hollow ring, and it isn't likely that they would be noticeably impressed by enlarged soup can labels palmed off as art. Art, in fact, is solidly based in New England, but it is usually representational in character and a tree is palpably a tree. Writing in a philosophical vein in 1837, Ralph Waldo Emerson took a typically New England view of the inconsistencies of politics. "From neither party, when in power," he wrote, "has the world any benefit to expect in science, art, or humanity, at all commensurate with the resources of the nation." The New Englander often sees gloomy prospects, but reason is usually with him.

A Many-Splendored Spring

The season that one usually associates with New England is autumn but this is an image that has been imposed upon the public consciousness by the tourist promotional people and does not at all mean that it is the finest time of the year there. I prefer the New England spring, but this is admittedly personal and I may be no closer to the truth—if it exists in this matter—than the tourist commissions. Spring comes to New England several weeks after it warms the Middle Atlantic states, and the countryside suddenly explodes. Lupine blooms wildly in the fields of Maine and Vermont, while elsewhere lilac and forsythia crown the land. The sun is warm, insects begin to hum, plows bite into the soil releasing the rich odor of the earth, and the farmers cautiously remove a layer of clothing. It is the time of reawakening, and it is exciting to experience. I shall never forget driving a jeep one spring morning along a country road in northern Connecticut. The top was off the jeep and because the sun was warm I had tossed my hat into the back. I was following a dirt road which meandered through a forest, and although the leaves were forming on the trees they were still too small to keep the sunlight from filtering through. Poets have written rhapsodically of the mottled sunlight of the Bois in Paris, but Connecticut that day would have made Paris look like a desert. Clumps of birch trees, their white bark sparkling in the clear light, loomed like ghosts among the oaks and spruce. Rocky paths led off into the woods, and lanes, still soft underfoot and filled with loose stones, came to the edge of the road and stopped. When the forest fell behind me, small farmhouses nestled close to the road, with dogs and pullets scampering about, and geese on the march. The odor of barnyards was in the air, and the scent of brush fires came and went. I don't think I possess any excessive admiration for the country, but the recollection of that spring morning will always haunt me.

The travel posters, of course, picture the forests of Vermont in the autumn, with the maples reddening, as representative of New England. This is an engaging sight, all right, but no more representative of the six states than the poplars turning yellow on the commons of a New Hampshire village, or the sight of waves beating against the foot of Pemaquid Light in Maine, or a fishing cove on Cape Cod. The states most certainly possess a homogenous quality and they share a great deal more than climate, yet it would be wrong to try to endow a Downeasterner from Eastport with the characteristics of a farmer from the Berkshire Mountains of western Massachusetts. City people tend to be more similar than country people—to generalize grandly—and there will be fewer visible differences between the people of Hartford and Boston and Providence and perhaps even Portland than among the rural residents of Connecticut, Massachusetts, Rhode Island or even Maine. Massachusetts will always mean Walden Pond and Concord to me, and I once drove out from Boston to see the place where Thoreau had built his hut and had spent two years watching the seasons pass. It was a disappointment, because since Thoreau moved on, civilization has come in the form of neon signs and beer cans, but something of the spirit of the unpredictable village radical hangs on. Rhode Island means clam chowder—the best in the world—and New Hampshire brings to mind a visit I paid to an aged artist who lived in the mountains near Hanover, close to the Vermont line. The artist was Maxfield Parrish and he was well in his eighties when I spent a summer day with him, talking of the country that he loved. "In the winter when the nights are long," he said, "I sit by my fireplace and doze, and occasionally I look up at the window and see the faces of two or three or four raccoons, who have climbed up the vine to peer in at me. The expression on their faces always seems to be one of astonishment at what queer things humans have in their burrows, and how unnecessary it all is." He looked at me quizzically. "Of course, they're right," he said.

Cultivated Men on Cultivated Land

Vermont is a special state because it is the only one of the New England group that has no access to the sea. Even New Hampshire has its tiny fifteen-mile long Atlantic coastline. But the Green Mountains, which extend from the Massachusetts line to the Canadian border, fall off to the west and give Vermont access to Lake Champlain, one of the prettiest bodies of water in the United states. The lake, in fact, constitutes the western boundary of the state for nearly half of its entire length. No one can say for certain whether the fact of being cut off from the sea has influenced the Vermonter's character in a way that is different from those of the other New England states, but I think it doubtful. The Vermonter is taciturn, serious, and industrious, but how does this cause him to differ from the man of Maine, or New Hampshire, or Massachusetts? Connecticut, of all the New England states, is the most varied and somewhere in its nearly 5,000 square miles one can find almost anything the heart yearns for. It has mountains, the ocean, plains, cities, villages, and open country. At its southern tip it is suburban New York City, but somehow the state manages to contain this area and I have the feeling that it is warily watched as though it were a plague spot that could spread.

There is a certain primitive quality to much of the country in southeast United States, especially in the bayou country of Louisiana and the burned out cotton lands of Mississippi and Alabama. But there is no trace of this characteristic in New England; rather there is the feeling that the country has been occupied a long time by people who knew what they were about, who organized well, who put the land in good condition and who intend to keep it that way. Even in the heavily-wooded and remote reaches of Maine, there is the feeling that someone has organized things adequately and left a heritage of good will and good intentions. There is oddity, sure enough, in the New England character, but it is not an erratic thing. There is a vast difference.

Gone from New England now is the stringent austerity of the early Calvinists, and the Shakers, once so influential, have almost vanished. The severity and immoderation of Colonial days, which led to the excesses of Salem, softened with time and with the immigration of people of other nationalities who brought new religions with them. Today, while Catholicism is strong because of the heavy Irish and Italian communities, churches of all faiths dot the countryside, mirroring the changing face of man's spiritual nature. Churches more than anything reveal the ethnic structure of today's New England villages; it's easy to see where the Scotch and Irish came to New Hampshire, the Irish and the Italians to Massachusetts, the German Catholics and the Italians who settled around Hartford, and the Portuguese who came to Gloucester. The lovely church of Our Lady of Good Voyage, in Gloucester, was built by the Portuguese fishermen who came primarily from the Azores, and today the statue of Our Lady stands between the twin blue towers of the church, her left arm cradling a full-rigged schooner. The extent that the fishermen look to this church for more than spiritual protection may be measured by the fact that even now when fishing vessels come into the harbor after dark the masters often ask that the statue be illuminated to serve as a beacon. It is unthinkable in New England that an object should serve only a single purpose, and signs of this harmony between man's spiritual and earthly requirements are not rare in this area.

Traditional—and Contemporary

Somehow New England has permitted the traditional to give way to the contemporary—a process that can be prevented about as easily as halting a glacier—with considerable grace. Perhaps another way of saying that is to cite the fact that the traditional does not clash with the contemporary, and to point out that quite a lot of both abound. The village greens, the clean, sharp church spires, the ancient buildings, all stand without compromise in an area that fully recognizes the complex requirements of an industrial society. The northeast states constitute perhaps the most industrially progressive section of the country, but Harvard's mellow Yard is totally uncorrupted by the Massachusetts Institute of Technology which sprawls beside it. Both mold man's brain for a better future, and one way or another this has been an important New England goal from the beginning.

The industrial sophistication of New England today undoubtedly grew out of colonial necessity and the skills which this necessity developed. New Hampshire and Maine manufacture paper and textiles, Vermont produces machine tools and cut stone, Massachusetts makes leather products and rubber and plastics, Connecticut is noted for airplane engines, electrical machinery, chemicals, and precision instruments, and Rhode Island is probably the nation's capital of jewelry and silverware production. And never forget, it was from an ironworks at Saugus, Massachusetts, that was set up by Governor John Winthrop, Jr., in 1645 that the gigantic iron and steel industry of the United States later descended.

The corrosions of progress seem less enveloping in New England than in other sections of the country. There is nothing that I know of there that has tortured the landscape like strip mining. Highways have been threaded through the verdant forests and fields of New England but the major roads of Connecticut, New Hampshire, and Maine are carefully-controlled turnpikes, while Massachusetts boasts of Route 128, by-passing Boston for north-south travelers, which also is a credit to the good taste of its planners. Hartford, Boston, and Providence, like all large industrial cities, possess slum areas, but this blight is being attacked by positive redevelopment programs in each of the cities.

There is no denying the lively character of New England politics, where quite often the playing gets rough and values have been known to become misguided. Politics is the breath of life to the Irish of Massachusetts and they left their stamp on the national scene long before the political ascendancy of the Kennedy family. If a school for political skill exists, it can be found in the predominantly Irish and Italian wards of Boston, Providence, and Hartford. Even New Hampshire and Maine, which for many years were quietly and respectably Republican, have now become politically yeasty and most certainly unpredictable.

How well does the New England of today meet the challenge of its tradition? The answer is that it meets it pretty well, and often in oblique but highly effective ways. The region is prosperous, proud, and productive. It is secure in the knowledge that it possesses some of the nation's greatest colleges and universities, and is thus projecting its influence far ahead into the future. But it has always done this. The winner of the Nobel Peace Prize in 1960, Albert Luthuli, was a graduate of a Durban, South Africa, college that was founded in 1838 by New England Congregationalists. It is a long way from New England to South Africa, and the past and present are curiously intermingled, but the fact speaks for itself.

Perhaps one of the best things that can be said about the New Englander is that his emotional economy contains no chauvinism. If you like the state in which he lives, and its people, and its customs, he is pleased. If you do not, he is not offended, nor does he appear to be troubled in the slightest. It is there, he feels, for those who like it. I have never heard a resident of Maine say to an outsider that "this is the greatest state in the union." I'm sure that the words have been spoken, but I think rarely, and never in my presence. Nor have I ever noticed any particular pleasure on the part of a New Englander when a visitor from another region goes out of the way to praise this section of the country. V. S. Pritchett, the English critic, says that more offense is caused by praise than blame, and I can't say whether this is true or not, but I do believe that the New Englander is more uneasy with overly fulsome praise than he is with criticism.

Have I said anything to indicate that New England is a temperate place? Its people are temperate, but its climate is not. Northeast gales, howling along the Atlantic coast in winter, can freeze the marrow in your bones. Ice storms can wreck power lines and topple trees, and snow piles up on old snow. Barns are attached to farmhouses to make sure that farmers can always get to their animals regardless of the weather. On clear nights in midwinter, panes in kitchen windows glaze over as steam and moisture turn to ice, and outside the still night air is so cold it seems to crackle. Yet the hottest day I have ever experienced occurred one July in Skowhegan, Maine, where the temperature soared over a hundred and not a breath of air stirred to relieve the fury of the sun. I have been in equatorial cities but no heat has touched me in the way that I suffered that day in Maine.

There is something majestic about the extremes of weather and the fury of the elements that sweep across the New England states. It is tremendously exciting to stand on the rocks of the coast and watch the sky darkening to a flat black grey, and to feel in advance of the storm the warm, moisture-laden air that hurries along to give warning. As the wind rises, scattered drops begin to fall from the dark clouds that move overhead. The first drops are big and they leave large spots on the rocks and they move the leaves violently on the trees. In a few moments the gentle patter has become an advancing wall of rain, and its tattoo increases until it has become a roar. Gusts tug at the trees and build great troughs in the sea. There is a terrifying flash of lightning and an instantaneous clap of thunder that rolls across the sky, booming and echoing until it fades away. It rains steadily in a grey sheet, with the thunder moving further and further in the distance. The clouds are low but they scud across the sea, and in a little while the fury is gone and only a gentle rain remains. The summer storm is over.

In New England, man built his isolation without meaning to and now some of that isolation has taken hold of his soul. But it has given him a serenity and sureness, and he is better for it. It serves him well in surmounting the exasperation, the frustration, the false admiration, and often the despair of a nation that sometimes seems quite old but is really very young. More than any other region of the country, New England bears a heavy load of history on its back but it bears it lightly, hopefully, and with good cheer.

FACTS AT YOUR FINGERTIPS

WHEN TO GO. Summer is the principal time for visiting New England, for drinking in its green and white (natural and man-made) beauty, its many vestiges of our heritage. The sun climbs early and sets late, leaving behind a trail of sun-filled days and cool nights. In summer Boston and environs can record temperatures higher than those in New York, and those in Portland, Maine, reach above those in Boston. But heat waves are fleeting, and sea and mountain breezes soon come along. Evenings are sweater-cool, and nights usually call for a blanket, sometimes two.

The so-called "season" for all of New England has been lengthening perceptibly over the past several decades. Even Maine, once thought of solely for the months of July and August, now attracts lake fishermen for months before and after those dates. Hunters are tracking the state's great wildernesses in ever-increasing numbers. Skiing facilities are growing impressively in western areas of the state.

The western regions of all the New England states now lure visitors virtually the year round. In late summer, visitors flock to country fairs. In autumn there's the brilliant blanket of fall foliage. From winter into spring there's skiing in over 100 developed areas. Late winter finds increasing numbers of people trekking into the beauty of these white and crystalline climes to watch sled dog races or to visit maple syrup operations and attend sugaring-off parties. In spring they come for the beauty of the blossoming fruit trees, dogwood, and rhododendron bushes.

PLANNING YOUR TRIP. Once you have decided where you are going, and when, it's time to get down to the details of hotel reservations, and if you are not traveling by car, ticket reservations. If you don't want to bother with reservations on your own, a travel agent can be of help. Using a travel agent, incidentally, won't cost you a cent, except for specific charges like telegrams. He gets his fee from the hotel or carrier he books for you. A travel agent can also be of help for those who would prefer to take their vacations on a "package tour"—thus keeping your own planning to a minimum; and in explaining the details of the "travel now, pay later" vacation possibilities offered by the nation's carriers.

If traveling by auto, enjoy the family fun of jointly discussing and mapping your route. You can ask your oil company touring service or an auto club to do it for you. (They will provide you with maps.) All can be of help for map routings and some offer emergency service on the road. If you plan to route yourself, make certain the map you purchase, or get from your local service station, is dated for the current year (highways and thruways are appearing and being extended at an astonishingly rapid rate). In addition, most states have their own maps, which pinpoint attractions, list historical sites, parks, etc. Write the *Tourist Information Dept., State Capital Bldg.,* in the state or states you plan to visit for a copy of current maps. City chambers of commerce are also good sources of information.

Plan to board the pets, discontinue paper and milk deliveries, and tell your local police and fire departments when you'll be leaving, when you expect to return. Ask a kindly neighbor to keep an eye on your house; fully protect your swimming pool against intruders. Have a neighbor keep your mail, or have it temporarily held at the post office. Consider having your telephone temporarily disconnected, if you plan to be away more than a few weeks. Look into the purchase of trip insurance (including baggage), and make certain your auto, re, and other policies are up-to-date. Convert the greater portion of your trip into travelers' checks. Arrange to have your lawn mowed at the usual times, and leave that kindly neighbor your itinerary (insofar as possible), car license number, and a key to your home (and tell police and firemen he has it).

PACKING. *What to take, what to wear.* Make a packing list for each member of the family. Then check off items as you pack them. It will save time, reduce confusion. Time-savers to carry along include extra photo film (plenty), suntan lotion, insect repellent, sufficient toothpaste, soap, etc. This will rule out your having to waste precious minutes driving into towns, parking, etc., in order to purchase them—time you could spend in holiday pursuits. Always carry an extra pair of glasses, including sunglasses, particularly if they're prescription ones. A travel iron is always a good tote-along, as are some transparent plastic film bags (small and large) for wet suits, socks, etc. They are also excellent, of course, for packing shoes, spillable cosmetics, and other easily-damaged items.

Fun extras to carry include binoculars, a compass, and a magnifying glass—to read some of those maps which must have been made by and for the wee people.

All members of the family should have a sturdy pair of shoes with non-slip soles. Keep them handy in the back of the car. You never know when you may want to stop and clamber along a rocky trail to some site. Carry the family rain gear in a separate bag, in the back of the car (so no one will have to get out and hunt for it in a downpour en route).

Women will probably want to stick to one or two basic colors for their holiday wardrobes, so that they can manage with one set of accessories. If possible, include one knit or jersey dress or suit, as they pack beautifully. The general consensus among well-traveled women is that a full-skirted traveling dress will show less wear and wrinkling. For dress-up evenings, take along a few "basic" dresses you can vary with a simple change of accessories. That way you can dress up or down to suit the occasion.

Be sure to check what temperatures will be like along the route. Traveling in mountains can mean cool evenings, even in summer—and so can traveling through the desert. An extra sweater is always a safe thing to pack, even if just to protect you from the airconditioning.

The man of the family will probably want a business suit along for dining out, possibly another wrinkle-proof suit or two, slacks or Bermudas, and a tweed or other informal jacket.

Planning a lot of sun time? Don't forget something sufficiently cover-up to wear over suits en route to the pool, beach, or lakefront, and for those first few days when you're getting reacquainted with sun on tender skin.

WHAT WILL IT COST? A single person can travel in the U.S. for as little as $21.00 a day (not counting gasoline or other transportation costs), as you can see in the table below. To find the cost for a couple, simply double the figures for all items *except* hotel rates. For this, add 25% to the cost of the single hotel room.

In some areas, such as Florida in spring or fall, you can cut expenses by traveling off season, when hotel rates are usually lower. The budget-minded traveler can also find bargain accommodations at tourist homes or family-style YMCA's and YWCA's. Some state and federal parks also provide inexpensive lodging.

Another way to cut down on the cost of your trip is to look for out-of-the-way resorts. Travelers are frequently rewarded by discovering very attractive areas which haven't as yet begun to draw quantities of people.

If you are budgeting your trip (who doesn't?), don't forget to set aside a realistic amount for the possible rental of sports equipment (perhaps including a boat or canoe), entrance fees to amusement and historical sites, etc. Put a little aside, too, for incidental medical fees: Junior just might step on a broken shell. Allow for tolls for bridges and super-highways (this can be a major item), extra film for cameras, and those souvenirs no one (well, hardly anyone) can resist when put to the test.

Typical expenses for one person

Room, at *reasonable** hotel or motel	$10.00
Breakfast at hotel or motel, including tip	1.25
Lunch at *inexpensive*† restaurant, including tip	1.25
Dinner at *reasonable** restaurant, including tip	4.00
One sightseeing bus tour	2.50
One evening drink	1.00
Admission to museum or historic site	1.00
	$21.00

* According to this book's system of categories, a "reasonable" hotel room ranges from $8.00 to $11.00; a "reasonable" restaurant from $3.50 to $5.00.

† An "inexpensive" restaurant means less than $3.00 in this book.

Picnicking will not only cut costs, but will also save looking for an eating place, parking, perhaps waiting in line—in other words, save time. Many states have set aside picnic and rest areas, even along big highways and thruways, so finding a stopping place shouldn't be difficult. A number of restaurants have take-out service (you can pick up lunch at breakfast). So buy or assemble a picnic kit before you leave home. Include several thermoses; it's a good idea to keep fresh water in one.

A plug-in water heater and a jar of instant coffee will, like picnics, serve a double purpose. It will take the gruff edge off any family member who is inclined to growl until a cup of the dark-brown brew has been imbibed. And, if you're staying in a motel, you might buy some easy-to-eat fruit and rolls or breakfast pastries the night before, thus saving on breakfast costs, and getting off-and-away that much sooner in the morning.

HOW TO GET THERE. *By car.* For southern New England, New York is the gateway. The city itself can be easily skirted by taking the George Washington Bridge, or the Tappan Zee Bridge across the Hudson River. Both connect with an extensive network of parkways and thruways. For northern New England, the main entry points are Hartford, Boston, and Albany, with the latter also a gateway to western Connecticut, Massachusetts, Vermont, and New Hampshire. Yearly, more and more turnpikes, thruways, and highways are being built and extended, making for swift, virtually uninterrupted motor trips to the doorstep or heart of vacationlands.

By train. New York Central trains to Albany will bring you near the western part of New England, including the various lake regions. Boston as a terminus brings you to New England's eastern and coastal regions, via the *Boston & Maine, N.Y. Central,* and *New Haven* railroads. Direct service from New York City to southern New England is maintained by the *New Haven.*

By bus. Continental Trailways and *Greyhound* bus routes form the warp and woof of a vast pattern of scheduled trips, allowing travelers from all parts of the U.S.A. to come close to their destinations, and, often, reach them directly. Check your travel agent or nearby Greyhound and Trailways office for information on the nearest point you can easily reach in the area where you wish to spend your holiday. Also ask your travel agent about *special bus tours* to the area you wish to visit. But keep in mind you can only spend as much time in any one place as is allotted by the tour itinerary. An extraordinary bargain for the traveler is offered by Greyhound, which sells a ticket for $99, which allows passengers to travel as long as 99 days to any of the 40,000 communities served by the company. You can see the entire country in this way.

By ship. Ferryboats, carrying both passengers and automobiles, run on regular schedule from Woods Hole, in southeastern Massachusetts, to the islands of Martha's Vineyard and Nantucket. It is advisable to reserve space for your car well ahead of time. Do so by writing *Nantucket Steamship Authority,* Woods Hole, Mass.

By air. Two major airports are the hub of New England's air network: Logan International Airport, at *Boston,* and Bradley Field, located midway between *Hartford, Conn.* and *Springfield, Mass.* Major airlines serving these metropolitan terminals include *Allegheny, American, Eastern, National, Northeast, TWA,* and *United. Mohawk* serves Boston only. If you plan to go to New England by air, you will probably book for one of these two entry points, and then, perhaps, change to a feeder line if your destination happens to be a smaller town some distance away. Frequent service is operated directly to smaller fields in the region from nearby points in New York and New Jersey, of course, so check with your local airport or travel agent for exact information. Boston's Logan Airport is a terminus of continuous shuttle service from Washington, Newark, and LaGuardia (New York) airports.

Most extensive airline service within the region is *Northeast,* which serves Burlington, Barre-Montpelier, and Rutland in Vermont; Keene, Berlin, Hanover, and Laconia in New Hampsire; and Portland, Auburn, Augusta, Rockland, Bar Harbor, Bangor, and Presque Isle in Maine.

HINTS TO THE MOTORIST. To the motorist accustomed to long, bare highways of the West, driving in New England can present a paradox. On the one hand, he will find he must accustom himself to slower speeds off the interstate highways and turnpikes as he tours the congested East with its seemingly endless array of services and facilities to entice him. And then, as he begins to feel free of the problems of desert driving and lonely mountain roads, he encounters a desolate stretch of highway, such as those in central and upper Maine, and begins to wonder if this is really civilization and where he is going to find the next service station. He soon learns that driving in the East can offer the same wide variety—albeit of a different kind—as driving in the West. He will encounter more than double the number of postings for speed limits for special conditions that he finds elsewhere. An illustration of these differences is seen in the official speed limits of *Maine.* You can tool along limited access highways at speeds up to 70 miles per hour. On other open highways it drops to 45. In *Rhode Island* the general maximums are 50 in daytime, 45 at night, with higher and lower speeds as posted. *Massachusetts* has the same limits, but raises them to 60 for turnpikes. *Vermont* allows 65 on interstate highways, 50 otherwise. *New Hampshire* has turnpike speeds of 60, and 50 on other open highways. *Connecticut* lets you go up to 70 on superhighways, parkways, and expressways, and up to 60 on other highways.

Neither AAA nor the ALA lists strict enforcement areas or speed traps for the New England states. Most use some sort of mechanical or electronic device for speed control. In *Connecticut* radar is used chiefly as a device to measure traffic flow, and only occasionally for enforcement—when warning signs are posted. In *Rhode Island,* where radar checks are made by some cities, no particular warning is given. *Massachusetts,* where cities and towns also check sometimes, gives posted warning. Sneaky *Vermont,* where state police check by radar, doesn't post warning signs. *New Hampshire* and *Maine* do, with Maine being especially generous by posting warnings within a quarter to one mile of the checkpoint.

Highway hypnosis—recognized by safety experts as contributing to many accidents—can be a problem in New England along the interstates, turnpikes, and other limited-access roads. It results from steady driving over long distances at set speeds. Principal symptoms are drowsiness and the inability to concentrate on what you're doing. The cure: Vary your speed occasionally, stop to stretch your legs, have a cup of coffee or tea, take a little exercise, take a brief nap. Driving such roads is decidedly different. The wise motorist studies in advance the exit and entrance points to avoid winding up beyond where he wants to go or entering the highway headed in the wrong direction. When you enter a limited-access highway, be sure to allow plenty of space between you and the onrushing cars before you merge into the right lane. Once on the freeway, keep your speed in tune with traffic. Keep an eye on cars in front and behind. If someone crowds your rear, slow down gradually and let him pass. Don't follow the car ahead too closely. Tailgating is the major cause of accidents on the freeway. And keep a keen eye on the signs, so you won't miss your exit. If you pass your exit, keep going. Don't back up to try again, and don't cross the center strip to turn around. Both are dangerous and are viewed dimly by the enforcement authorities. *A special tip:* Remember that after driving long stretches of high-speed roadway, you need to adjust to normal driving. Most common fault after leaving limited-access roads is to drive too fast on highways not engineered to high speeds. Slow down.

Mountain driving should be no problem in New England. These roads are well engineered—normally wide, well graded, and safe. Just keep an eye on the speed limits for curves. On steep grades, use your motor for downhill runs—second or low gear—to save your brakes.

If you get stuck—on an interstate highway, freeway, or country lane—use the universal rule of the road. Pull off the highway onto the shoulder, raise the hood, attach something white (a handkerchief, scarf, or piece of tissue) to the door handle on the driver's side, and sit inside and wait. This is especially effective on limited-access highways, usually patrolled vigilantly by state highway officers. A special warning to women stalled at night: Remain inside the car with the doors locked, and make sure the Good Samaritan is indeed a Good Samaritan. It's easier to find telephones these days along the major highways, since their locations are being marked more and more frequently. If you're a member of an automobile club, call the nearest garage listed. Or ask the Operator for help.

If you plan to pull a *trailer*—boat, camping, or house—and have never before done so, don't just hook up and set out. You need a whole new set of driving skills: starting, stopping, cornering, passing, *being* passed, and, most tricky of all, backing. Reading about it will help a little, but not much. Try to practice in an open field, but if this is not possible, take your maiden trip in light traffic. A few useful hints: In starting and stopping, do everything more slowly and gradually than normal; in cornering, swing wider than usual, remembering the trailer won't follow your rear wheels exactly. Too sharp a right turn will put your trailer wheels over the curb. Too sharp a left turn will squash a car waiting to let you make the turn. In passing, remember you're longer than usual. Allow more safe distance ahead to pull back into the right lane. A slight bit of extra steering will help if you're being passed by a large truck or bus. In these situations, the trailer is inclined to sway from air currents. Don't worsen it by slowing down. It's better to speed up slightly. In backing, the basic technique is to turn the steering wheel in the way opposite from that in which you would want the car to go if you were driving it alone. From there on, it's practice, practice, practice. Most states have special safety regulations for trailers. If you plan to haul it in several states, check with your automobile club, the police, or the state motor vehicle department about the rules. Also talk it over with the dealer from whom you buy or rent your trailer. Generally, speed limits for cars hauling trailers are lower, parking of trailers (and automobiles) is prohibited on expressways and freeways, and tunnels often bar trailers equipped with cooking units that use propane gas.

Budget your vacation-time as carefully as you do your money. It's no fun to go sightseeing after a neck-and-shoulder-wearying day behind the wheel. In the wide-open spaces, 300 miles a day is enough. Here in the East, stick to 250. Stop occasionally to stretch your legs, walk the dog, buy a postcard, or give the kids a nature lesson in the woods or a roadside wiener roast. Save the big push for business trips.

Traveling by car with your *pet* dog or cat? More and more motels and hotels accept them. Some turn them down, some want to look first, some offer special facilities. Check first before you register. If it's a first-time trip with your pet, accustom it to car travel by short trips in the neighborhood. And when you're packing, include its favorite food, bowls, and toys. Your dog may like to ride with its head out the window. Discourage this. Wind and dust particles could permanently damage your pet's eyes. Dogs are especially susceptible to heatstroke. Don't leave your dog alone in a parked car on a hot day while you dawdle over lunch.

In packing for a trip, the motorist is King Pin. He can *dress* as casually as he likes for the driving stint and has enough room to take along plenty of changes. One tip for frequent motel stops along the road is to pack two suitcases, one with the destination in mind, the other with items for overnight stops—pajamas, shaving gear, cosmetics, toothbrushes, fresh shirt, and dress. Put the overnight luggage into the trunk last, so it can be pulled out first on overnight stops. *A safety hint:* Don't string your suits and dresses on hangers along a chain or rod stretched across the back seat. This obstructs vision and can cause accidents.

HOTELS & MOTELS. *General Hints.* Don't be one of those travelers who persists in the practice of taking potluck for lodgings. You'll probably waste a lot of post-sunset hours hunting for a place, and often won't be happy with the accommodations you finally find. If you are without reservations, by all means begin looking early in the afternoon. If you have reservations, but expect to arrive later than five or six p.m., advise the hotel or motel in advance. Some places will not, unless advised, hold reservations after six p.m.

If you are planning to stay in a popular resort region, at the height of the season, be kind to your nerves, reserve well in advance. Include a deposit for all places except motels, (and for motels if they request one). Remember, too, that a city where you plan to stay—at any season—may be hosting a convention or special event. A number of chain or associated motels and hotels will make advance reservations for you at affiliated hostelries of your choosing along your route.

A number of hotels and motels have one-day laundry and dry cleaning services, and many motels have coin laundries. A surprising number of motels (and some hotels) allow pets.

Most motels, but not all, have telephones in the rooms. If you want to be sure of room service, however, better stay at an hotel.

Many motels have swimming pools, and even beachfront hotels frequently have a pool. Even some motels among those springing up in the heart of large cities have pools. An advantage at motels is the free parking. However, there's seldom a charge for parking at country and resort hotels.

Hotel and motel chains. In addition to the hundreds of excellent independent motels and hotels throughout the country, there are also many fine establishments in both categories that belong to national or regional chains. A major advantage of the chains, to many travelers, is the ease of making reservations en route, or at one fell swoop in advance. If you are a guest at a member hotel or motel one night, the management will be delighted to secure you a sure booking at one of his affiliated hotels for the coming evening—at no telephone or telegram costs to you. This, of course, saves you time, worry and money. In some chains, you have the added advantage of knowing what the standards are, of being sure that you will have "quality-controlled" accommodations all the way. The insistence on uniform standards of comfort, cleanliness and amenities is more common in motel than in hotel chains. (Easy to understand when you realize that most hotel chains are formed by simply buying up older, established hotels, while most motel chains have control of their units from the design stage up through the staffing.) This is not meant to denigrate the hotel chains; after all, individuality can be one of the great charms of a hotel—and uniformity can get to be a bore (some of America's finest luxury hotels, by the way, are members of chains).

Among the chains that assure standards of uniform quality are: *Downtowner Motor Inns; Hyatt Hotels, Chalets and Lodges; Imperial "400"; Holiday Inns; Howard Johnson's Ramada Inns;* and*TraveLodge*. At these inns you can expect such amenities as TV, telephones, airconditioning, wall-to-wall carpeting in your room, and often such extras as swimming pools, bellhop service, and free transportation to local airports.

Motel chains that act primarily as referral groups are: *American Motelodger; Best Eastern; Best Western; Quality Courts;* and *Superior.*

Leading hotel chains are: *Hilton, Hotel Corporation of America; Pick;* and *Sheraton.*

HOTEL AND MOTEL CATEGORIES

Hotels and motels in all the Fodor-Shell regional guidebooks are divided into five categories, arranged primarily by price but also taking into consideration the degree of comfort you can expect to enjoy, the amount of service you can anticipate, and the atmosphere which will surround you in the establishment of your choice. Occasionally, an establishment with deluxe prices will only offer first-class service or atmosphere, and so we will list it as first class. On the other hand, a hotel which charges only reasonable prices may offer superior comfort and service, so we will list it as first class. Our ratings are flexible and subject to change. We should also like to point out that failure to include certain establishments in our lists does not mean they are not worthwhile—many fine hotels and motels had to be omitted for lack of space. Conversely, a few establishments presently listed may be dropped in the future if better accommodations in their areas surpass the old hostelries in comfort, service, and atmosphere.

We should also point out to the careful reader interested in planning a trip that prices may vary substantially from one part of the country to another, and depending upon the size of the city or the type of community. Resort area hotels and motels are nearly always higher-priced than those establishments in small cities and towns catering to the business traveler; hostelries in the metropolitan areas, moreover, tend to be higher-priced than those in cities where the volume of traffic and business is less.

Super deluxe is a category reserved for only a few hotels (five in New York City, for example). In addition to giving the visitor all the amenities discussed under the deluxe category (below), the super deluxe hotel has a special atmosphere of glamor, good taste, and dignity. Its story will inevitably be full of many historical anecdotes, and it will probably be a favored meeting spot of local society. If an American president or a foreign princess comes to town, this hotel will probably shelter him or her. In short, super deluxe means the tops. Price averages: about $22 single, $30 double.

Deluxe means just what it says, but for a rough rule-of-thumb index, we suggest that generally speaking, the following minimum facilities must be present: all rooms with bath and shower, valet and laundry service, suites available, a well-appointed restaurant and a bar (where local law permits), room service, TV and telephone in room, airconditioning and heat (unless locale makes one or the other unnecessary), pleasing decor, and an atmosphere of luxury, calm, and elegance. Ample and personalized service. In a deluxe *motel,* there may be less service rendered by employees and more by machine or automation (such as refrigerators and ice-making machines in your room), but there should be a minimum of do-it-yourself in a truly deluxe establishment. Price range: about $18 single, $23 double.

First class: all rooms with bath or shower, valet and laundry service, restaurant and bar (local law permitting), limited room service, TV and telephone in room, heat and airconditioning (locale not precluding), pleasing decor. Although decor may be as good as that in deluxe establishments, hotels and motels in this category are frequently designed for commercial travelers or for families in a hurry and are somewhat impersonal in terms of service. As for *motels* in this category, valet and laundry service will probably be lacking; the units will be outstanding primarily for their convenient location and functional character, not for their attractive or comfortable qualities. Price range: about $14 single, $18 double.

(Note: We often list top-notch ultra-modern hotels in this first-class category, in spite of the fact that they have rates as high as deluxe hotels and motels. We do this because certain elements are missing in these hotels—usually, the missing element is service. In spite of automated devices such as ice-cube-making machines and message-signalling-buzzers, service in these hotels is not up to the standard by which we judge deluxe establishments. Room service is incredibly slow in some of these places and the entire atmosphere is often one of efficiency over convenience, economy of manpower and overhead taking precedence over the guest's comfort and peace of mind.)

Reasonable: attached bath or shower, restaurant *or* coffee shop, TV available, telephone in room, heat and airconditioning (locale not precluding), relatively convenient location, clean and comfortable rooms and public rooms. *Motels* in this category may not have attached bath or shower, may not have a restaurant or coffee shop (though one is usually nearby), and of course, may have no public rooms to speak of. Price range: average of $10 single, $12-$14 double.

Inexpensive: nearby bath or shower, telephone available, clean rooms. Price range: about $7.50 single, $11 double.

Free parking is assumed at all motels and motor hotels; you must pay for parking at most city hotels, though certain establishments have free parking, frequently for occupants of higher-than-minimum-rate rooms. *Baby sitter* lists are always available in good hotels and motels, and *cribs* for the children are always on hand—sometimes at no cost, but more frequently at a cost of $1 or $2. The cost of a *cot* in your room, to supplement the beds, will also be around $2 per night, but moving an *extra single bed* into a room will cost from $5 to $7 in better hotels and motels.

DINING OUT. For evening dining, the best advice is: make reservations wherever, and whenever, possible. Also note that hotels and farm vacation places usually have set dining hours. For motel-stayers, life is simpler, of course, if the motel has a restaurant. If it hasn't, try to stay at one that is near a restaurant, preferably within walking distance.

Except for roadside stands, turnpike restaurants and cafeterias, most restaurants are relatively fussy about how customers dress, particularly in the evening. Ladies in shorts and slacks are generally frowned on, except during the day at beach or informal resorts. In the evening, the general rule is dresses for women, neckties and jackets for men.

If you're traveling with children, you may want to find out if a restaurant has a children's menu, and commensurate prices (many do).

When figuring the tip on your check, base it on the total charges for the meal, not on the grand total, if and when that total includes a state sales tax. Why tip on a tax?

The restaurants mentioned in this volume which are located in large metropolitan areas are categorized by type of cuisine: French, Chinese, Armenian, etc., with restaurants of a general nature listed as American-International. Restaurants in less populous areas are divided price-wise into categories as follows: deluxe, first class, reasonable, inexpensive. As a general rule, expect restaurants in metropolitan areas to be higher in price. However, many restaurants that feature foreign cuisine are surprisingly inexpensive.

Wherever you go, be adventurous. Try some of the regional specialties: gumbo in the deep south, lime pie in Florida, abalone in California, lobster and Indian pudding in New England, and king crab in the northwest, for example.

RESTAURANT CATEGORIES

Restaurants and other eating places in our book are listed in two manners: in *large metropolitan areas,* we have usually grouped restaurants by type of cuisine *(French, Chinese, American,* etc.). Our category for general restaurants having no particular national specialties is *American-International,* indicating that they serve a wide variety of entrees, ranging from steaks to lobster, and onion soup to Indian pudding, perhaps. In *non-metropolitan areas,* we have classified restaurants by price category, also taking into consideration the general character of the establishment, its standards of service, and above all, its reputation for good food itself. A few words on our categories might be helpful to the reader:

Super deluxe: this category will probably be pertinent only to one or two metropolitan areas, like New York City. This indicates an outstanding restaurant which is lavishly decorated and which delights in the fear it inspires among the humble. Frequently over-priced and over-rated, it will charge the customer at least $10 for soup, entree, and dessert. The average price for the same is apt to be closer to $12.50. As in all our other categories, this price range does not include cocktails, wines, cover or table charges, tip, or extravagant house specialties and flaming desserts. The price range here indicates a typical roastbeef (prime ribs) type of dinner. The restaurant to be in this category must have a superb wine list, excellent service, immaculate kitchens, and a large, well-trained staff.

Deluxe: Many fine restaurants around the country fall into this category. This type of restaurant will have its own well-deserved reputation for excellence, perhaps a house specialty or two for which it is famous, and an atmosphere of elegance or some unique decor. It will have a good wine list where the law permits, and will be considered the best in town by the inhabitants. Clean kitchen and adequate staff. Price range here will be about $6.50 to $8.50 per person for soup (or *hors d'oeuvres),* main dish *(entrée),* and a dessert.

First class: its own menu (not a mass-produced menu used by every restaurant in town), one or two house specialties, wine list, and cocktails (where law permits), airconditioning (unless locale makes it unnecessary), a general reputation for very good food and an adequate staff with a general reputation for good service. An elegant decor and appropriately-dressed clientele. Clean kitchen. Price range about $5 to $7.50 for soup (or *hors d'oeuvres),* main dish *(entrée),* and dessert.

Reasonable: cocktails and/or beer where the law permits, airconditioning (locale not precluding), clean kitchen, adequate staff, better-than-average service. General reputation for good, wholesome food. Price range: about $3.50 to $5.00 for soup, steak, and dessert.

Inexpensive: the bargain place in town, clean, even if plain, decor; airconditioning (see above), tables (not a counter). A clean kitchen and an attempt to provide adequate service. Price range: $1.00 to $3.00 for soup (or *hors d'oeuvres),* main dish *(entrée),* and dessert.

Because prices vary widely throughout the country, these categories are subject to amendment in certain areas. In the far west, midwest, and south, for example, many establishments in the reasonable category are really first-class in everything save price, and many first-class restaurants, accordingly, offer deluxe service, atmosphere, and food for the lower prices. Try to consider the ratings as relative, and do not be disappointed if you cannot find a deluxe rating in the area where you intend to eat. It is quite possible that many of the first-class establishments will give you a deluxe evening for only a first-class price.

Inserted into this book is a form letter which you may wish to complete and mail to the publishers, with your impressions of the hotels, motels, and restaurants you have visited during your travels. We would be happy to have your criticism of establishments listed in the book (constructive or critical), your suggestions for other establishments to include in future annual revisions of the book, or your comments on this book itself. You can be sure that all your comments will be carefully considered by our editors and research staff, as you can also be sure of a quick reply from us.

BUSINESS HOURS & LOCAL TIME. All New England states and communities are on Eastern Daylight Saving Time from Apr. 25 to October 31. There is no worry here about being confused by time changes, accordingly. However, in some states, the law requires that liquor (or package) stores operate on Eastern Standard Time, so do your shopping of this nature early.

Business hours are generally 8 or 9 a.m. to 5 p.m., but some stores in the many communities used to catering to vacationers are likely to stay open later in the evening. Evening dining hours in New England are likely to begin at 6 p.m., with no seatings after 8 p.m. However, this is less likely to be true at the more exclusive resorts, at Chinese restaurants, and at restaurants frequented by guests from nearby motels.

SUMMER SPORTS. Over 5,000 miles of now sandy, now rocky, serrated shoreline edge eastern New England, making for a host of saltwater activities. There are many forms of *boating,* with their attendant races and regattas, including the world-famous America's Cup Race, held off Newport, Rhode Island. There's *small-craft sailing,* too. If you're not adept at the tiller, you can take lessons, or just be a contented passenger. *Surf casting* is done extensively, as is *deep-sea fishing*. Giant tuna, swordfish, white marlin, and blue marlin are plentiful, and charter boats for this type of fishing are available in Rhode Island, Massachusetts, southern Maine, and along New Hampshire's short but active seacoast.

Swimming is excellent in many areas along the coast. Not all swimmers, however, can take the frigid waters that lap the coast from Maine down to the south shore of Cape Cod. Then again, a surprising number can and do, and perversely complain that the waters of Connecticut's Long Island Sound are too tepid.

A number of *racetracks* draw people to see the thoroughbreds run; there are *sports* and *stock car races, tennis tournaments, horse shows,* and the classic *Yale-Harvard crew races* held in early June on the Thames River at New London, Conn.

Inland, all manner of sports abound, from *boating* and *canoeing,* to *hiking* and *mountain climbing. Lake swimming, tennis,* and *golf* are outstanding in many areas, and, in the northern areas, *rockhounds* can have a heyday. *Water skiing* is popular, as is *horseback riding* on numerous forest trails. Freshwater fish abound in many lakes and ponds, streams, and rivers (*fly-fishing* only is allowed on some streams), and favorite catches throughout the region are trout (lake, brook, brown, speckled, rainbow, and squaretailed), bass, perch, pike, pickerel, and land-locked salmon.

Many types of boats as well as canoes can be rented on a number of lakes and rivers, but for several-day or week-long canoe trips, it is best to bring your own. There are places, too, where you can rent water skis, and at some marinas there are water-ski towing boats for rent.

WINTER SPORTS. To many, "New England" has become almost synonymous with *skiing,* and with good reason. Facilities are excellent and are offered in a wide variety of areas, from virtually a few miles above Connecticut's southern border to the deep woods near Moosehead Lake in Maine. With skiing has come the resurgence of *ice-skating,* particularly on well-lighted rinks at night. *Sled dog races,* becoming very popular with spectators, are held during the first three months of the year in the northern New England states, and *ice fishing* is gaining a steadily increasing number of enthusiasts in this entire region.

Late fall *hunting* brings many people to New England, out after deer, bobcat, moose, and bear, and there is bow-and-arrow hunting in some areas. For hunters who can take frigid, rough, lake water, there are whistlers (goldeneye) and bluebills (scaup) for the taking from late November to early December, and on Cape Cod, waterfowl, quail, pheasant, and rabbit lure many a sportsman from late October through November.

For spectators, there are also fall *football* games (Ivy League and others), a number of *race tracks* are open through December, and for the first three months of the year, there are a number of *championship events* at the better-known ski resorts and at colleges and universities.

ROUGHING IT. More, and improved, camping facilities are springing up each year across the country, in national parks, national forests, state parks, in private camping areas, and trailer parks, which by now have become national institutions.

Pack trips are becoming increasingly popular, and there are, of course, such stalwart organizations as the *Appalachian Mountain Club,* and *American Youth Hostels.* The former maintains a chain of huts and trails and offers maps and guides; the latter has hotels of varying sorts, special tours, etc. Both are membership groups.

Canoe trips are extremely popular in some areas, while, here and there, travelers are making long vacation trips aboard their own motor cruisers.

Farm vacations continue to gain adherents, especially among families with children. Some are quite deluxe, some extremely simple. Here and there a farm has a swimming pool, while others have facilities for trailers and camping.

Useful Addresses: *National Parks Service,* U.S. Dept. of the Interior, Washington, D.C. 20025; *National Forest Service,* U.S. Dept. of Agriculture, Wash., D.C., 20025. For information on state parks, write *State Parks Dept., State Office Building,* in the capital of the state in which you are interested.

The *National Campers & Hikers Assoc.,* Box 451, Orange, New Jersey, 07051, is an informal organization of camping enthusiasts, as is the *New England Campers Assoc.,* 211 High Rd., Newbury, Mass., 01950. Commercial camping organizations include: *American Camping Assoc., Inc.,* Bradford Woods, Martinsville, Indiana, 46151, and *Camping Council,* 17 East 48 St., New York, N.Y., 10017.

Headquarters of the *Appalachian Mountain Club* is 5 Joy St., Boston, Mass., 02108; *American Youth Hostels,* 14 West 8 St., New York, N.Y., 10011.

For a listing of farms which take vacationers (including rates, accommodations, etc.), in addition to those listed in this book, write *Farm Vacations,* 36 East 57 St., New York, N.Y., 10022. Send $1.50 (prepaid) for their booklet (add 25¢ if you wish booklet sent by first-class mail).

TIPPING. These days, the going rate for tipping on *restaurant* service is 15%. For *bellboys,* 25¢ per bag is usual. However, if you load him down with all manner of bags, hatboxes, cameras, coats, etc., you might consider giving an extra quarter or two. In many places the help rely on tips for a goodly portion of their income. Unfortunate as this may be, it's a fact. So if you're staying in a *hotel or motel* more than a day, 50¢ per day per person should be left for the maid. If you are staying at an *American Plan* hostelry (meals included), $1.00 per day per person for the waiter or waitress is considered sufficient, and is left at the end of your stay. However, if you have been surrounded by an army of servants (one bringing relishes, another rolls, etc.), add an extra few dollars and give the lump sum to the captain or *maître d'hôtel* when you leave, asking him to allocate it.

Tipping at *counters* is not a universal practice. However, a number of customers do leave 10¢ on anything up to a dollar, and 10% on checks higher than $1.00.

Railroads suggest you leave a 10% to 15% tip in the *dining car* at each meal, and tip the *porter* (as you are leaving the train) 50¢ to 75¢ per person for each day spent on the train. Though many people are not aware of it, the 25¢ or 35¢ per bag you give the railway *station porter* is *not* a tip. At the end of the day he must hand in 25¢ or 35¢ for each bag he has carried, along with the stub of each luggage tag used. Therefore, his tip is only anything above 25¢ or 35¢ per bag. Best rule is probably to give him 50¢ per bag, and be grateful he was there to help you.

HINTS TO HANDICAPPED TRAVELERS. Happily, more and more hotels and motels are becoming aware of those things which make traveling simpler for the handicapped. Two publications which give valuable information about motels, hotels, and restaurants (rating them, telling about steps, table heights, door widths, etc.), are *Where Turning Wheels Stop,* published by Paralyzed Veterans of America, 3636 16th St., N.W., Washington, D.C. 20010, and *The Wheelchair Traveler,* 22480 Cass Ave., Woodland Hills, Calif. 91364.

KEEPING AMERICA BEAUTIFUL

While the much-discussed waste and disorganization of modern living combined with a population explosion, industrial expansion, and a careless citizenry threatens today to engulf the natural beauty of this country, there is at least one region of the country where they have been doing something about this growing problem for years. Long before "America the Beautiful" became a major national issue, New Englanders have, to a great extent, been succeeding admirably in preserving the natural beauty they have inherited.

Rich in tradition, and ever conscious of its early Colonial history, New England has been fortunate to have some enlightened state and local governments and organizations like the *National Society of the Colonial Dames of America,* the *D.A.R.,* and other civic-minded groups, working to preserve the beauty and Colonial flavor of many of its famous old "greens," streets, homes, and gardens. The restoration of 17th- and 18th-century homes has been a significant contribution to the overall effort to retain the beauty that New England has enjoyed from its very beginnings.

Outraged citizens are at least trying to do something to stem the great wave of desecration and decay which has set in by those who care nothing for preserving native beauty or keeping the historic remnants of the past unmarred for future generations. Town Meetings throughout New England echo more and more to cries in behalf of protecting this region's historic treasures.

Recently the President of the United States has stepped in to encourage the beautification of the nation by proposing bills designed to help create the "Great Society." President Johnson's *Housing and Urban Development Act of 1965* was sent to the Congress with the explanation that "we wish to create a city where men and women can feed the hunger of the spirit for beauty and have access to the best of man's work."

Another effort of the President's in this regard is his *Highway Beautification Act,* signed into law in October, 1965. Under the terms of that law, states are to receive funds for landscaping their highways, controlling outdoor advertising billboards, and for the control of junkyards. A state like Connecticut, for example, stands to receive $767,597 for landscaping, $15,000 for outdoor advertising control, and $16,981 for junkyard control. It is designed to eliminate billboards within 660 feet of designated highways and remove or hide junkyards from sight of busy highways.

As far as the cities are concerned, one of New England's oldest major cities, *Boston, Mass.,* has been facing up to the problem of urban blight with a $120 million urban renewal program. This has involved redevelopment of its aging waterfront area, remodelling the Copley Square area, and establishment of a multimillion dollar government center on famed Scollay Square, set amidst many historic buildings which are being carefully preserved. A *Citizens Committee for a Cleaner Boston* has conducted massive cleanup drives and the city even has a *Teen Age Organization for Urban Renewal* which has painted benches on Boston Common.

In another historic center of New England, *Hartford,* the capital of Connecticut, has been recognized by the American Institute of Architects for its excellence in community architecture. With the sponsorship of the *Travelers Insurance Company,* the city of Hartford has replaced a blighted downtown area with its new *Constitution Plaza,* consisting of a related group of commercial buildings occupying a 12-acre site near the business center of the city. Included are two office buildings, a hotel, broadcast building, brokerage building, research center, and two retail commercial buildings amidst a landscaped plaza designed for pedestrian traffic only.

Organizations like the *National Council of State Garden Clubs* and *National*

Clean Up—Paint Up—Fix Up Bureau continue to exert their influence as they have for many years in New England and in every other section of the country to make the public aware of its responsibilities in helping to beautify America.

Another agency active in this campaign is the *Keep America Beautiful* organization, whose purpose is to prevent litter throughout the country. Litter costs taxpayers an estimated $500 million annually, this agency estimates, to keep streets and highways clean. Considering that the average citizen today disposes of four pounds of trash daily, the work of such agencies is monumental.

"If the present trend continues unchecked," the Interior Department reports, "in another generation a trash pile or piece of junk will be within a stone's throw of any person standing anywhere on the American continent."

It seems certain that with the combined efforts of an alerted citizenry and the various agencies and organizations devoted to the preservation of beauty within this small northeastern corner of the United States, New England will continue its campaign to keep its traditions intact without marring its natural beauties.

THE HERITAGE TRAIL

New England's Heritage Trail, with more than 1,000 points of interest, was mapped out by the New England Hotel Association. Each year more than one million motorists travel the whole, or parts, of the 2,000-mile long Trail. Many side trails branch off the main route and rejoin it at other places. By following the main, and side trails a tourist can spend a day, a week, or a month seeing parts of New England and never retrace a mile of highway.

Being a circular route through the six New England states, it is possible to join the Trail at any point. We'll start the 2,000-mile trip in Boston.

Heritage Trail first makes a small circle, representing a one-day trip, from Boston toward the west, to visit Lexington and Concord, where the first armed resistance to British rule started the Revolutionary War. It returns to Boston by way of South Sudbury and a visit to Longfellow's *Wayside Inn.* Heading north now, the Trail travels along the seacoast to Gloucester and the artists' colony at Rockport. It continues north along the ocean, crosses into New Hampshire by the beaches of Hampton and Rye, and goes into Maine at Kittery. The famous rock-bound coast comes into view from here on as the Trail follows US 1 through the summer resort towns of Ogunquit and Kennebunkport to Portland. Again, we continue north on the same route, and bordering the Atlantic Ocean, come to Acadia National Park and Bar Harbor. From here, the Trail swings inland, through rich lumbering country, pleasant lakes and swift rivers to New Hampshire, at the northern reaches of the White Mountains. The route now makes a rough "W" through the most scenic area of the mountains and crosses the Vermont border for the spectacular scenery of the Green Mountains and, in particular, the ski center of Stowe. Here, a chair lift takes you to the top of Mt. Mansfield, Vermont's highest point.

Heritage Trail then swings south along Lake Champlain to Bennington, where it takes a short jog to the east to afford the fine views along the Molly Stark and Mohawk Trails. Still going south, it travels through the Massachusetts Berkshire Hills to the Connecticut coastline, where it detours, again, for the lovely Connecticut River valley. This detour enables tourists to enjoy seeing Amherst, Smith, and Mt. Holyoke colleges before returning to the coast by way of Old Sturbridge Village in Massachusetts. Once back on the coast, the Trail travels by Old Mystic Seaport, along the southern coast of Rhode Island and to Providence. Before returning to Boston, Heritage Trail visits the mansions at Newport, Rhode Island, the Whaling Museum in New Bedford, Massachusetts, and the cranberry-bog country of southeastern New England. Crossing the Cape Cod Canal, the visitor can enjoy this land of windmills, white beaches, and Cape Cod cottages before arriving at Provincetown, the site of the first Pilgrim landing in America. A boat tour follows, on the return trip, to the islands of Nantucket and Martha's Vineyard. Back on the mainland, the Trail follows Highway 3 through Plymouth (for a look at Plymouth Rock) to Boston.

Side trails should not be considered less important either from the standpoint of historical attractions or scenery. They were added to make the following of the various trails easier for the traveler and also to provide for connecting roads to shorten, or lengthen, the trip, depending on time available.

Because of the wide variety of route numbers and side roads used, travelers should obtain a specially-made road map before following Heritage Trail. These can be obtained from auto club offices, information booths, chambers of commerce, or by writing to the Heritage Trail Foundation, 131 Clarendon Street, Boston, Mass.

Opposite: The lusty days of sailing are recalled at Mystic Seaport Museum, Conn.
Photo: C. Schoefield–Rapho G.

Overleaf: Halifax, Vt. The white steeple and the red foliage dominate the New England palette.
Photo: E. Henderson

Facing page 33: Hartford's Constitution Plaza is a fine example of the surge toward urban rebirth.
Photo: B. G. Silberstein–Rapho G.

Schaefer's
SPOUTER
TAVERN

HERITAGE TRAIL

There are nearly 1,000 things to see and do on the Heritage Trail. The list below is only a small fraction of the attractions available:

1. **Norwalk-Westport.** Silvermine Exhibit and Art Colony.
2. **Bridgeport.** Barnum Memorabilia.
3. **Stratford.** American Shakespeare Theatre.
4. **New Haven.** Yale, Winchester Gun Museum.
5. **Branford.** Trolley Museum.

5a. **Wallingford.** Choate, Silver Center.

6. **Guilford.** Oldest Stone House, Colonial Museum.
7. **Wethersfield.** Webb House.
8. **Hartford.** Mark Twain Memorial, Colt Gun Collections.
9. **Farmington.** Museums.
10. **Bristol.** Clock Museum.
11. **Warehouse Point.** Trolley Museum.
12. **Springfield.** 5 Museums, "Muskrat Trail."
13. **West Springfield.** Old Storrowton Village.
14. **Northampton.** Smith College, Coolidge Home.
15. **Amherst.** U. of Mass., Amherst.
16. **Pioneer Valley.**
17. **Princeton.** Antique Autos.
18. **Worchester.** 2 Museums.
19. **Sturbridge.** Old Sturbridge Village.
20. **Woodstock.** Oldest school in U.S.A.
21. **Storrs.** U. of Conn.
22. **Lebanon.** Revolutionary War Office.
23. **East Haddam.** Gillette Castle, Nathan Hale School House.
24. **New London.** Coast Guard Academy, Old Griste Mill, Allyn Museum.
25. **Norwich.** Indian Burial Ground, Leffingwell Revolutionary War Inn.
26. **Groton.** Fort Griswold, Submarine Base, and Fort Museum.
27. **Stonington.** Old Lighthouse Museum, typical fishing village.
28. **Mystic Seaport.** Re-created Early American Seaport, old sailing vessels.
29. **Watch Hill.** Summer Resort.
30. **Westerly.** The Granite Quarries.
31. **West Kingston.** Great Swamp, U. of R. I.
32. **Wakefield.** Museum of Primitive Culture.
33. **Narragansett.** Popular Summer Resort.
34. **Point Judith.** Fishing Villages, Lighthouse, ferry to Block Island.
35. **Beaches.**
36. **Block Island.** Summer Resort.
37. **Wickford.** Smith's Castle, County Museum.
38. **Saunderstown.** Gilbert Stuart Birthplace.
39. **East Greenwich.** Varnum House.
40. **West Warwick.** Gen. Greene Homestead.
41. **Johnston.** Indian Quarry, Clemence Goddard Irons House.
42. **Providence.** Oldest House in R. I., Roger Williams Museum, Brown Library and Gallery, First Baptist Church in America, Brown U., Pembroke College.
43. **Pawtucket.** Old Slater Mill.
44. **Bristol.** Indian Museum.
45. **Middletown.** Purgatory Chasm.
46. **Newport.** "The Breakers" and other magnificent mansions, Oldest synagogue in America, Cliff Walk, America's Cup Races, Music Festivals.
47. **Fall River.** Battleship USS Massachusetts.
48. **New Bedford.** Whaling Museum.
49. **Woods Hole.** Aquarium, ferries for Martha's Vineyard and Nantucket.
50. **Martha's Vineyard.** Summer Resort.
51. **Nantucket.** Fishing ports, old homes, resort.
52. **Hyannis.** Summer Resort.
53. **Chatham.** Chatham Light.
54. **Provincetown.** Pilgrim Monument, Artist Colony.
55. **Brewster.** Drummer Boy Museum.
56. **Sandwich.** Sandwich Glass Displays, Christopher Wren Church, Dexter Gardens.
57. **Sagamore.** Sagamore Beach.
58. **Plymouth.** Plymouth Rock, Restored Pilgrim Village, Mayflower II, Museums.
59. **Edaville.** Steam Railway.
60. **Quincy.** Adams Homes, Granite Railway, Tombs of two Presidents.
61. **Boston.** Freedom Trail, Bunker Hill Monument, Paul Revere House, *Old Ironsides*, Beacon Hill, Faneuil Hall, Boston Common, Louisburg Square, Old North Church, Old South Meeting House, Fine Arts Museum, Boston College, Boston U.
62. **Cambridge.** Harvard U., Radcliffe College, *The Glass Flowers*, Fogg Art Museum, MIT, Longfellow's Home.
63. **Lexington.** Battle Green ("First Shot of Revolutionary War"), Minuteman Monument, Munroe and Buckman Taverns.
64. **Concord.** Concord Bridge (Scene of Battle of Concord), Antiquarian House, Emerson House.
65. **South Sudbury.** Longfellow's *Wayside Inn*, "Little Lamb" School, and the Old Grist Mill.
66. **Saugus.** Restored Iron Works.
67. **Salem.** Pioneer's Village, *House of Seven Gables*, Witch's House, National Maritime Historic Site.
68. **Marblehead.** Yachting Center.
69. **Beverly.** Cherry Hill Farm.
70. **Gloucester.** Fisherman's Memorial, Hammond Castle Museum, Beauport Mansion.
71. **Rockport.** "Most Painted Building in America," Paper House.
72. **Ipswich.** Crane's Beach.
73. **Haverhill.** Buttonwoods Museum, Whittier Homestead.
74. **Salem.** Mystery Hill Caves.
75. **Hudson.** Wild Animal Farm.
76. **Hampton.** Hampton Beach.
77. **Rye.** Rye Beach.
78. **Portsmouth.** John Paul Jones House, Thomas Bailey Aldrich House, Athenaeum, U.S. Naval Base, Strawbery Banke, Moffatt-Ladd House.
79. **Kittry.** Fort McClary.
80. **York.** Old Gaol Museum.
81. **Ogunquit.** Beach.
82. **Kennebunk.** Kennebunk Beach.
83. **Kennebunkport.** Trolley Museum.
84. **Old Orchard Beach.**
85. **Portland.** Wordsworth-Longfellow House, Calender Islands, Art Museum, Victory Mansion.
86. **Brunswick.** Art Museum, Bowdoin College.
87. **Popham Beach.** Fort Popham.
88. **Wiscasset.** Fort Edgecomb.
89. **Boothbay Harbor.** Summer Theatre.
90. **Monhegan Island.** Art Colony.
91. **Thomaston.** General Knox House.
92. **Rockland.** Lobster Festival, Art Museum, Owl's Head Light.
93. **Camden.** Artist's and Musician's Colony.
94. **Searsport.** Penobscot Marine Museum.
95. **Castine.** Fort George.
96. **Bar Harbor.** Entrance to Acadia National Park, Summer Resort, ferry to Nova Scotia.
97. **Bangor.** Paul Bunyan Statue.
98. **Orono.** U. of Maine.
99. **Old Town.** Indian Reservation.
100. **Eastport.**
101. **Aroostook County.** Potato Country.
102. **Fort Kent.** Old Block House.
103. **Lakewood.** Dramatic Stock Company.
104. **Waterville.** Colby College.
105. **Augusta.** Fort Western.
106. **Lewiston.** Bates College.
107. **Poland Spring.** Maine Exhibit.
108. **Gray.** Grave of Unknown Confederate Soldier.
109. **Naples.** Lake Resort Center.
110. **Bethel.** Fishing and Hunting Center.
111. **Dixville Notch.**
112. **Mt. Washington.** Highest Point in New England.
113. **Glen Ellis Falls.**
114. **North Conway.** Ski Country.
115. **Mirror Lake.** Libby Museum.
116. **Meredith.** Auto Museum.
117. **Polar Caves.**
118. **White Mountain Glacial Park.**
119. **Crawford Notch.**
120. **Franconia Notch Area.** Old Man of the Mountains, The Flume, Indian Head, Cannon Mt.
121. **St. Johnsbury.** Fairbanks Museum.
122. **Barre.** World's Largest Granite Quarries, Maple Syrup Museum.
123. **Montpelier.** State Capitol.
124. **Stowe.** Smuggler's Notch, Ski Resort.
125. **St. Albans.** Northernmost Battle of Civil War.
126. **Burlington.** U. of Vt., Fleming Museum, War of 1812 Battle Site.
127. **Shelburne.** Shelburne Museum.
128. **Proctor.** Marble Exhibit.
129. **Rutland.** Marble Quarrying Center, Art Exhibits.
130. **Dorset.** Oldest Golf Course in USA, Artist's and Writer's Colony, Famous Playhouse.
131. **Manchester.** Old Time Village, Skyline Drive.

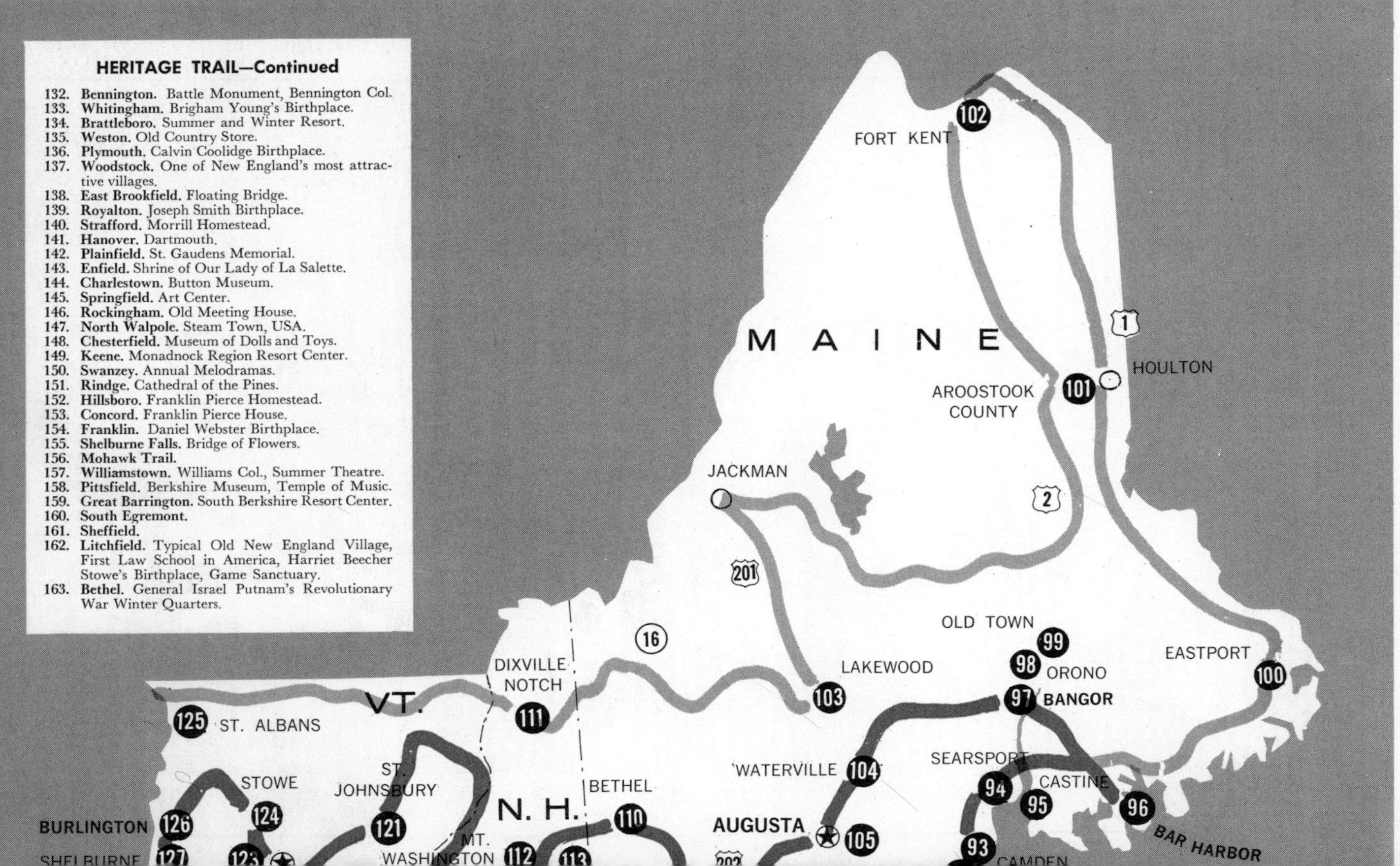

HERITAGE TRAIL—Continued

132. **Bennington.** Battle Monument, Bennington Col.
133. **Whitingham.** Brigham Young's Birthplace.
134. **Brattleboro.** Summer and Winter Resort.
135. **Weston.** Old Country Store.
136. **Plymouth.** Calvin Coolidge Birthplace.
137. **Woodstock.** One of New England's most attractive villages.
138. **East Brookfield.** Floating Bridge.
139. **Royalton.** Joseph Smith Birthplace.
140. **Strafford.** Morrill Homestead.
141. **Hanover.** Dartmouth.
142. **Plainfield.** St. Gaudens Memorial.
143. **Enfield.** Shrine of Our Lady of La Salette.
144. **Charlestown.** Button Museum.
145. **Springfield.** Art Center.
146. **Rockingham.** Old Meeting House.
147. **North Walpole.** Steam Town, USA.
148. **Chesterfield.** Museum of Dolls and Toys.
149. **Keene.** Monadnock Region Resort Center.
150. **Swanzey.** Annual Melodramas.
151. **Rindge.** Cathedral of the Pines.
152. **Hillsboro.** Franklin Pierce Homestead.
153. **Concord.** Franklin Pierce House.
154. **Franklin.** Daniel Webster Birthplace.
155. **Shelburne Falls.** Bridge of Flowers.
156. **Mohawk Trail.**
157. **Williamstown.** Williams Col., Summer Theatre.
158. **Pittsfield.** Berkshire Museum, Temple of Music.
159. **Great Barrington.** South Berkshire Resort Center.
160. **South Egremont.**
161. **Sheffield.**
162. **Litchfield.** Typical Old New England Village, First Law School in America, Harriet Beecher Stowe's Birthplace, Game Sanctuary.
163. **Bethel.** General Israel Putnam's Revolutionary War Winter Quarters.

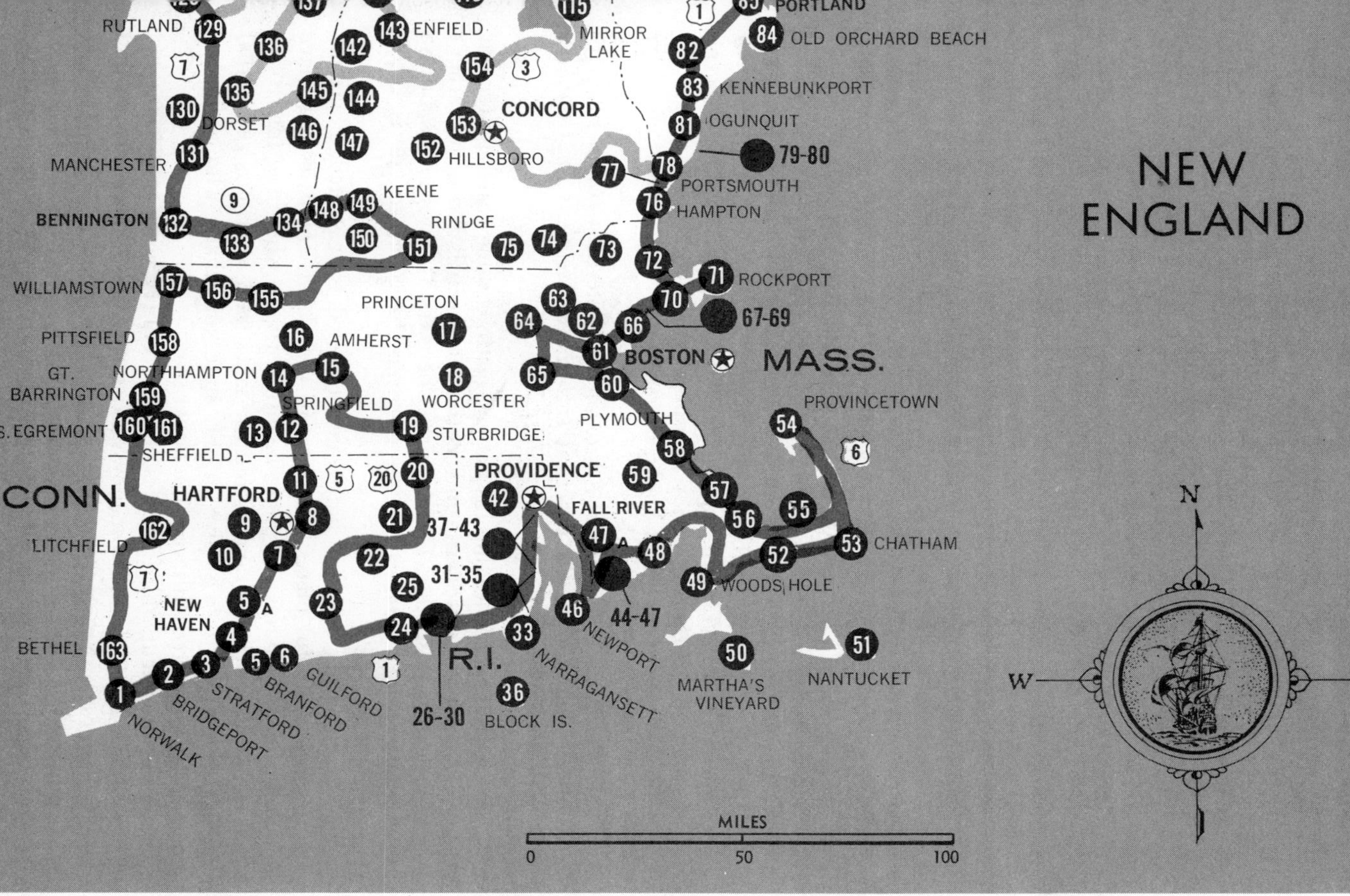
NEW ENGLAND
PORTLAND
OLD ORCHARD BEACH
KENNEBUNKPORT
OGUNQUIT
79-80
PORTSMOUTH
HAMPTON
ROCKPORT
67-69
BOSTON
MASS.
PROVINCETOWN
CHATHAM
WOODS HOLE
NANTUCKET
MARTHA'S VINEYARD
NEWPORT
44-47
NARRAGANSETT
BLOCK IS.
R.I.
26-30
31-35
37-43
FALL RIVER
PROVIDENCE
PLYMOUTH
STURBRIDGE
WORCESTER
PRINCETON
AMHERST
SPRINGFIELD
NORTHHAMPTON
RINDGE
KEENE
HILLSBORO
CONCORD
MIRROR LAKE
ENFIELD
RUTLAND
DORSET
MANCHESTER
BENNINGTON
WILLIAMSTOWN
PITTSFIELD
GT. BARRINGTON
S. EGREMONT
SHEFFIELD
CONN.
HARTFORD
LITCHFIELD
NEW HAVEN
BETHEL
NORWALK
BRIDGEPORT
STRATFORD
BRANFORD
GUILFORD
MILES
0
50
100
N
E
W

CONNECTICUT

Front Door to Yankeeland

by

BARNETT D. LASCHEVER

(A newspaperman since 1945, Mr. Laschever was travel editor of the New York Herald Tribune *for many years. Prior to that he also had served as travel editor of* The Hartford Times, *and as a correspondent for the U.S. Army newspaper* Stars and Stripes. *He is the author of five children's books. Presently, Mr. Laschever is an editor of* Fodor's Modern Guides.

(Sando Bologna, Travel Editor of the Waterbury *(Conn.)* Republican, *contributed the* Practical Information *sections for Connecticut, Vermont, and New Hampshire.)*

A young man leaving his native Hartford some years ago for one of the big midwestern universities was surprised by his father's parting words: "Son, I don't know where you'll travel in life, but no matter where you go, you'll discover that Connecticut is God's country."

The father, who had hardly ever traveled, exaggerated. There are more beautiful places elsewhere in the world, countries that have higher mountains and more beautiful rivers, where the forests are bigger, the views grander, and the lakes more spacious. Yet, withal there are those who live in this state—and many who wish they did—who agree with what the father said.

Connecticut, third smallest in the country with only 5,000 odd square miles of land, somehow excites a real pride in its citizens that is almost unmatched anywhere else in the country. Perhaps only in Virginia is pride in the state more intense.

There are little old ladies scattered around the state who have labored all their lives in dreary offices elsewhere in the country with their eyes ever on one bright star: an old Colonial home in Connecticut. And once they have moved into their old clapboarded homes with sagging doors, sloping wide-board floors, ineffective heating systems and few of the basic conveniences, nothing can get them to leave.

Pride in living in Connecticut extends to the tiniest communities and some feel it has turned its residents into insufferable snobs. Not loud and vociferous, but quiet, haughty snobs. Whereas the residents of some towns elsewhere in the country, towns that sit astride superhighways or alongside oil refineries, might have to extend themselves to say a prideful word about their area, practically everyone in Connecticut, whether he talks about it or not, thinks he is living in the best of all possible places.

And if citizens of Connecticut think that people who live anywhere else in the world are poor benighted souls, within the state itself they have a rigid pecking order that sees everyone looking down a bit on everyone else. If you accuse a resident of West Hartford of living in Hartford, you'll always be corrected: "Oh no, I live in WEST Hartford!" The people in Hartford proper look down on those living in East Hartford as "poor folks," while residents of Fairfield County, suburban-exurban bedroom to New York City, are not properly considered Connecticut Yankees by anyone else in the state. Indeed they themselves hardly know their own state. An officer in one of New York's biggest banks who lives in Wilton, Connecticut, recently admitted he didn't know where Litchfield, Connecticut, was located, although this lovely section of the state is little more than an hour's drive away.

For those who live in its gracious old Colonial homes, Litchfield is the *crème de la crème*. When the state government declared the village with its spectacularly beautiful North and South streets an historic site, the residents greeted the announcement with mixed feelings. They were delighted that the exterior architecture could never be changed, thus preserving the character of the village forever; but, they were chagrined that news of the State's action would spur tourists to come and visit and clog the roads and lanes. No matter, the visitors have been coming for years without any special urging from the State, particularly in the fall when the foliage stages its annual pyrotechnic display.

The Colonial Tradition

As one writer has noted, Connecticut has done more to preserve its old Colonial homes than any other state, and it's a rare woman who can ward off the disease of Colonialitis when planning to move into a rural area where gracious old buildings predominate. Really atrocious prices are paid for any home that has its share of exposed old beams, warped paneling, wide-board floors, damp basements covered with small stones, and inadequate heating systems, so long as they can put up a sign over the front door that reads 1774. And it doesn't take long before the new residents in the 1774 house drive past homes built in 1784 and sniff haughtily, "Newcomers."

The fact is, in most Colonial areas, the oldtimers call the newcomers, "Summer residents who stay year-round," until the newcomers have been around for at least three years and show some positive signs that their slumming days are over and they really mean to stay. Even then, there are residents of antique vintage who are given to such weighty pronouncements as "Around here, we don't consider anyone a Yankee unless they are at least third generation." In a similar vein the newcomers who have purchased and restored an old Colonial (which usually means installing new furnace, bathrooms, kitchens, and in extreme cases, shoring up the foundation) can not for the rest of their lives imagine how anyone can possibly live in a 20th-century split-level house or a modern ranch.

It has always been thus. From earliest days, one group of Connecticut residents has cast eyes on another—and, often gone a step further, and cast them out. First to come, in the years just following the settling of Plymouth and the Massachusetts Colony, were the Dutch who made their way up the Connecticut River and made a precarious toehold on what is now called Warehouse Point, on the southernmost limits of Hartford.

English settlers in Massachusetts who had fled persecution at home only to suffer more of the same from their own stiff-necked brethren broke away from the first colonies, and came down the Connecticut River where they found the happy Dutchmen. The Dutch were not to remain happy for long. In short order, the English made life sufficiently unpleasant so that the Dutch soon concluded, as did their compatriots at Nieuw Amsterdam, that the English obviously were more fit to rule.

Several groups of English made their way down to Connecticut from Massachusetts, but best known is the cavalcade led by the Rev. Thomas Hooker which made an abortive start one year, retired back to Newtown for the winter, and came down again in the spring of 1635, on foot, accompanied by an impressive herd of cows. The first cluster of settlements included Hartford (named after Hertford, England), Windsor, just to the North, and Wethersfield just to the South. These first towns banded together informally and drew up a governing document called the "Fundamental Orders" which contained many provisions later incorporated into the U.S.

Constitution. Since that time, Connecticut proudly has called itself "the Constitution State."

After the first settlements, a stockade was built at New Haven, a town which sprouted and grew rapidly. Until 1875, the capital of Connecticut was alternately located in Hartford and New Haven.

In the early days relations with the Indian were good, but only because the Indian didn't really understand what was happening to him. When a settler paid an Indian for land, he assumed that complete title now was in his hands. To the Indian, private ownership of communal land in whose forests everyone hunted and in whose streams everyone fished, was an abstraction he could not understand. By his way of thinking, giving the settler title to the land in return for a handful of trinkets was merely extending to the stranger the courtesy of living on land used by everyone. It was, therefore, incomprehensible to the redman for the white man to erect fences and barriers and deny the Indian access to his traditional hunting and fishing lands.

It took some years after friendly Massasoit died for one Indian at least, the chief's son, King Philip, to conclude that the white man was a true and serious menace to the future of the Indian. Philip was too wise. He alone understood that unless the white man was driven into the sea, the Indian of New England was doomed. He rallied other chiefs—and King Philip's War was on. The war raged in several states, and Connecticut men shouldered arms and joined the fray. The Indians fought valiantly—until their king was killed, and then losing the will to fight, evaporated into the forest. There had been other skirmishes with Indians in Connecticut in those early days—most notably the successful attack on the Pequot stockade at Norwich, but King Philip's War was conclusive. From then on it was downhill for the Indians. Many fled into New York or into the northern states of New England. The whites extended into every corner. Today there are only three tiny reservations with miniscule populations of Indians in Connecticut.

Indian Words, Biblical Feelings

The Indian lives on, of course, in the many place names in Connecticut adopted by the settlers, including the name of the state itself, meaning "beside the tidal river." These early God-fearing settlers (who wanted everyone else to fear God—but in their way) also drew heavily on the Bible when they named their little settlements. There's Goshen, Sharon, Canaan, and Bethlehem, to name a few. But most of the little stockade settlements were tabbed with nostalgic reminders of the homes they left behind: Cornwall,

Norfolk, Hartford, New London, and the Thames River (pronounced in Connecticut as it is written, not Tems, as in London).

As was to be expected, the English made a large and lasting imprint on the culture, the way of thinking, the way of living of the people of Connecticut. A visible reminder is the classic simple beauty of the white Congregational Church, seen throughout the state in communities that still treasure the heritage of their Colonial forebearers. The typical big American breakfast, instead of the simple French croissant and coffee, is a legacy of the British, as are the traditional stern attitudes toward sex and morality.

During the American Revolution, Connecticut soldiers were in the thick of every battle. It is said that General Israel Putnam, whom legend has it left his plow in its furrow when he heard the call to arms, would have led the American Army if George Washington had not accepted the assignment. Major battles of the Revolution were not fought in Connecticut—New York, New Jersey and Virginia can claim those honors—but the British on several occasions raided ports and some inland cities with fleet-based soldiers burning private homes and destroying food and other supplies, then retreating to their ships before American regulars could reach the scene. The raid on New London was led by General Benedict Arnold, the turncoat who now was wearing a redcoat. It was a particularly dastardly affair. The American commander of the garrison at nearby Fort Griswold surrendered, and when he had given up his sword, he and his men promptly were cut down, a senseless bloodletting.

When peace came upon the land and Americans set about the business of building a new country, Connecticut assumed a unique role. There was nothing in her topography—a central river valley surrounded on both sides by rolling, irregular, forested hills dotted with lovely lakes—that would appear to have been a determining factor in the nature of her people, except for the salient fact that really large-scale farming was not practicable. The valley, flat and fertile, was planted with tobacco, a strange crop one would think, for this Northern state where winters are rigorous. Yet it was a fruitful decision. Tobacco grown under wide cheesecloth tents, a colorful sight in summer, and tobacco grown in the open, are still staple crops in Connecticut. The highlands, with their rocky fields, were suitable mostly for dairy farming. Aside from that the soil would not support a growing population.

The Ingenious Yankees

Connecticut men, recognizing the limitations of farming, early displayed an inventive genius that helped propel America right into the Industrial Age, which meant factories and jobs for large numbers of workers. Perhaps the greatest debt is owed Eli Whitney. Not for his own inventions, but for discovering the basic principle of mass production: the interchangeability of parts. Before Whitney, guns were made by hand and the parts from one did not fit the other. Whitney changed all that. He took a giant step forward and made guns with parts that fit all other guns of the same design. Henceforth, manufactured goods no longer depended on the whims, the skills, the availability of individual craftsmen. Almost anyone could stand at a machine and make one part over and over again. This simple, but basic discovery, led directly to the assembly line. Manufacturing took its place alongside agriculture as basis of the American economy.

From then on, Connecticut has been known throughout the country for the skill of its factory workmen.

In guns alone Connecticut has made a loud report. The first revolver, the famous Colt .45 made in Hartford, was hung in the holster of every Western rider during the wild and woolly days following the Civil War. The Colt six-shooter earned a popular nickname, "The Peacemaker."

From New Haven came the Winchester repeating rifle, and it too helped win the West during those hectic days when every man was a law unto himself.

From Connecticut factories came other things. The more intricate, the more detailed the item—the more likely you'll still find it stamped, "Made in Connecticut." Fact is, one of Connecticut's informal nicknames is "The Gadget State." Clocks, nails, screw drivers, kitchen utensils, typewriters, ball bearings and numerous parts to fit other manufactured goods are made in this state. Latins cut their way through South American jungles with Collins machétes made in Collinsville. The Pope Company was making cars in Hartford before Detroit fashioned its first carburetor; bicycles were made in Connecticut, hats, too, at Danbury. Today, Connecticut still has a reputation for its skilled workers. At East Hartford, Pratt & Whitney makes most of the jet engines that power the world's airlines. Helicopters are made by Sikorsky and Kaman, brass and copper roll from the mills at Waterbury, while tools and appliances, parachutes, textiles, marine hardware and hundreds of other items are fabricated, woven, designed, assembled or produced in hundreds of factories, big and small, throughout the state. In finance, too, Connecticut is a leader. Hartford, with the home offices of more than 60 insurance companies, is known as America's "Insurance City."

Culturally, the people of Connecticut look both to the past and the present. The Wadsworth Atheneum in Hartford was the first municipal art museum in the country, forerunner of numerous excellent museums today. Art associations dot the state, displaying the best work of amateurs and professionals. Avid theatergoers, Connecticut residents think nothing of making regular excursions to Broadway or to Boston, or as is more likely, to New Haven where Broadway previews are still held. Summer theater—the straw-hat circuit—is popular in Connecticut.

If Connecticut residents do not boast, they also do not indulge themselves in such quaint speech patterns as "Yup" and "Nope" and "Thataway." They are sparing of speech, but they do like to talk.

Who are the Yankees of today? They are much changed from the Congregationalists who pushed their way through the woods from Newtown to Hartford with Thomas Hooker. Their lovely white churches still stand, but there are others. The great migrations of Europeans to the United States during the late 1800's and early 1900's saw large infusions of Latins, Germans, Eastern Europeans, and others into Connecticut.

The Yeast of Immigration

Italians make up a sizable proportion of Connecticut residents (in New Haven, 60 percent of the population is of Italian descent) and though most are concentrated in the cities, you can find a restaurant advertising pizza nearly everywhere in the state, even in the most remote villages.

The Italians, together with a heavy infusion of Irish, plus other groups from the Mediterranean area, have almost tipped the religious scale. Once wholly Protestant, Connecticut is now nearly 50 percent Catholic. In the cities there are flourishing Jewish groups.

The influx of newer immigrants with different religions and cultures has had a large impact on a state that at heart is still conservative, a conservatism, however, that does not preclude justice and fair play. It's interesting commentary on the basic fair-mindedness of the people of Connecticut to recall that not too long ago they overwhelmingly elected as Governor a Jewish politician, Abraham Ribicoff (now a U.S. Senator) over an old-line Yankee, John Lodge.

If Connecticut still has one foot in its Colonial past, carefully nurturing, tending and restoring its old houses, it has its other foot firmly in the future.

Hartford and New Haven are good examples. The great American author and humorist, Mark Twain, came out of the West and chose Hartford as his home, principally because his publisher was located there; but more than that, he wrote that he found its wide tree-lined streets pleasing and in general found its overall aspect attractive. (The unique house in which he lived and worked for nearly 25 years on Farmington Avenue is now maintained as a museum to the distinguished writer.)

As the years passed, downtown Hartford—and downtown New Haven—as it has happened to so many American cities, became dreary slums.

Not difficult to understand, since only a handful of American cities were planned; they just grew, like Topsy. And, unfortunately, as they aged, most grew old, not with charm and grace, but with all the wrinkles showing. Besides, during its formative years, America was little concerned with beauty—and only in 1965 did the Federal government itself become concerned with the fact that "America the Beautiful" was, in too many instances, becoming "America the Ugly." In Connecticut, the realization came much earlier. Back in the late 50's, under the leadership of far-seeing Mayor Richard C. Lee, New Haven took the lead, and embarked on a massive urban redevelopment plan that saw the wrecker's ball bash against building after building. Shiny new buildings started to rise when the rubble was cleared away. The program is not yet finished, but the grateful citizens of New Haven gave Mayor Lee a mandate to continue the good work by electing him in the 1965 elections to a seventh term.

Hartford was a late starter, but faster to the finish line. Its Front Street section, where Hartford was first settled, was completely razed, and with the backing of moneys from its great insurance companies, a new Constitution Plaza has arisen, a raised mall containing new office buildings, a hotel, restaurant, bookstore and exclusive shops, even trees, planted penthouse style in large enclosures of dirt, and, most striking, a glass skyscraper shaped like a ship (the Phoenix Mutual Insurance Company). Beneath the Mall is a large parking area. The Plaza has excited comment across the country, and redevelopment experts from many states have come to Hartford to study it. Mark Twain would not recognize downtown Hartford, but the setting around his old house has been preserved. Next door is the spacious home of Harriet Beecher Stowe, the woman Lincoln accused, in jest, of starting the Civil War.

Bridgeport, Connecticut's other major industrial city, long has been the butt of jokes by New York wits. Basest canard of all is that hoary gag: "When you leave New York, you've left the country; everything on the other side of the Hudson River is Bridgeport." Fact is, aside from a few sightseeing attractions connected with circus impresario P. T. Barnum, Bridgeport really doesn't have much to recommend it. Sorry, that's just the way it is. Its residential sections, Fairfield, Trumbull, et al., are pretty enough, but when someone asks you about Bridgeport, it's hard to come up with anything that will hold your listener for long. Factories it has. In abundance.

The Connecticut story is not yet quite told. Connecticut's attitude toward highways, for example, illustrates a point. For years the state has truculently refused to help its own citizens get anywhere by car. Except for one notable exception. Very early in the game, just shortly after the Pennsylvania Turnpike, the granddaddy of the big superhighways in the U.S., was built, Connecticut laid down the Merritt Parkway. The superhighway led from the New York border, past Bridgeport, New Haven, and then with a name change, continued past Hartford on a diagonal route to Massachusetts and on to Boston. But if citizens of Hartford had a notion to visit the beaches and resorts in the greater New London area, they had to fight the traffic all the way to the coast. Likewise, citizens in the western part of the state had overcrowded State 7 or State 8 to take them down toward the shore, and New York.

The next big highway project by Connecticut planners was the Connecticut Turnpike, which runs parallel to the Merritt Parkway until New Haven, and after that helps speed visitors entering from New York across and out of the state to Rhode Island and Massachusetts.

Connecticut residents heading west out of Hartford toward the Berkshire Hills still must take their lives in their hands on good old State 44. Perhaps that's the way the people really want it. After all, some argue, string superhighways from the really beautiful old rural areas in both the eastern and western parts of the state to the big population centers and you can expect, in a few years, people.

Fact is, Connecticut, tiny as it is, highly industrialized, a world center of insurance, and a prime vacation state, has managed to strike a nice balance between city and country living. More concrete spanning the hills could only spoil it.

And, finally, there's that little matter of education. Since early times, the people of Connecticut have been compulsive about schools. Yale University, and the fast-growing University of Connecticut, head a long list of outstanding colleges and universities that attract students from all over the world. Equally important are the many excellent preparatory schools from whose ivy-covered halls have come so many of America's political leaders (John F. Kennedy and Adlai Stevenson from Choate), writers, artists, teachers, business, industrial and financial leaders.

Unlike some of their other New England neighbors, the people of Connecticut have no really perceptible accent—except that you can always tag a Yankee when he says "idear" for "idea." However he talks, the Connecticut Yankee is friendly to strangers, but not in an overwhelming "How are you, honey" fashion, like the Westerner.

He may not smile first, but he responds quickly to a smile. It may take a little longer to become fast friends, but then in Connecticut, the people choose friends carefully. They place no big premium on knowing lots and lots of people, but once you've been befriended by a Connecticut Yankee, you've made a friend for life.

You too may discover, driving over the rolling hills, past dogwood and laurel and rhododendron in bloom, past lovely lakes and streams and forests, or along the shore with the tang of salt in the air, the truth a young college student's father knew intuitively, that here indeed is God's country.

PRACTICAL INFORMATION FOR CONNECTICUT

CONNECTICUT FACTS & FIGURES. Connecticut derives its name from the Mohegan Indian Quinnehtukquet, meaning "beside the long tidal river." It has three state nicknames: *Constitution State, Nutmeg State* and *Land of Steady Habits.* The state flower is the mountain laurel; state tree, the white oak; state bird, the robin. *Qui transtulit sustinet* ("He who transplanted still sustains") is the state motto. There is no official state song.

Hartford, the state capital, is also the biggest city in the state and the "insurance capital" of the country. The state population is 2,535,234.

Much of Connecticut is made up of rolling hills and pleasant valleys, dotted with picturesque old New England towns. The southern half of the state, bordering Long Island Sound, is a highly mixed area: summer resorts, factory towns, rural villages, old whaling ports, military bases, wealthy estates, and the sub- and ex-urbia of New York's "bedroom towns." Despite its plentiful rural charms, agriculture plays an unimportant role in the state's economy, and Connecticut is, in fact, a leading national industrial center. Hartford, where the country's first insurance company was founded in 1794, is headquarters for some 40 insurance companies.

The climate is moderate.

HOW TO GET AROUND WITHIN THE STATE. Excellent highways, frequent rail, air, and bus services provide quick access into Connecticut. More than 7,000 miles of state, interstate, and local roadways criss-cross the 5,000 square miles of Connecticut. Nautical-minded travelers arrive on yachts and motor boats (from Long Island) along the 235 miles of the Long Island Sound shoreline, dotted with marinas.

Most *motorists* drive in from New York on the Merritt Pkwy., Conn. Tpke., and Interstate 84 (still being constructed in the Hartford and Waterbury areas). The *New Haven Railroad* trains leave from New York's Grand Central Terminal; Boston-Washington trains depart from Pennsylvania Station. *Greyhound* and *Trailway* buses depart for Connecticut destinations from the Port Authority Terminal, 41st St. and 9th Ave., New York.

Majority of *air* arrivals are at Bradley Field, Windsor Locks (20 mi. n. of Hartford), served by seven airlines. Within the state are 23 airports (4 are state-owned, 5 are municipally operated), 4 seaplane bases, several heliports. Connecticut is a leading manufacturer of aircraft engines and helicopters.

Travelers arriving at Kennedy International Airport, LaGuardia Airport, and Newark Airport, can use *Connecticut Limousine Service* between these air ports,

Bradley Airport, Hartford, and other Conn. towns. Limousine schedules originate from major hotels and motor inns of large cities.

Avis Rent-A-Car, Hertz Rent-A-Car, and other car rental agencies are listed in telephone books. Auto ferry services are available across the Connecticut River below Middletown during summer.

Ferries, boat rides. *Bridgeport–Port Jefferson, L.I. Ferry:* from Calif. St., Bridgeport Dock (Exit 28 from Conn. Tpke. to Pembroke St., Calif. St.) from May 25 to Sept. 20, three boats daily; fourth boat, Sun. during summer. Fares: adult $2 one way; $3 round trip same day; $3.50 Sun. & holidays. Children under 12, half-fare. Automobiles, including driver, $8.50; maximum charge for car and all passengers, $10.

New London-Block Island, R.I. Ferry: From City Pier, New London, near Railroad Station, 11 a.m.; extra trip, Fri. & day after Labor Day, 7:30 p.m. Fares: adult $3 one way; round trip same day $4; children under 12, half-fare. Passenger car, $12. Car reservation must be made in advance with $5 deposit. Return trip from Block Island daily, 3:45 p.m.; extra trip, 7:30 a.m. Sat. & Tues. after Labor Day.

New London-Orient Point Ferry: From dock, 112 Pequot Ave., New London, 10 times daily (July 2 to Sept. 7), same return from Orient Point. Fares: Adult $2 one way; $3 round trip same day; children under 12, half-fare. Automobile, including driver, one way $8.50.

Conn. River Ferry: Rocky Hill-Glastonbury, oldest known ferry service in U.S. (started about 1650) and Chester-Hadlyme Ferry, both operated by State Highway Dept., from Apr. 1 to Dec. 1, from 6 a.m. to 10 p.m. Modest fares for crossing, which takes less than 5 min.

Conn. River Cruises: Dolly Madison and *Holly* operate daily from 159 Wethersfield Ave., Hartford (May 1 to Nov. 1), 10 a.m. to noon, adult $2; 2 to 6 p.m., $4; 8 to 10 p.m., $3. Children under 16 half-fare. Special rates for groups, 10 or more.

Thames River Tours: From Whaling City Dredges & Dock Co. Pier, 88 Fairview Ave., Groton (May 30 to Sept. 15), 50-passenger, open fiberglass boats, hourly, 9 a.m. to an hour before sunset; 7-mi. cruise with commentary, New London, Groton, submarine base, Coast Guard installation, industrial, and historic areas.

SEASONAL EVENTS. *Art:* year-'round special shows at Yale Art Gallery, New Haven; Wadsworth Atheneum, Hartford; Museum of American Art, New Britain; Silver Guild, New Canaan (Mar.–Nov.); Lyme Art Association, Old Lyme (June–Sept.).

Antique-flea markets. In most of Connecticut's 169 cities and towns, usually on week ends from May–Oct. Largest flea markets: Nichols (May); Old Saybrook (July), Guilford (July), New Haven Arena and Salisbury (both Oct.).

Christmas: Festival of Lights, Constitution Plaza, Hartford, from Thanksgiving to New Year's Day; Christmas Village, Torrington (Dec. 5 to 24); holiday programs, Mystic Seaport; special postal mark, Bethlehem Post Office.

Carnival: Barnum Festival in Bridgeport, 1966 from June 26–July 5; climax is huge street parade in Bridgeport, July 4.

Fairs: Harvest fairs in 20 or more towns; most famous is Danbury Fair, first week of Oct. (Schedule of fairs from *Conn. Development Commission,* State Office Building, Hartford.)

Fife and Drum: Muster of Eastern Corps, Deep River (July). Corps competitions on weekends in towns during summer.

Flower festivals: Laurel Festival, Winsted, third Sun. in June. Rose garden display, one of nation's best, Elizabeth Park, Hartford (latter part of June and first part of July); Rose Art Festival, Norwich (June).

Home tours: Middletown (May) house and garden; Hartford, for Hartford Art School (June); Litchfield historic homes (2d Sun. July) for Junior Republic.

Festivals of Arts, Song and Drama: New Haven Green (May); Constitution Plaza, Hartford (July); Waterbury Green (July).

Miss Connecticut Pageant: in July, different city each year. Local competitions in many towns.

Powder House Day: on New Haven Green (April) commemorates 1775 muster led by Capt. Benedict Arnold.

Theater: American Shakespeare Festival, Stratford (June–Sept.). During summer months, premieres and revivals, Goodspeed Opera House, East Haddam; summer stock, Canton Show Shop, Canton; Oval-in-the-Grove, Farmington; Ivoryton Playhouse, Ivoryton; Jorgensen Theater, University of Conn. campus, Storrs; Oakdale Musical Theater, Wallingford; Southbury Playhouse, Southbury; Westport Country Playhouse, Westport.

The Dance: American Dance Festival, started in 1947, held three days, second week of Aug., at Connecticut College, New London. Five performances, highlighted with famous artists, held in college's Palmer Auditorium. Visitors welcomed at six-week-School of the Dance, "America's summer center for modern dance study and performances," opens Jul. 7. Lectures, criticism, music, workshops, esthetics, and premieres.

Shows: *Auto races and exhibitions:* Auto Concourse, Westport (Aug.); sports cars, Thompson (Sept.); Antique Auto Meet, Ridgefield (Sept.).

Dog: State Armory, Hartford, sponsored by Governor's Foot Guard Athletic Assn. (Feb.)

Horse: from May through Sept. in various towns, on Sat. on Sun. Largest is at Westport (June, Aug., Sept.); Bethlehem (Aug.).

Travel: State Armory, Hartford, sponsored by the *Hartford Times* (Jan.).

TOURIST INFORMATION SERVICES. *Connecticut Development Commission,* State Office Building, Hartford, 06115 has a free *Vacation Guide,* special listings, etc.; *State Highway Dept.,* Wolcott Hill Rd., Wethersfield, 06109—highway map, road conditions; *State Park and Forest Commission,* 165 Capitol Ave., Hartford, 06115—campsites and camping applications; *State Board of Fisheries & Game,* State Office Building, Hartford—fishing information; *Conn. Motel Assn.* and *Associated Restaurants of Conn.,* 179 Allyn St., Hartford, 06103; *Convention & Visitors Bureau,* Greater Hartford Chamber of Commerce, 250 Constitution Plaza, Hartford.

DRINKING LAWS. Local option in towns: some towns, therefore, are "dry"; others permit beer only. Large towns and cities allow sale of beer, wine, and liquor in licensed restaurants and hotels. Women prohibited from standing at bars. No liquor served to young people under 21 years; they must show drivers' licenses or identification with birthdate if bartender requests it. Liquor, beer, and wine sold at licensed liquor stores and drug stores; beer only at grocery stores. A 1965 law, designed to curb teenage drinking and driving, provides for 60-day suspension of driver's license if beer or liquor found in car operated by minor.

STATE PARKS AND FORESTS. Connecticut, unlike other states, has neither a national park nor a national forest. Therefore, large sums of federal funds for park-forest purposes don't come to this state. Highly industrialized Connecticut, which is nearly 70 percent wooded, boasts 80 state parks (25,000 acres) and 28 state forests (125,964 acres in all). They are well-marked and in good condition for hiking, picnicking, and relaxing.

A motoring family can visit a different park every day. Within drives of from one-half hour to not more than 2½ hours, there are parks with salt water and fresh water bathing facilities. Varied in appeal and facilities, they range in size from one-acre *Minnie Island* in Salem, near New London, to sprawling *Macedonia Brook Park* of 1,845 acres in Northwestern Litchfield County. At Macedonia, three miles of excellent trout waters and two hills (over 1,200 ft.) offer scenic trails and panoramic views.

Hammonasett Beach at Madison attracts about 1 million people annually along miles of sandy beaches. *Gillette Castle Park,* Hadlyme, off Rte. 9, near Middletown, features a Rhenish fortress-like castle built by actor William Gillette from 1914 to 1919, overlooking the Conn. River. Open daily, 11 a.m. to 5 p.m. (from May 22 to Oct. 12). Admission 50¢. *Harkness Memorial Park* (between Niantic and New London), about 235 acres with a 42-room mansion, displaying Rex Brasher's famous watercolors of American birds. Admission, adults 50¢, children 25¢. Open May 22 to Sept. 26.

Fort Griswold State Park, Groton, highlighted by a granite obelisk commemorating the only Revolutionary War battlefield in Conn. (Sept. 6, 1781); *Sherwood State Park,* 203-acre island on Long Island Sound, near Westport; *Mohawk Mt. State Park and Forest,* in Northwestern Conn., a year-round playground where skiing and winter hike trails have been developed in recent years.

Recreation areas in state parks and forests are free of charge; open from 8 a.m. to one-half hour after sunset. Parking at nominal fees. Picnic areas.

State Highway Dept. maintains about 150 *roadside areas* (from one-quarter acre to four acres) with picnic tables; fireplaces at some areas. Four hundred miles of *marked trails* dot state's woodlands.

List of parks and forests may be obtained free from *State Park & Forest Commission,* Hartford, 15. List of roadside areas, motorist hints, and information booth sites, from *Conn. Highway Dept.,* Wolcott Hill Rd., Wethersfield, 06109.

WHERE TO GO. One can get lost and enjoy himself while driving through Conn. Some sections of highways, such as US 84, are so new that they are not listed on maps as being completed. The new super highways get motorists through areas quicker than the old two-lane roads, but the scenery is not as eye-catching as on the "town roads."

The countryside brightens up during May when the dogwood and other spring flowers are blooming, but Nature bursts out in June with the state flower, the mountain laurel, in great abundance.

Connecticut's greatest free show takes place in a blazing array during the foliage season (late Sept.–early Oct.) Best trips to see the leaves are in Litchfield and Windham counties, and along the Connecticut and Farmington River valleys.

The Constitution State is blessed with renowned and distinguished tourist attractions. Among them: America's only recreated 19th-century whaleport museum, *Mystic Seaport.* The nation's first medium-sized planetarium of its kind—*Museum of Art, Science and Industry,* Bridgeport.

Copy of *Elizabethan Globe Theatre* at Shakespeare Festival Theater, Stratford. Replica of world's *first commercial telephone exchange* (New Haven, 1878), at Southern New England Telephone Co., New Haven. One of the *oldest stone houses* in U.S. (1639), Whitfield House, Guilford.

First American law school, Tapping Reeve House (1773 and 1784), in Litchfield's Historic District. Site of election of *first Episcopal bishop* in U.S., Glebe House (circa 1690), Woodbury.

Connecticut's "Valley Forge" (winter 1778–79), Putnam Memorial State Park, Redding. *First state capitol* built after Declaration of Independence (1796), Old State House, Main St., Hartford.

Only U.S. *museum on clockmaking* (600 items), American Clock and Watch Museum, Bristol. Restored 10-room house of Revolutionary War hero, *Nathan Hale Homestead,* South Coventry. *Colonial War Office* (Washington conferred here) on Lebanon's historic Green. *Nation's first public municipal museum* (65 galleries), Wadsworth Atheneum (1842) Main St., Hartford.

Odd-shaped buildings: Two eye-catching modernistic buildings, eliciting international attention, are: the whale-shaped *David S. Ingalls Hockey Rink* on Yale University's campus, New Haven (opened 1959), and the 14-story ship-shaped *Phoenix Mutual Life Insurance Co. Building,* at Hartford's Constitution Plaza (dedicated in 1963). The Phoenix structure is the world's first elliptical office building (225 feet from bow to stern).

For hundreds of motoring families, New England's Heritage Trail begins in Connecticut. Entering the state from New York's Hutchinson River Pkwy, take the Merritt Pkwy., always a delightful highway, to *Norwalk* (Exit 39), turn into US 7, through the picturesque towns of *Wilton, Cannondale, Ridgefield,* and *Redding,* outstanding for their antique shops. Then to *Danbury, Brookfield Center, Candlewood Lake,* and *New Milford,* for side trips to Lake Waramaug, Lillinonah Lake, and the Housatonic River. Onward to *Kent,* a quaint town; Bull's Bridge, near the Schaghiticoke Indian Reservation, where a few Indians still live. Then, 6 miles n.e. of Kent, to Kent Falls State Park, to wade in chilly brooks and stroll in restful meadows; then on to *Cornwall Bridge* for a look at an excellent covered bridge. From here, take State 4 and 63 to *Litchfield* (settled 1720), a "Parlor Town" with well-preserved Colonial homes on North and South sts. Then go back on 63 to continue to US 7 to the Massachusetts line.

A fun-packed circle tour can also begin at *Norwalk,* scene of Silvermine Art Exhibitions; stay on Merritt Pkwy. to *Westport,* an affluent town with picturesque marinas and summer theater; to *Bridgeport,* for a view of Seaside Park and the expanding University of Bridgeport campus; to *New Haven,* for a walk on Yale's campus and historic Green shadowed by urban renewal buildings.

Take State 69 n. to *Bristol,* for a visit to the American Clock & Watch Museum; e. on States 72, 71 and 175 to Wethersfield for views of the Webb, Buttolph-Williams, and other historic homes on tree-shaded Main St.; to Hartford, with its splendid Constitution Plaza, museum buildings, State Capitol, and shopping district; then swing to Rte. 15 (Wilbur Cross Pkwy.), passing more scenic countryside and tobacco fields, to US 44A (Exit 92) for another scenic ride to the sprawling University of Connecticut at Storrs. Then onward to Willimantic on State 89; to Lebanon, another Colonial village with a long Green and Revolutionary period buildings; to East Haddam via State 16 and 149, for views of the Nathan Hale Homestead, Gillette Castle, and Goodspeed Opera House at the edge of the Connecticut River; down the riverside road (State 9) to the Connecticut Tpke., then to New London, for a quick survey of the Thames River, Submarine Base, Coast Guard Academy and Conn. College for Women campus. A short drive on I-95 leads to Mystic Seaport, where several hours are needed for an appreciation of this exciting recreated 18th-century seaport. This circle tour should be done in leisurely manner of two or three days at least, to ensure a truly memorable journey.

WHAT TO DO WITH CHILDREN. There's a wide variety of attractions and places for children and adults. Best *amusement parks* (open Memorial Day through mid-Sept.) are: Lake Quassapaug, Rte. 6A, Middlebury, and Lake Compounce, 3 mi. s. of Bristol's Center. Both lakes have excellent swimming areas, boating amusement rides, miniature train rides, and picnic groves. No admission charge to grounds. Plenty of parking.

Planetarium shows and scores of exhibits at Mystic Seaport, near New London; *Museum of Art, Science and Industry,* near Exit 47, Merritt Pkwy, Bridgeport; *Stamford Museum and Nature Center,* High Ridge & Scofield Town Rd., Stamford. Modest charges.

Nature lore featured, as well as trails, at *Mid-Fairfield County Youth Museum,* 10 Woodside Lane, Westport; *Children's Museum,* 950 Trout Brook Dr., West Hartford; *Audubon Center,* Riversville Rd., Greenwich, Exit 28, Merritt Pkwy.; *West Rock Nature Center,* Wintergreen Ave., New Haven; *Bruce Museum,* Steamboat Rd., Greenwich; *New Canaan Bird Sanctuary & Wildlife Preserve,* Old Stamford Rd., New Canaan.

Children love to visit trolley museums, open summer months at *Branford Trolley Museum,* near US Rte. 1, East Haven; *Conn. Electric Railway Trolley Museum,* Rte. 191, Warehouse Pt. Also *Gillette Castle* (May 30 to Oct. 12), off Rte. 148, East Haddam; *Old State House,* 800 Main St., Hartford; *Mark Twain Memorial,* 351 Farmington Ave., Hartford; *Mattatuck Junior Museum,* 119 West Main St., Waterbury, *Peabody Museum of Natural History,* Whitney Ave. and Sachem St., New Haven; *Museum of Transportation,* Rte. 95, Mystic; *Holy Land* at Pine Hill, replica of Jerusalem and Bethlehem, off US Rte. 84, Waterbury.

EXPLORING HARTFORD

A proper tour of Connecticut would not start with Hartford inasmuch as it is located in the center of the state. Most visitors will enter Connecticut from New York City, though there are other gateways for those coming from upstate New York, or from any of the other New England States. Nonetheless, because it is so rich in beauty, history, and sightseeing attractions, Hartford has been chosen as one of the 30 metropolitan areas which will receive special treatment in these *Fodor Shell Travel Guides to the USA.* Following the Hartford area tour, we will take a trip to see other points of interest.

Capital of the state, Hartford also is Connecticut's largest, prettiest—and most interesting city. For years its skyline has been dominated by the skyscraper home of the Travelers Insurance Company, tallest building in New England until the erection of the Prudential Tower in Boston in 1965, and Hartfordites returning to their city at night would know they were close to home when they spotted the warm green glow of the Travelers tower light. In recent years, other tall buildings, part of an extensive urban renewal project, have joined the Travelers in creating a new Hartford skyline.

Yet, the first building the visitor passes approaching the city from the south on Interstate 91 is only about five stories tall and is easily identified by its unique onion-shaped dome. The entire building once housed the Colt Patent Firearms Company which manufactured the famous Colt revolvers that "won the West," and are now slung in the holsters of nearly every movie and TV Western star. Only one end of the building is now used by the weapons company which has resumed limited manufacture of the Colt .45, but, more important, is currently making a new lightweight, high velocity rifle the U.S. Army has found so effective in the Viet Nam War.

Proceeding north along the Connecticut River, you approach a network of concrete spaghetti that leads cars in and out of Hartford, across the river, and to north and south expressways. Follow the sign to State Street. On the right is Constitution Plaza, Hartford's spanking new complex of office buildings, stores, radio-TV studio, specialty shops, restaurants, and a hotel, all centered on a raised mall landscaped with trees that are laced with thousands of tiny white lights during the Christmas season. Architecturally unique is the many-windowed Phoenix Mutual Insurance Company's skyscraper, which looks like a green-glass boat.

Past Constitution Plaza, you come to Connecticut's lovely Old State House (1796), a Colonial masterpiece in red brick with a white dome, designed by Charles Bulfinch. (Bulfinch also drew up the plans for the State House in Boston.) It is now open to the public as a museum. Period furniture in the building has been provided by the Daughters of the American Revolution. Of special interest in the building is the beautiful Council Chamber and a graceful unsupported spiral staircase. For many years the impressive front of the building, facing the river, was obstructed by an ugly post office building, which, thankfully, has been destroyed and its successor placed on another site.

The Charter Oak Incident

South on Main Street, you will come to the Travelers Insurance Company buildings. The 527-foot high tower may be visited on weekdays. A plaque on the front of the tower building marks the spot of the old Zachary Sanford Tavern, locale for a dramatic incident that saw the colonists outwit the English governor of all the New England colonies. On the night of October 31, 1687, Sir Edmund Andros, the Crown-appointed governor, arrived in Hartford with an armed escort, and at a meeting in the tavern (throughout the colonies in those days, taverns played an important role in the political life of the people) demanded the return of a liberal charter granted the Hartford Colony in 1662 by King Charles II. According to the story, the charter was produced, but before the Governor could put his hands on it, all the candles in the tavern were suddenly blown out. The charter, which had given the Hartford Colony its independence, was stolen in the darkness by Joseph Wadsworth and hidden in the truck of a great oak tree five blocks away. The irate Andros left Hartford without the precious document; two years later he was recalled to England, and the colony resumed government under the terms of the charter. The episode of the charter hiding, one of the first acts of resistance in the colonies to Great Britain, was the stuff of which legends are made, and its participants—including the tree—became larger than life. Henceforth, the tree became known as the Charter Oak, and the name became a brand name for every conceivable product. A plaque on Wyllys Street in the south end of the city marks the spot where the magnificent oak stood until 1856, when it crashed to the ground in a windstorm. Today, in various public buildings and museums, you can see gavels, chairs, and other objects that have been fashioned from the wood of the tree. Guidebook writers like to recall Mark Twain's comment on the subject. He said he had seen "a walking-stick, dog collar, needle-case, three-legged stool, bootjack, dinner table, tenpin alley, toothpick, and enough Charter Oak to build a plank road from Hartford to Salt Lake City."

Continue past the Travelers on Main Street to the Wadsworth Athenaeum (oldest city museum in the country), the Avery Art Memorial, and the adjoining Morgan Memorial, a museum with a fascinating gun room and an excellent collection of Middle Eastern and Oriental archeological relics, and one of the largest exhibits anywhere of Meissen china. The gun room (in the Colt Wing) displays muskets, rifles, and Colt revolvers, including a piece from the first wooden model of the revolver invented by Samuel Colt. The Avery boasts paintings by Daumier, Gilbert Stuart, Picasso, Goya, Giordano, Cézanne, Whistler, and Sargent, and its many special exhibitions are the occasion for social evenings that bring out Hartford society. (Money for the Morgan Memorial was a gift from the famous financier, J. P. Morgan, a Hartford boy, who chose not to join his father's business but went to New York to seek his fortune.)

The statue on the lawn in front of the Morgan Memorial honors the youthful Connecticut schoolteacher, Nathan Hale, who was caught by the British while spying on Long Island for Washington's forces and was hanged in New York City, uttering before his death, words that have become immortal in American history: "I regret I have but one life to give for my country."

At the next corner, going south, look toward the river. The striking building with the columned portico is the *Hartford Times,* leader in the afternoon newspaper field. The columns came from the front of the church of a crusading New York City preacher who was a contemporary of Lincoln Steffens. At Christmastime, the Times annually stages a huge Carol Sing that attracts thousands and is highlighted by a famous singer.

The next building on Main Street is the City Hall, and next to it, resting on huge steel girders—among the largest ever fashioned—is the new Public Library. The girders bridge four lanes of road that lead to the riverside superhighways. Thousands of cars daily pass beneath the library, but insulation muffles the noise.

Beautiful Capitol Hill

The present State Capitol, described by one visitor as a "Gothic Taj Mahal," sits dramatically atop the highest point in Bushnell Park, the Central Park of Hartford. While the Governor and top officials have their offices in the gold-domed Capitol, most state workers are housed in a new white building on the edge of the park. In the Capitol Building visitors can see Lafayette's camp bed, a canvas cot that folded into a trunk much like a Murphy bed slips into the wall. Battle flags carried by Connecticut soldiers in many wars line the wall of the exhibition room.

Across the street in the imposing State Library, you'll find another collection of early rifles and revolvers, including the Colt six-shooters carried by such distinguished Western types as Wild Bill Hickok, and the lawman-turned-newspaperman, Bat Masterson. (After he left the West, Masterson took a job on the sports desk of a New York newspaper. He died, some years later, not with his boots on, but at his typewriter.) The State Library also has some excellent oil paintings by renowned Colonial artists, including Gilbert Stuart's famous portrait of George Washington. In an alcove off the museum room sits the table upon which President Abraham Lincoln signed the Emancipation Proclamation that freed all slaves during the Civil War. A duplicate of the stolen Connecticut Charter is also on display.

Two other buildings of note stand in the Capitol Hill complex: the State Armory, and Bushnell Memorial. The Armory, to the west of the Capitol, is a large imposing building that's headquarters to Connecticut National Guard and military reserve units. Its spacious floor often is used for circuses, balls, sportsman's shows and other entertainments. Across the street from the Armory is the new home of the *Hartford Courant,* the oldest daily newspaper in the country in continuous publication. (Every state apparently has a newspaper that is the oldest *something*—"oldest east of the Alleghenies," "oldest west of the Rockies," etc., but the Courant really is the granddaddy of daily papers still publishing.)

The Bushnell Memorial, on the east flank of the Capitol, is a beautiful auditorium that serves as the cultural heart of a community that places a high premium on the theater and music. To the Bushnell come the world's top symphony orchestras, opera and ballet companies, Broadway plays, lectures, and travel movies. It's also the home of the Connecticut Opera Company.

In the south end of the city, high on a ridge of traprock, is

Trinity College, one of the most respected of the Ivy League colleges. Get out of your car and stroll along Trinity's "Long Walk," a tree-shaded campus sidewalk bordered by school buildings. The college chapel is a masterpiece of neo-gothic architecture. If you are interested in medieval manuscripts and books, stop at the Trinity Watkinson Library. Bird watchers will have a field day examining Audubon's masterwork, *Birds of America.* The folio is considered the second most valuable in the U.S. The college's natural history museum offers the usual exhibits of rocks, minerals, fossils and skeletons.

To explore the rest of Hartford, you must now return to midtown and head west on Farmington Avenue. On the left in the center of the small park you'll see the brick-red Aetna Insurance Building, the largest Colonial-style structure in the country. Across the street is the new, semi-modernistic Hartford Cathedral, built a few years ago to replace the old cathedral which was destroyed in a mysterious fire.

Tom Sawyer Lived Here

Further out, at 351 Farmington Ave., you come to what was once known as Nook Farm. On the few remaining acres of the tract, you'll find the grand old Victorian home of Mark Twain, and the neighboring house in which Harriet Beecher Stowe lived and worked. For many years, the lower floor of the Twain house was used as a branch of the Hartford Public Library, with the upstairs rented out as private apartments. Interested residents raised sufficient money to take over the house, and a very active Mark Twain Memorial Commission started the long process of bringing back to Hartford furniture, furnishings and belongings of the author and his family. Today, except for a few rooms still occupied by tenants, the venerable old house is much as it was when the Twain family lived here. The great author, whimsically, built the kitchen on the street side so that the servants could watch the annual circus parade go by while continuing with their work. (The parade never got that far up Farmington Avenue.)

The south portico of the house is shaped much like the wheelhouse of a Mississippi River steamboat, recalling for Mark Twain the happy years he spent on the river as a pilot. In a top floor room is the pool table upon which he worked when he wanted to escape the hubbub of the family below. And in the basement is the typesetting machine Twain financed. It was never a success and eventually plunged the author into bankruptcy. Not one to escape his debts that way, Twain went on a world lecture tour, eventually paying back every creditor.

Of the Hartford house in which he lived for more than 20 years, Mark Twain once wrote: "Our house was not unsentient matter—it had a heart, and a soul, and eyes to see us with; and approvals and solicitudes and deep sympathies; it was of us, and we were in its confidence and lived in its grace and in the peace of its benedictions. We never came home from an absence that its face did not light up and speak out in eloquent welcome—and we could not enter it unmoved."

The adjacent Harriet Beecher Stowe House, containing her family furnishings, was for many years the home of Miss Katharine S. Day, niece of the authoress. Miss Day played a leading role in the cultural life of the city and is well-remembered for her aid in preserving historical sites. She died several years ago, and it is now planned to open the Stowe House to the public.

Many of the large office buildings you pass in Hartford (including this part of the city) are the homes of some of America's leading insurance companies. And while Hartford is known throughout the country as the Insurance City, it is interesting to note that the total assets of all its companies do not equal the assets of one single company, the Metropolitan Life Insurance Company in New York City. Nonetheless, Connecticut companies long have been leaders in the field. The industry's proudest story tells of the representative of one fledgling company who hastened to Chicago while that city still was burning—remember Mrs. O'Leary's cow?—stood on a box at the edge of Lake Michigan, and announced: "Phoenix of Hartford will pay all claims." A wave of hope spread throughout the stricken city. After that, insurance business flowed into Hartford.

From the Stowe House, continue west, turn right on Woodland Street, then left on Asylum Street to Elizabeth Park, one of many beautiful parks in the city. Its spectacular rose gardens annually attract thousands of visitors from all over the country. You now are in West Hartford, one of the most beautiful residential communities in the country, with miles of tree-shaded streets and attractive houses with well-kept lawns and gardens. And there are more exclusive sections here, with expensive mansions. On South Main Street you can visit the modest little saltbox house in which Noah Webster, compiler of the first American dictionary, was born. The saltbox, an architectural form unique to New England, was evolved because of the tax policies of the first Colonies. Higher taxes were leveled on any building that had more than one full story. The Colonists who had one-floor homes but needed more room neatly solved the problem of avoiding taxes by building what essentially was a lean-to on top of the first floor. Thus, the slanted roof masked a second floor, satisfying both the homeowner and tax assessor. The name derived from its similarity to the design of the typical box housewives of the day used for storing salt.

The Children's Museum of Hartford, one of the most complete in the country, is located in West Hartford at 960 Trout Brook Drive. Youngsters will be fascinated with the numerous exhibits, ranging from Colonial artifacts to natural history displays.

Touring the Suburbs

Metropolitan Hartford encompasses a number of interesting attractions. Immediately south of the city you can tour the Webb House on the Wethersfield Green, one of the most beautiful village greens in the country. In the Webb House (1752), Washington and Count de Rochambeau, head of French forces in America, plotted the strategy that led to the Allied victory at Yorktown over the British under Lord Cornwallis. Wethersfield was a natural meeting place for the two commanders, being about halfway between the Frenchman's headquarters in Newport, R.I. and Washington's command posts in upstate New York. Numerous Continental officers had been welcomed by Joseph Webb and his charming wife, and the Webb House, a charming mansion, became known as "Hospitality Hall." The story is told that Madame Webb, like any good hostess, rushed to have an expensive wallpaper, just arrived from France, put up in the room she had prepared for her distinguished American guest. The original gaily-patterned red flock paper still looks down on the canopy bed in which Washington slept. Other points of interest are the kitchen, the graceful stairway, and the Council Room, in which the fateful battle plans were laid.

Researchers for the Connecticut Historical Commission discovered in Washington's diary his own account of the visit to the Webb House. The General left his headquarters on May 18 "for interview at Wethersfield with the Count de Rochambeau and Admiral Barras." On May 19, he wrote: "Breakfasted at Litchfield (at the Sheldon Tavern, where he spent the night), dined at Farmington and lodged at Wethersfield, at the house of Joseph Webb." May 20—"Had a good deal of private conversation with Governor Trumbull." May 21—"Count de Rochambeau with Chevalier de Chastellux arrived about noon. The appearance of the British fleet off Block Island prevented attendance of Count de Barras." May 22—"Fixed with Count de Rochambeau the plan of campaign."

The rest is history.

If the Webb House reflects the life of a wealthy Connecticut family during the Revolution, the nearby Buttolph-Williams House, built in 1692, shows how the Colonists lived under much sterner conditions nearly a century earlier. Typically, additions were made to the original building, a common practice in Colonial times, yet they were made to harmonize with the basic clean design of the dwellings. Most interesting in this house are the numerous artifacts in the big kitchen. The fire seat, a curved settee whose back acted as a heat reflector, looks inviting but actually is quite uncomfortable.

Other interesting old buildings on Wethersfield's Main Street, which borders the Green, are: Silas Deane House (1776), home of one of the special envoys sent to Europe by the Continental Congress, and the Old Academy Museum (1801), where household tools, utensils, and a loom are on display.

Across the Connecticut River, fast-growing East Hartford is the home of the Pratt & Whitney division of United Aircraft Corporation, makers of some 60 percent of all American airplane jet engines. UAC, which also maintains its headquarters here, has other divisions in Connecticut—Hamilton Standard in Windsor Locks (now engaged in the Apollo project), and Sikorsky Helicopters in Stratford—and is one of the largest employers in the state. The fact is, one out of every seven Connecticut factory workers is in the aviation industry.

Fields of Tobacco

Cross the river again on any one of the five bridges that span the Connecticut in the Hartford area, and head north to East Granby. In summertime, you'll pass by miles of fields covered with huge flat tents of white cheesecloth. You are witnessing a unique agricultural enterprise in action: the cultivation of shade-grown tobacco, prized as wrappers for cigars. The white tents maintain throughout the growing season an even warm temperature that is ideal for this type of tobacco. Biggest menace to the tents are summer hail storms that can tear the cloth in shreds and rip apart the tobacco leaves. Negroes, West Indians and, more recently, Puerto Ricans, comprise the field hands.

At East Granby, on Route 20, you can descend into the main shaft of an old copper mine at the infamous Newgate Prison, used during the Revolutionary War to incarcerate war prisoners and Tories.

Return to Hartford, stopping enroute in Windsor, a town which probably has more well-preserved pre-Revolutionary War houses than any other in the state. Only a few buildings are open to the public, but in them you can see examples of early architecture and early furnishings. For example, the Loomis Homestead, on the grounds of the Loomis School for Boys, an excellent prep school, boasts of its old walled cupboard and a fireback, believed to be one of the first brought to the Colonies from the Mother Country.

Bloomfield, near Granby, is the new home of the Connecticut Life Insurance Company, a strikingly modern building set in a huge park punctuated with ponds, groves of trees and shrubs, and highlighted by red monoliths sculpted by the noted Japanese-American artist, Isamu Noguchi. Formerly located in midtown Hartford, Connecticut General is the first of the big Hartford insurance companies to depart from conventional design when it built a new home. The Bloomfield building may be visited.

Farmington, on State 4 west of Hartford, is a lovely old community with many Colonial homes set on quiet streets and shaded by graceful elms. It's the home of Miss Porter's, one of the most exclusive finishing schools for girls in the country. Jacqueline Kennedy is one of the school's distinguished graduates. The school is housed in a building originally used as a hotel when the Farmington Canal opened. The Stanley-Whitman House (1660), now a museum, is one of the oldest frame houses in Connecticut. Prize of Farmington, however, is the Hill-Stead Museum (1901), a lovely mansion overlooking the valley. The front porch is somewhat reminiscent of Mt. Vernon, but the real attractions of the museum are the paintings collected by its wealthy owners during their world travels: works by Monet, Manet, Whistler, and many Japanese wood-block prints.

This completes the Hartford area tour.

PRACTICAL INFORMATION FOR HARTFORD

HOTELS AND MOTELS. Hartford, the capital city, has taken the lead in modern accommodations in recent years. The *Bond Hotel,* well-known for a couple of generations, shut down in 1965, but there are excellent replacements not far from that former downtown showplace.

First Class

Hotel America, in the heart of the new $40-million Constitution Plaza. Dedicated in May, 1964, the $5-million, 12-story building is the second Hotel America in the Hotel Corp. of America chain. Main entrance of the 310-room structure overlooking the Connecticut River, is at Columbus Blvd., close to the Interstate 91 access ramp. Nearby shopping, historic areas, insurance buildings, and theaters. Free parking in large underground garage, with direct access to lobby. Swimming pool is on the Constitution Plaza Mall. Presidential Suite has gold-plated plumbing fixtures; silk-covered walls. Subscription TV in all (air-conditioned) rooms. Elegant decor in the *Carlton Room* for banquets and meetings. *Rib Room* restaurant with cocktail lounge, is in Old English decor. *Tivoli Coffee House,* decorated in Scandinavian colors, with Nordic bric-a-brac. No charge for children under 14 years of age in parents' room.

Constitution Plaza (tel. 278–2000).

Reasonable

Diplomat Motor Hotel, medium-sized, with restaurant—cocktail lounge; meeting rooms. TV, telephones in air-conditioned rooms.

765 Asylum Ave. (tel. 525–5311).

Farmington Ave. Motor Lodge, small, near insurance company offices; TV, telephones in (air-conditioned) rooms. No pets.

226 Farmington Ave. (tel. 249–8531).

Howard Johnson's Motor Lodge, via Interstate 91, medium-sized place with TV/radio, telephones in (air-conditioned) rooms. In-room coffee, cocktail lounge. Swimming pool & conference rooms. Near Constitution Plaza. Courtesy car.

7 Weston St. (tel. 525–4441).

Shoreham-Oaks Motor Hotel. Nearly 100 air-conditioned rooms with TV and telephones; in downtown, near State Capitol, railroad station, bus stations. Three restaurants in varying decorations and varied menus. Near theaters, business and shopping districts.

440 Asylum St. (tel. 249–7611).

The Statler Hilton, facing Bushnell Park, 455 rooms with modern appointments. Family rates and free parking. Airlines representatives in ground floor shopping center. Barber and beauty shops also on first floor. *Terrace Dining Room* and *Four Kings Bar* are favorites with guests and the public for luncheon and dinner.

Ford & Pearl sts. (tel. 249–5611).

DINING OUT in Hartford is limited to a few good restaurants, unless you are in a hurry or want to economize at the nondescript places which abound everywhere. You may wish to travel out into the country to seek out one of the inns listed elsewhere, or you may even want to dine in your hotel or motel. Most of the better establishments offering rooms for the night have superior dining rooms. Because of space limitations, many restaurants which are suitable for inclusion are not listed here, and we give only a representative sampling of what Hartford has to offer.

First Class

Hearthstone Restaurant. Elegant dining place, serving American, Italian and French dishes. Specialties: veal, blue-ribbon steaks. Open daily 11 a.m. to midnight, Sun. noon to 9 p.m. Closed Sun. in July & Aug. Bar and cocktail lounge.

680 Maple Ave.

Reasonable

Honiss Oyster House. This seafood restaurant in downtown Hartford, established in 1845, still serves only fish and other seafoods. Old prints and photos adorn the walls. Saturated with atmosphere. Children's plates, half-price. Special seafood dinners served from 4:30 to 8 p.m., Sat. to 9 p.m. Closed Sun.

44 State St.

Inexpensive

Sagan Cafeteria. Variety of foods in pleasant environment. Open daily, except Sun.

90 State St., reached from Rte. 91 Exit in Hartford.

MUSIC. *Bushnell Symphony Series,* distinguished orchestras, Bushnell Memorial, Hartford (Oct.–Mar.); *Conn. Opera Assn. Series* (five operas with famous artists), Bushnell Memorial (Nov.–Apr.).

STAGE & REVUE. *Hartford Stage Show,* at Constitution Plaza, produces occasional plays. Bushnell Memorial, Hartford, also schedules opera, revues, and drama.

TOURS. Newest tours, proving quite popular with visitors, are conducted at the $40 million *Constitution Plaza,* where the modern high-rise buildings look down on the Old State House (1798), an outstanding landmark-museum. Plaza Deck Tours take about one-half hour. Tours can also be made through the elliptical *Phoenix Mutual Life Insurance Co. Building, Conn. Bank & Trust Co. Building* and *WTIC Broadcast House*. There is no charge.

Walking tours of downtown Hartford are suggested by the Coordinating Council for the Arts to such places as *Travelers Tower, Wadsworth Atheneum, State Capitol, State Library, Mark Twain Memorial, St. Joseph Cathedral,* and other places of interest. Detailed information from *Convention & Visitors Bureau,* Greater Hartford Chamber of Commerce, 250 Constitution Plaza. *Trinity College Campus Tours* are conducted free Sun. from Trinity College Chapel at 2, 3, and 4 p.m.

INDUSTRIAL TOURS AND MUSEUMS. Hartford: *Royal McBee Corp.,* 150 New Park Ave., typewriters & data processing equipment; *The Hartford Courant Building,* 285 Broad St. East Hartford: *Fuller Brush Co.,* 88 Long Hill St., world-famous brushes, brooms, mops, etc. West Hartford: Whitlock Mfg. Co., 101 South St., heat exchangers, coils.

Also in Hartford: *Colt Gun Collection,* State Library Building, 231 Capitol Ave., Hartford (across from State Capitol): world's best collection of Colt firearms. Open Mon. to Fri., 8:30 a.m. to 5 p.m.; Sat., 9 a.m. to 1 p.m. except holiday week ends: closed Sun. Free.

Insurance company tours: Hartford, as the "insurance city of the world," is visited by thousands of insurance salesmen and executives—and policyholders—who want to tour their favorite insurance headquarters. Here are the principal tours: *Travelers Insurance Companies,* 600 Main St., year-round tours; *Traveler Tower* visited from May through Sept. *Aetna Life Affiliated Companies,* Farmington Ave., home office hour-long tours from 9 a.m. to 3 p.m. on weekdays. *Conn. Mutual Life Insurance Co.,* 140 Garden St., see beautiful garden on north side of building during spring to late fall. *The Hartford Insurance Group, The Hartford Steam Boiler Inspection & Insurance Co., Phoenix Mutual Life Insurance Co., Mutual of Hartford Companies,* and *Security Insurance Group* all provide guides by advance appointment.

In Bloomfield, five miles from downtown Hartford, *Connecticut General Life Insurance Co.* offers free tours Mon. through Fri., from 9 a.m. to 3 p.m., Sun. from 2 to 5 p.m. Advance notice needed for weekday tours, but not for Sun. Beautifully landscaped grounds and modernistic home office building. Information on all tours and other matters may be obtained from the *Insurance Information Office of Connecticut,* 79 Farmington Ave., Hartford.

HISTORIC SITES. Listed as National Historic Landmarks in the *National Registry* of the *National Park Service* are: *Old State House* (1796), 800 Main St., Hartford; Bulfinch-designed brick and brownstone museum of state's legislative, government and judicial history. Open Tues. to Sat., noon to 4 p.m. Adults 50¢; children 10¢. Closed Mon.; holidays.

Mark Twain Memorial Building (1873), 351 Farmington Ave., Hartford, home of the famous author when he wrote his best sellers. Open Tues. to Sat., 10 a.m. to 5 p.m. Sun. 2 to 5 p.m. Closed Mon. and holidays. Adults 75¢; ages 15 to 18, 50¢ under 15, 25¢.

Noah Webster Birthplace, West Hartford, salt-box house (about 1676) now a town museum. Public welcomed.

MUSEUMS AND GALLERIES. *Wadsworth Atheneum* (590 Main St., Hartford), America's first public art gallery (founded 1842), with 65 galleries of worldwide collections; large expansion program of new facilities. Open Tues. to Fri., 10 a.m. to 5 p.m.; Sat., 9 a.m. to 5 p.m.; Sun., 1:30 to 5:30 p.m. Holidays, noon to 5 p.m. Closed Mon. & holidays (New Year's Day, Good Friday, July 4th, Labor Day weekend, Thanksgiving, Christmas). Admission free. *Old State House* (800 Main St., Hartford) nominal admission rates.

FAMOUS LIBRARIES. *Connecticut State Library,* 231 Capitol Ave., Hartford, across from State Capitol, contains countless records and memorabilia beginning with first General Court session Apr. 26, 1636. Open Mon. to Fri., 8:30 a.m. to 5 p.m.; Sat., 9 a.m. to 1 p.m., except holiday week ends. Closed Sun. and holidays. Free admission to above libraries.

GARDENS. *Elizabeth Park,* 915 Prospect Rd., Hartford, 99 acres of outstanding gardens, considered the most beautiful municipal rose gardens in this country. For best blooms, come in latter part of June.

SHOPPING. Department stores, specialty shops and shopping centers, offer the visitor to the Hartford area the opportunity to buy anything from antique andirons to the latest in woman's fashions. Best known among Hartford stores is *G. Fox & Company,* Main St., one of the outstanding department stores in New England, noted not only for the variety and quality of its goods, but for its personal service in an age where attention to the customer is a sometime thing. Men's and women's clothes are excellent here, as they are at the West Hartford branch of *Lord & Taylor's.* Another good men's store in the downtown area is *Stackpole Moore & Tryon,* 115 Asylum St., conservative but always in fashion. (The Tryon scion, Tom, forsook haberdashery and is a well-known TV and movie star.) In West Hartford, *Allen Collins,* 43 S. Main St., has an excellent selection of Ivy League clothes and English shoes; he is well regarded for its custom tailoring. *Lux, Bond & Green,* 70 Pratt St., Hartford, is best for jewelry, while around the corner, *Freed's Furs,* 20 Allyn St., has been making Connecticut women glamorous for decades. *Clapp & Treat,* 672 Farmington Ave., is a sporting goods haven, offering everything from tennis balls to trailers, and skis, boats and marine hardware. *Sports Limited,* 15 S. Main, W. Hartford, specializes in skiing and tennis. It's a branch of Sig Buchmayr of New York City. Two stores on the mall of the Constitution Plaza, both New York-based, should be visited: *Brentano's* for books, *W. and J. Sloane* for furniture and furnishings. For specialties, try two West Hartford stores: *Pascos,* 17 S. Main St., Swedish and Danish silver and contemporary furnishings, and the *Pottery Shed,* Bishop's Corner, pottery, figurines, bowls, plates, etc. *Lappen's,* 19 Main St., back in Hartford, has a wonderful selection of fireplace accessories, wrought iron furniture, hitching posts, and souvenirs.

WHAT TO DO WITH THE CHILDREN. Hartford's amusement park is *Keney Park,* on Main Street. Free admission includes playgrounds, swimming pool, zoo. The *Old State House,* at 800 Main St., and the *Mark Twain Memorial,* at 351 Farmington Ave., are both interesting to children. *West Hartford* has a *Children's Museum,* at 950 Trout Brook Dr.

EXPLORING CONNECTICUT

Two superhighways that run almost parallel along Long Island Sound for a while are the natural gateways to Connecticut from New York City. The older road, the Merritt Parkway, is the more scenic route and is more inland; it's a bit slower because only two lanes of highway run in each direction. Shortly before New Haven, the Merritt—named after the engineer who built it—becomes the Wilbur Cross Parkway, named after an extremely popular governor of the 'thirties. At this point, the road arches north toward Hartford, where it crosses the river and shoots on a diagonal up into Massachusetts. The newer road, the Connecticut Turnpike, sends three lanes in each direction fairly close to the shore, slicing through downtown portions of the major cities along the Sound. The views are less than entrancing: old factories, spouting chimneys, the wornout sections of towns. At New Haven, the Turnpike parts company with the Wilbur Cross and instead continues to hug the coast all the way to New London, where it finally takes a northerly turn, heads up the Thames River and finally, halfway up the state, turns abruptly east to connect with Rhode Island's highway system. Another major superhighway, Interstate 84, is under construction from Brewster, N.Y. and eventually will link that city with Waterbury, New Britain, and Hartford.

There are other bits and pieces of superhighway throughout the state, but for the most part, the rest of Connecticut's roads are ordinary two-lane highways that wind and twist, snake over mountains and around lakes, pierce forests, sometimes bog down in towns, but usually pass through some of the loveliest country in America. They are, of course, more difficult to drive.

A tour of Connecticut will traverse both the superhighways and the country roads. Being a small state with much to see, it's almost impossible to lay out a circular tour that is artistic and geometrical without missing some of the more interesting sights. We propose to wiggle and waggle, zig and zag, and backtrack occasionally when the attractions warrant it.

While our inclinations would cause us to make our entry into Connecticut on the more scenic Merritt Parkway, convenience puts us first on the more utilitarian Turnpike.

New York's "Bedroom Suburbs"

Immediately upon crossing the state line, you will pause in Greenwich, essentially a bedroom community for high bracket commuters to New York. Homes are more often estates; the people who live in them are captains of finance and industry; their wives' pictures appear regularly in the New York newspaper society pages. Country clubs, beach clubs, and yacht clubs are fashionable—and difficult to join. The average visitor will enjoy walking along the self-guided trail in the Greenwich Audubon Nature Center, or examining the 20,000 exhibits, the natural history dioramas, and the live animals in the Bruce Museum. Putnam Cottage, 243 East Putnam Avenue, was the scene of one of General Israel Putnam's legendary exploits. The doughty Revolutionary War hero, so the legend goes, was shearing his whiskers one morning, when something else besides his own face showed up in the mirror. Redcoats, by George III! The general dropped his razor, fled the house, lept on his horse and audaciously made his escape riding down a rocky slope, now known as "Putnam's Steps." There are other versions to this escape story, but none quite as interesting.

Proceed on the Turnpike to exit 5 and turn north toward Mianus, a nature preserve that still has stands of virgin timber, something rarely found elsewhere in the state. Although 60 percent of Connecticut still is covered with forests, today's trees hardly date back more than 50 years. Most are younger. This has come about because the first settlers cut down the trees to clear the land for farming. (It is reported by early travelers in Connecticut that spring skies were black with smoke in those days as the farmers burnt the trees they felled in huge bonfires.) Also, there always has been logging in Connecticut for lumber. Where, then, do today's trees come from? First, much of the farmland has been abandoned and reverted to nature itself. And then, once a stand of woods has been logged, the lumberman's axe is not heard in that spot for perhaps another 20 years.

From Mianus, make your way into Stamford, a bustling, progressive community that also is home to a significant number of New York commuters. The museum, at High Ridge and Scofield Town roads boasts a mixed bag, ranging from minerals to Indian relics, to a nature center and a planetarium.

The next towns up the road are Darien, close to the highway, and New Canaan, to the north. Both are exclusive residential communities. Other than fine homes—and the residents don't particularly care to have rubberneckers driving along their streets—there are only two attractions in the area. First is the famous Silvermine Guild of Artists, located off State 7. Open year-around, it stages regular exhibits of the works of its members, mostly artists who live in the Fairfield County area, and conducts a highly regarded school. The number of artists, sculptors, and ceramicists in residence swells in the summertime, when a small exodus of artists takes place out of

New York City. The other attraction is an excellent bird sanctuary in New Canaan's Mead Park.

Now, back to the superhighway—either one—and so on into Norwalk, a city whose depressing downtown section is ripe for urban renewal. One spot commands your attention: the Yankee Doodle House, East Avenue near Hendricks Avenue, where the lyrics were written to what became the most famous song of the Revolution, and which even today is sung with delight by schoolchildren. Unlike the *Battle Hymn of the Republic,* the solemn, heavy, ponderous marching song of the Civil War, *Yankee Doodle* had a light-hearted lilt that buoyed the spirits of the Colonial patriots, even though the words really carried no inspiring message.

Westport

Although there are some New York commuters who live deeper in Connecticut, Westport, the next city up the line, is about as far out as most people will go. For the visitor, there's the usual museum with nature trails, rocks, etc., and to the south, Sherwood Island State Park, which offers picnicking, fishing, and swimming in Long Island Sound. Fact is, as you proceed along the coastal roads toward Rhode Island, you'll find access to the bathing beaches on the Sound only through state parks, and an occasional town beach that allows non-residents (for a fee). Most beachfront property is in private hands, and most shore towns close to New York City have closed their beaches to strangers because they were being overcrowded by carloads of people from the metropolitan area.

If you are driving this way in May, don't miss the Green at Greenfield Hill, a small village just outside Bridgeport. During this period, hundreds of dogwood trees put forth masses of pink and white flowers, and the effect is almost as breathtaking as the Potomac River Basin when the Japanese cherry trees are in bloom. Only distraction will be the hundreds of other cars, bumper to bumper, out for the same view.

The fact is, if you are touring Connecticut in spring, avoid the unscenic Turnpike, and either shun-pike on back roads, or use the Merritt Parkway system. Laurel, rhododendron, and dogwood blossoms in profusion along most of Connecticut roads make driving a visual pleasure. Even more spectacular is the fall display, when the forests of maples and other hardwood trees put on many-colored coats of scarlet, russet, yellow, and orange. But remember, in areas where the foliage extravaganza is best, you'll again encounter bumper-to-bumper traffic on weekends. It's well worth the effort.

Bridgeport, third major city in the state, is principally a manufacturing center with such plants as Remington Arms, Singer Sewing Machine (the first sewing machines in the world were made here), General Electric, and Dictaphone. The city's Museum of Art, Science, and Industry should be of special interest to space-age visitors. On display is a huge scale model of the moon, and you can see the spot where our Ranger rockets crashed. There also are scientific and mechanical models that children can work, and other exhibits.

P. T. Barnum, the circus man who immortalized the phrase "There's a sucker born every minute," made a large impact on Bridgeport. His elaborate mansion stands opposite Seaside Park, which was a gift of his to the town; he established the Barnum Institute of Science and History which features mementos of Jenny Lind, the Swedish Nightingale; clothes of Tom Thumb and his wife, the famous midget couple; and other things collected by Barnum during his colorful career. You may visit Tom Thumb's House at 956 North Avenue. A Bridgeport tour should include a visit to Beardsley Park Zoo, the "biggest little zoo in New England." The collection includes the only pair of dwarf mongoose on the east coast, two spotted palm civet, an animal that's part dog and part cat, a fine collection of predatory birds, an elephant called "Fatso," and a barnyard where children can feed the ducks and chickens through a wire fence.

The park also has a Shakespearean garden containing the various plants mentioned in Shakespeare's plays. Which leads us to an even more tangible expression of Connecticut's regard for the Bard of Avon: the beautiful American Shakespeare Festival Theatre at Stratford. (Follow the signs off the Parkway, the Turnpike, or US 1.)

The theater building itself, modeled after the Globe Theatre in London, is the setting each summer for a series of Shakespearean plays, with occasional works by other dramatists. The lovely setting of the theater on the Housatonic River invites playgoers to *al fresco* dining on the lawn before performances. Most people attending the performances come by car, but many of the yachting set converge on the theater by boat, putting in at a nearby marina or tying up at friends' docks. The Judson House, 967 Academy Hill, built in 1723 and now a museum with featured exhibits of clothing worn by the Colonists and dolls that amused their children, also is worth visiting while in Stratford.

The previous site reminds us to caution the reader a bit. The prime sightseeing attractions throughout the state of Connecticut are the many preserved old Colonial houses, many of them the original homes of historic persons. Many are open to the public, but only in what is generally regarded as the regular vacation season.

This can vary from early or late spring, through the summer into early, or late fall. Few of these buildings, whether operated as private museums, or as the headquarters of historical societies, are open during the winter months, a thought to keep in mind when planning an automobile trip around Connecticut.

Now, on to Milford, and to the next historic house. (If you cross the Housatonic River on the Merritt Parkway, on the left you look down on the giant Sikorsky Helicopter plant. The adjoining hard-top field usually has several of the machines parked there, and often you can see them lifting off and flying around.) Veer off at exit 54 for a tour of the Eels-Stow House (1669). It's now the home of the local historical society. During the Revolution, sick prisoners of war were nursed back to health here.

New Haven

From Milford it's a short drive east to New Haven, Connecticut's second city and a treasure trove of things to see, most of them connected in some way with Yale University.

First, the more conventional sights. While Hartford has its extensive collection of Colt revolvers, New Haven is proud of a gun made here that joined the six-shooter in winning the West—the famous Winchester repeating rifle. The development, from 1866 to the present, of the Winchester rifles is shown through models in the Gun Museum, 275 Winchester Avenue. In addition, there's a massive collection of 5,000 pieces of war and hunting equipment, ranging from guns of every variety to bullets, bayonets, and bandoliers. The fact is, Connecticut's output of weapons in every war has earned the state another nickname: "The Nation's Arsenal."

There's hardly a Connecticut town without a wildlife sanctuary, refuge, formal garden, or at the very least, a nature trail. New Haven is no exception. On Wintergreen Avenue, the West Rock Nature Center has a zoo, ponds, picnic area, trails—and the Judges' Cave. And therein lies a tale. The story is told on a plaque bolted to a boulder.

"Here, May 15th, 1661 and for some weeks thereafter, Edward Whalley and his son-in-law William Goffe, members of parliament, General Officers in the Army of the Commonwealth and signers of the death warrant of King Charles First found shelter and concealment from the officers of the Crown after the Restoration." Then the final sentence: "Opposition to tyrants is Obedience to God!"

The two men who had sent the king to his death had fled England when their leader, Cromwell, had been deposed and King Charles II mounted the throne. The cave is high up on West Rock.

Back now to town, where a sweeping midtown facelifting is underway, involving the elimination of slums and blighted streets, followed by the construction of modern buildings, all this in an attempt to keep the heart of the city alive and flourishing as the business center. In 1965, Macy's opened a large department store in the redeveloped area to give the project a solid boost. The new New Haven is rising close to its historic Green, laid out on 16 acres of land by the first citizens and graced by churches, a library, and the Federal Building, which houses the U.S. District Court, U.S. Attorney's Office, and other offices of the Federal Government.

If Connecticut has achieved a reputation as a gadget state, in good part the credit belongs to New Haven, where many of these useful devices were first invented. Fishhooks? The Egyptians used slivers of bamboo. In New Haven the steel fishhook was invented, and the first meat grinder, the first corkscrew, and the first steamboat. Even the first lollipop was stuck on a stick in New Haven. A very early model telephone, and telephones you'll be speaking into in the near future, are on exhibit at the Southern New England Telephone Company, 227 Church Street, while in the New Haven Colony Historical Society, 114 Whitney Avenue, you can see Eli Whitney's cotton gin and the desk Webster used while gathering together all those words.

New Haven's Schubert Theater, undistinguished architecturally, even worse inside, nonetheless attracts playgoers from all over the state and from New York City, for it is still one of the principal tryout houses for new plays. Chances are good you can catch what soon afterwards will be a hit on Broadway for much less than it will cost in the big city.

While New Haven's nearly 200,000 citizens go about the business of making things, close to the old Village Green some 8,000 transients, students at Yale University, go about the business of learning. Not large as universities go, Yale nonetheless is one of the greatest institutions of higher learning in the country. (Traditionally, the students and the "townies" get along badly, and there doesn't seem to be much that can be done to engender good feeling between them.)

The visitor should get an overall view of the university by taking a free guided tour; then, extra time can be spent in any one of Yale's excellent museums and libraries. There's the Art Gallery, with a collection of masterworks from days of antiquity to the present. Particularly prized are the samples from Greece and Rome, and for Americans, the original Jonathan Trumbull paintings of the Revolution. You'll see the same scenes in the Capitol at Washington, D.C., copies painted especially for the people of

America by Trumbull. Yale's Peabody Museum of Natural History ranks with the best in the country, while for those with more specialized interests, there are the Yale Collection of Musical Instruments, the Rare Book and Manuscript Library, and the Yale University Library, which stages regular exhibits but is noted particularly for its German, Babylonian, and Western American collections, not to mention a Gutenberg Bible, and documents and papers of Benjamin Franklin. Harkness Tower, in neo-gothic style, is a Yale landmark.

En route to Hartford

From New Haven, rejoin the Wilbur Cross Parkway and head north to Hartford. A few worthwhile stops may be made enroute. Old furnishings and documents are on display in the Jonathan Dickerman House, built in 1770 and maintained by the Hamden Historical Society. It's located at the entrance to Sleeping Giant State Park, largest in Connecticut, with more than 1,000 acres devoted to hiking, camping, and picnicking. There's an excellent view of the surrounding countryside from a tower atop Mount Carmel. Wallingford, up the road, is the home of both a great industrial combine—and a well-known school. Its industry is Wallace Silversmiths, founded in 1835 to process minerals dug out of the ground in Idaho (the mines may be visited when you are in Wallace, in that western state). Merged with International Silver of nearby Meriden, Wallace now is one of the country's top producers of silverware. The school is Choate, and you'll enjoy walking about the campus, which is located in the center of town. Among its distinguished graduates were John F. Kennedy and Adlai Stevenson.

The first place where the Episcopalians worshipped in Connecticut, the Moses Andrews Homestead (1760), is located at 424 West Main Street, in Meriden. It's under the aegis of the local historical society, and may be visited on Sundays, and by appointment.

From Meriden, you can shoot straight north to Hartford, or take a sidetrip to New Britain, the "hardware city," home of the Stanley Works and other factories that make small tools, appliances, and other gadgets that help keep the wheels of the country turning. Its Museum of American Art, which also has a natural history section for children, features the *Arts in Life in America* murals by Thomas Hart Benton.

There are several parks. Walnut Hill on West Main Street has an outstanding rose garden and an illuminated 97-foot War Memorial shaft, while Stanley Quarter Park, North Stanley Street, offers an eight-acre lake for swimming and an 18-hole public golf course. The downtown section of New Britain stands in no danger of being selected as the subject for a calendar picture.

And so, on to Hartford (See *Exploring Hartford* section).

West of Hartford

From Hartford, we'll now start on loops around the state that may zig and zag to take in points of interest. For the western loop, head out on State 44 (Albany Avenue), up over Avon Mountain and down into Avon. Greater Hartford's growing population, already living on most of the available land in the Connecticut Valley, is slowly but surely pushing up the mountain, and the most expensive and most fashionable estates are now perched on the mountainside with magnificent views of the city in the distance below.

Avon Old Farms, at the bottom of the hill as you come off the mountain, is one of the better restaurant-inns in the state, a statement which is cause for another word to the reader. As a rule, service in Connecticut restaurants, cafes, and inns is adequate. It would be stretching the point to call it friendly. All this dates back to Colonial days when the government decreed that inns be established at regular intervals throughout the state—the distance being determined by the number of miles stagecoaches could travel comfortably between stops. The result was that many people who had no interest in the business, farmers in particular, were forced into innkeeping. The Marquis de Chastellux, in his intriguing *Travels in North America in the Years 1780, 1781 and 1782,* complains of the bad service he received at the hands of Connecticut innkeepers. The Marquis had plenty of opportunity to judge. A top-ranking member of the staff of Count de Rochambeau, he alone of the key French officers was fluent in English. As a result, the Marquis was sent on numerous liaison missions to the command posts of Washington and his generals. Enroute from Newport, Rhode Island to the American headquarters, he passed frequently through Connecticut. And as he put it, "Travelers are there considered as bringing more trouble than money." Things have changed quite perceptibly since those days, and service has been improved vastly; but don't expect the free and easy familiarity of waiters and waitresses in the West, nor the expertise of waiters in the better New York restaurants. Many of the inns and taverns that dotted the state no longer operate. Some are museums, others have been torn down, but a surprising number have become private residences.

In Avon you may want to make a quick tour of the Avon Old

Farms School for boys, because the buildings so much resemble a small English school in the Cotswolds in the 15th century. There are no special events scheduled here for the public, but visitors are welcome and can arrange for guides at the Alumni Office.

From Avon, continue on State 44 through Canton, a small village with a lively art colony and home of a popular summer theater, to State 181, which leads into Peoples State Forest, popular in summer months for camping, hiking, fishing, and picnicking. (No swimming.) But the real goal here is Riverton, on State 20 on the other side of the park, where the Hitchcock Chair Factory, founded in 1818, is still making chairs modeled after the original design. Visitors can watch the "rushing" operation on the seats of the chairs through glass windows and you may purchase Hitchcock chairs and other Colonial reproductions in the salesroom.

Continue south on State 8 through Winsted, a nondescript town known to sightseers only for its annual Laural Blossom Festival each spring. The same road brings you to Torrington, an industrial city with two small claims to fame: John Brown, the fanatical abolitionist, was born just north of town near State 4; while on State 8, toward Winsted, Miss Gail Borden concocted the world's first condensed milk. At Christmastime, a popular Santa's village draws parents and children from a wide area.

Litchfield and Its Hills

From the Torrington valley, State 25 now starts to climb sharply into the Litchfield hills, regarded by many as the most beautiful section of Connecticut. A drive of six miles brings you to the Litchfield Green, dominated by the beautiful white-steepled Congregational Church (a reconstruction of the original). While the lovely Green itself is a pleasant enough contrast to Torrington's midtown drabness, the two pearls of Litchfield are its North and South streets. On both sides of these two elm-tree lined streets are some of the most magnificent Colonial houses in America. No visitor fails to gasp with surprise and delight at the sight of these elegant white clapboarded homes with traditional black or green shutters. The area has been declared an Historic Site by the state, and no exterior changes may now be made; nor may owners drastically alter interiors by dividing big homes into busy rooming houses.

At 1173 South Street stands the Tapping Reeve House, one of Litchfield's prizes. But the eye of history is on another building on the same property, a small white structure that was America's first law school. Visitors can see the desks at which many distinguished American jurists studied, men like Aaron Burr (Tapping Reeve's brother-in-law) and John C. Calhoun, both Vice Presidents of the United States; former Supreme Court justices Henry Baldwin, Leir Woodbury, and Ward Hunt, six cabinet members, more than 100 congressmen, 28 senators, and numerous governors and chief justices of states. All these, and others, went forth from a one-room building in a remote Connecticut village.

The birthplaces of two more famous Americans, Harriet Beecher Stowe and Henry Ward Beecher, are located on North Street.

It might be wise at this time to check into an old inn and make Litchfield your headquarters for tours of this corner of the state. First trip will take you southwest on State 25 to Bantam, where a quick left on 209 brings you to Bantam Lake, largest natural lake in the state, and a popular summer playground. While there is much private property on the lakeside, there's a public beach; and at least half the lake is bordered by the 3,500-acre White Memorial Foundation, a bird and animal sanctuary that invites the public to hike, swim (at Sands Beach), picnic, camp, and ride its 27 miles of bridal paths. There's a launching ramp for boats, or you may rent rowboats.

Continue around the lake on 209 and turn south on State 61, which will land you in Bethlehem, a pleasant rural community of old Colonial homes, including the Bellamy House (1738), one of the country's first theological seminaries. In this building and in a nearby house, the Rev. Joseph Bellamy taught classes on religion. One of his pupils was Henry Ward Beecher of Litchfield. The public spotlight was focused on Bethlehem in 1948 when the story of the Regina Laudis Abbey was made into a popular movie starring Loretta Young and entitled, *Come to the Stable.* Today, visitors flock to the nunnery to see its magnificent crêche with 65 wooden figurines carved in the Sorrentine style. The crêche, located in a barn, is open from May through the Christmas season.

Washington, a Colonial Jewel

Now backtrack north on 61 and turn left on State 109. Drive southwest, and follow the signs to Washington. You've come here just to look at a jewel of a Colonial village—exquisite white houses around a small green, peopled with old elms. Here, as in many of the little towns in this part of the state, you'll often come upon one of the many prep schools that draw their enrollment from every state in the Union, and many foreign countries. The lovely settings of the beautiful schools cause many an adult to wish he were young again.

Otherwise, turn the car around and head north again, this time on State 47 to New Preston, and follow the signs to Lake Waramaug, where its spacious state park has facilities for camping, boating, and swimming. Billboards on the roads approaching the lake announce that on its shores are "Eight Friendly Inns."

From New Preston, it's a short ride south on State 25 to New Milford. Rockhounds may be able to obtain permission to poke around in the abandoned mica quarry near Merryall for samples of columbite, gem garnet, aquamarines, beryl, and other stones. Indian history buffs will be delighted to know that here, too, they tell that familiar old tale of the Indian Princess who plunged over a waterfall to "a watery grave" for any one of several reasons: either because her heart was broken, someone she didn't love was after her, or she had a white lover and Daddy didn't approve. In this case, the alleged incident took place in the Housatonic Gorge, just below New Milford on State 133, and the princess in question (you never hear of just ordinary Indian girls jumping over falls—just princesses) was Lilinoah, only daughter of Chief Waramaug. She was joined in the jump by her white lover, a man whose name historians failed to record. The cliff, naturally, is known as Lover's Leap.

After you've had your picnic lunch in the gorge, return to State 7 and continue on south toward Danbury. A spine of hills covered with trees accompanies you along the right side of the road. Beyond the hills lies Candlewood Lake, man-made and largest lake of all in the state. Again, much of the shore property is in private hands, but there are public marinas and beaches.

Danbury, once the country's hat city (not one hat company remains) is the scene each October of a country fair that's known throughout the East. The many permanent buildings on the fairgrounds can be seen from your car while driving on I-84. Danbury was one of the cities burned by British raiding parties during the Revolution. Several buildings, now part of the Scott-Fanton Museum and Historical Society, escaped the torch and may be visited. Hunting Hall, one of them, has art shows and displays of toys and dolls from all over the world. Before heading north around the lake, drop down State 58, through Bethel (birthplace of the great circus impressario Phineas T. Barnum) to Putnam Memorial State Park. During the winter of 1778–79, New Hampshire and Connecticut regulars under the command of General Israel Putnam suffered from cold, snow, and lack of provisions. Two blockhouses and a museum recall the hardships that earned this tract the title, "Valley Forge of Connecticut."

From Danbury, drive up along the western shore of Candlewood Lake to Squantz Pond State Park, which offers boating, swimming, fishing, and picnicking.

Just past Gaylordsville, after State 39 merges into State 7, you may cross the Housatonic River via Bulls Bridge, one of the few remaining covered bridges in Connecticut. The fact is, although covered bridges originated in the East, most have either rotted away or been replaced by more modern bridges, and today the state with the most covered bridges in the country is Indiana. At Kent Furnace, up the road, you can clamber around the ruins of what once was a major iron foundry, while still further up 7 is Kent Falls State Park, a 275-acre preserve with a beautiful 80-foot fall, over which no Indian princess ever plunged. (Too high, probably.)

Cornwall and Mohawk Mountain

Next stop is Cornwall; turn off 7 onto Route 4, and see still another classic Colonial town that belongs on a calendar or post-card. Its local bookstore gathers rare books and documents from all over the world—and has customers all over the world. Cornwall has attracted artists, writers, critics, and poets and is a delightful, congenial community. (Poet Mark Van Doren, critic Lewis Gannett and others live here.) The fact is, as you drive through this northwestern section of the state, you will find many names on rural post boxes that should be familiar to you. Many famous people work in New York and come up to Connecticut for the weekend. Others, such as William L. Shirer, live here year-round.

The far northwestern corner of Connecticut is dotted with lakes, mountains, state parks, and forests, and old Colonial towns with charming inns. Each of them usually has a historical society of some interest, or the ruins of an early forge or foundry, a ravine, a gorge, or a hiking trail. If you have time, you can continue your explorations in this area—and in summertime, perhaps, pass up into Massachusetts to attend one of the many cultural events that are staged there throughout the season: dance, art shows, antique shows, auctions, and most notably, the Tanglewood Festival.

But to continue our Connecticut tour from Cornwall, drive on State 4 into Mohawk Mountain State Park, a popular ski area with tows, lifts, ski school, and the usual shops and warming house. Since the area is in the lower snowbelt of New England, snow-making machines supplement nature. The tows and lifts do not operate in summer, when picnicking and hiking are popular.

Little Goshen, a farming village on State 4, has a pretty main street lined with white clapboarded houses. Tipping Rock, an 8-ton boulder, a calling card of the glaciers that may be moved slowly back and forth without falling from its perch, is on private property. State 63 will take you from Goshen back to Litchfield to complete your loop tour of this section of Connecticut. During your trip you've seen little industry, the absence of which, of course, is one of the charms of the area. Big farms abound here—in fact, half of all Connecticut's dairy farms are in the Litchfield area.

Aside from the farmers, who then lives in Litchfield? There's a sprinkling of executives from factories in nearby Torrington, the retired rich—and the so-called "summer residents," the title applied to the writers, artists, and businessmen who only live part-time in their Colonial homes.

Here, in this part of the country, democracy in its purest form, as practiced in the early days of the country, is still a way of life. Rules, regulations, and ordinances are proposed by selectmen, but approval must be obtained from the voters assembled in traditional town meetings, where each resident has his say. Visitors may watch a town meeting in action from the balcony or the rear.

But now, get back on the road. There is still much to see in the Constitution State. Connecticut residents don't much fancy the other nickname, Nutmeg State, because it recalls the time when Yankee peddlers were palming off wooden nutmegs on unsuspecting customers in place of the real thing. (Connecticut Yankees pride themselves as shrewd traders, but they don't like to be reminded of the time when they were.)

Clockmaking Towns

From Litchfield, head out east on State 254, which angles down through Thomaston, Terryville, and Bristol. This is clock country, with two of the towns taking their names from pioneer clockmakers. Seth Thomas started his clock works in Thomaston in 1812 after learning the trade with Eli Terry, who patented a clock with wooden works that became hugely successful. In Terryville, where Terry started ticking, one of his original wooden clocks still tells time in the tower of the Congregational Church. But the real clock bonanza is in Bristol, the next city on the route. Here, more than 600 clocks, some dating back to 1790, are on display in the American Clock & Watch Museum. The timepieces range from big grandfather clocks to a tiny watch, imbedded in a coin. Bristol Public Library is proud of its collection of 3,000 Indian relics. Some of the pottery—bowls, jugs, and dishes—were fashioned from foliated talc.

From Bristol, which also has a large General Motors factory, turn south on State 229. Lake Compounce, on the right, has a commercial public beach with a roller coaster and other amusements. Join up with Interstate 84 and glide into Waterbury, the city that copper built. Its Mattatuck Historical Society, 119 West Main Street, has Whistler etchings, plus the usual collection of pioneer relics found in museums of this type. Children enjoy playing druggist in the miniature apothecary shop of its Junior Museum. Some of the large copper foundries stage regular tours. Aside from these attractions, there is not much reason to tarry in Waterbury. State 8, southward to the shore, passes through Naugatuck State Forest to Beacon Falls, where there's a covered bridge, and a ravine for hikers. Old home buffs will want to visit the unusually large saltbox house in Ansonia built in 1748 by Reverend Richard Mansfield, first minister of the local Episcopal church, who served his parishioners 72 years. At Derby, pick up State 34 and follow it back through New Haven to the Connecticut Turnpike—and you are now ready to loop around the eastern half of the state.

From New Haven get back on the Turnpike and head east. Turn off at East Haven for the Trolley Museum, where you can give your youngsters a chance to ride a vehicle that has disappeared from most city streets in the country. Old-fashioned streetcars that were pulled by horses, the first electric cars, and all models in between, up to the most modern trolleys with cushioned seats and airflow design, are on display.

At Branford, next city on the pike, you may veer off, and in the summer ride the mailboat around and through the Thimble Islands. On Money Island, legend has it that Captain Kidd buried some treasure. The islands themselves are private property.

Old Guilford

Guilford is a town of history and beauty. The Henry Whitfield House, 1634, is believed to be the oldest stone house in the state. Now a museum, it has an excellent exhibit of antiques, and in the yard, an herb garden is replanted every year. The village has 150 old houses of various designs on original sites, many of them on the green. Among other buildings of interest are the Hyland House, (1639), Whitfield Street, whose five big old fireplaces are a feature, and the Thomas Griswold House and Farmer's Museum, with plows, rakes, hoes, and other tools used by the first farmers.

Guilford's Pinchbeck Greenhouse is 1,200 feet of glass, longest in the country. It's devoted principally to growing roses. The Congregational Church (1829) on the green is a perfect example of Greek Revival architecture.

Madison, five miles east, also has a beautiful Congregational Church on the village green. After you've looked at the church, however, get back on the road. Madison's fashionable beach and beach clubs are private.

At Hammonasset State Park, just east of Madison, you'll be welcome. Covering over 1,000 acres, the park has a long sandy beach, not as wide as those in New Jersey but more than adequate, a pavilion for picnics, fireplaces, and campsites. As at all the beaches along the Sound, the surf is gentle because Long Island itself, which stretches almost all the way to New London, acts as a giant breakwater for Connecticut.

Go back to the Turnpike, and on to Clinton for a walk through the Stanton House, where Lafayette spent a night during the Revolution. The building is located at 53 East Main Street and has the usual collection of antique goodies.

Old Saybrook, at the mouth of the Connecticut River, is a flourishing summer resort, a center for boating and fishing. The United States' first submarine was built here during the Revolution by David Bushnell and carried one man, who propelled the craft by hand. It was used against the *HMS Eagle* without much success. A Captain Morgan, a friend of Charles Dickens, lived in the Richmond William Hart House, now the Old Saybrook Inn. Morgan reputedly served as the model for Dickens' fictional Captain Jorgen in *A Message from the Sea.*

It's time to cross the Connecticut River; soon you will also bid a short farewell to the Turnpike. At Exit 72, turn right for Rocky Neck State Park, another oceanside beach where you can picnic, swim, and take the sun. The New Haven Railroad tracks separate the beach from the parking lot, and during the steam engine days bathers could count on a daily quota of fine coal ashes. Diesel engines have changed all that, and the trains whipping past now are a source of amusement to train buffs.

Pick up State 156 and continue to Niantic. Forget Black Point. It is private, with cottages owned mostly by Hartford area residents. Crescent Beach, a small but charming beach also frequented by Hartford folk, rents rooms for the day, so a visitor might find the chance here to take a swim on a hot summer day.

Niantic Bay, which you cross on a bridge that carried 156, is a snug harbor. You'll see many boats bobbing about at anchor or in the marinas. Niantic Bay scallops are a Connecticut delight, and as can be expected, may be sampled at most of the excellent seafood restaurants and inns that lie along the shore. In this long resort area that stretches from Greenwich to Rhode Island, you'll also find numerous art galleries that stage exhibits during the summer, and summer theaters. (Old Lyme has a flourishing art colony; also several fine old sea captains' homes.)

At Waterford, turn right onto State 213 for a visit to the Italian-style mansion in Harkness Memorial State Park. On exhibit are 900 life-size bird paintings in water color by the renowned Brooklyn-born artist, Rex Brasher. The formal gardens are interesting.

From here, it's but a few miles to Ocean Beach Park, maintained by the City of New London, but open to all visitors. Modeled after Jones Beach, on a much smaller scale, the beach nonetheless is spacious, and deservedly is one of the most popular in the eastern part of the state. The present pavilions, restaurants, recreation areas, and dressing facilities were built in the late 'thirties after the devastating hurricane of 1938 destroyed the boardwalk and most of the private cottages.

New London

New London, one of the earliest towns in Connecticut, has always looked to the sea for its sustenance. Along with Nantucket, New Bedford, and other famous New England ports, New London put forth upon the seas whaling ships that penetrated deep into the South Pacific in search of the elusive giants of the sea. New London whalers were in that hapless fleet, too, that was caught near Alaska during the Civil War by a dauntless Confederate raider. Most of the unarmed whalers, raked by cannon from the Rebel warship, were destroyed. It was the beginning of the end for the New England whaling business. The death blow came shortly after the Civil War when Americans started pumping oil out of the ground in Pennsylvania, and whale oil for lamps no longer was needed. (A limited amount of whale hunting still goes on today, mostly by the British, Russians, Japanese, and the Scandinavians.) During the heyday of whaling, however, fortunes were made and today in New London, you can see the luxurious mansions erected by Yankee sea captains when their ships came in. A small Whalers Museum is located in the Mariner's Savings Bank at 224 State Street.

Continuing its long tradition as a seafaring town, New London is the home of the U.S. Coast Guard Academy, one of our country's four military colleges. Visitors may tour the grounds, some of the buildings, and when it is in port, the *Eagle,* a bark used during summer months for cadet training cruises. The beautiful sailing vessel is quite a sight when it leaves the mouth of the Thames and heads out to sea. A former German ship named after the notorious Nazi, Horst Wessel, the bark was confiscated by the Americans as a war prize, renovated, and renamed. Battalion reviews attract visitors to the Academy during winter school months.

In the spring, the crew regatta on the Thames at New London, pitting Harvard against Yale, is a social as well as athletic event, surpassed only by the annual fall meeting of the same two schools on the football field. As might be expected, the New London County Historical Society is itself located in an historic building, the Shaw Mansion (1756), Bank and Blinman streets, a large stone building that attracted Washington and Nathan Hale during the Revolution when it was headquarters for the state's naval office. Other old buildings worth a visit are the Joshua Hempstead House (1678), the Deshon-Allyn House (1829), the Old Town Mill (1650, rebuilt in 1712), and the Lyman Allyn Museum, 100 Mohegan Ave., which is particularly proud of its early Chinese ceramics.

Where California has the Redwoods, those aged forest giants, Connecticut can boast only a few stands of virgin forest, one of them in New London. Here you can walk under the leaves of trees that are 400 years old in the 70-acre Connecticut Arboretum, across the street from Connecticut College for Women, a small girls' school not as well known as Vassar and Smith, but on a par with them scholastically and socially.

Groton, across the Thames River, is part of Greater New London. Headquarters of the North Atlantic submarine fleet is located in its vast U.S. Naval Base. The base is not open to visitors, but visitors enjoy watching the big subs passing up and down the river. For the history and lore of underwater craft, the Submarine Library and Museum, located in Gillmore Hall of the Naval Base, has ample research material. The library may be visited for research purposes by appointment. It traces the history of subs, from the replica of the glass barrel that Alexander the Great used for underwater observation in 332 B.C. to Admiral Hyman Rickover's first nuclear sub. There's also a working periscope. Most modern-day submarines are made at Groton's Electric Boat Division of General Dynamics. Groton's only old house worth visiting is the Ebenezer Avery Home, a makeshift hospital for wounded Continental soldiers during the Revolution. The 135-foot-high Groton Monument, offering a sweeping view of the harbor, marks the spot where American soldiers in Fort Griswold surrendered to traitor Benedict Arnold and his British cohorts, then were treacherously cut down to the last man. The last school in which Nathan Hale taught before going off to the war, and immortality, is located at Hempstead and Richards streets in New London.

Just beyond New London, the lusty, gusty days of sailing before the mast are recalled at Mystic Seaport Museum, one of the outstanding exhibitions of its kind in the country. Children particularly will love clambering about the old boats, climbing on cannons, and examining the numerous models and figureheads in the formal museum building. But Mystic is more than just an artfully arranged collection of relics and artifacts in a building; rather, it is a vivid depiction of what a typical seafaring village might have looked like in the early 19th century. Here on the shores of the Mystic River, there once was a shipbuilding firm, but that's all. The buildings you see today that line the cobblestoned street along the waterfront have been erected by Mystic Museum; some are original buildings moved from other parts of the state. Others, such as the tavern, are reproductions of buildings that certainly would have been found in a village of this sort.

Wonderful Mystic Seaport

Highlight of the museum for most visitors is the *Charles W. Morgan,* last of the great wooden whaling ships, and typical of the whalers that once sailed out of New England ports to the far corners of the world. The Morgan, now anchored in concrete, sailed for an incredible 80 years and during its life earned $2,000,000. You can climb about its decks, peer into the vats in which the blubber was melted down, then go 'tween decks and marvel that men could live for years at a time in such cramped and uncomfortable quarters. The year 1966 was designated by the Museum to commemorate the 125th anniversary of the Morgan's maiden voyage.

The *Joseph Conrad,* which is tied up to the docks, is a steel-hulled vessel and one of the last of the square riggers ever built. For a time it sailed under the command of Captain Alan Villers, the author-sailor who was master of *Mayflower II* during its commemorative voyage to the United States from Plymouth, England a few years ago. The Conrad is used as a training ship. A recent addition to the museum is a planetarium, with special performances that illustrate the art of navigation by the stars. Children will also enjoy shopping for licorice and other old-fashioned candies out of barrels in the stores.

The oldest bank building in Connecticut is located in Stonington. A unique flag with 16 stars and 16 stripes that was carried at the Battle of Stonington (1814) is on display. Main Street is one of the most beautiful in New England with its gracious old homes. A fascinating small museum of fishing gear, 19th-century portraits, weapons, and whaling equipment is maintained in The Old Stonington Lighthouse on the Point. If you go this far, retrace your steps and head north on any side road to Interstate 95, where you now will connect either with State 12, or State 32 across the river.

Turn north toward Norwich for the start of a loop around the eastern part of Connecticut, a section more rugged and less populated than the rest of the state. The fact is, airline pilots who regularly fly the commercial air routes up and down the East Coast of the United States report the northeastern part of Connecticut is the only real break in the megalopolis that stretches from Boston to Washington. Below their wings in this area are few lights, mostly darkness. And it is actually a betwixt and between area. In early days the main routes of commerce ran from Boston through Hartford to New Haven and west to New York. Industry grew up along the roads and the rivers in the central, western, and coastal areas, while eastern Connecticut cities fell asleep, and never quite woke up. Yet this part of the state has its special attractions, historic sites, recreation areas, and remembrances of days when the fierce Pequot Indians held sway here over all the other Indian tribes. Many state parks and forests are in this part of Connecticut.

First stop is in the area of Montville, rich in the lore of Uncas chief of the Mohegans who was born a Pequot. Outsiders, the Pequots invaded Connecticut and conquered the local Indians, then fearing the threat of the white settlers, turned upon them. The Indians were provoked. Misunderstandings also arose. The end result, however, war and massacre, was the same here just as it would be throughout the rest of the country in later years wherever the white man put down roots and squeezed the Indian off his lands. When the fighting had ended and the power of the Indians was broken, this spot would be remembered as Connecticut's bloodiest battleground. Reminders of Uncas are everywhere: at huge Cochegan Rock, a 6,000-ton mass of granite where legend says Uncas used to hide; Fort Hill, Uncas' stronghold; and Uncas Hill in Mohegan, where the cellar of Uncas' cabin can be seen. Uncas himself, it should be noted, disagreed with the Pequots and became "a friend to the whites." Near the Mohegan Congregational Church is a small museum of Indian relics, the Tantaquidgeon Indian Museum. In the yard, you may enjoy inspecting the frames of both a long house and a round house, the type of dwelling common to eastern Indians, who did not live in the buffalo hide teepee favored by the western Indians. After a day of sightseeing and exploring, stop for a swim and a picnic in Fort Shantok State Park. (Only the outline of the trenches of Fort Shantok remain.)

Norwich

Next stop is the city of Norwich, one of the earliest settlements in the state, that shares with its sister cities the unique Connecticut distinction of being first in the design of a small item that moved the world.

In Norwich, it was the lowly steel nail, cut for the first time in this country by an unknown, unsung blacksmith sometime before the Revolution. From then on, fastening boards together with wooden pegs became a thing of the past—until generations much later decided that nails were commonplace, and pegs were charming, sophisticated, and chic. After the Revolutionary War, Americans couldn't wait to cover what they thought were unsightly ceiling beams with plaster, and to move into homes with small fireplaces and efficient iron stoves. Today, of course, those old Colonial houses with the exposed beams and huge walk-in fireplaces are in most demand and command the highest prices.

Historic buildings in the Norwich area include the Joseph Carpenter Silversmith Shop (1772) in Norwichtown, still furnished as it was when Mr. Carpenter plied his trade; Rockwell House, 42 Rockwell Street, which has a fine collection of antiques; and the Leffingwell Inn, 344 Washington Street. Built in 1675, this once very active inn is now a museum of Colonial times. Continental officers often met here to plot war plans. Washington himself was a frequent guest. An excellent museum, particularly noted for its Indian and Japanese collections, is located on the grounds of Norwich Free Academy, an outstanding private high school. A memorial near the academy honors Samuel Reid, the soldier who in 1818 designed the present form of the Stars and Stripes.

The Yantic and Shetucket rivers join at Norwich to become the Thames River, which then flows southward to the sea. Indian sachems are buried in a special graveyard set aside by President Andrew Johnson and marked by the Uncas Monument on Sachem Street.

Near the Yantic River Falls is Indian Leap, so named because the Mohegan Indians drove the Narragansetts over the cliff in 1643 during the Battle of Great Plain. The rose gardens in a nearby park are worth seeing.

An express link will take you back to the Connecticut Turnpike where you turn right, heading first north and then east until Exit 85, where you turn right onto State 138 and proceed to Voluntown. From here, roads radiate into Pachaug State Forest, a 22,000-acre lake and forest preserve, the largest in the state. Little known to most Connecticut residents from other parts of the state, it's inked in brightly on the maps of fishermen. Collectors of odd and irrelevant bits of information will want to visit the Line Meeting House on the border between Ekonk and Sterling, off State 49. A bride and a groom cannot be married facing the pulpit in this building because the line between Connecticut and Rhode Island runs through the house and legally would cast them asunder. Many couples still enjoy the novelty of being married in this building. If the bride and groom are united on the Connecticut side, the marriage is legal. However, couples who take their vows on the Rhode Island side of the room then must repair to the nearby church in order to be legally wed in that state.

At Exit 90, leave the Connecticut Turnpike and continue on to State 52, to Old Furnace State Park where you can picnic, fish, or swim. Before reaching Danielson (an industrial town of no special interest except that one of the early mills was founded by a Tiffany, member of the family that became better known for its New York City jewelry store), turn off left on State 6 to Brooklyn.

We are now coming into Israel Putnam country, home of the doughty farmer-soldier who served the state and the country so well during the Revolutionary War, and who managed to surround himself with legends and fanciful stories which, if not true in their entirety, had strong kernels of truth.

Brooklyn, four miles west of Danielson, is the hometown of General Putnam. On the Green, surrounded by pleasant Colonial homes, is the town meetinghouse. Putnam Farm, north of the village near Pomfret, is the setting for a favorite tale about Putnam. As the story goes, Putnam was plowing his fields behind his large shingled farmhouse when a rider arrived with news of the battles of Lexington and Concord. Forthwith, the resolute Putnam dropped his plow in the furrow, stopped at his house just long enough to grab a musket, and rode off to war. Near Abington, west of Pomfret, Wolf Den State Park was the locale for an earlier feat of prowess by Putnam. Here, legend has it, Putnam grappled with a wolf in its lair with his bare hands—and won. If General Israel Putnam seems a bit larger than life, he did have some very lifelike problems, the same sort of problems that plagued the Montagues and Capulets—with a difference. Back in Brooklyn stands the Godfrey Malbone homestead, a lovely old home built in 1750. Malbone and Putnam, it seems, argued with each other violently, on many subjects: politics, religion and other matters. Later Putnam's handsome son, Daniel, married a Malbone girl and they lived happily ever after.

From Abington, two routes are open to the traveler now bound for Storrs, the seat of the University of Connecticut's main campus. The first choice, State 44 west, connects with 44A, which leads you to Mansfield, where America's first silk mill was built in 1829. There's nothing to see here, however, for Henry Ford scooped it up along with numerous other historic American buildings from other parts of the country and moved it to his Greenfield Village Museum at Dearborn, Michigan. Signs point to the university, a small "cow college" i.e. an agricultural school at the onset of World War II.

Today it's a bustling, ever-growing university with many faculties. The campus buildings are set on landscaped rolling hills, with ponds and streams between, an altogether pleasing effect. The agricultural school, in fact, is one of the oldest and most respected in the country. Branches of the university now can be found in cities throughout the state. (Most recent branch to open is located in Torrington.)

If you choose to drive to Storrs from Abington by the alternate route, drive south on State 97 and then follow US 6 to Willimantic, and turn right on 195 to Storrs. State 97 takes you through Hampton, where a charming story is told of the bride Sally Bowers, left alone and without a house, when her husband marched off with General Putnam to join the Continentals. The ingenious bride convinced a peg-legged carpenter, the only man left in the village, to supervise, whereupon Sally enlisted the aid of women in town and together they nailed, pinned and raised the roof. "The House That Women Built," as it is now known, is a mile north of the village on Route 97 and is still in use as a private residence.

Downtown Willimantic, a thread-making city, will never be selected by a discriminating artist for a postcard. Hurry through it to Storrs.

From the university, resume a westerly course on State 44A. Near Coventry you can turn off south for a visit to the homestead of the family of Nathan Hale, Washington's spy who was hanged by the British in Manhattan and buried in an unknown grave. The body of his brother Richard is in a grave on St. Eustatia where he died of consumption; and, while both brothers were separated in death by so many miles, they were united in the heart of their father, Deacon Hale, who expressed the love he had for his two sons on a cenotaph he erected in burial ground in Coventry, now known as the Nathan Hale Cemetery. The Revolutionary War collection in the Hale house is of interest.

Jonathan Trumbull of Lebanon

From here pick up State 87 for a short jaunt that will take you on a southeast tack to Lebanon, a village with a classic green—and a house of history. Here lived Jonathan Trumbull, a towering figure in the Revolution who won this praise from Washington: "But for Jonathan Trumbull, the war could not have been carried to a successful conclusion." Trumbull was governor of the Connecticut Colony when the war broke out; his sympathies were with the Revolutionaries, and he lent his prestige, his money, and his efforts to further the war effort. From a building near his house, the "War Office" of the Revolution, Trumbull marshalled supplies, men, and war materiel to keep the Army fighting. So efficient and effective was this man, that Washington often was heard to say, "Let us consult Brother Jonathan." According to the Connecticut Historical Commission, Trumbull succored Washington's starving troops at Valley Forge when he mounted a cattle drive of 300 steers to that sorely pressed winter encampment from Connecticut. Trumbull's house and the "War Office" may be visited. Trumbull became first Governor of the State of Connecticut. His son was a noted Colonial artist.

State 16 meanders southwest toward Colchester, where the restored Nathaniel Foote House, on the south side of Norwich Avenue and originally built in 1702, has an interesting exhibit of Colonial relics. For Hartford residents, Colchester always had been the roadblock on the way to the beaches in the New London–Niantic area. Between Colchester and New London there was a famous series of curves, ten in all, and back in the 'thirties children looked forward to counting them. On the seventh curve—or was it the ninth?—the features of a huge fish were painted onto a boulder that had the shape of a fishhead. Blasters and bulldozers have done their work—the ten curves, and the fish, are gone, and a superhighway from Hartford is inching its way past Colchester.

Before continuing on toward Middletown, you might want to take a sidetrip up into Salmon River State Forest. The drive along the river is beautiful, and you'll see the Comstock Covered Bridge, one of the few left in Connecticut. (The bridge is closed to traffic.) South of Salmon River lies Day Pond State Park, with facilities for swimming and fishing, and, of course, picnicking. At Winchester, State 149 breaks off and a short drive south brings you into the Moodus Hills, a summer vacation area with a sprinkling of resorts similar to those in the Catskills of New York and the Poconos of Pennsylvania.

Go back up on 149 and pick up 16 again for the last lap of your tour. Opposite Middletown, on the east side of the river, is Portland. From its brownstone quarries came most of the stone for the brownstone houses of New York City. Rockhounds flock to the nearby Strickland Quarry from all over the country, carefully chipping out beautiful specimens from the wide variety of minerals.

Middletown, on the west bank of the Connecticut, has several historic homes and an excellent historical society, but its major attraction is Wesleyan University, another of the top Ivy League schools. The home of the Honors College, built in 1828 by the Russell family, was one of the grandest mansions in the state. The General Mansfield House has the usual collection of furniture, but is only open on Wednesdays and by appointment.

For space-age scientists, the Wesleyan Olin Library is a shrine, for here are kept the original manuscripts of Albert Einstein's Theory of Relativity. The Davidson Art Center exhibits excellent examples of European and American art, while fossilized prehistoric footprints are on display in the Wesleyan Museums. The campus overlooks the town and the river. Once the largest city in the state, Middletown was soon surpassed by Hartford, New Haven, and Bridgeport. Today its major industry is the manufacture of marine hardware.

From Middletown, cross the Connecticut again for a tour down along the eastern bank. You'll pass by a succession of state parks, most of which offer swimming, boating, and fishing, until you reach East Haddam. Here a non-profit foundation has restored a most unusual building, the old Goodspeed Opera House, and performances are staged throughout the summer, reliving the days when Hartford opera lovers boarded Colonel Goodspeed's steamers at the foot of State Street and enjoyed an excursion down the Connecticut River to watch presentations put on by opera companies brought up from New York City. The church bell at St. Stephen's church was brought to this country from Spain and is believed to be the oldest in the country.

State 82, which runs east a bit before turning southwest, now leads to the Gillette Castle State Park, where one of the few authentic castles erected in America still stands. It was built by William Gillette, the actor who made a fortune playing over and over again the role of Sherlock Holmes.

Had you chosen to drive down along the Connecticut River on the west bank you could, had it struck your fancy, stopped at Shopboard Rock, on Route 9 past Higganum, a large boulder that got its name, according to the fanciful tale, after a tailor spread out a bolt of cloth on its flat top and, from it cut a suit. Why the rock top was more satisfactory than the work table in the tailor's shop goes unexplained.

Regardless of which side of the river you drive along, however, Gillette Castle is a must, and if necessary, near here, you can cross the Connecticut on the Hadlyme-Chester ferry.

Now, for the last leg of your Connecticut tour. Ivoryton on State 9 is an art center and the home of a summer theater that features top Broadway, movie, and TV stars. Head back to the river for a slight detour to Essex, one of the loveliest towns in the state, with a bustling marina and a beautiful old inn. This general area is fashionable with wealthy folk, and many sail up the Connecticut to Essex in very expensive yachts or sailboats.

From Essex, return to the Connecticut Turnpike. Turn west along the shore if you are returning to New York; or turn east and pass into Rhode Island to visit its sights, or continue on to fabled and fabulous Cape Cod.

The tour has not touched every town, nor has it led you through every state park or scenic area. There is much else of interest in Connecticut. In the western portion, for example, you might at some point want to rearrange your itinerary and take in the historic Glebe House at Woodbury, a town many feel is one of the most beautiful in the country. Or there's Redding, with its broad beautiful main street lined with elms. Roxbury, up near New Milford, is the home of Arthur Miller and a covey of kindred souls—writers, artists, and musicians. There are other fishing grounds, fairs to visit, museums, Indian caves, ravines, and waterfalls. All await the curious explorer on other trips around the state of Connecticut.

AROUND THE STATE

HOTELS AND MOTELS. Several excellent hotels and motor inns have been opened in recent years in downtown, redeveloped sections of Connecticut's largest cities. This trend of providing hotel accommodations in the central business areas, near the traditional green, is being intensified with the construction of interstate highways through or near the major cities. Meanwhile, new motor inns and motels, which have more handy facilities than old city hotels, have been rising in the outskirts of cities and near country towns.

Connecticut now boasts more than 10,000 rooms in various categories. Excellent motor inns, motor lodges and motor hotels line the Connecticut Turnpike, Merritt Parkway, Interstate 84, Interstate 91, and the Berlin Turnpike, or Wilbur Cross Highway.

Because of the competitive nature of roadside establishments, a goodly percentage now feature attractive dining facilities and lounges, as well as the swimming pools, which can be used only a couple of months each year. Many motor hotels also have large conference and meeting rooms for conventions, seminars, and conferences.

Popular resorts are found in the Moodus section of eastern Connecticut, which resembles a miniature Catskill area during July and August.

Long-term lodging facilities and cabins can be found in the more modest surroundings of such picturesque regions as Lake Waramaug, Bantam Lake, and the Twin Lakes of Litchfield County.

BRANFORD

Reasonable

Branford Motor Inn. Small. Swimming pool, TV, free continental breakfast. Near New Haven and Yale.

On US 1, ½ mi. e. of Exit 55, ½ mi. w. of Exit 56 (tel. 488–5442).

MacDonald's Motel. TV in some rooms, radio in others. Restaurant & cocktail lounge across street.

US 1, Boston Post Rd., few ft. off Exit 56 (tel. 488–4381).

Sunset Motel. Small but with kitchenettes and restaurant. TV in each room.

US 1 at Exit 54 & 55 (tel. 488–4035).

BRIDGEPORT (Fairfield)

First Class

Fairfield Motor Inn. A medium-sized tastefully decorated motel with seasonal rates May–Sept. Restaurant, room service, cocktail lounge. Swimming pool, spacious grounds with putting green.

417 Post Rd. in Fairfield (tel. 255–0491).

Reasonable

Bridgeport Motor Inn. Medium-sized with family rates. Air-conditioned rooms with TV & telephones. Three conference rooms. Dining facilities on premises, room service.

King's Highway, US 1A, Exit 24 on Conn. Turnpike (tel. 367–4404).

Stratfield Motor Inn, formerly the Stratfield Hotel. Extensively modernized, this large building is now more adaptable for receiving guests. Larger, finer dining and meeting rooms. Family rates (children in parents' room free). Swimming pool. Free parking.

Main & Chapel sts. (tel. 366–4321).

GROTON

Reasonable

Griswold Hotel and Country Club. A 170-acre resort with beach, on Long Island Sound, swimming pool, golf, water-skiing, cruising, tennis, shuffleboard, badminton and croquet. Free clambakes at Miles Standish Pier. Free dancing and entertainment in Paul Revere Tavern. Open from late May to Nov.

At Eastern Point, near New London (tel. 445–9701).

Groton Motor Inn (Knott Hotels Corp.). A medium-sized well-furnished motel with first-class rates in season June–Sept. Restaurant, room service, cocktail lounge. Swimming and wading pools. Spacious grounds.

At 95 & State 184. PO Box 807 (tel. 445–9784).

Holiday Inn. Large chain member with mystic nautical motif in cocktail lounge and dining rooms. Two heated swimming pools. Family rates (children in parents' room free). Seasonal rates May–Sept. First-class scale.

Broad St., just off US 1 & 95 (tel. 445–8141).

MILFORD

Reasonable

Connecticut Turnpike Motel. Small motel with each room air-conditioned and having TV and phones. Thermostat-controlled heat. Family rates. Seasonal rates May–Labor Day.

1083 Boston Post Rd., US 1 at Connecticut Turnpike Exit 39 w. (tel. 874–3216).

Holiday Inn. A large chain member conveniently located to Milford Harbor and downtown. Good choice of accommodations. Children in parents' room free. Restaurant, room service, cocktail lounge. Heated pool.

Boston Post Rd. at Conn. Turnpike Exit 39E (tel. 878–6561).

Howard Johnson's Motor Lodge. Medium-sized motel on spacious grounds. Restaurant, cocktail lounge on premises, in-room coffee. Swimming pool. Lower rates after Labor Day until June 1.

1052 Boston Post Rd., on US 1, at Conn. Turnpike Exit 39 w. (tel. 878–4611).

Howard Johnson's Parkway Motor Lodge. A medium-sized chain member located near Shakespearean Theatre and private golf course. Seasonal rates June-mid Sept. in first class range. Swimming and wading pools. Restaurant, cocktail lounge and in-room coffee.

Wheeler Farms Road, Exit 55 off Wilbur Cross Pkwy. (tel. 878–3521).

Inexpensive

Shoreline Motel. Small facility with family units, TV, telephone in each room, beaches nearby.

737 Boston Post Rd., US 1, Conn.

Turnpike Exit 37 e. & 36 w. (tel. 874–9975).

MOODUS

Reasonable

Banner Lodge & Country Club, comprehensive resort facilities. Olympic swimming pool. Air-conditioned accommodations. Rooms with telephones. Nightly entertainment. Open from May to Sept. Free golf clinics.
Tel. 873–8652.

The Grand View, hotel & cottages, stressing family vacationing with day camp. Sports activities, Olympic pool & golf course on premises. Some air-conditioned rooms available. Telephones in rooms. American-Jewish cuisine. Season is from last week of June to Labor Day. Dining room is air-conditioned.
Tel. 873–8151.

Ted Hilton's, a popular Moodus resort, on a 600-acre site with swimming pool, stream, and sports facilities. Cottages with good accommodations. Caters especially to young, lively folks.
Tel. 873–8641.

Klar Crest Resort & Day Camp, specializes in family vacationing during July & Aug. New, large swimming pool, pre-camp nursery, "teenagers' delight," lounge & playhouse. Air-conditioned dining room. Private lake on premises; free golf instructions. American-Jewish cuisine.
Tel. 873–8649.

NEW HAVEN

First Class

Midtown Motor Inn. Near Yale buildings. Large with well-furnished rooms and suites. Children in same room free. Restaurant, cocktail lounge, public dining room, heated indoor pool. No pets. Free garage.
1157 Chapel St., near Conn. Turnpike Exit 47 (tel. 864–4163).

New Haven Motor Inn. A large elegant motel with free continental breakfast. Swimming pool. Les Shaw's restaurant nearby.
100 Pond Lily Ave., Exit 59 Wilbur Cross Pkwy. (tel. 387–6651).

Reasonable

D'Andrea's "3" Acres Motel. Medium-sized with TV and telephone in each room. Restaurant and gas station on premises. Hideaway recreation room.
Litchfield Tpke., Woodbridge, nr. Wilbur Cross Pkwy. Exit 59 (tel. 387–1621).

Holiday Inns. Large chain members with good restaurants and cocktail lounges. Children under 12 in parents' room free. Swimming pool at each motel.
30 Whalley Ave., across from Broadway & Yale buildings (opened in 1965) (tel. 777–6221).
1605 Whalley Ave. (former Nathan Hale Inn, renovated, reopened in 1964), Wilbur Cross Pkwy. Exit 59 (tel. 389–9504).

Rip Van Winkle Motel. TV & telephone in each room, air-conditioned. Large outdoor lounge area. Swimming and wading pools.
1548 Whalley Ave. at Exit 59, Wilbur Cross Pkwy. (tel. 387–2557).

Hotel Taft, near Yale University, has been improved and modernized, as well as its adjacent *Hotel Adams.* TV and telephone in 449 rooms, some of which are air-conditioned. Dining facilities. Shops in area, now being redeveloped.
Chapel and College sts. (tel. 787–1121).

3 Judges Motor Lodge. TV; AM-FM radio in all rooms, air-conditioned, with telephones. Restaurant nearby. No pets.
1560 Whalley Ave. at Exit 59, Wilbur Cross Pkwy. (Rte. 15) (tel. 387–8761).

NEW LONDON

Reasonable

Lighthouse Inn and Motor Lodge, near Ocean Beach; three-story inn with an-

nex; TV in some rooms. Air-conditioned dining room. No children under 7 accepted during summer. Private beach nearby. Open year-round.
Lower Blvd. (tel. 443–8411).

Mohican Hotel and Motor Inn. Large, modernized, well-managed operation with roof garden and dining rooms. Free parking.
281 State St., in downtown section (tel. 443–4341).

New London Motel, TV and telephones in air-conditioned rooms; heated swimming pool. Terminal for Conn. Limousine service to N.Y. airports.
Jct. of US 1 and 95 (tel. 442–9441).

Schrafft's Motor Inn (Frank G. Shattuck Co.). Large motel with private lake and beach in front of place. 100 rooms air-conditioned. Telephone, TV, swimming pool. Four Kings Cocktail Lounge. Banquet facilities.
At US 1 & 95 (tel. 442–0631).

Inexpensive

Crocker House. Large, long-established downtown hotel with TV, telephone and air-conditioning in rooms. Restaurant & cocktail lounge. Free parking.
178 State St. (tel. 443–5371).

NEWTOWN

Reasonable

Hawley Manor Inn. Another nice small motel-inn-cottage arrangement on spacious grounds. TV & telephones in air-conditioned rooms of motel. Attractive restaurant, cocktail lounge. Pets welcomed.
19 Main St. (tel. 426–4456).

Housatonic Motel. Small facility; air-conditioned with TV and telephone in each room.
Sandy Hook, on Inter. 84, US 6 & Rte. 202 (tel. 426–4230).

Yankee Drover Inn. Small inn, with excellent dining facilities. Few guest rooms, cocktail lounge.
Jct. US 6, 202 & Rte. 25 (tel. 426–4401).

NIANTIC

Reasonable

Connecticut Yankee Motor Inn. Medium-sized. Air-conditioned rooms, TV. Restaurant, cocktail lounge with nightly entertainment. Telephones, swimming pool. Seasonal rates mid-May, mid-Oct.
At Conn. Turnpike Exit 74 (tel. 739–5483).

Niantic Motor Lodge. Large, individual heat & air-conditioning control, telephone, TV, stereo music, swimming pool. Two conference rooms, large banquet room, restaurant.
At Conn. Turnpike Exit 74 (tel. 739–5423).

Starlight Motor Inn. TV, telephone, air-conditioned. Swimming pool.
At Conn. Turnpike Exit 74 (tel. 739–5462).

NORWALK

Reasonable

Norwalk Motor Inn. Medium-sized motel with restaurant & cocktail lounge. Outdoor dining. Swimming and wading pool.
99 East Ave., at Conn. Turnpike Exit 16 (tel. 838–5531).

Silvermine Tavern. Authentic 200-yr.-old New England house with suburban atmosphere midst fine cuisine. Small in accommodations; no telephone, no TV, no radio in rooms. Showers. On grounds are *The Old Mill,* a tumbling waterfall; antique shops, & *Gatehouse Shop.*
Exit 15 on Conn. Tpke & Exit 38 on Merritt Pkwy. Tel. 847–4558.

Westporter Motel. Small with family units, TV & telephone in air-conditioned rooms. Swimming pool.
295 Westport Ave., nr. Conn. Turnpike Exits 16 & 17 (tel. 847–5827).

WATERBURY

First Class

Schrafft's Motor Inn (Frank G. Shattuck Co.). New hillside lodgings in Oriental motif with cocktail lounge, swimming pool, banquet room and restaurant.

At Scott Rd. Exit, off US 84 (tel. 756–8123).

Reasonable

Howard Johnson's Motor Lodge. Small with remote control TV. Free toothbrush and toothpaste for guests without them. Swimming pool.

South Main St., off Rte. 8 Exit (tel. 756–7961).

Roger Smith Hotel (Roger Smith Hotels Corp.). At the Green, downtown section. Air-conditioning and TV in some of the 160 large rooms. Copper Room Restaurant & cocktail lounge. Coffee shop. Meeting facilities.

30 West Main St. (tel. 753–2161).

Waterbury Motor Inn. Small new motel with TV, telephone, air-conditioning. Next to Hager's Steak House with nightly entertainment.

At Scott Rd. Exit, off US 84 (tel. 756–7925).

ELSEWHERE

AVON. *Avon Old Farms Motel.* First class. Medium-sized with New England decor. TV, telephones in air-conditioned rooms. In-room coffee, cocktail lounge. Swimming pool. Across street from Old Farms Inn. On Albany Tpke, US 44, w. of Hartford. Tel. 677–1651.

CLINTON. *Clinton Motel.* Reasonable. Small, with TV, telephone and in-room coffee in each room. Air-conditioned. Lower rates from 2d week of Sept. to last week of June. 3/4 mi. e. on US 1, at Jct. of Rte. 145. Tel. 669–8850.

Village Motel. Reasonable. Small with colonial atmosphere, TV, telephone and in-room coffee in each room. Restaurant nearby. Higher rates in July–Aug. East Main St., reached from US 1, Exit 63. Tel. 669–8403.

COLCHESTER. *Colchester Lodge,* Norwich Rd., Rte. 2. Family resort with day camp. Sports, fishing, square dancing, bridge and golf instructions. Open last week of June to Labor Day. Reasonable. Tel. 889–2377.

DANBURY. *Danbury Motor Inn,* formerly the *Danbury New Englander.* Reasonable. Large gracious establishment in 4-story building. All rooms have direct-dialing phones, TV & in-room coffee. Family rates (children under 6 free). *Surrey Room* for luncheon and dinner, *Mad Hatter Lounge* also. 198 Main St., in downtown Danbury. Tel. 744–1000.

DANIELSON. *Berris Motor Inn,* on US 6, 4 mi. w. of Conn. Tpke. Exit 90; small, air-conditioned; TV, telephones. Reasonable. Swimming pool; coffee shop, cocktail lounge. Tel. 774–9644.

DARIEN. *Howard Johnson's Motor Lodge.* Reasonable. A medium-sized member of this chain with family rates. Restaurant on premises, some room service, cocktail lounge. Swimming pool. Conn. Turnpike Exit 11 & US Rte. 1. Tel. 655–3933.

GREENWICH. *Greenwich Harbor Motor Inn.* First class. A medium-sized multi-story motel with spacious well-furnished rooms. Dock equipped to handle large boats. Seasonal rates May–Oct. Restaurant, room service, cocktail lounge—discotheque. Meeting facilities. 500 Steamboat Rd. near Conn. Turnpike Exit 3. Tel. 661–9800.

Greenwich New Englander Motor Hotel. Reasonable. A large modern motel with Surrey Room Restaurant and Gaslight Lounge. Children under 6 in parents' room free. In-room coffee. Swimming pool with sundeck. Complete meeting facilities. 1114 Post Rd. Tel. 637–3691.

HAMDEN. *Sleeping Giant Motel.* Small. TV and telephone in each room. Breakfast room. 3400 Whitney Ave., 3 min. from Exit 61 at Wilbur Cross Pkwy. Tel. 288–2505.

Howard Johnson's Motor Lodge. Large chain member. TV, phones and air-conditioning. Swimming pool. Restaurant. Near Yale. Limousine service to New York City and Newark Airports. 2260 Whitney Ave., at Wilbur Cross Pkwy. Exit 61. Tel. 288–3831.

EAST HARTFORD. *Howard Johnson's Motor Lodge.* Reasonable. Medium-sized member of this chain located near Pratt & Whitney, capital and museums. Restaurant on premises. In-room coffee. Swimming pool. Wilbur Cross Pkwy. at Exit 88, US 5, 490 Main St. Tel. 289–5404.

LAKEVILLE. *Interlaken Inn,* on Rte. 112, spacious comfortable old inn, with air-conditioned rooms. Reasonable. Open from July 4 to Labor Day. Lower rates from May 30 to July 3 and after Labor Day to Oct. 15. Closed rest of year. Sat. night dancing, golf privileges, fishing, all-round sports. Cocktail lounge, terrace and dining room are open to public. Tel. 435–2871.

Wake Robin Inn. Reasonable. Medium-sized lakeside resort on 26 acres. Sports, golf & swimming. Dining room, paneled bar & terraces. Opened from May 15 to Oct. 15. American and European Plans. Lower rates before July 1 & after Labor Day. 1 mi. s. on Rte. 3. Tel. 435–2000.

LITCHFIELD. *Westleigh Inn,* West St., small, but distinguished, inn at 200-yr.-old house on 9½-acre grounds. TV in bar; free parking. Reasonable. Excellent food in dining room. Private beach at nearby Bantam Lake for swimming & boating. Open year-round. Tel. 567–8744.

MERIDEN. *Holiday Inn.* First class. A large chain member conveniently located to this area's metal industry. Attractively furnished. Restaurant, room service and cocktail lounge. Swimming pool. Complete meeting facilities. Exit 67 Wilbur Cross Pkwy. & I-91. Jct. of Rts. I-91, 5, 15, 6A. 900 E. Main. Tel. 238–1211.

MYSTIC. *Mystic Motor Inn.* Reasonable. Medium-sized, old whale day's decor, with fine restaurant, cocktail lounge and conference rooms. Pool. Seasonal rates May–Oct. Jct. of US 1 & Rte. 27, 1 mi. from Mystic Seaport. Tel. 536–9604.

NEWINGTON. *Grantmoor Motor Lodge,* 3000 Berlin Tpke., US 5; country club atmosphere, large, with family suites; TV/radio, telephone in each room, valet service. Reasonable. Cocktail lounge and restaurant and large banquet room. Miniature golf course for children, driving range. Swimming pool, wading pool. Tel. 666–5481.

NEW PRESTON. *Loomarwick House & Motor Lodge,* on Lake Waramaug. Noted for years as family vacation spot, with sports, social programs. Reasonable. Family rates, with meals, lower than for individual guests. New lakeside motor lodge units. Open summer months. Tel. 868–2246.

NORWICH. *Wauregan Hotel.* Inexpensive. Large downtown hotel with bath and shower, telephone. Ball room. Free parking. 17 Broadway at Main St. Tel. 887–2587.

OLD SAYBROOK. *Terra Mar,* at Exit 67 of Conn. Tpke., a Long Island Sound motor hotel, with pool; air-conditioned rooms with TV & phones. Facilities for dining and conventions. Reasonable. Tel. 388–3444.

SALISBURY. *White Hart Inn & Motor Court.* Reasonable. Small cozy century-old inn with a few modern motel rooms plus those in Inn. All have private bath & telephones. Dining in air-conditioned dining room & patio. Cocktail lounge. Open year-round. Main St., on Rte. 25. Tel. 435–2511.

SOUTHPORT. *Pequot Motor Inn,* 3471 Boston Post Rd., US 1, Exit 19 on Conn. Tpke.; moderate-sized motel with air-conditioned rooms, TV, telephone & tile bathrooms. Reasonable. Conference rooms. Tel. 259–7885.

STAMFORD. *Roger Smith Motor Lodge Hotel* (Roger Smith Hotels Corp.). Reasonable. This large hotel is now on a motor inn operation. TV, phone & Muzak in rooms. Coffee maker also in motel section rooms, tile baths. Family rates (children under 14 free). Dining in three restaurants. 55 River St., reached from Merritt Pkwy. Exits 34 & 35, or Conn. Turnpike Exit 7. Tel. 323–2112.

Stamford House. Reasonable. Large older downtown hotel with TV & telephone in rooms. Pets limited. Restaurant and bar. Family rates. 86 West Park Pl., reached from Merritt Pkwy. Exit 35 or Conn. Turnpike Exit 7. Tel. 324–3113.

STRATFORD. *Stratford Motor Inn.* First class. Overlooking Housatonic River. Elegantly furnished, air-conditioned, 158 rooms. Children under 12 in parents' room free. Free coffee supplied for coffee maker in each room. 2 phones in every room and every room with balcony. Copy of Shakespeare's works to read. Shakespearean motif in Mermaid Tavern. Cocktail lounge with entertainment. Heated swimming pool, poolside service from snack bar. Near golf course. 6905 Main St., at Merritt Pkwy. Exit 53 N. Tel. 378–7351.

WALLINGFORD. *Yale Motor Inn.* First class. Large, well-run resort-type motel with family rates. In-room coffee. Swimming pool, free Sauna, putting green. Yankee Silversmith Inn (restaurant) is across road. Same ownership. At Exit 66, Rte. 15, Wilbur Cross Pkwy., 2½ mi. n. of Wallingford. Tel. 269–1491.

Exit 66 Motel, at Exit 66 of Wilbur Cross Pkwy. (Rte. 15) at Jct. of US 5; small establishment; TV, telephones in air-conditioned rooms, a few kitchenettes, tile baths. Reasonable. Near bowling alleys, summer theaters, fine restaurants. Tel. 269–3331.

WESTPORT. *Westport New Englander Motor Inn.* Reasonable. Medium-sized well-furnished motel with wide choice of accommodations. Children under 6 free. Sitter, laundry & valet services. Swimming pools, sun deck, cabana club, many sports. In-room coffee. Dining in pleasant *Surrey Room Restaurant. Gaslite Lounge.* 1595 East State St., US 1, Conn. Turnpike Exit 9. Tel. 259–5236.

WETHERSFIELD. *Towne House Motor Hotel,* 1730 Berlin Tpke., US 5; large; TV/radio, Muzak, air-conditioned, telephone, special bridal suites, conference rooms, heated swimming pool. Reasonable. Near restaurants. Tel. 529–8226.

WILSON. *Carville's Motor Lodge.* Reasonable. Large. TV and telephones in air-conditioned rooms. Heated swimming pool. Cocktails served in 1686 Forge Room. Conference rooms, banquet facilities. 25 Windsor Ave., Jct. of US 5A & Interstate 91. Tel. 525–1461.

WINDSOR. *Tobacco Valley Inn & Motor House* (Early American Inns Corp.). Reasonable. Distinctive New England atmosphere. Moderate-sized establishment, with TV & telephones in air-conditioned rooms. Swimming pool. Interstate 91, at Bloomfield Ave. Tel. 688–5221.

WINDSOR LOCKS. *Schine Airport Hotel & Motor Inn.* First class. Serving air passengers. Tastefully decorated rooms, TV, radio, telephones. Good dining facilities with overall view of airfield. Cocktail lounge. Courtesy car. At Bradley Airport. Tel. 623–2441.

Y **YOUTH HOSTELS.** *American Youth Hostels, Inc.,* has lodgings at East Shore Rd., Bantam Lake (Litchfield). Accommodations number 20 male, 20 female. $1 daily, except in winter, when it's $1.50. Tel. JO 7–9258. *Canton Hostel,* Sugar House, Canton (near Hartford) has room for six males, six females. $1 daily. Open May 1 to Oct. 1. Inexpensive accommodations for men are available at the *YMCA*'s in all large cities; for women in the *YWCA*'s in Hartford, New Haven and Bridgeport.

CAMPING OUT. Fourteen state parks and forests, six of them in northwestern Conn., are equipped with camp sites for short- and long-term camping. Fee, $1 per camp site daily. Connecticut residents may reserve them from 15 to 150 days prior to May 1. State and out-of-state residents may apply for short-term camping on the premises. Official camp season is from May 1 to Oct. 1. One *pet* is permitted for each camp site; dogs must be leashed at all times. Unmarried minors under 21 must be with an adult who accepts responsibility. The largest camp area, *Hammonasset Beach,* is on Long Island Sound at Madison; it has nearly 1,000 camp sites. Free folder from the State Park & Forest Commission, State Office Building, Hartford.

TRAILER TIPS. Trailers are permitted at all state camping places, except for Sleeping Giant and Mount Carmel.

DINING OUT. The bills of fare in Connecticut restaurants are, by and large, as varied and extensive as those in moderately-priced New York City establishments. The nice part of dining out in Connecticut, however, is the lower prices (as compared to New York City). Many old houses have been converted into "inns," all of which serve meals, but not all of which have rooms for the night. Some of these old homes are quite charming, and if you enjoy relaxed, comfortable dining, with a cheery fireplace in winter and a green, pastoral view in summer, get off the super highways and seek out some of the establishments listed here.

FAIRFIELD

Reasonable

Angus Steak House. Famous for steaks, beef and cocktails. Kitchen open until 10 p.m., bar until 1 a.m.

On Black Rock Tpke., 1 mi. from Merritt Pkwy., and Conn. Tpke. at Black Rock Tpke. Exit.

Continental. Meals served in that "just right" atmosphere. Continental cuisine. Steaks and chops. Lobster special Friday. Lunch and dinner daily. Music Wed. and Sat. nights. Closed Sun.

On Kings Highway, Rte. 1A, Exit 24 Conn. Tpke., or Exit 44 Merritt Pkwy.

Fairfield Motor Inn Restaurant. Dinner served from 5:30 to 10 p.m. Organ music nightly from 9 p.m. to 1 a.m. Cocktail lounge. Dancing Fri. & Sat. night.

Post Rd., US 1, near Exit 22 of Conn. Tpke.

NORWALK

Reasonable

Cove Marina. Picturesque dining where the harbor meets L.I. sound. Ocean-fresh seafood, prime steaks and chops, delicious specialties. Cocktail lounge. Docking facilities for boats. Open every day.

Beach Rd., 2 mi. from Exit 16 Conn. Tpke. in East Norwalk.

Dorlon's Shorehouse. An authentic shorehouse on L.I. Sound. Weekday lunch. Complete seafood and steak dinners. Chart room and cocktail lounge. Open noon to 10 p.m. Sat. 5 to 10 p.m. Closed Tues.

½ mi. s. of Exit 16 Conn. Tpke., Exit 39 Merritt Pkwy.

Jolly Fisherman Restaurant. A New England nautical atmosphere, serving seafood specialties, prime steaks. Piano music nightly from 8:30 p.m. to closing 1 a.m. Open daily from 11:30 a.m.

377 Main St., at Exit 39 Merritt Pkwy.

Gen. Putnam Inn. On the Village Green. Prime sirloin steaks, seafood specialties. Cocktail lounge. Lunch. Open daily to 9:30 p.m., Fri. and Sat. till 10, Sun. 1 to 8:30 p.m. Guest rooms.

East Ave. Conn. Tpke. Exit 16. Merritt Pkwy. Rte. 7, Exit 39.

Silvermine Tavern. An unusual collection of early American artifacts decorates the dining rooms. Summer terrace dining overlooking the river. Buffet dinner on Thurs. Variety on menu includes roast beef, fried chicken, lobster, seafoods, steak and chops, home-made breads and pastries.

At Perry & Silvermine aves. from Exit 40 Merritt Pkwy. & Exit 15 Conn. Tpke.

Valenti's. Gracious country dining in log cabin setting. Seafood, steaks and Italian dishes. Lunch and dinner daily. Cocktail lounge. Entertainment Fri. and Sat. Open every day.

Rte. 136, Exit 17 Conn. Tpke., turn right 1 mi. ahead.

Inexpensive

Phil Baker's. Traditional Italian menu, with foods served hot and carefully seasoned. Unusually fine pizza in this locally popular spot. They like children. Bar.

32 New Canaan Ave., off Rte. 7 or Rte. 123.

RIDGEFIELD

Deluxe

Stonehenge. Fine cuisine. *Druid Bar Parlour* for cocktails. Open for lunch and dinner. Entertainment at piano nightly. Guest accommodations. Facilities for private parties and receptions. Closed Mon.

N. on Rte. 7 from Merritt Pkwy. Exit 40.

First Class

Tode's Inn. One of Connecticut's most honored restaurants, serving fine French cuisine. Lunch, dinner, cocktails. Famed wine cellar. Private rooms.

West Lane, Rte. 35.

Reasonable

Luigi's. Features Italian dishes, baked lasagna, shrimp marinara, spaghetti combinations. Open daily 5 to 9:30 p.m., Fri. & Sat. until 10:30 p.m., Sun. from 2 to 8:30 p.m. Closed Tues.

Rte. 7, Branchville.

Rickshaw. Chinese-Polynesian food, many exotic specialties. Special family dinners. Cocktail lounge.

At Ridgefield Motor Inn on Rte. 7.

STAMFORD

Reasonable

Casa Maria Restaurant. Italian specialties are home-made manicotti and lobster fra diavolo. Cocktail lounge. Open daily noon to 9:30 p.m., Sun. to 10:30 p.m. Closed Mon.

680 Boston Post Rd., US 1, Conn. Tpke. Exit 6.

Chimney Corner Inn. Famous Colonial eating place. A tradition of hospitality and good food. Cocktail lounge. Open every day noon to 9:30 p.m.

At Exit 34 just off Merritt Pkwy.

Country Kitchen. Varied specialties of the house with an international flair. Lunch 12 to 2:30 p.m. Full-course dinners 6 to 10 p.m., Sun. 12 to 8:30 p.m. Cocktails.

Exit 34, Merritt Pkwy., 4 mi. n. on Long Ridge Rd. Rte. 104.

WATERBURY

Reasonable

Diorio's Restaurant. A favorite dining place in the area for over 50 years. Italian dishes and gourmet specialties served in Victorian dining room and lounge. Open daily until midnight. Closed Sun.

231 Bank St., downtown, off new I–84.

Hager's Steak House. Well-decorated restaurant featuring steak dinners and prime beef ribs. Adjoins *Waterbury Motor Inn.* Entertainment nightly in the cocktail lounge.

Off I–84 at Scott Rd. Exit.

Schrafft's. New restaurant with Oriental motif. American-style meals,

breakfast and lunch. Cocktail lounge, banquet facilities. Restaurant part of *Schrafft's Motor Inn.*
Off I–84 at Scott Rd. Exit.

WESTPORT

First Class

Cafe de la Plage. A cozy, unpretentious restaurant with L.I. Sound view. Customers from near and far enjoy San Francisco-type cuisine. Unusual entrees include Alaskan King crab in sherried caper sauce. Open daily. Dinner till 11:30 p.m. Reservations recommended.
223 Hillspoint Rd. at Compo Beach.

Reasonable

Cafe Barna. Specializes in Hungarian cuisine, kolbassi, goulash. Dancing Fri. and Sat. nights. Min. charge of $3 on these nights. Buffet dinner Mon. & Wed. 5 to 10 p.m.
630 East State St., nr. Exit 18 Conn. Tpke., Exit 42 Merritt Pkwy.

The Clam Box of Westport. Large number of seafood items and New England specialties, well prepared. Private dining rooms available.
833 State St., E. Boston Post Rd., nr. Exit 18 Conn. Tpke. & Exit 42 Merritt Pkwy.

Golden House. Chinese cuisine served in appropriate atmosphere. Lunch from 11:30 a.m. to 4 p.m. Dinner 4 to 9 p.m., Sun. from noon to 11:30 p.m. Cocktail lounge and bar harmonize with decor of dining room.
Compo Shopping Center, Main St.

Manero's Steak House. Open every day for lunch and dinner. Bar and cocktail lounge. New banquet facilities. *Artists and Writers* room.
Riverside Ave., Merritt Pkwy. Exit 41, Conn. Tpke. Exit 17.

The Red Barn Restaurant. Several dining rooms overlook attractive gardens. Accent is on beef and seafood in pleasant surroundings. Cocktail lounge.
Just off exit 41 Merritt Pkwy. on Rte. 33.

The Three Bears Inn. Historic Conn. atmosphere. Lunch, dinner, cocktail lounge. Piano nightly. Open every day.
On Wilton Rd., Rte. 33, Exit 41, 1/4 mi. off Merritt Pkwy., Exit 17 Conn. Tpke.

ELSEWHERE

AVON. *Old Farms Inn.* Reasonable. Intimate New England feeling in *Tavern Room, Grill Room;* gracious setting of *Coach Room;* original blacksmith shop appurtenances in *Forge Room* and Bar. Breakfast, lunch, dinner. Jct. of US 44 & Rte. 10.

BERLIN. *Hawthorne Inn.* Reasonable. Plush old English setting. Roast beef, lobster and steak dinners. Piano, organ interludes in *Ember Lounge.* Four banquet rooms for parties. 2421 Wilbur Cross Pkwy., Berlin Tpke.

BOLTON. *Fiano's Restaurant.* Reasonable. Features excellent lobster, rib beef and steak dinners. Cocktail lounge and men's bar. Dancing Sat. night. Open daily 10 a.m. to midnight, Sun. from noon to 9 p.m. Closed Mon. On Rts. 6 & 44A, e. of Manchester.

BRIDGEPORT. *Bru-Conte's Riviera.* First class. Italian atmosphere, including a view of Long Island Sound. Features Italian dishes, lobster and steak dinners. Dinner served until 10 p.m., liquor until 1 a.m. Dinner-dance music Fri. and Sat. 405 Seaview Ave., at Exit 29, Conn. Tpke.

BROOKFIELD. *White Turkey Inn.* Reasonable. Colonial-style inn with varied menu. Open from mid-May to mid-Oct. Closed Mon. On US 7, from Brookfield exit of I–84.

CHESHIRE. *Waverly Inn.* Reasonable. One of Conn.'s most noted restaurants, with continental as well as American cuisine. *Crystal, Saratoga,* and four other dining rooms serve up to 1,000 people. Open daily until midnight. Closed Mon. 286 Maple Ave., Rte. 10.

DARIEN. *Half-Way House.* Reasonable. American cuisine, seafood a specialty. Nicely decorated dining rooms and cocktail lounge. Open daily from 5 to 10 p.m., Sun. from noon to 8:30 p.m. 2748 Boston Post Rd., US 1 on Stamford–Darien line; Exit 9 on Conn. Tpke.

Red Coach Grill. Reasonable. Specializes in charcoal-broiled steaks, seafood. Lunch from noon a la carte. Dinner daily from 5 p.m. to midnight. *Tally-ho* cocktail lounge in keeping with early American decor of the inn. US 1, Exit 13 on Conn. Tpke.

ESSEX. *Griswold Inn.* Reasonable. Catering to travelers for over 150 years, the Inn specializes in baked stuffed lobster, steak and prime ribs of beef. Dinner week nights 6 to 9 p.m., Sat. 6 to 10 p.m., Sun. 1 to 8 p.m. Dancing Sat. Reached from Exits 65 or 67 Conn. Tpke.

Lord Essex. Reasonable. An attractive mid-19th-century mansion in historic Essex, with regional and continental fare. Bar and cocktail lounge. Lunch noon to 2 p.m., dinner 6 to 9:30 p.m., Sun. 1 to 8 p.m. Guest accommodations.

FORESTVILLE. *Johnny's Restaurant.* Reasonable. Four dining rooms, lounge. Dinners include steaks, lobsters, roast beef. On Rte. 3.

HAMDEN. *Carriage Drive Restaurant.* Reasonable, French and American cuisine. Complete luncheons and dinners. Cocktails in *Drum Lounge.* Open every day. At Exit 61 of Conn. Tpke.

Sanford Barn. Reasonable. Charcoal broiling a specialty. Lunch and dinner. Closed Sun. Exit 60, Wilbur Cross Pkwy. Turn right 1 mi. to Sanford St., Rte. 10.

LITCHFIELD. *Westleigh Inn.* Reasonable. Nestled on a knoll, this well-known inn excels in continental cuisine. Lunch noon to 2:30 p.m. Dinner served from 6 to 9:30 p.m. daily, Sun. from 12:30 to 8 p.m. Cocktail lounge. Guest accommodations. On Rte. 25.

MILFORD. *Donat's.* First class. *Taliesin Room* for fine French cuisine. Many specialties prepared at your table. *Mediterranean Room* supper club for dining, dancing and entertainment on Sat. Cocktail lounge. Closed Sun. On Boston Post Rd., Exit 39E, Conn. Tpke.

Tory Brook Inn. Reasonable. Colonial charm. Seafood, roast beef, steaks and specialties. Dinner from 5 to 9 p.m., Sun. from noon. Cocktails. 5 min. from Shakespeare Theatre. Closed Mon. On Boston Post Rd., Milford Exit from Merritt Pkwy., Conn. Tpke. Exit 36.

MYSTIC. *Flood Tide.* First class. Features regional favorites, clams, crabs and lobsters. Located in *Mystic Manor Inn,* near Mystic Seaport. Open for lunch and dinner to 10 p.m., except Sun. to 8:15 p.m. Bar and cocktail lounge. At Rte. 27 & US 1 Jct.

NEW HAVEN. *Les Shaw's Restaurant.* Reasonable. Popular eating place with attractive dining rooms. Open daily from 11:30 a.m. to 10 p.m. Sat. to 11 p.m., Sun. to 9 p.m. Dancing Sat. to 1 a.m. Off Wilbur Cross Pkwy., at 70 Pond Lily Ave.

NEWTOWN. *Newtown Inn.* Reasonable. An attractive inn, built in 1787. French-American cuisine. *Escargots, coq au vin,* clams casino and many other specialties. Cocktail lounge. Closed Mon. On Rte. 25.

PAWCATUCK. *Greenhaven Inn,* near the R.I. line at Westerly. First class. Three dining rooms (200 capacity) in 220-year-old Colonial manor house. Baked stuffed lobster and seafood are specialties, as well as prime sirloin. Lunch daily from noon to 3 p.m. Dinner from 5 to 10 p.m., Sun. from noon to 8 p.m. Closed Mon. S. off US 1, from Pawcatuck or Westerly.

PLAINVILLE. *Cooke's Tavern.* Reasonable. Lunch, dinner and Sun. breakfast served in the early American atmosphere of a 1789 home. 143 New Britain Ave., Rte. 72 at Cooke St., 1/4 mi. off Rte. 10.

REDDING. *Mark Twain Skandia.* Reasonable. Genuine Swedish smörgasbord, Scandinavian-American food. Fri. & Sat. 6 to 10 p.m. Sun. 1 to 8 p.m. Complete dinners daily. Cocktail lounge. Closed Mon. At crossroads of Rtes. 53 & 107.

REDDING RIDGE. *The Spinning Wheel.* Reasonable. A salt-box house with early Conn. atmosphere. Chicken, turkey tetrazzini, creamed chicken, and chopped steak specialties. Open Tues. to Sat. noon to 8:30 p.m., Sun. noon to 7:30 p.m. Closed Mon. Open holidays. Fresh flowers brighten the inn. At Black Rock Tpke., reached from exits 44 & 45 Merritt Pkwy.

RIVERTON. *Old Riverton Inn.* Inexpensive. An old inn with good American fare. Dinner daily from 5 to 8:30 p.m. Sun. from noon to 8 p.m. Cocktail lounge and bar. Rte. 20.

SALISBURY. *Ragamont.* Reasonable. A small country inn (1880), with tall trees and attractive landscaping. Candlelight in several dining rooms. Menu includes steaks, chops, seafood and poultry. Daily from 6 to 8:30 p.m., Sat. till 9 p.m., Sun. from noon to 8 p.m. Cocktail lounge. Guest accommodations. On Rte. 44.

STRATFORD. *Fagan's.* Reasonable. Overlooking the beautiful Housatonic, you will find hearty New England fare here. Cocktails. A mile from the Shakespeare Theatre. Closed Mon. 946 Ferry Blvd., nr. Exit 33 Conn. Tpke.

Mermaid Tavern, at *Stratford Motor Inn.* First class. Sumptuous fare in a pleasant Merrie England setting. Famous *Yard of Ale. Pub* cocktail lounge has piano entertainment. Party facilities. Open every day. At Exit 53N Merritt Pkwy.

WALLINGFORD. *Oakdale Tavern.* First class. Superb New England setting reminiscent of historic past. Specialties are Dover sole, stuffed shrimp and *sauerbraten.* Open daily until 1 a.m. Near the Oakdale Summer Theatre. Hartford Tpke., nr. Exit 64 Wilbur Cross Pkwy.

Yankee Silversmith Inn. Reasonable. Colonial Americana decor in 2-story inn. Excellent New England meals with good service. Cocktail lounge in railroad diner motif. Open daily from 8 a.m. to 10 p.m., Sat. to midnight, Sun. to 8 p.m. US 5 at Exit 66 of Wilbur Cross Pkwy.

WATERTOWN. *Armond's Restaurant.* Reasonable. Lobster and steaks are specialties in pleasant surroundings. Lunch served Tues., Thurs. & Fri. Rte. 63, at Waterbury–Middlebury town line.

WESTON. *Cobb's Mill Inn.* First class. A quaint old mill by a waterfall with varied food, served in rustic dining rooms. Open Mon. to Sat. from 5 to 11 p.m. Sun. from noon to 9 p.m. Charming cocktail rooms below the falls. Weston Rd., Rte. 37 from Exit 17 & 18 Conn. Tpke. or Exit 42 Merritt Pkwy.

WOODBURY. *Curtis House.* Reasonable. Reputedly Conn.'s oldest inn. Early American atmosphere. Famed specialties, sweetbreads, roast duck, seafood, steaks, roast beef. Lunch, dinner, cocktails. Open every day. On Rte. 6.

NIGHTCLUBS. The nightclub circuit in Connecticut has never amounted to much. The restaurant approaching the closest to a nightclub is the air-conditioned *Actors Colony* in *Seymour* (State 8). Stars of television, movies, and stage entertain there at two Sat. night shows. Evening entertainment is featured on other days. At the Thurs. and Fri. smorgasbord, you can eat all you want for $2.95.

MUSIC. From June through August the *New Haven Jaycees Pops Concerts* are presented at *Yale Bowl* in *West Haven;* there are *string concerts* at *Norfolk's Music Shed;* and Sunday afternoon *chamber-music concerts* are given at *Music Mountain* in *Falls Village.* The restored *Goodspeed Opera House* in *East Haddam* is a charming place in which to hear a performance.

STAGE AND REVUE. *Long Wharf Theater,* Frontage Rd., New Haven, the city's first resident repertory playhouse, opened July, 1965. Tickets are moderately priced. Also in New Haven, the *Shubert Theater,* on College St., is the scene of pre-Broadway performances. Tickets for evenings are $2 to $5.40; for matinees, $2 to $4. The *American Shakespeare Festival,* in Stratford, has admission prices comparable to Broadway during the summer season, but they are lower for spring and fall performances.

TOURS. One can get lost and still enjoy himself while driving through Connecticut. Sections of some highways, such as US 84, are so new that they are not listed on maps as being completed. And though the new super highways get motorists through areas quicker than the old two-lane roads, the scenery beside them is as eye-catching as that on the "town roads." The countryside brightens up during May when the dogwood and other spring flowers are blooming, but nature bursts out in June with the state flower, the mountain laurel, in great abundance. Connecticut's greatest free show, however, takes place with the blazing array of the *foliage season* (late Sept.–early Oct.). Best circle trips are recommended in *Litchfield* and *Windham Counties,* and along the *Connecticut* and *Farmington River valleys.*

Another kind of tour is provided by *Yale University* in New Haven. The general tour starts at Phelp's Gateway, College St.; Sat., 11 a.m., Sun. 1:30 and 3 p.m.; daily, 10:30 a.m., 1:30 and 3 p.m. Yale also has two special tours. The *Art and Architecture Tours* begins at lobby of the Art and Architecture Building, Chapel and York sts., daily at 3 p.m.; the *Engineering & Science Tour* starts at Woosley Hall lobby, Grove & College streets, weekdays, 10:30 a.m., Sun., 2:45 p.m. All are free.

Then there are *Thames River* tours from Whaling City Dredges & Dock Co. Pier, 88 Fairview Ave. Groton (May 30 to Sept. 15), on 50-passenger open fiberglass boats, hourly, 9 a.m. to an hour before sunset. These are 7-mi. cruises with commentary on the New London–Groton submarine, Coast Guard, industrial, and historic areas.

INDUSTRIAL MUSEUMS AND TOURS. Because Connecticut ranks tops in industry (4 out of 14 working residents earn livelihood in manufacturing), many visitors want to see various industrial plants and museums. There are relatively few tours and only four museums in this category. Reasons include government orders requiring strict security against visitors and operational methods which do not permit safe conduct of sightseers.

The *American Clock & Watch Museum,* 100 Maple St., Bristol: 600 Connecticut-made clocks and watches; memorabilia on area's famous clock industry. Open daily, except Mon., 1:30 to 5:30 p.m. Free admission. *Industrial Museum* at Mattatuck Historical Society Building, 119 West Main St., Waterbury: exhibits of brass products, buttons, watches, tools, machines. Open, Tues. to Sat., noon to 5 p.m.; Sun., 2 to 5 p.m.; closed Mon. No admission charge. *Winchester Gun Museum,* 275 Winchester Ave., New Haven: outstanding collection of Connecticut-made weapons. Open daily, 9 a.m. to 4 p.m., except Sun. and holidays. No admission charge.

Tours: Write a few weeks, in advance, if possible, to public relations departments of factories for tour appointments. State number of people in your group and time of arrival at plant. Reminder: production schedules may necessitate cancellation of visits. Tours, during working hours, daytime, listed alphabetically, by towns:

Bridgeport: *The Bullard Co.,* 286 Canfield Ave., machine tools. *Dictaphone Corp.,* 375 Howard Ave., dictating & recording machines. *Metropolitan Body Co.,* 151 Kossuth St., steel multi-stop trucks: *Warner Bros. Co.,* 325 Lafayette St., lingerie & bathing suits.

Fairfield: *J. L. Lucas & Sons, Inc.,* Post Rd., machine tools. Hamden: *Botwinik Bros., Inc.,* 33 Welton St., rebuilding of machine tools.

Manchester: *ABA Tool & Die Co.,* 1395 Tolland Tpke., plastic mold dies; fixtures. Milford: *U.S. Electrical Motors,* Old Gate Lane, electric motors. New Haven: *Winchester Western Div.,* Olin Mathieson Chemical Corp., 275 Winchester Ave., military & sporting guns. Putnam: *Belding Heminway Co.,* Providence & Main Sts., finished threads. Rocky Hill: *CSW Plastic Types, Inc.,* 1823 Silas Deane Highway, newspaper ad plates, printing plates.

Stafford Springs: *Cyril Johnson Woolen Co.,* 22 Furnace Ave., woolen fabrics. Stamford: *American Cyanamid Co.,* Central Research Div., 1937 West Main St., chemicals; *Pitney Bowes, Inc.,* Walnut & Pacific Sts., postal meters. Stratford: *Lycoming Div.,* Avco Corp., South Main St., gas turbine aircraft, engine & missile components. Terryville: *Eagle Lock Corp.,* 20 South Main St., all types of locks. Waterbury: *Bar-Work Mfg. Co.,* 1198 Highland Ave., screw machine products.

Newspaper building tours: *New Haven Register-Journal-Courier* Building, 367 Orange St., New Haven. The *Waterbury Republican-American* Building, 389 Meadow St., Waterbury. Guided tours (free) can be arranged by phoning newspaper office before coming to the building.

HISTORIC SITES. *Stanley-Whitman House* (circa 1665), High St., Farmington, architectural gem of its type; Colonial museum; Open Apr. 1 to Nov. 30, week days, ex. Mon, 10 a.m. to noon; 2 to 5 p.m.; Sun. 2 to 5 p.m.: Dec. 1 to Mar. 31, Fri. & Sat. 10 a.m. to noon; 2 to 5 p.m.; Sun. 2 to 5 p.m. Admission, adults 50¢; children under 12, 25¢.

Webb House (1752), Main St., Wethersfield, Gen. Washington and Count deRochambeau planned the Battle of Yorktown here in May, 1781. Open Mar. to Oct. weekdays, 10 a.m. to 5 p.m. Sun. 1 to 5 p.m., Nov. to Feb. weekdays, 10 a.m. to 3 p.m. Free.

Stephen Tyng Mather Homestead (1778), Brookside & Grand View Aves., Darien. Free.

Conn. Agricultural Experiment Station, nation's first facility of its kind, 123 Huntington Ave., New Haven. Open week days. Free.

Replica of the world's *first commercial telephone exchange* (1878), Southern New England Telephone Co., 227 Church St., New Haven, open week days from 8 a.m. to 4:30 p.m. Free.

Connecticut's architectural heritage has been preserved by establishment of *historic district* regulations, which cover Litchfield, Glastonbury, Norfolk, Wethersfield, Windsor, Farmington, and Fairfield. Principal streets in these towns lure many motorists. Historic districts are now being considered in Avon, Brookfield, Chaplin, Colebrook, Essex, New London, Ridgefield, Suffield, Tolland, and Wilton.

MUSEUMS & ART GALLERIES. History has been made and is being made in Connecticut. Since the mid-1600's, Yankee foresight has preserved much of historical interest in its homes, in museums, schools, and industrial plants. *Yale University* (founded 1701) has a treasurehouse of Connecticut arts, culture, documents, and memorabilia in its world-famed museums at New Haven. Visit its *Peabody Museum of Natural History* (Whitney Ave. & Sachem St.), with outstanding exhibits in zoology, geology, and development of the invertebrate to man. Open daily, 9 a.m. to 5 p.m. Admission, adults 25¢, children 10¢, on Tues., Thurs., Sat. & Sun. Free admission on other days. Closed holidays.

Yale Art Gallery (Chapel & High sts.), one of nation's best museums of fine arts, is always expanding and changing its exhibitions. Open, Tues. to Sat., 10 a.m. to 5 p.m.; Sunday, 2 to 5 p.m.; closed Mon. & holidays. Admission free.

Mystic Seaport, recreated 19th-century seaport, near New London, with six museum buildings on whaling and New England's sea-faring era; 37 exhibition buildings, planetarium, new *Seaman's Inne* (restaurant), new library building. Open daily, except Thanksgiving and Christmas, 9 a.m. to 5 p.m. Admission, adults $2.50; children under 16, 50¢, except Oct. 15 to Apr. 15, when rate for adults is $2. Special group rates.

Museum of American Art (56 Lexington St., New Britain) free admission; *Museum of Art, Science & Industry* (90 Acre Park, Bridgeport) near Exit 47, Merritt Pkwy., admission, adults $1; children 50¢; *American Clock & Watch Museum* (100 Maple St., Bristol), admission free. *Mattatuck Historical Society* (119 West Main St., on Green, Waterbury), general, industrial, junior museums, admission free.

All large cities, most towns, and some villages have historical societies, some with exhibitions of local interest. Ask for *Museums in Connecticut* list from *Conn. Development Commission,* State Office Building, Hartford, or from societies and chambers of commerce in respective towns.

FAMOUS LIBRARIES. The *Beinecke Rare Book and Manuscript Library* at Yale University, New Haven, dedicated in Oct. 1963. It's a $6 million "windowless," six-story building with 250 huge marble slabs comprising the facade. The six-tier, cathedral-like Exhibition Hall holds 160,000 valuable volumes. The building (capacity 800,000 volumes and 1 million manuscripts on 21.3 miles of shelves) connects with *Sterling Memorial Library* through underground tunnel. Gothic-styled Sterling Library is worth visiting for timely exhibits in the corridors and exhibition rooms; Mon.–Sat., 8:30 a.m. to 5 p.m. during school terms. Library closed on holidays and Sat. and Sun. during student vacations.

GARDENS. There's a rosy paradise at the two-acre greenhouse of *Nicholas Grillo,* Canal St., Southington, near Waterbury. Grillo is the originator of the thornless rose *(Briarclif Supreme)* whose flowers are grown under licensing arrangements throughout the U.S.A. and in other countries. Mountain Laurel, the state flower, is in bloom during latter part of June.

SHOPPING. Some of the best department stores and ladies' wear shops in the East are in Connecticut. Among them are *Read's,* Bridgeport and Trumbull; The *Mexican Room,* Darien; the *Edward Malley Co.* and *Macy's,* New Haven; *Howland's,* Fairfield; *W. & J. Sloane* and *Best & Co.,* Stamford; *Jones Morgan & Co.* and *Freedman's Inc.,* Waterbury.

SUMMER SPORTS. Connecticut is a year-round, sports-active state. The athletic fields on the college campuses and in town stadiums are beehives of competition from early spring to late fall. Yale Bowl at West Haven is the state's best known sports arena.

Boating and *deep sea fishing* attract hundreds of enthusiasts on Long Island

Sound. Others prefer the lakes and rivers. A total of 53,000 motor boats are registered with the Conn. Boating Safety Commission, as well as 10,000 sailboats, 25,000 rowboats, and an estimated 10,500 other boats. Connecticut-made Sunfish and Sailfish are popular. *Fall Cruising Sailboat Race Series* at New London in Sept.; *Conn. River Regatta* takes place on Memorial Day at Middletown; *Yale-Harvard Regatta* is run on Thames River around June 20. Expert *water skiing* events are featured at Bantam Lake. *Conn. River Shad Derby* takes place in May at Windsor.

Rifle ranges in various parts of state; competitions from May through Oct. at Blue Trail Range, Wallingford. National and regional *sports car races* are staged during summer at Lime Rock Track, in western Connecticut, and Thompson, in eastern section. *Softball,* one of most popular outdoors games, is played by top women amateur teams at Raybestos Memorial Field, Stratford. *Conn. Valley Bicycle Classic* at Colt Park, Hartford, in Sept.

Golfing ranks high in the leisure time habits of men and women. Thirty-five public golf courses are in or near the large cities; some 50 more "private" and membership courses also well-patronized. Golf tournaments are staged throughout summer; most widely known being the pro *Insurance City Open* at the Wethersfield Country Club in July. Many tourneys are sponsored by the Conn. State Amateur Golf Assn.

WINTER SPORTS. Although Conn. doesn't have the high slopes of other New England states, *skiing* and affiliated winter activities are increasingly popular. Of the eight ski areas, the largest is Mohawk Mt., near State 4, at Cornwall in northwestern Conn. Ten trails and four slopes challenge both novice and expert skiers. Public ski area list is available from *Conn. Development Commission,* State Office Building, Hartford.

Hunting, trapping and sport fishing: Rules and regulations and pertinent information are available in free booklet on over 500 lakes and ponds, 300 miles of streams for public uses, three major rivers, 250 miles of Long Island Sound coastline. Write: *Dept. of Agriculture and Natural Resources,* State Office Building, Hartford.

WHAT TO DO WITH THE CHILDREN. There's a wide variety of attractions for children. Best *amusement parks* (open Memorial Day through mid-September) are at *Quassapaug Pond,* US 6A, Middlebury, and *Lake Compounce,* 3 miles south of Bristol's Center. Both lakes have excellent swimming areas, boating, rides, and picnic groves. No admission charge, and there's plenty of parking.

All kinds of attractions having to do with seafaring life and the old whaling days are to be found at *Mystic Seaport,* near New London. Other science and nature museums and places of interest are *Bridgeport's Museum of Art, Science and Industry,* near Exit 47 on the Merritt Parkway; the *Stamford Museum and Nature Center,* High Ridge and Scofield Town roads; *Mid-Fairfield County Youth Museum,* 10 Woodside Lane, in *Westport;* in Greenwich (Exit 28 on the Merritt Parkway); the *Audubon Center,* on Riversville Rd., and the *Bruce Museum,* on Steamboat Rd.; *New Haven's West Rock Nature Center,* on Wintergreen Ave., and the *Peabody Museum of Natural History,* at Whitney Ave. and Sachem St.; the *New Canaan Bird Sanctuary and Wildlife Preserve,* on Old Stamford Rd.; and the *Mattatuck Junior Museum,* 119 West Main St., *Waterbury.* There are two *trolley museums:* the *Branford Trolley Museum,* near US 1 in *East Haven;* and the *Connecticut Electric Railway Trolley Museum,* State 140 in *Warehouse Point.* Both are open during the summer. *Gillette Castle,* off State 148, *East Haddam,* which is open May 30 to Oct. 12, is fascinating to children, as is the replica of Jerusalem and Bethlehem, *Holy Land at Pine Hill,* which is off US 84 in *Waterbury.*

RETIREMENT AREAS. *Fireside Apartments,* on Palisade Ave. in northeastern Bridgeport, is the nation's first apartment complex built with federal funds. It comprises three buildings and nearly 250 units, with rooms for retired persons. The rents are inexpensive. The project is the model for similar buildings for the elderly in other Connecticut cities. Senior-citizens' groups in large cities participate in special community events under private or municipal sponsorship. Housing for the elderly is being constructed with federal and state assistance, supervised by local housing authorities.

RECOMMENDED READING. *Connecticut* (1961) by state historian Prof. Albert E. VanDusen; Random House. *Pictorial Connecticut* (1962), by Lawrence F. Willard and Alvin V. Sizer; College and University Press, New Haven. *A Guide to Historic Sites in Connecticut* (1963), by Litchfield Associates; Wesleyan University Press, Middletown. *Connecticut Yankee* (1943), by former governor Wilbur L. Cross; Yale University Press. *A Political History of Connecticut* (1941), by Brother J. Robert Lane; The Catholic University of Connecticut Press.

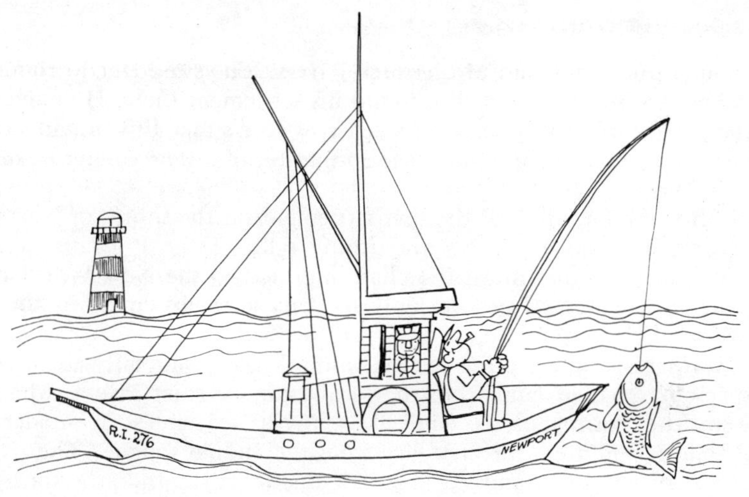

RHODE ISLAND

America's Smallest Bundle of Surprises

by

PHILIP WALLWORK

Mr. Wallwork is editor of The Automobilist, *official magazine of the American Legal Association, one of New England's major automobile clubs and editor of the association's guidebook. He is also author of the descriptive text on Massachusetts, following.*

(The Practical Information *section for the Rhode Island, Massachusetts, and Maine sections of this book were contributed by Florence Lemkowitz, former travel editor of the* Hartford Times.)

"Whereas Mr. Roger Williams, one of the elders of the church of Salem, hath broached and divulged new and dangerous opinions against the authority of magistrates; hath also writ letters of defamation, both of magistrates and churches here . . . it is therefore ordered that the said Mr. Williams shall depart out of this jurisdiction . . . not to return any more without license from the Court."

This order of banishment, issued in October, 1635, by the Puritan leaders of the Massachusetts Bay Colony, was one of the foundation stones of the State of Rhode Island. Roger Williams did depart. Unshaken in his strong convictions about religious liberty, and accompanied by a few followers, Williams fled Salem for the relatively unknown territory to the south. The following spring, a canoe bearing Williams and his party floated down the Seekonk River, rounded Fox Point and arrived at the confluence of the

Woonasquatucket and Moshassuck Rivers. The site looked promising, and Williams decided to found his settlement there. He named the place Providence, "having a sense of God's merciful providence unto me," and set in motion the formation of a new colony in the New World.

Thus the founding of the first settlement on the shores of Narragansett Bay was a curious and ironic echo of the Puritans' own experience. As dissenters, they had migrated to the New World in search of religious freedom, only to deny it to dissenters in their midst.

Williams, and the other settlers who followed, gradually acquired spacious tracts of land from the local Indians, chief among which were the Narragansetts. Indeed, many place-names in modern Rhode Island are a direct legacy from the Indian tongue. The city of Pawtucket, for example, takes its name from the Indian term for "waterfall place." Woonsocket, Apponaug, Pettaquamscutt, Conanicut, Narragansett—all these names and more add flavor to the Rhode Island of today and are an important link with its past.

Fittingly, the Narragansetts gave their name to the body of water that is Rhode Island's most significant geographical feature. Narragansett Bay, with its tributary rivers, extends 28 miles inland from the sea and virtually cuts the state into two thoroughly unequal parts. Thanks to its many subsidiary bays, coves, and inlets, Narragansett Bay gives the nation's smallest state (Rhode Island is 48 miles long and 37 miles wide) an impressive 250-mile-long coastline.

The island-studded waters of Narragansett Bay lap more than 100 beaches, some of them still undeveloped, and provide residents and visitors alike with ideal conditions for swimming, boating, and fishing. Giovanni di Verrazano, the Florentine explorer, surveyed its "islands of great fertility and beauty" in 1524 and pronounced it an excellent harbor. A hundred years later, the settlers of Providence thought so, too, as did those who followed them.

Another early visitor to Rhode Island was the Dutch fur trader and explorer, Adriaen Block, who made a careful survey of Narragansett Bay in 1614. Eight miles offshore, Captain Block sighted the island that still bears his name. Verrazano had noted the island, too, and had likened it to the island of Rhodes in the Mediterranean. However, the Florentine had shrewdly named the island Claudia, after the mother of Francis I of France, under whose colors he sailed. Some years afterward, his reference to the isle of Rhodes played a part in the official naming of the state.

Legally, Block Island's proper name is New Shoreham, but the designation is favored mainly by mapmakers. The old Dutchman's name stuck, and the island was admitted to the colony in 1664.

Today, Block Island is one of the state's major recreational areas.

Many salt-water and fresh-water ponds—some say there is one for each day of the year—dot this pear-shaped chunk of rolling countryside that sits marooned in the Atlantic Ocean. There are several good beaches along its shores, and its two fine harbors are popular havens for boatmen. One of the more spectacular vistas available in Rhode Island, by and large a rather flat and unspectacular portion of New England, rewards those who make their way to the top of Mohegan Bluffs. At 200 feet above sea level, the bluffs are the highest point on Block Island. The state's highest point is well inland. Jerimoth Hill, in the town of Foster in the northwest corner of Rhode Island, rises all of 812 feet above sea level.

After Providence, Portsmouth and Newport were the next Rhode Island towns to be founded. The new settlers bought from the Indians the largest island in Narragansett Bay. On the northern end of the island, then called Aquidneck, the community of Pocasset was established in 1638. A year later, Newport was founded at the island's southern end. Pocasset was soon renamed Portsmouth, and in 1644 Aquidneck itself was renamed the Isle of Rhodes, or Rhode Island, marking the first official use of that name in the growing colony. The fourth of the original settlements, Warwick, was founded on the mainland south of Providence in 1642.

Religious Freedom for All

The four towns sent Roger Williams to England in 1643, for the purpose of obtaining the colony's first charter. This was superseded in 1663 by a royal charter from Charles II, which guaranteed full religious freedom to the colony, an important step in largely intolerant New England. The charter served as a basis for Rhode Island's government until 1843, a span of 180 years.

From the year of the royal charter to the end of the 17th century, the colony's population grew very slowly. In the 18th century, a gradual transition from agricultural activities to commerce saw the colony experience a rapid growth in wealth and prosperity. It became part of the famous triangular trade, in which ships hauled rum from New England to Africa, slaves were transported from Africa to the West Indies, and molasses was shipped from the West Indies to New England for the profitable manufacture of rum.

Rhode Island's history after the middle of the 17th century is mainly concerned with military and naval affairs. In the Great Swamp fight of King Philip's War (1675–76), the winter camp of the Narragansett Indians, near South Kingston, was destroyed by troops from the New England colonies.

The Great Swamp is still one of Rhode Island's more unusual

areas. This 2,600-acre morass, now a wildlife reservation, offers nature lovers a chance to observe plants and animals in an environment virtually untouched by man.

In the winter of 1675, the Great Swamp was the scene of a bloody and decisive battle between the Indians and the growing number of settlers in the colony (the population of Providence had reached 1,000). The battle in the swamp was the major engagement of King Philip's War. Philip, son of Massasoit, was the leader of the Wampanoag tribe and feared the growing strength of white settlers. Long-simmering resentments had led the Wampanoags, along with the Nipmucks, to open hostilities against the settlers. They were joined, in turn, by the more powerful Narragansetts, and a full-fledged Indian uprising began. The Indians took refuge in the swamp, believing themselves secure, but the colonial troops took them by surprise and virtually ended their effectiveness as a fighting force. The Narragansetts, who lost more than 600 of their number, never recovered from the blow.

Today, a road leads into the swamp to the battle site, and a granite shaft marks the place where the Indian fortifications are believed to have stood. There are several picnic groves near the swamp's borders. To the north, within easy driving distance, is Smith's Castle, a trading post burned by the Indians after the great battle. Rebuilt in the 1680's, it is the oldest structure in southern Rhode Island and is the only existing house in the state known to have been visited by Roger Williams. The end of King Philip's War marked the rapid decline of the Indian in the affairs of Rhode Island.

Rhode Island did, however, take part in at least nine intercolonial wars between 1652 and the end of the Revolution. These struggles involved, at various times, the English, French, Dutch, Spanish, and their Indian allies. After the French and Indian War ended in 1763, Rhode Island became increasingly resistant to British authority. Because of limitations placed on the state's commerce, and the growing burden of taxation, the colonists attacked and scuttled the British revenue sloop, Liberty, at Newport in 1772. The following June, another British vessel, the Gaspee, was burned by the colonists at Providence.

On May 4, 1776, a year after British troops clashed with the Minutemen at Lexington and Concord, Rhode Island declared its independence from the British Crown. It was an act fully in keeping with the same motivations that moved Roger Williams. Rhode Island acted two months before the Declaration of Independence was approved by the Continental Congress in Philadelphia, giving it claim to the title of the oldest state in the union. After the Revolution, however, Rhode Island was plagued by severe economic strains. The state opposed the idea of a strong central government because of its fear of heavy taxation and further interference with trade. As a result, Rhode Island did not send delegates to the Constitutional Convention in 1787, nor did it ratify the Constitution until economic pressures forced it to act in 1790. Thus, although Rhode Island was the first of the 13 colonies to declare its independence, it was the last of the 13 to ratify the Constitution—and then by only two votes.

Few Revolutionary War battles were fought in Rhode Island, but the war left its mark upon the economy of the state and reduced one of its major cities to ruins. Newport, one of Rhode Island's four original settlements, had prospered during the years preceding the Revolution, reaching a peak of commercial splendor during the period 1740–75. The city's fine harbor brought in great quantities of shipping, and wealth began to transform the town into one of the showplaces of New England. Much of this wealth derived from the slave trade. In 1784, however, Rhode Island's slaves were emancipated and the further introduction of slaves was forbidden. In any case, only Boston and Philadelphia topped Newport as a trade center. Then as now, the city's climate and seaside location attracted numbers of wealthy summer visitors. Impressive homes were built, trees lined the avenues of the town, and a gay social life enlivened the hard-headed business atmosphere. Then, in December of 1776, a British fleet landed 9,000 troops in Newport, and the town remained in British hands until 1779.

Newport's Gilded Age

Newport under the occupation was bleak, but the British left it in still worse shape. Many homes and wharves were burned, trees were cut down, and properties were ransacked and destroyed. Many residents had fled during the war. Afterwards, the tide of commerce turned toward New York, and the town did not recover for some time. By the 1850's, Newport's role as a summer retreat for the well-to-do was becoming reestablished. The town's social life really began to regain some of its pre-Revolutionary glitter after the Civil War, when wealthy Northerners took a shine to the place.

Newport's gilded age, from the 1890's to the eve of the First World War, saw the art of entertainment rise to fantastically expensive heights. Among the hostesses of that Newport era was Mrs. Pembroke Jones, who, it was said, set aside no less than $300,000 for entertainment purposes at the beginning of every season. The names of millionaires—Astor, Belmont, Vanderbilt—became synonymous with Newport society, and Newport society, with a capital

S, was promoted untiringly by its chief spokesmen and drumbeaters, Ward McAllister and Harry Lehr. Supposedly, the designation for members of Society's Blue Book—The Four Hundred—was arrived at by Mrs. William Astor and Harry Lehr in the course of choosing the guest list for one of Mrs. Astor's famed annual balls. Her Newport ballroom could accommodate only 400 guests. That summer, only the elite made the grade and took title to the label.

After World War I, different money came to Newport, only to depart when the stock market dissolved in 1929. The age of huge dinner parties and cotillions had gone. Many of the baroque summer villas and chateaus that lined the shore—"cottages" they were called—were closed down or otherwise dispensed with. There is still wealth and society in Newport, but it is more discreet. Much of Newport's social, economic, political and religious history can be seen in its architecture. The diverse churches along with the Touro Synagogue, a National Historic Site, underscore the religious toleration of earlier days. The period when Newport was one of the most important cultural centers on the seacoast is relived at the Redwood Library. And the remaining millionaires' "cottages" are revealing clues to the nature of the town's Gilded Age.

Today, Newport's economy is strongly linked to the expenditures of the United States Navy ($99 million in 1964), which maintains a sprawling base there. The city also is the scene of an annual jazz and folk-music festival. As a major boating center, Newport has played host in 1958, 1962, and 1964, to the America's Cup yachting competition.

The New Immigrants

While Newport's fortunes limped along for many years after the Revolutionary War, the rest of Rhode Island began to change. Agriculture and shipping shrank in importance as the state became more and more industrialized. Successive waves of immigration brought French-Canadians, Portuguese, Irish and Italians to Rhode Island's cities. The old began to give way to the new. As an example, the importance of Rhode Island's seagoing commerce during the 18th century can be inferred from a single voyage of the ship *John Jay* in 1794. That vessel sailed from Providence with a $34,000 cargo of iron, rum, gin, pork, candles, and tobacco, and returned from Bombay carrying $250,000 worth of tea.

However, four years before the voyage of the *John Jay,* an English mechanic had arrived in Pawtucket with a secret that was to add an important new ingredient to the state's economy. The mechanic, Samuel Slater, brought with him details of the power spinning-frame, called the Arkwright process, and established himself in the textile business in Pawtucket. Textiles soon became a major factor in the growing industrialization of Rhode Island, and many of the new immigrants went to work at the looms. One of Slater's early mills, now a museum, still stands beside the Blackstone River in Pawtucket.

Growing urbanization has created new problems. The state's population shifted from about 20 percent urban in 1800 to nearly 90 percent urban in 1900. Because Rhode Island had poor urban representation in the legislature and no suffrage for non-landed citizens, Thomas Wilson Dorr led an armed revolt in the 19th century. Dorr's Rebellion led to the adoption of a new state constitution, the Freeman's Constitution, in 1842. This gave voting rights to all adult males of American birth who owned real property valued at $134, or who paid an annual tax of at least $1.

The state's industrialization continued to expand after the Civil War. In 1880, Rhode Island was first among the jewelry-producing states of the nation. By 1890, Providence was the second most important woolen-manufacturing city. After World War I, however, a marked change occurred in the state's industrial pattern. When many textile factories were moved to the Southern states in the 1920's, Rhode Island's textile industry underwent a severe decline. Forced to diversify its manufacturing activities, the state placed more emphasis upon the manufacture of machinery, machine tools, and metal products.

Today, Rhode Island's concentration of employment is found mainly in four industry groups—the metal trades, textiles, jewelry, and rubber and plastics. The United States Navy is another large industry in the state, employing thousands of civilians at its Newport naval base and elsewhere in Rhode Island. Total Navy disbursements in Rhode Island in 1964 topped $170 million. Rhode Islanders also are becoming aware of tourism's potential as an income-producing industry. The Rhode Island Development Council, a state agency, has increased the tempo of its campaign to publicize the state as America's First Vacationland. The state's annual income from tourism has increased from about $18 million in 1950 to about $35 million by current estimates.

Rhode Island may be the smallest state, and the most densely populated, but its natural recreational assets are varied and surprisingly unexploited. More than 80 percent of the state still consists of wooded and farmland areas. There are beaches and parks, fishing ports, harbors, historic homes and monuments, and pleasant rolling countryside. The climate, influenced by the Gulf Stream and Narragansett Bay, averages about 72 degrees in July and 50 degrees on a year-round basis.

Rhode Islanders also take pride in their state's educational history and facilities. In 1640, Robert Lenthal founded the first public school in the colonies in Rhode Island. Henry Barnard, in 1844, established the Rhode Island Institute of Instruction, the oldest association of its kind, in this state. And "the patron saint of the nation's public school system," Horace Mann, was educated at Brown University, founded in 1764 and the state's oldest institution of higher learning. Brown has been involved in an expansion and development program since the end of World War II, calling for the expenditure of nearly $60 million. The university's current program probably will continue for some years, thanks to many incoming grants.

Politically, Rhode Island's voting pattern has been far from consistent over the years. At first, the state tended to lean toward conservatism in Presidential elections. Then, in 1928, Alfred E. Smith carried the state for the Democratic Party. Rhode Island stayed with the Democratic nominee in every election thereafter until it went for Eisenhower in 1952 and 1956. Democratic candidates won the state in 1960 and 1964.

The political machinery of Rhode Island is, of course, in its capital. Providence is a curious mixture of many elements. There is history to be found during a walking tour of the older sections of the city, and its varied cultural heritage provides touches of cosmopolitan flavor. Providence also is an important deep-water port (the third-largest in New England in tonnage handled), an industrial complex, a legislative seat, and an educational center. Its schools include Brown University, Providence College, the Rhode Island College of Education, the Rhode Island School of Design and a number of private institutions.

One of the major landmarks in Providence is the State House, home of the Senate and the House of Representatives. Completed in 1904, the State House boasted the first marble dome in the United States. Numerous older buildings, some in acute disrepair, have survived the ravages of time and progress in Providence, but the city suffers esthetically from its rambling character. Its boundaries have spread, with no apparent logic, in all directions, and there is no sharply defined downtown area. This has been underlined, and perhaps aggravated, by the extensive highway program that has pushed a network of limited-access roadways through the most congested areas. Providence, once an endless ordeal for transient motorists, who had to zigzag endlessly along miles of local streets to get through town, no longer is a driver's nightmare. The city, like the state, is beginning to plan more determinedly for the future.

PRACTICAL INFORMATION FOR RHODE ISLAND

RHODE ISLAND FACTS & FIGURES. The state is named for the Isle of Rhodes in the Mediterranean. Its nickname is *Little Rhody*. The violet is the state flower, the maple, the state tree, the Rhode Island red, the state bird. "Hope" is the state motto. *Rhode Island* is the state song.

Providence is the state capital. The state population is 859,488.

The sea is the dominating factor in this tiny (the nation's smallest) north Atlantic state. In Colonial days, Rhode Island was a leading seafaring province. Today shipbuilding has declined, but the Atlantic beaches attract thousands of visitors to the coastal resorts (including the prestigious and elegant Newport), and tourism and the big Newport Naval Base are two of the major sources of state income. Textiles, which flourished in the 19th century, have seriously declined in importance, but remain the state's leading industry. Rhode Island contains many charming old towns, sleepy mementoes of the state's Colonial past. Inland, the state is a land of rolling hills and small lakes. The climate is cold in the winter, warm in summer. The weather is extremely variable, and marked by occasional hurricanes and tidal waves.

HOW TO GET AROUND. Rhode Island is easily reached by airline, railroad, bus, automobile, or private boat.

By *car* from New York the quickest route to Rhode Island is via the *New England Thruway* (I-95). Exit 76 leads to State 95 and *Providence.* For the *Narragansett* seashore, take exit at State 138, the Kingston Interchange. Signs mark the way to *Jamestown Bridge* and the *Newport Ferry*. State 1A is the scenic highway; US 1 from Westerly is known as the *Heritage Trail. Car ferries* operate between *Jamestown* and *Newport,* usually every half hour in summer; tel. Jamestown 423–0242 and Newport 846–8479. Car ferries daily to *Block Island.* Parking at the piers, *taxi service* at Block Island dock. Information from New London, Conn., tel. 442–7891; Point Judith, tel. Sterling 3–4613. Also daily ferry service between *Bristol* and *Prudence Island;* and summer ferry from *Warren* to *Rocky Point.*

Theodore Francis Green State Airport, is about 7 mi. from Providence; served by *Allegheny, American, Eastern, Mohawk, National, United.* Flight time from New York is about 45 min. Limousines from airport to downtown, about $1.50 for 30-min. drive. *Air charter* and *air taxi* service: *Travel Air Service, Executive Flight Service, Skylanes.*

*Car rentals—Avis, Hertz, National—*are available at the airport, the *Sheraton-Biltmore Hotel* in Providence, and locally.

For *boat charters,* write *Rhode Island Charter Boat Booking Service,* Snug Harbor Marina, Gooseberry Road, Wakefield. Tel. 783–7766. *Skiff rental: Fish's Bait Shop,* Galilee; *Kenyon's Boat and Bait Shop,* 489 Water St., Warren; *Babcock's Boat Yard,* Pond St., Wakefield; *Wickford Bait and Tackle,* 1 Phillips St., Wickford; *Watch Hill Boat Yard,* Watch Hill.

By *rail* Providence is served by the *New York, New Haven and Hartford Railroad.* From New York, train trip is about 3 hours; 1 hour from Boston. By *Bus: Greyhound* and *Trailways* serve Providence. Local bus service throughout the state.

SEASONAL EVENTS. One of the most important events is *Rhode Island Heritage Week,* an annual celebration commemorating the state's declaration of independence from Great Britain. Special ceremonies take place the first week in May. Information is free from the Heritage Week Committee, R.I. Development Council, Providence 8, R.I.

From May to Oct. the *Striped Bass Tournament* is open to all; in Newport. Details are at WADK, P.O. Box 367, Newport. Galilee is the scene of many *fishing tournaments:* the annual *Swordfishing Tournament* about the second week in July; the *Rhode Island Tuna Tournament,* about the first week in September, followed by the *Annual United States Atlantic Tuna Tournament,* and the *Annual Surf Casting Tournament.*

Country fairs begin in June thru the middle of September. One of the best is the *Rocky Hill State Fair* in East Greenwich, about the third week in August.

The *Navy Relief Carnival* features the Blue Angel aviators, at Quonset Naval Air Station, Quonset Point, July. *Parades* are varied in Rhode Island, from the *Italian Festa* late in July from St. Mary's Church in Cranston to the annual *V-J Day* parade Aug. 14, Providence.

The *Newport Motor Car Festival* is held the middle of June in Newport, and the *Narragansett Auto Fair* in Narragansett (the end of July). Newport has a steady stream of *yachting events,* climaxed by *America's Cup Races. Block Island Week Sailing Regatta* is held mid-July.

At the end of June, there are two *beauty pageants:* one for *Miss Rhode Island* at 8 p.m., Warwick Musical Theatre, Warwick; and one for *Little Miss Rhode Island Universe,* 7 p.m., Palladium Ballroom, Rocky Point Park.

The annual *Rhode Island Arts Festival,* Kennedy Plaza, downtown Providence, is held from the end of May to mid-June.

Shows: Antiques take the center of the stage about the end of Aug. in the annual *Antique Show and Sale,* Newport Casino, Newport.

The annual *Providence County Kennel Club Dog Show,* about the middle of Sept. is held at Cronin's Field, LaSalle Academy, Providence. From June to Oct., there are ten *horse shows.* The big one is late Aug. Rocky Hill Fairgrounds, State 2, East Greenwich.

Flower shows begin in May with the azalea displays in *Swan Point Cemetery,* 585 Blackstone Blvd., Providence and at the *Winsor Gardens,* 44 Marden St., Cranston. From June to Nov., the *Llys-Yr-Rhosyn Rose Gardens* have a free show at 93 Rumstick Road, Barrington. The free flower show prevails, also, at *Brownell Memorial Rose Gardens,* Little Compton, from late June to first frost.

TOURIST INFORMATION SERVICES. The *Rhode Island Development Council* leaves no stone unturned when the subject is tourism. An extremely efficient organization, the council supplies reams of brochures and literature. The *Rhode Island Tourist Guide* lists what to see, where to stay, what to do, a calendar of events, etc. The address is 49 Hayes St., Providence, R.I. 02908. The *Preservation Society of Newport County,* Washington Square, Newport, R.I. is very cooperative also and supplies informative literature. Just about every town has its own chamber of commerce, including the *Block Island Chamber of Commerce* on Block Island, for specific vacation information.

DRINKING LAWS. You have to be over 21 to order a drink or buy packaged liquor in local liquor stores. Legal hours, 6 a.m. to 1 a.m.; from noon Sun. No sales Christmas Day.

STATE PARKS. Little Rhody has big ideas in the recreation field—more than 8,000 acres for *state parks and forests.* Facilities are excellent, including toilets, fireplaces, picnic tables, and drinking water in the majority of the state parks listed here. Information and permits from the Division of Forests in Providence.

Arcadia State Park (Arcadia State Forest is alongside) in Richmond has 6 tent sites ($1 a night), 100 picnic tables, 54 fireplaces; also good for swimming and fishing. *Beach Pond State Park,* Exeter (State 165), offers swimming, fishing, and camping on about 3,000 acres. 120 picnic tables and 76 fireplaces. *Burlingame State Forest* adjoins *Burlingame State Park,* off US 1 near Charlestown. About 350 campsites are available. Swimming, boating, fishing in Watchaug Pond. *Kimball Bird Sanctuary* nearby. *Dawley State Park,* Richmond, offers log shelters; also more than 40 fireplaces and picnic tables.

Goddard Memorial State Park, about a mile from East Greenwich, is a favorite with children (amusements are the attraction). Summer and winter sports. More than 300 picnic tables, over 100 portable stove slabs and fireplaces. *Lincoln Woods State Park,* only 5 mi. from Providence offers huge Olney Pond for summer water sports and winter skating; 10 mi. of bridle paths; sports field. *Casimir Pulaski Memorial State Park,* and *Pulaski Memorial State Forest* are off US 44 in Gloucester. Swimming, fishing, and ice skating. Picnic tables, fireplaces. *George Washington Memorial State Forest,* also in Gloucester, US 44, offers some campsites with a promise of more to be constructed.

State beaches include *Block Island State Beach,* Block Island; *East Matunuck State Beach,* South Kingstown; *Misquamicut State Beach,* Westerly; *Sand Hill Cove State Beach,* Narragansett; *Scarborough State Beach,* Narragansett; *Tiverton Beach,* Tiverton.

INDIANS. Rhode Island was happy hunting grounds for the *Narragansett Indians* in the 17th-century. Canonicus, the Narragansett chief, sold Roger Williams the land on which he settled. The Narragansetts became allies of the colonists in the Pequot War, 1637. However, the Indian power in southern New England was destroyed in 1675 after the King Philip War. Their fort was attacked in Kingston (the Great Swamp Fight). The survivors migrated, some settling among the *Niantic Indians* near Charlestown. The combined group was named Narragansett.

The visitor will get a good look at—and even a taste of—Indian lore at the *Tomaquag Indian Memorial Museum,* a reconstructed Indian village, on the Old Hopkington—Burdickville Rd. in Ashaway, about a half-mile south of I-95. From spring to winter, there is usually a celebration every weekend, including clambakes on the Fourth of July and Labor Day. The museum features an Indian garden and the *Strawberry Festival* in June; the *String Bean Festival* in July; the *Gathering-of-Nuts* and *Cranberry Festival* in Oct. In Nov. there are *Hunter's Moon* and *Thanksgiving* ceremonies. The season ends in Dec. with a *Give Away Feast and Dance.*

WHERE TO GO. The 13th of the 13 original states has more than its share of famous birthplaces and Revolutionary period shrines. Following is a condensed tour of the cities and towns with interesting sights. *Barrington* is known for Barrington College, Barrington Yacht Club, Karl P. Jones' Rose Gardens, Rumstick Point and Nayatt Point. *Block Island* is famous for home of Arthur Penn, composer of the song *Smiling Through;* Settlers' Rock; Block Island Historical Society, Palatine Graves (historic cemetery), Salt Pond, Sandy Point State Park, Mohegan Bluffs, Block Island State Beach. In *Bristol,* see Colt Drive, Haffenreffer Museum of the American Indian, Poppasquash Neck, Bosworth House, the Lindens, Governor Bradford

House, Reynolds House, Lafayette's Headquarters, the Barrack House, Historical Society Museum and Library. *Burrillville* has Wallum Lake, Memorial Forest and State Park, and the Shrine of the Little Flower.

Central Falls contains Jenks Park, the Clock Tower, the Iron Umbrella, Adams Memorial Library. *Charlestown* is the site of Fort Ninigret, Royal Indian Burying Ground, General Stanton Monument, the United Nuclear Corporation, Salt Pond, Burlingame State Park, Kimball Bird Sanctuary. *Coventry,* with ten villages, has the home of General Nathanael Greene in *Anthony,* Haven's Tavern in *Pottersville,* Isaac Bowen Homestead, the Benjamin Carr Homestead, Tiogue Lake, the George B. Parker Woodland. *Cumberland* is the site of the 1635 William Blackstone House, Blackstone's grave, Diamond Hill Reservation and Ski Center.

East Greenwich has the Mitchell Varnum House, Varnum Memorial Armory, the Independent Company of Kentish Guards Armory, East Greenwich Academy, the Friends' Meeting House, Old Baptist Burying Ground, East Greenwich Yacht Club, Goddard Memorial State Park. *East Providence* is popular for Crescent Park, an amusement center. *Exeter* has geological formations such as *Wolf Rocks* at Yorker Hill; Queen's Fort; Arcadia State Forest; Arcadia State Park; and Beach Pond State Park.

Foster is the site of the Pardon Williams Homestead, the Wilcox Stone House, the Town House, and Jerimoth Hill, highest point in the state. *Gloucester* is the site of Acote's Hill in Chepachet, Dorr Monument, Durfee's Hill, Bowdish Reservoir, George Washington Memorial State Forest, Waterman's Lake, Smith and Sayles Reservoir, Killingly Pond, Spring Grove Pond. *Hopkinton* contains the Tomaquag Indian Museum, southern section of Arcadia Forest, Blue Pond, Ashville Pond, and Winchek Pond.

Jamestown Island has Sheffield Cove, Mackerel Cove, the Old Windmill, Friends Meeting House, Home of Captain Paine, Carr Homestead, John Greene House, Fire Museum, Marsh Meadows Wildlife Preserve, and Beaver Tail Lighthouse. *Johnston* has the old Indian Soapstone Quarry; the Clemence-Goddard House. *Lafayette* has a State Fish Hatchery.

Lincoln has Lincoln Downs Race Track, Lincoln Woods State Park, Great Road with famous colonial homes, and Limerock Quarry. *Little Compton* is the location of the ancient Commons burial grounds with Elizabeth Pabodie Monument; Wilbor House, Brownell Rose Gardens, the Pabodie House, the Rhode Island Red Hen Monument (at Adamsville), Sakonnet Yacht Club and Marina. *Middletown* is noted for Purgatory Chasm, Whitehall, and the Norman Bird Sanctuary. *Narragansett* has some of the state's best beaches; The Towers, Point Judith Lighthouse, Galilee Bird Sanctuary, fishing villages Galilee and Jerusalem, Fort Green State Park, Salt Pond, Scarborough State Beach, and Sand Hill Cove.

Newport has a wealth of elegant mansions, The Breakers; Belcourt Castle; The Elms; Marble House. Places to go in Newport are Ocean Drive, Cliff Walk, Abraham Rodrigues Rivera House, the Brick Market, National Tennis Hall of Fame, Newport Artillery Company and Museum, New England Naval and Maritime Museum, White Horse Tavern, Newport Historical Society, Old Colony House, Old Stone Mill, Redwood Library, Touro Synagogue, Trinity Church, Rochambeau Statue and Monument, Vernon House, Wanton-Lyman-Hazard House, World War I Memorial Tower in Miantonomi Memorial Park, U.S. Naval Base, Newport Harbor, Easton's Beach (public), Bailey's Beach (private).

North Kingstown is known for the birthplace of artist Gilbert Stuart, the 18th-century Snuff Mill, U.S. Naval Air Station at Quonset Point, Old Narragansett Church, South County Museum, colonial homes of Wickford Village, Wickford Marina, the Palmer-Northrup House, Smith's Castle at Cocumscussoc, the Trout Hatchery, Belleville Pond, Silver Spring Lake.

Pawtucket has Narragansett Race Track, Old Slater Mill Museum, Slater Park

Daggett House, Seekonk River State Park, Blackstone River Falls, Pidge Tavern. *Portsmouth* has five public beaches, four golf courses, Island Park Recreation Center, Old Stone Bridge and Marina, Founder's Brook, Butts Hill Fort, Portsmouth Priory, Portsmouth Historical Society.

Providence, the state capital, has the R.I. State House, Brown University, the Cathedral of SS Peter and Paul, Arcade Building, a mechanized post office, First Baptist Church, John Brown House, Stephen Hopkins House, John Hay Library, Museum of Art at Rhode Island School of Design, John Carter Brown Library, Providence Art Club, Providence College, John D. Rockefeller Library, Round Top Church, Prospect Terrace, Roger Williams Spring, Providence Public Library, Rhode Island Historical Society, Rhode Island Reds Hockey Hall of Fame, Shakespeare's Head Old State House, Market House, Episcopal Cathedral of St. John, Kennedy Plaza, Roger Williams Park, Pembroke College, North Burial Ground.

Richmond has Dawley Memorial State Park, Carolina State Forest, and Meadowbrook Golf Course. *Scituate* is the location of the Scituate Reservoir. *Smithfield* contains the Woonasquatucket and Stillwater reservoirs, the North Central State Reservoirs, the Half Way House, Daniel Angell Tavern, the Greenville Tavern, the Noah Farnum Homestead, the William Smith House, Captain Joseph Mowry's House.

South Kingtown is the home of Rhode Island University, Kingston; Pettiaquamscott Rock; site of the Jireh Bull Garrison House; the *Carter Killed Jackson* Monument; the Glebe House; the Helme House; the Museum of Primitive Culture in Peace Dale; the Great Swamp Wildlife Reservation, site of the Great Swamp Fight; Kingston Village; Matunuck (seven top beaches); Kenyon Grist Mill; Oliver Hazard Perry Home; John Potter's Great House; Edward Everett Hale's Wash Pond House, Point Judith Salt Pond.

Tiverton has four public beaches, General Lafayette's Headquarters, Tiverton Heights, the Captain Robert Grey House. *Warren* is the home of the Blount Marine Corporation. *Warwick* is the location of the Theodore Francis Green Airport, the Warwick Summer Musical Theatre, Gaspee Point, Oakland Beach, Rocky Point Amusement Park, Lincoln Park, and the Governor Greene House.

Westerly is famous for Watch Hill summer resort, the Flying Horse Carousel, Misquamicut State Beach, Weekapaug, Burlingame State Park, Granite Quarries, Old Whipping Post Farm. *West Greenwich* offers Lake Mishnock, Step Stone Falls, Wickaboxet State Park, Beach Pond State Park, the Alton Jones Campus of the University of Rhode Island. *Woonsocket* is the American headquarters of L'Union St. Jean Baptiste, and is near Diamond Hill State Park and Ski Center.

WHAT TO DO WITH THE CHILDREN. *Amusement Parks: Crescent Park,* Riverside, E. Providence, features Kiddieland, Iron Horse ride, turnpike ride, riverboat cruise. Free parking. *Rocky Point Park,* Warwick, has rides, games, amusements, huge saltwater pool (nightlighting). Free parking. UTC buses from downtown Providence. *Roger Williams Park,* Providence, features Kiddieland, merry-go-round, train, airplane, boat rides. Other amusement parks are: *Easton's Beach,* Newport; *Watch Hill Beach,* Watch Hill; *Lake Mishnock,* West Greenwich; *Goddard Memorial State Park,* Warwick; *Oakland Beach,* Warwick; *Slater Park,* Pawtucket.

Highland and Cider River Railroad, State 101, North Scituate, was built especially for children. Rides 25 cents; weekdays, 3 to 9; weekends, 12 to 9.

Zoos: Roger Williams Park Zoo allows children to pet animals in special area. Zoo animals, just for watching, are at their best during feeding time, 1 to 5 p.m. *Slater Park Zoo,* Pawtucket, is considered one of the best in New England. Park has picnic area, tennis courts, boat rental.

Museums: Smith's Castle, Cocumscussoc, US 1 (near Wickford), features a narrative tour of this 1678 house. Admission 10 cents, children; 50 cents, adults. Closed Thurs. *Tomaquag Valley Indian Museum,* Burdickville Rd., Ashaway, includes Indian village, garden, nature trail, and live Indian celebrations weekends. Summer hours from morning to dusk; winter, 1 to 5 p.m.

Children's Playhouse at the Breakers, Newport, once belonged to Vanderbilt children. Hostess. Open June to Oct. Admission to the Breakers, Playhouse, gardens is 75 cents for children; $1.75, adults.

'Twas the Night Before Christmas by the late Dr. Clement C. Moore, who resided at Catherine St. and Greenough Place, Newport. Now children may go all through the house, opened as a *toy museum.* Open weekends; 25 cents, children; 50 cents, adults.

The *Planetarium, Roger Williams Park,* Providence, welcomes starry-eyed youngsters. *University of Rhode Island* invites children and parents to the milking parlor, dairy barn, between 3 and 5 p.m. State 138, Kingston.

EXPLORING RHODE ISLAND

Your tour of Rhode Island should begin with a comprehensive exploration of Providence, the state's capital. You may obtain a useful pamphlet, *Seeing Providence,* at the Providence Journal Building, Providence Chamber of Commerce, Rhode Island Development Council, or automobile club offices.

The presence of the city's founder makes itself felt through a bust of Roger Williams situated over the main entrance to Providence City Hall. Across the street is the civic center, Exchange Place, reportedly the first, and one of the finest, central squares of its kind in the nation. Highlighting the square's many structures is the Industrial Trust Building, 416 feet high, which is capped by a huge lantern that can be seen at night from a distance of 40 miles.

Providence's Civic Center

The square, including City Hall Park, boasts several monuments which commemorate Rhode Island's participation in the nation's wars. A mounted figure of General Ambrose E. Burnside, Civil War commander, later Governor of Rhode Island and U.S. Senator, stands on the east end of the railroad station. Just west of here is *The Scout,* in memory of Major H. H. Young, chief of scouts to General Phil Sheridan. Other attractions in the square include a monument paying tribute to Civil War soldiers and sailors, and a Spanish War memorial, *The Hiker.* Don't miss the bronze fountain in City Hall Park.

From Exchange Place, drive east, passing the post office, into Memorial Square. Bear left by the World War I Memorial, a 115-foot granite shaft topped by an heroic figure symbolizing peace, turn right on Waterman Street, then left on North Main Street.

Here, you can see the First Baptist Meeting House. It is the oldest church of any denomination in the state and was the first Baptist Church in America. Founded by Roger Williams in 1638, the church has maintained a continuous existence ever since. Its beautiful interior is preserved in colonial form, including a crystal chandelier which was first lighted in 1792. The structure was built for a dual purpose: "for the publick worship of Almighty God; and also for holding Commencement in." Today, the church still serves both functions. If you desire a conducted tour, you can reach the office by the Waterman Street entrance.

Just left of the First Baptist Meeting House, at 11 Thomas Street, is the Providence Art Club. Inside the building, which was erected in 1793, are headquarters of the Providence Water Color Club. Its galleries host local art exhibitions, which are changed frequently. Adjacent to the art club, at 9 Thomas Street, is the Deacon Edward Taylor House, built about 1790 by a deacon of the First Congregational Church. Next, at number 7, is the Fleur de Lys Building, a studio building erected in 1886 by Sidney R. Burleigh, who was called dean of Rhode Island artists until his death in 1929. Its half-timbered design is of the 17th-century Norman and Breton style. Of particular interest are the ornate decorations in the wood and stucco.

Opposite the church, on Waterman Street, are buildings of the Rhode Island School of Design, which covers nearly the entire block. Opened in 1878, it is known as one of the finest schools of design in the country. At the corner of Waterman and North Main streets is the East Side bus tunnel. The entrance, which is marked by a bronze plaque, was the site of the first Town Meeting House of Providence, where, from 1644 to 1647, Roger Williams often presided over the freemen.

Continuing north on North Main Street, you will see the Joseph Russell House at number 118. An ambitious Providence merchant, Russell traded with the Far East, building the house in 1772. It has been raised to allow room for stores on the ground floor. Farther up the street, on the right, is a square wooden house, which was once designated by a sign of *Shakespear's Head.* Built in 1763, this was the residence of John Carter, at one time an apprentice of Benjamin Franklin. After Franklin, as Postmaster General, appointed Carter postmaster of Providence, the house became the post office. It was also used as a bookstore and popular meeting place. Supposedly, the house later served as a station of the "underground railroad" for runaway slaves.

On the opposite side of Meeting Street is the Brick School House (1769), which was used both as a school and a place for town meetings. In 1900, it became one of the four first free public schools, and just before the Civil War, the building was a school for Negroes. Continue up North Main Street for a block until reaching the Old State House, meeting place of the General Assembly from 1762 until 1900. Today, it serves the Sixth District Court. A little farther up North Main Street, on the left-hand side, you can see the Roger Williams Spring, which is enshrined in a little park. By a Proprietors' Grant in 1721, "liberty is reserved for the inhabitants to fetch water at this spring forever." A house across the street, at the corner of Howland Street, bears a tablet stating that "a few rods east of this spot stood the house of Roger Williams, founder of Providence, 1636."

Turn right on Church Street and then right again on Benefit Street. At the next corner, on the left-hand side, is the Sullivan Dorr House. A marked spot in the rear of the house indicates where Roger Williams was buried in 1683. Many years later, loam from his grave was transferred to an inscribed metal container in the main cemetery vault at North Burial Ground.

Continue on Benefit Street for several blocks, past the rear of First Baptist Church, and cross Waterman Street, coming to the School of Design Museum. Pendleton House, entered at 224 Benefit Street, has one room on the ground floor devoted to the arts of Rhode Island. Here, works of great Rhode Island cabinetmakers and a superb array of Rhode Island silver are on display. Collections of American, European, Oriental, and Aboriginal arts, which are shown in the Eliza Radeke Building, are arranged, for the most part, in chronological order so you can proceed from the arts of ancient Egypt through the arts of the present day. The second floor houses splendid Oriental collections. Study rooms and galleries for special exhibitions of prints, drawings, and the decorative arts can be seen on the floors below the entrance to the building.

Love in the Athenaeum

Follow south on Benefit Street to the corner of College Street. Here you will find the state's oldest library, the Providence Library. Erected in 1838, this ivy-covered building of the Greek Revival period houses a vast collection of valuable books in shelved alcoves of the main room. It was in these alcoves where Edgar Allan Poe and Sarah Helen Whitman carried on their courtship. You may also find the library's paintings of special interest. At the next corner, Hopkins Street, is the Stephen Hopkins House, whose occupant was governor of the state ten times and Chief Justice of its Supreme Court. General Washington was a guest in the house in 1776, after the evacuation of Boston, and again in 1781, when he came to Rhode Island to meet General Rochambeau.

One block farther on the left, at the corner of Benevolent Street, is the First Congregational Church. Built in 1723, the church is a beautiful example of early 19th-century ecclesiastic architecture. John Holden Greene, its designer, considered the church his masterpiece. The steeple holds the largest and heaviest bell cast in the foundry of Paul Revere and Son.

Turn left on Benevolent Street and left again through Megee Street, across George and into Prospect Street. On the right is the campus of Brown University. The seventh oldest of American colleges, Brown was chartered in 1764 as Rhode Island College. The first building, facing the front campus, is Rhode Island Hall, which was built in 1840. Slater Hall, a dormitory, is next in line. The central building is University Hall. In 1770, John Brown laid its cornerstone, and during the Revolution, the hall was used as a barracks and hospital for American and French soldiers. Guarding the main entrance to the campus are the beautiful Van Wickle Memorial Gates. On the other side of University Hall are Manning Hall (1835), a lecture hall, and a dormitory, Hope College (1822). Across the street, at the corner of College Street, is the John Hay Library. Built in 1910, it houses the university special collections and the Physical Sciences Library. Collections of particular interest include the Harris Collection of American Poetry and Plays, the Rider Collection of books and manuscripts about Rhode Island history, the McLellan Collection of Lincolniana (11,000 items, including 800 bearing the Great Emancipator's signature) and the Webster Knight stamp collection, containing U.S. stamps in blocks of four, uncancelled—one of the best of its kind in the country.

Proceed on Prospect Street until coming to the corner of Meeting Street, where stands the First Church of Christ, Scientist. The church's lofty green dome, completed in 1913, is a prominent feature of Providence's skyline. This dome, which is one of the highest spots in the city, was used for a beacon in 1669 to warn of Indian attack, and again in 1775, to give warning of British approach. The beacon was reportedly visible from as far as Cambridge, Massachusetts. Turn left on Meeting and right on Congdon Street. Here, at Prospect Terrace, you can obtain a panoramic view of the city. Established in the mid-1800's, the park is the site of the new Roger Williams Memorial Monument, where the ashes of Rhode Island's founder were deposited when the monument was dedicated in 1939.

From Congdon Street, turn right on Bowen Street and then right again on Thayer Street. Follow Thayer past the east side of Brown's campus until taking a right on George Street. Near the George Street gate to the university is John Carter Brown Library. This building of neo-classic design houses a collection of Americana, one of the very best in the world. John Carter Brown, grandson of John Carter, the printer, started this assemblage of printed books, surveying the literature of this hemisphere until the 19th century. Today, the collection numbers 30,000. The library's main reading room is constructed and furnished as a gentleman's library.

Across the street is The Wriston Quadrangle, encompassing the better part of two city blocks. In the largest single expansion program ever undertaken by the university, the quadrangle was added to Brown in 1951. It consists of ten buildings, including the Refectory, Rhode Island's largest dining hall, seating 1,800 students. After turning left on Brown Street, stop to view the Annmary Brown Memorial, a block down on the left. This building of simple classical style, which boasts two wrought bronze doors, houses that part of the university devoted to incunabula and Renaissance studies. Bibliophiles will be fascinated by the collection of literature from the end of the 15th century. The memorial also has a collection of portraits, paintings, family heirlooms, and Civil War relics.

Four Early Mansions

Continue to the end of Brown Street where, within a block of the spot, stand four mansions dating from the early days of the republic. On the left, at 66 Power Street, is the Thomas Poynton Ives House. Ives, for whom the house was built in 1806, was supposedly foremost among the citizens of Providence of his day. Turn right on Power Street where, at number 52, stands the John Brown House. Built in 1786, and one of the finest examples of Georgian design architecture, this house is presently the headquarters of the Rhode Island Historical Society. John Quincy Adams wrote of the house in 1789: "We only saw the outside of it, which is the most magnificent and elegant private mansion that I have ever seen on this continent." Three rooms on the first floor contain objects from the days of the Indians to the present time. The house also has a fine collection of furniture made by the famous Newport cabinet makers of the 18th century. Several architectural features set the house apart: four chimneys, rather than two; a slight projection, crowned by a pediment, in the center of the facade, with the open entrance porch set in the projection; and the Palladian window over the entrance.

Just around the corner to the left, at 357 Benefit Street, you can see the Joseph Nightingale House, one of the largest frame Colonial houses in existence. In this house, built around 1792, John Carter Brown assembled his famed collection of Americana. For this reason, the house is often referred to by his name. Follow Benefit

Street for a block and turn left on Williams Street. At number 66 can be seen the fourth of this noted group of mansions, the Edward Carrington House. The structure is of early Republican design, although its porch belongs to a later period. Erected in 1812, the house boasts many elegant Colonial furnishings and some valuable Chinese work collected by Edward Carrington, a shipping merchant, through his trade with the Orient.

Return to Benefit Street, turn left, and follow it past Arnold Street. On the right is the Tillinghast Burial Ground, named for Pardon Tillinghast, who came to Providence in 1643. In 1680, he built the first wharf on what later became a flourishing waterfront. In 1700, as a Baptist minister, he built the first church, at his own expense, "in the shape of a haycap, with a fireplace in the middle, the smoke escaping from a hole in the roof." He died in 1718 and is buried, with his family, on this land, his private burial ground.

Turn right on Transit Street and be sure to notice, at number 53, the old Lightning Splitter House. Its sharply-pitched gables suggest the steep roofs of medieval houses. Turn right onto South Main Street where, on the left at number 403, stands the Dolphin House. A sailing captain, Joseph Tillinghast, built the house about 1770. Its name is thought to stem from the building's use as a tavern for sailors during the days of the China trade. A few blocks farther on South Main, at the corner of Powell Street, is the Talma Theater. Erected as a church in 1883, this brick building with portico served as a morgue in the days of the Civil War. After the war, it was used as a theater by amateur companies, and in 1916, the building became the home of the Providence Boys' Club.

The farther corner of Planet Street is the site of Sabin Tavern. Built about 1763, the building served as the Providence depot for the first stagecoach line to Boston. A tablet on the side of the structure reads: ". . . upon this corner stood the Sabin Tavern in which on the evening of June 9th, 1772, the party met and organized to destroy H. B. M. Schooner *Gaspee,* in the destruction of which was shed the first blood in the American Revolution." At 50 South Main Street is the Joseph Brown House, designed and built in 1774 by Joseph Brown, one of four brothers whose efforts were largely responsible for the city's commercial progress. In the rear of the house, it is reported that, where there used to be a huge pear tree, "George Washington once sat and regaled himself with the luscious fruit." Follow South Main Street past Hopkins Street to the Providence County Court House (1933). Designed as an adaptation of Colonial-style architecture, it is unusually large. Built on the side of a hill, it has eight stories in front, six in the rear.

Across the street is the historic heart of the city, Market Square. As a market place in the colonial days, the square was a spot for political as well as commercial activities. Here, you can see the "world's widest bridge." Crawford Street Bridge is 1,147 feet wide, covering the Providence River from Crawford Street to the rear of the parcel post building at Exchange Street and Memorial Square. The central feature of the square is the Market House, which was completed in 1774. The lower floor served as a market. The second story was used as a banquet hall, barracks for French soldiers, and office of Samuel Bridgham, first mayor of the city. The third floor served as Masonic quarters. A tablet on the buildings marks the height of water reached in the great gale of 1815, when ships were thrown over the square. This mark was blurred when the 1938 hurricane forced tidal flood waters to an even higher level.

From Market Square, follow north on North Main Street, turn left on Waterman Street to Memorial Square. Head west on Westminster Street, one of the chief business and shopping streets of the city. But you cannot drive the entire distance—Providence's new half-million-dollar Mall has transformed Westminster Street from a narrow, congested, uninspiring thoroughfare into a pleasant and colorful shoppers' walkway 950 feet long. Stretching from Dorrance Street to Snow Street, the pedestrians-only mall includes a cross spur along two parts of Union Street. The Mall is tied to the city's other two major shopping streets, Washington and Weybosset, and to main bus lines. Proceeding on Westminster Street, you will see Turk's Head, which is the name given to the fork at Westminster and Weybosset streets. About 1750, a huge wood carving, originally a ship's figurehead, was mounted over the facade of Jacob Whitman's house. Today, an office building occupies this site, but a Turk's Head still appears in the belt course ornamentation of the present structure.

A Greek Revival Arcade

Continue on Westminster Street where, on the left, is The Arcade. Built in 1827, this building, which closely resembles a Greek temple, was a 19th-century Five and Ten cent store. It was a shoppers' paradise and a show place of the town. The Arcade is the last of the temple-like structures built in America during the Greek Revival period. Its columns, each weighing 12 tons, are said to be some of the largest monoliths in the country. Beyond Dorrance Street, where the Mall begins, is the center of the shopping district. Included among the many shops and stores is *Gladding's,* which claims to be the oldest dry goods store in America.

A few blocks farther on the left, on the corner of Mathewson Street, is Grace Church (Episcopal). This brownstone Victorian

Gothic building, consecrated in 1846, houses chimes that ring the quarter hours as well as an occasional melody throughout the city. From here, continue on Westminster Street and turn right on Empire. At the next corner, Washington Street, is the Providence Public Library, an Italian Renaissance edifice completed in 1900. This central library and its branches boast 480,000 volumes and many notable collections. From Empire Street, turn right on Fountain Street and proceed past the *Providence Journal* Building. Bear left at the end of the street, pass the railroad station, and go through the underpass. Turn right at the next corner and bear left at the Pershing Square rotary onto Stillman Street.

The Marble-Domed Capitol

You are now facing the State Capitol, considered one of the most beautiful in the nation. Made of white Georgian marble, the building is capped by the second largest among four famed marble domes in the world, the largest being the top of St. Peter's in Rome. The dome is particularly attractive at night, when it is illuminated by a battery of floodlights. The best approach is across the 14-acre lawn and up the terraced steps. If this thought doesn't appeal to you, turn right on Gaspee, left on Smith Street, and find parking space before returning to the south entrance. Bronze statues of General Nathanael Greene and Commodore Oliver Hazard Perry guard the entrance. But, before entering the building, you might want to know what is the statue on top of the dome. The figure watching over the liberties of the state from a height of 235 feet is a symbolic statue, *The Independent Man*.

The statue is of classic-heroic style and depicts a man, clothed only in a lion's skin, holding a spear in his extended right hand while his left hand rests on an anchor, the emblem of Rhode Island since 1647. The bronze figure is about 11 feet high and weighs around 500 pounds. In the great state reception room hang portraits of Washington, General Greene, and Commodore Perry. The governor's office and the halls display portraits of nearly every governor from colonial days to the present. Historical relics, battle flags, and other memorials can be seen at the building's many entrances. The most valuable historical relic, presently enshrined in the office of the Secretary of State, is the original parchment charter granted by King Charles II, July 8, 1663.

Across from the Capitol, on Smith Street, is the State Office Building, which houses the Department of Public Works. Be sure to obtain a state highway map from here before leaving the city on our tour of Rhode Island. To finish your route of Providence, however, turn left on Francis Street and follow it under the Union Station to Exchange Place, near the City Hall.

From Providence, take Interstate 195 east to State 114, which will lead you south to Barrington, a distinguished suburban community. This town boasts such attractions as Karl P. Jones' Rose Gardens and the Rhode Island Country Club. Many country estates are nearby, particularly at Nayatt Point and Rumstick Point on Narragansett Bay. From here, follow Asylum Road until taking Colt Drive, a scenic two-mile route along the shore with facilities for swimming and picnicking.

Continue on 114 to reach Bristol, one of the state's most historic towns. Although it was an important seaport for trading vessels for 150 years, Bristol's harbor today serves mostly pleasure craft. The Reynolds House, at 956 Hope Street, was used as headquarters by Lafayette in 1778. Mount Hope Farm, which is reached via Metacom Avenue, is where King Philip and his tribe made their home. On the farm is King Philip Museum, which contains a large collection of Indian relics, including many personal mementos of Philip. The Bristol Art Museum has several changing art exhibits and the historic coach of James DeWolf. The Haffenreffer Museum houses a collection of Indian artifacts and a Tribal Arts exhibit gathered from Africa, North America, and the Pacific.

Continue on State 114 out of Bristol, cross Mount Hope Bridge, and take the ferry to Portsmouth. This town, first settled in 1638, embraces the northern portion of the island named "Rhode Island." During the Revolution, many earthwork fortifications were erected in Bristol. Butts Hill Fort, off Sprague Street, is the site of the only major land battle in the state during the Revolutionary War, and you can still see scars from this conflict. Bristol Ferry Fort, not far from Mount Hope Bridge, also retains signs of the earthworks. Founder's Brook, located off Boyd's Lane, is where the first settlers from Boston landed in 1638. Another attraction you may find interesting is the Portsmouth Priory, a Benedictine monastery and preparatory school. This church of contemporary style houses a wire sculpture by Richard Lippold.

From Portsmouth, follow State 138 to Middletown, the central town on the island. Off Purgatory Road, be sure not to miss Purgatory, which is a huge chasm in the rocks. On Hanging Rock Road, a continuation of Purgatory Road, you can view the unusual "hanging rocks." Whitehall, a house built in 1729 by Dean George Berkeley, noted English philosopher and bishop, lays claim to being a shrine of American culture. The quaint, hipped-roof house contains an original fireplace, a small garden and many furnishings of the 18th century. Near the Portsmouth line, on Highway 114, is the Overing House. Here, British General Prescott was captured in a daring raid on July 9, 1777. Continue on 138 to Broadway, which will lead you to Newport.

Elegant Newport

Colonial Newport, one of the state's six cities, is probably best known for its magnificent "museum mansions." What is a "museum mansion"? It can best be defined as a former private home which, because of its historic value and architectural significance, has been preserved for current and future generations, and which is open to the public on a regular or semi-regular basis. Each one is a living record of a fabulous period in the history of the United States.

"The Breakers," on Ochre Point Avenue, is considered the most stunning summer residence in Newport. Originally designed for Cornelius Vanderbilt, it is a grandiose monument to a fabulous age. Its 70 rooms contain massive fireplaces, giant crystal chandeliers, mirrored walls, mosaic floors, a stained glass skylight, paintings, frescoes, carvings, tapestries, and furnishings that required the skills of two continents. In general, the design follows that of 16th-century northern palaces of Genoa and Turin. The house measures approximately 250 feet by 150 feet and its rooms are distributed among four floors, arranged symmetrically around a center hall. The first, or main, floor contains the formal rooms, and the second and third floors are devoted to sleeping apartments. Built for entertaining, the house shows off to its best advantage at night when illuminated by glittering chandeliers suspended from the high ceilings.

The most recently-opened museum mansion is "The Elms," beautiful Bellevue Avenue estate of the late E. J. Berwind, Philadelphia coal magnate. Designed by the famous architect, Horace Trumbauer, the estate was largely modeled after the Château d'Asnières, near Paris. The rooms on the first floor reflect the elegance of the mansions built in Newport at the turn of the century. The main hall boasts 18th-century paintings from the Palazzo Cornaro in Venice. You can see the opulence of the era in the Venetian-style dining room with its unusual furnishings, the breakfast room with large black and gold lacquer Chinese panels of the K'ang-hsi period (1662–1722), and the ball room with a crystal chandelier. The mansion is completely furnished with museum pieces, some of which are part of the original furnishings. Others were lent by museums and private collectors. A highlight of Newport is The Elms' grounds, boasting bronze and marble statues, playing fountains, gazebos, sprawling green lawns with trees and hedges trimmed in the French manner, and beautiful, formal, sunken French gardens. You may also enjoy viewing a rare collection of trees and shrubs from all over the world, all properly labeled.

Bellevue Avenue also boasts the "Marble House," which is often referred to as the "Sumptuous Palace by the Sea." Completed in 1892 for William K. Vanderbilt, the house was designed by Richard Morris Hunt, who also designed The Breakers. The Marble House takes its name from the many kinds of marble used in its construction and decoration. Many features of the Grand and Petit Trianon at Versailles are incorporated in the architecture and decor of this mansion. The wrought ironwork of the gates and driveway is modeled after the one at Versailles and is repeated in the entrance doors, staircase, and balcony railing of the central hall. The yellow marble in the hall comes from Sienna, Italy, and the formal walls of the dining room are made of deep pink Numidian marble.

You can easily distinguish the Marble House's Gothic Room from the rest of the mansion, which is characterized by its 17th- and 18th-century French style. The mantelpiece of Gothic figures was modeled in plaster by sculptors in Italy. Unquestionably, the most elaborate of the rooms is the ballroom, which is known as the "Gold Room" because of its extensive gold ornamentation. Candelabras in the form of bronze figures flank the stunning marble mantelpiece, in the center of which is a French clock, contrived to indicate the various times all over the world. Many emblems can be seen throughout the mansion, but particularly in the Gold Room, where you can see the face of *le Roi Soleil,* the Sun-King, Louis XIV. Stories from Greek mythology are depicted on four gold bas-reliefs on each side of the fireplace and on the opposite wall. The Marble House is completely furnished with the original pieces placed in the house when it was built.

Building Castles in Rhode Island

Another recommended visit is "Belcourt Castle," also on Bellevue Avenue, which was built by a descendant of Commodore Matthew Calbraith Perry, Oliver Hazard Perry Belmont. In 1891, Richard Morris Hunt designed the 52-room mansion, completed in 1894 at an estimated cost of three million dollars. Purchased in the 1950's by the Harold B. Tinney family for use as both a residence and a private museum, Belcourt Castle, with its King Louis XIII architecture, is enhanced by the Tinney collection of antiques and art treasures from 29 countries of the world. Within the castle, you can see what is considered the largest private collection of stained glass on earth. Included in the array are representative windows from throughout France, Germany, and America. European craftsmen were brought in to complete the magnificent wood carvings for which the estate is also noted. The Grand Stair is an authentic reproduction of the Francis I stair housed in the Musée de Cluny in Paris.

Be sure to see The Breakers' carriage house and stable, at the corner of Coggeshall and Bateman avenues. Here, you will view one of the largest collections of carriages and coaches owned by an American family. The stables have been maintained as they were at the turn of the century. Harness, livery, and other equipment are also displayed in their original setting. Return to Bellevue Avenue and continue north to the Newport Casino, on the corner of Memorial Boulevard. Designed in 1881, the casino houses the National Lawn Tennis Hall of Fame and Museum. The museum has four large rooms, and a "Hall of Fame" grass tennis court opposite the entrance. Each year, thousands of persons visit this shrine of American Tennis, to browse among the displays of tennis memorabilia and to enjoy the notable Stanford White architecture.

Turn right on Memorial Boulevard to reach Cliff Walk. Starting at Easton's Beach, it skirts the cliffs along the ocean for three miles, in front of the mansion museums, and ends at Bailey's Beach. Only portions of the walk can be traveled because much of it was ruined by the 1938 hurricane. After returning to Bellevue Avenue and turning right, you will come to a building housing the Art Association of Newport, which holds frequent exhibitions of paintings, and the Redwood Library, a national historic site. Designed by Peter Harrison in 1748, the library has the oldest reading room in continuous use in the country. You might take particular interest in its outstanding collection of American paintings. Across the street is the Old Stone Mill, concerning which much time and effort have been spent to determine its origin. Some maintain that the mill was built by Benedict Arnold while he was governor of the colony. But, the most popular theory is that this "mystery tower" was erected by Norsemen seven centuries ago.

A block away, at the corner of Church and Spring streets is Trinity Church, which has been called a supreme and matchless reminder of Colonial America. Built in 1726, the church is said to be more perfectly preserved than any other major wooden structure of early colonial days. The three-tier wine glass pulpit is the only one left in America. You can see many treasures that add to Trinity's fame, such as the simple table which serves as the altar, first used by a visiting missionary in 1698. The Kay Memorial Baptismal Bowl, hammered out of a single sheet of silver, is possibly the finest piece of silverware in the country. Since 1734, Trinity's babies have been baptized from this font. The bell in the Tower Room is dated 1702, and is thought to be the first church bell heard in New England. Another priceless relic is the original casework of

Bishop Berkeley, with its royal crown and Bishop's mitres. You can see the George Washington pew and the grave and memorial tablet of Admiral D'Arsac de Ternay, which are reminders of Newport's crucial part in the struggle for independence. The black and gold altarpiece has been in place since 1733, although the British Royal Arms which surmounted it was destroyed by a mob after the British troops evacuated Newport. This was the only damage sustained by the church during the Revolutionary War.

Follow north on Spring Street to Washington Square where, within short walking distance of the area, many more historic landmarks should be seen. The Newport Historical Society occupies a group of buildings, all connected, at 82 Touro Street. One of these is a colonial church, built in 1729, the oldest Seventh Day Baptist Church in America. Downstairs, to the right of the front entrance, you can visit the Marine Museum, which displays objects relating to the navy and its history in Newport, pictures illustrating the life of the Naval Academy when it was located at Newport during the Civil War, and models and pictures depicting the Merchant Marine. On the second floor are displayed rare furniture and china, memorials of the Civil War as well as miniatures, silhouettes, and special exhibits. Dresses and accessories of various periods, some dating back to the American Revolution, are shown in display cabinets here. On the walls hang portraits, rare prints, broadsides, samplers, and many other fine attractions. One of the most stunning displays in the building is the silver and glassware shown in the Prescott Lawrence Room. Another room, devoted to newspapers published in Newport, may also interest you.

America's Oldest Synagogue

Next door to the Newport Historical Society stands Touro Synagogue, a national historic site. A symbol of religious liberty since 1763, this is the oldest synagogue building in America. When Peter Harrison designed Touro Synagogue (often called his masterpiece), he used the Georgian style, but modified it to accommodate the Sephardic ritual. As was the custom of Sephardic Jews, the synagogue was inconspicuously located on a quiet street. It stands diagonally on its small plot so that worshippers standing in prayer before the Holy Ark face eastward toward Jerusalem. This symbolic placement gives an air of individuality to the building and subtly insulates it from its surroundings.

The plain brick exterior gives no idea of the richness you can find within the building. Twelve Ionic columns, representing the tribes of ancient Israel, support a gallery. Above these rise twelve Corin-

Above: The Mayflower II, which was sailed to America on a commemorative voyage under the command of Capt. Alan Villiers, is now permanently anchored at Plymouth, Mass.
(Photo—B. D. Laschever)

Overleaf: There is a lot of fun to be had on the frozen New England lake, on a crisp winter day.
(Wm. Tague)

Facing page 129: Antique-hunting in New Hampshire is a popular summer sport.
(Davis Pratt—Rapho Guillumette Agency)

thian columns supporting the dome ceiling. Five huge brass candelabra, dating back to the 18th century, hang from the ceiling. The Holy Ark at the east end of the room contains the Scrolls of the Law, or Torah. Hand-lettered with special ink by scribes of great skill, these scrolls are the most sacred of Jewish objects. On them are recorded the Five Books of Moses, the source of Jewish faith. The scrolls are mounted on wood rollers, two of which are decorated with exquisite silver belltops. Above the Ark, you can see a representation of the Ten Commandments in Hebrew, painted by the Newport artist, Benjamin Howland.

The Old Colony House (1739), on Washington Square, is one of the early government buildings of America. The house was the scene of inaugurations of governors for 150 years, and from its handsome second floor balcony, the acceptance of the Declaration of Independence by Rhode Island was proclaimed. The Vernon House, at 46 Clarke Street, is the well-preserved building which served as General Rochambeau's headquarters during the American Revolution. Built in 1758, the house is noted for its interior paneling and its curious 18th-century Chinese wall decorations. The Wanton-Lyman-Hazard House (1675), at 17 Broadway, is the oldest house in Newport and one of the finest Jacobean houses in New England. Of special interest is the small colonial garden in the rear of this national historic site. A block away, at the corner of Farewell and Marlborough streets, stands the White House Tavern, oldest tavern in the country. Erected in 1763, the building is restored as a combined museum and colonial tavern. Also on Marlborough Street is the Friends Meeting House. Built in 1699 on the site of an earlier meeting place, it now serves as the Community Center.

An outstanding example of Newport's pre-Revolutionary Golden Age is the Hunter House, on Washington Street. It was built in 1748 by Jonathan Nichols, Jr., a prosperous merchant of the period. During the hundred years from 1750 to 1850, the house was occupied successively by Nichols, Colonel Joseph Wanton, and William Hunter, a graduate of Brown University, United States Senator from Rhode Island, and Minister to Brazil. Now, fully restored to its 18th-century appearance, the Hunter House ranks among the ten best specimens of colonial residential architecture. It has five rooms fully-paneled from floor to ceiling, a rare feature that should not be missed. You can see fine examples of the cabinet-making skills of the Townsend and Goddard families of Newport. Silver, paintings, and furniture can also be seen in their appropriate settings. The last recommended stop before leaving Newport, at Washington Square, on the corner of Long Wharf and Thames Street, is The Brick Market. This national historic shrine is the home of *Newport*

Crafts, showroom of Historic Newport Reproductions, where furniture, china, and the like are for sale.

From Thames Street, turn right onto Mill Street, where you can take the ferry to Jamestown, on Conanicut Island. This entire island is devoted to recreation during the summer months. Some of the houses which escaped the British torch in 1775 can still be seen. Sportsmen will enjoy the facilities offered by the town, including swimming and fishing. Beavertail Lighthouse is where the original lighthouse was built in 1749, the third light established in America. The present tower, made of granite and erected in 1856, will afford you a superb view of the ocean along the New England coast if you climb it. For more good views, drive north on Ocean Avenue (East Shore Road) from Jamestown. About a mile from the village, just off the road, is the foundation of the Benedict Arnold House, built in 1693. You may be interested in the Old Windmill, erected in 1787. Located about a mile and a half from Jamestown, on North Road, the windmill has been restored to working condition. The Fire Museum on Narragansett Avenue displays a horse-drawn fire pumper and antique fire-fighting equipment. Back at the corner of Narragansett Avenue and North Road is the Old Burying Ground, which dates back to 1656.

Recreation at Narragansett Pier

Take Eldred Avenue over the Jamestown Bridge. Follow State 138 onto Highway Alternate (Scenic 1A) to reach Narragansett Pier, which was referred to by the *New York Times* recently as ". . . without a doubt, one of the finest beaches in the world." This narrow strip of seacoast on Rhode Island Sound has been a well known resort for years. Narragansett's crescent beaches are lined with luxurious summer residences and modest seashore cottages. "The Towers," designed and built in 1882 by Stanford White, is a landmark of the Pier. It is the only building in the United States that arches over a federal highway. Fishing is a chief recreational facility, as Narragansett boasts of being "world tuna headquarters." The United States Atlantic Tuna Tournament and Rhode Island Tuna Tournament are held here. You can surfcast, fish from shore, sail on any of dozens of boats with experienced skippers, or rent a skiff and motor. In addition to fishing, swimming, and boating, Narragansett offers a variety of vacation activities. Sprague Park has facilities for tennis, baseball, softball, practice golf, and horseshoes. Horse racing is available nearby at Narragansett Park and Lincoln Downs. In town, you can enjoy bowling, movies, a fine library, summer stock, and special exhibitions. The summer school of the University of Rhode Island features art shows, concerts, and cultural programs. Just south of the Pier is the Hannah Robinson House, on Boston Neck. Built in 1746, the building was a stop for Lafayette at one time. Follow Ocean Road past Scarborough State Beach to Point Judith.

Of special interest here is the Point Judith Lighthouse, an important beacon known to coastal mariners. The original lighthouse, a wooden structure built in 1806, was demolished in the great gale of September, 1815. Standing today on the same spot is an octagonal stone structure, erected in 1816. During the Revolution, a coast guard and tower beacon were maintained at the point. At the entrance of Point Judith Pond, known as "The Breachway," are the fishing villages of Galilee and Jerusalem. Commercial fishermen, lobstermen, and draggers ship their catches from these points, and the bulkheads are thronged with pleasure craft and charter boats. From the docks at the State Pier in Galilee, take the ferry to Block Island.

Block Island Refuge

About nine miles south of the mainland, Block Island is a summer resort and fishing center. Visitors spend many hours on the white sands of Crescent Beach or at the resorts where privately owned beaches are at the disposal of guests. Skin-divers and surf-fishermen feel at home here, where world records for fish are common. Deep-sea fishing is the primary interest. The waters off Block Island are plentiful with tuna, bluefish, cod, striped bass, and flounder. At the northern end of the island, you can see Mohegan Bluffs, spectacular cliffs of clay, which bear a strong resemblance to the chalk cliffs of Dover, England, rising more than 200 feet above sea level and stretching along the seacoast for about five miles. The bluffs are so named because in many places, they seem to resemble profiles of Indians.

Whittier's poem, *The Palatine Light,* commemorates the Palatine Graves area near Dickens Point, where the crew of an ill-fated German ship lie buried. In 1661, the settlers of Dickens Point arrived at Cow Cove; the well known Settler's Rock is inscribed with their name. For a superb view of the sea, go to the top of Beacon Hill on Beacon Hill Road, where you will be 234 feet above sea level.

A man-made harbor, New Harbor, graces the western shore of the island; it was constructed by connecting the Atlantic with the Great Salt Pond by means of digging a channel across the separating finger of land, no small task considering the tools available. Old

Harbor, on the other side of the island, is where much fish is caught before being shipped to eastern markets.

On the Mainland Again

After taking the ferry back to Point Judith, follow State 108 to the outskirts of Wakefield. In Peace Dale, just north of Wakefield, is the Museum of Primitive Culture. Here, you can see a collection of American Indian, South Seas, African, and other primitive weapons and tools. From Wakefield, take US 1 south to Matunuck Beach Road, to Browning Beach Road, to Moonstone Beach Road, to Matunuck School Road. The latter road, which changes to US 1, leads you to Charlestown. This drive affords splendid views along the shore, where there are many opportunities to swim and fish. Charlestown includes the summer resorts of Charlestown Beach and Quonochontaug Beach. Indian Burying Ground, just north of the town, is the burial ground of the Narragansett Indians. On the shore of Ninigret Pond, south of Charlestown, you may visit Fort Neck Lot. At an old fort built by early Dutch traders, Captain John Smith and his men camped here in 1637. Kimball Bird Sanctuary, on the shore of Watchaugh Pond, can be reached from US 1 by turning north about two miles west of the town. The General Stanton Monument, farther north of the sanctuary on US 1, was built in memory of Joseph Stanton, native of Charlestown who served in the French and Indian War as well as the Revolution.

From the Stanton Monument, follow US 1 onto Scenic 1A. Turn left at Old Shore Road to reach Weekapaug, where you can start a pleasant drive along the shore on Atlantic Avenue. A highlight of this route is Misquamicut Beach, unquestionably one of the finest in the state. Follow unnumbered roads to Avondale, where you can take Watch Hill Road to Watch Hill, a popular resort with a fine ocean beach. One point of interest is the Flying Horse Carousel, a merry-go-round well over 100 years old and still making the rounds day after day. On Bay Street, you can see Ninigret Statue, commissioned in Paris in memory of the chief of Rhode Island's Niantic Indians. A live Indian from Buffalo Bill's Wild West Show, in Paris at the time, was the model. Surf-bathing and fishing are popular at Watch Hill, and boats are available. Return to Avondale and follow Scenic 1A to Westerly, logically enough the most westerly town in the state, in what was the territory of Misquamicut prior to 1669. Before the War of 1812, Oliver Hazard Perry built gunboats here for the government. Westerly granite is known the world over and has been quarried in the town since 1846. The quarries on Granite Street may be visited.

From Westerly, take State 91 to the outskirts of Kenyon. Turn left onto State 2 and follow it until coming to the entrance to

Rhode Island's primitive Great Swamp, a 2,600-acre marsh carved by a glacier some 100 centuries ago. You can see an infinite number of harmless creatures walk, crawl, swim, guide, and fly amid vegetation of all types. To be sure, Mother Nature rules here. In the heat of summer, the swamp can be a steam bath, while in winter it can become an icebox. In fact, the Great Swamp became a part of Colonial history on a frigid day in 1675, when its waters turned to ice.

In that year, two Indian tribes, the Wampanoags and Nipmucks, were fighting desperately to win back their land from the British. The settlers were not faring well in the war, and as a result, they became increasingly wary of the nearby neutral, but powerful, Narragansett Indians. After Narragansett Indians finally joined in the fight, the New England Federation sent a thousand men to battle the tribe. The army assembled at Smith's Castle, a trading post and blockhouse in Wickford. When the men set out to attack the Indian village in the Great Swamp, on December 19, the Narragansetts were confident that the waters surrounding them would slow any aggression. But the swamp had frozen solid. The army found an opening in the Indians' strong defense, fired the wigwams, and the battle turned into a massacre. The site of this encounter is marked by a granite shaft in the small clearing where wigwams and fortifications are believed to have stood.

From the Great Swamp, follow Liberty Lane, then State 138 to Kingston, a small town dating from 1700. One of the town's many historic buildings is the Helme House, on Kingston Road. Erected in 1802, different shows of the South County Art Association are displayed here weekly. Kingston is also the home of the University of Rhode Island, established in 1892. You may have a guided tour of the school's grounds and other points of interest in the village by students during summer session. Old Kingston Court House (1775), on Kingston Hill, was the meeting place of the General Assembly from 1776 to 1807. Continue on State 138 to the junction of US 1. Nearby, west of Pettaquamscutt Road, lies Pettaquamscutt Rock, where the white settlers and Indians signed deeds.

Follow north on US 1 until turning right on Gilbert Stuart Road. Here, you can see the Gilbert Stuart Birthplace, which dates from 1751. Stuart, the best known of Colonial artists and one of America's foremost portrait painters (especially for his series on George Washington), was born in 1755. You might take particular interest in the period furnishings, water wheel, and a snuff mill. Not far from here is Samuel Casey Farm, a New England farmhouse and out-building, built around 1750. Return to Gilbert Stuart Road, turn right and follow it onto Scenic 1A, which will lead you to Wickford.

Main Street in Wickford Village contains an outstanding collection of houses dating from the late 18th and early 19th centuries. Some say that the village boasts the largest concentration of such houses in the country. One structure on Main Street that should not be missed is Old Narrangansett Church, erected in 1707, the oldest Episcopal Church building in use north of Philadelphia. It is one of four original Colonial parishes in Rhode Island and features Queen Anne communion silver service, box pews, a wine glass pulpit, and a slave gallery. On West Main Street, you can view Firemen's Memorial, home of the North Kingston Veteran Firemen's Association. It displays a restored, hand-pumped fire engine, built in 1875, as well as other antiquated fire-fighting equipment. A key to the building is available at the nearby Public Safety Building, on Tower Hill Road.

Domesticating the Lobster

Wickford's Main Street is also the site of the Lobster Hatchery, the only lobster rearing station in the nation. A lobster is hatched from an egg and passes a period of six to eight weeks before it assumes the appearance of its progenitors. Before this, it swims on the surface and is prey for fish. It then assumes the form of a lobster, less than an inch long, and sinks to the bottom. The Lobster Hatchery keeps the larvae until the bottom-seeking stage and then releases them. As many as 10,000 larvae are hanging around in the water at any given time in the hatchery.

A short distance north of Wickford, on US 1, is St. Paul's Church, built in 1707. Nearby is Smith's Castle, at Cocumscussoc. Erected in 1677 as a trading house by Richard Smith, it was used as a rendezvous for troops who fought in the Great Swamp Fight. The building, which features an 18th-century garden, is believed to be the only house standing in which Roger Williams preached. From here, follow Stony Lane to South County Museum on Quaker Lane. The museum houses a collection of articles from early New England life and industry, including tools, farming implements, vehicles, appliances, and mechanical devices. Return to US 1, turn left and follow it to Quonset Point, where signs will direct you to Quonset Point Naval Air Station. Here, you will be at the birthplace of the Navy's "Seabees" and the Quonset Hut.

Continue on US 1 to reach East Greenwich, one of Rhode Island's most attractive residential communities. Of the town's many Colonial buildings, the General James M. Varnum House, War. Washington, Lafayette, and Rochambeau are among those who were entertained at this mansion (1773), accented by memorabilia from the Revolutionary era and boasting rare paneling and wallpaper. Kent County Court House, at the corner of Main and Court streets, was erected in 1750 and enlarged in 1805. The Rhode Island Constitution was framed here in 1842, following Dorr's Rebellion. The Independent Company of Kentish Guards, chartered in 1774, is an armory well worth a visit. General Nathanael Greene, second-in-command of Revolutionary Army troops under Washington, was a member of this command. Greene's birthplace, built in 1684, can be reached via Forge Road. Varnum Memorial Armory's Military and Naval Museum can be seen at the corner of Division and Main streets. Erected in 1914, the building contains a collection of objects pertaining to all of the nation's wars. In the northern outskirts of East Greenwich, near Greenwich Cove, you may visit Goddard Memorial State Park. Featured attractions include recreational facilities and educational exhibits.

From the park, follow US 1 to Apponaug and turn left onto State 117, which will lead you to Anthony. This mill town is the site of the Nathanael Greene Homestead, at 48 Taft Street. Built in 1770, the 14-room house has been restored as a patriotic shrine in Greene's memory. Return west on State 117 and pass through Apponaug to Warwick. Rocky Point, reached via 117 and Rocky Point Road, is a pleasant shore resort famous for its seafood dinners. Warwick Neck Lighthouse can be seen following Warwick Neck Avenue from 117. You may enjoy fine salt-water bathing at Oakland Beach, at the end of Oakland Beach Avenue and at Nausauket Beach Reservation, just west of Buttonwood.

Pawtucket and Woonsocket

This tour, so far, has focused primarily on the shoreline areas of Rhode Island, along Block Island Sound, Narragansett Bay, and Rhode Island Sound, which are the best known parts of the state. As a result, these areas are usually the only places visited by vacationers. This is unfortunate because some of the state's most attractive sections are to the north and northwest—miles from the busy, salt-water shores.

Just north of Providence is Pawtucket, known as "the birthplace of America's cotton industry." Here, in 1790, Samuel Slater started North America's first successful cotton manufacturing plant operated by waterpower. You can see Old Slater Mill, Roosevelt Avenue, which was built by Slater in 1793. The mill has been restored to its mid-19th century appearance. Maintained as a museum, Old Slater Mill represents pioneer textile production in New England and the beginning of the American factory system. Included in displays are a cotton gin, hand loom, and tools used in the hand processing of flax, cotton, and wool. You can see demonstrations of hand spinning, weaving, and operation of early textile machines.

Pawtucket also boasts the Daggett House, originally built in 1644, which can be seen in Slater Park. This example of early Americana is completely furnished with outstanding antiques, including rare articles used by Samuel Slater. Lincoln Downs, Route 146, at Lincoln, and Narragansett Park, just off Alternate US 1A, can provide many hours of exciting entertainment for horse racing enthusiasts. Both tracks have pari-mutuel betting.

From Pawtucket, follow Highway 114 to the northeastern corner of Rhode Island. Here, music-lovers can enjoy outdoor Sunday festivals, during the summer, at Diamond Hill State Park's facilities in Cumberland. This area also provides some fine skiing during the winter months.

A few miles west of Diamond Hill is Woonsocket, where there are an unusual number of good community parks, with picnic and recreational accessories. You may take particular interest in Cold Spring Park, 25 acres along the Blackstone River, off Harris Street, which has a fine spring. Globe Park, at the south edge of town, has a pond and special facilities for children. The falls of the Blackstone River, in the center of the city, are scenic, and pot holes in the river bed can be seen from Globe Bridge. For a good view of northern Rhode Island, go to the top of Woonsocket Hill. A rough, dirt road runs from Union Village south from Route 146 over the shoulder and within 160 feet of the summit. At 22 Hamilton Avenue, you can see St. James Church (Episcopal), which was the first organized church in the city. Parts of the present structure date from 1883. St. Jean de Baptiste Society, 1 Social Street, houses one of the most complete French libraries in New England, specializing in French history and culture. Another point of interest may be Peleg Arnold Tavern, near the junction of Route 146 and St. Paul Street, which was an old Revolutionary gathering place, built in 1690.

The northwestern corner of Rhode Island (reached via Highways 146A, 102, through Harrisville and Pascoag, and Highway 100) is one of the most charming sections of the state, according to local residents. This corner, bounded on the north by Massachusetts, on the west by Connecticut, and on the southeast by a rough line drawn from Diamond Hill State Park to Arcadia State Forest, is a land of lakes, streams, state parks, forests, and farmlands. Pulaski Memorial State Forest, just west of Pascoag, has many scenic trails as well as fine facilities for swimming and sunbathing.

From Pulaski State Forest, take Highway 44 to Chepachet, where Thomas W. Dorr, leader of Dorr's Rebellion in 1840–1842, made his last stand on June 26, 1842. Dorr and his followers disappeared before Federal troops arrived. Out of his activities came the present Rhode Island constitution giving universal suffrage. Under the old constitution, only land owners and certain other privileged persons were entitled to vote.

Follow Highway 102 to Highway 12, which can start you on a fine scenic tour around Scituate Reservoir. From here, Highways 116, 117, and 3 will lead you to Arcadia State Forest, an ideal area for leisurely drives. Arcadia State Park has attractive facilities for swimming and beach fun. Another popular bathing beach is Beach Pond, on the western edge of the forest.

AROUND THE STATE

HOTELS. Accommodations range from family-style cottage to luxurious seaside resort. Providence Plantations hospitality is a tradition. Hotel and motel chains are *Holiday Inns* (Providence), *National Motels (Rhode Island Yankee* in Warwick), *American Hotel Corp. (Viking Hotel,* Newport), and the *Sheraton (Sheraton-Biltmore,* Providence).

BLOCK ISLAND

First Class

Narragansett Inn and the **Spring House.** These two ocean-view resort hotels have same management. Free transportation. Airy, pleasant dining rooms. Boat rentals. Dancing, entertainment. Modified American plan. Open June 1. Spring House, larger of the two, closes Labor Day; inn closes Sept. 16.

Tel. 466–2626.

Ocean View Resort Hotel claims to be largest on the island. Free tranportation. Charter plane service available. Most rooms face ocean. Evening entertainment, dancing. Open June to Sept. Rates include breakfast and dinner.

Located in Old Harbor, near village. (tel. 466–7780).

Reasonable

Ballard's Inn is small and popular; open from June to Sept.

Block Island Inn, another small and popular inn, is open from June to Sept.

Vaill Hotel and Country Club has a capacity for about 100 guests, and is open from June to Sept.

CHARLESTOWN

Reasonable

The Place Called Hathaways. This friendly cottage colony welcomes the overnight guest or vacationer. Near beaches, summer theater, movies. Open Apr. to Nov.

Near junction of Rtes. 1 & 2 (tel. 364–8269).

Sea View Motor Court. This is a family-style motel where electric-heated units have kitchens and cribs. Open Mar. 15 to Nov. 1.

On US 1 (tel. 364–6212).

Snow's Ranch Motel. Just a small set-up but there are beaches for swimming and fishing. Family units (electric heated) with kitchen.

Just off Rte. 1 (tel. 364–6726).

Sunset Motel. There are just six units but they are close to beaches and restaurant.

On US 1 (tel. 364–6042).

NARRAGANSETT

Reasonable

Blue-Lite Tourist Court. All the cottages and cabins are heated at this motel, just 5 minutes from the beach.

TV and radio. Season is from June to Oct.

21 Rhode Island Ave., off Ocean Rd. (tel. 783–4898).

Bonnet View Cottages. Near Bonnet Shore Beach, these heated family units have kitchenettes. Laundry on the premises a convenience. Open the year around.

Boston Neck Rd., US 1A (tel. ST 3–8203).

The Breakers. Beach privileges and summer sports are nearby to this small resort hotel. Season extends from June to Sept.

55 Ocean Rd. (tel. 783–2942).

Heden's Motel. For the vacationing family, there are several heated units—and the family pet is allowed, too. Prices go down between middle of Sept. to middle of June.

Boston Neck Rd., US 1 (tel. 783–4104).

Massasoit Hotel. At this popular, small resort hotel, home-style meals are included with rates on the American plan. Access to beach club and nearby attractions.

29 Mathewson St.

Narragansett Motel. This motel also offers a cut in price from Sept. 15 to June 15. Heated family units available.

Boston Neck Rd., US 1 (tel. ST-3512).

NEWPORT

First Class

Castle Hill Hotel. Overlooking the ocean, this former mansion has the advantage of a dramatic view. Private beach. Some apartments have a kitchen. Open summer only.

On Ocean Dr. (tel. 847–1913).

Shamrock Cliff House. Once a palatial residence, this resort hotel offers guests a magnificent view. Swimming pool, access to beach. Restaurant, cocktail lounge (weekend dancing). Season extends from July to Sept. with lower rates Apr., June and Oct.

On Ocean Dr. (tel. 847–5700).

Viking Hotel and adjacent **Viking Motor Inn.** Just about the most popular place in town with a choice of staying at the well-established redecorated hotel or the new motel. Swimming pool, access to beach. Family plan rates. Hotel dining room is top-rated. Coffee dispensers in motel rooms.

Tel. 847–3300.

Reasonable

Carlton Motel. Although this is not a big motel, the rooms are carpeted. Open all year around with reduced prices from Oct. to May. In season, price of room includes light breakfast. Coffee shop open 6 a.m. to 10 p.m.

On Route 138 (tel. 847–1593).

PROVIDENCE

Deluxe

Sheraton-Biltmore. Here, in the state's largest hotel free hospitality includes parking, continental breakfast, ice cubes. Pets welcome. Limousine to and from airport. Walk to bus and train terminals. Airline ticket offices, pharmacy, barber, deluxe restaurants and lounges, coffee shop. Family rates.

11 Dorrance St. (tel. 421–9200).

First Class

Holiday Inn. This attractive motel, one of a well-known chain, is actually in S. Attleboro, Mass. but within 7 mi. of Providence. King-size swimming pool. Dining room, cocktail lounge, coffee shop.

Drive in via US 1A (tel. 761–6660).

Reasonable

Colonial Motor Inn. Very attractive inside and outside, this motel has a big swimming pool. Popular cocktail lounge, dining room. Room service.

2750 Hartford Ave. on US 6 (less than 10 mi. from downtown) (tel. 647–3336).

Congress Inn Airport Motor Lodge. This two-level motel is conveniently located at the airport. Swimming pool is another attraction. Restaurant, cocktail lounge, and room service.
On US 1, 2082 Post Road.

New Yorker Motor Lodge. Price of room includes a continental breakfast at this two-level motel. Cocktail lounge.
400 Newport Ave., East Providence (tel. 434–8000).

Redwood Lodge. This motel is less than a half-mile from the airport. Pets welcome. Coffee shop open, breakfast only. Family plan for children under 12.
2282 Post Rd. (tel. 739–1150).

Inexpensive

Crown Hotel. This older hotel was redecorated recently. Two dining rooms and cocktail lounge. Free parking.
Downtown. (tel. 331–8200).

WESTERLY

First Class

Weekapaug Inn. This attractive resort with ocean view features the fun of water sports. Price of room includes delicious meals. Summer season only.
Rte. 1 (tel. 322–0301).

Reasonable

Blue Star Motel. This is a pleasant place to stay with easy access to the beach. During summer price includes light breakfast. Prices reduced after Labor Day. Individual heat control.
US 1 (tel. 596–2891).

Pine Lodge Motel. The secluded location offers traffic-free relaxation, just minutes from the beach. Some heated cottages, plus a few family units with kitchen.
US 1 (tel. 322–0333).

Pony Barn Motel. Togetherness family style is featured here, complete with recreation area for children and picnic grounds. Pets welcome. Just a very small motel; open summer only.
Shore Rd. (tel. 348–8216).

Traveltel. One of a fast-rising group of the same name, this 2-level motel has all the comforts for the budget-conscious traveler. Families will enjoy picnicking on premises.
US 1 (tel. 596–7475).

WICKFORD

First Class

Gray's Motor Village. This little resort, complete with pool and lifeguard, is convenient to Quonset Naval Air Station. Family accommodations. Room rate includes continental breakfast. Rates reduced at end of season.
7835 Post Rd. (tel. 294–9551).

Reasonable

Bob Bean Motor Court. A very comfortable motel just a few miles from the Quonset Naval Air Station. Some units have kitchens. Restaurant.
600 Boston Neck Rd. (tel. 294–4571).

Cold Spring House. Hospitality prevails at this friendly small resort, overlooking Narragansett Bay. Good beach. Room rates with and without meals. Restaurant and cocktail lounge open to public also.
36 Beach St. (tel. 294–9651).

ELSEWHERE

CRANSTON. *Colony*. Deluxe. Here, minutes from Providence, the accent is on resort atmosphere. Pool, patio, cabanas. Marco Polo Cocktail Lounge, Marco Polo Restaurant, and coffee shop. Pets welcome. Airport limousine. Free ice. 1150 Narragansett Blvd. Tel. HO 7–8800.

Hillside Motor Lodge. Reasonable. This motel is only about 4 mi. from Providence. Carpeted rooms have TV. Right near shopping center and restaurant. On Routes 2 and 3. Tel. 942–4200.

EAST GREENWICH. *Greenwich Hotel* is an older hotel right in the center of the town's business and shopping area. Located very near to a variety of cafes, snack bars and restaurants. Inexpensive. 162 Main St.

FOSTER. *Hi-Star Motel.* Reasonable. Although small, this motel offers picnic and playground facilities. Some family units, too—heated. Weekend auctions nearby. On Highway 101. Tel. 647–3932.

JAMESTOWN. *Bay Voyage Inn.* Reasonable. This delightful well-established inn has seaside appeal. American plan rates. Open from June to Sept. Just a little north of Jamestown on Route 138.

LINCOLN. *Clover Leaf Motel.* Inexpensive. This small motel is heated and has free TV. Open all year around. On George Washington Highway (junction of 146 and 116). Open all year around. Tel. Pawtucket 2–2087.

LITTLE COMPTON. *Old Meeting House Inn.* Reasonable. This interesting, historic house, open from June to Sept., has a few rooms. Cozy colonial dining rooms are open for lunch and dinner daily except Tues. Gift shop. On the Common.

PAWTUCKET. *Roger Williams Hotel.* Reasonable. This friendly hotel is modern, centrally located, and air conditioned. Parking is free. 179 Main St.

State Line Motor Inn. Reasonable. Along with all the comforts, this motel features color TV in lobby. Restaurant next door is open from breakfast to midnight snack. On Rte. 1. Tel. 761–4825.

TIVERTON. *The Stone Bridge Inn* has a few accommodations, and is open all year around. However, the dining rooms and terrace seat hundreds. Open daily. Reasonable. Junction of routes 138 & 177.

WAKEFIELD. *Larchwood Inn.* Reasonable. A well-kept landscape distinguishes this small inn situated near the ocean. Year around restaurant offers good food and grog. Only a small number of rooms; reservations are important. 176 Main St. Tel. 783–5454.

Hillside Tourist Court. Reasonable. Although this motel may have just a few units, it's a pleasant place to stay. Just off US 1 on Tower Hill Rd. Tel. 783–5890.

WATCH HILL. *Ocean House.* Reasonable. Lots of family fun at this resort hotel, especially good for beach sports. Weekend dancing. Excellent food and drinks. Meals included with rates. Summer only. Bluff Ave. Tel. 348–8161.

WOONSOCKET. *Hi-View Motel.* Reasonable. Here skiers will find convenient access to Diamond Hill State Park. Rooms have free coffee dispensers. Dine any hour as nearby restaurant never closes. On Route 146. Tel. 762–9631.

YOUTH HOSTELS. The YWCA, 254 Washington St., Providence, has facilities for eight girls. Reservations are required. Call the Resident Director, 421–8770.

FARM VACATIONS AND GUEST RANCHES. *Wionkhiege Valley Farm,* about 10 miles from Providence, encompasses 200 acres. Vacation includes horseback riding, swimming, fishing, square dancing. Open July to Labor Day. American Plan rates, $55 a week; $35 for children. Reservations by writing to the Lathams, RFD, Esmond 17, R.I. Tel. 231–0417.

CAMPING OUT. The largest camping facilities are at *Burlingame State Park,* near Westerly, via US 1, with more than 350 campsites; tents and trailers are permitted. Season begins Apr. 1, ends Nov. 30. Fee is $1 a night. Permits (two-week maximum) are issued by the Division of Parks and Recreation, 100 North Main St., Providence. *George Wash-*

ington State Park in Foster offers about six camp sites. *Beach Pond Campground,* in the Exeter–West Greenwich area, via State 165, has 48 overnight cabins. *Little Rhody Campgrounds,* off State 165, in *Arcadia State Forest,* permits trailers. There are about 40 campsites. Rates, $2 a night; $12 a week (seasonal rates also). 128 Greylawn Ave., Warwick. Tel. 539–7636. *Happy Valley Tent Camping,* in the State 165 area, on Escoheag Hill Road, Escoheag, is near good fishing. Trailers are allowed. For information, write Happy Valley, Inc., Escoheag Hill Road, Escoheag.

TRAILER TIPS. Visitors do not require a permit for a legal-size trailer 50 feet in length, not exceeded by 12 feet in width. Permits from Division of Roads and Bridges, Dept. of Public Works, State Office Bldg., Providence 2. Tel. JA 1–7100, ext. 494. Trailers are allowed in *Burlingame State Park* and in privately-owned *Little Rhody Campgrounds.* There are many trailer parks throughout the state where rental is on a permanent basis. Here are a few names, and the visitor may inquire directly about transient rental: *Border Hill Trailer Park,* South County Trail, Charlestown; *Davis Mobile Homes Park,* Tourtellot Hill Road, Foster; *Trailer Park,* US 6, Johnston; *Helen's Mobile Home Park,* US 1, North Kingstown; *Harris Trailer Park,* 200 Courtney Ave., Pawtucket; *Oliveira Trailers,* State 138, Portsmouth. *Fair Haven Trailer Park,* Seascape Ave., Middletown (about two miles from Newport) is a seasonal trailer park.

DINING OUT. For three centuries, the oldest eating tradition along the rockbound New England coast is the clambake. The Indians taught the early settlers how to cook green corn, clams, and fish covered in seawood over white-hot stones. Now, bakemasters have their own method of arranging firewood in a shallow pit over layers of big stones, covering these with seaweed; then adding the seafood, ears of corn, fish, sausages, broiler chickens, sweet potatoes, more seaweed, and a canvas cover. Clambakes are featured at many church celebrations throughout the state. There are clambakes every Sunday at 1 p.m. from June to Labor Day at *East Warren Rod and Gun Club* in Warren; an annual clambake in July at the *First Baptist Church* in Block Island. Clam cakes, chowder, clam pie, Block Island swordfish, johnnycake (corn bread), blueberry slump, and barbecued chicken (Rhode Island Red, of course) are other food specialties for the visitor to enjoy.

Many restaurants in the state feature all the specialties in season, with excellent selections of seafood all the year around.

BRISTOL

First Class

The Castle. This is actually a castle-shaped building overlooking Narragansett Bay. Boating patrons may dock right there. Parking area for those who drive. Steaks and lobster highlight the menu. The Castle has its own wine cellar, also a glassed-in sunken bar and cocktail lounge. Open every day, lunch is served Mon. through Fri.

On Poppasquash Rd.

Reasonable

The Lobster Pot. Lots of lobsters are boiled in the pot here. Try their chowder, too. Cocktail lounge. Special America's Cup exhibit. Waterfront location is next to Herreshoff Boat Yard. Closed Mon.

119–121 Hope St.

Inexpensive

Tweet Balzano's Cafe. Very informal and very inexpensive, to say the least.

Heaping big bowls of steamed clams are unbelievably priced at $1. You order spaghetti by the pound; a pound is $1 and serves four. The sauce is delicious.

180 Mt. Hope Ave.

LINCOLN

Reasonable

The Harness Room is the rustic dining room of the *Kirkbrae*. Although this is a private country club, the dining room is open to the public from 12 to 2:30 p.m., 6 to 10 p.m., Sat. to 11 p.m., Sun. from 12 to 9 p.m. There are special plates for children. An orchestra plays for dancing Sat.

Old River Rd.

Johnny's Shadow. Features steak on the menu. A waterfall adds to the decor and valet parking adds to the service. Lunch served 11 a.m. to 3:30 p.m., dinner 5:30 to 10 p.m. Sun. the bar is open but no meals are served.

On Washington Highway.

The Lindsey Tavern was visited by Washington and Lafayette during the Revolution. A pianist plays relaxing music in the cocktail lounge. Menu features lobster, fisherman style, and other favorite seafoods. Children's plates are served. Open daily, except Mon., for dinner only.

609 Smithfield Ave.

NEWPORT

First Class

The Pier. Whether you order a seafood specialty such as the clambake, or steak, you will be pleased. Both restaurant and bar are very popular. Dinner reservations necessary. Open for lunch and dinner daily; Sun. dinner only from noon. Accessible by boat or car. Floating dock.

In Williams and Manchester Shipyard.

Reasonable

McGann's Restaurant. Here you will find rustic atmosphere and home-style cooking. Sizzling steak platter is a specialty. Very tempting desserts. Liquor served. Popular with local citizens and tourists.

102 Connell Highway.

Viking Hotel. The Sun. buffet is a sumptuous feast. Look for the daily specials. Double lobster plate is excellent. Open for breakfast, lunch, and dinner. Cocktails. No charge for parking.

9 Bellevue Ave.

PROVIDENCE

First Class

The Sheraton-Biltmore Hotel. Formal Williamsburg colonial dining in the *Mansion House* or the more informal 16th-century tavern atmosphere of the *Falstaff Room* provide double dining pleasure. Both dining rooms are distinctly different. Mansion House serves many gourmet dishes with a flaming flair. Hearty roast beef is the *piece de resistance* in the Falstaff Room. Lunch and dinner daily, except Sat. when dinner only is served. Mansion House is closed Sun.; Falstaff Room serves from 5:30 p.m. Sun.

Dorrance St.

Sullivan's Steak House. This is one of the most popular restaurants in town. Steaks cooked to order are the specialty, of course, with club steak and filet mignon topping the list. Menu is *à la carte*. Rolls, bread, pies, and cakes are baked on the premises. Reservations are important on Sat. nights. Open from 4 to 11 p.m., Sat. until 1 a.m.

1303 No. Main St.

George Winkler's Steak House. Reservations are required, especially for dinner, as this is a very popular restaurant. Steaks, chops and lobster are highlighted on the menu, and the continental dishes are excellent (especially breast of chicken Cordon Bleu). Hours are from 11:30 to 1 a.m. daily. Closed Sun., also Thanksgiving, Christmas Day and first two weeks in July.

34 Middle St.

Reasonable

Camille's Roman Gardens. Just about anything under the Italian sun on the menu—all this, and a fountain in the dining room, too. This restaurant has been in business about 50 years. Lunch and dinner every day of the week except Monday.
71 Bradford St.

Chalet Restaurant. Yes, it's built like a chalet, with the menu leaning toward the Italian border area of Switzerland. Children's menu, too. Cocktail lounge. Open for lunch and dinner.
1021 Mineral Spring Ave.

The Copper Galley. This is a bright, new combination of restaurant, Polynesian village night club, and marina. Lots of parking for cars and boats. Snacks, meals, and cocktails served from lunchtime to after midnight.
At Shipyard Marina, Cranston.

Johnson's Hummocks Restaurant. The miniature clambake is a feast. Choose your lobster from the special tank. *Prime Rib Room* for the meat-and-potatoes man. Children's menu. Friendly cocktail lounge. No charge for parking. One of the most famous restaurants in town.
245 Allens Ave.

Luke's. Cantonese and Polynesian dishes share the spotlight. Exotic drinks are an attraction. Relaxing island atmosphere in *The Hut*. Open from 11 a.m. to 10:30 p.m.
59 Eddy St.

Ming Garden. Savory chicken wings *a la Ming Garden* are a specialty here; also sweet-sour chicken, and fried wonton with lobster and vegetables. Open for lunch and dinner.
141 Westminster St.

Inexpensive

Carr's. If you like quaint 19th-century tea rooms, this is your cup of tea. Tea-time is 2:30 p.m. Tasty casseroles are the big attraction at lunch-time. Closed Sun. Check on summer closing hours. Conveniently near Brown University.
107 Angell St.

Crescent Park Shore Dinner Hall. This is one of the largest shore dinner halls in the world, open from May 30 to early Sept. The bill of fare offers a clambake feast for about $2.75 and $3.75; about $1.60 and $2.10 for children under 12.
In Crescent Park.

Miss Dutton's. This tea room serves more than tea—breakfast, lunch, and dinner attract a steady clientele. Tempting children's menu, too. Closed Sun.
48 Washington St.

TIVERTON

Reasonable

Chanticleer. Here in this small country restaurant, lobster is the big attraction. Roast beef a specialty, too. Sometimes, eight vegetables accompany dinner. Guests may bring own wine and liquor for set-ups.
Near Tiverton-4-Corners.

The Coachman. Dinners are served in an attractive, converted home. One claim to fame is that Frank Sinatra dined there in summer of 1965.
Near Tiverton-4-Corners.

Sunderland's. This rambling farm house features country-style dining. Home cooking and baking have maintained popularity through the years. Cocktails. Open for lunch and dinner in summer, dinner only autumn and winter. Usually closed from after New Year's Day to March.
2753 Main Rd.

ELSEWHERE

BLOCK ISLAND. *Narragansett Inn and Spring House.* Reasonable. Both pleasant resort hotels have the same management. The dining rooms offer *a la carte* menus for visitors. Vegetables are from the garden. The *Spring House* closes Labor Day; the *Narragansett* closes Sept. 16. Open for the season in late spring.

Red's Lunch, Ernie's, and *Smugglers Cove.* All reasonable. Three island restaurants which stay open beyond the summer season.

CRANSTON. *Coffee's Cafe and Restaurant.* Inexpensive. Italian. Whether you order the white clam sauce or the red clam sauce, you'll proclaim it's delicious. Big portions at little prices. Open 7 days a week from 9 a.m. to 1 a.m. 357 Dyer St.

Twin Oaks. Inexpensive. Such good food in big portions at small prices that there are usually customers waiting to enter the dining room. Combination of veal, peppers and sausage with spaghetti is little over a dollar. The steak sandwich is like filet mignon and costs about $2.25. Open for lunch and dinner. Closed Mon. 100 Sabra St.

FOSTER. *Shady Acres Restaurant.* Inexpensive. Families will find that this is a good drive-in with reasonable prices and good service. Menu includes everything from hamburger to steak. On Route 6, about a mile east of the Conn. Turnpike.

NORTH KINGSTOWN. *Kingstown Inn.* Reasonable. This attractive inn is famous for the bountiful Sun. afternoon and evening smorgasbord. Open for dinner every day but Mon. Children's menu is available. Dance band on weekends. Piano bar is popular. Set back from highway on 6275 Post Rd.

SCITUATE. *Burger Corner* is a good drive-in, specializing in fried clams and extra-long hotdogs. Inexpensive. Open from May to Oct. At intersection of Rtes. 116 & 101.

Highland Orchards. Inexpensive. At this roadside restaurant you may order anything from a sandwich to steak grilled on the open charcoal pit. Restaurant adjoins children's amusement area with steam train ride and self-drive auto ride. Rte. 101.

WARREN. *Fore 'N Aft.* Reasonable. This is an attractive restaurant with nautical decor and fireplaces. New England cooking is featured. Open from noon to 11 p.m. for lunch and dinner. Own wine cellar and lobster pool. 1070 Main St.

Wharf Tavern. Reasonable. Select your own lobster from the pool. Then it's prepared your favorite way. Charcoal-broiled steaks are delicious, too. Open daily and Sun. for dinner only. Water St.

WARWICK. *Holland House.* Reasonable. Once known as the *Frog Farm,* the restaurant still serves frogs' legs occasionally as a specialty. Wide selection includes Chicken Holland. Rambling house overlooks pond. Popular at lunch and dinner. Closed Tues. 1473 Warwick Ave.

Rocky Point Shore Dinner Hall. Inexpensive. Overlooking Narragansett Bay, the immense dining room offers the shore dinner menu of relishes, clam chowder, New England brown bread, clam cakes, baked sausage, baked fish, corn on the cob, boiled lobster, potatoes, watermelon, and Indian pudding. Open from May 30 to early Sept. In Rocky Point Amusement Park.

WESTERLY. *Greenhaven Inn.* First class. Excellent service is provided by waiters wearing madras jackets. Delicious food and generous drinks. Rustic decor, complete with fireplace, is rivaled by ocean view. Open for lunch and dinner. Closed Mon. and holidays. Just over border to Greenhaven Rd., Pawcatuck, Conn.

WICKFORD. *Cold Spring House.* Reasonable. This cozy little resort is located on Narragansett Bay. Yankee fare is the specialty, including clambakes. Children's menu. Breakfast, lunch and dinner daily. Decor is brightened by interesting art display. 36 Beach St.

Marina House. First class. Here dining is enhanced by the picturesque view of Wickford Harbor dotted with sailboats. Menu is varied with seafood and beef. Bar is as popular as the dining room. Dinner only. Open from Apr. to end of Sept. Check on dates. 135 Steamboat Ave.

BARS. The *Falstaff Room* in the *Sheraton-Biltmore Hotel,* downtown Providence, is one of the most popular at cocktail time. On weekends especially, the bar at *Kingstown Inn,* 6275 Post Road, North Kingstown, is a lively spot. There's a piano bar for guests, a combination of Naval officers and local gentry. A good jazz combo is an attraction at *Hurley's* bar in Newport. Don't forget that the legal age for drinking in Rhode Island is 21. Drinking time, until 1 a.m.

NIGHTCLUBS. *El Marocco,* outside of Providence, is considered the leading nightclub for stage shows and dinner. The address is 1291 Hartford Ave., Johnston. The *Gaiety-Go-Go* is *très* gay at 533 Broadway, in Pawtucket. This lively discotheque features girls in cages dancing the latest gyrations. If you want more of the same, *Ziggie's Lounge,* across the street, at 530 Broadway, also has the caged dancing girls and discotheque. For a night out on the town in Newport, the jazz combo is terrific in *Hurley's Lounge,* 110 Levin St., or stop in at any of these: *Strike Zone Lounge,* 173 East Main Rd., Middletown; *Sully's Publik House,* 108 William St., Newport; the *Tavern,* 3 Memorial Boulevard, Newport.

COFFEE HOUSES AND OUTDOOR CAFES. Good coffee and good conversation have kept things perking at the *Tête-a-Tête,* 226 Thayer St., Providence. No liquor is available. Sometimes in summer, pastry is served. Hours are weekdays from 8 to 12 p.m.; weekends, 8 p.m. to 1 a.m.

MUSIC. The annual *Newport Jazz Festival* dominates the Rhode Island musical world, around the Fourth of July, followed by the *Newport Folk Music Festival.* Both festivals last three days, with afternoon and evening sessions in Freebody Park, Newport. Information and tickets available by writing to Newport Jazz Festival (or Folk Music Festival), Newport, R.I.

The state has two philharmonic orchestras, the *Rhode Island Philharmonic* and the *Providence Philharmonic;* also a 35-piece *Plantations Modern Symphonic Pops Orchestra.* Programs are announced in advance. There are concerts by the *Brown University Music Department Orchestra;* also by professors and students at *Barrington College School of Music.* The *Peloquin Chorale* has appeared on national television. They perform regularly at the Cathedral of SS Peter and Paul, downtown Providence.

The annual three-day *Bach Festival* is usually held first week in May. Performed by the *Rhode Island Civic Chorale,* this is the only Bach Festival in the New England–New York State region.

A calendar of musical events is free from the Rhode Island Fine Arts Council, C/O Rhode Island Development Council, 49 Hayes St., Providence, R.I.

STAGE AND REVUES. The *Sock & Buskin Players* of *Brown University,* Providence, perform for a full season series Oct. thru May. The *Barker Players,* the oldest of the state's little theater groups, perform in five major productions a year at 400 Benefit St., Providence. *Trinity Players* is a new repertory theater group.

TOURS. From June thru Sept., *Viking Tours* of Newport feature a 22-mile guided tour of historic Newport. At least 150 points of interest are pointed out, such as the famous Newport mansions, the Touro Synagogue, Wanton-Lyman-Hazard House, Naval War College, the Old Colony House, Hunter House, Trinity Church, the Old Stone Mill, Redwood Library, Newport Casino, Pirate Point, Hammersmith Farm (the former Summer White House), etc. The trip includes the 10-mile Ocean Drive. Then you have your choice of a trip through either one of these fabulous mansions, The Breakers or The Elms. Tickets are available from the driver at Hotel Viking. The main office of Viking Tours is at 4 Bush St., Newport. The phone number is 847–6921. For adults the ticket is $4 a person; children from 6 to 16, $2. Special arrangements are made for groups and parties. Tours leave Hotel Viking at 9:30 a.m. and 1:30 p.m. In May and Oct., the tour is on weekends only, at 1:30 p.m.

Walking tours of colonial *Newport* are featured by *Viking Tours,* also. The schedule is daily from June thru Sept.; weekends only May and Oct. Tours leave from the Chamber of Commerce Information Center, Eisenhower Park, downtown Newport, at 3:30 p.m. The adult ticket is $1.50, with special discounts for military personnel in uniform.

INDUSTRIAL TOURS. The welcome mat is out at many Rhode Island companies. All they ask is a phone call well in advance. In North Kingstown, *Browne & Sharpe Manufacturing Co.* shows visitors around their precision and machine tool plant on Frenchtown Rd. One-hour tours Fri., 1:30 to 4:30. The *California Artificial Flower Co.* showrooms are open from 8:30 a.m. to 5:30 p.m.; Thurs. until 9 p.m., at 400 Reservoir Ave., Providence.

Want to see a watercress farm? *Colonial Mill Farm,* Moonstone Beach Rd., So. Kingstown, offers 30-min. tours, Sat. only, from June thru Sept. Stained glass window techniques are demonstrated at *Decorative Window Studio,* 90 Aldrich St., Providence. 45-min. tour is by appointment only (except in summer). A week's notice is required for the 90-minute tour of *Gorham Mfg. Co.,* 333 Adelaide Ave., Providence. This was one of the earliest silversmiths in the country. For an hour's tour to see hand-printing on linen towels, visit *Kay-Dee Handprints, Inc.,* Skunk Hill Rd., Hope Valley. Five days' notice is necessary for a 90-min. tour of *Narragansett Brewing Co.,* New Depot Ave., Cranston. Tour days are Mon. thru Thur., 10 a.m. to noon. Tel. 942–7000.

At least a week's notice is necessary for the 45-min. tour at *Newport Creamery, Inc.,* 208 W. Main Rd., Middletown. For demonstrations of hand-spinning, weaving, and operation of early textile machines, visit *Old Slater Mill,* Roosevelt Ave., Pawtucket. Open Tues. to Sat. from 10 a.m. to 5 p.m.; Sun. from 2 to 5 p.m. Fiberglass sailing yachts are built at *Pearson Yachts,* Div. of Grumman Allied Industries, Burnside St., Bristol. One week's notice is required for the 1½-hour tour Thur. at 2 p.m. A newsworthy tour is offered by the *Providence Journal-Bulletin* and *Radio Station WEAN,* 75 Fountain St., Providence. The *U.S. Automated Post Office,* 24 Corliss St., Providence, has 20-min. tours by appointment only, except in Dec. Contact Postmaster's office. The *US Naval Base* in Newport observes Open House on Armed Forces Day, third Sat. in May, and Navy Day (Oct. 27). Special tours are arranged by the Public Information Officer.

HISTORIC SITES. History began for Rhode Island when Roger Williams stepped ashore from his canoe in 1636, near what is now a little park bounded by Power, Williams and Gano sts., Providence. Here visitors will see what is known as the *Roger Williams Rock,* but actually a monument. The site of the original Providence settlement, *Roger Williams Spring,* is enshrined in a small park on North Main St. Across the street, on the corner of Howland St., a plaque proclaims that Roger Williams lived there in 1636. The *First Baptist Meeting House,* a landmark of old Providence, was founded by Roger Williams in 1638. Church office, on the Waterman St. entrance, welcomes visitors from 10 a.m. to 4 p.m. daily, May 1 to Oct. 31, and 11 a.m. to 4 p.m. Nov. 1 to Apr. 30. Sundays, there is one tour only, after the 11 a.m. services. The Roger Williams story ends at the site of the *Roger*

Williams Memorial, Prospect St., where there is also a panoramic view of Providence.

Because Providence was founded in 1636, historical homes dot the city. One belonged to *Stephen Hopkins,* a signer of the Declaration of Independence. The house is opposite the Court House on Hopkins St. and is open for visitors on Wed. and Sat. from 1 to 4 p.m. The *John Brown House,* now headquarters of the *Rhode Island Historical Society,* is at 52 Power St. George Washington was entertained there. Visiting hours are Mon. thru Fri. from 9 a.m. to 5 p.m.; Sun. from 3 to 5 p.m., except summer months. Closed on holidays and holiday weekends.

Although the *Old State House* on North Main St. has its place in history since 1762 (it's open weekdays), the present *State House* dominates the city. Built of white Georgia marble, it boasts the second largest of the four marble domes in the world. Inside is a prize historical relic, the original parchment charter granted by King Charles II in 1663. The famous full-length portrait of George Washington by Gilbert Stuart hangs in the reception room.

Newport has its share of national historic landmarks. One is *Touro Synagogue,* 72 Touro St., the oldest synagogue in America. Built in 1763 by America's first architect, Peter Harrison, it is considered a colonial masterpiece. Admission is free, guides also. Open daily except Sat., July 1 to Sept. 6, from 10 a.m. to 5 p.m. At other times, open Sun. from 2:30 to 4 p.m., or by appointment weekdays. Another national historic landmark of Newport, designed by the same architect in 1762, is the *Brick Market* in Washington Square, open Mon. thru Sat., 9:30 a.m. to 5 p.m. The oldest house in Newport, dating back to 1675, is also a national historic landmark. The *Wanton-Lyman-Hazard House,* 17 Broadway, has been restored and furnished by the Newport Historical Society. Open daily from 10 a.m. to 5 p.m., July 1 to Labor Day. Admission 50 cents; 25 cents, children.

Redwood Library on Bellevue Ave. is another national historic landmark in Newport. Designed by Peter Harrison, it is considered the oldest library room in continuous use in the United States. The collection of American paintings is exceptional. Admission free. Open daily, except Sun. The *Colony House,* Washington Square, Newport, is a national historic landmark. Government building dates back to 1739. Open Mon. thru Fri., 9:30 a.m. to 4:30 p.m.; Sat. 9:30 a.m. to noon. Admission free.

And, for a conversation piece, the *Old Stone Mill,* Touro Park, Newport, is a mystery site. No one really knows whether it was built by the Norsemen seven centuries ago or by the colonists sometime in 1673.

LIBRARIES. *Providence Public Library,* 150 Empire St., is New England's second largest library. Collections: whaling, printing, Civil War, early children's books, Irish and Italian culture. Hours, 9 a.m. to 8 p.m. Mon. thru Fri.; 9 a.m. to 6 p.m., Sat.

GARDENS. The formal sunken garden at *The Elms* in Newport is a fantasy of fountains, lights, and music on Sun. evenings, July and Aug., from 8 p.m. to 10 p.m. Admission $1, 50 cents for children. The Elms is modeled on the Chateau d'Asnieres near Paris, France. Combination admission $1.75; 75 cents, children. Mansion and gardens are open weekends only Apr. 18 to May 30; daily from May 31 to Oct. 31.

SHOPPING. Stores are open Mon. thru Sat., and both Tues. and Thurs. evenings in Providence. *Gladdings,* downtown Providence, claims to be the oldest local department store and features women's and children's fashions. Newly redecorated, the *Outlet,* 176 Weybosset St., has just about anything from tires to bedroom sets. Another medium-priced store that has everything from soup to nuts and bolts is *City Hall Store,* 150 Washington St.

In East Greenwich, *Browning's,* on Main St., has an excellent line of gifts. *Country Clothes,* also Main St., features top fashions and sportswear. The *Art Shanty,* at the end of Cyprus St., Wickford, sells nautical note paper and books for the yachtsman. There are at least 16 *antique dealers* in South County. *James E. Scudder,* State 112, Carolina, deals in Early American antique furniture. *Early Rhode Island Shop,* on State 138, four miles west of intersection of Routes 2 and 138, antiques consist of beams, hinges, hasps, mantels, windows, doors, etc. for restoring Early American houses. The *Brick Market* in Newport features Newport reproductions in furniture, bedspreads, lamps, wallpaper, china, and accessories for Newport decor.

SUMMER SPORTS. Fifteen *golf courses* are open to the public, including *Louisquisset* in North Providence, with night-lighting. For the spectator, one of the golfing events is the *Annual Northeast Amateur Invitation Golf Tournament,* usually the last week in June. Information from the *Providence Journal-Bulletin,* one of the sponsors.

You can count on thousands of spectator boats in Newport during the *America's Cup Races,* and June's *Bermuda Race.* The yacht-watcher is always assured that there are white sails in the summer sunset. There are 28 local *yacht clubs;* weekly races are scheduled all summer. Yachting and boating facilities are detailed in the free brochure *Boating in Rhode Island,* from the Rhode Island Development Council, Roger Williams Building, Providence, R.I.

Fishing is excellent in the state, from surfcasting (no license) to inland streams (license required). Spectators will catch much of the excitement at the many *fishing tournaments,* climaxed by the annual *United States Atlantic Tuna Tournament* at Galilee in Sept. Individual record catches have been caught in Rhode Island waters: striped bass, bluefish, tautog, cod, flounder. The U.S. record bluefin tuna was caught in Rhode Island (961½ pounds). There are two *party and charter boat associations* operating out of Point Judith. Contact Snug Harbor Marina, Gooseberry Road, Wakefield (tel. 783–7766). The Division of Fish and Game stocks more than 60 outlets with trout (season from mid-Apr. to mid-Oct.).

There are many saltwater and freshwater *beaches* for swimming and sailing; *parks* for picnics and camping; and *tennis courts* in and around the towns. Tennis matches at Newport rank in prestige with Wimbledon and Forest Hills.

WINTER SPORTS. *Professional hockey* (the *Providence Reds)* and *professional football* are spectator sports in autumn and winter. College teams compete in football and basketball games.

The short *hunting season* requires a license, about $10 for a nonresident and $3.25 for members of the armed forces and active U.S. merchant marine personnel. From Nov. 15 to Feb. 1, there is open season on muskrat, mink, and otter. For partridge, quail, and cock pheasant, the dates are Nov. 1 to Dec. 31. Rhode Island hunting regulations from the Department of Natural Resources, Veterans Memorial Building, Providence, R.I.

Ice fishing is restricted to daylight hours, and a license is necessary.

Skiing in Rhode Island is part of winter fun at *Diamond Hill State Park,* Cumberland. The snow machine guarantees skiing from Dec. through Mar. A warming hut is on the premises, a food concession, and restrooms. Skis may be rented. There are ski tows for beginners and advanced skiers. At night, the area is lighted. This includes the nearby *skating pond,* the *sledding area,* and the 500-foot *toboggan chutes* (all free). Ski tow fees are $1.50, adults and teenagers; $1, children. Special family rates. Parking, 50 cents.

Adjacent *Ski Valley* is privately owned, with snow-making machine, four slopes, two trails, four rope tows. Open from 2 to 10 p.m. daily; from 10 a.m. Wed., Sat., Sun., and holidays. The tow fee is the same as Diamond Hill State Park; free parking. Six instructors charge $2 an hour, racing lessons free Sat., 10 a.m. Ski rental, 95 cents an hour (skis, boots, and poles). Ski shop on premises, also a chalet warming hut.

From Sept. 11 to Dec. 12, two race tracks offer more than 120 days (or nights) of pari-mutuel *horse racing*. Both *Narragansett Park* in Pawtucket and *Lincoln Downs* in Lincoln schedule night racing as well as daytime programs. Lincoln Downs is on State 146, north of Providence. Narragansett Park, off alternate US 1A, is in East Providence.

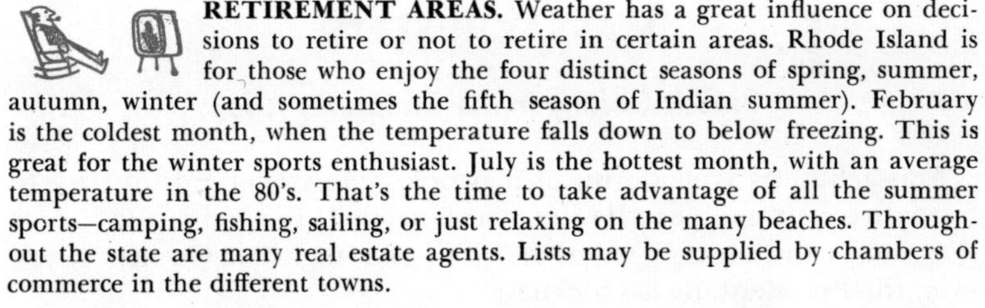

RETIREMENT AREAS. Weather has a great influence on decisions to retire or not to retire in certain areas. Rhode Island is for those who enjoy the four distinct seasons of spring, summer, autumn, winter (and sometimes the fifth season of Indian summer). February is the coldest month, when the temperature falls down to below freezing. This is great for the winter sports enthusiast. July is the hottest month, with an average temperature in the 80's. That's the time to take advantage of all the summer sports—camping, fishing, sailing, or just relaxing on the many beaches. Throughout the state are many real estate agents. Lists may be supplied by chambers of commerce in the different towns.

RECOMMENDED READING. Here are some suggestions: *Sachems of the Narragansetts,* by Howard M. Chapin; *Early Houses of the King's Province in the Narragansett Country,* by William D. Miller; *The America's Cup Races,* by Herbert L. Stone; *A Pictorial Guide to American Gardens,* by Louis H. Frohman; *The Star-Crossed Woman,* by Maribelle Cormack.

MASSACHUSETTS

Classic Colony in the Computer Age

Massachusetts is made up of a people who prefer informality to formality, can exercise dignity when needed, but generally are so down-to-earth that they see no harm in greeting their Governor, yes, even the President, by his nickname.

This is illustrated by an incident Senator Leverett Saltonstall says happened when he was Governor of the commonwealth. On a number of occasions while walking from the State House to the Harvard Club, he would meet Godfrey Cabot. Mr. Cabot, an old-line Yankee, would doff his hat and bow low—not to honor Mr. Saltonstall, but the office which he held.

One day, Senator Saltonstall recalls, right after one of Mr. Cabot's lowest bows, a cab driver pulled up with screeching brakes, leaned out of his window, and yelled: "Can I give you a lift, Salty?"

This type of greeting, most Bay Staters feel, is more sincere and reflects greater respect than the deep bow and doffing of hat by Mr. Godfrey Cabot. Indeed, it reflects the sincere friendliness of the man in the street; his generosity and thoughtfulness toward another.

Bay Staters are noted for their generosity and are the first to reach in their pockets to aid the less fortunate. Each year thousands of dollars are raised for the Jimmy Fund to help doctors not only ease the sufferings of children with cancer but to find a cure. The United Fund drive always reaches its goal.

This generosity of the Bay Staters comes down from the Pilgrim fathers who, at their first Thanksgiving feast in Plymouth, invited all of the neighboring Indians to share their abundance.

It was these Pilgrims who sailed into Massachusetts Bay in 1620, and to a larger extent, the Puritans who arrived eight years later, who produced a major effect on the cultural, social, and economic life of the state. Much of the conservatism the early settlers practiced prevails in the Bay State today to such a degree that it has remained an outstanding factor in the life of the commonwealth today.

It is such conservative thinking that has added to the general belief that Massachusetts people are cold and inhospitable. It is true that it takes a lot to draw them out but when one does it is like a drink of water from a cold bubbling spring.

The Bay Stater's character first and foremost is individualistic. He possesses many skills, is shrewd at making bargains, possesses stubbornness, and has a tendency to conform—"provided he thinks conformity his own idea."

But there are times when the Bay Stater's conservatism gives way to radical social reforms. In 1836 the state enacted the child labor law. Later, it established the first state board of health; the first minimum wage law for women and children, and provided the first state tuberculosis sanatorium.

Cradle of Culture

Massachusetts is an open, living history book. Such patriots as Paul Revere, James Otis, John Hancock, and Samuel Adams successfully rallied the citizens of the small colony against the British to defend their right to worship freely and to have taxation with representation.

The state has contributed more than its share of great men and women to positions of national and international prominence. From its ranks have come four presidents—John Adams; his son, John Quincy Adams; Calvin Coolidge, and John F. Kennedy.

Massachusetts women whose names loom large, include Mary Lyon, Mary Livermore, Lucy Stone, Susan Anthony, Lydia Maria Child, and Margaret Fuller, all champions of women's rights. Louisa Morton Greene was the first woman to rebel against the discrimination suffered by women in industry when she refused to do a man's work at a Dedham woolen mill unless she was paid a man's wages. She was also active in the anti-slavery cause, industrial reform, and women's suffrage.

Clara Barton, Massachusetts born, was an early organizer of the Red Cross and its first president. Phillis Wheatley was one of a long line of Negro women of Massachusetts who contributed to the state's literature, art, and social movements.

In literature alone, the state has a world-wide reputation. Among its best known writers are Jonathan Edwards, Benjamin Franklin, Emerson, Thoreau, Hawthorne, Longfellow, Lowell, Melville, Holmes, Whittier, Emily Dickinson, and Henry Adams.

Massachusetts educational institutions of higher learning rank with the best in the world. Within an area of 25 miles from downtown Boston are Harvard, Massachusetts Institute of Technology, Brandeis, Boston University, Radcliffe, Boston College, Tufts, Northeastern, and Wellesley, to list a few. The first free public school supported by taxation was opened in Dedham in 1649; the first college commencement in the U.S. was held at Harvard in 1642.

One of the great medical centers of the world is in Boston and to it come children from as far away as Thailand; a king from Saudi Arabia; and statesmen from Great Britain and other countries for treatment.

Long before the *Mayflower* made its tedious journey across a stormy Atlantic the shoreline of Massachusetts had been charted by such early explorers as Leif Ericson and his Norsemen around the year 1000. John Cabot, in 1497 and 1498, carried on explorations of the area on which England based its claim to North America. A British navigator, Bartholomew Gosnold, sailed through the many islands of Vineyard Sound and Buzzards Bay in 1602. He established a colony on Cuttyhunk, one of the Elizabeth Islands, and the main town bears his name today. He returned to England with a cargo of sassafras. Gosnold also is given credit for the first reference to Cape Cod because of the fish that swarmed about it.

When the Pilgrims sailed from England they literally were running for their lives. The Protestant Reformation, from which the religious dissension of the reign of Henry VIII can be traced, drove Pilgrim and Puritan to Massachusetts in quest of freedom to worship as they pleased. A small, determined group of them obtained financial support from London financiers and obtained a grant (1619) to settle on the James River in Virginia. It was for this point that the *Mayflower* set sail in 1620. But storms and strong winds blew them off course and they finally dropped anchor in Provincetown harbor on Cape Cod.

While in Provincetown, the Pilgrims drew up the *Mayflower Compact,* an agreement binding all to conform to the will of the majority. A pattern was thus cast which was to serve the first Massachusetts colony well during the coming winter and allowed the colony to experience a slow but steady growth.

The land on that section of Cape Cod was so barren that the group set sail and arrived at Plymouth harbor. The little settlement soon prospered and the London backers were paid off. Thus did the Pilgrims prove that a colony could be self-supporting. This encouraged others to leave their homeland and cross the sea. It was in Plymouth that the first Thanksgiving was celebrated in November, 1621.

More important, perhaps, was the arrival of the Puritans in 1628 who received, a year later, a royal charter granting them the right to govern the colonies. The charter provided for two general courts, one composed of freemen who would then elect the members of the other, which was composed of a governor, deputy governor, and 18 assistants. This formed the basis of the state and federal government in the United States as we know it today.

From Farming to Shipping

The Puritans landed at Salem, a small fishing village, elected John Winthrop their first governor, and then moved temporarily to Charlestown. In September, 1630, they crossed the Charles River and founded Boston. The colony expanded rapidly and prospered.

The early colonists found the soil in Massachusetts to be poor for extensive farming and turned, instead, to shipping and general commerce because of the abundance of good wood for ships and the fine harbors. They embarked on ventures that were to make Massachusetts the carrier of the young nation. It established the triangular trade by which sugar and molasses were brought from the West Indies in return for lumber, codfish, and livestock. Molasses was made into rum and sent to Africa in return for slaves who were sold to the Indies for gold used to buy English luxuries.

England wanted exclusive trade with its new colony. But this would have put Massachusetts at a decided economic disadvantage with wealthy England. Thus followed a series (Sugar Act, 1764; Stamp Act, 1765; Tea Act, 1773) of restrictions on the rebellious colony. The Boston Massacre of 1770, when British soldiers fired on a taunting crowd of citizens, was an ominous hint of the Revolution which was to follow.

Soon after the Boston Tea Party (1773), reprisals and restrictions became unbearable to the colonists. They held a meeting of the Continental Congress behind locked doors while General Gage, the British commander, shouted through the keyhole that the Congress be dissolved. The Congress ordered a boycott of all British goods. On April 19, 1775, the embattled farmers, warned by the historic rides of Paul Revere and William Dawes, engaged the British regulars at Concord and Lexington. There followed, in short order, the colonists' siege of Boston, the Battle of Bunker Hill and, on March 17, 1776, the British evacuation. Massachusetts, where the first blood of the Revolution was shed, had won its most important victory and never again was any enemy to cross its borders.

Each year on April 19th Paul Revere's ride is recreated from Charlestown to Concord. The riders are dressed in Colonial costume; there are parades, band concerts, speeches, and general celebration. The observance of such an important event in American history is little known even outside of Middlesex County in Massachusetts. No promotion on a national scale is done. Massachusetts' conservative reluctance to blow its own horn dominates even an event of national importance. The celebration of the British evacuation of Boston is similarly celebrated by a city holiday and a local parade. Tourist promotional officials look with envy on the gigantic celebrations which less conservative states, such as Florida and California, would stage had these two events occurred there.

Despite half-hearted efforts at promotion, the vacation industry in Massachusetts is becoming big business—even bigger than manufacturing. People from all over the country feel thay are coming "home" when they visit the Bay State. For here their ancestors had their roots before leaving for more expansive regions of the country.

Diversification of scenery, ranging from a twisting sea coast to the green, gently rolling hills of the Berkshires in the western part of the state, rich in historical lore, and vast recreational opportunities are among the lures which bring visitors to the Bay State from all over the world.

The south shore of Cape Cod is washed by the warm waters of the Gulf Stream as it swings eastward toward Europe and during the summer months swimming and sun bathing are popular activities for thousands. Cape Cod was the summer White House for President John F. Kennedy and the streets of Hyannis became crowded with tourists when it was known the Kennedy family would be "at home." Even today, long after President Kennedy's assassination, the Hyannis home is a prime tourist attraction.

Massachusetts Bay, as well as the North shore through Marblehead and Gloucester, with nearby Rockport, an artist colony of national repute, provide some of the best sailing opportunities in the state.

Every Massachusetts village, town, or city, possesses historical sites worthy to be examined by visitors interested in how their country was formed and the trials and sacrifices made by those founding fathers.

Most of the large cities are in the eastern section of the state where there are cultural, social, and educational advantages. There are 79-degree awarding colleges and universities within the state, most of which are located in the populous eastern section. Summer sessions at many of these colleges and universities attract thousands of visitors.

The broad, sometimes turbulent, Connecticut River bisects Massachusetts from north to south. Nourished by the flow of water this fertile valley is a rich agricultural area. Cities such as Springfield, scene annually of an agricultural exposition, Holyoke, and Greenfield, thrive on industry and farming. The western section of the state is hilly and, consequently, another major vacation area. Mount Greylock in the Berkshires has an altitude of 3,491 feet and many others rise over 2,000 feet.

Massachusetts is a four-season vacationland. The summer months are the busiest for the entire state from mountains to seashore. The coming of autumn brings on the region's foliage spectacle. Because of the mixture of climate, soil, and frosts, the entire New England area is a riot of color for almost the entire month of October. This rare combination brings visitors by the thousands to enjoy the color, cool evenings, and warm days. With the arrival of snow the ski season swings into action, primarily in the Berkshire Hills where most of the facilities in the state are located.

When spring fills the streams and lakes with melted snow, the fishing season comes to the state.

Industrial Renaissance

Because of the demands for goods and services brought about by the tourist business, Massachusetts industry has expanded to meet the demand. Millions of dollars worth of recreational goods are produced every year. Included are golf balls and clubs, bathing suits, boats of all descriptions, a wide variety of sport shoes and sneakers, sporting guns, camping gear as well as equipment for all types of competitive sports. Radios and television sets, carpeting light fixtures, beds and bedding are also used in large amounts by the booming Massachusetts hotel and motel industry.

The state's economic and industrial development, with many ups and downs, is at present experiencing an unprecedented boom. Shipping and general commerce were the mainstay of the state's economy during the early days when Massachusetts-built ships and goods were seen throughout the world. However, President Jefferson's Embargo Act, imposed as retaliation for the interference of France and Britain on American shipping, and the War of 1812, took a heavy toll of the state's lucrative trade. Also, the state did not keep pace with the shipbuilding industry when ships changed from wood to iron, distance from the source of supply being the main reason.

These factors forced the state to manufacture many of the goods previously brought in through trade. Waterpower was plentiful, farmers trained in handcraft were available, and capital was looking for new investments. In 1814, Francis Cabot Lowell set up his perfected power loom in Waltham which was to transform Lawrence, Lowell, Fall River, New Bedford, and others into great textile centers. At the close of the 19th century, Massachusetts factories were producing more than one-third of the nation's cotton and woolen textile goods. The boot and shoe industry, and the associated leather and tanning industry, took root in Lynn, Brockton, Worcester, Haverhill and other cities until Massachusetts was producing half of the boots and shoes worn in the entire country.

The industrial opportunities in the cities brought a flood of immigrants to transform the once predominantly English population into a mixture of national strains. In 1930, 65 percent of the inhabitants were either foreign-born or of foreign and mixed parentage. Today large groups of Italians, Irish, Finns, Lithuanians, Poles, Germans, and others cast their lots with descendants of the Pilgrims and Puritans. In the nation-wide 1929 depression there was a trend toward industrial decentralization and a movement of industry closer to sources of raw material. As a result, Massachusetts lost much of its textile industry to Southern states and its leather industry to the West. New industry soon took its place, particularly research plants.

When World War II began in Europe in 1939, the state flexed its muscles and went to work. As of 1960, there were 460 licensed users of radio active material, including a nuclear reactor, two research reactors and one training reactor. Sixteen colleges offer courses dealing with nucleonics.

Massachusetts has played an important role in the scientific advancements necessary to the winning of World War II, the Korean conflict and, still later, the waging of the Viet Nam conflict.

The improved network of roads, brought about by the Federal Interstate Highway Program, has contributed substantially to the state's present-day industrial growth. Boston, and its suburbs, were slowly being choked by automobile traffic. The circumferential highway (State 128), which connects points in the north with those west and south, has become a model for similar city-avoiding highways throughout the country. It also attracted the electronics industry. Today, 128's 64-mile length is lined with laboratories and factories. This influx of industry bordering a new superhighway is being repeated as each new mile of Interstate road opens. Interstate 495 north and west of Boston, connecting the industrial cities of Lowell, Lawrence, and Haverhill with markets to the west, is developing fast and bringing new business life to those cities which had lost their textile industry to Southern states. Interstate 91 running north and south through the Connecticut River valley is bringing the same benefits to Springfield, Northampton, and Holyoke. This latter route is also expected to increase the tourist business from Canada for this part of the state.

Cape Cod, a sand spit jutting 70 miles out into the Atlantic Ocean in the shape of an upturned arm bent at the elbow, is the state's busiest summer vacation area. Heaped up by glaciers long ago, then molded by winds and currents, Cape Cod has been endowed with plant and animal life in wide variety. Surf pounds the eastern headland while calmer waters wash the northern and southern shores. Between these shores are marsh, woodlands, and ruffling ponds left behind by the glaciers. For three centuries, the Cape was spared the great industrial buildup of our eastern coast. Combined with a seafaring way of life and a rich heritage, this isolation produced a picturesque scene, small villages, the well-known gray-weathered cottages, windmills and lighthouses.

Until recently, its charm had been preserved by town and county governments but the Cape's vast tourist business threatened to destroy much of its old-time flavor. Establishment of the Cape Cod National Seashore, in 1961, permanently assures protection against the inroads of modern commercialism. The Seashore will cover roughly 27,000 acres and extend from the town of Chatham, at the Cape's elbow, to Provincetown, at its fist.

To protect as much of Massachusetts' rich historical past as possible for future Americans, the Federal government recently established another similar park west of Boston. This is called the Minute Man National Monument and parallels the route of retreat taken by the British from Lexington to Concord on that fateful opening day of the Revolutionary War.

The Massachusetts citizen is many things, but perhaps his most distinctive characteristic is pride, not necessarily in himself, but in his state. This pride brings a surprisingly large portion of its people, who have strayed for one reason or another, back within the state's borders from places all over the world.

Massachusetts history, brief as this account is, explains its people and thus explains Massachusetts.

PRACTICAL INFORMATION FOR MASSACHUSETTS

MASSACHUSETTS FACTS & FIGURES. The experts aren't sure, but they think the meaning of the state's name, which comes from Massachuset Indian, means something like "at (or near) the great hill." The state's many nicknames are easier to understand: *Bay State; Old Bay State; Old Colony State; Baked Bean State; Puritan State.* The mayflower is the state flower; the American elm, the state tree; the chickadee, the state bird. *Ense petit placidam sub libertate quietem* ("By the sword she seeks peace, but peace only under liberty") is the state motto. *Hail Massachusetts* is the "unofficial" state song.

Boston is the state capital. The state population is 5,148,578.

Heavily populated in most areas, Massachusetts is one of the leading industrial states. Boston, mother of Harvard University (in nearby Cambridge) and the state's biggest city, is New England's leading port as well as cultural center. The state's many historical sites and resort areas, particularly the Cape Cod peninsula, attract many visitors yearly. From its low Atlantic coastline (whose fishing fleets yearly bring in about a third of the nation's annual fish catch), Massachusetts rises to a hilly plateau in the center of the state and to the scenic Berkshire Hills and Taconic Mountains in the west.

It is a state of sharp climatic changes—cold winters and warm summers.

HOW TO GET AROUND. The *Massachusetts Turnpike* is the newest and most important superhighway in the state. This toll expressway, from the new *Boston Extension* west to the *New York* state line, leads into the *New York Thruway*. The *Southeast Expressway* and *State 3* travels from *Boston* to *Cape Cod's Sagamore Bridge;* then *US 6* to *Hyannis. State 128* expressway circles *Boston* from *Gloucester* on the North Shore to *Braintree* on the South Shore. *State 15* links the *Wilbur Cross Parkway* from Hartford, Conn. with the *Mass. Turnpike* at *Sturbridge. Route 9* links *Boston* with *Worcester* if you do not use the Mass. Turnpike. For leisurely driving, the scenic *Mohawk Trail* is on *State 2.*

Both *Trailways* and *Greyhound* bus companies serve the state. Local bus service is good everywhere. *Taxi service* is no problem; local companies are listed in telephone directories. For *car rentals, Avis, Hertz* and *National* have offices located in all the key localities.

Northeast flies to *Nantucket, Martha's Vineyard, New Bedford, Lawrence,* and *Worcester* from Boston. *Yankee Airlines* flies from *New York* to *Pittsfield Airport. Berkshire Aviation Enterprises* flies from *Great Barrington* to *Boston, Martha's Vineyard, Nantucket,* etc. An *air-taxi service, New England Flyer's Air Service,* is located at *Beverly Airport,* Beverly.

The *Alert* sails daily in summer from *New Bedford* to *Cuttyhunk Island.* There are *sailboat rentals* at *Community Boating,* Boston shore of Charles River; *Wollaston Beach,* Wollaston; *Winthrop Beach,* Winthrop. *Norwood Chris-Craft,* US 1, Norwood (15 mi. from Boston), has chartered boats by week or month. Tel. 762–2452. Their marina is 24 Ericson St., Neponset. Tel. 288–1000. Boat and canoe rentals are no problem in the *Berkshires.* Just about anywhere there is a stream, you will find a boat livery.

Hiking trails are in *Westfield,* bordered with laurel late June. Hiking is the only way to get to the top of *Monument Mountain* in Stockbridge–Great Barrington area. Two foot trails. Parking facilities are at foot of mountain. Climb to the tower at the summit of *Mount Everett,* So. Egremont. There are special historic walking tours of *Boston, Cambridge,* and *Salem.* Maps available from local chambers of commerce.

Horseback riding is popular in *Milton* (Blue Hills Reservation) and the *Berkshires.* Check locally for stables.

TOURIST INFORMATION SERVICES. Free folders, brochures, and maps may be obtained from the *New England Council, Inc.,* Statler Office Building, Boston, Mass. 02116; *Massachusetts Department of Commerce,* 150 Causeway St., Boston, Mass. 02114; *Division of Forests*

SEASONAL EVENTS. In all four seasons, plus Indian summer, Massachusetts offers a variety of events. *Autumn* is heigh-ho-come-to-the-fair time. *Fairs* include: *Barrington Fair* (8 days), Sept., Barrington; *Eastern States Exposition* (7 days), Sept., Springfield; *Tri-County Fair,* Sept., Northampton; *Topsfield Fair* (6 days), Sept., Topsfield; *Franklin County Fair,* Sept., Greenfield.

Festivals: Boston Art Festival, June–July, Boston Common; *Berkshire Music Festival,* July–Aug., Tanglewood in Lenox; *St. Peter's Fiesta,* late June, blessing of the fishing fleet, Gloucester; *Blessing of the fishing fleet,* late June, Provincetown; *Dance Festival at Jacob's Pillow,* late Aug., Lee; *Festival of Arts,* first wk. of July in Marblehead, mid-July in Hyannis and Provincetown, late Aug. in Gloucester; *Scallop Festival,* early Aug., New Bedford; *Bridge of Flowers Art Festival,* late Aug., Shelbourne Falls; *Artists' Costume Ball,* mid-Aug., Rockport; *Rockport Amateur Arts Festival,* first wk. in Oct., Rockport; *Foliage Festival,* early Oct. in Greenfield, late Sept. to early Oct. in North Adams; *Winter Carnival,* early Feb., Greenfield.

Special days: Thanksgiving Day, Pilgrim Procession enacted, Plymouth; *April 19,* parades in Lexington and Concord; *May 30,* Memorial Day parades and ceremonies; *Muster Day,* mid-June, Old Sturbridge Village, Sturbridge; *Civic Days,* early July, Fitchburg; *Fourth of July,* fireworks, parades; Indian Pow-Wow, early July, Mashpee.

Races: Auto races, from mid-June, Riverside Park, Agawam; *greyhound races,* spring and summer, Raynham Park, Raynham, and Wonderland Park, Revere, parti-mutuel betting; *horse races,* late June to July, Suffolk Downs, Revere, Berkshire Downs, Hancock, and Brockton Fair, Brockton; *harness racing,* end of June, Foxboro Raceway, Foxboro; *marathon race,* April 19, world marathon runners compete, Boston; *regattas,* sailboat regatta, July 4, in Gloucester, late July in Edgartown (Martha's Vineyard); *Race Week,* 1,000 sailboats, late July, Marblehead; *tournaments,* striped bass and bluefish derby, middle of Sept. to Oct., Martha's Vineyard; *parachute* jumping, summer, Sport Parachuting Center, Orange, lessons Sun.

The dance: Many fine, world-renowned ballet companies perform in Boston and newspapers should be checked for schedules at the theaters. The groups are announced well in advance.

Shows: Massachusetts is always in the limelight with a variety of shows. *Antiques: Village Fair Antique Show,* about June 20, Phillipston; *Antique Show,* early Aug., Chatham; *Antique Fair,* last wk. July, National Guard Armory, Hyannis. *Dog Show:* early June, Framingham. *Horses: Horse Show,* late May, at Racelands, Framingham; *Class A Horse Show,* all divisions, early July, Great Barrington; *Grange Horse Show,* late Aug., Williamstown; *Eastern States Exposition,* about Sept. 12 to 19, always includes horse shows. *Flowers: Annual Flower Show,* mid-March, Wonderland Park, Revere; *Laurel Week,* third wk. July, Westfield (trails announced); *Flower Show,* late July, Chatham; *October Harvest and Chrysanthemum Show,* Horticultural Hall, Boston.

Boats: Boston Herald Traveler sponsors a boat show annually, date announced; *Travel: Boston Herald Traveler* sponsors a travel show, date announced; *Air Show: Annual Navy Air Show,* mid-Sept., Naval Air Station, South Weymouth.
and Parks, 15 Ashburton Place, Boston, Mass., 02108; *Cape Cod Chamber of Commerce,* Hyannis, Massachusetts 02601; *Berkshire Hills Conference,* 100 North St., Pittsfield, Mass.; *Greater Boston Chamber of Commerce,* 125 High St., Boston, Mass. 02110; *Pioneer Valley Association,* 38 Gothic St., Northampton, Mass.; *Mohawk Trail Association,* Charlemont, Mass.; *Essex County Tourist Council,* Village Green Motor Inn, Danvers, Mass.; *Nantucket Chamber of Commerce,* Nantucket, Mass.; *Martha's Vineyard Chamber of Commerce,* Martha's Vineyard, Mass.

DRINKING LAWS. Drinks may be ordered until 1 a.m. daily; until midnight Sat. Sun. serving hours: 1 p.m. to 1 a.m. Packaged liquor sold until 11 p.m. in package stores; no sales Sun. Legal drinking age is 21.

NATIONAL PARKS. Spectacular describes *Cape Cod National Seashore* in Eastham, authorized as a national park in 1961. Eventually the National Seashore will encompass 27,000 acres from Chatham to Provincetown. Now four areas are open to the public all year around: *Province Lands, Pilgrim Heights, Marconi Station, Coast Guard Beach,* all accessible by paved roads from US 6. Although camping is limited, inquiries may be addressed to: Superintendent, Cape Cod National Seashore, P.O. Box 428, Eastham.

Visitors to the National Seashore will enjoy the *guided walking tours* and evening *lectures* July through Oct. Self-guided trails are open all year for a good look at wildlife and birds.

A visitor's information center is located in *Orleans* on US 6.

Picnicking is allowed on all the beaches, protected by lifeguards in summer from morning to 6 p.m.

Seasonal *hunting* must conform to regulations. Freshwater and shell *fishing* require license; not necessary for saltwater fishing.

Beach buggies are allowed on the sand routes; some dunes are about 75 feet high. Views of pounding surf are spectacular.

Privately-owned campgrounds in nearby towns, all with trailer sites, are: *Horton's Park,* tel. Provincetown 1220; *North of Highland Camping Area,* tel. Provincetown 1191–W–1; *North Truro Camping Area,* tel. Provincetown 1847–M; *Dune's Edge Camp Ground,* tel. 8604; *Maurice's Tent & Trailer Park,* tel. South Wellfleet 349–2029.

STATE PARKS. From May to Oct., the approximately 50 state parks and forests are open daylight hours. Usually trailer and tent sites are available; picnicking is allowed. There's a two-week limitation on campsites, $1.50 a night. *Beartown State Forest,* access from State 23 or 102, near Great Barrington. Camp and swim at Benedict Pond. Ski in winter. More than 8,000 acres include Mt. Wilcox, Sky Peak, Livermore Peak, Beartown Mountain. *Brimfield State Forest,* US 20, near Worcester and Springfield. Fish in Woodman Pond. Swim in Dean Pond. Hike on Mt. Waddaquadduck. *Erving State Forest,* State 2, near Erving and West Orange. Hunting, fishing, camping, and swimming here. *Horseneck Beach Reservation,* access from US 6 and State 88, near Fall River. Stroll on sand dunes; enjoy surf-fishing and swimming. *Mohawk Trail State Forest,* State 2, near Charlemont. Fish for trout; take outstanding scenic photographs. *Mount Greylock State Reservation,* near North Adams. Mt. Greylock, highest Massachusetts mountain, is here, with Massachusetts War Memorial Beacon. Hunt, ride, camp, and ski on more than 8,000 acres. *Mount Tom State Reservation,* access from US 5, Holyoke. Good fishing. Excellent, privately-owned ski area open to public. *October Mountain State Forest,* near Lee. Good camping (trailers). Visit Schermerhorn Gorge; fish in Shaker Mill Pond. Largest Massachusetts forest, almost 15,000 acres. *Myles Standish State Forest,* near Plymouth. Swim in ponds; hunt, fish. Camping (trailers); cabins for rental. *Pittsfield State Forest,* near Pittsfield. Sports galore, including skiing. *Salisbury Beach State Reservation,* access on State 1A, near Newburyport. Miles of ocean for swimming. Camping. *Spencer State Forest,* State 31, Spencer. Monument to inventor Elias Howe and family here. Swim, fish in Howe Pond. *Walden Pond State Reservation,* State 126, near Concord. Summer sports in pond area. Thoreau lived here. *Willard Brook State Forest,* State 119, near Fitchburg. Scenic waterfalls; Damon Pond Beach. Camping (trailers).

INDIANS. Massachusetts is named for the Massachuset Indians, who occupied the Massachusetts Bay Territory in the early 17th century. The Massachuset tribe also owned and occupied the site of Boston. Although they numbered about 3,000, the tribe was reduced to less than 500 by 1631. Soon after, the Indians converted to Christianity and their tribal life diminished. Now there is no accurate record of just how many persons of Indian descent live in Massachusetts; but it is believed the count is about 2,000. Indian Day is Aug. 12 in Massachusetts, a quiet observance. That was the date in 1676 when the famous Indian leader King Philip was killed by an Indian informer. King Philip was the son of Massasoit. A powerful Indian ruler and chief of the Wampanoag tribe, Massasoit signed the peace treaty of 1621 with the Pilgrims of Plymouth. He kept his vow faithfully.

Neighboring Indians participated in the first Thanksgiving Day feast with the Pilgrims in 1621. The colonists were grateful for all that the Indians taught them about farming and survival in New England.

Russell Gardner of South Hanson is the present chief of the Wampanoags' Mattakeesett Band and vice-president of the Federated Eastern Indian League.

Early July is the date of the annual *Indian Pow-Wow* in *Mashpee.* In *South Mashpee,* tourists may visit the *Indian Village* and be greeted by Princess Evening Star. Handmade Indian gifts are sold. It's open every day from 10 a.m. to 5 p.m. (State 28 and State 151, halfway between Falmouth and Hyannis).

WHERE TO GO. *Boston:* Top views from *Prudential Tower Skywalk, John Hancock Building, U.S. Custom House, Bunker Hill Monument. Gardens:* Arnold Arboretum, The Fenway, Public Garden, Boston Common. *Historic:* Freedom Trail (Boston Tea Party Site, *Old Ironsides,* Revere House, etc.), Beacon Hill homes. *Libraries:* Boston Public Library. *Museums:* Museum of Fine Arts, Boston University Gallery, Isabella Stewart Gardner Museum, Museum of Science and Planetarium. *Scenic:* Charles River Reservation.

There are many other points of interest in the *Boston vicinity. Cambridge:* Harvard University, Harvard Library, Harvard University museums; Massachusetts Institute of Technology; Radcliffe College; Longfellow House; Cambridge Common; sculling, boating on Charles River. *Dedham:* Fairbanks House (1636). *Framingham:* Shoppers World; Cary Memorial Building and Library; Carousel Theatre. *Hingham:* Old Ship Church (1681); Samuel Lincoln House (1741); Old Ordinary (1650). *Hull:* Nantasket State Beach; Paragon Amusement Park. *Lexington:* Minute Man Statue; Buckman and Munroe Taverns; Hancock-Clarke House (1698); Old Cemetery (1690). *Medford:* Peter Tufts House (1678); Tufts University. *Milton:* Blue Hills Reservation (Houghton's Pond). *Newton:* Boston College. *Quincy:* birthplace homes of John Adams (1663) and John Quincy Adams (1675). *Sudbury:* Wayside Inn. *Waltham:* Brandeis University. *Watertown:* Mt. Auburn Cemetery (Mary Baker Eddy, Longfellow, Lowell, Louis Agassiz). *Wellesley:* Wellesley College; Jewett Arts Center; Coleman Map Building (Babson Institute); Babson World Globe.

South Shore to Cape. Attleboro: Shrine of Our Lady of LaSalette. *Cohasset:* Minot Light. *Duxbury:* Home sites of John and Priscilla Alden and Myles Standish; Old Burying Ground. *Foxboro:* Bay State Raceway. *Kingston:* John Bradford House; Old Burying Ground. *Mattapoisett:* old whaling town. *New Bedford:* was whaling center; now biggest scallop port; Moby Dick tour. *Norton:* Wheaton College. *Plymouth:* Plymouth Rock; Plimouth Plantation; *Mayflower II. South Carver:* Edaville Railroad rides; cranberry bogs. *Taunton:* King Philip Oak; greyhound racing; Old Colony Historical Society. *Wareham:* Ocean Spray Cranberry Museum; beaches. *Weymouth:* Naval Air Station; Abigail Smith Adams House.

Cape Cod. Bourne: Cape Cod Canal; beaches; fishing; Otis Air Force Base. *Chatham:* watch incoming fishing fleet at Lydia's Cove; Old Wind Mill; Marine Shell Museum; beaches. *Dennis:* Cape Playhouse; beaches. *Eastham:* Old Windmill; beaches. *Falmouth:* Falmouth Playhouse; Falmouth Historical Society; beaches. *Hyannis:* late President Kennedy's summer home; shopping center; beaches. *Mashpee:* Old Indian Church and Cemetery; Indian powwows. *Orleans:* beaches; information center for Cape Cod National Seashore; beach buggy rides. *Provincetown:* beaches; surf-casting; dunes tours; Chrysler Art Musum; Marine Aquarium; Pilgrim Monument. *Sandwich:* home of Sandwich Glass (exhibited in Historical Society Museum); Old Grist Mill; oldest Cape Cod town. *Truro:* Pilgrim Spring (part of National Seashore); Corn Hill Beach; ancient gravestones. *Wellfleet:* Cape Cod National Seashore displays; beaches; Audubon Bird Sanctuary (tours); Marconi wireless site. *Woods Hole:* U.S. Commercial Fisheries Aquarium; Oeanographic Institution and Marine Biological Laboratories. *Yarmouth:* Winslow-Crocker House; beaches.

Cuttyhunk Island: excellent swimming, fishing; bird-watching; boat trips from New Bedford via *Alert. Martha's Vineyard:* Gay Head Indian Museum; Dukes County Historical Museum; Old Whalers' Church; Memorial to Praying Indians; Methodist Camp Ground (Grand Illumination Aug.); beaches. *Nantucket Island:* Old Windmill; Old Gaol; Old Fire Hose Cart House; Whaling Museum; Jethro Coffin House; Maria Mitchell House; Friends Meeting House; Great Point Light; beaches; The Moors.

Cape Ann area. Beverly: Old Waterfront; Hale House; Balch House (1636); beaches. *Gloucester:* Fishermen's Memorial Monument; Our Lady of Good Voyage Church; Hammond Museum; North Shore Arts Association. *Ipswich:* Crane Memorial Reservation (Castle Hill Estate summer concerts); Crane's Beach; 17th-century houses; Ipswich clams. *Magnolia:* Reef of Norman's Woe (in Longfellow's poem *The Wreck of the Hesperus);* Rafe's Chasm; scenic drive. *Manchester:* unusual rocks (Agassiz Rock Reservations). *Rockport:* art colony; scenic harbor.

Essex County (North Shore). *Amesbury:* historic homes: John Greenleaf Whittier; Mary Baker Eddy; Macy-Colby. *Andover:* Phillips Academy, Addison Gallery of American Art, Peabody Foundation for Archaeology, Memorial Hall Library; Merrimack Valley Textile Museum. *Danvers:* historic homes: Rebecca Nurse House; Jeremiah Page; Samuel Fowler. *Haverhill:* John Greenleaf Whittier Homestead; Winnikenni Castle. *Lowell:* Whistler House, Parke Gallery. *Lynn:* Mary Baker Eddy House; Lynn Woods. *Marblehead:* yachting center; Fort Sewall; Powder House; Old Burial Hill; St. Michael's Church; Abbot Hall; Jeremiah Lee Mansion; King Hooper Mansion. *Newburyport:* Tristram Coffin House; old shipbuilding center. *Peabody:* Northshore Shopping Center. *Pepperell:* covered bridge. *Salem:* House of Seven Gables; Witch House; marked Historical Trail from Hawthorne Hotel; Pingree House; Essex Institute; Pioneer Village; Charter St. Burying Ground; Derby Wharf; Salem Willows. *Salisbury Beach:* amusement park; state beach. *Saugus:* The Ironworks Restoration; Old Ironmaster's House. *Swampscott:* beaches; Mary Baker Eddy Historical House. *Topsfield:* Fairgrounds (Fair early Sept.); Topsfield-Ipswich River Wildlife Sanctuary. *Wakefield:* Pleasure Island, amusement park.

Pioneer Valley. Agawam: Riverside Park (car races, amusements). *Amherst:* Amherst College; Mead Art Gallery; University of Massachusetts; Emily Dickinson home; Robert Frost and Eugene Field homes not open to public. *Belchertown:* Quabbin Reservoir. *Cummington:* birthplace of poet William Cullen Bryant. *Deerfield:* site of Indian massacres; Indian House Memorial; Memorial Hall Colonial Museum; Old Graveyard; Frary House; Hall Tavern; Asa Stebbins House; Wright House; Old Deerfield Inn; Main St. drive. *Easthampton:* Mt. Tom Reservation; Arcadia Wildlife Sanctuary of Massachusetts Audubon Society. *Holyoke:* Mt. Tom Reservation (ski area, chair lift views); Mountain Park; Holyoke Museum. *Northampton:* Smith College (guided tours); Smith College Museum of Art; Wiggins Tavern. *South Hadley:* Mt. Holyoke College. *Springfield:* George Walter Vincent Smith Art Museum; Science Museum and Planetarium; Small Arms Museum; Forest Park. *West Springfield:* Storrowtown Village; Storrowtown Music Fair; Eastern States Exposition Grounds (Fair mid-Sept.). *Westfield:* Shaker Farms; Jasper Rand Art Museum; Athenaeum houses. *Wilbraham:* state game farm. *Worthington:* cascade. *Westfield:* laurel tours; Grandmother's Garden; Stanley Park, Carillon.

Berkshires. Adams: Savoy Mt. and Mohawk Trail State Forests; Ashley Falls; Col. Ashley House; Bartholomew's Cobble. *Becket:* Jacob's Pillow Summer Dance

Festival; Happyland. *Dalton:* Crane Paper Museum. *Egremont:* site of Shay's Rebellion. *South Egremont:* Jug End Barn resort; Catamount ski lift (summer sightseeing rides). *Great Barrington:* Beartown State Forest; Monument Mountain reservation. *Hancock:* Shaker community; Berkshire Downs. *Hartsville:* Federal Hatchery. *Florida:* views of Hairpin Turn. *Rowe:* Atomic energy plant (guided tours). *Charlemont:* Antique Auto Museum; *Hail to the Sunrise* statue; Thunder Mountain ski area (summer chair lift); covered bridge. *Shelburne Falls:* Salmon Falls; potholes; Bridge of Flowers. *Lenox:* 8-week Berkshire Music Festival, Tanglewood (July–Aug.); Berkshire Music Bar, folk music, jazz (July–Aug.); Pleasant Valley Wildlife Sanctuary and Trailside Museum. *Mt. Washington:* Bish Bash Falls. *Greenfield:* Sept. Franklin County Agricultural Fair; 1400-foot pool; Oct. Foliage Festival; Poet's Seat Tower; covered bridge. *Millers Falls:* French King Bridge. *New Marlborough:* Red Fox Music Barn, chamber music festivals. *North Adams:* Natural Bridge (marble); Mt. Greylock, War Memorial Tower; ski slopes; Oct. Fall Foliage Festival. *Pittsfield:* South Mountain Concerts; Berkshire Athenäeum; Berkshire Museum; lakes. *Sheffield:* Shay's Rebellion Monument; covered bridge. *Stockbridge:* Village Cemetery; Chesterwood; Berkshire Garden Center; Naumkeag Gardens (Choate Estate); Berkshire Playhouse; Mission House. *Tyringham:* Shaker Colony Shaking Ground; Tyringham Art Galleries. *Colrain:* covered bridge. *Orange:* Sports Parachuting Center; Lake Mattawa (skin-diving). *Williamstown:* Sterling and Francine Clark Art Institute; Williams College; Williams College Museum of Art; Chapin Library; Williamstown Summer Theatre.

South Central. Fitchburg: Lake Whalom Playhouse; Damon Pond; Fitchburg Art Museum; *Groton:* Groton School; Lawrence Academy; Old Burying Ground. *Harvard:* Fruitlands Museum; Old Shaker House; American Indian Museum; Harvard Astronomical Observatory. *Lancaster:* Birthplace of naturalist Luther Burbank. *Leominster:* Johnny Appleseed Festival (June); Johnny Appleseed birthplace. *Millville:* covered bridge. *Princeton:* Redemption Rock; Museum of Antique Automobiles; Mt. Wachusett. *Royalston:* cascades. *Spencer:* Howe Park, Spencer State Forest; home of inventor Elias Howe. *Sturbridge:* Old Sturbridge Village. *Webster:* Webster Lake (water-ski center). *Worcester:* Worcester Art Museum; Science Museum; Worcester Polytechnic Institute; Worcester County Horticultural Society.

WHAT TO DO WITH THE CHILDREN. For the young set, there are summer *amusement parks* at *Revere Beach,* Revere; *Paragon Park,* Nantasket Beach, Nantasket; *Salisbury Beach,* Salisbury; *Mountain Park,* Holyoke. *Pleasure Island,* Wakefield includes a pirate boat ride, train ride, etc. Admission includes all rides: $1.75 children under 12; $2.25 adults. Summer only. *Storyland,* State 132, Hyannis, has amusements and Mother Goose Village, summer only. Children 60 cents; adults $1. *Happyland,* US 20, Becket, is Disneyland-inspired. Summer only. *Edaville Railroad,* South Carver, features a train chugging through Cranberryland. Daily in summer; after Labor Day, weekends only. Closed from Jan. 3 to June 20. Chicken barbecue restaurant and picnic grounds on premises. Children 40 cents; adults 90 cents.

Zoos. Franklin Park Zoo, Blue Hill Ave., Dorchester, is open all year; free. There are thousands of animals and hundreds of birds on more than 50 acres. Buildings open 10 a.m. to 4:45 p.m.; grounds open from 8 a.m. to 7 p.m. Children may pet animals in special area; 25 cents admission. Picnic grounds on premises. *Forest Park,* Springfield, has an interesting zoo; picnic grounds.

Old Sturbridge Village, US 20 and State 15, is a re-created 18th-century farming village. Children will see craftsmen making horseshoes, dipping candles, baking bread. In winter there are sleigh rides. Open daily from 9:30 a.m. to 5:30 p.m. Apr. thru Nov. Guided summer tours Mon. thru Fri. at 10 a.m. and 2 p.m.

From Nov. on, the Village is closed at 4:30. Restaurant on the premises. Admission $2.50 adults; $1 children 8 to 17; under 8 free. Closed Christmas Day and New Year's Day. *Dinosaur Land* is in So. Hadley (off Amherst St.). The museum exhibits assorted dinosaur prints. Open daily from 9 a.m. to 6 p.m. Adults 50 cents; children 25 cents. Children should also visit *Plimouth Plantation* in Plymouth and *Mayflower II*. The reconstructed Pilgrim village costs $1 for adults, 50 cents for children under 14, children under 5 free. Open daily from 9 a.m. to 5 p.m., Apr. thru Nov. 29. Boarding the *Mayflower II* costs 75 cents; 50 cents for children 5 to 14; under 5 free.

EXPLORING BOSTON

A tour of Massachusetts properly starts in Boston—and on foot. That's because most historical sites are located along Freedom Trail, a well-planned walk of only 1½ miles. After parking your car, take any subway car marked Park Street for the official start of the Trail.

First stop is the Park Street Church, built in 1809. Henry James called it, "The most interesting mass of brick and mortar in America." It was here that William Lloyd Garrison gave his first anti-slavery address (1828) and that *America* was first sung (1832), both on July 4th. The corner on which the church stands is known as Brimstone Corner because at the time of the War of 1812, brimstone was stored in the church. Interesting short walks jutting off from various points along the Freedom Trail are called Freedom Paths.

An important Freedom Path leaves the Park Street Church and leads to the State House, Louisburg Square, the Central Burying Ground and returns through Boston Common. The State House, built on what was John Hancock's cow pasture, is an excellent example of Colonial architect Charles Bulfinch's work. Memorial Hall, with its torn and bloodstained battle flags, located within the State House, is interesting. Louisburg Square looks much as it did 130 years ago with its charming bow-windowed brick houses and privately-owned central park. The Square has been the home of many notables, such as Louisa May Alcott who lived and wrote at number 10. Boston Common, of course, belongs to the people. The town bought it from a hermit, Rev. William Blaxton, in 1634. Originally, the land was set aside for the training of the local militia and the common grazing of cattle. It still allows citizens of Boston to graze their cows—if they have any and are so inclined. Freedom of speech is a tradition on the Common and anyone with a grievance or a message can set up a soapbox and orate. The Central Burying Ground appears to be a part of the Common but actually was a Col. Finch's pasture before the city took it over in 1756. The great artist Gilbert Stuart is buried here.

From the Park Street Church, the Freedom Trail heads north along Tremont Street. On the left is the Granary Burying Ground, the second stop on the Trail. The site was the location of Boston's granary which gave its name to the cemetery. The graves of John Hancock, Robert Treat Paine, and Samuel Adams, all signers of the Declaration of Independence, are here along with Paul Revere, Peter Faneuil, James Otis, many governors, Benjamin Franklin's parents and victims of the Boston Massacre. A stone marked Mary Goose is believed by many to be the grave of *Mother Goose*. There is much debate over the identity of Mother Goose. There was, in the early part of the 18th century, an Elizabeth Vergoose living in Boston. The French claim that Mother Goose was really Queen Bertha, and in England a woman called Mother Goose sold flowers on the streets of Oxford. Take your pick.

At the corner of Tremont and School Streets, turn right down the hill to King's Chapel, Boston's very first Episcopalian church. The present building was completed in 1754, although the congregation was organized in 1686. In Colonial days the church was a royal favorite. Queen Anne gave its red cushions and George III its communion plate. The burying ground beside the church was the early colony's only cemetery for many years and contains the graves of Governor Winthrop and William Dawes, Jr. On the opposite corner is the *Parker House* hotel where its well-known rolls are served with a flourish.

On the left, as you head down School Street is Boston's City Hall. A schoolhouse built near the hall became Public Latin School, the first public school in the country. The Rev. Cotton Mather, Emerson, Hancock and Samuel Adams are a few who studied there and went on to make their mark on American history. On the lawn of City Hall is a statue of Benjamin Franklin and it was the first (1856) such statue erected in Boston. One side of Franklin's face is smiling while the other is sober . . . the impression of the sculptor Richard S. Greenough.

On the left where School Street meets Washington Street is the Old Corner Bookstore. Built in 1712-1715, the building was first an apothecary shop, then a bookstore. It became a busy meeting place for literary greats of the day and today it is maintained by *The Boston Globe* as a downtown office and a museum containing first editions and pamphlets of historical interest. The *Globe* restored the building in 1960.

The Tea Went Overboard

If you glance to the right from the front of the bookstore and across Washington Street, the Old South Meeting House can be seen. Here, the colonists held many mass meetings that culminated in the Revolutionary War. The plot for the Boston Tea Party took shape here and the building was used during the war as a lively bar while the Royal Light Dragoons used the main floor as a riding school. Returning along Washington Street to the north turn right on State Street and enter the Old State House on the corner. From its balcony citizens of Boston heard the news that King George III had just been crowned. Below the balcony, mobs burned symbols of the hated British, and Generals Gage, Clinton, and Howe planned the strategy for the battle of Bunker Hill in the building. Across State Street from the Old State House is a circle of cobblestones marking the site of the Boston Massacre when British soldiers fired into a taunting mob of colonists, killing five men. In a rare show of co-operation, the British agreed to a trial of their soldiers involved in the massacre and, not to be outdone, the Colonists provided John Adams and Josiah Quincy, Jr., to conduct the defense. All but two were acquitted, and those convicted of manslaughter were branded on the hand and discharged from the army.

Continue down State Street and turn left at North Street. Dock Square and Faneuil Hall will be in front of you. The hall, originally built by Peter Faneuil as a market, is called the "Cradle of Liberty" because so many meetings were held here by advocates of American freedom. The building later was presented to the city and now houses a museum of flags, photographs and weapons of the Ancient and Honorable Artillery Company of Boston. The ground floor of this historic Colonial structure still contains food and produce stalls where much of Boston still does its marketing. Atop the building is a unique grasshopper weathervane—and therein lies a tale.

The Baby and the Grasshoppers

Hector Campbell, superintendent of the artillery museum, says there are several stories that explain why the weathervane was shaped in the form of a grasshopper. One version merely states that the grasshopper was an old agricultural symbol, making it eminently suitable for a market. But the story Mr. Campbell likes best goes like this:

"It is said that in the year 1519 a group of children were chasing grasshoppers in a field outside London when they found an abandoned baby lying in the grass. They took the infant to a nearby church where he was sheltered. The child grew up to become Sir Thomas Gresham, financial adviser to Queen Elizabeth and founder of the Royal Exchange of London. In gratitude, Sir Thomas had a grasshopper placed on the Exchange Building.

"Two centuries later, Peter Faneuil became a member of this

same Exchange Building and as the legend goes, he became fascinated both by the shape of the building weathervane and its attending tale.

"When he gave Faneuil Hall to the Town of Boston he had a large grasshopper placed above the cupola."

The next point on the Freedom Trail is the most popular with tourists. Stay on North Street, cross under the Expressway, to the Paul Revere House. Revere lived here from 1770 to 1800 and presumably left from here for the Boston Tea Party, dressed as an Indian. And, of course, he was living here when he set out on his historic ride to Lexington in April, 1775. The house, probably the oldest in Boston, was built in the 1670's and the interior and furnishings present an excellent insight into the mode of living during those times. Gracing the small park before the house is the Cyrus Dallin equestrian statue of Paul Revere and located around the park, on bronze tablets, is the story of the part played by the North End and its people during Boston's beginnings.

From the Revere House it is a short walk (via Prince, Hanover, Bennett, and Salem streets) to the Old North Church, or Christ Church. The two lanterns, hung from its steeple on the night of April 18, 1775, signaled that the Redcoats were leaving for Lexington and Concord and started Paul Revere on his ride. The old bells in the steeple rang out the good news, in 1781, that Cornwallis had surrendered at Yorktown. It is, incidentally, the oldest church in the city and was built in 1723. Just down Hull Street from the church is Copp's Hill Burying Ground where the British set up heavy cannons trained on Breed's Hill and Charlestown. It had been used as a burying ground, however, since 1660 and resting there are the remains of Rev. Cotton Mather and Edmund Hartt, who constructed the legendary warship, the *Constitution*.

Charlestown, the Bunker Hill Monument, and the *Constitution (Old Ironsides)* are on a Freedom Path, a good distance from the Copp's Hill site. Take a cab, or drive across the Charlestown Bridge and follow local signs to the Bunker Hill Monument. The actual battle, while a defeat for the American forces who were badly outnumbered, showed a remarkable degree of courage which proved a great morale factor for the coming long war. At the bottom of the hill can be seen the docks of the Charlestown Navy Yard and the tall masts of the *Constitution*. There are adequate parking facilities at the ship if you are driving. Walk up the gangplank onto the wonderfully preserved ship that never lost a fight. Nicknamed *Old Ironsides,* the 44-gun frigate, first put to sea in 1798 and is still an officially commissioned ship of the U.S. Navy.

Boston is an old city. Yet you may be surprised to find sections of the city as new as tomorrow. There's the new Government Center

15 16

Places of Interest

3. Archives Building C-17
6a Benjamin Franklin's Birthplace, Site C-18
6b Benjamin Franklin's Statue C-17
12. Boston Athenaeum C-17
15. Boston Garden and North Station A-17
16. Boston Massacre, Site C-18
19. Boston Tea Party, Site C-19
28. Calvin Coolidge College C-17
30. Central Burying Ground D-17
32. Chamber of Commerce C-18
32a Chamber of Commerce Convention and Visitors Building C-18
37. City Hall (Boston) C-17
44. Community Boating, Inc. B-15
46. Congregational House C-17
48. Copps Hill Burying Ground A-18
50. Court House (Boston) B-17
55. Custom House B-18
59. Edward Hatch Mem. Shell C-15
59a Emerson College C-15
62. Faneuil Hall B-18
63. Federal Office Building B-18
64. Federal Reserve Bank C-18
66. First Church in Boston C-15
68. First Post Office in America, Site C-18
68a First Public School, Site C-17
72. Government Center (Under Construction) B-18
73. Great Elm Site C-17
75a Harrison Gray Otis House B-16
92. John Hancock House, Site C-17
93. King's Chapel and Burying Ground C-17
94. Kirstein Memorial Library Building C-18
95. Lafayette Lodging C-17
97. Liberty Tree, Site D-17
98. Lincoln Monument D-16
107. Massachusetts Department of Public Works Building A-17
109. Massachusetts General Hospital B-16
122. Museum of Science A-16
123a New England College of Pharmacy C-16
128. New England Museum B-17
129a North Station A-17
133. Old Corner Book Store C-18
134. Old Granary Burying Ground C-17
136. Old North Church A-18
137. Old South Meeting House C-18
138. Old State House C-18
141. Parkman Band Stand, Boston Common C-17
141a Park Street Church C-17
142. Paul Revere House B-18
147. Post Office (Boston) C-18
161. Quincy Market B-18
167. Robert Gould Shaw Memorial C-17
170. St. Pauls Cathedral C-17
171. St. Thomas More Oratory C-17
173. Samuel Adams House C-17
176. Soldiers and Sailors Monument C-16
182. South Station D-18
183. State House B-17
183a State Office Building B-17
184. Suffolk County Jail B-16
185. Suffolk University B-17
188. Trailways Bus Terminal D-16
192. Union Rowing Club C-15
194. Unitarian Headquarters C-17
195. United States Appraisers Stores C-19
203. Washington Monument (Public Garden) C-16
205a Welfare Department (Boston) B-17

Hotels

213a Avery Hotel D-17
214. Beacon Chambers Hotel B-17
215. Bellevue Hotel C-17
223. Essex Hotel D-18
230. Lincolnshire Hotel C-16
232. Madison Hotel A-17
234. Parker House C-17
235. Ritz-Carlton Hotel D-16
241. Touraine Hotel D-17

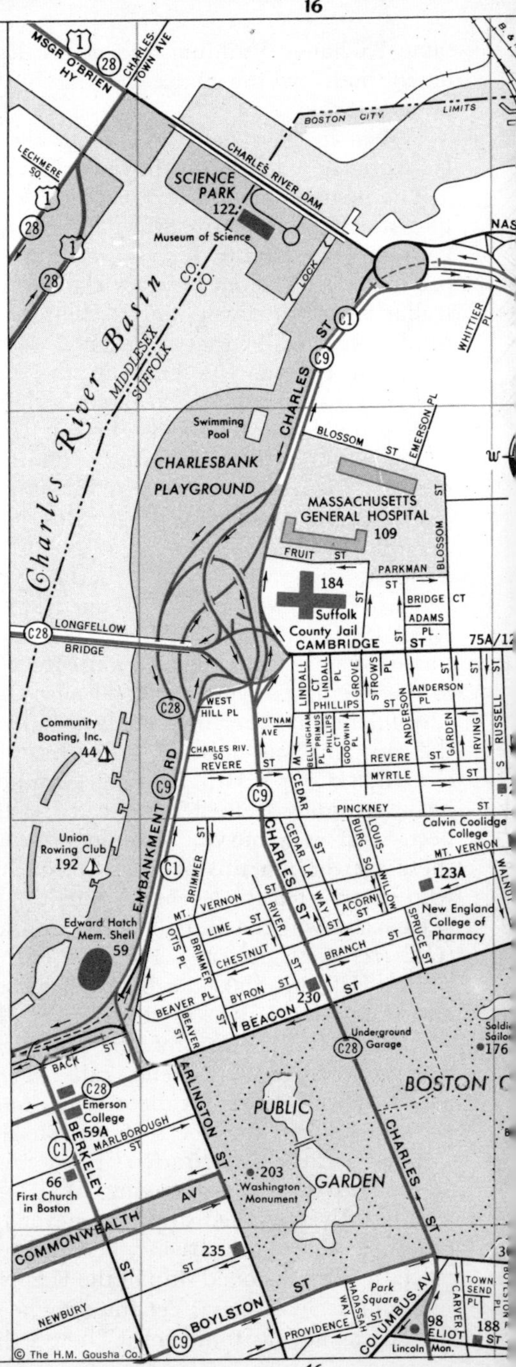

A B C D

15 16

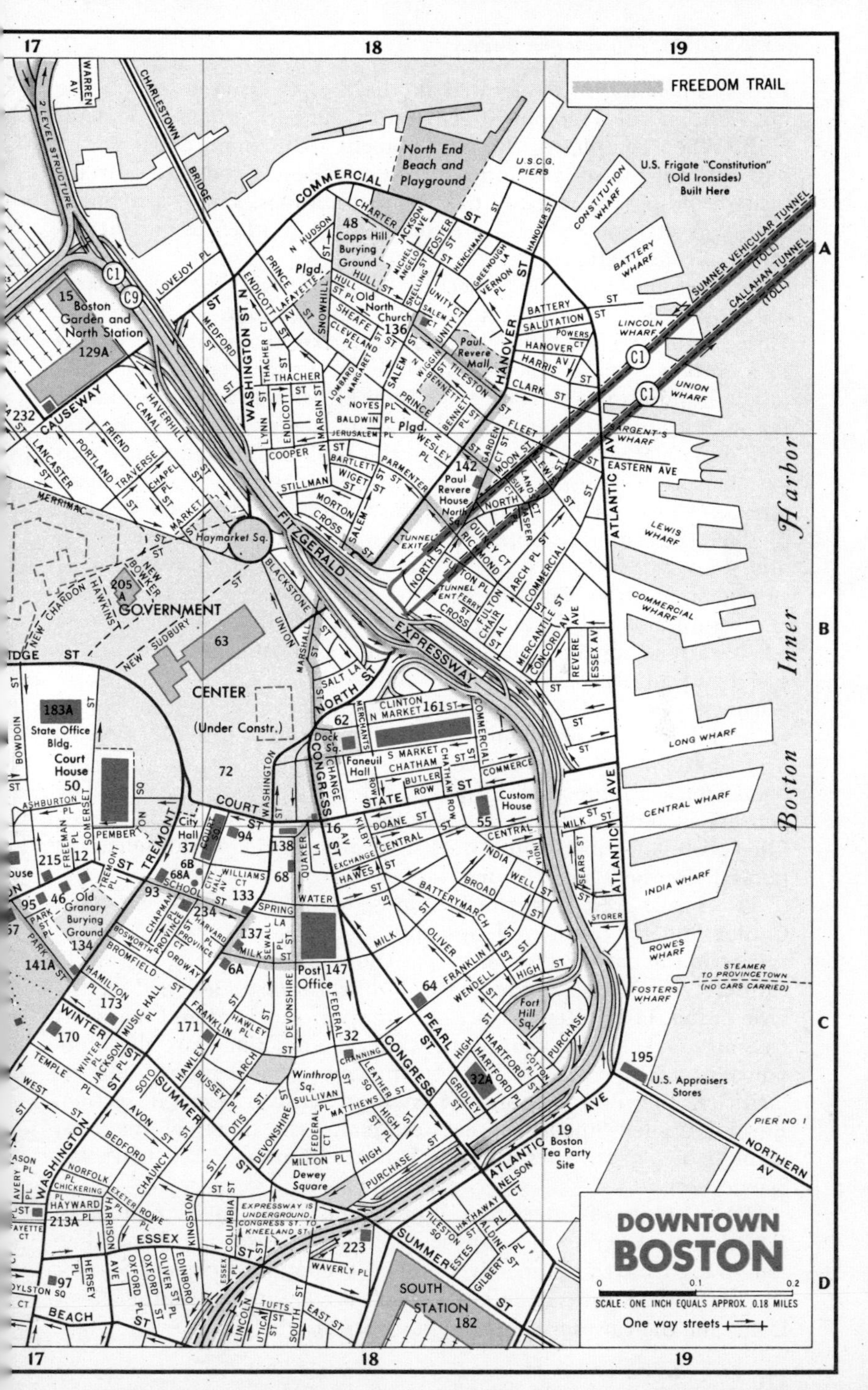

DOWNTOWN BOSTON
SCALE: ONE INCH EQUALS APPROX. 0.18 MILES
One way streets
FREEDOM TRAIL
Boston Inner Harbor
North End Beach and Playground
U.S. Frigate "Constitution" (Old Ironsides) Built Here
U.S.C.G. PIERS
Copps Hill Burying Ground
Old North Church
Paul Revere Mall
Paul Revere House
Boston Garden and North Station
Haymarket Sq.
GOVERNMENT CENTER (Under Constr.)
State Office Bldg.
Court House
City Hall
Old Granary Burying Ground
Faneuil Hall
Dock Sq.
Custom House
Post Office
Winthrop Sq.
Dewey Square
Fort Hill Sq.
Boston Tea Party Site
U.S. Appraisers Stores
SOUTH STATION
STEAMER TO PROVINCETOWN (NO CARS CARRIED)
EXPRESSWAY IS UNDERGROUND, CONGRESS ST. TO KNEELAND ST.
SUMNER VEHICULAR TUNNEL (TOLL)
CALLAHAN TUNNEL (TOLL)
FITZGERALD EXPRESSWAY
CONSTITUTION WHARF
BATTERY WHARF
LINCOLN WHARF
UNION WHARF
SARGENT'S WHARF
LEWIS WHARF
COMMERCIAL WHARF
LONG WHARF
CENTRAL WHARF
INDIA WHARF
ROWES WHARF
FOSTERS WHARF
PIER NO 1

Redevelopment Project located in the Scollay Square area at the northern end of Tremont Street against the background of Faneuil Hall. When completed, the development will extend down to the harbor from the square and will contain federal and state government buildings, a new city hall, office buildings, shops, apartment buildings, etc. Some already are completed and others are in various stages of construction.

Another gleaming new project that contrasts with the red brick of old Boston is in the streets west of Copley Square in Back Bay. Here, built over the Massachusetts Turnpike Extension, is the new Prudential Center. At the present time, the Prudential Tower is the tallest building in the country outside of Manhattan (though that borough contains eight other buildings higher than the Boston Prudential). Rising 52 stories high, the building contains an observation deck, a gourmet restaurant on top, as well as the northeastern home office of the Prudential Insurance Company. By the end of 1965, the center also included a new War Memorial Auditorium and the new *Sheraton Boston Hotel,* the first major hotel built in Boston in 30 years. Commercial buildings, apartment houses, shops and restaurants will be added to the center. Because of the center's 5,800-seat auditorium, the Back Bay area of Boston is becoming its social and cultural center.

You should not think, however, that you have really seen Boston after walking the Freedom Trail and having viewed the modern new Boston. As an example, children will enjoy a ride on the Swan boats which ply the artificial pond within the Boston Garden. The Garden is about one-half the size of the Boston Common and is filled with flowering shrubs, trees from all over the world, reflecting pools, flower beds, and curving walkways.

Two blocks west from the Boston Gardens on Boylston Street, is Copley Square, considered by many as the most attractive public square in the nation. On the left, as you enter the square, is Trinity Church. Across the square is the Public Library, designed in the style of the Italian Renaissance. An interior courtyard and many art treasures make a visit here worthwhile. To accommodate the thousands of college and university students who regularly use its facilities, the Boston library has an extensive research section. Beyond Copley Square to the west looms the dome of the First Church of Christ, Scientist, the Mother Church of the Christian Science sect.

Other points of interest in Boston are: Museum of Fine Arts, Huntington Avenue; the Gardner Museum, Fenway and Worthington Street; Church of the Advent, Mt. Vernon and Brimmer Streets; Science Park, northerly end of Charles Street, at the Charles River Dam; and the Custom House on State Street.

PRACTICAL INFORMATION FOR BOSTON

HOTELS AND MOTELS. Boston's reputation for fine hotels remains undimmed, but the glamor of the Ritz, the Parker House, and the old Copley Plaza (now the Sheraton-Plaza) is frequently forsaken by motor-minded travelers who prefer to stay in the many excellent motels in the suburbs and in outlying towns. For those who enjoy walking tours of old Boston and Cambridge, nothing can beat the downtown hostelries, while those who intend to remain auto-bound will no doubt choose to stick close to the car in the well-furnished and conveniently located motor inns all around the area.

Deluxe

Ritz Carlton Hotel. Royalty has stayed at this impressive hotel. Superb service. Crystal chandeliers; plush decor. Gourmet's restaurant, cocktail lounge. Barber, beautician. Boston Public Garden view.

Arlington St. (tel. KE 6–5700).

Sheraton-Boston. This is a new hotel in Boston, and the talk of the town. Pool, health club. Poolside lanai rooms. Unusual restaurants, cocktail lounges. Pets welcome. Free parking. Airport service. Several wide rooms for wheelchair guests.

In new Prudential Center. (tel. 236–2000).

Sheraton-Plaza. A tradition of Boston elegance has been maintained here. Blend of old (the *Copley Plaza*) and new. Coffee shop, gourmet restaurant, famous *Merry-Go-Round Bar.* Pets welcome. Barber, beautician. Free parking.

Copley Square. (tel. CO 7–5300).

First Class

Fenway. Baseball fans take note: this Quality Courts motel is a hop, skip, and jump from Fenway Park. Free use of typewriter, iron. Pets welcome. Pool. Restaurant; cocktail lounge.

1271 Boylston St. (tel. 262–1558).

Fenway-Commonwealth. Here you have beautifully-appointed rooms and convenience to Boston University and Lahey Clinic. Access to pool. Pets welcome. Restaurant; cocktail lounge. Quality Court motel.

575 Commonwealth Ave. (tel. CO 7–3100).

Fenway North. This resort motel features a king-size pool and Sat. night dancing. Pets welcome. Restaurant; cocktail lounge. Quality Court motel.

407 Squire Rd., Revere (less than 10 mi. from downtown Boston) (tel. 284–7200).

Hamilton House. This new hotel features kitchenettes in most rooms. High living on rooftop: pool, health club, *Kismet Lounge* (dancing, entertainment). Restaurant open for breakfast, lunch, dinner. Valet parking.

1110 Commonwealth Ave. (tel. RE 4–7400).

Hotel Kenmore. Most professional ball teams stay here (Fenway Park within walking distance). Pets welcome. Family plan. Wheel-chair ramps. *Hearthside, Beef 'N Bird* restaurants; *Gaslight Room* lounge (entertainment).

490 Commonwealth Ave. (tel. KE 6–2770).

Hotel Lenox. New Prudential Center is next door neighbor here. Nice walk to Copley Square and downtown Boston. Pets welcome. Free parking. Coffee shop, restaurant, cocktail lounge.

64 Exeter St. (tel. KE 6–5300).

Logan International Hotel. The free airport bus will take you right to this

terminal motel. Family plan. Room rate includes coffee. Pool. Restaurant; cocktail lounge, dancing.
Logan Airport (tel. LO 9–9300).

Midtown Motor Inn. After checking in, take a swim; relax in steam and massage room. Pool and patio. Restaurant, coffee shop. Family plan. Near Prudential Center.
220 Huntington Ave. (tel. CO 2–1000).

Parker House. Everyone knows this hotel as the home of the Parker House roll. Restaurants; rooftop cocktail lounge. Amplified phones and special facilities for handicapped. Barber, beautician. Nearby parking. Pets welcome. On historic Freedom Trail.
60 School St., at Tremont (tel. CA 7–8600).

Ramada-on-the-Charles. *Magnifico* describes this brand new Spanish-decorated motor inn (opened Feb. 1966). Hand-carved furniture. Pool. Family plan. Restaurant; cocktail lounge. Free parking.
1234 Soldiers Field Rd., off Storrow Dr. (tel. 254–1234).

Hotel Somerset. This hotel is especially famous for the *Rib Room* and *Polynesian Village*. Pool. Limited free parking. Popular cocktail lounge.
400 Commonwealth Ave.

Statler Hilton. Redecorating has given this well-established hotel a glamorous new look. New *Trader Vic's Restaurant;* new *Captain's Bar*. Also *Hungry Pilgrim; Thirsty Pilgrim*. Barber, beautician, shopping arcade. Pets welcome.
Park Square (tel. HA 6–2000).

1200 Beacon St. Motor Hotel. Within 10 minutes, you will be in downtown Boston from this convenient motel. Well-equipped rooms. Wheelchairs available. Restaurant; *The Barn* cocktail lounge.
Tel. BE 2–7979.

Hotel Vendome. *My Apartment* is the fun place here—cocktail lounge with dancing. Convenient to new Prudential Center, museums, Back Bay shops. Two restaurants.
160 Commonwealth Ave. (tel. CO 6–4700).

Reasonable

Hotel Avery. Theater fans and shoppers will like this conveniently-located hotel. Pets welcome. Restaurant and cocktail lounge.
24 Avery St. (tel. HU 2–8000).

Hotel Beaconsfield. Just a few minutes from downtown, this hotel is also convenient to Brookline and Framingham shopping centers. Pool. Restaurant.
1731 Beacon St. (tel. AS 7–6800).

Hotel Bostonian. Here you are within walking distance of museums, Symphony Hall, and Fenway Park. Coffee shop and cocktail lounge. Free parking.
1138 Boylston St. (tel. KE 6–1200).

Hotel Bradford. Play-goers who stay here will be in the center of the theater district. Family plans; package tour rates. Free parking nearby. Steak house, coffee shop, cocktail lounge.
275 Tremont St. (tel. HA 6–1400).

Hotel Essex. This well-established hotel is opposite South Station railroad terminal, and just off end of Mass. Turnpike and Southeast Expressway. Free parking nearby. Coffee shop, restaurant, cocktail lounge. Pets welcome.
695 Atlantic Ave. (tel. HU 2–9000).

Hotel Madison. This pleasant hotel adjoins North Station and Boston Garden. Motor entrance for free parking. Pets welcome. Coffee shop, dining room, cocktail lounge.
Causeway St. (tel. 227–2600).

HOW TO GET AROUND. *Logan International Airport,* about 3 mi. from Boston, is served by Air-Canada, Air France, Alitalia, American Airlines, British Overseas Airways Corp., Eastern Airlines, El Al, Irish International, KLM, Lufthansa, Mohawk, National, Northeast, Northwest Orient, Pan American, Sabena, SAS, Swissair, TWA, United. Taxi from airport to downtown Boston costs about $1.60; about $1.25 by private bus line; 30 cents by subway or bus. Flight time from New York to Boston is about an hour. *Provincetown-Boston Airline* flies from Logan Airport to *Provincetown Airport. Northeast* flies to *Nantucket, Martha's Vineyard, New Bedford, Lawrence,* and *Worcester.*

Boat service from Boston to *Provincetown* is provided daily in summer, leaving from *Rowe's Wharf.* Boats also leave Rowe's Wharf to *Nantasket Beach. Sailboat rentals* may be made at *Community Boating* on the Boston shore of the Charles River.

Boston is served by the *Boston & Maine Railroad* at North Station. Tel. CA 7–5070; the *New York, New Haven, Hartford Railroad* at South Station. Tel. HU 2–6800; *New York Central Railroad,* South Station. Tel. HU 2–6800.

Local *subway* and *bus service* is efficient in Boston, on the *MBTA* line, operating daily from 5 a.m. to 1 a.m. Information booth in Park St. Station, downstairs in the subway. Tel. 522–5700.

DINING OUT. Some of the world's best chefs apparently discovered Boston on *their* travels and stayed. It's a good place for gourmet dining—and wining. Don't neglect the Parker House rolls, or, if you're adventurous, the Ward Eight cocktail (basic ingredients: whiskey, lemon juice, and grenadine), both invented here. There are also good places to eat in the neighboring areas of Brookline, Cambridge, Newton, and Malden, which you can find listed under *Dining Out* in Massachusetts.

AMERICAN-INTERNATIONAL

Super Deluxe

Locke-Ober. Since 1875, this has been a gourmet rendezvous. World-famous award winner. Ward Eight cocktail invented here. Lobster Savannah superb. Victorian decor, royal service. Outstanding wine cellar. Private men's bar. Even if you can't afford the prices, splurge—you can't afford to miss this dining experience. Lunch, dinner, except Sun., and holidays.
3 Winter Pl.

Ritz-Carlton. Gorgeous dining salon with Public Garden view is considered the epitome of proper Boston dining. National awards winner. Gourmet menu. Formally-dressed waiters. Excellent cocktails and wines. Lunch, dinner. Cafe downstairs open from breakfast on.
15 Arlington St.

Deluxe

Joseph's. If you say this restaurant is as good as Locke-Ober's, you are right —management is the same. Superb menu, wines. Excellent service. Lunch, dinner daily, except Sun. and holidays.
279 Dartmouth St.

Nick's. Walls are covered by photos of the famous who dined here. Very popular bar. Children's menu. Open daily, lunch, dinner, Sat. from 4 p.m. Closed Sun., Christmas Day, and New Year's Day.
100 Warrenton St.

Nine Knox. Out of this world and way out. Stanley and Staples are chefs, waiters, entertainers. No menu—*prix fixes.* Magnificent antiques. Dinner only. Closed July and Aug. Reservations required.

Yes, this restaurant is at 9 Knox St. (tel. HU 2–3494).

First Class

Anthony's Pier 4. Here there is elegance at the Fish Pier. Romantic setting in cocktail lounge. Nautical collections, Early American motif. Menu slightly more expensive than Anthony's other restaurants in Lynn and Swampscott. Lunch, dinner. Free parking.
140 Northern Ave.

Beef 'n Bird. Enjoy hearty roast beef (or even duckling *bigarade)* in Old English atmosphere. No charge for parking. Open for lunch and dinner, Sun. from 1 p.m.
Kenmore Sq., in Hotel Kenmore.

Black Angus. Hospitality highlighted here with free wine and fresh fruit with dinner. Notice illuminated wall mural of Old Boston. Delicious roast beef. Free parking. Open daily for dinner at 5 p.m., Sun. at 1 p.m.
42 Stuart St.

The Charles. Sumptuous buffet dinners from hors d'oeuvres to do-it-yourself desserts are a big attraction here. Children's prices. Lunch, dinner. Cocktails. Closed Mon., closed Sun. in summer. Boston Common Garage for parking.
75A Chestnut St.

Executive Suite. Elegance prevails here with 19th-century cavalier decor. Plush *Embassy Room, Scarlet Salon, Crystal Lounge*. Interesting menu. Entertainment nightly. Lunch, dinner, a la carte.
21 Broad St.

Falstaff Room. Hearty roast beef is always on the menu in this romantically dim English chophouse. Iced tea flavored with cranberries. Lunch, dinner. Cocktails.
Prudential Ctr. in new Sheraton-Boston.

Golden Swan. View of Charles River is as impressive as the menu—sirloin cutlet Cleopatra, shrimp Calcutta. Continental service carts. Mediterranean decor. Piano music. Valet parking. Lunch, dinner. Cocktails.
10 Emerson Place (Charles River Park).

Hearthside. This is another delicious addition to the little world of dining in Hotel Kenmore. Meats and seafoods grilled on copper-hooded, open hearth. Lunch, dinner. Cocktails. Free parking.
Kenmore Sq.

Hungry Pilgrim. Plymouth atmosphere prevails here. Waitresses are customed like Pilgrims. Suggestions: clam chowder, broiled lobster. Breakfast, lunch, dinner daily and Sun.
Park Sq., in Statler Hilton Hotel.

Jimmy's Harbor Side. Excellent Yankee foods have won countless awards for Jimmy. Boat-shaped bar, dining room with harbor view. Clam chowder has been sent to Washington upon Senator's request. Children's menu. Lunch, dinner, except Sun. Cocktails.
240 Northern Ave.

Red Coach Grill. This Red Coach is very popular. Lively bar. Children's menu. Charcoal-broiled meats and lobster excellent. Lunch, dinner. Closed Christmas. Other Red Coach Grills in Mass. at Framingham, Saugus, Wayland, Braintree, Hyannis.
43 Stanhope St.

Rib Room. Beefeater bonanza here with gourmet Adam rib cut and Beefeater's martinis. Delicious Yorkshire pudding, potato *sonesta*. Fish, lobster included Fridays. Beef carved at table. Rich, red leather decor. Lunch, dinner.
400 Commonwealth Ave., in Somerset Hotel.

Sheraton Plaza Hotel. The *Cafe Plaza* is one of the most elegant dining rooms in town. Special dinners. *Town Room* downstairs more moderately priced. Seafood smorgasbord and buffet dinners. Children's menu. Breakfast, lunch, dinner.
Copley Sq.

Yankee Fisherman. This waterfront restaurant serves a Yankee clambake in an individual pot complete with real sea water and seaweed inside. Baked stuffed clam appetizer. Noteworthy salad. Varied menu. Cocktail lounge. Valet parking. Lunch, dinner, except Christmas Day.

100 Atlantic Ave.

Reasonable–First Class

Cobb's. King-size drinks and a free fruit basket with dinner are two attractions at this century-old restaurant. Lunch, dinner.

32 Tremont St., nr. historic King's Chapel.

Steuben's. This is a popular restaurant for both family dining and couples attending pre-theater parties. Upstairs dining room less expensive. Supper Club downstairs. Cafe Midnight open to 3 a.m. Lunch, dinner.

114 Boylston St., next to Colonial Theatre.

Union Oyster House. Original restaurant in group of 3 has been at 41 Union St. since 1769. Also at 122 Canal St. and recently enlarged one at 143 Stuart St. Quaint, nautical decor. Delicious seafood from scrod to Alaskan king crab. Steaks, chops, poultry. Lemon meringue and apple pies baked here. Lunch, dinner daily.

Reasonable

Dini's. Here the specialty is Boston's famous scrod—young codfish boned, baked, and browned. Large restaurant also serves good steaks. Right on the Freedom Trail walking tour. Luncheon, dinner. Cocktails.

94 Tremont St.

Dinty Moore's. You might say that good food is right up their alley. Well-known restaurant is in two alleys, one off Avery St., other off Washington St. Corned beef and cabbage a specialty. Lively cocktail lounge. Lunch, dinner except Sun. and holidays. Free parking (dinner).

22 Avery St.

Durgin-Park. Just about every tourist makes sure he dines at this unusual restaurant. Historic and culinary landmark. Gigantic portions. Mixed groups sit at long tables. Have a drink in *Gas Light Pub* (first floor), go up back stairs, show receipt, and seating is immediate. Lunch, dinner, except Sun. and holidays.

30 N. Market St.

Jacob Wirth's. At this century-old sawdust-on-the-floor restaurant, satisfy your craving for pigs' knuckles, homemade sauerkraut, and dark beer. New England boiled dinner also. Mahogany bar. Children's menu. Quick service. Parking lot next door. Lunch, dinner, except Sun.

33 Stuart St.

Ken's. This delicatessen with balony has a great variety of sandwiches, pancakes. No liquor. Very popular at late, late snacktime. Breakfast, lunch, dinner. Open to 3 a.m.

549 Boylston St., Copley Sq.

Parker House. This is the home of the Parker House roll. Main dining room emphasizes elegant dining. Variety on menu from Cape scallops en brochette to broiled tripe. *Revere Room* less expensive. Breakfast, lunch, dinner. Free parking.

60 School St.

Patten's. Here you will dine on good Yankee cooking in Colonial atmosphere complete with antiques. Famous homemade chowders, Boston baked beans. Cocktails. Lunch, dinner, except for breakfast, lunch, dinner, except Sun. and holidays.

173 Milk St.

Pavilion Coffee Shop. Whether you want a meal or just a delicious cup of coffee, you will be pleased here. Children's menu has painted cartoons, matching china. Breakfast, lunch, dinner, snacks.

Plaza level of new Sheraton-Boston, Prudential Ctr.

Pieroni's Sea Grills. There are 3 of these dependable seafood restaurants. Cocktails. Good service. Open daily for lunch and dinner, except Christmas.
7 Park Sq.; 601 Washington St.; 13 Stuart St.

Place for Steak. Just the place for steak but there are other goodies too: broiled chicken, jumbo shrimps, etc. Exceptionally quick service. Near theaters. Luch, dinner daily, except Sun.
Lobby level, Hotel Bradford.

Ramada on the Charles. *Si, señor,* Spanish specialties are featured at this beautiful, new restaurant (opened Feb., 1966). American favorites, too. Costumed waitresses. Children's menu. Lunch, dinner. Cocktails. Free parking.
12345 Soldiers Field Rd., off Storrow Dr.

St. Clair's. Pleasant chain serving good variety. Children's menu. Open daily for breakfast, lunch, dinner, except Christmas Day.
1651 Massachusetts Ave. and 92 Summer St.

Warmuth's Port Side. Select your own lobster from the tank. Home-baked rolls and pies. Children's menu. Cocktails. Lunch, dinner, except Sun. and holidays. Closed Sat. in July.
280 Devonshire St.

Inexpensive

Filene's. Bargain-basement shoppers know that the upstairs restaurant is a bargain, too. Omelettes are a specialty. Children's menu. Open for lunch and early dinner. Closed Sun. and holidays.
Washington and Summer sts.

Kum-Up-Tu. Here is home-style cooking that Mother never makes since she probably uses canned or frozen foods. Only fresh vegetables and seafood in season cooked here. Lunch and dinner. Closed Sun.
55 Falmouth St., nr. Christian Science Mother Church.

CHINESE-POLYNESIAN

First Class

Bob Lee's Islander. From the waterfall outside to tropical murals inside, the stage is set for exotic dining. Suggestions: *pu-pu* platter, flaming ambrosia. Island drinks. Bob Lee's personal hospitality. Lunch, dinner daily, Sun.
20 Tyler St., Chinatown.

Cathay House. Here you will discover just about any dish under the Chinese sun, even to a Cathay House gourmet special. Cocktails. Dinner only. Open till 3 a.m. including Sun.
70 Beach St., Chinatown.

Kon Tiki Ports. This is the newest Polynesian port in town, actually 4 restaurants in one many-splendored area. Exquisite gold and silk decor reminiscent of movie setting for *Anna and the King of Siam.* Exotic foods, dramatic drinks. Open until the wee hours.
Lobby level of new Sheraton-Boston Hotel, Prudential Ctr.

Polynesian Village. Here you will discover romance island-style, including oversized cocktail with two straws for sweethearts. Exotic Cantonese and Polynesian specialties. Dramatic decor. Dinner only.
400 Commonwealth Ave., in Hotel Somerset.

Trader Vic's. South Sea Island enchantment is predominant in this new addition to the Statler Hilton Hotel. Spectacular cocktails and flaming dishes in the internationally known Trader Vic style. Lunch, dinner daily, Sun.
Park Sq.

Reasonable

Gamsun. "Gold Mountain" is the translation of this restaurant's name. Hong Kong smorgasbord is a mountain of food. A la carte delicacies. Complete luncheons and dinners. Children's menu. No cocktails. Daily, Sun. noon to midnight.
21 Hudson St., Chinatown.

South Seas. Relax with a delicious island drink or arrange a big luau party in this attractive restaurant. Everything cooked to order from a la carte specialties to complete tropical dinners. Lunch and dinner, to 3 a.m.
21 Harrison St., Chinatown.

FRENCH

Deluxe

French Room. Here everything is *magnifique* from ambiance to menu. Usually ensemble serenades at dinner. Gourmet dishes from pressed duck to crepes suzette. Lunch, dinner.
160 Commonwealth Ave., in Hotel Vendome.

First Class

Au Beauchamp. This well-known Parisian restaurant serves tastiest frogs' legs this side of the River Seine. Vintage wines. Lunch, dinner. Sun. dinner only. Closed holidays. Guests may park at Boston Common Garage.
99 Mt. Vernon St.

Les Tuileries. This restaurant has a French alliance with Au Beauchamp on Beacon Hill—both have same owner. Excellent *quiche lorraine*. Impressive Parisian murals. Lunch, dinner daily. Sun., dinner only. Closed holidays.
370 Commonwealth Ave., in Hotel Eliot.

GREEK

Reasonable

Athens-Olympia Cafe. From *dolma* to *baklava,* generations of Bostonians have satisfied their hankering for Greek dishes here. Cocktails. Lunch, dinner. In theater district.
One flight up at 51 Stuart St.

ITALIAN

First Class

Café Amalfi. For years, this has been one of the favorite restaurants Italian style. Try the *scaloppine Amalfi*. After 9 p.m., menu is a la carte. Open for lunch, cocktails, dinner.
10A Westland Ave., nr. Symphony Hall.

Casa Barbi. *La dolce vita* here includes pizza and cafe espresso on the patio in summer. Dining room is formal with gourmet Italian specialties on menu. Rare vinos. Open for dinner from 4 p.m. Sun. and holidays from 1 p.m.
1277 Commonwealth Ave.

Reasonable

Felicia's. Follow Felicia into the kitchen and watch her prepare *scampi à la Felicia.* Children's menu. Good wines. Gay with musical background. Dinner only. Lunch is served on Fri. only.
145A Richmond St., nr. Paul Revere House.

Giro's. Mile-long menu features lobster *fra diavolo*. Cocktails. Children's menu. No charge for parking. Lunch, dinner.
464 Hanover St., nr. Paul Revere House and Old North Church.

Marliave. Informality Italian-style is accented here. Alfresco roof garden in summer. Lounge intercom announcements for tables. Good vinos. Children's menu. Lunch, dinner, except Sun. and holidays.
11 Bosworth St.

Stella. The Polcari family is proud of 40 Italian specialties and famous clientele. Roman-style meals for 35 years. Cocktail lounge and bar. Free parking. Lunch, dinner daily to 1 a.m. and Sun.
9 Fleet St., North End.

Inexpensive

European. Here they are past masters at being pasta masters. Considered Boston's oldest Italian restaurant. Everything from delicious pizza to baked stuffed shrimp. Seats hundreds. Open for lunch, dinner, cocktails.
218 Hanover St., nr. Paul Revere House.

MIDDLE EASTERN

Reasonable

The Nile. When King Saud visited Boston, he ordered food here. Middle East specialties—*lah'm,* flat Syrian bread, homemade salad dressing, *baklava.* Exotic carpets, brass chandeliers. Lunch, dinner.

76 Broadway, off Stuart St.

SCANDINAVIAN

Reasonable

Ola. Small, cozy dining room in centuries-old home features immense smorgasbord table. Summer dining in old-fashioned courtyard. Authentic specialties from Ola's Norwegian cookbook. Bring own wine. Lunch, dinner.

14 Carver St., nr. Park Sq.

BARS. These are just a few of the popular bars in Boston: *The Mermaid Bar.* Quaint decor, stand-up captain tables. Waiters wear French merchant marine uniform. In Sheraton-Boston Hotel in new Prudential Center. *Persian Lounge.* Waitresses wear harem costumes and serve unique drinks. Also in Sheraton-Boston Hotel. *Cobb's 1860 Bar.* Double-size drinks; free hors d'oeuvres; entertainment. 30 Tremont St. *Gaslight Room.* Jazz by Basin St. Boys. Hotel Kenmore, Kenmore Square. *Darbury Room.* Sophisticated rendezvous; entertainment. 271 Dartmouth St. *Merry-Go-Round Bar.* Carousel really turns. Smart, gay setting. Sheraton-Plaza Hotel, Copley Square. *Number Three Lounge.* Popular with executives. 3 Providence St. *Red Coach Grill.* Popular bar. 43 Stanhope St. *The Barn.* Really a transplanted barn. Opens 4 p.m.; entertainment. 1200 Beacon St. *Your Father's Moustache.* Beer and banjo music. Open 8 p.m. to 1 a.m. Sat. from 8 to 12 p.m.

NIGHTCLUBS. Daytime hours may tick seriously in Boston; but the pendulum swings to the light side after dark until 1 a.m.; until midnight Sat. *Dancing* in rooftop lounges may be enjoyed at *Parker House,* Tremont St.; *Hamilton House Hotel,* 1110 Commonwealth Ave. *Blinstrub's Village.* This huge supper club features top artists, and show business greats. One of two largest theater-restaurants in country (1500 seats). No cover charge. Broadway, So. Boston (about 4 min. drive from Park Square). *Caesar's Monticello.* Top show-business names perform on a 1500-square-foot stage at this supper club. State 9, Framingham (15 min. drive from downtown Boston). *Steuben's.* Good variety shows nightly at this popular supper club. Popular family place. 114 Boylston St. *Club Khiam.* Arabic, Greek, Armenian, and Turkish dancing is featured here. 3 Appleton St. *La Discotheque Nicole au Club Henri IV.* You have to be 21 years of age for dancing here, nightly (except Sun.). 96 Winthrop St. *The Forum.* Greek-accented discotheque complete with toga-clad waitresses. 464 Commonwealth Ave. *Your Father's Moustache.* Gay '90's fun is complete with banjo music, peanuts, pitchers of beer. 74 Warrenton St. *Bavarian Hofbrau.* Costumed, singing waiters and waitresses perform, plus two shows every night but Mon. 100 Dartmouth St. *The Hawaiian.* Free hula lessons Wed. night. Shows, dinner, dancing nightly. 146 Boylston St.

COFFEE HOUSES AND OUTDOOR CAFES. One might say that Boston coffee houses have grounds for fame—Joan Baez began her folk singing career here. Most coffee houses are in the Newbury St. and Charles St. areas, and in the university areas of Cambridge. *Turk's Head Coffee House.* European coffees and snacks.

Nightly folk entertainment. No cover charge. 71½ Charles St. *The Loft.* Coffee; folk music. Open 8 p.m. to 12 p.m. 54 Charles St. *Cafe Florian.* Exotic coffees and teas; pastries; luncheon. Open daily 12 to 12; Sat. 8 p.m. to 1 a.m.; Sun. 5 p.m. to midnight. Sidewalk cafe in summer. 85 Newbury St.

MUSIC. Boston hits a high note in the music world with the *Boston Symphony Orchestra*. Erich Leinsdorf is musical director. The winter season begins the end of Sept. with concerts in *Symphony Hall* (Massachusetts and Huntington Aves.) Fri. afternoon, Sat. evening, and some Sun., Mon., Tues. concerts. Several rehearsals are open. There is also a *Boston Women's Symphony Orchestra. Pops concerts* in Symphony Hall are from end of Apr. to end of June, conducted by Arthur Fiedler. He also conducts the outdoor Esplanade concerts in Hatch Shell, along the Charles River, from end of June until middle of July. Boston newspapers announce schedules, also programs for John Hancock Hall, New England Mutual Hall, Boston University Concert Hall, Jordan Hall, Museum of Fine Arts, Isabella Stewart Gardner Museum.

The oldest U.S. active choral group is Boston's *Handel and Haydn Society,* performing in Boston and Philharmonic Hall, New York. The recent spring *opera* season had its debut in the new War Memorial Auditorium, in Prudential Center, featuring the Metropolitan Opera. The winter opera season is always important in Boston; programs announced in newspapers. Summer *band concerts* are usually from 12 to 2 p.m. daily at Parkman Bandstand, Boston Common. During the *Boston Arts Festival,* June–July, there's a music-filled program on Boston Common.

STAGE AND REVUES. *Boston* has three downtown theaters famous for pre-Broadway premieres. The *Wilbur Theatre, Shubert,* and *Colonial* begin their season soon after the first week in Sept. Engagements, with top stars, last two or three weeks. Check newspapers for matinee and evening performances.

TOURS. There are many package tours for the visitor. *Gray Line* of Boston, in the Sheraton Plaza Hotel, has a number of good tours. *Tour No. 1,* takes about 2 hours, and covers historical and business sections. The bus circles Bunker Hill Monument, stops at Christ Church (Old North Church), Paul Revere House, Old Ironsides. There are morning and afternoon tours; the fare is about $3.25. A year-round tour. *Tour No. 2* is an educational tour of Boston for two hours. The bus drives along Back Bay, Fenway, and residential areas to the James Russell Lowell Home, Museum of Fine Arts, Radcliffe College. The bus stops at Christian Science Publishing House to view the Mapparium, at Longfellow House, Harvard University campus, and at Agassiz Museum to see the glass flowers. This fare is about $3.25, and it's a seasonal tour. *Tour No. 3* takes about 4 hours and visits the birthplace of famous authors —Longfellow, Lowell, Hawthorne, Emerson, Louisa May Alcott. Then the bus follows the route taken by Paul Revere and the British troops. There are stops at Concord Battleground, Old North Bridge, and the stops of Tour No. 2. This package costs about $5.50 and is a year-round tour. For the nighttime, Gray Line has a tour *Evening Under the Stars* which tours Boston for two hours, July and Aug., for $3.25. For other Gray Line Tours originating in Boston, see *Tours* under Massachusetts and Cape Cod *Practical Information sections.*

Copley Motor Tours travel around historic Boston, Cambridge, Lexington, and Concord. Office is at Sheraton Plaza Hotel.

SPECIAL INTEREST TOURS. *Harbor:* A windjammer Boston Harbor cruise sails in summer from *India Wharf,* 320 Atlantic Ave. Three-hour tour on the *Spray* is about $3.50 for adults; children, $2. Lunchboat harbor cruises leave *Rowe's Wharf,* Atlantic Ave., Mon. thru Fri. at 12:15 and 1:15 for a 40-minute tour. Lunch may be purchased aboard. Fare 50 cents. River excursion boats cruise up the Charles River to

Watertown and back, from pier behind Hatch Shell on Esplanade (starting June 1). Fare 50 cents; children 25 cents.

Walking: The most popular walking tour in *Boston* is the *Freedom Trail,* a 1½-mi. walk, with 15 historic sites. Free souvenir guide booklets are distributed at any of the sites along the way. Trail is clearly marked and begins at the edge of Boston Common, Park and Tremont Sts. Take a walk around *Faneuil Market* area on Fri. or Sat. for a colorful look at open-air stalls, where just about every food under the sun is sold European style. A walk through Boston's *Chinatown* is interesting. Wednesday is a good day for a walking tour of Boston's *Beacon Hill.* Mansions are open; luncheon may be arranged. At night, the visitor should not miss a visit to the glass-enclosed *Skywalk* on the 50th floor of the Prudential Tower in new Prudential Center. Open to 10 p.m. daily and Sun. Adults 50 cents; children 25 cents.

INDUSTRIAL TOURS. *The Boston Globe,* 135 Morrissey Blvd., shows the details of newspaper publishing, Mon. thru Fri. at 9:30, 10:30, 11:30 a.m. and 1:30, 2:30, 3:30 p.m.; Sat., 9 a.m. and 1 p.m.

HISTORIC SITES. For instant history, just walk along Boston's *Freedom Trail* which begins at the State House, Beacon and Park sts. You will see the *Park Street Church* where gunpowder was hidden during the War of 1812; the *Granary Burying Ground* where many patriots were buried (including Paul Revere). Stop in to see *Faneuil Hall,* where pre-Revolutionary meetings were held. It's open weekdays from 9 a.m. to 5 p.m.; Sat. from 9 a.m. to noon; Sun. from 1 p.m. Closed Thanksgiving and Christmas. Admission free. The *Paul Revere House,* on North Sq., is open daily except Sun. and holidays, from 10 a.m. to 4 p.m. Admission is 25¢. The *Old North Church,* where the lantern signaled Paul Revere, is open from 10 a.m. to 4 p.m. daily. In *Copp's Hill Burying Ground* are tombstones dating back to 1660. You will want to see the *USS Constitution,* called *Old Ironsides,* at *Boston Naval Shipyard,* Charlestown. Admission is free; hours are 9:30 a.m. to 4 p.m. daily. The ship is but a few blocks away from *Bunker Hill Monument,* off Main St., Charlestown. This granite obelisk commemorates the battle of Bunker Hill, fought in 1775. Admission is 10¢. Hours are from 9 a.m. to 5 p.m. daily. Closed Christmas Day.

MUSEUMS AND GALLERIES. Boston has some of the best museums to be found anywhere. *The Museum of Fine Arts:* Leading Asian art collection of western world; thousands of oil paintings, watercolors, sculpture, furnished period rooms, tapestries, costumes. Restaurant, reference library, free guides, gallery talks, art classes, children's programs. Open daily, except Mon. Closed Holidays. Free admission. 465 Huntington Ave. *Isabella Stewart Gardner Museum.* A treasure trove of art housed in a Venetian palace with garden courtyard. At least 300 paintings; more than 250 sculptures. Recital programs. Open Tues., Thurs., Sat., 10 a.m. to 4 p.m. Sun., 2 to 5 p.m. Closed Aug. and holidays. Free admission. *Museum of Science,* Science Park, Boston. Charles Hayden Planetarium is included. Unusual exhibitions: Talking Transparent Woman Demonstration; How Your Heart Works; live animals. Skyline Room restaurant. Free parking. Science Park station for MBTA service. Planetarium shows. Closed Mon., holidays. Admission: $1 adults, children under 12, 25¢; 12–16, 50¢. Planetarium, add. 50¢.

LIBRARIES. *Boston Public Library,* at Copley Square, is an impressive Italian Renaissance building with rare book collections, priceless paintings, and the only Chavannes murals outside of France. Open daily from 9 a.m. to 9 p.m.; from 9 a.m. to 6 p.m. Sat.; Sun.

from 2 to 6 p.m. in winter. From June thru Sept. the library is closed. Admission is free. The site of the *John F. Kennedy Memorial Library,* designed by Ieoh Ming Pei, will be located on the Boston bank of the Charles River, near the Harvard Business School.

GARDENS. Bostonians are proud of their *Public Garden,* separated from Boston Garden by Charles St. Seasonal floral displays (30,000 spring tulips). Swan boat rides on lagoon.

SHOPPING. In *Boston,* stores are open daily from 9:15 a.m. to 5:30 p.m. and usually until 8:30 p.m. Mon. and Wed., except summertime. No doubt *Boston's* most famous store is *Filene's,* a first-class department store which includes Filene's Basement, the bargain-hunter's paradise. Shoppers may buy anything from mittens to minks at automatically reduced prices. *Raymond's* on Tremont St. is another department store for bargain hunters. *Jordan-Marsh Co.,* Washington St., has everything from records to designer dresses. The heart of Boston's shopping district is Washington, Winter, and Summer sts. The Newbury St. area is Boston's *art world* (at least 25 art galleries in four blocks. *Specialty dress shops* are located here, also. *S. S. Pierce,* Tremont St., is a gourmet's paradise. Gift packages are mailed anywhere.

WHAT TO DO WITH THE CHILDREN. *Playgrounds* (seven) are available at the *Charles River Reservation.* The *Boston Children's Theatre* presents matinees Sat., 2:30 p.m. Prices from 75 cents to $1.75. New England Life Hall, 225 Clarendon St. The famous *swan boats* which sail along the *Public Garden* lagoon are 25 cents for adults, 15 cents for children. Rides are from April to last Sun. in Sept.

Children's museums. The Children's Museum, 60 Burroughs St., is open Tues. thru Sat., 9 a.m. to 5 p.m.; Sun. from 1 p.m. to 5 p.m. (closed Mon.). Admission 25 cents. Free nature walks every Sat., weather permitting. Tel. 524-6472. *The Children's Art Center,* 36 Rutland St., is open weekdays from 9 a.m. to 5 p.m.; Sat. to noon. *Boston Museum of Science* at Science Park features a talking transparent woman in the Wright medical theater. Open Tues. through Sat., 10 a.m. to 5 p.m.; Sun. 1 to 5 p.m. Closed Mon. Adults $1; children 12 to 16, 50 cents; under 12, 25 cents. The Skyline Room Cafeteria is open for lunch Tues. thru Sat. and for Fri. dinner (museum is open until 10 p.m. Fri.). *Charles Hayden Planetarium,* at Museum of Science, features shows Tues. thru Fri. at 11 a.m. and 3 p.m.; Fri. at 8 p.m.; Sat. at 11 a.m., 1:45, and 3 p.m.; Sun., 1:45, 3, and 4:15 p.m. No children under 5 in Planetarium only. Admission 50 cents for everyone.

SPORTS. *Spectator:* Baseball is a favorite spectator sport in the good old summertime. *Boston Red Sox* play American League games at Fenway Park, Jersey St., nr. Kenmore Sq. *Thoroughbred horse racing* (pari-mutuels) takes place at *Suffolk Downs,* East Boston, from Apr. 20 to July 4; then again from late Sept. to late Oct. There is also *night harness racing* at *Suffolk Downs,* from the middle of Oct. to late Nov. Winter finds the spectator at *Bruins hockey games, Celtics basketball games* (Boston Garden), or *Patriots pro football games* (Boston University field).

Participant: For *bicyclists,* there's a marked 5-mile route in Cambridge from Eliot Bridge to Longfellow Bridge. *Committee of Safe Bicycling, Inc.* is located in Boston. *Skiers* will find *Blue Hills Reservation,* in Milton, just outside Boston. The Blue Hills Reservation also has eight stables for *horseback riders.*

EXPLORING CAPE COD

The next tour from Boston again combines history and spectacular scenery and should take two days. Head south from Boston on the Southeast Expressway to Neponset Circle. Follow the exit ramp and go under the expressway. Turn right across a small bridge and follow Hancock Street into Quincy. This is the only city in America where you can see the birthplaces, homes, and final resting places of two Presidents. On Hancock Street, at the corner of Washington, is the First Parish Church, which was built in 1828 of Quincy granite, and contains the crypt of the Adams family. Here are buried the remains of John Adams and his wife, Abigail, as well as those of John Quincy Adams and his wife, Louisa Catherine. A little beyond the church on Hancock Street, turn right on Franklin Street for the Adams National Historic Site, the home of four generations of the Adams family. It is filled with priceless heirlooms and antiques and is open to the public. The family presented the home to the United States Government in 1946. Also located on Hancock Street, is the home of Dorothy Quincy, the wife of John Hancock. The Quincy family, long associated with the cause of freedom, harbored patriots in a secret room in the home which visitors can now see.

Quincy, in its early days, was well-known for its granite, with which the Bunker Hill Monument was built. Quincy's largest industry, the Quincy Shipyard, continues the tradition of shipbuilding which started here in 1696. The yards can be seen as you leave the city on Washington Street, heading south. The Southeast Expressway and later the divided highway, Route 3, also goes to Cape Cod from Quincy, but tourists will enjoy remaining on Route 3 Alternate, through the pleasant seaside towns of Hingham, Cohasset, Greenbush, and Marshfield. This route is rarely over a mile from the ocean and many public beaches can be enjoyed by turning left on almost any of the small roads. Route 3 Alternate rejoins, and crosses, the superhighway (Route 3), but visitors should stay on the smaller road to Kingston. The history of this town almost coincides with that of Plymouth, of which it was a part until 1726. The Bradford House contains many of the original furnishings dating back to 1674, when it was built. Route 3 Alternate continues four more miles to Plymouth.

Plymouth is a thriving and busy city. It is also the city of the Pilgrims. These two Plymouths are separate and distinct areas and you will do well to save modern Plymouth until last. To enjoy this town you must first close your eyes and picture the little ship, *Mayflower,* with 102 souls aboard, sailing fearfully into the quiet harbor to what they hoped would be their new home in a new, and unknown, country. With this picture in mind, turn off Route 3

Alternate, on North Park Avenue, to the left, and follow it to the waterfront, where Plymouth Rock now rests under a canopy of granite to protect it from souvenir hunters.

A few yards from the hallowed boulder is the *Mayflower II,* an exact replica of the original ship. It was built in England from plans prepared by naval architect William Baker and sailed across the Atlantic in 1957 under the command of Captain Alan Villiers. Visitors are welcome aboard. From the Rock, climb the stairway leading to Cole's Hill. This is where the Pilgrims buried their dead during the night so that the Indians could not determine how many people were left in the village the next day. More than half the original band died that first winter. If it had not been for the friendship of Massasoit, the great chief of the Wampanoags, they would all have perished. A statue of him stands near the sepulchre. On Chilton Street is Pilgrim Hall, which has an interesting collection of Pilgrim relics and paintings. On Leydon Street is the First Parish Church, which was the church organization of the Pilgrims. The original building on this site was erected in 1683 and the present church is the fifth to be built. Walk up the stone steps beside the church to Burial Hill, which overlooks the Square. The fort was built in 1621 and contained five cannon. It was also used as a meeting house and as a burial ground. Marked plainly are the graves of the early settlers, including Governor Bradford, Edward Gray, Thomas Clark, and John Cotton. Also of interest is the town brook, which furnished water for the Pilgrims. The town purchased the land along here and established Brewster Gardens, which are on the site of the original gardens of the settlers.

After leaving the waterfront of Plymouth, follow Route 3 Alternate south about one half mile to Plimouth Plantation. This re-creation of the original Pilgrim colony as it looked in 1627 has been built from records. In that year, the herd of cattle which, up to that time had been owned in common, was divided. Also in that year, the first census was taken and from these two events it was possible to know who lived in each of the houses. Young men and women in costume carry on the day-to-day activities of the Pilgrims. Next follow Route 3, cross the Cape Cod Canal, first proposed by Washington but not dug until much later, and you're on Cape Cod.

Everyone's Vacationland

For many years the Cape was a thriving industrial center. It had the first commercial salt works in the country along with a large shipbuilding, farming, and fishing industry. But, with improvements in transportation, particularly the automobile, Americans rediscovered the Cape as an ideal vacationland. Tourism is now, by far, the most important source of revenue. At the traffic circle after the bridge, turn off on Route 6 Alternate, which follows the northern shore toward the east. The first town is Sandwich.

It is the site of the first town on the Cape, and was named for Sandwich, England. From 1825 to 1888, it was famous for its beautifully colored glass made from a secret formula, now lost The Historical Museum on Main Street contains relics of the early history of the town as well as an outstanding collection of pressed and lace glass. Continuing on Route 6 Alternate, you will come to Barnstable and the site, on its village green, of the Liberty Pole. Here the Colonists held many freedom meetings. When the pole disappeared, one Aunt Freeman, a defiant Tory, was accused because of her previous threat of tearing up the old tree. She was tarred, feathered, and ridden out of town on a pole. Barnstable is now a lovely town of large old homes, which still survive from its once-large trade in codfish, rum and molasses. Great salt marshes extend into the bay. Sturgis Library, dating to 1645, is a fine example of the Cape Cod house.

Seven miles beyond Barnstable is the little town of Dennis, which once boasted a thriving salt industry. Turn left in Dennis center, just past the post office, for Scargo Hill, the highest spot in the area. From here the view of the bay is spectacular. The town of Brewster follows quickly on Route 6 Alternate. Luxurious homes built by shipping fortunes line Main Street. While touring the Cape, visit the town landings, if you have time, and watch the local fishermen unload their catches. All along Route 6 Alternate, signs point to these landings. In this way, you can see many parts of the Cape which are rarely seen by the average tourist.

All three major Cape roads, Routes 6 Alternate, US 6, and Highway 28, join in Orleans. From here US 6 continues northward to Provincetown. In Orleans, follow Rock Harbor Road (left) to the town landing. Here, in 1814, the militia of Orleans routed a British landing party. The Captain Linnell House on this road resembles a country home in southern France. From Orleans, on Nauset Beach Road, is Nauset Beach, one of the finest along the eastern seaboard. It is the anchor end of a stretch of 40 miles of beach, extending to Provincetown. The beach is part of the new Cape Cod National Seashore Park.

Three miles north on US 6 is the town of Eastham and, on the right just beyond the village, is the headquarters building of the Cape Cod National Seashore Park. It contains a large auditorium for nature lectures, displays, and literature racks. Turn right here to the Coast Guard Beach area and the Nauset Beach Lighthouse. The beach, maintained by the Park Service, has parking and bathhouse facilities. During the season, daily nature walks and lectures are given by Park guides. Views from the high bluffs near the lighthouse are excellent.

Five miles beyond, on the same route, is the Marconi Station Area of the park. Here are the remains of the first transatlantic wireless station erected on the mainland of the United States. From here, Marconi sent a radio message to Europe on Jan. 19, 1901. Earlier, a wireless message was sent across the Atlantic from Newfoundland. As you approach the tip of the Cape, water will appear on both sides of the road. Watch for a sign (right) leading to the Pilgrim Heights Area of the park. Lectures on the early history of this section are given daily at the Interpretative Shelter and there are parking and picnic areas. Close by is the spring from which the Pilgrims refilled their casks before sailing on to Plymouth. There are many nature trails through the salt meadows and over the dunes that may be explored in beach buggies. Next follow US 6 to the Province Lands Area of the park, or US 6 Alternate, to Provincetown. The Province Lands Area contains the Coast Guard station and Race Point Lighthouse. There are also bathhouses and excellent bathing. A circular road runs through the park area and returns to Provincetown.

Pilgrims' First Landfall

Historically, P-town, as it is called by Cape Codders, has an ancient bone to pick with Plymouth. The Pilgrims' first landfall in the New World was at the tip end of Cape Cod. The *Mayflower* remained off shore for four or five weeks. P-towners then ask, "Why should Plymouth, which was a Pilgrim afterthought, get all the glory and fame?" So the town has done just about everything a town could do to make people think of the Pilgrims and Provincetown at the same time. They erected a 252-foot stone tower called the Pilgrim Monument; the actual landing spot of the Pilgrims has been marked, at the junction of Commercial Street and Beach Highway; an historical museum was built to house an excellent collection of early relics; and dozens of plaques mark other sites connected with the Pilgrims.

Provincetown, in summer, attracts a lively and sometimes unorthodox crowd of artists, playwrights, novelists and poets . . . and an almost equally large crowd of tourists who come to watch the bohemians at work and play. Souvenir shops and art galleries are jammed together along the narrow main street. And the summer theater in which Eugene O'Neill presented his first plays is still active.

Over all hang the smells and sounds of the sea as, essentially, Provincetown is still a fishing village and the majority of its year 'round residents are fishermen. The excellent beaches around Provincetown are enjoyed by residents and tourists alike.

On the return trip, retrace your route south to the traffic circle at the outskirts of Orleans. Go around the circle and bear left on Route 28 for Chatham. At its outskirts, where Route 28 turns sharp right, continue straight ahead along the shore to Chatham Lighthouse. There are excellent sea views from the parking space between the lighthouse and the cliffs which lead down to a sandy beach. Monomoy Island stretches, low and flat, about ten miles out into the ocean from here. Chatham is a typical Cape Cod village, but without much of the commercialism which detracts from many towns and villages on the south shore of the Cape. Rigid zoning laws have done much to keep Chatham the way it was at the turn of the century. It also boasts the largest public bathing beaches on the Cape. Every Friday night during the summer, the Chatham band gives a concert in a natural amphitheater located just off Main Street. Children will enjoy the concert which is planned, in part, for them. Festivities start at 8:00 p.m.

Leave Chatham on Route 28, heading west. You will enjoy the views and beaches located at the end of both Ridgevale and Cockle Cove roads. Both roads turn left off Route 28, in South Chatham about two miles from the center.

Continue west on Route 28 through South Harwich and Harwich Port to Hyannis.

The commercial hub of Cape Cod, Hyannis contains branches of many of the better Boston and New York stores. Turn left in the center and follow Ocean Street, which runs south along Lewis Bay and which is a focal point for boating activity in the Hyannis area. Continue along the oceanfront, bearing left whenever possible. On Irving Street, in Hyannis Port, is the Kennedy family compound with the summer home of the late President. Tourists are not allowed near the compound, which is surrounded by a high fence. Nonetheless, traffic is heavy with sightseers. After passing Craigville Beach, Ocean Street returns to Route 28. Turn off this route just before East Falmouth center on Central Avenue, to the left. This road runs south to the ocean and continues through the seaside centers of Davisville, Mara Vista, and Acapesket, to Falmouth. This is also a major resort area and commercial center. Falmouth is an old town, having been settled in 1660, and was an active shipping center. The Congregational Church, opposite the green, has a Paul Revere bell. Out of Falmouth, head south, following local signs to Woods Hole.

Two Lovely Islands

Woods Hole is the location of the U.S. Bureau of Fisheries and Aquarium, as well as the Woods Hole Oceanographic Institute.

Ferries leave from here for Martha's Vineyard and Nantucket islands and if you are planning to spend several days on the islands it would be well to take your car. Several sailings a day make long waits unnecessary but reservations, for cars, are helpful during the summer.

History says that Martha's Vineyard was discovered by Bartholomew Gosnold, in 1602, but the island may well have been the "Vinland the Good," mentioned in early sagas of the Norsemen. For many years, villages on the island were the home ports of whaling vessels which roamed the seven seas. Now, much like Cape Cod, the main industry is tourism, particularly during the summer months. A circular road tours the island, the villages of which still retain their whaling-days flavor and atmosphere. Among the island's several centers are Oak Bluffs, Edgartown (the oldest settlement with an excellent public museum of early relics), and Menemsha, a famous rendezvous for yachtsmen and sport fishermen. Gay Head, a former Indian reservation, was described by Herman Melville in *Moby Dick* as "a village which has long supplied the neighboring island of Nantucket with her most daring harpooners." Don't miss the view from the vari-colored cliffs at the edge of the sea.

Historic Nantucket Island, 30 miles out to sea and 40 miles east of Martha's Vineyard, was also discovered by Gosnold. The point at which he spotted the island is marked by a lighthouse wearing a distinct red cummerbund. The great saga of whaling began when Nantucketers caught their first whale, in 1672, off the shores of the island. Old South Wharf still stands as a nostalgic landmark of Nantucket's colorful whaling era, when it was the greatest whaling port in the world. Along Main Street, you will see the many white clapboard mansions built by whaling captains, which reflect the affluence of more than a century ago. On Old Mill Hill stands the Old Mill, built by Nathan Wilbur after the design of those he had seen in Holland. The Jethro House, oldest on Nantucket and home of Maria Mitchell, the island's famous astronomer, may be visited. Also of interest are the museum and adjacent Quaker Meeting House on Fair Street. Both islands have managed to develop thriving tourist businesses without ruining the attractive early American atmosphere. There are a few motels, but very few. Most visitors stay in small country inns or hotels which were once the homes of seafaring people.

After debarking from the ferry at Woods Hole, head north on Route 28, 15 miles to Bourne, at the western end of the Cape Cod Canal and cross the bridge to the mainland.

Before leaving Cape Cod, mention should be made of one major road which we have not traveled. It is the Mid-Cape Highway running through the center of the Cape from the Sagamore Bridge to Orleans and can be used whenever you are in a hurry. Scenically, however, it is not satisfying.

When leaving the Bourne Bridge, follow US 6 through Onset and Wareham. There are many cranberry bogs along this stretch of road and, if you are lucky, you might see workers harvesting the berries in special rake baskets. These, incidentally, make unusual and attractive magazine racks for homes and offices. Continue on US 6 to Fairhaven and cross the river to New Bedford, successor to Nantucket as the country's most important whaling port.

On Johnny Cake Hill, high above the tides of Buzzards Bay, visitors can get the feel of whaling days of a century ago by walking the decks of the largest ship model ever built. The *Lagoda*, in the Bourne Whaling Museum, is a completely accurate, half-scale model of an 1850 whaling bark and is the keynote exhibit in the museum. Allied exhibits include a valuable collection of whaling relics and replicas of various shops which were part of the city's vast whaling industry. Ship carvers of New England were well-known throughout the world and the museum has many fine examples of their work: figureheads, billetheads, stern boards, a mast sheath and many other pieces. Also on display are many fine examples of scrimshaw, which are carvings in whalebone and teeth by whaling sailors. Across the street from the museum is Seaman's Bethel, opened in 1832, which contains murals and cenotaphs described by Herman Melville in *Moby Dick*. He said that the brave houses and flowery gardens of New Bedford were all harpooned and dragged up from the bottom of the sea.

Although whaling is no longer a factor in New Bedford's economy, the city led all other New England ports last year in poundage of food fish produced.

Cuttyhunk, the most westerly of the Elizabeth Islands, is a small island 14 miles south of New Bedford. Once the home of the whaling fleet pilots, it is now a headquarters for sports fishermen. A boat leaves Pier 3, in New Bedford, daily at 10 p.m. When leaving the city, follow US 6 again, 13 miles to Fall River.

On to Narragansett Bay

Fall River was, for many years prior to World War I, one of the largest textile producing cities in the country. When that industry moved to southern states, Fall River almost became a ghost town with its once-busy mill buildings now gaunt and empty. But Fall River is looking to a bright future in the tourist business. It is located on the eastern shores of Narragansett Bay, well-known for its good sailing waters and is only 15 miles north of Newport, Rhode Island. Interstate Route 195, linking New York City with

Cape Cod, goes right through the city from east to west with appropriate interchanges. A new superhighway, Route 24, now links it with Boston and other cities to the north. Fall River also recently acquired a new tourist attraction which, in its first month of operation, attracted more than 40,000 tourists. The battleship, *USS Massachusetts,* was brought from Norfolk, Virginia, to a permanent berth on the Taunton River at the foot of the new bridge crossing the river from Providence on Interstate Route 195. Visitors can board the ship daily for a small fee. It represents the only official World War II memorial of the state. When returning to Boston, cross the Taunton River and follow Highway 138. It is faster to follow the new Highway 24 but not as rewarding in scenery, particularly along the river.

AROUND THE CAPE

HOTELS AND MOTELS. Accommodations on the Cape range from the splendiferous sublime to the salty ridiculous. You can live like the not-so-starving artists in a rickety shack on Provincetown's waterfront and pay $100 a week for the privilege of associating with the bearded and bedraggled elite, or you can pay the same price for a very comfortable, but terribly bourgeois, motel room on a side street. One of the best bets are the smaller establishments in the reasonable category. Another good bet can't be listed here—these are the rooms in private houses, frequently let out only on recommendation of a friend who's already been there. But if you haven't a friend, or don't trust his or her advice in any event, or if you just want to make up your own mind about where to stay, read on, gentle reader . . .

BUZZARDS BAY

First Class

Buzzards Bay Motor Lodge. Summertime easy living here with private beach, rafts, boat dock. Some cottages with kitchens. Open from first week in May to middle of Oct.
Route 28 (tel. 759–3466).

Woodchips Motor Inn. Always something to do at this lively motel, near beach and golf courses. Interesting restaurant features luaus and smorgasbord certain nights. Open Mar. to Nov.
Route 28 (tel. 295–0210).

Reasonable

Austria Motel. Pleasant to sit back and relax on the screened porch (with all rooms). Pets welcome. Convenient restaurant. Open all year around.
Cranberry Highway (tel. 295–0483).

Redwood Motel. This friendly motel is near beach, shops, churches, restaurants, golf course. Pool. Pets welcome.
Route 28 (tel. 759–3892).

Trading Post Motel. Picnicking families will enjoy the use of private picnic grounds here. Pets welcome. TV free in each room.
Bourne Bridge, Cape side (tel. 759–3883).

CHATHAM

First Class

Dolphin Court Motel. You will like the restful, secluded location away from highway noise. Convenient beach; near restaurant. Extended summer season.
352 Main St. (tel. 945–0070).

Reliance Motel. No problem here of cars whizzing by—motel is away from

highway. Carpeted rooms are heated. Outdoor recreation area. Near beaches and restaurants.
Route 28 (tel. 945–0710).

Reasonable

Seafarer Motel. New deluxe units with Williamsburg colonial accent have been added. Short distance to beach and restaurants.
Main St. (tel. 432–1739).

DENNIS PORT

First Class

Colony Beach Motel. This is a popular oceanfront resort motel. Pool, beach. Children under 6 not permitted. Near restaurants. Seasonal.
Old Wharf Rd. and Depot St. (tel. 398–2217).

Edgewater Motor Lodge. This good-looking motel is a next-door neighbor to Belmont Hotel. Ocean-view balconies. Recreation area. Near restaurant. At height of season, children under 10 not permitted.
Chase Ave. (tel. 398–6922).

Motel Oriental. Japanese sliding doors open to a view of oriental gardens here. Pretty, carpeted rooms. Near restaurant. Open extended season.
Lower County Rd. (tel. 398–3841).

New Spouter Whale Motor Inn. This new oceanfront resort motel is noteworthy for soundproof, fireproof walls. Beach. Room rate includes continental breakfast. Open extended season.
286 Old Wharf Rd. (tel. 398–8010).

Shifting Sands Motel. Ocean-view rooms are an attraction at this oceanfront motel. Beach. Short walk to restaurant. Transportation to and from airport or bus.
Chase Ave. (tel. 398–9145).

The Soundings. In season, the minimum stay here is three days. Popular oceanfront location; beach, pool. Most rooms have ocean-view balconies. At height of season, children must be over 10 years old. Summer to Oct.
Chase Ave. (tel. 398–2205).

Reasonable

By The Sea. Most rooms at this oceanfront lodge have an ocean view. Recreation room; color TV. Beach sports.
Chase Ave. and Inman Rd. (tel. 398–6895).

Captain William's House. This cozy colonial inn is a restful place to stay. Room rate includes breakfast and dinner. Public invited to dining room.
Depot St. (tel. 398–3910).

Inexpensive

Loydon Inn. There's a good view of Nantucket Sound from here. Restaurant nearby. Near beach. Transportation to and from airport or bus terminal.
Tel. 398–2631.

EASTHAM

Reasonable

Route 6 Motel. Each carpeted room has TV and morning coffee, free. Pool. Near restaurant. Back from highway.
Route 6 (tel. 255–1132).

Salt Pond Motel. Here you will have a view of the famous salt pond. Swimming, boating, fishing on beach. Room rate includes continental breakfast. Pets welcome. Open from May to Oct.
Route 6 (tel. 255–2100).

Inexpensive

Whalewalk. This old captain's estate includes some housekeeping cottages for families; also pleasant rooms in inn. Breakfast service. Near restaurant. Early season opening.
Bridge Rd. (tel. 255–0617).

FALMOUTH

Deluxe

Cape Codder Hotel. This oceanside resort features just about every summer sport under the sun, and nightly entertainment. Beach. Transportation to and from airport to bus.

Sippewissett Road (tel. 548–9777).

Clauson's Inn and Golf Resort. This is a favorite with golfers, of course, who compete on 18-hole championship course. All sports from riding to water-skiing. Open all year around. Seasonal rates.

Next to Falmouth Playhouse (tel. 563–2255).

Coonamessett Inn. This famous resort has been a favorite place to stay. All the comforts, even poolside service. Beautiful gardens and lake. Cape Cod style buildings. Gourmet restaurant; sidewalk cafe. Cocktail lounge.

Tel. 548–2300.

First Class

Alden Tower Motel. Hospitality here includes continental breakfast with room. Water sports on beach. Pool. Free golf. Extended season.

Grand Ave. (tel. 548–4443).

Falmouth Marina. The picturesque harbor view is just one reason why this motel is so popular. Room rate includes continental breakfast. Pool.

Robbins Rd. (tel. 548–4300).

Trade Winds. Located on Falmouth Harbor, this motel is near beaches, golf course, shops, restaurants, theaters. Coffee dispenser in rooms. Open all year around. Off-season rates.

12 Robbins Rd. (tel. 548–4575).

Reasonable

The Capewind. A lakeside setting adds to the attractions here. Best of all, the motel is away from highway traffic. Recreation and picnic area. Some kitchen units. Open all year around.

Route 28, Maravista Ave. Ext. (tel. 548–1449).

Red Horse Inn Motel. You will find convenience here to Martha's Vineyard boat, beaches, shops, restaurants, theaters. Big, carpeted rooms. Half-price off-season rates.

28 Falmouth Heights Rd. (tel. 548–0053).

HARWICH

Deluxe

The Belmont. Fun and games here with social director's program. Beautiful ocean-front location. Beach. Pool and patio. Access to golf course. Room rate includes meals. Children's dining room. Beautician. Summer season.

Tel. 432–1120.

Wequassett Inn and Cottages. Here you have a private beach, and swimming pool for vacation fun. Hospitality includes free canapes in cocktail lounge. Gourmet restaurant. Open May through Sept. Pleasant Bay.

East Harwich (tel. 432–1740).

Reasonable

Moby Dick Motel. This family-style motel features a pine-grove setting. Pool. Picnic grounds with fireplace. Recreation area. Near beach. Room coffee dispenser. Restaurant nearby.

Route 28, So. Harwich (tel. 432–1434).

Red River Motel. Here there is peace and quiet in a residential area but near the beach. Convenient to restaurants, shops, golf course, theaters, churches. Extended season.

Route 28, So. Harwich (tel. 432–1474).

HYANNIS

First Class

Candlelight Motor Lodge. This quality motel is convenient to restaurants, theaters, and vacation activity center. Well-equipped rooms. Open year around; off-season rates.

447 Main St. (tel. 775–3000).

Charles Motor Lodge. Just a few minutes from Craigville Beach, this hos-

pitable motel features a new coffee shop, restaurant, cocktail lounge. Pool; poolside service. Special weekly rates. Open for extended summer season.
662 Main St. (tel. 775–5600).

Harbor Village. Stay in your own Cape Cod cottage equipped with electric kitchen, living room with fireplace—and maid service. View of Nantucket Sound. Summer season.
Sea St. (tel. 775–9744).

Howard Johnson's Motor Lodge. Deluxe, carpeted rooms have twin lavatories. Whirlpools, sauna baths. Enclosed pool. Restaurant; cocktail lounge (entertainment).
Downtown Hyannis (tel. 775–8600).

Hyannis Harborview Motel. A 5-min. walk from here will bring you to Hyannis Center. Pool. Access to boating. Restaurant open from breakfast to wee hours. Cocktail lounge; entertainment.
213 Ocean St. (tel. 775–4420).

Hyannis Holiday Motel. Rooms have an excellent view of the harbor. Two-level new motel has balconies. Walk to center of town. Near beaches, restaurant. Pool, sundeck. Summer season.
131 Ocean St. (tel. 775–1639).

Hyannis Inn Motel. This new motel features two water shows nightly in season. Convenient to shops, beaches, excursion boat. Pool. Breakfast and dining rooms; cocktail lounge. Open year around.
473 Main St. (tel. 775–0255).

Lamplighter Motel. Watch the fun in the pool from your private porch. Tennis and badminton. Custom-decorated rooms.
Route 132 (tel. 775–3330).

Lewis Bay Lodge Motel and Hotel. The waterfront location is picturesque, yet convenient to excursion boats, shops, theaters, and summer sports areas. Two double beds in each luxury room. Pool. Dining room; cocktail lounge.
Tel. 775–0041.

Rainbow Resort Motel. Here you have a scenic combination of lake and countryside. Pool, kiddie pool, beach. Free boating and fishing. Nearby theaters and beaches. Coffee shop.
Route 132 (tel. 362–3217).

Yachtsman Motor Inn. Here the accent is on the boating enthusiast, including a Regatta dining room. Pool. Cocktail Lounge; entertainment. Pets welcome. Near excursion boats.
500 Ocean St. (tel. 775–4600).

Reasonable

The Angel Motel. This friendly motel, near the airport, has family accommodations as well as some singles. Pool. Near beaches, shops. Off-season rates.
Route 132 (tel. 775–2440).

Belle Ingram Motel. Here you will find convenience to the center of town and Craigville Beach. Inquire about weekly rates.
Centerville Rd. (tel. 775–0028).

Country Lake Motel. There's fun here on the private lakeside beach. Pool. Recreation area. Near restaurants, stores, theaters.
Route 132 (tel. 362–6455).

Hyannis Star Motel. Family fun is emphasized here—some units have housekeeping setups. Pool. Recreation area. Coffee shop. Pets welcome.
Route 132 (tel. 775–2835).

Summerside Motel. This friendly motel is only a couple of blocks from Main St. Convenient to restaurants, beaches, entertainment. Off-season rates.
Summerside Lane (tel. 775–4284).

MARTHA'S VINEYARD

First Class

Harbor View. Old-fashioned hospitality of this Treadway Inn is a tradition. This includes good food and grog. Summer sports on beach and five-acres of inn. Seasonal.
North Water St. (tel. 444).

Harborside Inn. Take advantage of sailing instructions here—inn has its own fleet. Some rooms with balconies for pool and garden view. *Boathouse Bar. Navigator restaurant.*
South Water St. (tel. 415).

Katama Shores Motor Inn. Lots of room for roving and recreation on the 100 acres. Pets welcome. Beach. Cocktail lounge. Restaurant.
Tel. 1081.

Menemsha Inn & Cottages. A variety of summer activities here includes water-skiing. Pine grove cottages for families (children over 3 years old). Lively recreation room. Room rate includes meals.
Tel. MI 5–2521.

Reasonable

The Captain's House. Family atmosphere prevails here. Breakfast buffet in season; continental breakfast off-season included in room rate. Beach.
Upper Main St. (tel. 221).

Daggett House. Sailing enthusiasts may arrange for boats at private dock. Recreation area. Breakfast included with rates.
North Water St. (tel. 46).

NANTUCKET

Luxurious

White Elephant Inn and Cottages. This attractive Treadway Inn has everything from a marina to a croquet game. Deluxe rooms with harbor view. Pool; patio. Gourmet restaurant. Cocktail lounge.
Harbor View Way (tel. 228–2500).

First Class

Beachside. This new motel offers family rates. Outdoor recreation area. Convenient to restaurants. Continental breakfast may be ordered.
North Beach St. (tel. 228–2241).

Gordon Folger Hotel and Cottages. Take your choice of American or European plan here. Picturesque view of harbor. Restaurant.
Easton St. (tel. 228–0313).

Harbor House. This Treadway Inn resort is known for hospitality, lovely gardens, and the *Bamboo Room* restaurant. Cocktail Lounge. Entertainment; dancing. Access to golf course. Beautician.
Beach St. (tel. 228–1500).

Reasonable

Moby Dick Inn and Cottages. Rose-covered cottages with ocean view are typically Nantucket. Pool. Snack bar. Breakfast included with room rate. Recreation area.
Tel. 257–6297.

Sea Cliff Inn. You will admire the view from your pleasant room. Selection of European or modified American plans. Children's rates.
Cliff Rd. (tel. 228–0250).

Wauwinet House and Cottages. Here at Nantucket Harbor you will enjoy water sports. Pets welcome. Restaurant features shore dinners. Cocktail lounge; dancing every night—never on Sun.
Tel. 228—0145.

ORLEANS

First Class

Cove Motel. Scenic Town Cove is the site of this good-looking motel. Beach. Pool. Restaurants, stores nearby. Light breakfast served. Open all year; special off-season prices.
Routes 6A and 28 (tel. 255–1203).

Governor Prence Motor Lodge. You're practically at the door of Cape Cod National Seashore here. Pool. Recreation area. Lively cocktail lounge. Restaurant across the way.
Routes 6A and 28 (tel. 255–1216).

Olde Tavern Motel. Thoreau visited site over a century ago. Now modern motel has colonial-style rooms. No charge for continental breakfast. Near restaurant. Open Apr. to Nov.
Route 6A (tel. Orleans 1565).

Orleans Holiday Motel. Here you are near the gateway to National Seashore Park. Pool. Restaurant. Open all year around; lower off-season rates.
Opposite Town Cove (tel. 255–1514).

Seashore Park Motor Inn. This new motel is outstanding with balconies for each room. Access to golf, boating, fishing. Pool. Coffee shop. No charge for continental breakfast.
At entrance to National Seashore Park (tel. 255–2500).

PROVINCETOWN

First Class

Breakwater Motel. Real relaxation here on the private beach or on the sundeck. Luxury in two penthouse suites. Cape Cod Bay view. Near restaurants, sport centers, theater. Open Apr. to Nov.
Route 6A (tel. Provincetown 1134).

Chateau Motel. Large, attractive rooms have view of bay, town, and sand dunes. Pool. Restaurant nearby. Off-season prices.
Bradford St. (tel. Provincetown 1286).

Coral Sands Motel. This new ocean-front motel also has a few efficiency units. Beach. Nearby restaurant. Off-season prices.
Shore Route 6A (tel. Provincetown 1410).

Governor Prence Motor Lodge. From the hilltop, you can see Cape Cod Bay and Provincetown Harbor. Pool; pool bar. Cocktail lounge, entertainment. Restaurant. Recreation area.
Route 6 (tel. Provincetown 629).

The Inn At The Mews. Here you will find an unusual, continental arrangement of waterfront accommodations in a setting of gardens and art galleries. Some housekeeping rooms. Beach. Open all year. Off-season rates.
Commercial St. (tel. Provincetown 1500 or 714).

The Moors Motel. Pleasant luxury in these carpeted rooms complete with piped-in music and view of Cape Cod Bay. Pool. Pets welcome. Transportation to and from terminals.
Beach Highway (tel. Provincetown 1030).

Provincetown Inn Motel. Enjoy the ocean view from your room. Pool; children's pool. Recreation area. Coffee shop; dining room; cocktail lounge. Open Apr. to Nov. Off-season prices.
1 Commercial St. (tel. Provincetown 1030).

Surfside Arms Motor Inn. These new, carpeted rooms have a view of Provincetown Harbor. Beach. Pool. Near theaters, shops, galleries. Restaurant; cocktail lounge. Elevator.
542 Commercial St. (tel. Provincetown 1726).

The Tides Motor Inn. Pleasant idea to have private patio or balcony for each room. Beach. Pool. Recreation area. Coffee shop. Open May to Oct.
Route 6A (tel. Provincetown 1045).

White Dory Inn. You will like the convenience to the art colony, theaters, restaurants. Beach. Breakfast may be ordered. Off-season prices.
616 Commercial St. (tel. Provincetown 224–W).

Anchor Inn. This all year around inn is convenient to theaters, museums, restaurants. Room rate includes continental breakfast. Off-season prices. Beach.
175 Commercial St. at harbor (tel. Provincetown 432).

Blue Sea Motel. This pleasant motel offers a beautiful beach or swimming pool. Recreation area. Some family units with kitchen. Open May to Nov.
Route 6A (tel. Provincetown 1041).

Bradford House and Motel. Acquire a tan on the sundeck or enjoy the view of the harbor. Rooms in house furnished Cape Cod style. Near restaurant.
41 Bradford St. (tel. Provincetown 173).

The Buccaneer Motel. Here you have your choice of beach or pool. Practice putting green. Near restaurants, and vacation activities. Right on beach.
Tel. Provincetown 1144.

Cape Colony Inn. This new motel is convenient to Town Wharf. Pool. Recreation area. Coffee shop. Pets welcome. Transportation to and from airport or bus.
280 Bradford St. (tel. Provincetown 1755).

SANDWICH

Reasonable

Daniel Webster Inn. This is known as the oldest inn in the oldest Cape Cod town. Open all year. Restaurant. Cocktail lounge.
Main St. (tel. 888–0020).

Sandy Neck Motel. This small but pleasant motel offers lower rates off-season. Pets welcome. Open June to Oct. In secluded area.
State 6A (tel. 362–3992).

Scorton River Motel. This two-level motel features sundecks with view of salt marshes. Pool. Near beach. Open Apr. to Nov.
Tel. 888–0710.

WOODS HOLE

First Class

Nautilus Motor Inn. Beautiful gardens and Vineyard Sound provide a double-feature view from the rooms here. Vacation centers nearby; access to beach and golf course. Pool.
Route 28 (tel. 548–1525).

Sands of Time Motor Inn. Here you have a sweeping view of the ocean plus convenient location to ferries. Pool. Light breakfast served.
Woods Hole Road (tel. 548–6300).

Reasonable

Woods Hole Inn. From this year around inn, you may walk to ferries, restaurants, churches, etc. Off-season prices.
Tel. 548–9763.

YARMOUTH

First Class

Beach 'N Towne. The family will enjoy the lawn games here. Pool. Nearby restaurant. Lower prices in off-season.
State 28 (tel. 398–2311).

Jolly Captain Motor Lodge. You will have a jolly time here. Top deck of bi-level motel has balconies. Pool. Nearby restaurant. No charge for continental breakfast.
State 28 (tel. 398–2253).

Reasonable

Cummaquid Inn. Swimming, boating and golfing are nearby to this friendly inn. Choose from motel rooms or housekeeping cottages. Breakfast included with rates. Dinner and cocktails served.
Route 6A (tel. 362–3191).

Inexpensive

Old Yarmouth Inn. Comfortable rooms here for the budget-minded. Food, liquors. Open from end of May to end of Sept. Off-season prices.
Route 6A (tel. 362–3191).

ELSEWHERE

BASS RIVER. *Blue Water Motel.* First class. Everything conducive to summer relaxation here—including sauna baths. Pool, beach. Children under 10 not accepted at season's height. South Shore Dr. Tel. 398–2288.
Surf and Sand Beach Resort Motel. First class. Enjoy the ocean view here from your own balcony. No children under 10. Own beach. So. Shore Dr. Tel. 398–2341.

BOURNE. *Mashnee Village.* First class. This year-round resort offers daytime sports and night-time entertainment. Beach and boat dock. Snacks;

cocktails. Pets welcome. Tel. 759–3384.

Panorama Motor Lodge. Reasonable. The Panorama includes view of bridge and Cape Cod Canal. Pets welcome. Cocktail lounge. Restaurant nearby. Open year around. South Bourne Bridge Rotary. Tel. 759–4401.

BREWSTER. *Skyline Motel.* Reasonable. No frills but pleasant—especially good for family on budget. Open end of May to Oct. 15. Route 6A. Tel. 385–3707.

CENTERVILLE. *Craig Village By The Sea.* First class. This popular cottage colony has four motel units. Near golf course; fishing. Shops nearby. Off-season rates. Open Apr. to Nov. Craigville Beach. Tel. 775–0350.

Trade-Winds. First class. Resort attractions are combined here with New England's seaside charm. Dining room; cocktail lounge. Room rate includes breakfast and dinner in summer season. Closed Dec. through March. Craigville Beach Rd. Tel. 775–0365.

HARWICH PORT. *The Harwich Port Motel.* First class. This new motel is open all year around. Near beach, golf course, shops, theaters. Restaurant next door. Pool. Off-season rates. Main St. Tel. 432–2424.

Lincoln Lodge and Mary Todd Court. Reasonable. Just minutes from the beach, this motel resort has acres of landscaped grounds for relaxation and playtime. Pool. Restaurant. Room rates with or without meals. Near Allen's Harbor. Tel. 432–0657.

SAGAMORE. *Wind-Mill Motel.* Inexpensive. Families enjoy staying here. Pool. Recreation area. Free use of bicycles. No charge for continental breakfast. Open Apr. to Nov. US 6. Tel. 888–9779.

HOW TO GET AROUND. *Provincetown–Boston Airline* flies from Logan Airport to Provincetown Airport. *Cape & Islands Flight Service* has flights to *Nantucket,* charter to all points from *Hyannis Airport,* Hyannis. *Car ferries* are regularly scheduled all year to *Martha's Vineyard* and *Nantucket* from *Woods Hole.* Information from Woods Hole, Martha's Vineyard, Nantucket Steamship Authority, P.O. Box 284, Woods Hole. In 1965, the new car-ferry *Uncatena* was added. Pier parking for ferry passengers. Two new 70-passenger hydrofoils leave from *Falmouth Harbor* to *Martha's Vineyard* and *Nantucket.* Tel. Woods Hole KI 8–5011. Three ships cruise to *Nantucket* and *Martha's Vineyard* from Pleasant St. Wharf, *Hyannis.* Tel. Hyannis 775–1222. There is boat service daily in summer from *Rowe's Wharf, Boston,* to *Provincetown.* In addition, Cape Cod has boat liveries galore and excellent marinas.

DINING OUT. The birthplace of cranberry sauce is liberally dotted with interesting inns. The fact that many sea captains retired to this part of Massachusetts will be obvious to diners enjoying quahog chowder and duckling à l'orange amid the appurtenances of whaling. Although most restaurants are closed after the summer season, there are some open the year round for those interested in seeing the Cape after the sun-worshippers have all gone. Listings are given under each town, that is, under *East* Harwich or *West* Harwich, rather than under a general Harwich heading.

CHATHAM

First Class

Christopher Ryder House. In this quaint home, superb New England foods are served—lobster and seafoods, as well as continental specialties. There's a clam bar, too. Children's menu. Cocktails. Fun place with dancing in the *Opera House* nightly. Open summer only, for dinner.

N. on State 28.

Reasonable

Chatham Arms. One of the best buys at this fairly new restaurant is the roast beef dinner. Children's menu. Pleasant, hospitable atmosphere. Open for breakfast, lunch, dinner. Cocktails. Parking area.
Main St.

Chatham Wayside Inn. This pleasant old inn features favorites on a varied menu—roast beef, lobster, etc. Cocktails served. Open for breakfast, luncheon, dinner. Sun. dinner only.
512 Main St.

Queen Anne Inn. The native Chatham bluefish is exceptionally well done here. Vegetables are all garden-fresh. Open for breakfast, luncheon, dinner.
Queen Anne Rd. nr. Oyster Pond.

Rose Acres Inn. Beautiful gardens and lawns distinguish this well-known inn. Delicious boneless stuffed chicken as well as Cape Cod lobster. Cocktails. Open for breakfast, lunch, dinner all year round.
Cross St.

Inexpensive

Captain's Table. Informal atmosphere here is especially good for family dining. Complete meals and sandwiches. Tasty lobster salad. Home-baked orange bread is different. Open for lunch and dinner except Mon., March to Nov.
580 Main St.

DENNIS PORT

Reasonable

Beachcombers. Relax with a drink and peruse the beach mural. Then dine on French-fried lobster or any of the delicious specialties. Homemade pecan rolls. A la carte or complete dinners.
Lower County Rd.

Ebb Tide Restaurant. Try the Cape Cod scallop-and-lobster casserole. Big relish tray. Children's menu. Cocktails in quaint lounge (sea captain's home). Open for breakfast, lunch, dinner.

Captain William's House. Just as a sea captain would return with worldly recipes, the chef prepares curried shrimp and lobster, Rock Cornish hen with black cherry sauce, filet of sole with wine sauce. Traditional Yankee dishes, also. Open for breakfast and dinner, summer only.
Depot St.

FALMOUTH

First Class

Coonamessett Inn. This distinctively decorated restaurant features a gourmet menu, excellent service, and a panoramic view. Popular cocktail lounge. Open for breakfast, lunch, dinner.
Gifford St. and Jones Rd.

Falmouth Playhouse Restaurant. You are welcome to dine here whether or not you attend the theater. Theater and dinner special. Cocktails. Musical revue nightly, 11 p.m. Dinner only.
Falmouth Playhouse.

Flying Bridge Restaurant. Take your choice of open-hearth dining downstairs or more formal dining upstairs. Suggestion: baked stuffed lobster. View of *Falmouth Marina*. Lively cocktail lounge. Open extended summer season, noon to 10:30 p.m.
Scranton Ave.

HYANNIS

First Class

Neptune Room. Flaming Cape Cod duckling and flaming desserts are attractions in this glamorous dining room. Cocktail lounge opens at noon, nightly entertainment. Dinners only from 4 p.m., from noon Sun. and holidays. Closed Nov. to March.
In Airport Admin. Bldg., n.w. of State 28.

Reasonable

Beachwood Inn. A Cape Cod sea captain once lived in this gracious home. Tasty New England specialties on menu. Hot-from-the-oven breads, rolls, and pies. Outdoor terrace.
415 Main St.

Harborside Seafood. The shore dinner is a seafood feast here. Lengthy menu also includes steaks and poultry. Children's dinners. Dinners from noon to 10 p.m. Good view of harbor.
132 Bayview St.

Hill's Dining Room. Visit the garden where vegetables are picked fresh for dinner. Children's menu. Home-style cooking. Open from 4:30 to 8 p.m. daily except Tues., from 12 to 8 p.m., Sun. and Labor Day.
530 W. Main St.

Hyannis Inn. Friendly atmosphere prevails at this all-year-round inn. Good home-style cooking. Popular cocktail lounge. Open for breakfast, lunch, dinner. Free parking.
209 Main St.

Mildred's Chowder House. From tasty chowders, Mildred's menu has expanded to Cape Cod seafoods, chicken, steak. Entertainment in cocktail lounge. Open for lunch and dinner. Closed Thanksgiving Day and Christmas Day.
1 mi. n. on State 28.

Priscilla Alden Dining Room. It's difficult to choose between the gourmet buffet or the special lobster platter. Sophisticated Colonial atmosphere here. Cocktails. Open for dinner only.
Main St. and Barnstable Rd.

Slades of Hyannis. Surprise—Southern cooking in the heart of Hyannis. Tasty chicken, corn bread, sweet potato pie. Seafoods, too. *Plantation Lounge* for cocktails and entertainment. Open for lunch and dinner.
720 Main St.

MARTHA'S VINEYARD

Reasonable

Home Port. Boat enthusiasts are attracted to this friendly restaurant. Everything from a sandwich to baked stuffed lobster. Open for lunch and dinner. Summer season only.
Menemsha Rd.

Munro's of Martha's Vineyard. Enjoy your lobster or roast beef on the old-fashioned porch. Cocktails. Dinner only. Open for extended summer season.
122 Circuit St., Oak Bluffs.

Seafood Shanty. Yacht-dotted harbor view and good Yankee fare add up to dining enjoyment here. Variety from sandwich to baked stuffed shrimp. Cocktails. Children's menu. Open for lunch and dinner. Summer season only.
Dock St., Edgartown.

NANTUCKET ISLAND

First Class

Jared Coffin House. Gracious dining is a tradition here. Delicious shrimp-stuffed lobster, blueberry-glazed cheesecake. Cocktails. Breakfast, lunch, dinner. Open all year round.
Broad and Center sts.

Opera House. The Gay 90's are gayer here. *Scampi à l'Opera* a dinner favorite. Cocktails. Open for lunch and dinner for summer season only.
4 S. Water St.

The White Elephant. Formal dining at this Treadway inn is enhanced by artistic decor and continental cuisine. Cocktails. Piano music. Open summer season only, for breakfast, lunch, dinner.
Harbor View Way and Easton St.

Reasonable

Chanticleer. It's pleasant to dine in the garden here. Own recipe for quahog chowder. Breads and pastries fresh from oven. Children's menu. Open

for breakfast, lunch, dinner; summer only.
New St.

Harbor House Bamboo Room. South Sea Island atmosphere comes to Nantucket Island in this Treadway restaurant. Varied menu. Open for breakfast and dinner, summer only.
Beach St.

PROVINCETOWN

First Class

The Mews Cafe. This new restaurant, on premises of *Inn at the Mews,* features a gourmet menu that runs the gamut of French bouillabaisse to Portuguese seafood specialties. Opposite Chrysler Art Museum. Dinner only. Seasonal.
Commercial and Center sts.

Reasonable–First Class

Ciro and Sal's. Romantic garden atmosphere, beautiful recorded music, and candle glow are highlights here. All this and gourmet Italian cuisine, too. Good wines. Open dinner only, summer season.
4 Kiley Ct.

S'il Vous Plait. This top-rated restaurant glorifies roast duck with tangerine sauce. Haute cuisine in an unusual five-course dinner. Artistic French decor. Take along your favorite wine (host will chill it). Open for dinner only.
193 Commercial St.

Reasonable

Bonnie Doone. This wee bit of Scotland in Yankee territory features a generous menu. Knotty pine dining rooms. Cocktails. No charge for parking. Open for late breakfast, lunch, dinner, summer only.
35 Bradford St.

Colonial Inn. Shrimp Colonial is a delicious, different casserole at this old-fashioned inn. Home-baked rolls and muffins. Cocktails, entertainment. Open for breakfast and dinner.
603 Commercial St.

The Flagship. Salvaged shipwreck timber built this waterfront restaurant. Bar is fishing dory. Lobsters, steaks broiled over open pit. Open for lunch and dinner, until 1 a.m. Seasonal.
463 Commercial St.

The Moors. Unusual Portuguese seafood dishes and pirate atmosphere are intriguing here. Yankee fare, too. Snacks. Children's menu. Cocktails, entertainment. Open for lunch and dinner. Seasonal.
Beach Rd. and Bradford St. Extension.

Provincetown Inn. Dining is pleasant at this motel-resort. Complete dinners or à la carte. Broiled lobster is specialty. Cocktails. Open for lunch and dinner, coffee shop for breakfast on. Open Apr. through Oct.
1 Commercial St.

Inexpensive–Reasonable

Everbreeze Restaurant. This is the town's oldest restaurant. Picturesque harbor location. Delicious strawberry pancakes. Sandwiches; complete meals. Open for breakfast, lunch, dinner. Closed 3:30 to 6 p.m.
433 Commercial St.

Inexpensive

Plain and Fancy. Everything here from Portuguese flippers to *matzo brie.* Fancy foods include shrimp curry. On plain side, order soft-shell crabs. Snacks. Open 8 a.m. to 2 a.m.
334 Commercial St.

WEST YARMOUTH

First Class

The Rooster. Here the specialty is Hungarian *Palatschinken à la Vienois.* Cape seafoods, too. Cocktails, entertainment. Open all year.
State 28.

Reasonable–First Class

Casa Barbi. Same elegant restaurant located in Boston; this one has patio, too. Superb lobster Fra Diavolo. Native seafoods. Cocktails. Dinner only; Sun. from 1 p.m.
State 28.

Reasonable

The Gay Nineties. This is a fun place with costumed waitresses, songfests, gaslights, and cracker barrel. Informality at clam bar. Broiled lobster is specialty. Children's menu. Open for dinner only. Seasonal. Next to Cranberry Village.
State 28.

Inexpensive

Lobster in the Rough. You will have a picnic here with delicious cracked lobster served hot with melted butter, French-fried potatoes, cole slaw. Play area for the children. Watch lobsters boiling outside. Open for lunch and dinner. Seasonal.
State 28.

ELSEWHERE

BARNSTABLE. *Bacon Farm.* Reasonable. Special complete dinner offered daily, plus International Buffet, attracts patrons to this hilltop home overlooking harbor. Scandinavian fare includes delicious Finnish coffee bread. A la carte and complete dinners. Children's menu. Open summer only, for dinner, daily and Sun. State 6A.

Capt. Grey's Swedish Smorgasbord. Reasonable. There are 50 choices on the groaning board in this quaint sea captain's house with bay view. Also complete dinners to choose from. Swedish pancakes with lingonberries and whipped cream. Cocktails. Dinner daily and Sun. State 6A.

BASS RIVER. *Petrillo's Italian Kitchen.* Inexpensive to reasonable. From enormous sandwiches Italian-style to homemade manicotti, you will find variety here. Good *calamari* (squid) with sauce. All this and pizza, too. Homey atmosphere. Early morning to midnight daily. State 28.

BREWSTER. *Latham's.* Reasonable. Every evening something different is on the menu in this old sea captain's home. Delicious popovers, strawberry ice-cream meringue pie. Dinner only, except Mon. Summer only. State 6A.

BUZZARD'S BAY. *Bourne Mill.* Reasonable. All year round you may enjoy the charcoal-broiled meats and ocean-fresh seafood here. Pleasant cocktail lounge. Right at Bourne Bridge Rotary, State 28.

CRAIGVILLE. *Craigville Inn.* Inexpensive. Although the atmosphere is informal, no shorts or slacks are allowed for ladies; men are asked to wear jackets. Different dinner each day, usually $2.50 complete ($1.50 for children). Two dining rooms with lily pond or beach view. Dinner daily and Sun. Lake Elizabeth Dr.

CUMMAQUID. *Cape Cod Ranch.* Inexpensive. The bountiful smorgasbord dinner is so popular that this attractive restaurant has 5 very different dining rooms to accommodate hundreds. Unusual collection of brass and copper enhances decor. Beautiful silver service. Artistic, nautical cocktail lounge. Open dinner only, summer season. Bone Hill Rd.

DENNIS. *Bayside Inn.* Reasonable. Here in this Victorian home you will enjoy hearty Yankee cooking, with offers of second helpings. Specials each evening along with regular menu. State 6A.

EAST BREWSTER. *Chillingsworth.* Deluxe. Dinner is a gourmet's delight in this elegant home. Unusual specialties with French flair. Choice vintage wines. Dinner sittings by reservation only. Summer season. Closed Mon. State 6A. Tel. 896–3640.

EASTHAM. *Gristmill Restaurant.* Reasonable. For a real Cape Cod treat, order clam chowder and the Fisherman's Platter. Beef for the nonconformists. Home-baked breads and pies. Dinner only, daily and Sun. US 6.

EAST HARWICH. *Wequasset Inn.* Reasonable. Dining is delightful on the alfresco *Terrace Room* with sunken garden. Variety from lobster to duckling *à la bigarade.* Open for breakfast, lunch, dinner. Cocktails. Seasonal. On Pleasant Bay.

ORLEANS. *Nauset Inn.* Reasonable. Here you have your choice of indoor or outdoor dining. Roast duckling with wild rice a favorite on varied menu. Sandwiches and salads at lunch. Cocktails. Open from breakfast through dinner daily, Sun. from noon to 10 p.m. Cove Rd.

Orleans Inn. Reasonable. Delightful informality here, especially on the outdoor patio with seaside view. Lengthy menu highlights shore dinner. Children's menu. Cocktail lounge with nightly entertainment. Open all year for lunch and dinner. State 6A.

SANDWICH. *Daniel Webster Inn.* Reasonable. Daniel Webster slept here. This is the Cape's oldest inn. *Devil 'n' Dan Tavern* for cocktails. Children's menu. He-man sirloin, lobster stuffed with lobster are specialties. Open lunch and dinner. Main St.

Yankee Clipper. Reasonable. This restaurant has been popular for many summer moons. Extensive menu includes Cape Cod duck and lobster. Cocktails. Children's menu. Open for lunch and dinner. From Apr. to Dec. Right on State 6A.

SOUTH YARMOUTH. *Riverway Lobster House.* Reasonable to first-class. The gourmet dressing here is famous. Roast beef, steaks, chops on varied menu. Children's menu. Open dinner only, all year round. Closed Mon. in winter. State 28.

WELLFLEET. *Holiday House.* Reasonable. A whaling skipper once lived here. Interesting antiques. Cocktails in *Chart Room.* Specials daily. Delicious lobster pie and quahog chowder. Sun. buffet. E. Main St.

WEST DENNIS. *The Columns.* First class. Dinners have a delightful French accent, but you will also enjoy American favorites here. Children's menu. Cocktails. Beautiful century-old Georgian estate. Dinner only. Summer season. State 28.

WEST HARWICH. *Bishop's Terrace.* First class. Leisurely dining is emphasized in this sea captain's home. Luscious coffee ice-cream pie. Outdoor dining patio. Cocktails. Reservations necessary. Main St. Tel. 432–0253.

Cape Half House. Reasonable. Here the setting has old-fashioned garden charm. Interesting sandwiches at lunch. Cocktails. Variety of complete dinners. Lunch, dinner. State 28.

WOODS HOLE. *The Dome.* Reasonable. On a hill above Little Harbor, this interesting restaurant features open-hearth broiling. Entertainment in cocktail lounge. Open for breakfast, lunch, dinner. At Nautilus Motor Inn, State 28.

Landfall. Reasonable. Right on waterfront, window wall overlooks busy harbor. Broiled lobster, steaks, and chops are specialties. Portuguese bread. Cocktails, entertainment. Open for lunch and dinner. Water St.

YARMOUTH. *Blacksmith Shop Restaurant.* Reasonable. Steaks have special flavor when charcoal-broiled on forge. Seafoods, too. Cocktails. Lunch, dinner. Truro Rd.

YARMOUTH PORT. *The Cranberry Goose.* Reasonable to first class. Where else but in this old Cape Cod cottage could you order Pious Goose Mousse for dessert? Good wines. Delicious pan-fried chicken au vin, duckling à l'orange, lobster maison. Open for luncheon buffet, afternoon tea, dinner. Dinner only on Sun. Closed Tues. State 6A, Cranberry Hwy.

MUSIC. On Cape Cod, the Wareham-Onset area presents Thurs. night *band concerts* and Fri. night community *sing-along.* Chatham features band concerts Fri. evening. Provincetown has its own *Provincetown Symphony Orchestra.* On Martha's Vineyard, summer *chamber music* concerts are presented in Edgartown. Nantucket Island has *band concerts* on Main St., 8 p.m., also classical concerts, July and Aug., by *Nantucket Musical Arts Society.*

STAGE AND REVUES. The Cape is thick with good summer theaters. Among them are: the *Cape Playhouse,* Dennis; *Falmouth Playhouse,* Falmouth; *Cape Cod Melody Tent,* Hyannis; *Straight Wharf Theatre,* Nantucket; *Provincetown Playhouse,* Provincetown; and the *Yarmouth Summer Playhouse,* Yarmouth.

TOURS. *Gray Line* of Boston, located in the Sheraton Plaza Hotel, conducts a 3-day tour in July and Aug. covering the Pilgrim Shore, Cape Cod, and Martha's Vineyard, also Provincetown. The cost is about $65 a person and includes everything but 2 lunches, meal tips, and admissions. For information tel. KE 6–2470. *Parker Motorcoach Tours* feature a 7-day tour to Martha's Vineyard, Nantucket, 3 nights at the Yachtsman Hotel in Hyannis, summer theater, Provincetown, etc. Information may be obtained from Parker Tours, 125 West 43rd St., New York City. *Trailways of New England* has day trips to Hyannis which include a lectured boat trip to Nantucket. This trip leaves Boston at 8 a.m. and returns at 7:30 p.m., summer only. Ticket is $11; children $5.75.

A combination sightseeing plan includes a bus ride from Greyhound Terminal, 10 St. James St., Boston to Hyannis; then a trip to Nantucket on the cruise ship *Siaconset,* followed by a sightseeing bus tour of Nantucket Island, or the visitor may stay in Hyannis overnight and take the boat the next morning. For information, write *Plymouth and Brockton St. Railway,* 112 Sandwich St., Plymouth 6, Mass., or phone LI 2–3532 or HU 2–9000. Round trip costs about $13 for adults; half price for children.

Nantucket has two sightseeing services: *Barrett's Gray Line Sightseeing* (tel. 228–0174) and *Island Sightseeing Tours, Inc.* (tel. 228–0334.).

Tauck Tours, 475 Fifth Ave., New York City, provides escorted tours to Cape Cod, Martha's Vineyard, and Nantucket.

SPECIAL INTEREST TOURS. *Museums: Drummer Boy Museum,* US 6A, Brewster, features guided tours every 30 minutes daily. Life-size scenes of American Revolution. There is a *whaling museum* on Broad St., Nantucket. *Audubon:* Bird-watchers have something to sing about; free tours are arranged at these sanctuaries all year around: *Ashumet Wildlife Sanctuary,* Ashumet Rd., Hatchville (Falmouth). Tel. 563–6390. *Wellfleet Bay Wildlife Sanctuary,* US 6, South Wellfleet (beach buggy wildlife tours, also). Reservations by writing to Box 171, South Wellfleet. Tel. 349–2615.

Underwater: The skin-diver will have to arrange his own underwater tour. There is excellent skin-diving in *Cape Cod* waters, filled with interesting marine life. Some of the best places are: Corporation Beach, Dennis; West Dennis Beach, West Dennis; The Spindle (entrance to Hyannis outer harbor); Springhill Beach, Sandwich; Scussett Beach, Sagamore; Nantucket outer harbor; Martha's Vineyard (off West Chop).

Hourly harbor *sightseeing cruises* between Hyannis and Nantucket are scheduled on the motor ship *Siasconset,* from Ocean St. Dock, Hyannis. Tel. 775–1885.

MUSEUMS AND GALLERIES. *Chrysler Art Museum.* At 354 Commercial St., Provincetown, this museum has excellent collections of American and European art, art nouveau, Egyptian sculpture, etc. Open daily, except Mon. Admission, adults $1; children 25 cents. *Provincetown Historical Museum,* on the hill near the Pilgrim Monument, displays artifacts of Admiral Donald MacMillan's Polar Expedition, Sandwich glass, early American pewter, and P'town's oldest fire engine. Open daily mid-Apr. to mid-Nov., 9 a.m. to 5 p.m. (to 6 p.m. in July and August). Adults 75¢, children under 12, 25¢. *The Drummer Boy Museum,* near Brewster on State 6A, has several large paintings depicting the Revolution's major battles, including Bunker Hill. Open July and August to 6 p.m. $1.50 adults, 75¢ for children.

SHOPPING. *Salt and Pepper Gift Shoppe,* West Dennis, has all sorts of salt and pepper shakers. *Wood & Wood,* Provincetown, stock casual and high-fashion summer apparel. There are many fascinating shops offering unusual items, sometimes kooky, sometimes chic, along Provincetown's main drag. Wild hats, antiques and junk, and every conceivable kind of knick-knack, bibelot, gew-gaw, and gadget are offered at prices ranging from ridiculously low to just plain ridiculous. Among the outstanding establishments appealing to the collector is the *Shell Shop,* 188 Commercial St., with shell jewelry and novelties, as well as artfully-twisted (by nature) driftwood.

SPORTS. Striped bass fishing began three hundred years ago on Cape Cod and is at its best along Cuttyhunk Island and Martha's Vineyard. (*Vineyard Striped Bass Derby* from Sept. 15 to Oct. 15). Surf-casting is popular in Nantucket, at Madaket. Daily charters on the Cape, for game-fishing, cost from $40 to $75. No fishing license is needed. On Cape Cod, two 18-hole *golf courses* welcome guests: *Bass River Golf Club,* So. Yarmouth, tel. 398–9079; *Pocasset Golf Club,* Pocasset, tel. 563–9851 (ladies' day Thur.). There are many free tennis courts from Bourne to Provincetown.

Bicycle rentals are no problem throughout Cape Cod. On Nantucket Island, figure about 5 a week for rental. *Beach buggies,* the fun way to ride over sand dunes, are a Cape Cod trademark and may be rented at Provincetown, Orleans, and at the Audubon Society's Wellfleet Bay Wildlife Sanctuary. Cape Cod features both saltwater and freshwater beaches, the most spectacular at *Cape Cod National Seashore.* For would-be water-skiers there's a *Mayfair Water Skiing School,* Kelley's Bay, South Dennis.

WHAT TO DO WITH THE CHILDREN. *Bassett Wild Animal Farm,* Tubman Rd., Brewster, has an animal contact zoo where children may pet their favorites. Pony rides; picnic facilities. Open daily, summer only. Children 30 cents; adults 50 cents. *Yesteryear's Doll Museum* in Sandwich has thousands of dolls, dollhouses, and miniatures. Open from 10 a.m. to 5 p.m.; Sun. from 1 to 5 p.m. Admission 75 cents; children 25 cents. *The 1865 Cranberry Express,* Orleans–Eastham Rotary on US 6, is in Cranberry Cove. Summer only; daily to 11 p.m. Restaurant features make-it-yourself sundae buffet with ice creams, sherbets.

EXPLORING MASSACHUSETTS

Across the Charles River from Boston is Cambridge, best reached by the Harvard Bridge (Route 2) running north from Boston's Commonwealth Avenue. Directly in front as you cross the bridge are the buildings of the Massachusetts Institute of Technology, whose initials, MIT, are known throughout the scientific and educational world. Only a few miles to the west along the river, the Larz Anderson Bridge leads to Harvard University. Connecting MIT and Harvard is Memorial Drive, which runs along the Charles River. At the junction of the Larz Anderson Bridge and Memorial Drive, turn right to Harvard Square, where there are adequate parking facilities for a walking tour of the Harvard campus with students as guides. Of major interest is the exhibit of glass flowers in the University Museum at Oxford and Jarvis streets. Other buildings at Harvard, such as the Widener Library and the Fogg Art Museum, also should be seen.

On the northern edges of Harvard Square and its common is Radcliffe College for Women. It was named in honor of Lady Radcliffe, an early benefactor of Harvard and was incorporated in 1832. Many classes and courses are now held jointly with Harvard.

Just beyond the Radcliffe buildings is the Longfellow House, on Brattle Street. The house had been owned by Dr. Andrew Craigie and, upon his death, his wife took in boarders, one of whom was Henry Wadsworth Longfellow. Longfellow, then a young Harvard instructor, eventually bought the house in 1843. He lived in it until his death in 1882 and most of his well-known works were written there. The house, open to the public, is a fine example of Colonial architecture and is maintained by the Longfellow Trust, set up by his descendants.

Following Paul Revere

A popular one-day trip out of Boston takes you to Lexington and Concord, with a return stop at Sudbury.

Leaving Boston, cross the Charles River to Memorial Drive, which is US 3, and turn west. By following this route you will come to Arlington center in about 15 minutes. Go straight ahead on Massachusetts Avenue. At the first traffic light beyond the center, turn left on Jason Street, and stop at the Jason Russell House. As the British soldiers headed for Lexington, on April 19, 1775, they passed along Massachusetts Avenue, and engaged a group of Colonists close by this house. It was the first battle of that fateful day. A number of the Minutemen, almost surrounded by the British, retreated to the

Russell home. Russell and 11 others were killed on the first floor oι the house. Bullet holes can still be seen.

Continue west on Massachusetts Avenue, through Arlington Heights and East Lexington, to Lexington and its green, where you can park. Here the Minutemen stood on April 19, 1775, and the Minuteman statue faces the line of British march. Behind the statue is the green and a large boulder marking the line of the Colonists. On the stone is inscribed the command: "Stand your ground. Don't fire unless fired upon. But if they mean to have war, let it begin here."

On the right side of the green is Buckman Tavern, where the Minutemen gathered and waited for the British. The Hancock-Clark House, on Hancock Street, a short way from the green, is also open to the public. Here, the Rev. John Hancock was staying when Paul Revere rode into Lexington warning that the British were coming from Boston. Samuel Adams, also in the house at the time, and Hancock fled to avoid capture. The house contains a notable collection of historical articles and is open the same days and hours as the Buckman Tavern.

Leave Lexington on Massachusetts Avenue, which bears left from the green and connects with Route 2A to Concord. On the right is the so-called Grapevine Cottage where the Concord grape first was grown. A little beyond, again on the right, is The Wayside, which was the only house ever owned by Nathaniel Hawthorne. It was also the early girlhood home of Louisa May Alcott and, later, the home of Margaret Sidney, who wrote *Five Little Peppers*. A little further on the right is the Louisa May Alcott House, which was the second home of the authoress. Here she wrote *Little Women* and *Little Men*.

On the left as you follow Route 2A almost into Concord center is The Antiquarian House, one of the most important museums in Concord. It contains several authentic early New England rooms, in which are displayed furniture, glass, china, wainscoting, fireplaces and other articles of the period.

Entering the center of Concord, you will see Monument Square, which has three war memorials on its green. Turn right on Monument Street toward the battleground. On the right is the Bullet-Hole House, where Elisha Jones, a Minuteman, guarded supplies stored in the basement. When the British began their retreat, Jones appeared in the doorway with his flintlock and was fired upon. The shot missed him but the hole is still to be seen. On the left, just before the battleground and bridge, is the Old Manse, home of Ralph Waldo Emerson. The battleground, itself, consists mostly of the bridge and the pleasant shaded pathway leading to it. Along this path, the British marched to be met by shots from the Minutemen on the other side of the bridge where now stands the Concord Minuteman statue. Along the pathway are the graves of the unknown British soldiers who fell on that day.

She Had a Little Lamb

Leave Concord the way you came (Route 2A) and turn right on a connecting road marked Wayland, left on Walden Street. This crosses Route 2 and becomes Highway 126. On the right will be Walden Pond, where Thoreau lived for two years before he wrote his famous book *Walden*. The site of his cabin can be reached along a wooded path to the right at the north end of the pond. Directly across the lake in a lovely wooded grove is a public picnic area, while on still another shore of the tranquil lake is a town bathing beach.

Route 126 soon joins US 20, where you should turn right and drive six miles to South Sudbury. A sign on the right points to the *Wayside Inn*. The inn, which has been providing food and lodging to travelers for almost 280 years, was originally known as *Howe's Tavern* and later *Red Horse Tavern*. It acquired its present name after Longfellow made it the scene of his *Tales of a Wayside Inn*. In 1923, it was bought by Henry Ford who preserved it through a national trust. It burned almost to the ground in 1955 but was restored. The gardens are extensive and interesting and contain the schoolhouse attended by the Mary of *Mary Had a Little Lamb*.

The schoolhouse actually was located 40 miles away, and was brought to its present location in 1926 by Henry Ford. The first part of the little poem was written in 1822 by John Roulston, Jr., a freshman at Harvard University, for a little friend of his, Mary Tyler. The poem was finished in 1830 by Sarah Josephus Hale.

For the return trip to Boston, turn around on US 20 and head east. This road joins Commonwealth Avenue, runs past the massive buildings of Boston University and winds up in downtown Boston.

Down to the Sea

The next tour combines history with rugged coastline, smooth beaches, sailing, and fishing. Leave Boston on Route C 1, which leads through the Callahan Tunnel under Boston harbor and borders Logan International Airport. At the traffic circle near Revere, turn right on to Route 1A, which travels along Revere Beach and into the city of Lynn. Visit Nahant beaches. The drive along the shore is particularly beautiful. Head north again, bearing always to the right and you will join Atlantic Avenue, which leads to Marblehead.

The town of Marblehead was settled in 1629 by fishermen from the Channel Islands and Cornwall. While fishing is still important, the magnificent harbor has become a yachting center. Race Week, usually the last full week in July, brings boats from all over the Atlantic seaboard.

Abbot Hall, the seat of town government, houses the famous painting *The Spirit of '76,* considered to be the most patriotic painting in America. It was painted by A. M. Willard in 1876. Also to be seen is the original deed to the town by the Nanepashemet Indians, dated 1684. To get the full flavor of an early New England seacoast town, park your car in the public lot and walk along the narrow, winding streets lined with ancient elms and the mansions of 18th-century ship captains. The Old Town House on Mugford Street was built in 1727, and St. Michael's Church, 1714, still uses a bell cast by Paul Revere. Before leaving, visit Marblehead Neck and the lighthouse at the harbor entrance. This is reached by following the Ocean Avenue Causeway from Atlantic Avenue. Still hugging the sea, leave Marblehead on Route 114 to Salem, only three miles away.

Salem would probably be known today merely as the birthplace of Nathaniel Hawthorne if it hadn't been for a West Indian slave named Tituba. A servant of the Rev. Samuel Parris, Tituba had a talent for storytelling which she exercised well but not wisely. Her listeners, frequently, were two impressionable young girls who, quite naturally, would have a screaming and shuddering nightmare when getting into bed after one of Tituba's better stories. The girls were declared witches and shortly accused Tituba and two other unpopular old women in the town of acquainting them with the Devil. Coupled with such goings-on was the spread of witchcraft stories which were, at the time, spreading from Europe to America. No one in Salem was safe and before the hysteria ended, in 1693, nineteen persons had been hanged on Gallows Hill. Contrary to popular belief, however, no one was burned at the stake. Hawthorne helped spread the word of the Salem witches with his story, *The House of the Seven Gables.* The house is located at 54 Turner Street and is open to the public.

The Chamber of Commerce of Salem has plotted many points of interest onto an Historic Trail map and has erected signs for easy following. A copy of the map can be obtained at information booths as well as the chamber's offices. Of particular interest on the trail is the Witch House. It is the restored home of Jonathan Corwin, judge of the Witchcraft Court. The witchcraft trials came to an end when the wife of Governor Phips, and the saintly Mrs. Hale, wife of a minister, were accused. This, indeed, was going too far. The terrible witchcraft period ended as quickly as it began.

When leaving Salem, go north on Route 1A, cross the bridge over the harbor, and turn right on Route 127 to Beverly. Beverly is known as the birthplace of the American Navy and, according to official records in the Library of Congress, the schooner *Hannah,* which was docked at Glover's Wharf, was converted to an armed vessel of war and set sail on Sept. 5, 1775. Two days later, the *Hannah* returned with its first British prize. A Beverly resident, George Cabot, was named as first Secretary of the Navy by President Adams. Also of interest in Beverly is the Balch House, 448 Cabot Street, which was built in 1638.

Continue on Route 127 to Beverly Farms, Pride's Crossing, Manchester-by-the-Sea, and Magnolia. By taking Hesperus Avenue, in Magnolia, you can see Norman's Woe rock which was made famous in Longfellow's *The Wreck of the Hesperus.* Hesperus Avenue rejoins Route 127 and crosses the Annisquam River into Gloucester. Park your car along the seawall.

Facing the sea is the Gloucester Fisherman statue, a memorial to Gloucestermen lost at sea. Each August a memorial service is held along the seawall and flowers tossed on the water disappear on the outgoing tide. Beyond the statue on the right are the fishing wharves and picturesque fishing vessels which help to make Gloucester one of the most famous fishing ports in the world and the largest lobster distributor in America.

Rockport—Artists' Delight

Rather than head directly to Rockport on Route 127, take the scenic shore drive which is Route 127 Alternate. This leads down to East Gloucester and Eastern Point lighthouse. There is good fishing from the breakwater leading out from the light. Route 127 Alternate winds along the shore, passing places with such interesting names as: Bass Rocks, Loblolly Cove, Gap Head, Good Harbor Beach, and Brier Neck. At Rockport, park your car in the square and walk out on Bearskin Neck where you can see the lobster shack known as "Motif No. 1" because it has been painted for generations by artists from the world over. Rockport has numerous art galleries and souvenir shops and attracts thousands of people daily throughout the summer. Some drive up, jump out of their cars, snap a picture of the famous shack, return to their cars—and roar away. They've "done" Rockport!

Continuing on Route 127, you will come to Pigeon Cove and, unless you look sharp, you'll miss a small sign on the left pointing to the Paper House, which was started in 1922. Since that time more than 100,000 copies of newspapers have been used in the construction of the house and furniture.

Route 127 continues along the shore from Rockport, passes

Halibut Point, and runs down the western shore of Cape Ann, affording fine views of the sea every mile of the way. It joins Route 128 at a large traffic circle. Turn right on Route 128, cross the Annisquam River, turn right again (Highway 133) toward the town of Essex, which was an early shipbuilding center and is still in operation, and drive into Ipswich, four miles beyond.

Colonial Ipswich is said to have more 17th-century houses, still standing and lived in, than any town in America. It was settled in 1633. The Whipple House, built around 1640, is the showpiece of the town and is furnished with many antiques. It is located at the junction of Route 133 and 1 Alternate. Argilla Road leads out of the town square to the Crane Memorial Reservation, a 10-mile stretch of sandy public beach. Located here, also, is Castle Hill, the home of Mrs. Richard T. Crane, Jr. During the summer months many public concerts and lectures are held at this estate.

From Ipswich, follow Topsfield Road to US 1 for the return trip to Boston. At Saugus, visit the restoration of the nation's first iron works. A pleasant alternate return from Ipswich, for lovers of early New England homes, follows Route 1A north, for 12 miles, to Newburyport.

US 1 returns to Boston through Topsfield, the scene of the oldest public fair in the country.

The Yankee Village

New England has many villages which have been reconstructed to demonstrate the mode of life in the early days of the country. Old Sturbridge Village, southwest of Worcester, is the most popular and a visit here makes an interesting and pleasant one-day trip from Boston. Leave Boston on the Massachusetts Turnpike. The village is at the junction of the turnpike and Highway 15. The 56-mile trip takes an hour.

Visitors to Old Sturbridge meet history face to face: watching an historic newspaper pulled from a 200-year-old printing press, seeing a horseshoe shaped under a blacksmith's hammer, learning to recognize useful herbs from the garden, or visiting a traditional meeting house. Horses draw a carry-all for visitors to ride, an ox cart plies the village lanes, and a flock of photogenic geese guard the mill-pond. You can sit in the shade of a maple tree on the village green and listen to a strolling minstrel sing his story-songs. In the village are found the homes, shops, general store, schoolhouse, tavern and pillory of an average New England village of the early 1800's. Craftsmen recreate the life lived in these buildings, demonstrating spinning, weaving, printing, the making of pottery, the skills of the pewtersmith and tinsmith, as well as the family arts of fireplace cooking, herb gardening and candle dipping.

Many of the original buildings—there's a total of 38 in the village—have been brought to Old Sturbridge from different parts of New England. Meals and lodging and a large parking lot are available. No cars are allowed within the village but walking distances between buildings are not great.

If you decide to stay overnight at Old Sturbridge Village, return to Boston over a different route. Follow US 20 to Charleton City and turn north on Highway 31 to Princeton. Miles of apple orchards line this route and it is most scenic, particularly in the spring of the year when the apple blossoms are out. From Princeton, follow local signs to the road leading to the top of Mt. Wachusett. While not high by usual mountain standards, Mt. Wachusett looms over the surrounding flat countryside and provides excellent views. A snack bar and picnic facilities are provided. Returning to the bottom of the mountain, turn right on Highway 140 and left on Highway 31 to Route 2. Turn right to Boston.

Land of Colleges

Four roads in western Massachusetts form a rough square starting at the Connecticut River, running north and south across the state, and extending to the New York border. US 5 runs north, from the Massachusetts Turnpike at Springfield to Greenfield, a distance of 32 miles. Route 2 travels west, along the Mohawk Trail, to Williamstown, from where US 7 heads south to Great Barrington. Highway 23 returns east to the general Springfield area. We will start this tour from the junction of the Massachusetts Turnpike and US 5. This point can be reached by following the turnpike from Boston, a drive of two hours.

Five miles north on US 5 is Holyoke. The well-known women's college, Mt. Holyoke, is only four miles from this busy industrial city on Highway 116. The grounds and buildings of the college are spacious and attractive and the Dwight Memorial Art Museum, on the campus, is open weekdays. It contains many excellent collections. Just north of the small town of South Hadley, in which the college is actually located, is Dinosaur Land, an interesting display of the fossil tracks of pre-historic animals. Leave South Hadley on Highway 47 to the junction of the mountain road, about three miles from the village. The road leads through the Pass of Thermopylae, a narrow, winding pass, and under Titan's Piazza, an interesting outcropping of rock. From the summit of the mountain road, return to Highway 47 and continue to Hadley. Turn left to Northampton. This town is the site of the famous Smith College, for women. On the campus, visit the Tryon Art Gallery; it is open to the public on weekdays and Sunday afternoons. Three miles south of Northampton, off US 5, is Mt. Tom, having an elevation of 1,214 feet. A mountain road runs to the top and it is a major ski center during the winter months.

Continuing north, drive 12 miles on US 5 to the village of Old Deerfield, an authentic settlement that dates back before the Revolution. Today, Deerfield is not so much a town as it is the ghost of a town, its dimness almost transparent, its quiet almost a cessation. Yet, it is one of the most fascinating ghosts of its kind in America. Other New England communities have had more importance, but Deerfield is, and will probably always remain, the perfect and beautiful statement of the tragic and creative moment when one civilization is destroyed by another. In fact, nothing has happened there for more than two hundred years, with the whole history of its greatness crowded into those violent and dreadful years from 1672 to 1704, when it was the northwest frontier of New England. Although part of Dedham in 1663, no Dedhamite had settled there until 1669, when Samuel Hinsdell, a squatter, began cultivation of the fertile soil where the Pocumtuck Indians had grown their corn, tobacco and pumpkins. By 1672, however, Samson Frary and others had joined Hinsdell, until the population numbered 125. This was, according to the Pocumtucks, carrying encroachment too far and one dark night three years later, they struck. The fight, called the Bloody Brook Massacre, either killed or drove off to more southern hamlets every single white person. For seven years Deerfield's houses were empty. Slowly, through the years, the settlers returned to their homes and in 1686, Deerfield held its first town meeting. The Indians attacked again in 1704, putting to torch more than half the town's buildings, capturing over 100 men, women, and children for slaves, and killing 50 others who tried to resist. With this great raid, Deerfield ended its active life. But its memory still is bright and vivid. The Deerfield Historical Society has restored many of the original buildings from the 17th and 18th centuries to their former glory.

Memorial Hall contains, along with many relics of early days, the front door of one of the Deerfield houses which survived the great raid of 1704. The door still clearly shows a hole caused by a tomahawk. The Frary House is well worth a visit, along with the Indian House with its second- and third-story overhangs illustrating the earliest Colonial architecture. Many other delightful early homes are open for inspection along Old Deerfield Street. Continue north from Old Deerfield, on US 5, to Greenfield and the start of the Mohawk Trail going west. Before leaving Greenfield, you may find a drive through the town interesting. Follow Maple Street to the top of Rocky Mountain for good views of the Berkshire Hills to the west and the farmlands to the east. Greenfield is a summer and winter sports center for the Pioneer Valley area.

The Mohawk Trail

The 67 miles of Route 2 from the New York state line to the junction of Highway 63 just east of Greenfield, has been officially recognized by the Massachusetts Legislature as the Mohawk Trail. Strategically important because it connects the great water routes of New York and Massachusetts, the Trail has been historically significant since Indian times. It was first an Indian path that stretched from New York's Finger Lakes region to the villages of western and central Massachusetts. Later, as the settlers moved west in their covered wagons, it became the first road over the mountains and the lifeline for garrisons along New York's Hudson River. In 1786, the Trail became America's first free road. Prior to that time, most roads were under private ownership and a toll was charged. During the 19th century, the Trail became a symbol of America's westward expansion and was the route followed by the stagecoaches. In 1875, the Hoosac Railroad Tunnel, which crosses the Trail north of the town of Florida, was completed and linked the railroads of the east and west. In 1913, the Trail was engineered for automobile travel with many off-road parking areas for scenic vistas and historical markers.

Leave Greenfield on the Mohawk Trail (Route 2) heading west toward Shelburne Falls. Follow the road marked By-pass to the Bridge of Flowers. Planted and maintained by the Women's Association since 1929, the 400-foot bridge is a riot of color in the spring, summer and early fall. It is the only bridge of its kind in the country. Close by are the so-called Indian Potholes and Salmon Falls, both of which are interesting. The town of Shelburne was established in 1756 and was the birthplace of Linus Yale, the founder of the Yale Lock Company. Further along the Trail, on the right, is the old Oak Meeting Ground, a pre-Revolutionary War shrine.

Midway point on the Trail is Charlemont, about three miles beyond the Campground. It focuses attention on the beauties of the Deerfield River and the many unusual off-Trail drives to the north and south. The Indian statue, Hail to the Sunrise, is just west of the new bridge at the junction of the road to Monroe Bridge and Monroe. Also of interest is the Buttonball Tree and the watering trough at its base, which was made in 1760 as a token of friendship for the Indians. The Bissell Bridge, a modern covered bridge, is also located here.

On the right, close to the Indian statue, is an off-Trail road to the village of Zoar and to Rowe, site of the $60,000,000 atomic power plant built by the Yankee Atomic Electric Company. An interesting and pleasant return trip to the Trail is via Monroe Bridge, south along the Deerfield River and by the entrance to the Hoosac Tunnel.

Camping and Hiking

The Trail now runs through the Mohawk Trail State Forest. Attractive scenery and many different camping sites provide a pleasant stopping place. Boy Scouts camp at the junction of the Cold and Deerfield rivers, where Indians once held their war councils. The recreational facility covers 50,000 acres. Several off-Trail drives radiate from the top of Forbidden Mountain. One circles through Savoy Mountain State Forest (follow local signs) and travels by Tannery Falls, Balance Rock, and Beaver Pond. Cabins and camping facilities are available here. The off-Trail route also goes by the building housing the blowers for the Hoosac Tunnel's 1,028-foot central shaft, which took 22 years to build.

Whitcomb Summit, the highest point on the Trail, presents fine views of the Deerfield River and overlooks the Tunnel entrance. The B.P.O.E. Memorial Elk is also located here. A short drive beyond is Western Summit, offering excellent views of North Adams, Williamstown, and Mt. Greylock. The most memorable part of the Trail is just ahead at the Hairpin Turn. At the parking area here, there is a small gift and snack shop. The Trail, from here, travels down from the mountains to North Adams. Turn right in the center of the city and drive a mile to New England's only Natural Bridge. West of the city, just beyond the village of Braytonville, is the site of old Fort Massachusetts. South of the city is Mt. Greylock Reservation.

A scenic road leads to the top of the mountain and this road can be reached either directly from North Adams or from Adams, located six miles south on Highway 8. Mt. Greylock, the state's highest mountain at 3,491 feet, overlooks western Massachusetts, the Hudson River Valley of New York and the Green Mountains of lower Vermont. A 90-foot granite tower, a memorial to Massachusetts' veterans of all wars, is located at the top of the mountain. Stairs lead to the top of the tower to an observation spot directly beneath a glass-enclosed beacon. The Thunderbolt ski run, part of a large ski development on the mountain, plunges down the face of the mountain into the town, 2,000 feet below. Many foot trails cross the summit, including the Appalachian Trail, and the more hardy tourists will find an hour wandering on these trails close to the summit to be rewarding. After driving down the mountain, return to North Adams and continue west on Route 2.

Five miles west of North Adams is Williamstown, one of the loveliest communities in New England. It lies between the Taconic Range on the west of the village and the Hoosac Range to its east. To the south are the Berkshire Hills. Williams College started here as a free school but became a college in 1793. The campus is well worth a walking tour because of its attractive grounds.

The college's Thompson Memorial Chapel, a Gothic structure built in 1904, is on the north side of Main Street. Its stained glass windows are seen to best advantage from inside the chapel. Diagonally across the street is the Lawrence Art Museum, recognized by its octagonal form and Grecian Rotunda. The museum houses fine collections of glass, pottery, bronzes, and sculpture. On South Street, just west of the center of town, is the Sterling and Francine Clark Art Institute, one of the finest small art museums in the country. It boasts great paintings, rare silver, furniture and china, most of which was collected by Mr. and Mrs. Clark. They founded the Art Institute to share what they loved with others. Located also in Williamstown is an excellent summer theater.

The Berkshire Hills

From Williamstown, turn south on US 7, into what is popularly known as the Berkshire Hills area. Its heritage comes not only from the Puritans and Pilgrims of eastern Massachusetts, but from the Dutch, who settled New York City and the upper reaches of the Hudson River valley. Because the Berkshires are small in area (55 miles north to south and 40 miles east to west) tourists are apt to roam the area rather than travel through it. Every side road running off US 7 holds something of interest and every such road, by means of connecting roads, circles back to the main north-south route. In the Berkshires, visitors may see the homes or birthplaces of William Cullen Bryant, Oliver Wendell Holmes, Edith Wharton, Susan B. Anthony, Josh Billings, Herman Melville, Norman Rockwell, and Daniel Chester French, sculptor of the famous statue of Abraham Lincoln in the Lincoln Memorial at Washington, D.C. Tourists also may visit Tanglewood, site of the renowned Berkshire Music Festival and summer home of the Boston Symphony Orchestra. Dance enthusiasts will enjoy Ted Shawn's Jacob's Pillow Dance Festival.

As is the case with Cape Cod and many other sections of Massachusetts and New England, the main industry of the Berkshires is tourism but the pace of vacation life is far different here than in the others. Living is more relaxed and the pleasures simpler. Still, there is more than adequate day and nighttime activity for the younger people, but this, to a large extent, is confined to the several large resorts in the area.

Because of its high elevation, snow generally comes early to the Berkshires and stays late, bringing joy to the operators of 12 major ski areas. When the snow leaves, the many mountain streams jump with trout and the countryside and hills take on varying shades of green.

Continue your tour south from Williamstown on US 7 to Lanesboro, a distance of 15 miles. This is the birthplace of Josh Billings, the American humorist. Turn left on Berkshire Road, just north of the cemetery. This road leads through farm country and joins Highway 8, which rises slowly, affording fine views, to the village of Cheshire. After this tiny hamlet's farmers sent President Jefferson a 1,235-pound cheese, Cheshire cheese became extremely popular in America. Continue north on Highway 8 to Adams, the birthplace of Susan B. Anthony, pioneer suffragette. The house, now a private home, is at Bowen's Corners on East Road. Follow this road to Highway 116 and bear right to the mountain village of Savoy. At the southern limit of the scattering of homes, a well-marked road turns to the right, leading to the Jambs in the Windsor State Forest. A left turn at the dam, where there are swimming facilities, leads to the Jambs, which is a deep flume or gorge cut through solid rock. The forest road soon joins Route 9. About a half mile to the left off Route 9 is Cummington Road and the William Cullen Bryant Homestead, open to the public. A small fee is charged. Go west on Route 9. The ride down from the hills approaching the town of Dalton offers excellent views, particularly during the fall foliage season. At the foot of the hills, a well-marked road on the left leads to Wahconah Falls, a state park created around a waterfall in a clear, cold mountain stream. There is swimming and picnicking at the foot of the falls. Continue west on Route 9, through Dalton to Pittsfield.

On the east side of South Street, just before Park Square, is the Berkshire Museum, a fine small museum of art and natural history. In a corner of the museum grounds is a marker on the site of Eaton's Tavern, where plans were laid in 1775 for the capture of Fort Ticonderoga in upper New York state.

Heritage of the Shakers

Leave Pittsfield on US 20 and drive west about five miles to the Hancock Shaker Village. The Shakers first began to gather at Hancock in the early 1780's when Mother Lee, the English-born founder of the movement, was still alive. The community was organized under the principles of separation from the world, common property, confession of sin, and celibacy. At its numerical height, in the 1830's, there were six "families" at Hancock, each with its elders, eldresses, and deacons. Total membership was about 300 brethren and sisters. The last two Shakers left the Church Family in 1960. Since that time, a group inspired by the Shaker heritage has resolved to restore the village as a memorial to the Shaker community's contribution to the religious, social, and economic life of early America.

Eighteen buildings are now restored and open to the public. Of particular interest are the Garden House, Brethren Shop, the Round Barn, Meeting House, and Laundry Shop. Three bountiful fall dinners, on succeeding Saturdays toward the end of September, are open to the public. Just beyond the village turn left, on Highway 41 to Richmond, and visit the ruins of an early iron foundry. Turn left on Lenox Road for Tanglewood.

Tanglewood is, in reality, a music school. Here, every June and July, students, world-renowned soloists and artists, the Boston Symphony Orchestra, and just plain music lovers gather to learn, enjoy and perform. The main Music Shed seats 6,000 people for the large concerts, the Theater Concert Hall is used for small orchestra and chamber music concerts, and the Chamber Music Hall seats 300 and is used for small chamber music groups, lectures and large classes. While the various classes are in session, tourists are asked to tour the area in the company of guides. At the time of the Berkshire Festival concerts by the Boston Symphony Orchestra, usually July 1 through the first week in August, with Friday and Saturday evening and Sunday afternoon concerts, admission is by ticket only. Also on the grounds is the cottage in which Nathaniel Hawthorne lived while he wrote *The House of the Seven Gables* and *Tanglewood Tales.* The dwelling is open to the public before each concert.

From Tanglewood, travel east on Highway 183 to the town of Lenox. Nearby is the Pleasant Valley Wildlife Sanctuary. Open in the summer, the sanctuary has hundreds of live specimens of the area's plant and animal life. Return to Lenox, where the main library has an excellent collection of rare books, and continue south on US 20 to Lee. Beyond the town, Ted Shawn draws followers of the dance to his Jacob's Pillow Dance Festival every summer. There are regular performances by visiting dancers and dance companies from around the world. The University of the Dance is operated by Ted Shawn for resident students. From Lee, return on Highway 102 to Stockbridge and turn left on US 7 to Great Barrington.

Great Barrington is the largest town and the economic center of Southern Berkshire County. One of the early acts of the townspeople was to seize the courthouse from the British in August, 1774, which was, they claim, the first act of open resistance to British rule in America. Continue south through the town and turn right on Highway 23 to the small village of South Egremont, just beyond which is the junction of Highway 41 to the left. At this small junction is Smiley's Pond, a protected sanctuary for wild life, and there is usually a family of ducks, or beavers, to be seen. Turn left on Highway 41 and then right beyond Smiley's Pond for the short trip to Bash Bish Fall Reservation.

A large parking area is provided and a short, pleasant footpath leads to the falls and picnic area. Following a gorge cut deep into solid rock, the Bash Bish Brook plunges 50 feet into a deep, clear, rock-bottom pool. According to the story, seemingly told at all the falls in North America, an Indian maiden, unhappy in love, jumped to her death in the pool from the rocks above. Her tortured spirit, of course, haunts the falls.

Retrace the route to Great Barrington and head east, on Highway 23, to US 20, which will take you to Westfield and Springfield. Settlement here began as early as 1636. The Springfield Arsenal was the first in the country and its site was selected by George Washington in 1794. It is the home of the famed Springfield rifle, and the M1 of World War II. The arsenal, located on State Street, has a fine museum with a collection of early firearms. Forest Park, entrance from Sumner Ave., has picnic areas and a zoo for children.

AROUND THE STATE

HOTELS AND MOTELS. The high standard of Massachusetts hostelries is matched only by the general reputation for hospitality, though to the non-Yankee, the latter may seem too completely cloaked in traditional taciturn demeanor. The charming inns of western and southern Massachusetts and the comfortable resorts in the Berkshires are traditional havens for the weary New Englander who doesn't wish to go very far for relaxation. These, and the up-to-date hotels and motels around the larger cities and along the pikes are considered to be among the best in the country, category by category.

ANDOVER

First Class

Sheraton Rolling Green Motor Inn. Swim, have lunch by the pool, and relax in this attractive motel. Resort atmosphere. Family plan. Medieval restaurant, breakfast, lunch, dinner. Cocktails.

Lowell St. (tel. 475–5400).

Reasonable

Andover Inn. This Treadway Inn is conveniently situated on the Phillips Academy campus. Pets welcome. Parking free. Typewriter loan service. Restaurant serves breakfast, lunch, cocktails, dinner.

Tel. 475–5903.

Merrimack Valley Motor Inn. Contemporary colonial charm is prevalent here. Pool. Pets welcome. Restaurant serves breakfast, lunch, cocktails, dinner.
Chickering Rd. (tel. 688–1851).

CAMBRIDGE

First Class

Charterhouse Motor Hotel. You can look across the Charles River to Boston here. Pool and patio. Pets welcome. *Five Chateaux* restaurant; cocktail lounge. Hotel Corp. of America owned.
Tel. 491–3600.

Treadway Motor House. Traditional Treadway Inn hospitality here with complimentary continental breakfast. Pets welcome. Good for families. Short drive to downtown Boston.
110 Mt. Auburn St. (tel. UN 4–5200).

Reasonable

Continental Hotel. Just minutes away from downtown Boston, this comfortable hotel is known for *Piccadilly Inn* restaurant—good food and grog. Pets welcome.
Near Harvard Square (tel. KI 7–6100).

Sheraton Commander Hotel. Some rooms have kitchenettes here. Convenient to historic sites and colleges. *Golden Steer Restaurant;* cocktails. Free parking. Pets welcome. Barber, beautician.
Cambridge Common (tel. 499–9215).

CONCORD

First Class

Colonial Inn. This historic landmark was built in 1716. Restaurant, cocktail lounge, men's bar. No charge for parking.
Monument Square (tel. EM 9–4600).

Concordian. Country estate setting adds to the beauty of this motel. Pool. Pets welcome. No charge for continental breakfast.
Hosmer St. (tel. 263–7765).

Howard Johnson's Motor Lodge. This new, chain-owned motel is always a dependable place to stay. Pool. Pets welcome. Restaurant. Cocktail lounge.
Elm St. (tel. 369–6100).

FRAMINGHAM

Deluxe

Fonda del Corro. "Inn of the friendly circle" is the translation for this Spanish-accented motel; dramatic decor. Pool. Elevators. Famous *Maridor* restaurant part of motel.
Route 9 (tel. 872–6503).

First Class

Caesar's Monticello. This lively motel has a plush supper club featuring top name performers. Across from *Shopper's World.* 15 min. drive to Boston. Restaurant.
Route 9 (tel. 875–1394).

Holiday Inn. This chain-operated, attractive motel emphasizes hospitality with free coffee dispensers in rooms. Pool. Family plan. Pets welcome. Restaurant. Cocktail lounge.
30 Worcester Rd. Route 9 (tel. 875–0053).

GLOUCESTER

First Class

Atlantis Motor Inn. Enjoy the ocean view from your room, or patio. Pool. Access to golf. Closed Dec. to Feb. Off-season prices.
Atlantic Rd., Bass Rocks (tel. 283–0014).

Bass Rocks Motor Inn. Surrounded by a grand expanse of land, this new motel has an outstanding view of the ocean. Pool; sundeck. Light breakfast. Near restaurant. Closed Nov. to Mar.
Scenic Shore Dr. (tel. 283–7600).

Good Harbor Beach Inn. Bask in the sun and enjoy the cool ocean breezes on your patio. Room rate includes continental breakfast. Snack bar. Cozy lounge. Summer season.
Brier Neck (tel. 283–1489).

Rockaway Hotel. Here the room rate includes breakfast and dinner. *Beauport Room* open to public also. Cocktail lounge. Free parking. Access to marina. Open extended summer season.
7 Rockcliff St. (tel. 283–7466).

Reasonable

The Anchorage Hotel. Take your skin-diving gear along—there's a school nearby. Pleasant family vacation spot. Picnic grounds; recreation area. Free parking. Open summer season.
5 Hawthorne Lane (tel. 283–4788).

GREAT BARRINGTON

First Class

Jug End In the Berkshires. Sports galore are featured on the 1,600 acres of this popular all-year round resort. Top-notch skiing facilities. Pool. Fishing. Tennis instructors. Sauna. Restaurant, cocktail lounge, entertainment.
So. Egremont (tel. Great Barrington 434).

Reasonable

Barrington House. There's a fresh, new look now that this well-established hotel has been re-decorated. Restaurant; cocktail lounge. Barber, beautician, pharmacy. Free parking.
Route 7 (tel. 1840).

Briarcliff Motor Lodge. Pleasant for families here—even the family pet. Recreation area. Near restaurant. Low off-season prices.
Route 7 (tel. 1950).

Brookbend Inn. This cozy historic inn features art exhibits. Choice of room rates with or without meals. Restaurant; cocktails.
General Knox Trail, Monterey (tel. 528–2300).

Fairfield Inn. Here at this old-fashioned inn, you may admire the many antiques. Children under 14 not permitted. Restaurant. Access to golf.
S. Egremont Rd. (tel. 706).

The Flying Cloud Motel. This all-year resort features seasonal sports, with emphasis on tennis. Fresh-water pond for swimming, rink for ice-skating. Room rate includes meals. Hundreds of acres.
New Marlboro (tel. 229–2113).

Golden Eagle Motel. Expect higher prices during Tanglewood weekends here. Off-season prices are low. Colonial motif with carpeting. Pets welcome. Near restaurant.
Route 7 (tel. 574).

Monument Mountain Motel. You will like the hospitable touch of electric blankets in most rooms. Recreation and picnic area. Family plan.
Route 7 (tel. 134).

Mountain View Motel. Pleasant custom of free juice and coffee in the morning here. Pets welcome. Good skiing about a mile away.
Route 23 (tel. 969).

HOLYOKE

First Class

Howard Johnson's Motor Lodge. This bright and cheerful motel, is one of a dependable chain. Family plan. Free coffee dispensers. Restaurant. Pool.
Tel. JE 6–1440.

Reasonable

Riviera Motel. Skiers take note: Mt. Tom Ski area is nearby. Pretty river view. Play area. Breakfast only. Nearby restaurant.
Route 5 (tel. 536–3377).

Yankee Pedlar Inn. Just a few guest rooms in this colonial inn, but they are comfortable and attractive. Excellent restaurant; cocktail lounge. One of Early American Inns, Inc.
Route 5 (tel. 532–9494).

LENOX

First Class

The Edgewood Motel. In summer, you are near music festival grounds; in winter, ski areas. Free coffee dispensers. Pool. Coffee shop from 5 to 12 p.m. Cocktail lounge. Near restaurant open from 6:30 a.m.

Route 7 (tel. 637–3000).

Reasonable

Avaloch Inn. This country inn resort, open all year, is across the road from Tanglewood. Lively *Five Seasons Steak and Ale House*. Dancing in gazebo. Poolside barbecues. Ski trails.

Tel. 637–9706.

Curtis Hotel. Although you are in the center of town, pool and patio provide resort atmosphere. Variety of sports. Pets welcome. Restaurant, cocktail lounge. Room rates with or without meals.

Tel. 637–0016.

Eastover. This year-around resort presents a program of summer and winter sports. Indoor and outdoor pools. Top ski area. Pets welcome—horses, too. Entertainment. Popular with single set. Rates include meals.

Tel. 637–0625.

MALDEN

Reasonable

New Englander Motor Court. Pleasant hotel with hospitable service of free light breakfast. Family rates. Pets welcome.

551 Broadway (tel. 321–0505).

Robin Hood Motor Lodge. This popular motel has many conveniences, including beautician, free coffee dispensers, no charge for cribs or irons. Special family plan. King-size pool.

321 Broadway (tel. 324–8500).

Town Line Motel. Relax at this attractive motel with extra-large swimming pool and play area. Family plan. Pets welcome.

735 Broadway (tel. 324–7400).

NEW BEDFORD

Reasonable

Capri Motel. Courteous service here includes free continental breakfast. Pool. Seasonal rates.

Route 6 (tel. 997–7877).

Chateau Motel. Many of the rooms have a good hillside view. Room rate includes continental breakfast. Pets welcome. Restaurant for dinner and late snacks; cocktails from 8 p.m.

829 American Legion Highway (tel. 636–2235).

New Bedford Hotel. You will enjoy New England hospitality here. Family plans. Pets welcome. Barber, beautician. *Spouter Inn-Jolly Whaler Bar* popular restaurant.

725 Pleasant St. (tel. WY 6–8521).

Young's Court. Privacy from the highway is accented here. Play area. Continental breakfast service. Restaurant nearby.

Tel. ME 6–2776.

NORTHAMPTON

First Class

Schine Northampton Inn. Old New England is emphasized at this hospitable hotel. Pets welcome. Family plan. *Wiggins Tavern* restaurant; cocktail lounge.

36 King St. (tel. JU 4–3100).

Reasonable

Country Belle. This charming motel presents a warm welcome with fireplace in entrance. Family plan. Pool. Nearby restaurant.

Route 9 (tel. JU 6–0715).

The Jenny Lind Motel. This pleasant motel has free coffee dispensers in each room. Family rates. Pool.

Route 5 (tel. 247–5502).

PITTSFIELD

First Class

The Springs Motor Inn. This motel has a very popular restaurant. Free

coffee dispensers in rooms. Pool. Game area.
Route 7 (tel. GL 8–5945).

Wendell-Sherwood. You will find the convenience of barber, beautician, and pharmacy right in this hotel. Rates go up during Berkshire Music Festival weekends. Free parking. Pets welcome. Family plan. Popular restaurant; cocktail lounge.
Route 7 (tel. 443–9334).

Reasonable

Golden Key. This well-equipped motel welcomes pets. Pool. Rates go up from July to Labor Day. Restaurant nearby.
1055 South St. (tel. 443–4714).

PLYMOUTH

Reasonable

Pilgrim Sands Motel. This new motel has its own beach. Nearby restaurant. Open Apr. to Nov.
Warren Ave. (tel. 746–4360).

Yankee Traveler. As an added inducement during the off-season, this pleasant motel serves a continental breakfast gratis. Pets welcome. Play area.
Warren Ave. (tel. PI 6–3000).

Inexpensive

Cadillac Motel. Some of these pretty, pine-panelled rooms have wider doorways to accommodate wheelchairs. Pets welcome. Rates go down after Labor Day. Nearby restaurant.
Route 3 (tel. PI 6–1900).

ROCKPORT

Reasonable

Peg Leg Motel. This popular motel owns a famous restaurant by the same name, about a block away. Nice-size rooms here.
10 Beach St. (tel. 546–6945).

Seaward Inn. Here artists and photographers will be inspired by the beautiful ocean view and bird-sanctuary. Access to golf course, tennis courts. Room rate includes meals. Open May to Oct.
Marmion Way (tel. 546–6792).

Straitsmouth Inn. Here you have a good ocean view and access to beach. Family plan. Room rates with and without meals. Pets welcome. *Golden Oar Restaurant* features seafood.
Gap Head Rd. (tel. 546–2900).

Yankee Clipper Inn. Many rooms here have a beautiful view of the ocean and gardens. Pool. Free parking. Room rates with and without meals. Very good dining room. Open Apr. to Nov.
127 Granite St. (tel. 546–3407).

SPRINGFIELD

First Class

Arrow Head Motel. Any time you want a meal or snack, the nearby restaurant is open around the clock. Pools; play area. Pets welcome. Coffee shop for breakfast only. Off-season prices.
1573 Riverdale St. (tel. 736–5416).

The Schine Inn. Here you have a little city in itself—restaurants, cocktail lounges, barber, beautician, bowling, ice-skating. Pool. Patio service.
Mass. Turnpike Exit 6 (tel. LY 2–7751).

Reasonable

Black Horse Motel. Here you have a convenient location to the Eastern States Exposition grounds. Pool. Play area. Family plan. Off-season prices. Nearby restaurant.
Route 5 (tel. RE 3–2161).

Corral Motel. Away from highway noise, this pleasant hotel has a pool and picnic facilities. Pets welcome—or horse boarded. Breakfast only.
Route 5 (tel. 732–6272).

Federal Plaza Motel. On top of Federal Hill, this motel features pool, restaurant, cocktail lounge—and con-

venience to downtown. Pets welcome. Family plan.
50 Federal St. (tel. ST 8–7371).

Howard Johnson's Motor Lodge. This large motel is one of a very dependable chain dotting the U.S.A. Pets welcome. Pool. Game area. Restaurant.
333 Columbus Ave. (tel. 734–8211).

Seven Gables. So pleasant to go boating, swimming, or water-skiing on the lake. Picnic facilities. Pets welcome. Pool. Restaurant.
1356 Boston Rd. (tel. 782–2351).

Sheraton Motor Inn. Service clubs meet at this popular motel. Free coffee dispensers in rooms. Pets welcome. Restaurant; cocktail lounge, entertainment. Laundry, too.
70 Chestnut St. (tel. RE 4–3141).

Westover Motel. This well-equipped motel is convenient to Westover Air Force Base. Family plan. Pool.
Mass. Turnpike Exit 5 (tel. 536–0570).

West Springfield Motel. Friendly atmosphere prevails here. Breakfast and lunch in coffee shop. Nearby restaurant never closes. Pool.
437 Riverdale St. (tel. ST 5–5365).

STURBRIDGE

Deluxe

Sturbridge Orchard Inn. On a hillside away from highway noise, this beautiful motel has both a swimming pool and wading pool. Play area. Pets welcome. Rooms for wheelchairs. Restaurant; cocktails.
Haynes St., Route 15. (tel. 347–9555).

First Class

Treadway-Sturbridge Motor Inn. If you happen to stay here any time from Nov. to May, remember free breakfast is served. Pets welcome. Away from highway noise. Nearby restaurant.
Route 15 (tel. 347–3391).

Reasonable

Colonial Motel. Relaxation is the keynote here. Pool, play area, picnic grounds. Restaurant. Off-season prices.
Route 20 (tel. 347–3306).

Liberty Gap Motel. This motel is at the Old Sturbridge Village entrance, and next door to *Governor Lincoln House Restaurant.* Off-season prices.
Route 20 (tel. 347–3327).

Publick House. This well-known Treadway Inn has old-fashioned, comfortable rooms with modern conveniences. Pets welcome. Free parking. Dining room; cocktail lounge.
Main St. (tel. 347–3313).

WILLIAMSTOWN

First Class

1896 Motel. Relax on the porch at this peacefully-situated motel. Less expensive from Nov. to May. 1896 House restaurant very popular; cocktails.
Cold Spring Rd. (tel. GL 8–5935).

Reasonable

Berkshire Hills Motel. It's a good idea to reserve ahead for Tanglewood weekends (rates go up then, too). Complimentary coffee. Pool. Rates go down off-season. Nearby restaurant.
Tel. 458–3950.

Elwal Pines Motor Inn. Inn and motel are combined here. Complimentary coffee dispensers in motel rooms. Pets welcome in inn only. Pool. Play area. Excellent restaurant.
Cold Spring Rd. (tel. 458–4267).

Williams Inn. This beautiful, rambling inn has well-decorated colonial rooms with views of Williams College campus and garden bird sanctuary. Family plan. Dining room; cocktail lounge. Pets welcome. Convenient to Tanglewood, Sterling Clark Art Institute, Green Mountain Raceway.
Tel. 458–5711.

WORCESTER

First Class

Howard Johnson's Motor Lodge. One of a famous chain, this motel is new. Pools. Family plan. Restaurant.

181 W. Boylston St. (tel. 835–4456).

Yankee Drummer Motor House. One of the well-known Early American Inns, Inc., this motel has decorator-furnished rooms. Pool. Yankee atmosphere in restaurant; cocktail lounge.

Mass. Turnpike Exit 10, Auburn (tel. 832–3221).

Reasonable

Holiday Inn. One of a well-known chain, this motel is convenient to downtown. Pool. Dining room, cocktail lounge.

Myrtle and Southbridge sts. (tel. 791–2291).

Pleasant Valley Motor Lodge. This new, handsome motel provides country club privileges. Access to pool. Dining room; cocktails.

Route 146 (tel. 865–5222).

ELSEWHERE

AMHERST. *Amherst Motel.* Reasonable. Hospitality includes room coffee dispenser and continental breakfast, free. Pool. Convenient restaurant. Family foursome rates. Northhampton Rd. Tel. 253–2509.

Lord Jeffery. The innkeeper makes sure guests are happy at this Treadway Inn. Dining room for breakfast, lunch, dinner. Cocktail lounge. Historic *Plimpton* papers in parlor. Old-fashioned charm. On Village Green. Tel. AL 3–2576.

BRAINTREE. *Charter House.* First class. This resort-style motel is especially attractive in summer with gay patio and pool activity. Restaurant, cocktail lounge. Pets welcome. About 10 mi. from Boston. Route 128. Tel. 848–0600.

DALTON. *Crane Inn.* Reasonable. The sports enthusiast will like the convenience here to riding, swimming, golfing, and skiing areas. Pets welcome. Free coffee dispensers. Restaurant. Cocktail lounge. Free parking. Main St. Tel. 684–2814.

DANVERS. *King's Grant Motor Inn.* First class. Here the accent is on hospitality. Family plan. No charge for continental breakfast. Pool. Restaurant. Cocktail lounge; weekend dancing. Route 128. Tel. 774–6800.

Village Green Motor Inn. First class. This attractive motel features two pools —one for children. Pets welcome. Continental breakfast served free. Restaurant; cocktail lounge (weekend dancing). Tel. 774–6550.

DEDHAM. *Hotel 128.* First class. Arrive in style in a helicopter from Logan Airport! Little city in itself with barber, beautician, health club, pool, coffee shop, restaurant, cocktail lounge. Coffee dispensers in rooms. Deluxe suites. Dancing weekends. Elm St. Tel. DA 6–6700.

DEERFIELD. *Deerfield Inn.* Reasonable. This typical New England inn is part of Old Deerfield Village restoration. Relax with book or watch television in parlor. Dining room. Closed middle of Dec. to first week in Jan. Village St. Tel. 773–3838.

FALL RIVER. *4-D Motel.* Reasonable. This is a pleasant place to stay and wake up to a complimentary continental breakfast. Nearby restaurant. Park at door. Route 6. Tel. 678–9071.

FITCHBURG. *Coach House Inn.* Reasonable. Recently, this traditional inn was renovated and refurbished. Pool. Play area. Access to golf course. Restaurant; cocktails. Routes 2A and 13.

Thunderbird Motor Lodge. Reasonable. This is a good place for families to stay. Pool. Play area. Light breakfast served. Cocktail lounge. 299 Lunenburg St. Tel. 342–6001.

GREENFIELD. *Candle Light Motel.* Reasonable. Here you have an excellent location on the Mohawk Trail. Restaurant nearby. Family plan. Route 2. Tel. 772–0101.

Oxbow Motel. Reasonable. Lots of fun for the family here with playground, golf-course, pool. Pleasant restaurant and cocktail lounge. Route 2. Tel. 625–6729.

LAWRENCE. *Holiday Inn.* Reasonable. Here you will enjoy all the comforts of this well-known motel chain. Pool. Pets welcome. Family plan. Coffee shop never closes. Restaurant, cocktail lounge. 333 Winthrop Ave. Tel. 686–9411.

Lamplighter Motel. Reasonable. This two-level motel is a pleasant place to stay—take along the family pet, too. Restaurant, cocktail lounge. Family plan. Route 28. Tel. 686–3901.

LEE. *Laurel Hill Motel.* Reasonable. Here you have convenience to summer sport areas. Free coffee dispensers. Prices go up Tanglewood festival weekends. Nearby restaurant never closes. Laurel St. Tel. 243–0813.

Oak 'N' Spruce. Reasonable to first class. This hotel-motel resort offers a choice of rooms from plain-but-pleasant to hillside Japanese-style units. Pool. Organized activities. Social skiing. Variety of sports. Restaurant, cocktail lounge, entertainment. Tel. 243–3500.

LEOMINSTER. *Leominster Motel.* Reasonable. Relax under the oak trees, or take a dip in the pool at this pleasant motel. Breakfast, snack bar. 665 Central St. Tel. KE 7–1741.

LEXINGTON. *Battle Green Motor Inn.* First class. This attractive motel has more comforts than home—color TV in lounge, pool, beautician, heated garages (free). Popular Heritage Room restaurant. 1720 Mass. Ave. Tel. VO 2–6100.

Lexington Motor Inn. First class. Families enjoy staying at this beautifully-landscaped motel, as it's near new Minute Men National Park. Pets welcome. Restaurant. Marrett Rd. Tel. 862–8700.

LOWELL. *Howard Johnson's Motor Lodge.* First class. Practice on the putting green here or swim in the pool. Free coffee dispensers. Family plan. Pets welcome. Restaurant. Tel. 256–6584.

LYNN. *Charter House Motor Hotel.* First class. Here you have bay view plus attractive rooms. Pool; play area. Pets welcome. Family plan. Restaurant, cocktail lounge. 830 The Lynnway. Tel. 598–6080.

NATICK. *Natick Travelodge.* This two-level motel has both swimming pool and lifeguard. Family plan. Restaurant is close by. Also near shopping center. 1350 Worcester St. Tel. 655–2222.

NEEDHAM. *Hotel 128.* First class. Fly to Logan Airport on chartered helicopter from here. Facilities include barber. Pool. Free coffee dispensers in rooms. Family plan. Restaurant; cocktails. 100 Cabot St. Tel. 444–8900.

NEWBURYPORT. *Wayside Motel.* Reasonable. These well-equipped rooms feature free coffee dispensers. Play area. Restaurant for breakfast and dinner; cocktail lounge. Central St. Tel. 462–4704.

NEWTON. *Charter House Motor Hotel.* First class. Some rooms are poolside at this well-decorated motel. Family plan. Pets welcome. Restaurant; cocktail lounge. 160 Boylston St. Tel. 527–9000.

NORTHFIELD. *The Northfield Inn.* Reasonable. This informal family resort is open all year around with a diversified sports program—everything from tennis to skiing. Planned entertainment. Pool. Room rate includes meals. Free parking. Tel. 498–5341.

PEABODY. *The Carriage House.* Reasonable. Here you have the protection of a lifeguard at the king-size pool. Room rate includes continental breakfast. Pets welcome. 111 Newbury St. Tel. 535–1300.

The Victorian Motor Inn. Reasonable. Children have their own little pool here—the big one is for grownups. Pets welcome. Play area. Nearby restaurant. Seasonal rates. 233 Andover St. Tel. 531–8800.

QUINCY. *Sheraton Motor Inn.* First class. There's elevator service in this attractive motel. Pets welcome. Good restaurant and cocktail lounge. Pool. 29 Hancock St. Tel. GR 1–1500.

Presidents' City Motel. Reasonable. Here you have the advantage of Winfield House, the motel's famous dining room. Cocktail lounge. Play area for children. 845 Hancock St. Tel. GR 9–6500.

SALEM. *Hawthorne Hotel.* Reasonable. Here you have the historic location of Salem Common. Notice antiques in dining room. Family plan. Free parking. 18 Washington Square. Tel. 744–4080.

Pilgrim Motel. Reasonable. This fairly new motel has some units with kitchens. Pool. Restaurant nearby. Rates go down off-season. 40 Bridge St. Tel. 745–2000.

SALISBURY. *Henry's Tourist Court* and *Sun 'N Sand Motel.* Reasonable. Take your choice—motel room or cottage with kitchen. Play area. Pool. Picnic grounds. Pets welcome. Off-season prices go down. Restaurant. Just a short drive to Salisbury Beach. 250 Beach Rd. Tel. 462–6341.

SAUGUS. *Dean's.* Reasonable. Here you have convenience to shops and restaurant. Family plan. Free coffee dispenser in rooms. Rates go down off-season. 718 Broadway. Tel. 233–1717.

SHEFFIELD. *Blue Belton Resort and Motor Lodge.* Reasonable. Fun for the entire family here—wading pool and play area for children; a diversified sports program for adults. Nearby skiing. Resort rates include meals; motel rates, without meals. Restaurant, cocktail lounge and motel open summer only. Route 7. Tel. 229–2162.

Stagecoach Hill Inn. Reasonable. This friendly country inn is open all year around. Comfortable rooms. Interesting restaurant; cocktails. Route 41. Tel. 229–2012.

STOCKBRIDGE. *Red Lion & Motor Lodge.* Reasonable. Old-fashioned atmosphere prevails at this summer resort. Modern facilities include pool. Pets welcome. Rooms with or without meals. Free parking. Restaurant and cocktail lounge open to public. Tel. 298–5545.

SUDBURY. *Longfellow's Wayside Inn.* Reasonable. This is a fascinating inn, the oldest operating inn in the U.S.A. About 10 rooms. Antique-filled public rooms. Authentic colonial recipes served in restaurant. Free parking. On more than 100 acres. Mass. Turnpike Exit 12. Tel. HI 3–8846.

SWAMPSCOTT. *New Ocean House.* Deluxe. Whether you stay in the main house or cottages, vacations are fun here. King size pool, lifeguard. Patio snack bar. Directors for sports and entertainment. Dance lessons, health club, barber, beautician. Room rate with meals in summer; without meals off-season. Restaurant; cocktails. 216 Puritan Rd. Tel. 592–6500.

Colony Motor Hotel. First class. From your balcony, enjoy the ocean view (private beach). Pools, play area. Patio. Restaurant; cocktail lounge (entertainment). 441 Atlantic Ave. Tel. 593–6600.

WAKEFIELD. *Lord Wakefield Motor Hotel.* Reasonable. The scenic lakeside location is an advantage here. Pool; game area. Coffee shop and dining room. 595 North Ave. Tel. 245–6100.

WALTHAM. *Charter House Motel.* First class. Businessmen will like the advantage of a heliport here. Pool, play area. Pets welcome. Family plan. Open-hearth restaurant. Winter St. Tel. TW 9–8700.

Holiday Inn (formerly *Waltham Motor Inn*). First class. Charter a helicopter here to expedite your trip. Pool. Family plan. *Gourmet Room* restaurant, cocktail lounge, entertainment weekends. Totten Pond Rd. Tel. 899–3000.

WEST BROOKFIELD. *Copper Lantern Motor Lodge.* Reasonable. Take your fishing gear along and try your luck in lake across the way. Free coffee dispensers in rooms. Pets welcome. Restaurant nearby. Route 9. Tel. 867–6441.

WESTFIELD. *Berkshire Hills Motel.* Reasonable. Summertime hospitality here includes continental breakfast with the room rate. Pool. Access to golf course. Rates go down off-season. Coffee shop for breakfast only. Route 20. Tel. LO 8–8157.

Westfield Motor Lodge. Reasonable. Balconies add distinction to this two-level motel. Pool. Pets welcome. Restaurant for breakfast and dinner; just breakfast Sun. Route 202. Tel. LO 8–8611.

WESTMINSTER. *Westminster Village.* Reasonable prices, first class mood. In keeping with the colonial motif, this motel features fireplaces in some rooms. Pool. Play area. Coffee shop for breakfast. *Old Mill Restaurant* nearby (same management). Route 2. Tel. 874–5911.

YOUTH HOSTELS. The *Greater Boston Council of Youth Hostels* is located at 683 Atlantic Ave., Room 355, Boston. Tel. HA 6–8595. This is a listing of some hostels, rate about $1 to $1.50 a night: *Boston,* Christ Church Youth Hostel, 1620 Dorchester Ave. Open June 22 to Sept. 8. *Eastham,* Smith's Seashore Shelters Youth Hostel, Bridge Rd. Open Apr. 19 to Oct. 12. *East Sandwich,* Skiff House Youth Hostel, US 6A. Open June 15 to Oct. 1. *Gloucester,* Louise S. Spring Memorial Park Youth Hostel, Atlantic St. Open June 20 to Labor Day. *Granville,* Old Lilacs Youth Hostel, off State 179. Open May 15 to Sept. 15. *Great Barrington,* Taylemme, off State 23. Open year round. *Harvard,* Friendly Crossways Youth Hostel (off Old Littleton County and Schoolhouse Rds.). Open year round. *Nantucket,* Star of the Sea Youth Hostel. At Atlantic Ave. and Surfside Rd. June 10 to Labor Day. *New Bedford,* YMCA Day Camp, The Shining Tides Youth Hostel. Off US 6, Mattapoisett. Open June to Sept. *Pittsfield,* Pittsfield YMCA Day Camp Youth Hostel. Off US 7. Open May 15 to Sept. 15. *Sheffield,* Mount Everett Youth Hostel, State 41. Open May 15 to Oct. 15. *Springfield,* Springfield College Camp Youth Hostel, 701 Wilbraham Rd. Open July 1 to Sept. 1. *Sudbury,* Elbanobscot Foundation, Inc. On Weir Hill Rd. Open June 15 to Sept. 5. *Sunderland,* Little Meadow Youth Hostel, off State 47. Open June to Sept. *Swansea,* Hayloft Youth Hostel. Open May 30 to Oct. 15. *Martha's Vineyard,* West Tisbury, Lillian Manter Memorial Youth Hostel. Open May 1 to Sept. 15, and by arrangement. *Yarmouth,* Captain Hallet Youth Hostel, 165 Main St. Open May to Oct.

FARM VACATIONS AND GUEST RANCHES. *Evergreen Farm.* For reservations in any of the three double rooms, contact the Easterbrooks, Dudley Farm, Dudley. Near *Sturbridge Village.* Adults $50 with meals; children $35 to $40 a week with meals. *Sea View Farm.* This 100-acre dairy farm and dude ranch is on *Cape Ann.* Four housekeeping apartments. $70 a week without meals. Contact the Lanes, Sea View Farm, Rockport. *Lost Wilderness Ranch.* About 90 rooms are available at this 1,000-acre ranch. Rates from $75 to $120 a week with ranch-style meals. Contact Gladys Cavellier, Lost Wilderness Ranch, Sandisfield.

CAMPING OUT. Campers are in luck in Massachusetts, with more than 50 places for overnight camping. From May 1 to Oct. 15, tent and trailer sites are available at $1.50 per day. The time limit for camping out at one place is two weeks. If you don't have your own tent, state-owned tents on platforms are $3 a day; tent platforms are $2.

The *Mohawk Trail State Forest* is in Charlemont on State 2, along the Mohawk Trail. Tent or trailer sites are available, also overnight cabins on some 6,000 acres. *Mount Greylock State Reservation,* south of North Adams, contains Mt. Greylock, highest mountain in Massachusetts. Campers will find a lodge for meals on the mountain. *Mount Tom State Reservation* near Holyoke, on US 5, has ten campsites and four trailer sites. Gates close at 9 p.m. Plymouth has *Myles Standish State Forest* with tent sites, trailer sites, and cabins on more than 10,000 acres.

A privately-owned campground is in *Provincetown,* Cape Cod. *Dunes' Edge Camp Ground* on US 6 has 75 campsites, 12 trailer sites, and all facilities (pets on leash allowed). Reservations are accepted; tel. 8604. The campgrounds are open from May 15 to Oct. 1. *Cape Cod* also is the site of *Bourne Scenic Park* near Buzzards Bay where 150 tent sites are available, also trailer sites, and many facilities.

TRAILER TIPS. Legal trailer size (without permits) is 33 feet (for mobile home) length, 8 feet wide at the base. No regulation as to height. Permits, information from Burton C. Parker, Maintenance Engineer, Mass. Dept. of Public Works, 100 Nashua St., Boston 14, Mass. Tel. CA 7–7800 (ext. 520).

In Charlemont, the *Mohawk Trail State Forest* on State 2 has trailer and tent sites. *Mount Tom State Reservation,* Holyoke, has room for 4 trailers and 10 campsites. *Crystal Springs Campground* in Bolton has 60 trailer sites and 120 campsites, electricity, toilets, showers, swimming; pets allowed on leash. The fee is $2 for four. This is privately-owned. *North Truro Camping Area,* North Truro, on Cape Cod has 50 trailer sites; 150 campsites. Open all year round. Rates are $2 a day for 1 to 3 persons, or $13 a week. There is no hook-up for regular house trailers (only camp trailers). The camp has hot showers, lavatories, and a laundromat. *Maurice's Tent & Trailer Park* on US 6, South Wellfleet, Cape Cod, has 50 trailer sites, toilets, electricity, drinking water. Fee is $2 for 3.

Rand McNally's *Guidebook to Campgrounds* is a complete directory of family camping.

DINING OUT. Although the culinary world is well-represented in the state from Oriental delicacies in Boston's Chinatown to Portuguese specialties on Cape Cod, typical foods are Cape scallops, Ipswich clams, Cotuit oysters, native lobster, scrod (baby codfish), codfish, halibut, swordfish, haddock, flounder. Typical meals are fish cakes, brown bread, Boston baked beans (on Saturday night), and New England boiled dinner (corned beef simmered with cabbage, potatoes, turnips, and onions). Baked Indian pudding is a favorite dessert. In summer, it's blueberry pie with native berries.

ANDOVER

Reasonable–First Class

Ivanhoe Room. No knight ever had it so good—charcoal-broiled steak impaled on flaming sword. Heraldic decor. Children's menu. Cocktails. Breakfast, lunch, dinner.

In Sheraton Rolling Green Motel, Lowell St., jct. State 133 and Interstate 93.

Reasonable

Andover Inn. Yankee hospitality, good food and grog combine for enjoyable dining in this well-decorated Treadway Inn. Children's menu. Open for breakfast, lunch, dinner. Near Phillips Academy.

Chapel Ave., s. off State 28.

Fieldstones. New England favorites with a gourmet flair are graciously served in rustic farmhouse. Unusual

vegetable recipes. Delicious home-baked breads. Cocktails, also. Children's menu. Open at noon for lunch and dinner.
400 S. Main St., State 28.

CAMBRIDGE

First Class

Five Chateaux. An award winner, and rightly so. A lovely view of the Charles River and Boston skyline adds to dining pleasure. Lunch, dinner. Cocktails. Mon. through Fri. Dinner only, Sat. and Sun. Parking free.
In Charter House Hotel, Cambridge Pkwy.

Reasonable–First Class

Chez Dreyfus. French specialties, such as *escalopes de veau cordon bleu,* are delicious. Cocktails. Lunch, dinner. Closed Sun. Dinner patrons have free parking.
44 Church St., Harvard Sq.

Reasonable

Window Shop. Don't forget to look into this restaurant, presumably the home of the Village Blacksmith (Dexter Pratt) in Longfellow's poem. Excellent menu from wiener schnitzel to tempting pastries. Summer dining in garden. Cocktails. Lunch, dinner daily, except Sun. in winter season.
56 Brattle St.

Yard of Ale. Here they not only serve ale (by the yard in the elongated glass) but also cook with it—shrimps in ale batter. Pleasant, costumed waitresses. Chophouse motif. Lunch, dinner, including Sun.
9 Brattle St., Harvard Sq.

Inexpensive–Reasonable

St. Clair's. This pleasant restaurant, one of a chain, has everything from blueberry pancakes to Irish coffee. Children's menu. Open daily for breakfast, lunch, dinner, except Christmas Day.
9 Brattle St.

FRAMINGHAM

First Class

Abner Wheeler House. Pre-Revolutionary mansion features Southern-style pan-fried chicken, pecan rolls, pecan pie. Extensive menu. Cocktails. Open for lunch and dinner.
State 9.

1812 House. Traditional Colonial atmosphere and Yankee cooking are the highlights here. Pan-fried chicken is a specialty. Cocktails. Children's menu. Lunch, dinner.
11 Salem End Rd., State 9.

Ken's Steak House. This replica of a Normandy farmhouse has 5 dining rooms. Open hearth for steak and lobster in *Cafe Five* room. Own recipe for pecan pie. Cocktails. Lunch, dinner.
State 9.

Maridor. This glamorous restaurant has a variety from seafood platters to shish kebab. Lunch specials. Sun. is Family Day. Dancing nightly in cocktail lounge. Lunch, dinner daily. Next to *Fonda del Corro* inn.
State 9.

Red Coach Grill. This excellent chain-operated restaurant has the extra attraction of a lake view. Charcoal-broiled steaks a specialty. Cocktails. Rustic decor. Lunch, dinner. Closed Christmas Day.
State 9.

Reasonable–First Class

Sea 'n Surf. Briny-deep atmosphere is luxurious with new carpeting and new furniture. *Yacht Club Lounge.* T-bone steak and chicken specials. Lobster pound (plans to double the size). Open lunch, dinner, cocktails.
State 9.

GLOUCESTER

First Class

Blacksmith Shop Inn. Unusual specialties here include cold blueberry soup —refreshing. Hearty shore dinner. Chil-

dren's menu. Luncheon buffet. Home-baked pies. Open for lunch and dinner. Cocktails. Closed Dec. to March.
87 Atlantic Ave., Bass Rocks.

Reasonable

Finnerty's Lobster & Steak House. Select your lobster from the pool. Children's menu. Cocktails. On landing for river boat ride. Open for lunch and dinner. Seasonal.
Rocky Neck Ave.

Gloucester House Restaurant. While enjoying seafood at this wharfside restaurant, watch the fishing boats from the window. Suggestions: shore dinner, fried Ipswich clams. Home-baked pies. Cocktails. Lunch, dinner, except Mon. Extended summer season.
Seven Seas Wharf.

HOLYOKE

Reasonable–First Class

River Lodge. This attractive restaurant was a private, river-bank estate. Suggestions: escargots, Dover sole. Cocktails. Dinner only, Sun. from 1 p.m. Closed Mon. Also closed from end of Nov. to Good Fri.
Follow sign at corner of State 33 and State 116.

Reasonable

Log Cabin. Hillside view and interior decoration with seasonal flowers are part of enjoyable dining here. Cocktail chuck wagon on patio in summer. New England dishes. Open for lunch and dinner.
Easthampton Rd.

Yankee Pedlar Inn. This is the original of the excellent Early American Inns, Inc. Antique decor. Yankee cooking. Home-baked pastries. Cocktails. Open for lunch and dinner. Closed Christmas Day.
1866 Northampton St.

LENOX

Reasonable

Curtis Hotel. This well-known resort hotel is near Tanglewood. *Old Stage Grill* popular. Breakfast, lunch, dinner—and poolside snacks.
Walker and Main Sts.

Five Reasons Steak and Ale House. One reason for popularity is the 30 varieties of imported beer. Half-pound charcoal-broiled hamburgers and steaks. Entertainment. Open all year.
In Avaloch Inn, opposite Tanglewood.

Lenox House. New in 1963, this restaurant has quickly become popular. Suggestions: scampi, roast beef. Homemade relishes, rolls, pies. Children's menu. Cocktails. Open for lunch and dinner.
1 mi. n. on US 7.

The Potting Shed. Once a countess' greenhouse, now a supper club featuring north Italian cuisine. Top folk and jazz entertainment. Dinner only. Closed Mon. Usually opens July 3 for summer—check ahead.
Next to Berkshire Music Barn (tel. 637–3313).

PITTSFIELD

First Class

Ida and John's. Whether you win or lose at nearby Berkshire Downs Raceway, you will enjoy dining here. Recipient of dining awards. Lunch, dinner, cocktails till 1 a.m. in racing season. Otherwise, open at 5 p.m., Sun. from noon.
4 mi. w. on US 20.

The Springs. There are at least 30 entrées on the menu, prepared to order. Oven-fresh rolls and pies. Children's menu. Cocktails. Open for lunch and dinner. Closed Christmas Day.
9 mi. n. on US 7.

Reasonable–First Class

Copper Pin. Diversified dining here with a *French Room* for continental dishes; Oriental cocktail lounge. Snack bar next to bowling lanes. Dancing by swimming pool in *Bubble Room.* Canopy held high by climate-controlled air. Different.
E. at Lyman St.

Reasonable

Berkshire Restaurant. The specialty here is a tasty clam sauce served on spaghetti. King-size cocktails. Children's menu. Lunch and dinner, except Mon.
143 West St.

Yellow Aster. This attractive restaurant has a varied menu and home-like atmosphere. Suggestions: trout, roast duckling. Cocktails. Lunch and dinner, except Tues., Sun. dinner from noon on. Usually closed from Dec. to Apr.
Pittsfield-Lenox Rd.

SHEFFIELD

Reasonable

Stagecoach Hill. Once a stagecoach stop, quaint atmosphere is enhanced by glowing fireplaces. Dart board for pub motif. Suggestion: steak and kidney pie. Cocktails. Lunch and dinner in summer. Dinner only, in winter, except Tues. Closed Mar.
State 41.

The Riverside. Gourmets who yearn for beef Wellington may order a day ahead for groups of five or more. Suggestions: cheddar cheese soup, chicken *margengo.* Homemade desserts. Cocktails. Lunch, dinner, except Tues.
US 7.

Inexpensive

F-2 Restaurant. Watch the specials every day for menu bargains. *Sheffield Lounge* new addition. Also new dining room for beef tenderloin en brochette. Breakfast, lunch, dinner.
US 7.

WILLIAMSTOWN

First Class

Mill on the Floss. The open kitchen decorated with copper pots is typically French—so is the French provincial dining here. Suggestions: sweetbreads *aux câpres,* tournedos. Choice wines. Dinner only. Sun. from 1 p.m.
8 mi. s. on US 7.

Reasonable

Country Restaurant. This is a bit of Brittany in the Berkshires. Suggestion: *escalope de veau Oscar.* Piano bar. Bi-level dining room. Lunch, dinner, late supper. New, so check ahead for closing days and vacation months.
US 7 (tel. 458–4000).

1896 House. This is an interesting place to dine, woodland setting and all. Suggestion: turkey Villeroy. Children's menu. Home-baked breads and pies. Cocktails. Lunch, dinner. Open noontime Sun. and holidays. Closed Mon. after summer season.
Cold Spring Rd., 2 mi. s. on US 7.

Elwal Pines. Here you will enjoy such unusual dishes as chicken Tahiti and turkey Dieppe. Children's menu. Cocktails. Indoor waterfall. Breakfast, lunch, dinner daily. Sun., open at 12:30 p.m. Open March to Dec.
Cold Spring Rd., s. on US 7.

Williams Inn. In summer, sip your cocktail in the garden; in winter, in front of the fireplace. Good New England meals. Children's menu. Breakfast, lunch, dinner. Sun. from 12:30 p.m.
College Pl.

ELSEWHERE

AGAWAM. *Federal Hill Club.* First class. Mine host recites the menu in this elegant Colonial home. Dinner only. Attractive cocktail lounge. Closed Sun., July 4, Dec. 25. 135 Cooper St.
Tinti's. Reasonable. Spacious pink-and-green, mirrored dining rooms are informal. Try lobster with spaghetti

special. Children's menu. 22 King St. nr. Eastern States Exposition Grounds.

AMHERST. *Lord Jeffrey*. Reasonable. Gracious dining and Yankee cooking are highlighted in this Treadway Inn. Good grog, too. Note *Plimpton Papers* collection in parlor. Open for breakfast, lunch, dinner. 30 Boltwood Ave. nr. Amherst College campus.

Mill Valley Grist Mill. Reasonable. You'll enjoy the quaint setting of this reconverted Colonial mill. Delicious food (and great martinis). Open lunch and dinner. Closed Mon. State 116.

AUBURN. *Yankee Drummer Inn*. Reasonable. Friendly atmosphere prevails, as in all Early American Inns, Inc. New England foods. Colonial dining room. *Spirit of '76 Tap Room*. Breakfast, lunch, dinner. State 12, Exit 10 on Mass. Tpke.

BEVERLY. *The Commodore*. Reasonable to first class. Lots of atmosphere with gas lamps, rotating waterwheel, beamed ceilings. Circular oyster bar, open hearth. Suggestion: Alaskan crab legs. Luncheon, dinner. Cocktail lounge. Free parking. 45 Enon St., State 1A.

BROOKLINE. *Jack and Marion's*. Reasonable. Tremendous menu features tremendous sandwiches. Complete meals and salads, too. Delicious blintzes with sour cream. Fruit-glazed cheesecake dessert. Cocktail lounge. Breakfast, lunch, dinner to 3 a.m. 299 Harvard St.

Novak's Towne Terrace. Here you will find beef stroganoff, sauerbraten, and Lazy Man's Lobster. Unusual baked Alaska dessert. Sophisticated atmosphere. Lunch, dinner. Closed Christmas Eve, Christmas Day. 1700 Beacon St.

CHICOPEE. *Schine Inn*. First class. The *Wiggins Tavern* dining room has contemporary colonial furnishings, including gigantic chandeliers. Extensive menu. Cocktails. This is a fairly new complex of motor inn, swimming pool, various dining rooms. 297 Burnett St.

COHASSET. *Hugo's Lighthouse*. First class. This restaurant is an award-winner. Fireplaces for cozy warmth in winter. Ocean-fresh seafoods; steaks and chops, too. Children's menu. Cocktails. Open for lunch and dinner. 44 Border St., at Cohasset Harbor.

CONCORD. *Colonial Inn*. Reasonable. Lobster pie is a favorite here. Varied menu. Home-style baking. Cocktails. Open for breakfast, lunch, dinner. 11 Monument Sq.

DALTON. *Crane Inn*. Reasonable. The chef has a continental touch here —beef stroganoff, baked sole filet stuffed with lobster. Sandwiches, too. Cocktails. Open breakfast, lunch, dinner. Main St.

DEERFIELD. *Deerfield Inn*. Reasonable. Gleaming silver, rich furniture, pretty china and good food add up to fine dining at this country inn. Children's menu. Open for breakfast, lunch, dinner. Mon., breakfast only. Closed from about Dec. 15 to Jan. Village St.

FOXBORO. *Lafayette House*. Reasonable. This old tavern began serving guests soon after the Revolutionary War. Delicious roast beef. Cocktails. Children's menu. Open for lunch and dinner, except Mon. US 1.

Lord Fox. Reasonable. This impressive mansion specializes in bountiful buffets, including Sun. buffet. Breakfast from 9 a.m. to noon. Buffet every evening, also regular menu. Luncheon fashion show Thurs. Cocktails, entertainment. Washington St., US 1.

LEE. *Morgan House*. Reasonable. Here in cozy Colonial atmosphere you will enjoy the homemade soups, breads, and desserts. Cocktails. Snacks. Lunch and dinner. Closed Mon. Main St.

Oak n' Spruce. Reasonable. This year-round resort has an attractive, informal dining room open to the public. Cocktail lounge. Reservations at height of season. Breakfast, lunch, dinner. 3 mi. s. off State 102.

LEICESTER. *Major's.* Reasonable. Julius Caesar would be proud of the shrimp *à la Giuliu Cesare* here. Good wines. Open for dinner only. Sun. open 11:30 a.m. Closed Mon., also Thanksgiving, Christmas, Good Friday, and Feb. At 6 So. Main St.

LONGMEADOW. *Friendly Steak and Sundae Shop.* Inexpensive. Really friendly with cozy colonial dining room for daily specials; counter for snacks. Lunch, dinner. Closed Christmas Day. Chain-operated. 732 Bliss Rd.

LYNN. *Anthony's Hawthorne Restaurant.* Reasonable to first class. Anthony became so famous here that he opened more restaurants, including Boston's new *Pier 4*. Lobster stuffed with lobster. Popovers. Salad tossed at table. Homemade dressing. Lunch and dinner. 95 Oxford St.

LYNNFIELD. *The Ship.* Reasonable. Once you step aboard this jolly red ship (a 1790 brig), you will be greeted by costumed attendants. Buffets, fashion shows, dancing on busy year-round program. Children's menu. Cocktails. Lunch and dinner. On US 1, Newburyport Tpke.

Towne Lyne House. Reasonable. In this lovely mansion overlooking Lake Suntaug, you will enjoy gracious dining. Suggestion: chicken amandine. Cocktails. Open for lunch and dinner. On US 1.

MAGNOLIA. *The Patio.* Reasonable. When you dine outdoors and order *escargots,* it's almost like being in Paris. Open for dinner only, for extended summer season. Usually closes end of Nov. 2 Lexington Ave.

The Surf. Reasonable. Watch the surf from The Surf. Suggestions: chicken Kiev, baked stuffed lobster. Children's menu. Snacks. Sun. buffets from Oct. through Feb. Cocktails. Dinner only. Closed Dec. 24 and 25. 56 Raymond St.

MALDEN. *Kernwood Restaurant.* Reasonable. Four big dining rooms here offer quick service or leisurely dining. Baked stuffed lobster is the attraction. Cocktail lounge. Open for breakfast, lunch, dinner. Closed Sun. 7 Dartmouth St.

MARBLEHEAD. *Adams House.* Reasonable. You are welcome to select your own lobster from the tank. Steaks, poultry on menu also. Picturesque harbor view. Cocktails. Lunch, dinner. Summer only. 147 Front St.

The Molly Waldo. Reasonable. Unusual room divider here: fish tanks. Varied menu. Popular with tourists. Cocktails. Lunch, dinner. 12 School St.

NEW BEDFORD. *Spouter Inn—Jolly Whaler Bar.* Reasonable. This jolly place commemorates whaling days with whaling ship motif. Suggestion: charcoal-broiled fish. Cocktails. Breakfast, lunch, dinner, Sun. from 1 p.m. In New Bedford Hotel, 725 Pleasant St.

NEWTON. *Simpson House.* Reasonable to first class. Stone fireplace is focal point of decor here, but all eyes are on flaming baked Alaska dessert. Suggestion: roast duckling. Children's menu. Lunch and dinner, from 1 p.m. Sun. 1114 Beacon St., Newton Highlands.

South Pacific. Reasonable. Tropical islands inspired the decor, menu, and drinks here. Suggestion: chicken Bali Hai. Open for lunch, dinner, until 2 a.m. 1152 Beacon St., Newton Highlands.

NORTH ATTLEBORO. *Brook Manor.* Reasonable. Pleasant dining in this small mansion. Suggestion: roast prime ribs of beef. Cocktails. Open for lunch and dinner. Closed Christmas Day. 116 Elm St.

Millstone. Reasonable. Rustic charm is enhanced by woodland location of this popular restaurant. Suggestion: lobster supreme. Cocktails. Children's menu. Dinner only, Sun. from noon. Mt. Hope St.

NORTHAMPTON. *Wiggins Tavern.* Reasonable. New England atmosphere prevails in this over-a-century-old landmark. Candlelight dinner. Varied menu. Cocktails. Breakfast, lunch, dinner. In Schine Northampton Inn, 36 King St.

PEABODY. *Century House.* Reasonable. This popular restaurant is located on historic Governor Endicott's Plain. Varied menu. Dessert suggestion: home-baked lemon meringue pie. Children's menu. Cocktails. Lunch and dinner, except Mon. State 114, near Northshore Shopping Ctr.

PLYMOUTH. *Currier's.* Reasonable. This attractive restaurant is just a 5-minute walk from *Plymouth Rock.* Suggestion: Pilgrim Dinner. Delicious sundaes (ice cream made on premises). Children's menu. Breakfast, lunch, dinner. Sun. from 11 a.m. Closed Wed., Thanksgiving, and Christmas Day. 61 Main St.

The 1740 Willis House. Reasonable. Waitresses are costumed like Priscilla Alden. Own farm supplies fruits, vegetables. Delicious breads, pies. Favorite dessert: ice cream pie. Lunch, dinner Sun. and holidays from 12 to 8 p.m. Closed Nov. to Apr. 15 Summer St., Kingston.

ROCKPORT. *Blacksmith Shop.* Reasonable. Where else would you find braised celery with mushrooms, or Indian pudding baked in a beanpot? Lobster, chicken, beef broiled on forge. All this and harbor view, too. Lunch and dinner. Seasonal. 23 Mt. Pleasant St.

Oleana-by-the-Sea. Reasonable. Smorgasbord and smorgas-plate are highlighted here, or you may order from regular menu. Tempting Scandinavian desserts. Breakfast, lunch, dinner, except Mon. in winter. Closed for a month from Dec. 19. 23 Main St.

SALEM. *China Sails.* Reasonable. This is one of three Dave Wong restaurants. Other China Sails in Peabody, Revere, Brookline. Chinese specialties, Polynesian drinks. Free parking. Open from 11:30 a.m. to 1 a.m. 516 Loring Ave., State 1A.

Main Brace & Essex Room. Reasonable. Very good (and popular) buffets are served here Fri., Sat., Sun. Beautiful antiques. Cocktails. Breakfast, lunch, dinner. 18 Washington Sq., State 1A, in Hawthorne Hotel.

SAUGUS. *Chickland.* Reasonable. This landscaped, rambling restaurant is very popular with families. Hearty portions of tasty barbecued chicken at inexpensive prices. Regular menu, too. Cocktails. Open all year round, lunch and dinner. US 1.

SEEKONK. *Old Grist Mill.* Reasonable. At this quaint, authentic mill, complete with millpond, you will enjoy a typically New England meal. Johnnycake, breads, rolls, pies baked on premises. Cocktails. Especially delightful Thanksgiving Day. Lunch and dinner, except Mon. Closed Christmas Day. 390 Fall River Ave.

SHELBURNE FALLS. *The Sweetheart.* Reasonable. This truly is a sweetheart of a restaurant in a gracious Colonial mansion. Pink linens, pink rose china. Suggestion: boned fried chicken with waffles. Cocktails. Luncheon, dinner. Closed Nov. to Apr. 19. State 2.

SOUTH EGREMONT. *Jug End.* Reasonable. Hospitality prevails for country-style dining in *Egremont Room* or *Dutch Jugendkeller* at this lively, all-year-round resort. Sat. is steak night, Sun., roast beef. Cocktails. Check ahead for menu and entertainment. Off State 23 and State 41. Tel. Great Barrington 434.

SOUTH HADLEY. *Hadleigh House.* Reasonable. With Colonial motif inside and out, this new restaurant seems to be a long-time landmark. Good food and grog. Lunch, dinner, cocktails. US 202, about 3 mi. from Holyoke.

SOUTH SUDBURY. *Longfellow's Wayside Inn.* Reasonable, but first class. This is the oldest United States inn, dating back to 1686. Authentic Colonial recipes. 100-acre complex includes museum rooms. Breakfast, lunch, dinner. Cocktails. Closed Christmas. Wayside Inn Rd.

SPRINGFIELD. *The Gunnery.* Reasonable. This is your target for good food and fun downtown. An Early American Inns, Inc. restaurant. Lively *Gunnery Pub.* Jazz concerts; discotheque. Lunch, dinner, cocktails.

At Kimball Towers, Chestnut and Bridge Sts.

Student Prince and the Fort. Reasonable. This citadel of fine food and German beers (on draught) has a grand stein collection. Old Heidelberg-style stained-glass window. Very popular. Children's menu. Lunch, dinner.

8 Fort St.

STOCKBRIDGE. *Red Lion Inn.* Reasonable. *The Lion's Den* and *The Gate* are for grog; the dining room for hearty food (notice fine antiques). Guests welcome at this American-plan resort. Summer season. Main St.

STURBRIDGE. *Publick House.* Reasonable. There's good, old-fashioned Yankee fare at this Treadway Inn; also authentic Colonial atmosphere. Children's menu. Cocktails. Breakfast, lunch, dinner. Main St.

Village Tavern. Inexpensive. Food is priced right for the family touring Old Sturbridge Village. Buffet luncheon. Cafeteria downstairs. Children's prices. Closed after 4 p.m.; also Dec. to Mar. but cafeteria is open weekends then. Right in Village.

SWAMPSCOTT. *General Glover Inn.* First class. This was the home of General John Glover, father of U.S. Navy. Steaks broiled on open hearth. Delicious roast beef. Cocktails. Delightful atmosphere. Same ownership as Anthony's in Lynn (below), Swampscott, Boston—but with personality all its own. Free parking. Dinner only. Salem St.

Hawthorne-by-the-Sea. Reasonable. Anthony's famous Hawthorne lobster stuffed with lobster is featured at his waterfront restaurant. Same specialties as in Lynn. Lunch, dinner. Free parking. 153 Humphrey St.

WAYLAND. *Red Coach Grill.* Reasonable to first class. Maybe this one seems more romantic because it's the original of the East Coast chain. Low lights, soft music, fireplaces. Excellent steaks. Cocktails. Dinner only. Sun. and holidays from noon. Post Rd.

WEST BROOKFIELD. *Salem Cross Inn.* Reasonable. Salem witch hex signs, a cross on the latches, may be seen in this historic house. Cozy cocktail lounge. Excellent food. Lunch, dinner, except Mon. and Christmas Day. State 9.

WESTMINSTER. *Old Mill.* Reasonable, but first class. This is one of the prettiest restaurants in New England. Authentic Colonial dining rooms have view of millpond and ducks. Cocktails, exotic drinks. Family dinner specials, buffets. Breakfast, lunch, dinner. Closed Christmas Day. State 2A.

WEST SPRINGFIELD. *Old Storrowtown Tavern.* Reasonable. Here you have another antique-decorated Early American Inns, Inc. restaurant. Delicious New England specialties. Cocktails. Lunch, dinner, except Sun. In Storrowtown Village, on Eastern States Exposition Grounds.

Vincent's Steak House. Reasonable to first class. This restaurant is so popular that more dining rooms and parking areas are added. *Oyster Bar.* Excellent menu. Tempting breads. Dinner only. Closed Sun. and Mon. US 5.

WHITMAN. *Toll House.* Reasonable, but first class. This is the beautiful home of the Toll House cooky. Delicious meals—try boneless fried chicken. Cocktails. Old-fashioned garden. Children's menu. Lunch, dinner, except Mon. Not open Jan. 362 Bedford St.

WORCESTER. *Putnam & Thurston.* Reasonable. Several attractive dining rooms insure prompt seating at this popular restaurant. New England favorites as well as latest Polynesian specialties. Cocktails. Breakfast, lunch, dinner, except Sun. July and Aug. 27 Mechanic St.

BARS. In *Cambridge,* popular bars are in the *Charter House Motor Hotel* (5 Cambridge Parkway), the pub-style *Yard of Ale* (Harvard Square), *Cronin's* (the famous gathering place of Harvard men at 114 Mt. Auburn St.), and the *Wursthaus* (4 Boylston St., just off Harvard Square).

MUSIC. The *Berkshire Festival,* on the Tanglewood estate in Lenox, is a world-famous event. The eight-week festival begins July; performances, 8 p.m. Fri. and Sat.; 2:30 p.m. Sun. in the Music Shed. Admission to open rehearsal Sat. morning, $1.50 adults; 50 cents, children. Programs in Music Shed, from $3.50 to $7 Listening outside on the lawn (picnicking permitted) costs $2.50. Ticket information: Tel. Lenox 637–1600. *Berkshire Music Barn,* Lenox, features *folk-singers* and *jazz groups* from first week in July to first week in Sept. Tickets, $2.75 to $4.40. Tel. 637–0919.

The *Red Fox Music Barn,* New Marlborough, features *solo* and *chamber music* series on summer Sat. nights. Famous performers participate. The *South Mountain concert series,* July to early Oct. weekends, features *chamber music,* sometimes *jazz;* in Pittsfield. Worcester features an Oct. *Music Festival. Castle Hill concerts,* July and Aug., Fri. and Sat., are featured at Castle Hill Estate, Ipswich. The *Chamber Music Society of Cape Ann,* Rockport, presents Sun. evening concerts for a summer series. *Cape Ann Symphony Orchestra* performs also. The spirit of '76 is revived with *fife and drum groups.* They play for competitions and local celebrations, April 19 in Concord and Lexington.

STAGE AND REVUES. There are excellent *summer theaters* throughout the state. These include *Carousel Theatre,* State 9, Framingham; *Loeb Drama Center,* 64 Brattle St., Cambridge; *North Shore Music Theatre,* Beverly; *South Shore Music Circus,* Cohasset; *Lake Whalom Playhouse,* Fitchburg; *Mt. Tom Playhouse,* Holyoke; *Berkshire Playhouse,* Stockbridge; *Merry-Go-Round,* Sturbridge; *Storrowtown Music Fair,* West Springfield; *Williamstown Theatre,* Williamstown; and the *Brandeis Theatre,* Waltham.

TOURS. *Gray Line* of Boston, in the Sheraton Plaza Hotel, Boston, conducts tours to other parts of the state as well as in Boston proper. *Tour No. 4* is an evening tour, for 5 hours, to *Salem* and *Marblehead* including dinner (fish, chicken, or lobster). The tour visits the North Shore beaches, Castle Rock, Old Marblehead, the Witch City, House of Seven Gables. The all-inclusive fee is $7.50. (Daytime rates are half for children, but not on this tour). Gray Line's *Tour No. 5* takes about 9 hours, is seasonal, and visits *Plymouth* and *Cape Cod Canal.* Tourists will see the birthplace and home of John Quincy Adams, Old Stone Church, Tomb of the Presidents, John and Priscilla Alden home, Plymouth Rock, Forefathers' Monument, Burial Hill, and *Mayflower II.* This costs about $9; half-fare for children.

There are also combination tours, four-night packages for trips to *North Shore* and *South Shore.* A double room with bath on the comprehensive four-night tour costs $55 a person, approximately, with no meals included. Gray Line also has tours to Wayside Inn for $7 to $9, depending on whether it is the 6-hour or 8-hour tour. There is also a grand tour, for 3 hours, of historic, literary and educational Boston and Cambridge for $5.50. For more information on Gray Line Tours, tel. KE 6–2470.

Michaud Bus Lines, 250 Jefferson St., Salem, conducts guided tours of the North Shore in radio- and microphone-equipped, air-conditioned coaches. Tel. 744–1207. *Tauck Tours,* 475 Fifth Ave., New York City, features a motorcoach vacation from New York to Concord-Lexington-Sturbridge, and another from

Washington, D.C. to Lexington Green, Concord Bridge, Walden Pond, and Old Sturbridge Village. Both tours cost a minimum of about $70.

Trailways of New England travels to Old Sturbridge Village from Boston, daily at 10:30 a.m. (summer and fall) and returns about 7:30 p.m. This trip costs about $7; children half-price. There are also hourly trips to Longfellow's Wayside Inn the year round. The price is $2.40; $1.25 for children. Trailways is located at 10 Park Square. *Continental Trailways Tours, Inc.* has packaged an escorted tour of historical Boston, Marblehead, Salem, etc., all the way from Salt Lake City.

Cambridge has a *Heritage Trail* beginning at Cambridge Common. Student-guided tours leave from Admissions Office of Massachusetts Institute of Technology, 77 Massachusetts Ave., Building 3, Room 108, Mon. thru Fri., 10 a.m. and 2 p.m. Free.

SPECIAL INTEREST TOURS. *Hammond Museum,* Hesperus Ave., Gloucester, exhibits famous organ built by John Hays Hammond, Jr. Organ concerts July, Aug. Guided tours. *Whaling Museums* are on Broad St., Nantucket and 18 Johnny Cake Hill, New Bedford. *Pilgrim Hall,* Plymouth, presents electronic guided tours. *Worcester Art Museum,* 55 Salisbury St., Worcester, presents lectures and gallery discussions. *Harvard University Museums,* Cambridge, offer guidance to foreign visitors. Information Center on Dunster St. Guidebooks printed in French, German, Spanish; a Japanese guide is planned. Office open Mon. thru Sat. 9 to 5; Sun., 1 to 4. Brandeis University, Waltham, offers guided tours from the Information Booth to *Rose Art Museum* and *Goldfarb Library.*

Archeological: Peabody Museum of Archaeology, Harvard University, Divinity Ave., has an excellent collection of American Indian lore. Guided tour arranged.

Night: Copley Motor Tours leaves from Boston Public Library for a night tour of North Shore. Summer only. Tel. CO 6–3500 for details.

Historical Societies: These cities have their own historical societies, usually in an historic house: Boston, Billerica, Cambridge, Dedham, Fall River, Falmouth, Martha's Vineyard, Mattapoisett, Northampton, Petersham, Rockport, Sandwich, Somerville, South Natick, Taunton, Templeton, Wellesley, Worcester. *Massachusetts Historical Society,* 1154 Boylston St., Boston, is open all year round; admission free. Visitors are always welcome in Historical Society homes.

Music, Art Tours: The visitor will enjoy charting his own music and art tours with all the cultural events scheduled in the state. Museum offices will arrange for guidance. *New England Council and Museum of Fine Arts* publishes a free folder *New England Museums and Historic Houses* which lists every art collection. Write New England Council, Statler Office Building, Boston.

Photography Tours: The state offers many scenic shots for the photographer; the autumn foliage season is the most colorful. *Thru The Lens Tours,* new in 1965, is a 14-day escorted tour in autumn. Price is all-inclusive, round-trip by jet, from Los Angeles, Chicago, Miami, Dallas, Toronto. Address is 12456 Magnolia Blvd., North Hollywood, Calif.

INDUSTRIAL TOURS. New England hospitality prevails in industrial life, too. These are some of the companies with tours for visitors. *General Motors,* Framingham, shows the assembly of Chevrolets Mon. thru Thur. However, be sure to register before 1:15 p.m., as the tour begins 1:30 p.m. Children under 12 years of age are not allowed on the tour. *Gorton's,* in Gloucester, has a special observation platform for watching the process of freezing seafood. Tours are Mon., Thur., and Fri. from 9 a.m. to 11 a.m., then noon to 2 p.m., and 2:30 to 4 p.m. *John H. Breck, Inc.,* 115 Dwight St., Springfield, is the place to see how shampoos and rinses are manufactured. Tours are by appointment only, Mon. thru Fri., 9 a.m. to 4 p.m. *Worcester*

Pressed Steel, 100 Barber Ave., Worcester, has a combination industrial-museum tour Mon. thru Fri., 9 a.m. to 4 p.m. The information center of the *Yankee Atomic Electric Co.* is in Rowe, in the Berkshires, also the site of a big nuclear power reactor open to the public Wed. through Sun. from noon to 5 p.m. Write in advance to Charles Keenan, vice-president, Yankee Atomic Energy Co., 441 Stuart St., Boston 16.

HISTORIC SITES. Let's begin with *Plymouth,* where the history of Massachusetts began when the Pilgrims arrived on the *Mayflower*. Plymouth Rock, duly inscribed 1620, marks the spot. Board a replica of the *Mayflower* at State Pier. The charge, complete with guide, is 75 cents for adults; 50 cents for children; open every day from 9 a.m. to 5 p.m., Apr. thru Nov. Plimoth Plantation has same schedule. This is a replica of the original homes and gardens.

The Minute Man statue in *Concord* commemorates the farmer–Revolutionary soldier of 1775. This was a battle site, as well as the Battle Green in adjoining town of *Lexington*. Both Concord and Lexington are historically important, with homes dating back to pre-Revolutionary times, old taverns, and old cemeteries. *The Minute Man* statue on the Lexington Green, by Henry H. Kitson, is supposed to be the likeness of Captain John Parker, a Revolutionary leader.

Deerfield is a town of historic interest, the site of the great Indian Massacres of 1675 and 1704. There are at least six colonial homes to visit, including the Frary House dating back to 1689, museums, the old graveyard. Combination tickets for $4.50 may be purchased. Buildings are open from May to Nov. The Information Center is in Hall Tavern, open Mon. thru Sat., 9:30 to 4:30; Sun., 1:30 to 4:30.

The *Witch House* in *Salem* dates back to 1642. This was the home of Judge Jonathan Corwin who questioned those accused of witchcraft. From June to Labor Day the house is open daily from 10 a.m. to 6 p.m. After Labor Day to Nov., from 10 a.m. to 5 p.m. Adults 40 cents; 15 cents for children.

MUSEUMS AND GALLERIES. *Addison Gallery of American Art,* Andover. This noteworthy museum includes works of American artists, glassware, sculpture, ship models. Open daily; free. *Rockport Art Association Exhibition Galleries,* Rockport. Collections are exhibited in the Old Tavern, 12 Main St., daily all year round. No charge.

Chesterwood in Stockbridge is the studio of Daniel Chester French, sculptor of *The Minute Man of Concord,* at Concord, and *Lincoln Statue,* Washington, D.C. Plaster casts are exhibited. A Barn Gallery is included. Open daily in summer; weekends only from Labor Day to Oct. 15. Admission, $1; children, 25 cents. *Tyringham Art Galleries* (Gingerbread House) was home and studio of late sculptor Henry Hudson Kitson. Primitive art, paintings, etchings exhibited. Open daily. Admission. Children free. South Lee exit on Mass. Turnpike to Tyringham Rd., Tyringham.

Museum of Fine Arts, Chestnut and State sts., Springfield, is a museum complex including collections of American, European, and Far Eastern paintings, sculpture. Admission is free to all buildings. Open daily, except Mon. Closed Aug. Tel. REpublic 2–4317. *Sterling and Francine Clark Art Institute* in Williamstown. This scientifically illuminated museum is well worth the trip. The impressive marble building is a showplace for 33 Renoirs, Sargents, Corots, and many other masterpieces. Rare treasures exhibited also. Free admission. Open daily, except Mon. Closed Feb.

Harvard University Art Museums (Cambridge) include Busch-Reisinger Museum, Fogg Art Museum, University Museum (Museum of Comparative Zoology; Peabody Museum of Archaeology and Ethnology; Botanical, Mineralogical, Geological museums). The fabulous Ware glass flowers are exhibited in the latter museum complex. Free guided tours, summer only. Inquire at Harvard Yard. During school year, inquire at Marshall's office, Wadsworth House. Of course you are welcome to visit any and all of these museums, on your own, free. Open Mon. thru Sat., 9 a.m. to 4:30 p.m.; Sun., 1 to 4:30 p.m.

Harvard Library. This is considered one of the greatest university libraries. Rare books *(Gutenberg Bible)* are in exhibition cases. Free. Open daily weekdays, 8:45 a.m. to 10 p.m.; Sat., to 5:30; closed Sun., holidays.

Carpenter Center for the Visual Arts. This Harvard University (Cambridge) exhibition is housed in a building by Le Corbusier which is controversial, to say the least. Open daily, free admission.

Charles Hayden Memorial Library at Massachusetts Institute of Technology, Cambridge, has important and varied free art exhibitions in a new gallery. Open 7 days a week; closed summer. Inquire at Administrative Office, 77 Massachusetts Ave. Tel. UN 4–6900.

LIBRARIES. At Harvard University, Cambridge, the *Widener Library* is the largest university library anywhere, with two million books. You can visit the public rooms here, and see the Gutenberg Bible and first Shakespeare folios in the Widener Room at the top of the main stairs. Next door is the Houghton Library of Rare Manuscripts, not open to the public, and next to that, the Lamont Library (for undergraduates). Another library of importance on the campus is the Far Eastern Library.

GARDENS. Not too far away from Boston, *Arnold Arboretum* in Jamaica Plain features about 6,000 species and varieties of trees, shrubs, vines. Open sunrise to sunset; free. *Naumkeag Gardens,* Stockbridge, are exotic with Chinese motif, moongate. Admission to mansion (belonged to Joseph Choate, ambassador to England) and gardens, $1.50. Open July thru Labor Day, except Mon., Sat. and Sun. only from Labor Day thru Oct. 1.

SHOPPING. *Shopper's World,* State 9, Framingham, includes famous department stores. The *Northshore Shopping Center,* Peabody, claims to be the largest in New England. *Deerskin Trading Post,* US 1, Danvers features deerskin moccasins, gloves, jackets, etc. *Johnny Appleseed's Store,* Danvers, sells everything from food delicacies to hunting equipment (building constructed 1687). *The Pewter Shop,* Bearskin Neck, Rockport, designs fine, hand metalwork on the premises. *Country Curtains,* Main St., Stockbridge, specializes in unbleached muslin and ball fringe for colonial curtains. The famous Sheffield Pottery can be found at the *Sheffield Pottery Barn* on State 7, s. of Great Barrington, in the town of Sheffield.

SUMMER SPORTS. *Boating* is a popular summer sport. Charter and party boats are available at all major ports. Larger lakes and ponds have launching ramps; boats or outboards may be rented. Spectators may watch morning departures and afternoon returns of commercial fishing fleets in Boston and Cape Cod. Charles River is dotted with sailboats in summer; also Gloucester, Marblehead, and Cape Cod.

Both freshwater and saltwater *fishing* are excellent. Division of Fish and Game stocks the streams. The Berkshires is an excellent fishing area, especially for trout in the many lakes and streams.

As for *golf,* there are 222 clubs; most welcome visitors. The governing body is Mass. Golf Association, 40 Trinity Place, Boston. In the Berkshires, *Taconic Golf Club* in Williamstown is outstanding. Tel. GL 8–3997. The home of *tennis* is at *Longwood Cricket Club,* Brookline, with annual National Doubles late Aug. *Horseback riding* is popular; inquire locally about stables. *Aspinwall Stables,* Pittsfield–Lenox Rd., Lenox, offers year-round riding indoors, plus about 40 miles of wooded trails. Tel. 637–0245. Just outside of Boston, *Blue Hills Reservation,* Milton, has 8 stables.

Water skiing has increased in popularity. The best lake for water skiing in the state is Lake Chargoggagaugmanchaugagoggchaubunagungamaugg. It's a 1,400-acre lake with a name as long as its shoreline—the site of the 1964 National Water Ski Championships. Location is Webster (exit 10 on Mass. Turnpike, then State 12). Just ask for Ben's Cove. With so many *beaches,* both fresh- and saltwater, visitors will enjoy basking in the sun or swimming. Right outside of Boston, beaches are located in South Boston, Wollaston, Nantasket. The North Shore, outside of Boston, includes Revere, Marblehead, Lynn, Swampscott, Gloucester, Rockport. In the Berkshires, ponds and lakes provide good swimming. Greenfield has a 1,400-ft. outdoor swimming pool on Green River.

Spectator sports are plentiful. *Soccer* is seen at its best in Ludlow, where Portuguese-American families have developed the sport into championship teams. Wherever there are university fields, spectators are welcome to watch sport practice sessions and games at Harvard, Tufts, Northeastern, Boston University, Brandeis, Massachusetts Institute of Technology, Boston College.

One of the most exciting sports to watch or participate in is *sport parachuting* in Orange, at the *Sport Parachuting Center.* The participation cost is $35 for 3 hours for instruction, rented equipment, and first jump. For exhibitions and meets, write to the center, Box 96, Orange, Mass. 01364.

Professional *baseball* is played at *Wahconah Park,* Pittsfield. There are no gambling casinos in Massachusetts. However, the visitor may try his luck at *horse races* and *dog races.* From mid-April to mid-June, pari-mutuel dog racing takes place at *Raynham Park,* Raynham (near Taunton). Pari-mutuel dog racing is on the schedule at *Wonderland Park,* Revere, from early May to Aug. 31. There is also pari-mutuel horse racing at *Berkshire Downs,* Hancock, from middle to late June, plus a July schedule. *Harness racing* is the attraction at *Foxboro* where pari-mutuel races are on the program from late June to late July. Remember that schedules are subject to change, and it is best to check dates with the sport pages in local or Boston newspapers.

WINTER SPORTS. There are many *ice-skating* rinks, *toboggan* chutes, and hills for *sledding.* Visitors who want to watch ice-skaters, or try the sport, should go to *North Shore Sports Center,* 30 Boston St., Lynn. Claimed to be New England's largest ice-skating arena, it's open all year. Lessons and rentals, too. Tel. 598–2550.

Skiing is the most popular winter sport, with ski areas right outside big cities, such as *Blue Hills Reservation* near Boston and *Mt. Tom Ski* area (night skiing also) near Holyoke and Springfield. These are some of the *Berkshire* ski areas: *Berkshire Snow Basin,* West Cummington, tel. 634–8808; *Brodie Mt. Ski Area,* US 7, near Pittsfield; *Bousquet Ski Area,* Pittsfield, tel. Hillcrest 2–3664; *Butternut Basin Ski Area,* State 23, near Great Barrington; *Catamount,* State 23, So. Egremont, tel. 325–7800; *Eastover,* Lenox, tel. 637–0625; *Jiminy Peak,* Hancock, tel. HAncock 4–4663; *Jug End* in the Berkshires, State 23 and 41, So. Egremont, tel. 434; *Happyland,* US 20, Chester; *Otis Ridge Ski Area,* Otis, tel Colfax 9–3761; *Thunder Mountain,* State 2, Mohawk Trail, Charlemont, tel. Edgewood 9–4986.

From about Oct. 20 to Nov. 30, *hunters* will have open season on pheasant, quail, gray squirrel, rabbit, hare, deer, all with special limitations. Bow and arrow hunting for deer. Visitor's hunting license, $15.25. Write to Division of Forests and Parks, 15 Ashburton Place, Boston. Also, *Sportsman's Guide to Cape Cod* from Chamber of Commerce, Hyannis.

RECOMMENDED READING. These books will give the visitor an insight into Boston and the rest of the state: *Boston-Ways: Hi, By, and Folk* by George Weston; *About Boston Sight, Insight, Sound, and Inflection,* by David McCord; *The Late George Apley,* by John Marquand; also *Massachusetts, a Guide to Its Places and People,* published by Houghton Mifflin, one of the American Guide Series.

On Cape Cod: *Cape Cod,* by Thoreau.

RETIREMENT AREAS. Evidently there is much interest shown in retirement on *Cape Cod.* The Chamber of Commerce prints a brochure, *A Wonderful Way of Life,* with all the necessary information. Weather on Cape Cod is divided into the four seasons plus Indian Summer, into November. Cold weather does not arrive on the Cape until January; zero temperatures are not usual. Facilities for retirement include new high rise apartments such as *Admiralty Apartments* at Marina Harbor, Falmouth. Rentals are from $145 monthly. Real estate agents are pleased to show more economical living quarters. Real estate taxes are low on the Cape; cost is estimated to be less than living in principal metropolitan areas.

Retirement homesites on the Cape can cost as little as $1,000 or as high as $25,000. Homes vary from a $3,000 do-it-yourself package for a shell to a $75,000 showplace. In most cases, the cost of the site does not include the home.

There are three modern hospitals, medical centers, good doctors, and a recently enlarged Hyannis Hospital with specialists. In emergencies, Cape Cod's Rescue Squads speed patients as far as Boston, on 24-hour call.

The Cape has retiree's clubs, bridge clubs, arts, boating, dancing, social clubs, sportsmen's clubs, women's clubs, garden clubs for men and women. Bird watchers will find bird sanctuaries such as the Audubon Sanctuary at Wellfleet. Golf is a year-round sport (17 courses), as snow never stays for more than a day or two.

VERMONT

The Green Mountain State

by

EUGENIA BEDELL

(Skiing, schooling and traveling in New England built up such pleasant memories that when, traveling in some far-off land, New Jerseyite Eugenia Bedell gets homesick, it is for New England. Her work has appeared in many national publications, including the New York Times *and* Saturday Review. *In addition to this chapter, she is also the author of the narrative sections on New Hampshire and Maine, following.)*

It was in 1609 that the French gentleman-explorer Samuel de Champlain discovered both Vermont and Lake Champlain. He probably should have let it go at that, remaining a mere explorer. But he didn't. One day, that same year, he and his Algonquin allies eyed some Iroquois on Champlain's shores, didn't like what they saw, and introduced the Iroquois to the effects of European firearms. This deadly demonstration incurred such an undying enmity for the French among the Iroquois that, still burning strong a century or so later, it made things much easier for the British when they began shoving the French off American colonial soil.

After a few decades, the Indians decided they didn't like all those encroachments of the white man to the southeast along the Atlantic Coast. Since there wasn't anyone to harass in Vermont territory, they used the state as a sort of highway on their way south and east to raid.

In 1724 another fort was built in Vermont, down in the southeast corner. It turned out to be Vermont's first settlement, though no one knew it at the time, as it was built by Massachusetts to protect some of its own settlements nearby.

To anyone with a bird's-eye view, it might have begun to look as though Vermont might just never make it as a state. But off in Portsmouth, New Hampshire, and over in England, things were happening which would put Vermont and its citizenry-to-be right smack in the middle of a walloping, big tug-of-war.

In 1741, King George III sent across word that Benning Wentworth, Governor of New Hampshire, could have all the territory extending due west across the Merrimack River "till it meets with other governments." That seemed sensible enough at first glance. But there was a small oversight. No one had ever told New York where its eastern boundary was to be. If Benning Wentworth knew this, he ignored it, and began parceling out land as far to the west as the Connecticut and Massachusetts borders ran in that direction. He also personally founded Bennington, deep in present-day Vermont's northeast corner. New York's Governor Clinton didn't like this and told Wentworth so. Instead of hiding his head in the sand over the matter, Wentworth wrapped the whole thing up in a ball of red tape by suggesting the Crown solve the problem. He knew any answer would take ages, especially with transatlantic communications in the state they were. Meanwhile, he went on granting territory in what is present-day Vermont.

It wasn't red tape, however, that foiled New York's Governor Clinton. Across the Atlantic, England and France went to war. On this side of the Atlantic, the French forthwith thought it was time for another French and Indian war. It looked to them like a good opportunity to drop on south and lop off some colonial territory. So they dug in at Fort Ticonderoga and Crown Point, on the New York side of Lake Champlain. All of this caused everyone's attention to be diverted from problems of boundaries, at least until British troops finally ousted the French from these two positions in 1759.

During all this time, more and more people, under the aegis of Governor Wentworth, were clearing land and settling in Vermont. Then, in 1764, a bombshell exploded. King George announced that henceforth the Connecticut River was to form the boundary between New Hampshire and New York. New York, gleeful, immediately assumed Wentworth's grants had been worthless. Now, in addition to making a number of new grants within what is now Vermont, the Yorkers also began telling longtime settlers they had gotten the wrong message. If the settlers wanted to stay where they were, the New Yorkers told them, they would have to pay New York for the land. Most of the settlers didn't happen to have that much loose cash lying around. Besides, they had already paid for the land once.

The injustice of the situation had an interesting effect. Prior to this time there had been very little communication between the Vermont settlers, as those along the Connecticut River seldom clambered west over the Green Mountains to the Lake Champlain side and vice versa. Now the bullying of New York knit most of the settlers into a tight little pugnacious band.

Ethan Allen's "Bennington Mob"

About the only thing their anger needed was a leader or two. These soon showed up in the persons of Ethan Allen, his brother Ira, Remember Baker, and Matthew Lyon. Of them all, Ethan Allen was the most outspoken, active, and colorful. Under the aegis of these men, a loose-knit military group called the Green Mountain Boys was soon formed. In 1770–71 the Green Mountain Boys, called by New Yorkers "the Bennington Mob," harassed settlers who had come to Vermont under grants from the Province of New York. They even dipped into New York territory with their house burnings and public whippings. However, the Boys neither killed nor seriously injured anyone. But they got a bad name among the Yorkers, who posted a bounty for Ethan Allen and some of his cohorts.

Just about then the Battle of Lexington and Concord occurred, and the Allens were quick to realize the British were sitting right on their doorstep, just across Lake Champlain, at Ticonderoga and Crown Point. They also realized the lake could act as a virtual funnel for the British who wished to enter Colonial territory from nearby Canada. The Continental Army, aware of this, too, sent Benedict Arnold along to Vermont. With Ethan Allen and his men, Arnold and his army went over and captured Ticonderoga. Seth Warner did the same at nearby Crown Point. Not only did the Green Mountain Boys take the forts, they also sealed off this northern gateway, and, further, supplied George Washington with over 100 British cannons, which were to come in mighty handy in the Boston area the following winter.

Even so, Vermonters weren't forgetting their other revolution—against New York. Following the Declaration of Independence in 1776, they seized upon the notion that since the British no longer had a voice in American affairs, just about all the granting that had gone on heretofore was nullified. Certainly the land that had been summarily turned over to New York (all land west of the Connecticut River) just plain didn't belong to New York. It belonged, rather, to the people who had settled under the New Hampshire

Grants of Benning Wentworth. Wouldn't it make sense, they reasoned further, to make a separate state of these grants?

After a series of lesser conventions, 70-some delegates met at Windsor, Vermont, in July of 1777, adopted a constitution of their own, and declared their independence. So independent Vermont became, and independent it remained until 1791. Vermont men went on fighting in the Revolution, but as an independent Republic they were also busy issuing bills of credit, coining money, corresponding with foreign governments, and naturalizing citizens of other states and countries.

Meantime, while the delegates were meeting at Windsor, General Burgoyne was inching down Lake Champlain. He took Ticonderoga, and then some of his troops tangled with Seth Warner and some of the Green Mountain Boys at Hubbardton, and Burgoyne was slowed in that direction. But things didn't look good for the Americans. Many expected Burgoyne would shortly be joining other British forces at Albany. That would mean the British would have accomplished what they'd long tried to do: completely cut off New England from the rest of the colonies.

Just one thing was keeping Burgoyne from reaching Albany. He badly needed supplies. He knew where he could get them, too—at Bennington. The Colonies, now desperate to stop Burgoyne's advance, ordered veteran Colonel John Stark out of retirement. He was soon marching off toward Bennington with a number of troops. Meantime, Burgoyne sent a force out to capture the supplies at Bennington, a force which didn't know of Stark's presence, nor of the scrapping spirit of the volunteers from all areas of Vermont who had come to back up Stark.

The Battle of Bennington began, and just at a time when things looked hopeless for the Americans, 300 of Seth Warner's boys showed up, after a march from Manchester. Victory was soon the Americans'.

Deprived of his supplies, his morale bent, Burgoyne lost the ensuing Battle of Saratoga to the Americans. Bennington, meanwhile, had already been noted as one of the few times in world history when regular, trained soldiers had been beaten by so-called improvised troops. Burgoyne, in a letter to England after the battle wrote, "The Hampshire Grants in particular—a country unpeopled and almost unknown in the last war—now abounds with the most active and rebellious race on the continent, and hangs, like a gathering storm, on my left."

By 1790, from the day 30 years earlier when its people had begun to flex their muscles, the state's population had grown from 300 to 85,425. In 1791, Vermont joined the Union, and its private war with New York ended. It had virtually ended the year before, when

New York had agreed to accept $30,000 for some territory that had still been in dispute.

In Again, Out Again Vermont

Vermont's admission to the Union, had not, however, been smooth. First Congress had seemed willing, then not. Sometimes Vermont seemed willing, and sometimes not. At one point George Washington even believed Vermont might have to be subdued by arms. As late as 1782 Vermonters arrested and ejected a New York sheriff and his men, for violating the Vermont border. The U.S. Congress, urged on by influential New York citizens, set up a howl. They ordered Vermont to allow such intrusions. Vermont thereupon made war-like noises and refused. Not only did the national government waver, and eventually not fight, it also never again questioned Vermont's authority within its own borders. Finally, peaceably, Vermont added the 14th star to Old Glory. However, there are people to this day who will jokingly tell you that, in the end, it was the Union which joined Vermont, and not vice-versa.

While Vermont was still a Republic, a bridge was built at Bellows Falls, the first of any type, it is said, to be built across the Connecticut River, and in 1785, the first marble quarry was opened, in the southwest, at Dorset. In 1805, Montpelier was established as the State Capital, and the steamship *Vermont* was proudly nosing her way through the waters of Lake Champlain, the second regularly operated commercial steamship in the world.

In 1810, an ex-diplomat, who had served in Portugal, introduced the famous Merino sheep of Spain into Vermont. Sheep-raising soon became so popular that in ensuing years there were six sheep to every citizen in the state. And in 1825, one of America's all-time-favorite imports, the Marquis de Lafayette, toured Vermont to the delight of the citizenry.

In 1805, Joseph Smith, founder of the Mormon faith, was born near Sharon, Vermont (Brigham Young, who was to later lead Smith's people to Utah, had been born four years earlier at Whitingham). The baby Chester A. Arthur, who was born at Fairfield in 1830, grew up to be America's 21st president. Admiral George Dewey, born 1837 in Montpelier, went on to his famous encounter with the Spanish at Manila Bay, and Charles Clark, born in Bradford in 1843, became another naval hero of this same war. From San Francisco he took the battleship *Oregon* through the Straits of Magellan, which no other battleship had previously entered. Up the east coast of South America he steamed to Cuba, where he aided William Sampson in destroying the Spanish fleet as it was attempting to escape from Santiago.

In World War I, over 16,000 men from this tiny state were in service and Vermont lost over 600 men. After the Armistice, things were quiet in the Green Mountains for a long time.

In 1927, floods caused millions of dollars worth of damage, took 60 lives, and completely wiped out many roads and railroads. But aside from the economic drain such natural disasters bring, Vermont's economy has remained remarkably even, little affected by the ups and downs of the American economy over the years. Agriculture, with emphasis on the dairy industry, has long provided a leveling agent.

Following World War II, more and more firms, such as IBM, General Electric and Standard Register have set up small operations in the state, while many long-established local firms have steadily expanded. Along with these, a number of small, independent businesses have sprung and are springing up, some only two- and three-man operations. These include the reviving of some of the old crafts, several publishing ventures, a wire and cable company, a farm which raises Sardinian and Sicilian donkeys, and a picture-framing business that has become so famous it does work for clients in all the surrounding states and elsewhere. A retriever-training center is doing a land-office business, and there are now 42 full-fledged ski resorts in the state.

Today's Vermonters quietly continue to work together. It was not an idle gesture when they chose "Freedom and Unity" as their State Motto. For a long time now there have been no Indians, Yorkers, French or British to fight on their home soil, but still the Vermonters go on together. Some observers feel it is subtly evident that what Vermonters are building now is a new way of life, a deceptively simple way of life which could perhaps shine as a beacon to all who would live free. In this effort many problems must be dealt with daily, within each individual's own sphere—not just at appointed times, at appointed places. Vermonters know the going is, and will be, tough. But that isn't going to stop them.

PRACTICAL INFORMATION FOR VERMONT

VERMONT FACTS & FIGURES. Vermont's name is derived from the French for "green mountain"—*vert mont*. Its nickname is *Green Mountain State*. The red clover is the state flower, the sugar maple, the state tree, the hermit thrush, the state bird. "Freedom and Unity" is the state motto. *Hail, Vermont* the state song.

Montpelier is the state capital. The state population is 389,881.

Much of Vermont is mountainous, and these mountains are the source of the state's major wealth: the thousands of visitors who flock to Vermont's 41 ski centers during the winter months. The mountains also provide the granite and marble for which the state is famous. The rocky soil makes farming a difficult task, but the hardy, taciturn Vermont farmer manages to make a living out of dairy produce, hay, and apples, and to turn out the nation's biggest supply of maple syrup. Vermont has long, cold and snowy winters; short, warm summers.

HOW TO GET AROUND. With the opening of new sections of Interstate 91, the flow of traffic into Vermont moves in greater safety without loss of the scenic countryside. Major highways are maintained in excellent condition. Driving time to the ski areas and picturesque villages has been diminished in recent years. The winding roads through the quaint towns and the rolling farmlands and woods are being widened and improved. Vermont is easier to reach now from Boston and New York.

Air travel. Major airfields in Vermont are *Burlington* and *Montpelier,* served by *Mohawk* and *Northeast* airlines from New York, Boston, and other fields. Private airfields for skiers and vacationists, year-round, at *Stowe* and at *Basin Harbor–Champlain.* Twin-engine flights to major ski areas from Kennedy, LaGuardia, Newark, White Plains, N.Y., Teterboro, N.J., and Red Bank, N.J., furnished by *Ski Air Service* of *Vermont International.* Seventeen other private airports in Vermont. Airport Chart available on request from Vermont Aeronautics Board, Montpelier. Taxi service for air passengers is provided by *Vermont Flying Service, Inc.,* to and from Barre-Montpelier Airport and the two cities.

Boat cruises. *Lake Champlain* ferry crossings: Two-hour scenic rides aboard Lake Champlain Transportation Co. ferries between Burlington, Vt., and Port Kent, N.Y.; Grand Isle, Vt., and Plattsburg, N.Y.; Charlotte, Vt., and Essex, N.Y.

Buses. *Vermont Transit Lines* have well-organized bus routes throughout the state, connecting with Greyhound buses in other states.

Mountain rides in summer months. First automatic gondola telecabin lift in the U.S. at *Mt. Snow Ski Area;* highest chairlift in the East, a 2½-mi. round trip, at *Killington Ski Area;* double chairlift on *Mt. Mansfield,* Stowe; aerial gondola tramway of 9,300 ft. to summit of *Lincoln Mountain,* Sugarbush Valley; 7,300-ft.-long double chairlifts to summit of *Jay Peak* near Canadian border.

Railways. *Boston & Maine Corp.* service, Springfield, Mass., and White River Junction; *Central Vermont Railway* service, White River Junction and Montreal, via Montpelier, Burlington and St. Albans. Four daily trains between Montreal and Washington, via *New Haven Railroad, Pennsylvania Railroad,* and *Canadian National Railroads.*

There are *Hertz Rent-A-Car* agencies in Burlington, Montpelier, and Rutland.

SEASONAL EVENTS. Throughout the year, the villages of Vermont, as well as the large vacation resorts, are bustling with activities to please the discriminating tastes of Vermonters and visitors.

A heavy emphasis is placed on skiing and other sports activities during the winter resort season, usually from late Nov. to mid-April. There are special events that attract national attention. *National Ski Week* is celebrated during the third week of January. A *Winter Week End* is held for former servicemen and their families during the *Veterans Derby and Carnival* at Okemo Mountain, also in January. Another exciting program is the February *Winter Snow Bowl Carnival* at the Middlebury College campus in Middlebury. Also starting in the fall, the cultural atmosphere is enhanced by the *Vermont Symphony Orchestra* as it makes its music-appreciation tour, village to village, from November to July. The *Vermont Stateside Show* is held in Barre in February.

Being the leading state in the East for maple syrup and maple syrup products,

Vermont honors that industry with public recognition programs during the spring. St. Albans celebrates with a well-organized *Maple Syrup Festival* in May. Also in this spring month are *Hardwick's Tulip Festival* and the *Blue Mountain Riding Club*'s horse show, at Windsor.

Summer brings antique shows and special *art shows* by Vermont and out-of-state artists during July and August at the *Fleming Museum* on the University of Vermont campus, Burlington, and at the *Southern Vermont Art Center,* near Manchester. Since 1951, world-famous musicians have participated in the *Marlboro Music Festival* at Marlboro College campus, Marlboro, during July and Aug. The *Champlain Shakespeare Festival,* staged by professional actors, starts during the last week of July and runs through August in the *University of Vermont Arena Theater,* Burlington. Summer stock is presented at a half-dozen theaters, the best known being the *Dorset Playhouse* in Dorset and the *Weston Community Club* in Weston.

Aquatic competitions are held during the summer on Lake Champlain and at many of the 400 lakes. Outing and canoe clubs sponsor *slalom championships* on West River. There is a horse show by the *Vermont Horse Assn.* in August, and horsemen are in for a treat at the various events of the *Green Mountain Horse Assn.* One of its principal affairs is the *100-Mile Trail Ride* (since 1935), which originates at South Woodstock during the first week of Sept.

Autumn fairs and foliage are prime festival occasions in all parts of Vermont. Some fairs are held in late Aug. before the summer folks head homeward. Others are held in Sept. and Oct., to celebrate the bountiful harvest. Community programs are planned in connection with the brilliant foliage season, usually from Sept. 25 to Oct. 15. An outstanding regional festival is the *Fall Foliage Festival* of Northeast Kingdom, involving the villages of Walden, Cabot, Marshfield, Peacham, Barnet Center, and Groton. *Trotting* races are run at *Green Mountain Park,* Pownal, while singing groups participate in the *Stowe Folk Festival* at Stowe during the last week of September. Vermonters also participate enthusiastically in *Forest Festival Week* at the end of September to dramatize the need for conservation of their beautiful green woodlands. In October there is the popular *Bennington Art Show.*

TOURIST INFORMATION SERVICES. Vermont's well-organized network of information services for visitors is expanded with the new *Welcome Center* on the eastern side of Interstate 91, about ½ mi. n. of the Vermont-Mass. line in Guilford. Approved by the Federal Bureau of Public Roads, the $42,500 one-story structure is the first of its kind on a U.S. interstate highway. Funds from Vermont business and travel companies were subscribed by the Vermont Development Department and the Greater Vermont Association. State funds will be used to staff and maintain the center year-round. Similar centers are proposed for Interstate 91 sites at White River Junction, St. Johnsbury, Newport, St. Albans, Rutland, and Bennington.

Twenty-six *information booths* are in focal points of 26 communities. The wealth of travel literature in each booth is provided by the Vermont Development Department, a state agency, which inspired the respective chambers of commerce to set up the summer booth information system.

Brochures are also furnished by the *Greater Vermont Association,* Box 37, Montpelier, which also mails free literature on request. Travel suggestions on many subjects are mailed free by the *Vermont Development Department,* Montpelier. Free literature is also available from *Vermont Attractions,* Shelburne; *Lake Champlain Islands Assn.,* South Hero; *Northeastern Vermont Development Assn.,* Lyndonville; *Stowe Area Association,* Stowe.

DRINKING LAWS. Bars are illegal in Vermont. What *are* legal are what state authorities call *"counters."* Most counters are open until midnight or 1 a.m., closing hour. Drinks are sold with meals in hotels and restaurants having first- and third-class licenses, daily and on Sun. from noon to 9 p.m. A few counters with live entertainment are allowed to be open until 2 a.m. Mon. through Fri. Persons under 21 years of age are not permitted to be served at counters or to buy at licensed liquor stores and agencies.

Bottled *beer* and light *wine* are sold at stores with second-class licenses. They are open from 8 a.m. to 10 p.m. Mon. through Sat., and on Sun. from noon to 9 p.m. Bottled *liquor* is sold at state liquor stores and agencies. Local option forbids the sale of liquor in some Vermont towns. However it is okay to bring in your own liquor and to buy setups.

NATIONAL PARKS. *Green Mountain National Forest,* in central and southern Vermont, follows the main ranges of the Green Mountains. Established in 1928, the forest comprises 232,464 acres, flanked or traversed by US 4, US 7, and Rtes. 11 and 100.

Winter sports predominate at the well-developed private facilities within the forest: *Snow Valley, Mt. Snow, Big Bromley, Stratton Mountain,* and *Sugarbush Valley.*

Summer camping and picnicking are featured at *Hapgood Pond, Greendale, White Rocks,* and *Texas Falls.* These areas, built and operated by the Forest Service, are on a first-come, first-served basis. No reservations accepted; no fees charged. Fourteen-day stay is maximum in summer per family. Campfire permits are required outside of developed areas without fireplaces. Fishing and hunting licenses may be obtained at town clerks' offices. Adirondack shelters for overnight lodging are at 6-mi. intervals along the 255-mi. *Long Trail,* celebrated hiking route of which 80 mi. are within the forest. Horseback riding trails and good roads wind through rich scenic spots. Trout is stocked in 3,233 acres of lakes and ponds and in 349 mi. of streams. Information on the forest is provided free by Forest Supervisor, Rutland; Vermont Development Dept., Montpelier. Forest officers are stationed in Middlebury, Rochester, and Manchester Center.

STATE PARKS. Vermont received its name from early French explorers after they saw the northern tip of the Appalachian chain and dubbed the area "green mountain" *(verd mont*—in French, of course). Some people say the area is sometimes blue, sometimes white. Most of Vermont remains green, particularly in the 96,359 acres of the 30 state parks and 29 state forests. These special naturelands are in close proximity to the 232,464 acres of the Green Mountain National Forest. The parks and forests, covering fertile valleys of the Connecticut River and the countless streams, are open to the public year-round for recreational purposes. The forests, however, are mostly for forestry and conservation uses.

There's much variety for the outdoor folks. Skiers and hikers thrill to the rugged forested lure of *Mt. Mansfield State Forest* (20,936 acres), with the state's loftiest peak (4,393 ft.). Here is perhaps the East's best ski region, capped with *Smugglers' Notch,* the gorge through which smugglers were supposed to have taken goods from Canada en route to Boston during the War of 1812. *Allis State Park* (485 acres), a great recreation paradise, is reached via Rte. 14 over the Brookfield Floating Bridge. *D.A.R. State Park,* at Lake Champlain (Rte. 17), contains a historic area dating from before the Revolutionary War. Now it is used for picnic and shelter purposes. *Monroe State Park,* at the eastern base of *Camel's Hump* (in the Green Mountains), is maintained partly as a bird sanctuary and a plant and game preserve. A beautiful sandy beach sparkles at

Branbury State Park along the eastern shore of Lake Dunmore, between Middlebury and Brandon. The *Killington Ski Center* is a focal section of the *Calvin Coolidge State Forest,* which also preserves the *Calvin Coolidge Farm.*

Camping reservations may be made with the Department of Forests and Parks, Montpelier, for not less than 4 nights or more than 3 weeks. Requests should be sent from Jan. 1 to May 1. No reservations are needed after Labor Day. Nominal fees are asked for camping and lean-to shelter privileges. A fee of about 25¢ is charged daily to every person entering a park or forest. They are open from 10 a.m. to 9 p.m. from late May through Labor Day; thereafter until 8 p.m., except to campers with permission. Ski areas close at 5 p.m. Brochures on the areas may be obtained free from the Department of Forests and Parks or the Vermont Development Department, both in Montpelier.

WHERE TO GO. Vermont claims a fair share of outstanding scenic, historic, cultural, and recreational appeals. World's largest, most complete *ski resort—Mt. Snow Ski Area,* near West Dover (Rte. 100). World's largest *granite quarries*—Barre's *Rock of Ages* quarry and *Craftsman Center,* open for free tours. *"Maple Center of the World"—Maple Grove Maple Museum,* free guided tour of world's largest maple-candy factory, St. Johnsbury (Rte. 2). Vermont's *"Little Grand Canyon"*—a mile-long chasm, *Quechee Gorge,* on Ottauquechee River, at Quechee (US 4). America's largest aerial *gondola lift*—thrilling ascent to *Lincoln Peak, Sugarbush Valley Ski Area,* Warren (Rte. 100). *Bennington Battle Monument*—Revolutionary War memorial on Monument Ave., Bennington, dedicated in 1891, with elevator to summit of 306-ft. shaft for view of historic battlefield and three states. *Shelburne Museum* —created village of New England Americana within 35 buildings in Shelburne, 7 mi. south of Burlington (Rte. 7).

WHAT TO DO WITH THE CHILDREN. Biggest attractions for children in Vermont are the *Green Mountains*—with extensive winter and summer facilities, ranging from nature paths to sensational ski lifts. Also, leisure-time areas are plentiful, from simple roadside picnic sites to plush mountainside resorts. They are usually geared to entertain children as well as adults.

Popular fun-places for children are conveniently located on principal highways. Among the outstanding ones are: *Quechee Gorge*—at Quechee (US 4), free camping and recreation areas near Vermont's "most unique natural wonder"—a mile-long chasm through which flows the Ottauquechee River at 162 feet below highway bridge. Open daily from May until Dec. 1. *Rare Bird and Animal Farm* —at Fairlee (US 5), where children enjoy feeding and petting animals. Open daily, from May until mid-Oct. *Santa's Land, U.S.A.*—north of Putney (US 5), a Christmas fairyland in summertime. Hungry animals wait to be fed; one-half mi. of Santa's *Alpine Railroad.* Open from May to Nov. 1 daily, from 9:30 a.m. to 5:30 p.m. Adm. for adults, 95¢; for children 6 to 12, 35¢, under 6, free. *Shelburne Museum*—in Shelburne (Rte. 7), contains exhibitions of Americana appealing to youngsters. Latest of 35 buildings is devoted to circus era, featuring extensive miniature circus. Museum grounds are open from May 15 to Oct. 20, daily from 9 a.m. to 5 p.m. Adm. for adults, $2.25; for students, $1. *Steamtown U.S.A.*—2 mi. n. of Bellows Falls (US 5), a 26 mi. ride on an old steam excursion train between Bellows Falls and Chester. Three daily excursions; extra run on Sun. and holidays. Train ride and visit to steam era museum at North Walpole, N.H., across the Connecticut River. Adults, $2.50; children $1.25. Open from May through Nov.

EXPLORING VERMONT

Everywhere the traveler looks in Vermont, he is confronted with sudden, almost capricious variations and contrasts in the character of the country and constant glimpses, strikingly anachronistic, of old America. For this *is* old America: it is the root and stock of hardiness and independence, the embodiment of the pioneering spirit. The early settlers were the pioneers of their day, pushing north from Connecticut and Massachusetts and west from New Hampshire, over the mountains and up the narrow valleys.

This spirit is nostalgically evident today. One old hill farmer still tells of his ancestors, among the first to make their way into the then rugged wilderness. "They come up into this country to get away from all the crowds down there around Boston," he says. "When they got far enough up here in the woods, they found a green valley and old Sam'l, he says, 'This here's the place. We'll make camp and tomorrow we'll scout the lay of the country for a place to build the cabin.'

"Well, just about daybreak, when they were makin' a fire to cook breakfast, all of a sudden—from off over the ridge—they heard a cock crow.

" 'Gol durn it,' says old Sam'l, 'we got neighbors!'

"So they picked themselves up and pushed on up here into the hills, until they found a place where they could look off in any direction and not see the smoke from any other cabin nor hear a cock crow."

There are few such views left for the traveler of today. Instead, he will find a remarkable panorama spread before him: the Green Mountains, white churches etched against a blue-blue sky, sturdy little meetinghouses, village greens, leafy country lanes, pastoral hillsides with sleek cows looking proverbially contented (joking remarks to the contrary, there are more people than cows in Vermont). There are red barns and white barns, stands of white birches, grazing sheep, rakish split-rail fences. In some seasons there are the fruit trees' feathery blooms, or the russets, reds, and golds of turning leaves, or meadows bright with buttercups, daisies, and red clover, the humble, yet lovely state flower.

Almost everyone knows the story about the stranger, motoring through Vermont, who stopped to ask a farmer directions to a certain settlement. The farmer thought for awhile and said, "Well, I reckon you can't get there from here." Actually you can get everywhere from "here" in the Green Mountain State, but the way may sometimes be roundabout. Perhaps that's all to the good. Sometimes going by a circuitous route, sometimes even backtracking for a bit, you're rewarded with just that much more of the spectacle that is Vermont.

Bennington and its Battlefield

One of the most pleasant introductions to Vermont is by way of State 7, north from Massachusetts. There, below to your left, as you drive up a steep hill, lies the calendar-picture Pownal Valley. Just beyond, you come to Bennington, home of the Bennington Museum, considered one of America's outstanding regional museums, though in many ways it speaks for all of America. You'll find it on State 9.

On March 1, 1966, the museum put on display the largest collection of Bennington pottery and porcelain in the world. It includes the famous Parian porcelain, made to imitate Parian marble. The museum also has the largest collection of patterned glass-goblets in the country, and fine examples of Vermont glass, colored Sandwich glass, and Tiffany art glass. The museum also has outstanding groups of toys and dolls, early tools, and some fine American and European paintings. Its great pride is the Bennington Flag, the oldest Stars-and-Stripes flag in existence. Centered beneath its 11 stars are the numerals '76. It came from the battle of Bennington, as did the museum's four cannons, which were taken from the British in that same battle, fought on August 16, 1777.

Actually, despite all the bickering and near warfare between New York and Vermont over boundaries, the Bennington Battlefield lies within the borders of New York State. But the Bennington Battle Monument (306 feet and with an elevator) is here, just beyond the museum. Near the monument you'll see a statue of Seth Warner, leader of the Green Mountain Boys who turned the tide of battle that day in 1777 at Bennington.

On the way to the monument (the museum's folder has a good map of the area) stop by the Old First Church, a classic among American churches. See its square pews, made this way so that a warmer, placed in the center, would give some comfort to all the occupants on bitter days.

On from the battle monument you can find one or more of Bennington's covered bridges: Paper Mill, Bert Henry, and Silk Pond. Bennington College is also on the outskirts. A four-year women's college, it has been recognized for its distinctive curriculum and methods since it first opened its doors in 1932.

Back in the center of town you'll find the Bennington Potters, which is in no way to be confused with earlier firms of that name which made some of the classic pieces now in museums throughout the world. However, you may be intrigued with some of the modern-day wares put out by this firm.

From Bennington take State 7 north to Shaftsbury. The Gerlachs, famous bookbinders, who do work for customers all over the world, live and work here. Vermont's first Baptist church was built here in 1768, and Jonas Galusha, who early in the state's history was governor for nine terms, lived here in a handsome Georgian house. You'll see this and other notable structures along here, as well as some typical New England mountain scenery.

Farther north on State 7 is Arlington. The late Dorothy Canfield Fisher lived here, as did illustrator Norman Rockwell, and, for a period, Robert Frost. Current residents include Herbert Wheaton Congdon, author of *Old Vermont Houses* and *The Covered Bridge,* and artist George Hughes, whose covers are familiar to *Saturday Evening Post* readers. Long ago, Green Mountain Boys' leaders Remember Baker and Seth Warner called Arlington home.

Left on State 313, is West Arlington, with a lovely village green, and nearby, a latticed covered bridge. East of Arlington, on an unnumbered road, you'll find the Candle Mill at East Arlington. Here you can see candles being made in original, tin candle molds, and the Mill has a wide selection of candles from many foreign lands.

Returning to State 7, continue north. At the roadside here is the Basket Barn, reputed to be one of the world's largest basket stores. Just beyond is Manchester, with its wide, elm-shaded streets, and marble sidewalks. Long a summer resort, it once attracted such vacationing notables as Mrs. Abraham Lincoln and Mrs. Ulysses S. Grant.

Manchester

Manchester, Manchester Center, and Manchester Depot form a complex here. Though the arrangement may seem confusing, there is plenty to see. If you have a large house, or piles of money, or both, drop in on Sam Ogden, Jr., who does some remarkable chandeliers and other objects of wrought iron. Stop at the Johnny Appleseed Bookshop, too. Perhaps you'll catch a glimpse of, or have a chat with, its famous poet-proprietor Walter Hard, Sr., author of *A Matter of Fifty Houses, Vermont Neighbors,* etc. Carl Sandburg once said of him, "Walter Hard is poet, annalist, anecdote finder. He and I believe that an anecdote of sufficient pith and portent is in essence a poem." Some of Walter Hard's best poetic anecdotes are gathered in a recently published book entitled *Vermont Sampler.* No self-respecting fisherman would dare visit Manchester without dropping by the showrooms of the Charles F. Orvis Company. This famous fishing rod firm has been in business since 1856.

By all means visit the Manchester Art Center (also called the

Southern Vermont Art Center on some direction signs). Here you'll find Vermont talent exhibited in paintings, sculpture, and photography. If you plan to be around the Manchester area for a few days, ask for a copy of the center's program of concerts and dance recitals. The noted artist Luigi Lucioni is a familiar figure in Manchester, and Pearl Buck, who has a home here, spends quite a bit of time in the area.

Equinox House here is a famous old inn. The *Sky Line Inn* atop Mt. Equinox is upstaging it these days, at least in modernity. You'll see the latter if you take the trip up Mt. Equinox on the Sky Line Drive, a toll road. It's a 5½-mile drive to the summit of 3,816-foot Mt. Equinox, for spectacular views of lakes, other mountains, and glimpses into New York, New Hampshire, and Massachusetts.

North from Manchester, take State 30 to Dorset. It's a hideaway haunt of writers and artists, and the Caravan Players at the Dorset Playhouse are a popular summer attraction. The Enchanted Doll House here has a wide selection of dolls and Vermont-made wooden toys.

Farther along on State 30 is Pawlet. You may find it hard to believe this sleepy hamlet was once a thriving mill town. Long before that, prominent pioneer and Green Mountain Boy Remember Baker had a gristmill here (1768), and in 1777 Herrick's Rangers, later to become known as the Terror of the Tories, was organized at this spot. (Herrick was another prominent leader in the Battle of Bennington.) In 1855, native son Joshua C. Stoddard not only originated the horse-drawn rake but, much more exciting, the steam calliope.

North of Pawlet is Poultney, where you'll find the beautiful campus of Green Mountain College. The nearby *Two Editors Inn* is named in honor of Horace Greeley and Raymond Jones, both of whom learned the printing trade at neighboring East Poultney. As everyone knows, Horace ("Go west, young man") Greeley later founded the New York *Tribune* (now the *Herald Tribune*). Raymond Jones, whose name is not as familiar as Greeley's, founded the New York *Daily Times* (now the *Times*). Jones' partner was, oddly enough, one George Jones (no relation), of Poultney. George, who was business manager, professed no journalistic leanings. However, when Raymond died, George took over for awhile as editor, launched the *Times'* famous crusade against the notorious Boss Tweed and his gang, and made the pages of history by summarily turning down the $5-million bribe offered him to drop the whole affair.

A famous toast was given in East Poultney, back in Revolutionary times, by Captain William Watson. He startled his confreres by beginning, "To the enemies of our country!" He went on, "May they have cobweb breeches, a porcupine saddle, a hard-trotting horse and an eternal journey."

The curious piles of rubble you see along State 30, derrick riggings and booms sticking up from them, are old slate-quarry dumps.

Continue on State 30 to Castleton Corners, turning right (east) on State 4 to Castleton, which has several interesting examples of the Greek Revival style in architecture. It was in Castleton, at Zadock Remington's Tavern, that Ethan Allen, Seth Warner, and their men are said to have planned the successful attacks on Fort Ticonderoga and Crown Point. And the founder of America's oil industry was born here. Edwin L. Drake, after years of heartbreaking setbacks, finally drilled America's first successful oil well, at Titusville, Pennsylvania.

Hubbardton Battlefield

Continuing east on State 4, watch for signs for the Hubbardton Battlefield (a left turn). Here the only battle of the Revolution which took place entirely on Vermont soil was fought. Military buffs will be delighted with this area. There's a big battle monument, a museum with both a diorama of early stages of the battle, and a large, animated relief map of the battlefield, with a running commentary of the actual battle.

Returning to State 4, turn left, then watch for West Proctor Road and signs for Wilson Castle. This complex of 16 buildings is of Flemish design, and the furnishings of the hilltop castle are worth beholding. Many of them (some are museum pieces) have been gathered (as well as a number of *objets d'art*) throughout the world by Colonel Wilson, present owner of the castle. Much of the paneling and many of the ceilings and fireplaces are quite elaborate.

Continuing north on West Proctor Road, you come to Proctor and the Vermont Marble Company. Among the many exhibits is a carving, from a solid block of marble, of *The Last Supper*. The Gallery of Presidents, bas-reliefs of many of our presidents, were carved by an Italian-born sculptor. In the town itself you'll see sidewalks, retaining walls, buildings, a bridge, and other construction, all of marble.

From Proctor, take State 3 south, and turn left where it joins State 4. You'll come to Rutland, one of only three places in Vermont where you'll find what could rightfully be called an industrial city. Burlington and Barre are the other two. Despite its bustle, Rutland, like Burlington, is a pretty place.

Where State 4 joins State 7, within the city, take the latter north, looking for a country road (paved) which bears off to the right. It's just beyond an old, red-brick powerhouse on your left. This road will take you to Chittenden. In area, this is Vermont's largest town. However, in number of buildings, it's one of the smallest. It was named for Vermont's first governor, Thomas Chittenden. Cross the little bridge at the left and follow signs to *Mountain Top Inn.* You'll find a glorious view and one of the country's better known hostelries. Members of the famous Grace Steamship Company family often vacation here, and its most famous guest to date has been trout-fisherman Dwight Eisenhower.

Returning to State 7, continue north to Pittsford. Covered-bridge fanciers will probably already know this was the home of Nicholas M. Powers, the state's master builder of these bridges. You can see his Cooley Bridge here, over Furnace Brook, and there's a model of one of his bridges at the Powers' store in town.

Farther north on State 7 is lovely, serene Brandon. It wasn't always given to producing serene citizens though, as you'll realize when you visit the cottage of Stephen A. Douglas, debater of Abraham Lincoln. The Little Giant was born here over 150 years ago.

Another local man of note was Thomas Davenport who, though he died poor and unheralded, invented and patented the first electric motor. He also made a model of the first streetcar, now preserved in the Smithsonian Institution. Brandon is very art conscious, and in summer a look at the local paper will probably disclose an art exhibit going on somewhere in town.

Next on State 7 is Leicester, but it's such a small settlement you might not know you're there. You'll want to turn left here on an unnumbered road (there should be small signs here pointing to the Fort Ticonderoga Ferry). This road will take you to Whiting and on to Shoreham Center, with views of rolling country, the Adirondack Mountains in the distance to the west, and scatterings of cows on green hillsides. This is big, important, dairy country.

Beyond Shoreham Center turn north (right) briefly, to Shoreham, taking State 74 left (west) here to Larrabees Point. Here you'll find the little ferry that crosses Lake Champlain to Fort Ticonderoga.

Opposite: This slice of skyline reflects Boston's allegiance to both tradition and progress.
Photo: E. Fodor

Overleaf: Maine's hidden beauty spots call lovers of the outdoors.
Photo: Maine Publicity Bureau

Facing page 257: Going down to the sea from Gloucester, Mass. remains the heritage of its rugged fishermen.
Photo: Rapho G.

You may just want to look, or you may want to ride over and back on the six-minute crossing. Larrabees Point is where Ethan Allen and his Green Mountain Boys embarked in May of 1775 to take Fort Ticonderoga and Crown Point, and you may want to visit Ticonderoga from here.

Hand's Cove, near here, was named for Augustus Cincinnatus Hand, whose grandson Learned Hand was one of America's most famous jurists.

Middlebury's Cultural Delights

Returning on State 74, you'll find this road continues north to Middlebury, an interesting region where you may want to spend some time. Middlebury College, founded in 1800, has a charming campus and excellent collections of both Robert Frost and Thoreau in its library. Despite its relatively small size, Middlebury has one of the country's largest campuses, thanks to a somewhat eccentric millionaire named Colonel Joseph Battell. He left 30,000 acres of forest land to the college. Battell loved mountains and Morgan horses, and he hated automobiles. He had a resort hotel, *Bread Loaf Inn,* and anyone who dared to drive up to the door in an auto was immediately turned away, reservation or no. He filled a weekly paper he published with detailed accounts of automobile accidents.

Middlebury College, well known as it is, is probably better known for its three summer activities: the summer language schools (French, Spanish, Italian, German, Russian), the Bread Loaf School of English (advanced study), and the Bread Loaf Writers' Conference. All three draw large groups each summer, and among those whose names are closely connected with the conference are poet-critic John Ciardi, novelist Nancy Hale, and for a number of years, the late Robert Frost.

Middlebury's Congregational Church, with its 136-foot bell tower, is among Vermont's loveliest and most photographed. Among prominent residents are Mrs. Chester Way, famous flower arranger, and Dike Blair, writer and owner-proprietor of the Vermont Book Store. It's difficult to know where the personality of Blair leaves off and the store's contents take over, but for whatever reason, countless visitors to the Middlebury area make a beeline for Dike's door. His Vermont store also does a huge mail-order business.

The Sheldon Museum here (not to be confused with the Shelburne Museum, farther north) is considered by many as one of the finest small museums in New England. Certainly many visitors claim they emerge with the feeling that they've just been guests at a lovely old home. By 1882 the house's owner, Henry Sheldon, had opened his Sheldon Art Museum, Archeological and Historical

Society, the first incorporated village museum in America. The present-day visitor can be grateful for Sheldon's predilection for collecting, as many of his treasures and finds are currently displayed in lovely room settings.

Skiers, and those who would like to see Bread Loaf, should drive out east of town on State 125, to Ripton. It was long the hometown of Robert Frost, and this is where Middlebury College's famous Snow Bowl is located.

If you're a fan of the drama, there's summer theater at the Bread Loaf Little Theatre, the College Playhouse, and at the various schools of language (in French, German, Italian, and Spanish).

From Ripton return to Middlebury and continue west on State 125, watching for signs to the University of Vermont Morgan Horse Farm, at Weybridge. You'll recognize the farm by the handsome statue of a Morgan horse on the lawn, a familiar sight to actor James Cagney, a frequent visitor here who has bought several Morgans.

The farm was begun in 1907, when the eccentric Colonel Battell gave some of this land to the U.S. Government in the hopes it would continue and improve the Morgan horse. In 1951 the government, in turn, gave the farm to the University of Vermont. Now, not only Morgan horses, but also sheep and cattle are raised here. Visitors are welcome during the summer, at the barns, along pasture fences.

The Morgan horse's exact bloodlines are somewhat clouded, though it is generally believed the original was of Arabian stock. Brought to Vermont by its owner, schoolteacher Justin Morgan, the original horse sired so many notable offspring (as they, in turn, did) that the first horse not only became known as Justin Morgan, but also was named Vermont's State Animal in 1961. Experts say the Morgan blood was instrumental in founding, among several other American breeds, the standardbred and the Tennessee walking horse.

Returning to State 125, continue west to State 22-A, turning right (north) here to Addison. You can visit the brick mansion built here by General John Strong. It's furnished in the period of the late 1800's. Nearby is the Dead Creek Wild Life Refuge, and farther along on State 17 is Chimney Point, where, historians say, Samuel de Champlain stood on the July day in 1609 when he modestly named the huge lake that lay before him. The French at one time had a settlement here, but they abandoned it in 1759, fearing an Indian attack. Well they might. The Iroquois, at least, had the French on their blacklist.

About 2 miles north of Chimney Point, on State 17, turn left onto the unnumbered road that skirts the lake en route to Panton. In 1776 Benedict Arnold—still on our side at that time—burned the remnants of his fleet here. He'd just been defeated by the British farther north at Valcour Island. There's an excellent account of this event in Kenneth Roberts' *Rabble in Arms.*

From Panton, another unnumbered road takes you to Basin Harbor. In 1814 the British attacked a fort here, anxious to get on up Otter Creek to destroy the fleet being built there by American forces. They were roundly defeated.

From Basin Harbor drive east (again on an unnumbered road), following signs to Vergennes. It's the third oldest incorporated city in America with a population of just under 2,000 and it covers 1,200 acres. This is where the fleet was being built which the British were trying to get at when they attacked at Basin Harbor. Later that same year the fleet sailed out of hiding and defeated superior British forces in Plattsburgh Bay, N.Y.

At Vergennes you can see copies of early American woodenware and other items being made at Kennedy Brothers, and there are excellent Vermontiana collections at the Bixby Free Library here.

Lake Champlain and Shelburne

By now you've gotten a pretty good look at Lake Champlain (you'll see it at its widest just north of Burlington). The lake forms Vermont's western border for almost 100 miles of its 125-mile length. The lake is shared by Vermont, New York, and Canada's Quebec Province and is 14 miles wide at its broadest point.

From Vergennes take State 7 north to Shelburne. At Charlotte, along the way, you'll see the Charlotte Congregational Church on your right. It's one of the few Greek Revival buildings in the state.

Shelburne is, of course, most noted for the Shelburne Museum, a village of old houses and buildings, many of them moved here from other areas. Its charms are legion, with literally something for everyone. For complete details, read *The Story of the Shelburne Museum* by Ralph Nading Hill and Lilian Baker Carlisle.

Even the highlights of the museum are almost too numerous to name. There are over 36 handsome buildings, a covered bridge at the entrance, a collection of quilts, excellent paintings (including a superb Andrew Wyeth), cigar-store Indians, carousel figures, weather vanes, old carriages and coaches, figureheads, stencils, one of the last of the 10-wheel steam locomotives, and the last side-wheeler to cross Lake Champlain, the *Ticonderoga.* There are old toys, old farmhouses, an early meetinghouse, a weaving display, pewter, glass, and ceramics. *Antiques* magazine said of it, "It is not a reconstructed village, it is, rather, a collection of collections." To get some idea of what a treat is in store for you, and some thoughts about your itinerary here, write ahead for a folder.

From Shelburne continue north on State 7 to Burlington. It's a lovely city, ideally situated above Lake Champlain. Maybe you'll get a little lost wandering about in it, but its residential sections are so pleasant you'll scarcely mind.

The Robert Hull Fleming Museum (Colchester Ave.), the art museum of the University of Vermont, has exciting collections covering history from prehistoric to modern times. There are also special collections of Americana, primitive, ancient, and oriental art, and changing exhibits of contemporary art. In this last category you may be lucky enough to see some of the works of Vermont painter Francis Colburn, who lives in Burlington.

The University of Vermont is located here. Both it and the city were founded by Ira Allen, a less peripatetic fellow than his brother Ethan. The university holds an annual Shakespeare festival in August. American philosopher John Dewey was born here, and among present-day notables is Ralph Nading Hill, author of *Sidewheeler Saga, The Winooski* (Rivers of America Series), *Yankee Kingdom: Vermont and New Hampshire,* and other books.

At Battery Park (Pearl St.) a British landing was foiled during the War of 1812. A visit here will reward you with fine views of Lake Champlain and the Adirondack Mountains. General Ethan Allen's burial place is in Burlington (Colchester Ave.), and there's a monument to Vermont's hero at the site of the old Ethan Allen farm, now a park site (North Ave.).

North of Burlington

From Burlington continue north on State 7 to State 2. Turning left at State 2, you cross a portion of Lake Champlain to Grand Isle. North of South Hero is the Hyde Log Cabin, the oldest original log cabin left standing in Vermont. It was built of hand-hewn logs, in 1783, by Jedediah Hyde, Jr., a soldier of the Revolution and a surveyor of this north country. The Grand Isle County Historical Society has a museum at the cabin.

As you drive along State 2, you'll see a number of split-rail fences. This type of enclosure was originally built at a time when there weren't any nails or wire to be had. Before people clearing new land had time to split trees and build these fences, however, walls or fences of old tree stumps often had to suffice. Split-rail fences are often built nowadays where small rocks are difficult to come by in quantity.

All along here there are great vistas of Lake Champlain and of the Adirondacks to the west. People who love to watch sunsets and to fish are particularly attracted to this area, as well as to South Alburg, farther along. Off State 2 you will want to take a left turn onto State 129 if you plan to visit the Shrine of Ste. Anne, at Isle La Motte. Though the isle's population is small, thousands of people come here each summer to visit the shrine where the first Mass in Vermont was said, in 1666, at the time when some French troops settled in here.

Back on State 2 continue north to its junction with State 78. Turn right here, following signs for Swanton. When Swanton celebrated its bicentennial several years ago, Queen Elizabeth sent over some swans to help the celebrations along (ask where these can be seen). Most sober souls believe Swanton is just a little over 200 years old. But there's an interesting local legend that suggests Swanton's history goes a lot farther back. On the banks of the river here, in 1835, someone found a lead pipe. In it was a piece of paper, with a message that read, "Nov. 29 A D 1564—This is the solme day I must now dies this is the 90th day since we lef the Ship all have parished and on the Banks of this River I die to farewell may future Posteritye know our end—John Graye." Some people surmise Graye was the last survivor of one of Martin Frobisher's expeditions, which came to this region in 1577 and 1578, seeking gold. However, Frobisher himself returned to England after each of these expeditions.

From Swanton, drive south on State 7 to St. Albans. Not only was this peaceful settlement a smuggling center during the War of 1812, it was also the site of the northernmost engagement of the Civil War. You can see relics and drawings of this 1864 raid at the Franklin County Bank, one of the three raided by the band of 22 Confederate soldiers who later escaped into Canada.

Continue south on State 7 to State 104-A to Fairfax. You'll pass an impressive hydroelectric installation (on your left). This area is one of the state's maple sugar centers. Vermont produces more maple syrup than any other state in the U.S.; some travelers visit here from March to mid-April, to see the sap being taken from the groves, to watch the sap being boiled down, and to attend maple sugar parties.

Continuing on State 104, you come to Cambridge. There are three covered bridges here, as well as covered railroad bridges. The river you see all along here is the Lamoille. From Cambridge continue east on State 15 to Jeffersonville and turn left onto the main street. At the end of the street you'll find a pony farm that the young fry will find especially intriguing.

Beyond Jeffersonville is Johnson, with its unusual post office that was once a church. Farther along is Hyde Park, named after the surveyor Jedediah Hyde (whose log cabin is at Grand Isle). He made out the charter for this settlement. Though this is a small town, the C. H. Dana Company here does a worldwide business in special equipment for cattle.

This is an area where you will probably see quite a few sheep. Sheep raising, which was once a popular Vermont industry, dropped off perceptibly in the early 1900's, but is now being revived. Among breeds you may see are the Shropshire, Hampshire, Romney, and Southdown.

Morrisville, the next town, is noted for its historical museum. Housed in a brick mansion built in 1820, its collections include over 2,000 pitchers, antique wallpapers, dolls, mementos of the first settlers, etc.

Stowe Ski Country

At Morrisville turn right (south) on to State 100. This takes you to the famous ski area of Stowe and the attractive village of that name. Some consider that its Community church has the most outstanding spire in the state. America's first Community church, incidentally, was a Vermont one, built over a century and a half ago. There are a number of good, attractive hotels, motels, inns, and restaurants in this area, as well as some intriguing shops.

At the junction with State 108, take this route north. You'll pass the modern Catholic church along here. It commemorates Stowe's Brother Joseph Dutton who worked at the Molokai leper colony in Hawaii.

Along 108 look for signs to the *Trapp Family Lodge,* presided over by the renowned Baroness Maria Augusta von Trapp. It is her story and that of her family which was so fascinatingly told by Rodgers and Hammerstein in *The Sound of Music.* Part of the two-mile road into the *Lodge* is unpaved, but the trip is worth it, to see the Austrian alpine buildings and the magnificent view from the high ridge.

Returning to State 108 (turn left), you come into the heart of Stowe's ski country. Much of this area's development is attributable to the presence and enthusiasm of the ex-Austrian skier Sepp Ruschp. In 1938 he came to Stowe, soon started a ski school, and talked local authorities into building a rope tow.

By 1940, the first chair lift in the eastern U.S. went into operation here. During World War II, Skimeister Ruschp went off to fly for the U.S. Army Air Force. After 1945, he was back at Stowe, teaching and advising on further developments. Today the company for which he works has a total ski-lift capacity of over 7,000 skiers per hour on Mount Mansfield and Spruce Peak, and outstanding skiers, such as Olympic champion Betsy Snite, have been attracted to the area as year-round residents.

In summer the chair lift is run at Mt. Mansfield a little more slowly than in winter, giving riders a better chance to take in the view. Standing at 4,393 feet, Mt. Mansfield is the Green Mountains' highest peak. Travelers can also drive up the 4½-mile toll road, up, up through cool forests, for the view of three states, Canada's Quebec Province, and big, long Lake Champlain.

Just beyond the toll road is another reason for Stowe's fame: *The Lodge* at Smugglers' Notch. Its guests have included the Kennedys, N.Y. Mayor John Lindsay, Walter Cronkite. Lowell Thomas liked it so much that he talked his employers into letting him do some of his broadcasts from here. Guests come, not only for *The Lodge*'s fine accommodations, facilities, and majestic scenery, but also for its French cuisine.

Just beyond the Lodge the road begins to snake up, up into Smugglers' Notch. This is an exciting area, not only for its rugged beauty, but for its history as well. In the olden days only a footpath and horse trail wound up into the 2,162-foot notch, with 1,000-foot cliffs towering over it. When the Embargo Act came along, followed by the War of 1812, thanks to the remoteness of the notch, trade, illicit though it was, continued between Vermont and its nearby Canadian neighbors. Many a cow and bull was urged up through the steep pass, far from the eyes of any revenue officers.

The Big Spring, with its 39 degree water, is an attraction at the Notch, as are the natural rock formations Elephant Head, Hunter and His Dog, and the Singing Bird. And there's King Rock, a 6,000-ton boulder that crashed down in 1910. Here, too, is the Smugglers' Cave, a rock formation called the Smuggler's Face, and a rock crevice that emits air at 49 degrees no matter how hot the day.

Beyond the Notch

Beyond the Notch, turn left into State 15 for several miles, then left again where 15 dips south to Jericho, a pleasant town, with a number of red-brick buildings. Its claim to fame is the late Wilson A. Bentley, who became internationally renowned for the 5,300 snowflakes he microphotographed over a period of 50 years. The Brown's River firm here makes maple products and welcomes visitors.

At Essex Junction take State 2-A south to State 2, paralleling Interstate 89, to Richmond, where are located Harringtons', nationally known for their smoked hams and other meats. You can visit a smokehouse here and, if you're like most visitors, drool over the many fine food products displayed.

Leaving Harringtons', return a few miles on State 2 to Interstate 89. Take 89 east toward Waterbury. Even the most confirmed shunpiker may have to admit he's glad he took this highway. It is most unusual and seems the sort of thing that perhaps could happen only in Vermont. All along are stunning rock formations in shapes and sizes that ought to make any abstract sculptor turn green from head to toe. Here and there, too, note the sides of the highway are of unusual, pink-granite gravel.

At Waterbury leave 89 and take State 2 a short distance east to State 100 to Waitsfield. Look for the unusual round barn on the right. Waitsfield is the site of the Bundy Museum, which, though it may seem out of line with most people's concepts of Vermont, has a permanent collection of modern art, including sculpture in an outdoor garden. Of interest to ski enthusiasts are the nearby ski areas of Mad River Glen, Glen Ellen, and Sugarbush.

Returning north from Waitsfield on 100, bear right into State 100-B. Where this route joins State 2, turn east (right) to Montpelier, Vermont's capital. The gold-leaf-domed Capitol Building is an attraction here, as is the rather poorly housed museum of the Vermont Historical Society. Exhibits include the nation's first printing press and memorabilia of Admiral George (battle of Manila Bay) Dewey, who was born here. At the National Life Insurance Company there's a huge mural by Vermont artist Paul Sample, a tour, and a sound-color film on Vermont.

From Montpelier take State 302 to Barre. It's a city you'll probably want to putter around in for awhile. Barre was settled mainly by Scotch, Italians, and French, and the memorial statue of Scotch poet Robert Burns you'll see here was designed by Scotsmen and executed by local Italian artisans in honor of their Scotch-American fellow workers. There are several granite quarries to visit and tour (Rock of Ages and Jones Brothers) and a good collection of antique sugaring equipment at John Shelby's Maple Museum. The Windy Wood Orchards here invites visitors. They are the first to have made red apple syrup, and few people can visit Barre without thinking of apples, one of the state's major crops.

From Barre take State 14 north to East Montpelier, and from there State 2, northeast to Marshfield. A private covered bridge here is a favorite of photographers. Continuing on 2, you'll come to Danville, site of what is called the country's biggest crossroads bank. In 1952 the *Wall Street Journal,* writing about this bank, in a community with a population of some 400, headlined its article: "'Biggest Crossroads Bank' Thrives on Cattle Loans Competitors Don't Want." The Caledonia National Bank has been in existence since 1825. Danville also has the distinction of being the site of the annual National Dowsers' Convention.

St. Johnsbury

From Danville continue east on State 2 to St. Johnsbury, long noted for its wide main street, fine homes, and unusual octagonal house. The Maple Grove products people here welcome visitors, who get a guided tour of the factory, sugarhouse, and maple museum. Increasingly popular is the Fairbanks Museum of Natural Science, with its planetarium and collection of Polynesian and African arts. Thaddeus Fairbanks invented the platform scale here in 1830.

The St. Johnsbury Athenaeum has a number of canvases of the Hudson River School, as well as good copies of many European masterpieces. The big trucks marked *St. Johnsbury* that rove all of America's highways do come from here, home base for New England's largest trucking firm.

Any covered bridge fancier will be delighted with Lyndon and Lyndonville, north of here, on State 5. There are five covered bridges in and about this area.

From St. Johnsbury return west on State 2 to Danville, there taking the unnumbered road at the village square to Ewells Mill and Peacham. At Peacham, on your left, look for the local post office (and its sign), surely one of the sweetest and most unusual in America. Oliver Johnson, who learned printing here, went on to become the influential editor of the *Anti-Slavery Standard.* Peacham Academy, still going strong, was founded here way back in 1795.

There are sweeping views all along this road and, at the end, a very steep hill. Although Vermont usually tells travelers what route they're on, and in which direction they should go, it doesn't here. Turn left at the bottom of the hill. You'll be on State 302. Continue east on this road to Wells River, an early Scotch settlement. Here take State 5 south. Just beyond the town, there is another of those unusual round barns.

Farther south on 5 is Newbury, one of Vermont's most photographed towns, with its fine old church and old homes. Indian Joe and Indian Molly are buried here at the Ox-Bow Cemetery. Joe and his squaw Molly were so friendly to the first people to come into this area that George Washington wrote Joe a letter, thanking him for all his help to the settlers.

South of Newbury

Just south of Newbury look for a handsome, yellow-painted farm to your left. A sign here will direct you to the Bedell Bridge, but continue on to the next left turning. It's a better road, easier on the axles. This bridge has long been a favorite with color photographers. There is a little red house near the western entrance to the bridge, and since the people who used to live there were a bit remiss about keeping the house well painted, some of the photographers took matters into their own hands. From time to time they'd arrive, not only with cameras, but with cans of paint. Asking for, and getting permission from the owners, they'd set to work with their brushes—the house would look better in their photos.

Returning to State 5, you come to Bradford, just south of here. Note there's a sign on almost every house in this settlement, giving the year it was built. James Wilson of this town, after 11 years of arduous work, produced the first geographical globes made in this country. Another photogenic village is East Corinth, northwest of Bradford on State 25.

South on State 5 is Fairlee, site of the Walker Museum and Lake Morey. The Walker Museum includes a Persian bazaar, a Japanese room, religious art dating from the time of Abraham, two floors of Americana, and other exciting exhibits. Lake Morey was named for Captain Samuel Morey, who lived here. He built a steam-driven boat, which he ran on the Connecticut River 15 years before Fulton's *Clermont* was launched. This area has a number of boys' and girls' summer camps, of which there are over a hundred in the state.

South of here, still on State 5, is the Rare Bird and Animal Farm, which the youngsters will enjoy. Beyond, you pass through the Thetford area, where a celebrated pioneer woman once lived. Mrs. Richard Wallace worked her farm singlehanded while her husband was off fighting in the Revolution. Though she didn't know it at the time, he was one of two soldiers who swam all the way across Lake Champlain, right through a British fleet, to deliver some important messages.

At Norwich, farther south on 5, live the famous puppeteer Basil Milovsoroff and the well-known watercolorist Paul Sample. Norwich University was founded here in 1819, but when a number of buildings burned in 1866, its site was moved to Northfield.

Continuing south on State 5, at the junction with State 4, you'll see at the station *Old 464,* a retired steam engine preserved by some of the local citizenry. Take State 4 right to Woodstock. On the way, stop and look down into Quechee Gorge, 162 feet deep. At Woodstock you'll find one of Vermont's most memorable towns. It's filled with fine houses and public buildings, and has more Paul Revere bells (four) in its churches than any other community in America.

Among outstanding shops here are those of Dorothy Bulmer (custom lamps and shades) and The Vermont Workshop, one of the finest gift shops in New England. Proprietor Nancy Wickham Boyd, a world-known ceramist, has won many a national and international prize for her unique work.

Memorable Woodstock

The late Dorothy Thompson once lived near here, as did Sinclair Lewis and Anne Batchelder, long-famous through the pages of the *Ladies Home Journal.* Byron Thomas, Ivan Albright, Tad Bailey, and Bruce Penny are among the artists living here. Woodstock, long known for its artists, numbers among its native sons Hiram Powers, a sculptor of the mid-1800's. He was famous for his *Greek Slave,* a copy of which is in the Corcoran Gallery in Washington, D.C. His bust of John Marshall and statues of Franklin and Jefferson are in the National Capitol Building.

If you should see a Stanley Steamer putt-putting about town, don't be surprised. It's a local feature, restored by two Woodstock lads. You, too, can take a turn about town in it, or a longer trip, depending on your budget, inclination, and amount of free time.

There are a number of side trips possible out of Woodstock. One goes north to Mount Tom and Suicide Six, site of the first ski tow in America (1934). At Windsor, where movie actress Marie *(Tugboat Annie)* Dressler had a summer home, you'll find Old Constitution House, sometimes called the birthplace of Vermont. A group of delegates met here in 1777 to draw up the constitution for the proposed Independent Republic of Vermont. It was at this time, too, that the suggestion was adopted that the state drop the name of New Connecticut, which it then had, and adopt Vermont as its name.

Other side trips from Woodstock might include a visit to Dartmouth College and its exciting Hopkins Center (across the Connecticut River in Hanover, N.H.), or a trip to Sharon, birthplace of Joseph Smith, founder of the Mormon faith. The Smith Monument is supposedly the world's largest (37½ feet tall) single shaft of polished granite. And at Strafford you can visit the birthplace of Justin Smith Morrill. He won a place in the annals of the history of education by authoring the Morrill Acts (Lincoln signed them in 1862). These acts established America's land-grant colleges and universities, a definite boost to higher education in America.

From Woodstock take State 4 west to its junction with State 100-A, turning south here to Plymouth Notch, site of Calvin Coolidge's birthplace. You may visit the little white house where he was born. The Wilder House next door, the home of President Coolidge's mother until she married Colonel John Coolidge, is also open to the public and serves as a hospitality center. At the Wilder Barn—now called the Vermont Farmer's Museum—there's a large display of old farm tools and other implements used on early farms. Thousands of people visit Plymouth Notch each year, and many stop by the Plymouth Cheese Company, store of President Coolidge's son, John.

Continue south from here on State 100 and 103 to Chester. This fetching settlement is especially noted for its stone houses, built mainly in the mid-1800's. The map-making firm National Survey is located here.

From Chester take State 11 west to Londonderry. Along here are both the Magic Mountain and Glebe Mountain ski areas. At Londonderry, turn right on State 100, to Weston, where is located the nationally known Vermont Country Store, whose catalog is avidly read by many fans from coast to coast. Each issue carries an editorial, written by Vrest Orton. Sometimes these are salty or sentimental, and sometimes he sounds off, thusly: ". . . I believe we have deprived many of our young folk of this classic American right to fail by bolstering them up with all manner of guarantee and subsidy . . . and by various methods arrange matters so the young-ones *can't* possibly fail. And then if, perchance, they do fail, we immediately spring into the breech and with our mature powers try to fix things so the kids won't get hurt as the result of their failure."

The Vermont Country Store carries everything from penny candy to calico, from spinning wheels to spruce gum, deerskin gloves to kerosene lamps—and many other old-fashioned items in between.

Weston, a highly popular summer and autumn resort, has a number of attractive shops, the interestingly furnished Farrar-Mansur House (a museum), the Vermont Guild of Old Time Crafts and Industries, and Playhouse on the Green, a theater which alternates between drama and musical concerts.

Artists' and Writers' Haven

Returning to Londonderry on 100, take State 11 to the west to Peru. Many artists live throughout this area, among the better known being Thomas R. Dibble and Hazel Kitts Wires. Peru's name originally was Bromley, but some publicity-minded types decided that if it were changed to Peru (shades of Inca gold, etc.), the little hilltop settlement would attract more residents. It did, but then along came "1800-and-froze-to-death," and not only the newcomers but also some of the regulars moved out. Vermont's weather has been described as "ten months of clear, sparkling winter, and two months of damn poor sleddin'." During the froze-to-death year of 1816 none of New England had any summer, there was snow on the mountains and little rain. Crop after crop failed. It was a phenomenon, felt as far south as Virginia, perhaps caused by sunspots so enormous they could be seen by the naked eye (the first time in recorded history). Today, such joking remarks as, "When do you have summer?" "Oh, that was last Monday," are just that, jokes. And despite its cold winters, as Vermonters glowingly point out, there's very little humidity.

Just beyond Peru is the Big Bromley ski area, where you can take a chair-lift ride (the lift operates in summer) to the mountain's 3,260-foot top for magnificent views. Beyond Bromley, turn left onto State 30 and follow the signs at Bondville for Stratton Mountain. Here, in an alpine settlement, is another of the great ski centers of America.

Returning to 30, continue east to East Jamaica, taking State 100 here into the Valley of the Inns, with its three ski areas of Mount Snow, Corinthia, and Haystack Mountain, with chair lift or gondola usually operating in summer at Mount Snow.

From here, just south of West Dover, turn left on an unnumbered road to Dover. Continue on this road east past Williamsville, turning left into State 30, to Newfane. It is another of Vermont's outstanding towns. The poet Eugene Field *(Wynken, Blynken and Nod; Little Boy Blue)* was born and brought up in Newfane, and Teddy Roosevelt was a well-known visitor here. The town's courthouse is unique, a four-pillared building of the Greek Revival period. The *Newfane Inn,* opened in 1787, has had its continental cuisine praised throughout the country. You'll probably enjoy visiting the Old Village Store here and the British Clockmaker, where Joseph Bates does a lively business in repairing and restoring clocks for customers from all over the U.S.

Returning south on State 30, take the unnumbered road at West Dummerston to Dummerston. Rudyard Kipling lived here for four years (his wife was an American), during which time he wrote *Captains Courageous,* the *Just So Stories,* and the two *Jungle Books*.

Steamtown, U.S.A. is north of here at Bellows Falls (40 steam locomotives; *Big Boy,* the largest locomotive ever built; a 1½-hour steam train excursion, etc.), but rumors were so strong in early 1966 that Steamtown would have to relocate, because of proposed highway construction, that it's best to check in Dummerston or nearby

Putney before heading north. The children may also wish to take in *Santa's Land,* a commercial venture, four miles north of Putney, on State 5. Returning south on 5, look for signs for Tamarlei Morgans. If you missed seeing Morgan horses in Weybridge, you can see them here.

The Molly Stark Trail

Farther south on 5 is Brattleboro. The city's native sons include William Morris Hunt, a noted artist of his day, and his younger brother, Richard Morris Hunt, who built the central portion of the Metropolitan Museum of Art in New York. He also did the New York houses of John Jacob Astor and William K. Vanderbilt and the Newport residences of Oliver Belmont, Cornelius Vanderbilt, and others. West from Brattleboro take State 9. It is called the Molly Stark Trail, in honor of the wife of General John Stark, hero of the battle of Bennington. General Stark, on the occasion of that battle, is said to have called to his troops, by way of inspiration, "There stand the Redcoats, and they are ours, or this night Molly Stark sleeps a widow."

Marlboro, just west of Brattleboro, is noted for a number of attractions. In summer the chief one is undoubtedly the Marlboro Music Festival, headed by the famed pianist Rudolf Serkin. The festival is held in the wooded, hilltop town, site of Marlboro College, which was founded in 1946. In winter, the main attraction is Hogback Mountain, where skiers can begin their day, not by taking a tow or lift uphill, but at the top of the slope, at the edge of Route 9. All year around the view from Hogback is tremendous. It's said to encompass a hundred miles and is at its very best from the *Skyline Restaurant,* just above the highway.

Farther along on 9 you come to Wilmington, another of those places burgeoning with hostelries for skiers. Many of these now stay open in summer, too. Clarence Budington Kelland, who lived here, patterned his town of Cold River, in his Scattergood Baines stories, after Wilmington. If you haven't as yet visited a maple sugarhouse, there's an interesting one here. Called Coomb's Beaver Brook Sugarhouse, it's said to be Vermont's largest authentic sugarhouse.

Continuing on State 9, you'll come to the Prospect Mountain ski area, which claims that, in season, it often has as many as 110 inches of snow. Beyond is Bennington, with a number of routes leading west and south, out of the state. But perhaps you'll first want to have another look around, for instance, at the museum. Maybe you'll want to have another look at some of the collections, now seeing them in a new light. Did you notice the copy of one of Coolidge's speeches when you were there before? The late President made the speech at Bennington, in 1938. In it he said, in part, "I love Vermont because of her hills and valleys, her scenery and invigorating climate, but most of all, because of her indomitable people. They are a race of pioneers who have almost beggared themselves to serve others. If the spirit of liberty should vanish in other parts of the union and support of our institutions should languish, it could all be replenished from the generous store held by the people of this brave little state of Vermont."

AROUND THE STATE

HOTELS AND MOTELS. Accommodations in Vermont are excellent, generally speaking, many of the establishments gearing their entire range of services to the winter sportsman and the summer loafer. Recreation facilities, broad vistas of the lakes and mountains, and best of all, strategically-sited locations make these hotels, lodges, and motels perfect bases for vacation activities.

BARRE

Reasonable

Heiress Motel, attractive, new, small motel. All rooms with combination or shower baths, thermostatic central heat. TV, telephones, radios. In-room coffee. Opposite Barre's Skyline ski area. Pets allowed. Lower rates from Oct. 16 to May 29.
US 302 (tel. 476–4109).

Howard Johnson's Vermonter Motel, midway between Barre & Montpelier. Small motel near ski area, golf courses, bowling center, shops. Restaurant. Open year-round.
US 302 (tel. 476–8541).

Sir Anthony Motel, on Rte. 14; new facility, small; with TV, phones, wall-to-wall carpeting, thermostat-controlled heat, combination bath-shower. Near restaurants, quarries,
173 South Main St. (tel. 476–3438).

BENNINGTON

Reasonable

Darling Kelly's Motel. Small motel located on spacious grounds. Conveniences, including TV, air-conditioning, combination bath, phones. Pool. Near restaurant, gift shop. Year-round, lower rates from Nov. 1 to May 25.
On US 7 (tel. 442–2322).

New Englander Motor Inn. Medium-sized motel. TV, phones, thermostatic heat, combination baths in air-conditioned rooms. Small restaurant, in-room coffee. Swimming pool and playground on premises. Open all year, lower rates from Oct. 20 to late June.
2 mi. n. of Bennington (tel. 442–6311).

Paradise Motor Inn. A new medium-sized, very attractive, motel with restaurant and cocktail lounge. Free continental breakfast. Swimming pool. Children under 12 in same room as parents free. Lower rates Nov.–May.
141 W. Main St. (tel. 442–5419).

Inexpensive

Walloomsac Inn. Large comfortable rooms in 1764 inn at historic Old Bennington. Not far from Bennington & Municipal Airport. Dining room. Free parking.
Tel. 442–4865.

BURLINGTON

Reasonable

Cupola Motel, with restaurant & lounge, adjacent to University of Vermont. A large facility with TV, telephones in rooms. Four dining rooms; cocktail lounge. Swimming pool & children's playground. Open year-round, lower rates Nov.–Apr.

Intersection of US 2 & Interstate 89 (tel. 862–6576).

Harbor Sunset Motel. Small motel with family accommodations featured. TV, air-conditioned, thermostatic-controlled heat. Pets welcomed. Restaurant next door. Open from Easter to Nov. 15.

On US 7, 3 mi. s. of Burlington business section and 3 mi. n. of Shelburne Museum (tel. 864–5080).

Holiday Inn. New, large, motor hotel. 30 mi. to Stowe and Sugarbush ski areas. All air-conditioned rooms with TV, telephones, tiled baths, valet & laundry services. Free ice and free kennels for pets. Swimming pool, baby sitter list. Merrie England decor in *Crimson Hearth Restaurant & Ye Olde Fox and Hound Lounge*. Open year-round.

At US 2 & Interstate 89, South Burlington (tel. 863–4726).

Howard Johnson's Motor Lodge. Two-story motor lodge; 89 air-conditioned rooms with TV, telephones, controlled heat, combination baths. Rates vary seasonally. Swimming pool.

US 2 & Interstate 89 (tel. 863–5541).

Redwood Motel. Medium size. TV, radio, telephone, thermostats, & air-conditioning in well-appointed rooms; penthouse & suite. Heated swimming pool. Near colleges, golf course, Shelburne Museum. No pets. Lower rates from Nov. 5 to May 15.

1016 Shelburne Rd., near Jct. US 7 & Interstate 89 (tel. 864–5525).

Inexpensive

Hotel Huntington. Downtown medium-size hotel, near theaters, restaurants, & stores. Self-service elevator. Room telephones, TV available.

St. Paul & Main Sts. (tel. 862–6565).

KILLINGTON

First Class

Summit Lodge. Large rooms for skiers & skaters. Outdoor sports in area. Fine dining facilities. Modified American Plan. Open mid-June to mid-Oct.; mid-Dec. to mid-Apr.

US 4, s. of Killington Access Rd. (tel. 422–3300).

Reasonable

Skol Haus Motel & Lodge, near Killington ski lifts. Medium-sized lodge. Private units with bath; combination bath; wall-to-wall carpet, unit-controlled heat. Fireplace & TV lounge. Year-round accommodations. *Skol Shed* dining room, Mod. AP in winter. EP in summer.

On Killington Access Rd., 2 mi. off US 4 (tel. 422–3305).

Inexpensive

Mountain Meadows Lodge, above Kent Lake. Fishing, boating, hunting, horseback riding, hiking, etc. Private pool. Dining room & lounge. 5 mi. to Killington. 2 mi. to Pico Peak.

E. of Jct. of US 4 & Rte. 100 (tel. 773–3595).

MANCHESTER

First Class

Equinox House & Villas. Congenial country club setting on 1,600 acres with 275 rooms and 175 motel units having heat, combination bath. Excellent dining room. Olympic size swimming pool, private trout lake, championship 18-hole golf course. Planned social activities, nightly dancing, except Sun. Not far from Southern Vermont Art Center, summer theater. Free parking. Open from mid-May to mid-Oct. Modified American Plan.

Tel. 362–1640.

Reasonable

Avalanche Motor Lodge. Open year-round, small motel with deluxe rooms, TV, telephones, combination bath, thermostat heat. Dining room & cocktail lounge. Nightly entertainment in winter season. Game room, sauna, swimming pool. Modified American Plan in winter, ski week specials. Lower rates April 16–Dec. 14.
On Rte. 11 (Manchester Depot) 2 mi. e. of Manchester Center (tel. 362–2622).

Erdman's Eyrie Motel. Small modern well-furnished motel. Relaxing setting of 200 acres of meadow and woodland. Tastefully decorated rooms with combination bath, thermostat-controlled heat. Family rates. Lower rates off-season. Restaurant, Ski Lounge, playroom and pool. Closed Nov. & April.
On US 7 about 7 mi. no. of Manchester (tel. 362–1208).

Manchester Motor Court. Small with scenic Green Mountains view. Central hot water heat, combination bath. Open all year. Golf, skiing, trout fishing, hunting.
On US 7, 2 mi. n. of Manchester Center (tel. 363–2739).

Stamford Motel. Small motel with central hot-water heat, ceramic tile bath, TV. Well off highway, with view of Mt. Equinox. Year-round vacation spot with nearby sports, recreation & cultural activities. Restaurant short drive away.
US 7, 1½ mi. n. of Manchester Center (tel. 362–2342).

MIDDLEBURY

Reasonable

Middlebury Inn. Year-round Colonial inn on the Green with 75 comfortable rooms, most with bath, some air-conditioned. TV & telephones. Main dining room & Morgan Room cocktail lounge. Near Middlebury College. Lots of activities nearby.
Tel. 388–4961.

Inexpensive

Maple Manor Motel. Small motel; eight cabins. Spacious grounds. TV & room coffee, electric heat.
US 7, just s. of town (tel. 388–2193).

Waybury Inn. Colonial place (1810), at foot of Green Mountains. Small all year country inn with all rooms having bath. Family rates and free parking. Club Room & Old Washington Room with fireplaces.
On Rte. 125 (tel. 388–4372).

MONTPELIER

Reasonable

Montpelier Tavern Motor Inn. Attractive rooms, most with baths, some rooms TV. Medium-sized with family rates. Sprinkler-protected. Air-conditioned lounge, two fine dining rooms. Free parking.
On US 2 near State Capitol (tel. 223–5252).

Toytown Motor Court. Small motel, modern cabins with showers, electric heat. Some TV. Replica of Capitol on lawn. Open from May 1 to Nov. 1.
On US 2, 1½ mi. w. of Montpelier (tel. 223–9038).

Inexpensive

Pavilion Hotel, next to State Capitol, old, but distinctive-looking large hotel. With TV/radio, air-conditioning in some rooms. Restaurant-cocktail lounge. Sprinkler-protected. Free parking. Open year-round.
State St. (tel. 223–3411).

NEWPORT

Reasonable

Camp Elizabeth Motor Inn. Rooms in main lodge and in larger cottages are for two or more persons. Sports & water activities. Capacity 60. Modified American Plan. Lounge. Open from July 1 to Sept. 7.
Off US 5 on Lake Memphremagog (8 mi. from Canada) (tel. 334–8157).

Roy's Newport City Motel. A small sound-proof attractive motel. Restaurant & diner nearby. Only ½ mi. to Lake Memphremagog & golf course. Open year-round. Lower rates Sept.–June.

996 East Main St. (tel. 334–8558).

Inexpensive

Hotel Newport. Medium-sized hotel with most rooms having private baths. Dining room. European Plan. Open all year.

On Main St. nr. railroad station (tel. 334–6573).

RUTLAND

Reasonable

Edelweiss Motel. Small new motel with shower or combination baths, thermostat-controlled heat. Playground, lounge, restaurant. Near Pico Peak Ski Area & entrance to Killington Basin. Modified American Plan. Open year-round.

On US 4, 8 mi. e. of Rutland (Mendon, Vt.) (tel. 775–5577).

Howard Johnson's Motor Lodge. New, 48-unit lodge with TV, telephones, air-conditioned, thermostat-controlled heat in rooms. Near ski facility & Calvin Coolidge Homestead. Heated swimming pool. Open all year. Rates vary seasonally. As usual, near restaurant.

US 7, about 1 mi. s. of US 4 (tel. 775–4303).

Long Trail Lodge. Rustic mountain lodge is a Treadway Inn, medium-sized but with a wide variety of accommodations—lodge and chalet rooms, dorm rooms and 1 & 2-bedroom cottages. Lots of activities. Swimming pool. Excellent dining room, cocktail lounge. Adjoins Pico-Killington ski areas. Seasons from June 10 to Oct. 15; from Dec. 20 to Apr. 10.

On US 4 at Sherburne Pass (tel. 773–6310).

Sun-Set Motel. New, two-story, medium-sized building. Modern, TV, room telephones; some air-conditioned rooms. Large TV lounge & playground for kiddies. Restaurant. Caters to families. Open all year. Special lower rates from Nov. 1 to June 15.

US 7, at 238 South Main St. (tel. 773–2784).

White Birch Motel, 41 North Main St., at Jct. of US 7 & 4; 16 deluxe motel rooms; plus a few housekeeping apts. TV, central steam heat in rooms. Good restaurant next door; shopping center. Open all year.

Tel. 773–9128.

Inexpensive

Bardwell Hotel & Motor Inn. A large hotel in business section. Rooms modernized; new dining room, cocktail lounge & coffee shop. TV/radio. Sprinkler, fire-proofed. Special group rates.

Tel. 773–3341.

ST. JOHNSBURY

Reasonable

Maple Center Motel. Colonial ranch-style medium-sized place. Rooms with TV, showers, thermostat-controlled heat. Near skiing, golfing, shopping. On premises is swank Candlelight Restaurant. Open year-round. Lower rates Nov.–May.

20 Hastings St., on US 2 & 5 (tel. 748–9798).

Rabbit Hill Motor Inn. A small very attractive converted inn in a rustic setting. Open from June 1 to mid-Oct. Restaurant.

Rt. 18 e. (tel. 748–9766).

Yankee Traveler Motel. Colonial-style medium-sized motel with attractive furnishings, TV, guest-controlled heat, sound-proofed. Diner next door, restaurants nearby. Lower rates from Oct. 15 to June 1.

65 Portland St. (tel. 748–3157).

Inexpensive

St. Johnsbury House. A medium-sized modernized classic inn open all year.

Family rates. Colonial dining room. Complete meeting facilities.

44 Main St. (Rts. 2 & 5) (tel. 748–3181).

SHELBURNE

Reasonable

Champlain Motor Lodge. Medium-sized motel with air-conditioned rooms, combination bath. Efficiency setup in motel & cottages. Early American restaurant & lounge. Recreational activities. Near Shelburne Museum. Open year-round.

3000 Shelburne Rd. (tel. 864–5777).

Shelburne Hotel. Small. Decor in keeping with nearby Shelburne Museum. Outdoor theater, golfing, fishing, bathing—all close by. Season, from May 1 to Nov. 1.

US 7 (tel. 862–1661).

Yankee Doodle Motel. On 35 acres with 14 pine-paneled units, air-conditioners, electric baseboard heat, TV, tub-shower. Colonial motif. Heated pool. Restaurant short drive away. Open May 20 to Oct. 20.

On US 7, 1 mi. n. of Shelburne Museum (tel. 864–9597).

SPRINGFIELD

Springfield is the center of the area known as "Precision Valley," so named because of the many machine-tool factories located along the banks of the Black River. Waterfalls, natural and man-made, flow through Springfield, lending charm to its already lovely setting.

Reasonable

The Hartness House. A former residence of a governor, now a small tastefully decorated inn, plus 10 modern motel units. Unusual Underground Lounge. Restaurant. American Plan. Open year-round. Pets allowed. Free parking.

30 Orchard St. (tel. 885–2115).

Howard Johnson's Motor Lodge. Typically excellent chain motel with restaurant & swimming pool. Within an hour's drive to 16 ski areas. Rates vary seasonally. Open year-round.

Jct. of Interstate 91, US 5 & Rte. 11 (tel. 885–4516).

Precision Valley Motel. Attractive, new, small motel, well-furnished. Continental breakfast. TV. Playground, picnic area on 25-acre grounds. Open year-round. Favorite with skiers.

Jct. of Rte. 104 & 10 (tel. 886–2707).

STOWE

First Class

The Lodge. Topnotch medium-sized resort at foot of lofty Mt. Mansfield. Renowned for excellent French cuisine & epicurean wines. Heated pool, 7 tennis courts, riding stables, 18-hole golf course nearby. Dancing, summer theater. Elegant rooms with TV, telephones, thermostat-controlled heat, combination bath. American and European Plans. Weekly and family rates (June–mid Oct.) American Plan only in season. Open June 15 to Oct. 15, Dec. 15 to April 15.

At Smugglers Notch (tel. 253–7311).

Toll House Inn. Distinguished medium-sized year-round motor inn with new rooms. Same ownership as The Lodge. At base of excellent Green Mountain ski trails. Each room fully furnished with balcony as an extra. Rustic dining room, cocktail lounge, big sundeck, 7 tennis courts, swimming pool, riding stable, 18-hole golf course nearby, summer theater. American Plan.

Tel. 253–7311.

Reasonable

Alpine Motor Lodge. Small, year-round mountain lodge, attractive accommodations. Large heated pool. Spacious grounds. TV, game room & Alpine lounge. Restaurant. American Plan in winter. Lower rates from April 15 to

July 1, Oct. 20 to Dec. 15. Not far from ski lifts, sports, cultural centers.

On Rte. 10 (tel. 253–7700).

Mountaineer Motor Inn. Medium, nicely decorated informal establishment. TV in lobby, game room, indoor heated swimming pool, cocktail lounge. Restaurant. Modified American or European Plans. Family rates. Open June 1 to mid-Oct., Dec. 15 to Apr. 15.

On Rte. 108, 4½ mi. n. of Stowe (tel. 253–7525).

Scandinavia Inn. Modern contemporary small lodge, 2 mi. from Mt. Mansfield & Spruce Park. Fine restaurant. TV-stereo lounge, game room. Sauna bath. Modified American Plan. Open Dec. to Apr. 30, Sept. 11 to Oct. 16.

Mt. Mansfield Rd. (tel. 253–7792).

Stowe Motel. A small motel with TV, radio, tub-showers, self-controlled heat. Swimming pool. Grand view of Mt. Mansfield from spacious grounds. Short distance to ski trails, horseback riding, summer theater, sports. Pets welcomed.

Smuggler's Notch Rd., Rte. 106 (tel. 253–7629).

Trapp Family Lodge. Medium-sized resort with Tyrolean old-world atmosphere, operated by Baroness Maria A. Trapp. Viennese-American cuisine, at 3 dining rooms. Tyrolean Bar. Heated pool. Nearby golf, tennis. Short drive from Mt. Mansfield ski slopcs. Open May 1 to Oct. 20 & Dec. 15 to Apr. 15. American Plan during summer period, modified American Plan winter.

Luce Hill, Rte. 108 (tel. 253–7545).

WAITSFIELD

Reasonable

Alpen Inn. Varied types of accommodations; chalets, dormitories; large dining room and cocktail lounge. Summer & winter sports (including pool) and entertainment on spacious grounds, only 1 mi. n. of Sugarbush Entry Rd. Inn is associated with Sugarbush Soaring Co. Mod. AP in winter. Open from June 15 to Oct. 15; Dec. 20 to Apr. 15.

Rte. 100, 3 mi. s. of Waitsfield (tel. 496–3401).

Bagatelle, charming ski lodge with 108 accommodations in various price categories. Continental breakfast optional. Not far from Mad River Glen & Sugarbush Valley. Open from Dec. 1 to May 1.

Tel. 496–3979.

Four Seasons Lodge, stragetically located within reach of four major ski areas. Swimming pool & horse riding on premises. Rooms are well appointed, overlooking picturesque mountain valley. Open all year.

Tel. 496–3656.

ELSEWHERE

BRATTLEBORO. *Holiday Motel.* Reasonable. Well-decorated medium-sized facility with air-conditioned, thermostatically-controlled heated rooms, with TV, telephones, combination bath. Heated swimming pool. Restaurant nearby. Lower rates from Nov. 1 to June 1. On US 5 near Interstate 91 interchange, 2 mi. n. of Brattleboro Tel. 254–2307.

Theatre Motor Lodge (Superior Motel). Medium-sized motel with some kitchen units. Can see movies from air-conditioned rooms with TV & telephones and in-room coffee. Heated swimming pool. Restaurant, cocktail lounge. Year-round operation. Lower rates from Sept. 1 to June 1. On US 5 & Rte. 9, 2 mi. n. of Brattleboro (Tel. 254–4483).

CHITTENDEN. *Mountain Top Inn Cottages and Club,* off US 7, 10 mi. n.e. of Rutland. Secluded 600-acre lakeside resort bordering Green Mt. National Forest. All sports, horses, free golf in June and Sept. Housekeeping cottages. Lounge and recreation rooms in Inn. AP. Skiing from mid-Dec. to spring. Reasonable. Tel. 483–2311.

DORSET. *Dorset Inn.* Reasonable. Medium-sized with bath or combination bath. American Plan. Restaurant. Terrace for steak cookouts. Near Dorset Field (golf) Club and summer theater. Swimming pool. Open June 18 to Oct. 20. Church & Main Sts. on Rt. 30 (tel. 867–5500).

ENOSBURG FALLS. *Dairy Center Motel,* on Rte. 105, 8 mi. to Canada border. Inexpensive. Family & housekeeping units in medium motel. Home-styled cooking for dining room; swimming pool. Electric heat in each room, combination bath. Tel. 933–2030.

FAIRLEE. *Lake Morey Inn & Club,* off US 5, on Lake Morey. First class. Over 300-acre estate, with sports, including riding & skiing. 18-hole golf course, home of Vermont State Open. Glass-enclosed dining room; cocktail lounge. Phone & electric heat in each room. Open early June to Oct. 13. Tel. 333–4311.

Bonnie Oaks Lodge & Bungalows. Reasonable. Resort of two main inns plus 35 bungalows with baths, fireplaces. American Plan, family rates, with lower rates for week or more. Lakeside dining room and open decking. Features family activities and water sports. New 9-hole golf course. Open early June to mid-Oct. Tel. 333–4302.

GRAFTON. *Tavern* and *Tavern Homestead,* an 1801 stagecoach inn, small; semi-private baths, 3 pleasant dining rooms; 5 acres, natural swimming pool, sports. Reasonable. EP. *Tavern* open May 15 to Oct. 15. *Tavern Homestead* open Jan. 15 to Nov. 15. Tel. Saxtons River 3400.

ISLE LA MOTTE. *Ruthcliffe Lodge & Motel Resort,* on Lake Champlain isle where first white settlement in Vt. was made. Inexpensive. Attractive, small lodge with new motel units having private baths. Swimming, fishing & boating. AP. Open from June 25 to Sept. 15. Tel. 798–8276.

JEFFERSONVILLE. *Highlander Motel,* on Rte. 108 at Smugglers Notch, is a small place on spacious grounds with natural pool. Fishing, hunting nearby. Restaurants about 1 mi. away. Madonna & Sterling mountains, 5 mi. away. Lower rates from Apr. 15 to Dec. 1. Tel. 644–2725.

LAKE BOMOSEEN. *Prospect House,* on lakeside, is a large facility with dining, golf, fishing, swimming, boating, tennis, dancing, other activities. Open from May to Nov. EP in spring and fall. TV, electric heat in rooms. Rt. 30. Reasonable. Tel. 468–5581.

Edgewater Inn & Motel, medium-sized motel with heated rooms. Central lobby with TV & fireplace. Meals with rooms. Inexpensive. Private docks & boats for fishing. Housekeeping units. Open from May 1 to Nov. 1. Tel. 468–2403.

LAKE ST. CATHERINE. *Lake St. Catherine Inn,* a picturesque inn on lake of same name. New building with showers & combination baths. Marina for 25 boats; outdoor sports. American-Jewish cuisine, AP. Open from May 20 to Labor Day. Reasonable. Tel. 287–9347.

LONDONDERRY. *Dostal's Motor Lodge,* medium-sized motel with deluxe units, private baths. Two dining rooms; cocktail lounge; playground. Swimming pool. Near Magic Mountain slopes. Reasonable. Tel. 824–6700.

University House, on Rte. 11, near Magic Mountain; 6 mi. to Big Bromley. Luxury rooms. Central lounge with old brick fireplace. Open all year. AP. Tel. 824–5433.

LUDLOW. *Bolton Homestead,* 12 Commonwealth Ave., near Rte. 103; large old home converted into small lodging place. 1 mi. to Okemo ski slopes. Walking distance to business, theater sections. Open during ski season; other dates by reservation only. Inexpensive.

Deeplawn Lodge. 53 Main St., small motel and lodge. Thermostat heat, combination baths. TV. Okemo ski area nearby. Inexpensive. Open year-round. Tel. 228–3841.

LYNDONVILLE. *Lynburke Motel.* Reasonable. Deluxe units with thermostat controlled heat, combination baths & TV. Central lounge, swimming and wading pools. Burke Mt. ski area, 7 mi. away. Lower rates Nov.–May. Junction of US 5 & Rte. 114. Tel. 626–3346.

Redwood Motel. Small rustic motel with heated pools. Family rates. Lower rates Oct. 16–June 14. Some food service. Rte. 5. Tel. 626–5112.

MALLETTS BAY. *Marble Island Club,* on Lake Champlain, with new golf & yacht club; luxurious accommodations. All-weather tennis courts, heated pool; 200-foot beach, & marina. Formal dining room, patio, snack bar & lounge with fireplace. Deluxe. Tel. 863–4501.

MARLBORO. *Marlboro Inn,* small motel & cabins at 2,350 ft. elevation; view of Hogback Mt. Reasonable. Open all year. Short drive to Marlboro Music Festival, shopping, swimming. EP. Tel. 464–5494.

MT. SNOW. *Snow Lake Lodge,* an outstanding resort owned by Mt. Snow Development Corp., with 120 rooms; year-round operation; Mod. AP, with reduced summer rates. Reasonable. All rooms with private bath, individually-controlled heat. Large dining room; excellent menus. Aerial tramway nearby to ski area. *Snow Barn,* converted farm building, used for accommodations during ski season. Tel. 464–3333.

NORTH HERO. *Shore Acres Resort-Motel.* Reasonable. A 46-acre resort on Lake Champlain with small motel capacity. TV room. Swimming, driving range. European and Modified American Plans. Restaurant. Open from May 20 to Oct. 20. Lower rates after Labor Day. On US 2. Tel. North Hero 382.

NORWICH. *Norwich Inn & Motel.* Family & ski groups especially welcomed at this medium-sized country inn with motel units. Restaurant with Vermont cooking featured. TV in most rooms. Free parking. Year-round operation. 1 mi. from Dartmouth College. Tel. 649–1143.

PERU. *Mountain Motor Lodge,* small lodge with private baths, individual-controlled heat. Continental breakfast. This Green Mountain motel is open year round. Inexpensive. Tel. 824–9581.

Wiley Inn, small, comfortable country inn & motel on Bromley Mountain. Inexpensive. Open from May 20 to Nov. 1; Dec. 15 to end of spring ski season. Special skiers' rates. Dining room, lounge & game room. Tel. 824–6600.

POWNAL. *Ladd Brook Motor Inn,* a new, small, well-appointed motel overlooking Pownal Valley on US 7, near Green Mountain Park race track. Reasonable. Equipped with TV, air-conditioning, tile baths with tubs, controlled hot water heat. Next to *Ladd Brook Restaurant.* Open from Apr. to Dec. Tel. 823–7341.

PUTNEY. *Putney Inn & 91 Motor Lodge.* Reasonable. A small motel with family rates; air-conditioned, TV, telephones. Warmly-decorated restaurant with excellent food, room service, cocktail lounge. Open year-round. At Interstate 91. Tel. 387–5502.

ST. ALBANS. *Cadillac Motel.* Reasonable. Modern medium-sized motor court. TV, telephone, combination bath, controlled heat & air-conditioning. Swimming pool, fishing, golf course, state beach within 4 mi. Open year-round. Lower rates from Oct. 25 to June 15. On US 7 (tel. 524–2191).

Rashaw's Motel. Short distance to shopping, golf, beaches, restaurants. The 30 units have TV/radio, heat by thermostat-control. In-room coffee. Open all year. Lower rates Sept.–May. On US 7. Tel. 524–5956.

VERGENNES. *Basin Harbor Club,* on Lake Champlain, distinguished resort on 700 acres. Deluxe. Used as summer home of about 300 members;

guests use some of 50 rooms with bath and 65 deluxe cottages. Comprehensive land and water sports. Large heated swimming pool; 18-hole golf course. Fine restaurant-cocktail lounge. Open from June 4 to Oct. 13. Tel. 877–2961.

WARREN. *Christmas Tree Inn.* Small inn with fine Continental cuisine in dining room & lounge. Weekend entertainment in Sled Room and Red Nose Room. Golf course & ski area within 2 mi., fishing & hunting also nearby. Pool. Modified American Plan. Open Dec. 15 to mid-Apr., Apr. 16–mid-Dec. European Plan. On Sugarbush Access Rd., Rte. 100. Tel. 496–3941.

Sugarbush Inn. Popular and reasonable. Recently rebuilt in Colonial-style decor with chalets for families, recreation room, heated swimming pool. New 18-hole golf course. Restaurant & cocktail lounge with dancing. Open Dec. 12 to Apr. 4 (Modified American Plan), June 4 to Oct. 31 (European Plan). Package plans available. On Sugarbush Rd. Tel. 496–3301.

WOODSTOCK. *Woodstock Inn,* an historic landmark on the town's Green, recently refurbished. Reasonable. Outdoor sports nearby, including golf course. Double rooms with bath. Restaurant. Pool. Year-round operation. The Green, Rte. 4 (tel. 457–1100).

Woodstock Motel (Superior Motels). A small motor court with units having TV & private bath. Near restaurants and outdoor sports places. Open from early Apr. to late Nov. On US 4 & Rte. 12. Tel. 457–2500.

YOUTH HOSTELS. Fourteen American Youth Hostels are situated in various parts of Vermont. Largest, most active one is the *School Hostel,* 146 Main St., in Rochester (70 beds), excellent accommodations, sponsored by the Metropolitan N.Y. Council. Year-round hostels (7) are so indicated in the listing; the others are open for the summer only. Rates are $1 a day in summer, $1.50 in winter. Brattleboro—*Orchard Hill* (20), Upper Dummerston Rd., 5 mi. n. of Brattleboro, via Rte. 30. Jamaica—*Jamaica Hotel,* center of village, Rte. 30. Lowell—*Lowell Youth Hostel* (20) off Rte. 100, year-round. Ludlow—*Pickabode Youth Hostel* (50) 1½ mi. e. of Ludlow, Rte. 103, year-round. Mendon—*Clear View Lodge* (22), 4½ mi. e. of Rutland, Rte. 4, year-round. Newport—*Newport City Youth Hostel* (16), 3 mi. from village, at Lake Memphremagog, 75¢ for daily lodging. North Hero—*Camp Abnaki Youth Hostel* (16), 30 mi. n. of Burlington, YMCA sponsor. Putney—*Putney School Youth Hostel* (18), 2 mi. w. of Putney. *Richford Youth Hostels* (35), open by advanced reservations, year-round. St. Johnsbury—*Three Brooks Tree Farm Youth Hostel* (14), North Danville Rd., 3 mi. w. of St. Johnsbury, year-round. Shelburne—*Shelburne Hostel,* under leadership only. Warren—*Old Homestead Youth Hostel* (40), 2½ mi. e. of Warren, off Rte. 100. Waterbury Center—*Ski Hostel Lodge Youth Hostel,* 4 mi. s. of Stowe, Rte. 100, year-round. Used as ski lodge only from Nov. to May.

TRAILER TIPS. It may disappoint trailer-vacationing families that there are a limited number of trailer sites in Vermont. This situation is probably due to the well-organized, successful ski and lakeside resorts that have sprung up during the past 30 years. The Department of Forests and Parks lists trailer sites at *Allis, Ascutney, Bomoseen, Brighton, D.A.R. Emerald Lake, Gifford Woods, Grand Isle, New Discovery, Stillwater, Rickers, Molly Stark, Little River,* and *Sandbar*. A few private vacation places also provide trailer sites.

CAMPING OUT: Vermont, with 12,000 farms in its 14 counties, encourages vacationing families to stop, see and stay at their places. Thirty organizations in agriculture sponsor the *Vermont*

Red Clover Trail, including 49 dairies, orchards, breeders, beekeepers, and maple sugar farms. Each "trail" host is identified by a "red clover" welcome sign. Some dairies and farms accept vacationists with room and board facilities. Among those with vacation lodgings are: *Sherryland Farm,* dairy, at Danville; *Bis-May Farm,* dairy, at Moretown; *White Farm,* dairy, at Ryegate; *Maple Avenue Farm,* dairy and maple products, at Waitsfield; *Upland Meadows,* dairy and riding horses, at Tyson. Reservations must be made in advance. List of agriculture hosts is available from the Vermont Department of Agriculture, Montpelier.

DINING OUT. Restaurants in Vermont take pride in several local specialties, such as roast turkey, clam chowder, griddle cakes with maple syrup, maple-cured ham, maple butternut pie, rum pie, and country-style sausage. Restaurants are listed here as follows: large towns first, alphabetically and by price category; then smaller towns, alphabetically.

BURLINGTON

Reasonable

Colony. Featuring roast beef and steak daily to 10 p.m. Summer Sun. buffet. Bar.
In Hotel Vermont at 131 Main St.

Conrad's. French-style lunches and dinners are served in *Parisienne Cellar.* Home-made bread and pastries. Open from 7 a.m. to midnight. Closed last week of Aug.
185 Pearl St.

Cupola Restaurant. Dine on the terrace and enjoy the superb Green Mt. view. Cocktails. Open daily until midnight from Mar. to Dec.
At cloverleaf of US 2 and I-89.

Holiday Inn. A good selection of dishes in Crimson Hearth Restaurant. *Ye Olde Fox and Hound Lounge* has Shakespearean motif and wide variety of wines and liqueurs.
On Williston Rd., at cloverleaf of US 2 & I-89.

Old Board Restaurant. Distinctive restaurant with excellent steak and roast beef dinners. Large cocktail lounge. Nightly dancing, with entertainment on Fri. & Sat. Open daily from 11 a.m. to 1 a.m.
520 Shelburne St.

Victorian Motor Inn. Overlooking Shelburne Bay on Lake Champlain, this inn features family dinners with six or more entrees. Specialties are shish kebab and Victorian pudding. Open from 7 a.m. to 11 p.m.
Shelburne Rd., on US 7, s. of Burlington.

Inexpensive

Lotus Restaurant. Features Chinese and American dishes in Oriental atmosphere. Bamboo lounge. Open daily from 11 a.m. to midnight.
114 Church St.

DORSET

Reasonable

Andirons. Rural atmosphere in dining room and main lodge. Specialties steak and lobster. Open daily from 6 to 8 p.m.
West Dover.

Barrow's House. A 1790 home used as an inn since 1900. Specializing in roast beef, cream-baked chicken, lobster bisque. Children's plates. Open daily to 8 p.m.
Rte. 30, 6 mi. N. of Manchester.

Dorset Inn. New England meals. Wed. steak cookouts, Sun. buffet. Children's plates. Open from mid-June to mid-

Oct. daily from 6:30 to 7:30 p.m.
On Rte. 30, 6 mi. s. of Manchester.

MANCHESTER

First Class

L'Auberge. French cuisine served in French provincial inn. Bar and cocktail terrace. Open Dec. 22 to Apr. 1; May 22 to Oct. 31. Closed Sun. Closed Wed. in Oct. and winter.
On US 7, about 1½ mi. s. of Manchester.

Reasonable

Avalanche Motor Lodge. New England meals in nice dining room and cocktail lounge. Entertainment and dancing during winter. Open year-round.
On Rtes. 11 & 30, 2 mi. e. of Manchester Center.

Equinox House. Traditional Vermont dishes are the rule in this white-columned resort, gracing a 1,600-acre estate. Dining room and garden lounge; also cocktails and dancing. Open daily to 9 p.m.
On US 7.

Harvest Inn Restaurant. Continental fare, with own baking. Liquor privileges. Open daily for lunch and dinner. Season is from late May to late Oct.
On US 7, 1 mi. s. of Jct. of Rte. 11.

Toll Gate Lodge. Dining by a brook in a forest setting. Specializes in Continental and French Alpine cuisine. Wine list. Dinner served daily from 6:30 to 10 p.m., Sun. & holidays from noon to 8 p.m. Open from May 28 to mid-Oct.
Just off Rte. 11, 4 mi. e. of Manchester.

Inexpensive

Quality Restaurant. Wide choice of New England cooking, featuring steak, chicken or fish. Children's plates. Liquor privileges. Open daily to midnight. Closed Tues. from Nov. to May.
735 Main St.

RUTLAND

Reasonable

Fairmont. Highly rated restaurant, featuring steak, chops, lobster, Italian dishes. Cocktail lounge. Open from 11 a.m. to midnight. Sun. noon to 8 p.m. Closed Mon.
On US 7, 1 mi. s. of Rutland.

Prouse's Restaurant. Steaks, lobsters and Italian dishes are served in the *Large Mural Lounge* and *Ye Olde Surrey Room*. Children's plates. *Red Goblet* cocktail lounge. Open all year daily until midnight. Closed Sun.
22 Center St.

Royal's Hearthside Restaurant. Specializing in lobster, charcoal broiled steak, baked stuffed shrimp, roast prime ribs of beef. Cocktail lounge. Gift shop. Restaurant open daily from 11 a.m. to 9 p.m.
37 No. Main St.

STOWE

First Class

The Lodge at Smugglers Notch. Top-notch Tyrolean dining room with superb French cuisine, well-stocked wine cellar. Specialties include filet of sole. Music, dancing and entertainment. Open year-round daily to 8 p.m.
At foot of Mt. Mansfield on Rte. 108.

Toll House Motor Inn. As is *The Lodge* (above), this is operated by Mt. Mansfield Co. Varied menus served in *Rib, Carriage* and *Town* rooms. Dancing and entertainment. Cocktail lounge. Open to midnight.
Mt. Mansfield Rd.

Reasonable

The Trapp Family Lodge. European-Alpine atmosphere in three dining rooms and Tyrolean bar. This "Family of Song" plans a variety of Austrian meals. Children's menu. Spacious lounge and coffee house. Open daily to 8 p.m. Closed from Oct. 16 to Dec. 14, April 16 to May 14.
Off Rte. 108.

Inexpensive

Tony's Restaurant. Serves own special soups and pastries, sandwiches, prime Western beef, chops, roasts, fish and Italian dishes. Entertainment and dancing in winter and spring at *Lounge* night club. Open daily to 10 p.m. Closed in Nov.

Located in Stowe Village.

ELSEWHERE

ARLINGTON. *West Mountain Farm.* Reasonable. A cozy inn on a 145-acre estate. Roast beef and steak dinners are specialties from 6 to 8 p.m., Sun. from 12:30 to 3 p.m. Ask for New England cooking at breakfast and lunch. Children's plates. Open year-round but closed Tues. Off Rte. 313, 1 mi. w. of Arlington.

BARRE. *Country House.* Inexpensive. Luncheons and dinners emphasize Italian home meals. Open daily from 11 a.m. to 10 p.m. Closed Sun. and week of July 4th. 276 North Main St., Rte. 14 & US 302.

Dugout Restaurant. Inexpensive. Family-type establishment, specializing in steaks, lobsters, chicken and Italian cuisine. Children's menu. Open daily from 5 to 11 p.m., Sun. 5 to 9 p.m. Closed Mon. On US 302.

BENNINGTON. *Four Chimneys.* Reasonable. Airconditioned restaurant in a former mansion. Continental cooking, featuring lobster. Lounge and wine cellar. Open from noon to 10 p.m. May 1 to Nov. 1. West Rd., on Rte. 9.

New Englander Restaurant. Reasonable. Small family restaurant, proud of its Vermont dishes, especially the roast turkey. Clam chowder also featured on Fri. Open all year. On US 7, 1½ mi. n. of Bennington.

BRANDON. *Adams.* Reasonable. This restaurant in picturesque Otter Valley serves a varied menu with its own pastries. Children's plates. Open daily to 8 p.m. Sun. from 12:30 to 2:30 p.m. Closed from mid-Oct. to mid-June. On US 7, 1 mi. s. of Brandon.

Brandon Inn. Reasonable. New England dishes served amid formal charm. Specialties are roast beef and compote of hot fruit. Cocktails. Open daily to 8 p.m. 20 Park St. on US 7.

BRATTLEBORO. *Stone Fence Inn.* Reasonable. Restaurant in pleasant setting, offering New England cuisine. Open for breakfast and lunch and for dinner from 5 to 9 p.m. Children's plates. Cocktail lounge. On Rte. 9 & US 5, 2 mi. n. of Brattleboro.

Town & Country Inn. Inexpensive, Large mansion for leisurely dining, specializing in charcoal-broiled steak. Children's plates. Breakfast. Open daily from 5 to 9 p.m. On US 5 & Rte. 9.

GRAFTON. *The Tavern.* Reasonable. A delightful old country inn, with 1801 homestead as focal point. Year-round dining with New England beef and chicken specialties. Opens at 7:30 a.m. for breakfast; dinner from 6:30 to 8 p.m. Liquor privileges. On Rtes. 121 & 35.

KILLINGTON. *Killington Restaurants.* Reasonable. Two complete restaurants with limited menus for Killington Mt. tourists. Open from Dec. to May, 8 a.m. to 5 p.m.; from June to mid-Oct. from 9 a.m. to 5 p.m. At Rte. 100 & US 4, 14 mi. e. of Rutland.

Valmont Restaurant. Reasonable. A variety of foods are served in this Colonial-type restaurant. Open daily from 7:30 a.m. to 8 p.m. Closed Tues. in winter; closed after fall foliage, reopens Dec. 26; also closed 4 weeks after ski season. On US 4, 10 mi. e. of Rutland.

LAKE MOREY. *Bonnie Oaks Lodge.* Reasonable. Dining room and lounge in main lodge open to public. Varied meals with children's dishes in this family resort. Open June 1 to Oct. 20. Off Rte. 5, 2 mi. from Fairlee.

Lake Morey Inn. First class. This large resort features traditional New England fare with Continental flourishes. Sun. night buffet. Open daily until 8 p.m. from early June to mid-Oct. Off Rte. 5.

LUDLOW. *Bavarian Castle.* Reasonable. Austrian and German fare. Goulash soup a specialty. Bavarian lounge. Open all year. A favorite with skiers. At Jct. of Rtes. 103 & 131, 2 mi. s. of Ludlow.

Valente's Restaurant. Reasonable. Pleasant setting accommodating up to 200 for New England specialties. Cocktail lounge, dancing and occasional entertainment. 190 Main St.

MARLBORO. *Marlboro House.* Reasonable. Small country inn on high hill with commanding scenic view. Popular dining room with varied New England meals. Open year-round. Near Marlboro Summer Festival and Hogback Mt. On Rte. 9.

Skyline Restaurant. Reasonable. At summit of Hogback Mt., opposite *Marlboro Inn.* Features Vermont specialties from breakfast to dinner in all-season establishment. For a treat, try the waffles or griddle cakes with homemade sausage. On Rte. 9.

MIDDLEBURY. *Middlebury Inn.* Reasonable. Situated on the Green, this Colonial inn has been a long-time favorite with Middlebury College famlies. Children's portions. Cocktails in *Snow Bowl* and *Pine Room.* Open all year. On Rte. 7.

Smith's Park Restaurant. Reasonable. A restaurant that is proud of its popular, home-like meals. Open daily, summer from 6 a.m. to 1 a.m.; winter from 6 a.m. to 11 p.m. Merchants Row, off US 7.

MONTGOMERY CENTER. *On the Rocks.* Reasonable. An out-of-the-way, but excellent small restaurant with Scandinavian tableware. There is an exciting view of Jay Peak. Among specialties are onion soup, lobster thermidor, frogs' legs and sirloin steak. Wine list. Open daily for lunch and dinner. Cocktails. Suggest reservations. Hazen's Notch, 8 mi. N.E. on Rte. 58.

MONTPELIER. *Lobster Pot.* Reasonable. Large restaurant featuring lobster, seafood and chicken specialties. Cocktails. Open week-days from 8 a.m. to 11 p.m. Open Sun. in July, Aug. & Sept. 118 Main St.

Tavern Motor Inn. Reasonable. Long a favorite dining spot of state officials and visitors. Vermont and Continental cuisine are featured in the *Justin Morgan Room* (cocktail lounge), *Thomas Chittenden Dining Room* (strictly New England), and *Governor's Coffee House,* open from early a.m. to late p.m. *Governor's Suite* and other dining room for special occasions. Near State Capitol.

NEWFANE. *Newfane Inn.* Reasonable. Distinguished 1787 inn with superb French cuisine. Attractive dining room with brick fireplace and harmonizing appointment. Featured on menu, appetizing onion soup, lobster Newburg, chicken in wine, sliced tenderloin bordelaise. Lunch and dinner daily, until 9 p.m. Open from June 20 to Oct. 20 and from Dec. 20 to Apr. 10. On Rte. 30.

NEWPORT. *Frank's Steak House.* Inexpensive. Continental cuisine is featured in new *Trophy Room.* Cocktails. Steak House is open daily to 11 p.m. Sun. to 10 p.m. 45 Main St.

Governor Prouty Inn. Inexpensive. Very old restored home on shore of Lake Memphremagog. Specializes in roast beef, lobster thermidor, homemade pastries. Cocktails. Open from 4 to 11 p.m. Sun. to 8 p.m. 115 Main St.

NORTHFIELD. *The Little House & Pantry.* Inexpensive. Home-cooked meals and baked goods in New England dining room. Maple-centered dishes are specialties. Open daily from 7:30 a.m. to 8 p.m. Thurs. buffet in summer. 40 So. Main St.

NORWICH. *Norwich Inn & Motel.* Reasonable. This Colonial country establishment is open year-round with Vermont foods as specialties, including maple-cured ham, country sausage and pancakes in *Four Seasons Dining Terrace.* Open from 7:30 a.m. to 8 p.m. 1 mi. from Dartmouth College.

PERU. *Bromley House.* Reasonable. Popular dining room featuring New England dishes. Children's plates. Open from 8 a.m. to 8 p.m. Closed from Oct. 16 to May 27.

ST. JOHNSBURY. *Candlelight.* Reasonable. Located in *Maple Center Motel.* Serving specialties such as lobster, roast beef, deep dish apple pie. Children's plates. Wine list. Open from 7 a.m. to 9:30 p.m. 22 Hastings St.

SHELBURNE. *Shelburne Inn.* Reasonable. Dine in grandeur on an old country estate overlooking Lake Champlain. Continental cooking. Features are shrimp scampi, shish kebab. Children's plates. Closed from Oct. 21 to May 9. On Harbor Rd., 4 mi. w. of Shelburne, off US 7.

SPRINGFIELD. *Hartness House.* Reasonable. Country inn on former residence of Gov. James Hartness. New England meals are served daily from 6 to 9 p.m. Cocktails. Buffet on Tues. & Wed. Look for the *Underground Lounge.* 30 Orchard St.

VERGENNES. *Basin Harbor Club.* Reasonable. Wide range of dishes served in resort's spacious dining room and cocktail area. Dinner from 6:30 to 8 p.m. Breakfast and lunch also served. Closed from mid-Oct. to mid-June. At Lake Champlain, 6 mi. w. of Rte. 22A.

Stewart's Restaurant. Inexpensive. Dining room, counter and booth service. Ask for Vermont roast turkey. Breakfast menu also features Vermont foods, maple syrup. Open daily from 6 a.m. to 9:30 p.m. At US 7, 1½ mi. n. of Vergennes.

WARREN (SUGARBUSH VALLEY). *The Christmas Tree Inn.* Reasonable. Excellent Continental cuisine in dining room and stube lounge. Week-end entertainment in *Sled* and *Red Nose* rooms. At entrance to Sugarbush Valley.

Sugarbush Inn. Reasonable. Large Colonial-style dining room and terrace, two lounges. Dinner features roast duckling and beef dishes. Children's plates. Open from 6 to 9 p.m. Closed from Oct. 16 to Dec. 14, Apr. 16 to June 14. On Sugarbush Rd.

WEST DOVER. *The Hermitage.* Reasonable. Leisurely dining in pleasant environment. Fine Continental cooking with distinctive veal specialties. Open daily to 9:30 p.m. Sun. and holidays to 8 p.m. Closed Tues., also Apr. to May 9, Nov. 12 to Dec. 11. Cold Brook Rd.

Snow Mountain Inn. Reasonable. An elegant resort restaurant with spacious lounge. Continental meals with a French accent. Dinner from 6 to 8:30 p.m. Closed from Oct. 21 to Dec. 5, Apr. 22 to June 20. 1½ mi. n.w. from Rte. 100.

WESTON. *Vermont Country Store Restaurant.* Inexpensive. Old-fashioned dining rooms with Victorian decor, specializing in Vermont foods (chicken, sausage, ham and griddle cakes). Open June through Oct. from 8:30 a.m. to 6 p.m. On Rte. 100.

WOODSTOCK. *White Cupboard Inn.* Reasonable. Specializing in New England cooking with such items as roast beef, steak and Mollie's rum pie. Dinner served to 8 p.m. Also open for breakfast and lunch. Children's plates. Open Sun. 12:30 to 3 p.m. On the Green.

Woodstock Inn. Reasonable. This charming historic landmark has recently been refurbished. New England dinners are served to music in dignified surroundings from 6 to 8 p.m. Cocktails, wine list. Breakfast and buffet lunch also served daily. Open year-round. On the Green.

NIGHTCLUBS. During the past few years, nightclubs have sprung up along Rte. 100, which leads to major Vermont ski areas. In these places, there are lots of folk-singing and fast-swinging combos, in addition to shows by out-of-state entertainers. Skiers can join in on folk-songs or catch up with the latest dance craze at such exotic places as the *Keg and Kettle,* located in the *Mt. Snow Base Lodge.* They might devote leisure time to the *Ski School's Tyrolean Evening* in *Stratton Ski Area.* Late into the night, things are jumping at the *Five Flys* at *Manchester Center,* the *Wobbly Barn* at *Killington,* and within the *Blue Tooth* at *Mad River Valley. Stowe* is still the greatest purveyor of night-sport (pardon, night-spot) activities. Among the bright (or dimmed) establishments are: The *After Hours Club, Town and Country Motor Lodge, Center Lodge, Sister Kate's,* the original *Five Flys,* and *Tony's Restaurant.*

MUSIC. Since 1950 the *Marlboro Music Festival* has attracted some of the world's best-known musicians to the campus of *Marlboro College* in Marlboro, not far from Bennington and Brattleboro. Sixteen weekend concerts of contemporary and classical chamber music are held during July and Aug. Rudolf Serkin is the artistic director of this important series. Cellist Pablo Casals has been Festival Orchestra conductor since 1960. The *Vermont Symphony Orchestra* presents concerts during the summer in various villages. The *Stowe Folk Festival* of lively music, yodeling, and dance, in Stowe during the fourth weekend of Sept., has been held as a foliage event since 1959.

STAGE AND REVUES. The *Champlain Shakespeare Festival,* organized in 1959, offers three Shakespeare plays by young professional actors during late July and all of August. They are presented in the *Arena Theater* in the *Fleming Museum* on the University of Vermont campus, Burlington. The 250 seats are the fading velvet ones taken from the Old Boston Opera House. The festival is the only major Shakespeare series given in a theater-in-the-round, and is associated with the new Institute on Elizabethan Arts and Literature on campus. *Summer theater* productions are staged in several Vermont towns, the best known being the *Weston Playhouse* in Weston on Rte. 100 and the *Dorset Playhouse* in Dorset.

SPECIAL INTEREST TOURS. Vermont, blessed with beautiful countryside, picturesque towns, and green forestlands, is an ideal place for self-conducted tours. The most popular *motoring tours* are held during the *foliage* period, usually from Sept. 25 to about Oct. 15. The coloration begins in the upper reaches of the Green Mountains and continues southward to the Massachusetts line, its progress depending on the various climatic conditions that affect the coloring processes.

The Vermont Development Department publishes a brochure with 13 proposed scenic tours which take the motorists efficiently along marked hardtop roads with scenic grandeur. Adequate housing accommodations are available in these areas. A typical tour in Southern Vermont might be outlined as follows: Start in Brattleboro, go to Poultney over Rte. 30, then head for Wallingford via Rte. 140, onward to Bennington over US 7, and to Brattleboro along Rte. 9, a total of some 180 miles. *Rte. 9,* popularly referred to as the *Molly Stark Trail,* is considered by some people to be Vermont's most scenic highway. It perpetuates the memory of the wife of Gen. Stark, who became famous for her legendary heroism in fighting the Indians.

Six villages in the *Northeast Kingdom* of Northern Vermont are so proud of the coloration in their area that they stage a *Fall Foliage Festival* during the last week of Sept. and the first week of Oct.

Being friendly people, Vermont *farmers and dairymen* welcome visitors to watch them at work. About 50 agricultural places display "welcome" signs. Each sign states: "See Vermont Agriculture." Some hosts are horse breeders, some beekeepers, others maple-syrup producers. A few farms accept vacation guests by reservation. Some places provide meals. The list of Vermont agriculture hosts may be obtained free from the Greater Vermont Association, Montpelier.

An intimate appreciation of the true nature of the New England atmosphere may be enjoyed by self-conducted *walking tours* in the villages. Among the more delightful settings are the towns which have large greens and college campuses. Top on the list of recommended "walking towns" are *Woodstock, Middlebury, Dorset, Putney, Bennington, Montpelier, Stowe, Burlington* and *Brattleboro.*

INDUSTRIAL TOURS. *Granite* and *maple-syrup products* are associated with Vermont. The doors are open for free guided tours at the world's largest granite center in Barre and at maple-syrup plants and museums. Tours in *Barre* (area pop. 10,400), in north central Vermont on US 302 and Rte. 14, are: *Rock of Ages* quarry, daily, from May 1 to Oct. 31, from 8:30 a.m. to 5 p.m.; *Craftsman Center,* Mon. to Fri., from 8:30 a.m. to 4 p.m.; *Wells-Lamson Quarry,* Jones Bros. Co. granite plant, Barre, daily, May 15 to Oct. 15, from 8:30 a.m. to 5 p.m.; *Vermont Marble Co.*'s world's largest marble exhibit, at Proctor, Rte. 3, daily, from May 21 to Oct. 17, 8:30 a.m. to 5:30 p.m., during July and Aug., until 8 p.m.; *John Shelby's Maple Museum* off US 302 in Barre, tour of modern processing plant and showplace of maple products. *Maple Grove, Inc., Museum* and world's largest maple-candy factory, at St. Johnsbury, daily, from mid-June to mid-Oct., from 8 a.m. to 5 p.m.; *National Life Insurance Co.,* Montpelier, near State Capitol, free guided tours of modern building, half-hour color movie on Vermont, souvenirs. Tours, Mon. to Fri., from 8 a.m. to 3:30 p.m.

HISTORIC SITES. Proud of their heritage, Vermonters established in 1961 the Vermont Board of Historic Sites, empowered to set up metal markers at historic places and buildings. A total of 91 historic signs are now posted. No. 1 is at *Chimney Point,* Addison, where first white settlement was stockaded in 1690; No. 91 is at *Woodstock* (Rte. 12), where the first ski tow in U.S. was launched in 1934. These sites are described in an official guidebook which also has a listing of Vermont's museums, a chronological list of important dates in Vermont history, and a special map.

Also described are the nine state-owned historic places, including the *State Capitol* (1859), with its beautiful Doric portico; the 306-foot *Battle Monument* at Bennington, erected in 1891 as a memorial to Vermonters who fought in the Revolutionary War; the *birthplace of Calvin Coolidge at Plymouth Notch,* where he was sworn in as the 21st President on Aug. 3, 1923; a 1783 structure on *Grand Isle,* considered to be the oldest log cabin in the nation still in its original condition; the *birthplace of President Chester A. Arthur in Northfield; Old Constitution House* in Windsor where state of Vermont received independence from New Hampshire; and the location of first U.S. *canal in Bellows Falls.*

The Official Guide Book may be obtained free from the Vermont Development Department, Montpelier.

MUSEUMS AND GALLERIES. Vermont's cultural, historic and artistic memorabilia are preserved in several museums in various parts of the state. Among the largest, best-staffed museums are: *Bennington Historical Museum and Art Gallery*—in Bennington, (Rte. 9), large collections of Bennington pottery and American glass; military relics of American wars, including the oldest Stars and Stripes in this country; largest genealogical library in state, paintings of Vermont artists. Open during summer months, daily from 9 a.m. to 6 p.m. Closed winter holidays, Sun. in Dec. and Jan., and all of Feb. At other times in winter, open daily from 9 a.m. to 4:30 p.m. Adm. for adults 50¢; children with parents, free. *Vermont State Museum* and *Library of the Vermont Historical Society* in State Administration Building, near the

State Capitol, Montpelier, has displays of three centuries of Vermontiana, featuring the famous *Stephen Daye Press,* which printed Vermont's first newspaper in 1781 at Westminster. Open daily, except Sat., Sun., and holidays, from 8 a.m. to 4:30 p.m. Adm. free. *Athenaeum Art Gallery and Library* in St. Johnsbury possesses collections of 19th-century paintings, as well as Bierstadt's "Domes of Yosemite." Open daily, except Sun., from 10 a.m. to 5 p.m.; also evenings, Mon., Wed., and Fri. to 9 p.m. Adm. free. *Robert Hull Fleming Museum* of the *University of Vermont at Burlington,* with collections of Americana and contemporary, primitive, ancient, and oriental art. Open Mon. to Fri. from 9 a.m. to 4 p.m.; Sun. from 2 to 5 p.m. Adm. free. *Southern Vermont Art Center,* two mi. from Manchester, is on a 350-acre site which has been developing regional exhibits of art and sculpture, summer programs of the performing and cultural arts. Open from mid-June to mid-Oct. from Tues. through Sat., 10 a.m. to 5 p.m.; Sun. from 1 to 5 p.m. Adm. for adults, 50¢, children, free. *Shelburne Museum*—Shelburne, on US 7, comprised of 35 buildings containing items of Americana of past three centuries, with focus on New England. Also on 45 acres are *Gallery of Art,* the sidewheeler *Ticonderoga* (on land), railroadiana and circusiana. Open from May 15 to Oct. 20, daily from 9 a.m. to 5 p.m. Adm. for adults $2.25, students $1.

SHOPPING. Although Vermont, with a population of not quite 400,000, may be limited in large shopping centers, there are many excellent shops to please the taste of milady. The various college towns and the winter resort areas are two reasons for the top-rate department and ladies' stores. Among the best-known shops are: Bennington, *Drysdale's;* Barre, *The Village Fair* and *Montgomery Ward & Co.;* Brattleboro, *The Casual Shop;* Burlington, *Abernethy, Clarkson Wright, Inc.;* Middlebury, *The College Shop;* Montpelier, *The Goodrich Store* and *The Oxford Shop;* Rutland, *Charles Sterns & Co.; and* Stowe, *Trapp Family Shop.*

SUMMER SPORTS. There's a concerted movement in Vermont to get more people into the Green Mountains during the summer. Sports is the magic lure. With more than 2,000 lodging and eating establishments along Rte. 100, which converges on many winter sports centers, many operators are remaining open during the non-snow months. This year-round business trend has been partly responsible for the annual income at the recreation and resorts areas, which goes beyond the $200 million mark. At *Mt. Mansfield,* for example, many ambitious hikers take the double chairlift to the 3,850-ft. level. Then they walk up to the 4,393 ft. summit (state's highest peak) for extraordinary panoramic views which extend to 100 miles or more in all directions on clear days.

New *golf courses* are being located near the winter sports centers. Now Vermont offers 39 golf courses in some of the most scenic spots of the Northeast. Among the biggest competitions are the *Vermont State Open* at *Fairlee* in June and the *Women's Tournament* in *Manchester* during July.

Thrills galore are experienced by drivers and spectators at the *International Motorcycle Scramble* held in July at *Perley Bell's Ranch,* Grafton.

Boating is another popular pastime that is expanding on many of Vermont's 400 or more lakes. Particular emphasis is being placed on this sport on the 136-mile-long *Lake Champlain.* Thousands of boats, from rowboats to huge yachts, dock at Champlain's piers. About 60 marina locations are listed at Vermont's lakes, where water skiing and cruising are on the increase. *Sailboat racing* is held at *Lake Bomoseen* and *Lake Dunmore;* lightning-class championships are staged at Lake Champlain's *Shelburne Bay.*

Hiking is being stimulated by such organizations as the *Green Mountain Club,* which maintains 250 miles of foot trails in the Green Mountains. The *Long Trail* has been a perennial favorite with hardy hikers, especially during the foliage season.

Horse racing received a boost in 1964 with the opening of the state's first pari-mutuel track, the $6-million *Green Mountain Park* at Pownal, in southwestern Vermont. The grandstand is the first to be entirely covered. Sixty thousand fans can be accommodated. The thoroughbred and night harness racing take place from May through July and from Aug. through Oct. Many events are sponsored by the *Green Mountain Horse Association* in South Woodstock, Vermont's "blue-grass region." The association maintains 1,000 miles of bridle paths throughout the United States.

WINTER SPORTS. Vermont is appropriately called "the Ski State of the East." A substantial percentage of the $200 million or more that is rung up in the state annually at recreation and tourist places is received at the ski areas. Plentiful snow, crisp weather, and well-developed slopes, surrounded with modern accommodations and recreational diversities, combine to please the countless thousands who participate in winter sports events. The snow belt within the Green Mountain ranges is often white-crowned from late Nov. to April, or even May.

Forty large ski areas form the chain of resorts, easily reached along Route 100, that attract enthusiasts from all parts of the U.S., Canada, and Europe. *Mt. Snow Ski Area* claims to be the world's largest, most complete ski resort. Still a favorite spot for many skiers is the *Mt. Tom Ski Area* at Woodstock, where the first ski tow in the United States was strung up in the depression year of 1934.

Most skiers travel to Vermont by auto over easily accessible multilaned highways from New York, Boston, Conn. and the provinces of Quebec and Ontario. Others come from metropolitan sections in chartered buses, while many travel in the four-a-day New York–Montreal trains of the Central Vermont Railway. In recent years, an increasing number of winter sports people have been arriving in Vermont aboard *"ski planes,"* landing at the airfields at Stowe and Sugarbush Valley, as well as at the private airfields and the commercial airports at Burlington and Barre-Montpelier.

Newspapers, television and radio carry daily *snow reports* during the ski season. Ski conditions are dispatched by the Vermont Development Department and the Greater Vermont Association, both in Montpelier, after they are received from the ski sections. Frequent reports are also available at the New York office of the Vermont Development Department, the Vermont Information Center at Montreal, and at the New England Vacation Center in Cleveland, Ohio.

Principal ski centers are *Big Bromley, Burrington Hill, Dutch Hill, Glen Ellen, High Pond, Hogback, Jay Peak, Inc., Killington, Mad River Glen, Mt. Ascutney, Mt. Mansfield Co.* at Stowe, *Mt. Snow, Mt. Tom, Madonna Mountain, Pico Peak, Sky Line, Stratton Mountain,* and *Sugarbush Valley.*

Brochures on facilities and accommodations may be obtained by writing the Vermont Development Department, Montpelier, or the Greater Vermont Association. The ski areas also have brochures.

RECOMMENDED READING. *Let Me Show You Vermont,* by Charles Edward Crane; *Green Mountain Farm,* by Elliott Merrick; *Vermont Tradition,* by Dorothy Canfield Fisher; *Nostalgia, The Waterbury Story,* and *Adventure in Retirement,* all by R. L. Duffus.

NEW HAMPSHIRE

A Playland Built on Granite

New Hampshire is the state of the White Mountains—a series of undulating peaks topped by more-than-a-mile-high Mt. Washington. It is a state of rich granite deposits and thereby takes as its nickname the *Granite State.*

The people of New Hampshire are as solid as the granite blocks which they quarry, in their ideals, beliefs, and convictions. It takes a charge of dynamite to change a New Hampshirite's opinion once he has made up his mind.

For years presidential political aspirants have used New Hampshire's primary elections as a testing ground to their popularity. In national elections the little town of Washington, the people sitting up until midnight on the eve of voting, was one of the first to send in its returns.

But it is its mountains which Granite Staters look to with pride and admiring eye. It is to the Presidential Range, the Franconias, Chocorua, Kearsarge, and Monadnock visitors flock each year, during all seasons, for recreational opportunities. It is on Mt. Washington the Cog Railway operates throughout the summer, carrying thousands to its peak. It was the first railway of its kind in the world and since 1869 has chugged up the steep ascent without injury to a paying passenger.

Granite Staters are not a people to boast and for reason of this, perhaps, some of its great men and women are not so well identified with the state nationally and internationally. New Hampshire contributed Franklin Pierce as 14th President of the United States. Other Granite State men who won their place in history included Horace Greeley, founder of the New York *Tribune;* Daniel Webster, the great orator; and Joseph E. Worcester, compiler of one of the first American dictionaries of the English language, published in 1830.

Among the women deserving a place in history, but little known, was Mrs. Sarah Josepha Buell Hale, who successfully campaigned to make Thanksgiving Day a national holiday. She also is credited with being the author of *Mary Had a Little Lamb.*

Unknown to millions of TV viewers watching "westerns" the stagecoaches were Concordmade. These wagons were used by migrating families to the West.

New Hampshire might also be likened to the sweet, dignified, little old lady who, when the necessity arose one night, pounded a burglar into semi-consciousness. It's more than likely she also sat on his prone form, quietly humming to herself, until the police arrived.

It isn't that New Hampshirites were or are natural-born scrappers. But, pushed to the wall, when the occasion demands, they come out swinging, either physically or verbally. From scraps and scrapes with the Indians and their French friends, to solving what might have proved disastrous economic problems, New Hampshire has gone into the thick of the fray, often emerging not so much bloody, but unbowed, as just plain unbowed.

None of this, of course, was apparent overnight, historically speaking. In fact, it took quite awhile, just as the settlement of the state did.

A Record of Free-Spirited Action

Before its colonization, New Hampshire, like Maine, Massachusetts, and other coastal states, was sailed along and poked about in by an assortment of explorers. Martin Pring, Samuel de Champlain, and John Smith all had a look at the Piscataqua River and Bay, liked what they saw, and said so when they got back home. But it wasn't until 1623, a decade or so later, that the first settlement was made. This was at, or near, present-day Portsmouth. The settlers arrived with their pots, tools, seeds, clothing, guns, and powder, and a few wilting lilac bushes that seemed of no particular import at the time. They planted the bushes on what is now the property of the Wentworth-Gardiner House in Portsmouth (they can still be seen today). Unlike the first colony, the lilacs prospered, in time people began taking slips from these bushes, and one day someone suggested it be made the State Flower. And it was done.

New Hampshire's somewhat slow settlement found the population by 1641 a mere 1,000. It wasn't altogether the weather, although, if you'll read Toynbee's *A Study of History* you'll see that that Englishman suggests New Hampshire is north of "the optimum climatic area," and thus, in his opinion, fit only for hunters, trappers, and the like. Even 90 years later, in 1732, the population was only 12,500. But it wasn't the weather and the marauding Indians. It was also very much involved with loose, often contradictory, land grants. There weren't many people who wanted to buy land and go to the back-breaking trouble of clearing it and settling down only to have someone come along and tell them to get off the land, that it wasn't legally theirs.

In the beginning, things had indeed been loose. In 1620, a charter obtained for the Council of New England granted all lands between the 40th and 48th latitudes (roughly between the midriff of present-day New Jersey and the Canadian border). East to west it was more far-flung, encompassing land "from the Atlantic Ocean to the South Sea." Since few people in those days knew their geography very well, it's doubtful that London merchant Capt. John Mason and Sir Ferdinando Gorges, Governor of Plymouth, England, who were given large grants under the charter, knew exactly what a piece of real estate they'd been handed.

At any rate, things had become a little more realistic by 1629, when Captain Mason received a clear grant to what is basically present-day New Hampshire. He soon set about sending out settlers, and deeding over bits and pieces of property here and there to others. But things weren't going to remain that simple, as later events showed.

In 1631, the first saw and gristmills were built at Portsmouth. By 1638 Dover and Exeter had been founded, and fishing, shipbuilding, lumbering, and fur-trading were the principal business activities. By 1635, tiny though it was, the state had already begun to show its sweet-old-lady character. In that year the general court ordered the men who had brought a colored man from Africa as a slave to return him immediately to his native land. In 1649, thoroughly annoyed at men who wore their hair long, the colony stated firmly, "Foreasmuch as the wearing of long hair, after the manner of ruffians and barbarous Indians, has begun to invade New England, contrary to the rule of God's word, which says it is a shame for men to wear long hair . . . (we) do declare and manifest our dislike and detestation . . ."

In 1673 Nashua, the first town to be considered in the interior of the state, was founded, and though the French and Indian Wars followed soon after, the state suffered little.

Land Grants Galore

Earlier, in 1641, realizing their state was too small and too sparsely populated to protect itself, New Hampshire had asked to be taken under the wing of Massachusetts. Now, in 1679, expressing deep annoyance at the fact Massachusetts had purportedly been illegally doling out land to settlers in New Hampshire, one of Captain Mason's descendants talked King Charles II into making the state a royal province. New Hampshirites smarted under this blow for six years, bearing up under what they considered tyrannical royal governors. Finally revolting, in 1685, they again allied themselves with Massachusetts, sharing its governor, but having its own legislature and council.

Though New Hampshire was not seriously affected by any of the French and Indian Wars, its citizenry was never free from Indian ambushes. And during this time many New Hampshire men took part in conflicts, including the famous expedition which took Louisbourg from the French in Nova Scotia. Of even greater fame were the exploits of Rogers and his Rangers. In addition to a number of other campaigns, they drove the St. Francis Indians back to Quebec during the war that took place from 1754 to 1763.

In 1741, Benning Wentworth, who was appointed royal governor, began as a popular figure. However, by the time he had finished, he had made a jigsaw puzzle of New Hampshire real estate. Every time he granted tracts of land to anyone, he included a personally-selected lot of 500 acres for himself. By the end of his term he had a neat little 100,000 acres scattered about. In 1766 he was asked to resign by George III, and his nephew, John Wentworth, was appointed governor.

It was while John was governor that Eleazar Wheelock founded Dartmouth College at Hanover, helped in his fund-raising by the governor. The school was founded for the Indians, but most of them shortly became drop-outs. However, the college continued, situated on 500 acres of land provided by ex-Governor Benning Wentworth.

Although Governor John Wentworth was popular, and opposed such regulations as the Stamp Act, things began to get too warm for him. In 1774, a riot broke out when an attempt was made to land a cargo of tea at Portsmouth, and in December a force of locals captured a large store of munitions from the British at nearby Fort William and Mary.

Declaration of Independence Precipitated

John Wentworth removed himself from the scene in 1775, and a Provincial Congress drew up a temporary constitution. Adopting this, in January of 1776, sweet-old-lady New Hampshire became independent of Britain seven months before the U.S. openly announced its similar intention! In November of 1776, New Hampshire's delegates to the Continental Congress signed the U.S. Declaration of Independence, and New Hampshire slipped quietly into the fold.

Three regiments of the state's militia had scurried to the front in June of 1775 (Battle of Bunker Hill), and throughout the Revolution New Hampshire maintained this strength in the Continental Army. In 1777 John Stark (later General) defeated the British at Bennington. The Redcoats were after supplies, and many historians say that if these had not been kept from them Burgoyne just might have won the Battle of Saratoga.

During the Revolution Portsmouth bustled with maritime activity. More than 100 New Hampshire men engaged in privateering, aiding in the defeat of the British at sea, and from 1775 to 1778 the *Raleigh, America,* and *Ranger* (made so famous by John Paul Jones) were built at the seaport.

In 1794 a one-half-mile-long bridge was built across the Piscataqua, from Portsmouth to Maine, and in 1796 the first New Hampshire turnpike company was chartered. These seemingly small events signaled a wholly-new era. From then on there would be more travel by land: not everyone would depend on river and sea transport. And by the mid-1800's the Concord Coach would emerge to write several exciting chapters in the history of America's expansion west.

The first textile mill in the state was built at New Ipswich in 1804, a forerunner of the great mills to follow, and in 1808 the State Capital was located at Concord. New Hampshire was moving inland.

In the War of 1812, 35,000 New Hampshire men went off to fight the British (more than 16% of the population). In 1818 Daniel Webster went off to do battle before the U.S. Supreme Court for Dartmouth College. His fight was a milestone in American judicial history, not only because of his oft-quoted, "It is, sir, as I have said, a small college, and yet there are those who love it," but also because the court's decision established non-interference by federal or state government with charters of either public or private corporations.

In 1819 the power loom was introduced at the great textile mills in Manchester, and in 1847 the state adopted the first 10-hour-day law for factory workers in the U.S.

Meantime, from 1820 on, anti-slavery societies mushroomed everywhere and continued strong. Loud protests went up from one end of the state to the other when Congress passed the Compromise of 1850. New Hampshirites considered it favored slavery. In October of 1853, 14 leading citizens with various political backgrounds, met and organized a new anti-slavery political party. They called the new party Republican. Four years later the new party elected its first governor, and in the presidential election of 1860 a sizeable majority of the state's citizenry voted Republican.

During the Civil War, New Hampshire sent 39,000 men to the front, more than 10% of its total population.

By 1871 the Industrial Revolution had gotten into full stride in the state and school attendance had become compulsory.

First Ski Club

In 1872, up north in the city of Berlin, a small incident occurred which was to play a surprisingly large part in the state's future. A group of Norwegian-Americans founded the Nansen Ski Club, believed the first such organization in America. Then in 1909 the Dartmouth Outing Club was organized at Hanover. Until then there had never been a club of this type on an American college campus. Following the D.O.C.'s beginnings, it started Winter Carnival, again a first. Now countless colleges and communities throughout the country hold such events annually.

Meantime, by the early 1900's, New Hampshire had become a full-fledged industrial state, with water power drawing many manufacturing firms.

Men 20,000 strong marched off to World War I, while others helped make Portsmouth a highly-important shipbuilding center.

Following the war, a number of strikes slowed the textile industry to a virtual halt, and eight years later the depression struck. Wages slumped and unemployment jumped. Things looked hopeless. The Amoskeag Textile Mill declared bankruptcy. Floods in March of 1936 destroyed $7 million worth of property throughout the state.

Once again the sweet-little-old-lady mien of the state came to the fore. Businessmen pooled their resources, bought the big Amoskeag Mill complex and began renting it out to smaller firms, piecemeal. In time these businesses, combined, were employing more workers than the mill ever had.

In 1938 New Hampshire's predilection for outdoor winter sports surged ahead. A Skimobile was built at Cranmore Mountain, North Conway, and a leading ski center was born. The same year an aerial tramway, the first in the United States, at Cannon Mountain in the Franconia Notch area was built. Suddenly there were 14 ski tows snaking their way up New Hampshire's hillsides. At other spots early ski enthusiasts were still getting uphill by herringbone—an almost lost art today.

In the year 1949, eying the decrease in employment which followed World War II with deep concern, then-Governor Sherman Adams appointed an eight-man Industrial Development Committee. By 1965, the state's industrial growth showed that "on the basis of percentage of population employed in manufacturing," New Hampshire ranked second as the most industrialized in the U.S. In the early 1950's she had ranked ninth among the then 48 states.

In 1964 the orders to phase out the Portsmouth Navy Yard came as a chilling bit of news. Would the shipbuilding industry that had been born here over 300 years ago, and been going on apace ever since, come to a final halt? Would the state be allowed to purchase the yard and pull it up, too, by its bootstraps? The general impression, after the initial shock, was that New Hampshire again would come out fighting.

The Current Scene

In addition to its long-time manufacturing operations the electronics industry is new and growing fast in New Hampshire these days. Nine new schools, opened since the war, have brought the total to 17 colleges and 17 outstanding private schools within the state, a number in both categories being world-known. A long-time, top crop continues to produce approximately 1,300,000 bushels of apples annually. Though most of these are consumed through Boston and New York markets, some 15% are exported each year to England and European markets.

What began small with the Nansen Ski Club in the late 1800's, grew with the activities of the Dartmouth Outing Club, and burgeoned with the opening up of Cranmore and Cannon Mountains, has built up to over 70 lifts and tramways throughout the state, as well as over 100 rope tows. What was begun in the late 1930's for skiers is attracting more and more summer visitors, who can take advantage of the greater variety of accommodations offered and the numerous chairlift and tramway rides to great heights and panoramic views.

New Hampshire has been the most progressive among the six New England states in building express highways to its major vacation areas. And it is over these safe, fast roads that motorists can reach the mountain and lake resorts in about half the time it used to take.

Equally important to New Hampshire's mountains as tourist attractions are the state's many fine lakes. The largest, Lake Winnipesaukee, called by the Indians, "the smile of the Great Spirit," has hundreds of cottages along its shores and is said to have as many islands as there are days in the year. Many notable boating events take place on it yearly but perhaps the most notable was in 1852 when the first race between the crews of Harvard and Yale was held.

Coupled with the time-honored Mt. Washington, where winds have been recorded to blow harder than any other place in the world, the Presidential Range, the many towns of calendar-picture calibre, the fine museums, art centers, summer theaters, the history, lore—all of these add up to tourism currently accounting for approximately 20 percent of New Hampshire's yearly income.

PRACTICAL INFORMATION FOR NEW HAMPSHIRE

NEW HAMPSHIRE FACTS & FIGURES. The state borrowed its name from Hampshire County, England. Its nickname is *Granite State.* The purple lilac is the state flower; the white birch, the state tree; the purple finch, the state bird. "Live Free or Die" is the state motto. *Old New Hampshire* is the state song.

Concord is the state capital. The state population is 606,921.

Tourism is fast becoming the major industry of this scenic New England state. Handsome forests, New Hampshire's chief natural resource, cover 80 percent of the land of this mountainous, lake-dotted state. The mountains attract visitors throughout the year, and especially in the fall, for hunting and foliage-viewing, and in the winter, to the many ski resorts. Pretty and historic old colonial towns are also among the state's attractions, and the coastal lowlands in the southeast provide several attractive Atlantic summer resorts. Industry is on a small scale, and farming not of great importance. Winters are cold and snowy, summers mild and brief.

HOW TO GET AROUND. "Photoscenic" is the word coined for New Hampshire highways and country roads. About 165 miles of four-lane expressways speed the motorists to six tourist regions. Four national awards have been won for the beautiful stretches of state turnpikes.

Air: principal airport, *Grenier Field,* Manchester (18 miles from Concord); daily service to Boston and New York; service also from Keene, Laconia, and Lebanon; 31 other airfields. *Boat cruises:* summer schedules on Lake Winnipesaukee, Lake Sunapee, and Portsmouth to Isles of Shoals. *Buses: Greyhound* and *Trailways* services, year round, with extra buses during summer and ski season.

Mountain rides: for thrilling panoramic vistas, take *Cannon Mt. Aerial Passenger Tramway,* Franconia Notch, US 3 (May 30 to mid-Oct. and ski season). *Mt. Cranmore Skimobile,* North Conway (State 16 and US 302), summer and winter. *Mt. Washington Cog Railway* (off US 302, north of Crawford Notch), steam-powered rail trip; May 30 to Oct. 12. *Wildcat Mt. Gondola Lift,* Pinkham Notch (State 16) in White Mt. National Forest, two-passenger gondolas rise to 6,800-ft. summit. Open from late May to mid-Oct.

Rail: New Haven Railroad service between New York and Montreal, through Vermont and New Hampshire. Passengers can board at Claremont Junction, N.H., Bellows Falls, Vt., Brattleboro, Vt., and White River Junction, Vt.; *Boston & Maine* railroad service; daily commuter trains, Boston and Concord; Boston and Dover, N.H. *Taxi:* service from airports to nearby towns. *Rent-a-Car* office at Grenier Field.

SEASONAL EVENTS. New England traditions of sociability, competition, and folklore pervade the seasonal activities in the villages and resort areas. Winter festivals attract thousands of skiers and spectators from all over the U.S. and from overseas. The colorful foliage weeks of late Sept. and early Oct. also lure countless thousands of visitors.

Spring: N.H. Art Assn. Traveling Exhibition, Exeter, Sharon, Mt. Sunapee State Park (Apr. thru Aug.); *Nashua Arts Festival,* Nashua National Guard Armory (June); *antique shows,* Manchester (Apr.), Exeter (June), Concord (June); *Dog Show,* Rockingham County Kennel Club, Portsmouth (May 30); *Trade and Beauty Show,* Concord (June).

Summer: antique shows, Wolfeboro (July), Keene (July), Concord (June and Aug.); *Craftsmen's Fair,* Mt. Sunapee State Park (Aug.); *Flower Show,* Whitefield (Aug.). *Old Home Week,* throughout the state (third week of Aug.); *Lobster Festival,* East Kingston (Aug.); *folk drama* revival (since 1942), *The Old Homestead,* Swanzey Center (July); *summer theatre,* Hampton, Dartmouth campus (Hanover), and the University of New Hampshire (Durham); *Cheshire County Fair,* Keene (Aug.).

Fall: foliage spectacular, with regional tours and festivities, *county fairs,* and *harvest suppers,* all over the state from late Sept. to early Oct.; *Button Show,* Concord (Oct.); *N.H. Heritage Forum and Antique Show,* Highway Hotel, Concord (Sept.); *Air Show,* Dillant-Hopkins Airport, North Swanzey (Sept.). *Antique Show,* Peterborough Town Hall (Oct.). Among most popular *fairs: Essex Fair,* Lancaster (Sept.); *Rochester Fair* (Sept.); *Sandwich Fair* (Oct.).

Winter: Dartmouth College Winter Carnival, Hanover (Feb.); *World's Sled Dog Championships,* Laconia (Feb.); *Alpine Ski Championships,* Mt. Cranmore, Wildcat Mt., Cannon Mt., Franconia Notch (Mar.).

TOURIST INFORMATION SERVICES. Excellent sources provide free information on New Hampshire and its tourist and sports attractions. A handy map, recreation calendar, and many pamphlets (fishing, boating, hunting, etc.) are furnished by the N.H. Division of Economic Development, Concord, N.H. 03301. *Free literature* is also available for the six tourist regions: Dartmouth–Lake Sunapee Region, Box 246, Lebanon, N.H. 03766; Lakes Region, Wolfeboro, N.H. 03894; Merrimack Valley Region, Box 634, Manchester, N.H. 03105; Monadnock Region, Peterborough, N.H. 03458; Seacoast Region, Box 807, Portsmouth, N.H. 03802; White Mountains Region, Lancaster, N.H. 03584. Year-round *information services* are at Turnpike Plazas in Dover, Hampton, Hooksett, Merrimack, and Rochester. Thirty-five tourist booths are on various highways during summer.

DRINKING LAWS. Liquor is sold only in 49 stores within the state, operated under the control of the State Liquor Commission. Local approval by voters may be voted every two years. Beer and ale may be sold for off-the-premises consumption by grocers and druggists having proper permits; consumption, by the glass, of liquor and beer is permitted at licensed hotels, restaurants and clubs, daily. State stores normally operate from 10 a.m. to 5:30 p.m., weekdays. They are closed on election days. No beer or liquor should be purchased by persons under 21 years of age. Golf club and cocktail lounges are closed Sunday, except in a few places.

NATIONAL PARKS AND FORESTS. The *White Mountain National Forest,* established in May, 1918, contains 724,000 acres of spectacular scenery, unspoiled wilderness, first-rate winter sports areas, lofty peaks, and silent valleys. The mountain slopes are crisscrossed by excellent highways and by marked hiking trails which are maintained by the U.S. Forest Service and the Appalachian Mountain Club. About 678,000 acres of the forest are in north-central New Hampshire; the rest is in western Maine.

Some 100 miles of Forest Service roads provide fast access to about 1,000 miles of foot trails and ski runs. Among the more popular highways are: Franconia Notch Highway (US. 3), Crawford Notch Highway (U.S. 302), Pinkham Notch Highway (Maine 113). Some of New England's most scenic drives are along Bear Notch Rd., Tripoli Rd., and Kancamagus Highway.

The roads lead to 15 national camp areas, 47 lakes and ponds, and 650 miles of fishable streams. The entire forest is open for fishing and hunting, during the regular state open seasons. Wildlife includes deer, bear, moose, grouse, raccoon, wildcat, and lynx.

From July 1 to Sept. 10 an *entrance fee* is required for the driver and occupants of each noncommercial car at designated recreational areas. A sticker, costing $7, entitles the holder and the occupants of his car an unlimited number of visits to any federal recreational area in the U.S., until the following Mar. 31. Seasonal permits of $1.25 per person, 16 years or older, are also sold. Entrance fees at nominal costs for each person over 16 years of age are also made for picnic and camping privileges. Vehicles with more than nine people in them are considered commercial vehicles. These drivers should obtain appropriate permits from Forest Service officers or area attendants.

The U.S. Forest Service warns that "storms of incredible violence" sometimes occur in summer months above the timberline. Hikers are reminded that ice-coated rocks, winds of hurricane force, and subfreezing temperatures may endanger their lives. Forest rangers, conservation officers, and game wardens are on constant patrol. Safety rules are urged at all times for hikers, hunters, and fishermen.

Campground facilities are available on first-come, first-served basis. No reservations accepted. Nominal fees are charged in most areas. No special facilities are provided for trailers but they may park in all camp areas, except at Dugway and Waterville. Sleeping in cars is permissible, but dressing must not be in the open. Dogs are permitted in the forest if they are leashed. The campsites at Dolly Copp, Russell Pond, and Compton are usually open from late May to late Sept. Other areas are open year round, but water and other facilities are not maintained from late Sept. to early May.

Picnicking is allowed in 12 areas having tables, drinking water, and sanitary facilities. Nominal fees are charged in some of these areas. *Campfire permits* are required at improved roadside campgrounds. They are given free by district rangers at Plymouth, Littleton, Gorham, and Conway.

Extraordinary panoramic views, on clear days, may be enjoyed on the 4,100-ft. summit of Wildcat Mt., toward the Presidential Range, called the "backbone of New England." Two-passenger gondola lifts take spectators to the top of Wildcat. Many visitor are thrilled with the scenery along the Mt. Washington Road; countless others have chosen to reach the lofty peak of Mt. Washington by the cog railway, first of its kind in this country.

Outstanding *winter sports* are scheduled at Pinkham Notch, Waterville, Valley, Attitash, and Mittersill. Tuckerman Ravine, at the 6,288-ft. level of Mt. Washington, highest point in the East, has alpine skiing sometimes until mid-June. Details on the national forest may be obtained free from Forest Supervisor, White Mountain National Park, Laconia.

STATE PARKS. Few states in the East can boast of the scenic splendors and fun spots that sparkle most of New Hampshire's 29 state parks. Swimming, picnicking, hiking, and boating are featured at 14 lakeside parks. Among the most popular for Hampshirites and for visitors is *Crawford Notch State Park,* with 10 miles of unspoiled rugged beauty and incomparable views of Crawford Flume and the Presidential Range (US 302). There are more scenic excitements at *Mt. Sunapee State Park* (at Newbury), a major recreation area with 125 acres of ski slopes and trails, gondola lifts, well-developed beach, and other facilities.

Franconia Notch State Park (at Franconia and Lincoln), is a deep valley of 6,552 acres between towering Franconia and Kinsman Mountain ranges. Unforgettable spectacles are the Flume Gorge, an 800-ft. natural chasm; Cannon Mt. Tramway, Echo Lake, and *The Old Man of the Mountains* rock profile. At *Rhododendron State Park* (in Fitzwilliam), some 16 acres of wild *Rhododendron maximum* burst out in mid-July.

White Lake State Park (at Tamworth) and *Monadnock State Park* (at Jaffrey) are among the 10 parks with public campgrounds for tenting and trails for hiking, especially for families and organized youth groups. Ocean bathing is the featured attraction at the newest state park, *Wallis Sands* (at Rye), which has a large beach house. A short drive away is *Hampton State Beach* with two miles of sandy beach along the Atlantic Ocean and a modern recreational complex.

Most state parks are open through the fall foliage season when the warm Indian summer days draw thousands to the outdoors. Major ski areas are operated by the New Hampshire Division of Parks at Franconia's Cannon Mountain and at Mt. Sunapee State Park. Free folders with state park information are sent, on request, by the New Hampshire Division of Economic Development, Concord.

WHERE TO GO. With the opening of new interstate highways and the extension of multilane state roads, New Hampshire is now in easy reach of New York and Boston, as well as of the West and Canada. A wide range of natural and man-made attractions is waiting for all members of the vacationing family. About 40 tourist information booths at strategic crossroad towns and in resort towns are stocked with brochures of a wide choice of places to stay, to visit, and to shop.

Here are some highspots to whet the appetites of motoring families bound for fun and memorable experiences:

Aerial lifts and mountain rides: Cannon Mt. Tramway, Franconia Notch, US 3, thrilling mile-long ride, operates from May 30 to mid-Oct., and in ski season. *Cog railway to Mt. Washington* rises 3 miles to "top of New England"; operates from May 30 to Oct. 12. *Gondola lifts* at *Wildcat Mt.* in White Mountain National Forest, State 16; *Mt. Sunapee State Park,* off State 103, at Newbury; *Mt. Whittier,* at West Ossipee near junction of States 16 and 25, all operating from May 30 to mid-Oct.; *Skimobile* at *Mt. Cranmore,* North Conway, State 16 and US 302, scenic ride to family ski area during winter and summer.

Commercial attractions: craft shops of the *League of New Hampshire Arts and Crafts,* open year round in Concord, Hanover, Manchester, and North Conway. Seasonal shops also in many other towns.

Historical homes: Daniel Webster Birthplace, between Salisbury and Franklin, on State 127. *Franklin Pierce's Homestead,* n. of Hillsboro, State 31, house (1804) of New Hampshire's only son to be chosen to the White House. *Horace Greeley's Birthplace,* Amherst, home of editor who advised young men to "go west."

Memorial: Cathedral of the Pines, Rindge, outdoor shrine for religious and patriotic services; open for all groups from May thru Oct.

Museums: Shaker Inventions and Handicrafts, 12 mi. n.e. of Concord, off State 106, open June 1 to Labor Day. *New Hampshire Historical Society* museum-library, near State Capitol, Concord. *Hopkins Center, Baker Memorial Library,* and *College Museum,* all on Dartmouth College campus, Hanover.

Natural wonder: Old Man of the Mountains, familiar stone profile, presiding over Profile Lake at Franconia Notch, US 3. *Lost River,* a series of glacial caverns along stream that disappears at Kinsman Notch, White Mountains, w. of North Woodstock. *Polar Caves,* glacial caverns and mineral displays, Rumney, near Plymouth, State 25, open from late May to mid-Oct.

Restoration: Strawbery Banke, multimillion-dollar project to restore 27 Colonial period buildings. Daily tours and surrey rides during summer. Also, summer tours at 10 historic homes in Portsmouth.

Sightseeing in towns: strolling along tree-shaded walks of New Hampshire villages and towns is a relaxing pastime, especially during the summer and the foliage season. The village greens, flanked by small shops, churches, and residential homes of other eras, are still preserved in the New England tradition. Campuses of preparatory schools and institutions of higher learning are also interesting places to walk about for an hour or two. Recommended for walking excursions are *Concord*'s historic square, shadowed by the State Capitol; *Portsmouth,* with its sea captains' and merchants' homes, *Manchester, Exeter,* and *Hanover,* all reflecting the quiet dignity of old New England.

WHAT TO DO WITH THE CHILDREN. Attractions and fun places for children vary from beaches to White Mountain slopes. Most places for kiddies are open during summer months, particularly at lake and shore resorts. *Hampton Beach,* reached by US 1 and I-95 from Mass., features children's playground, 3-mi. ocean boardwalk, free entertainment and shopping in new $350,000 Beach Sea Shell. Free guide book: Chamber of Commerce, 55 Ocean Blvd., Hampton Beach. *Animal Forest,* Laconia-Weirs Beach, US 3, herds of deer, hand-fed and pet-loose animals. Open June 15 to Oct. 15. Adults $1, children 50¢.

Lockehaven School House Museum, Lockehaven, State 4A, furnishings and books of century-old classrooms. Open mid-June to mid-Oct., 2 to 5 p.m. Free admission. *Parks, circus acts,* Nashua. This town, at confluence of Merrimack & Nashua rivers, boasts seven parks and playgrounds. *Benson's Wild Animal Farm* nearby on State 111, with outdoor circus acts. Open Apr. 15 to Nov.; Mon. to Sat., 10 a.m. to 6 p.m.; Sun. and holidays, to 7 p.m. Adults 80¢, children 40¢. *Polar Caves,* Rumney, State 25, 4 mi. w. of Plymouth. Tours, wild waterfowl exhibits, nature trails, picnic area. Open May 22 to Oct. 12. Adults $1.25; children under 12, 50¢; under 6 free.

Santa's Village, Jefferson, off US 2. Christmas setting in summer. Open June 20 to Oct. 17, daily, 9 a.m. to 6 p.m.; Sun., 10 a.m. to 7 p.m. Adults $1; children under 12, 50¢; under 6 free. *Storyland,* Glen, 7 mi. n. of North Conway. Children's well-known tales related in living displays. Pumpkin coach and steam train rides. Open from mid-June to mid-Oct., 9 a.m. to 10 p.m.

Children also like to see the *Old Man of the Mountains,* 40-ft.-high stone profile overlooking Profile Lake, at Franconia Notch (US 3). It is New Hampshire's most famous natural landmark. The "face" is formed by five ledges looking out from a 1,200-ft. elevation. It decorates the state emblem, the masthead of the *Manchester Union Leader,* state publications on travel attractions, and appears on other tourist literature.

Daniel Webster, one of New Hampshire's most famous sons, said of "The Old Man": "Men hang out signs indicative of their respective trades. Shoemakers hang out a gigantic shoe, jewelers a monster watch, and the dentist hangs out a gold tooth. But in the mountains of New Hampshire, God Almighty has hung out a sign to show that there He makes men."

EXPLORING NEW HAMPSHIRE

Probably the best way to begin exploring New Hampshire is much as the earliest seafarers and settlers did, along the coast. In distance there's little to go on here—only 18 miles—but in Americana, there's a heap of exploring to be done toward the north.

After Portsmouth, which has been building ships and rearing sailors (some of them privateers) since the early 1600's, one can begin to dip inland, as the early settlers did, to Exeter and beyond. Gradually, then, one works his way north, fortunately not slowed by severe winter weather, as the settlers were, nor downright hampered by hostile Indians and unfriendly French.

Up the Coastline

Coming in to New Hampshire near the coast, on Interstate 95 or US 1, turn east on State 86 for Seabrook Beach, where you should turn left onto State 1A. Here you'll head north, along the coast. If it's a bright summer day you may find you're pushing your way slowly through pedestrians and traffic. This is a very popular area—including Seabrook, Hampton Beach, Great Boars Head—which attracts literally hundreds of thousands in warm weather.

Don't give up, though, as things thin out quite a bit as you approach Little Boar's Head, with its magnificent summer mansions. All along, on your right, the sea slips or pounds its way into shore and there are a number of turn-outs where you can stop for a better look at the Atlantic. Those lovely islands off there, hazy on the horizon, are the Isles of Shoals. John Smith, early explorer and, later, husband of Pocahontas, saw them in 1614 and, to no one's surprise, named them Smith's Isles. Early fishermen, noting the shoaling or schooling of fish near their shores, and probably never having heard of John Smith, began calling them by their present name.

Lobster boats usually bob on the sea here, and a workaday freighter may be nosing its way toward the harbor at Portsmouth, perhaps blasting out a call for a harbor pilot.

On your right, just beyond a small military reservation, you'll see big, white Wentworth-by-the-Sea, a summer resort famous since its first day, in 1874, when carriages began rolling up to its front door. Further along you'll see signs for State 1B. Turn right here, to circle several of the islands that lie at the mouth of the Piscataqua River.

This road will take you past the resplendent Wentworth-by-the-Sea and on to New Castle, one of the lovelier settlements of New Hampshire. If you are driving slowly (it's almost guaranteed that if you're not, the alert, local constable will have something to say about it), you'll see, down a side street, an historical marker. Even if you're not given to reading these little squibs, this one is well worth it, for it says, "William & Mary Raids, Dec. 14–15, 1774, several hundred men overpowered the small British garrison at Castle William & Mary, now Fort Constitution, New Castle, and removed quantities of military supplies. These raids, set off by Paul Revere's ride to Portsmouth on Dec. 13, were among the first overt acts of the American Revolution."

State 1B circles back into Portsmouth, which is crammed with so much Americana it ought to give the traveler pause—perhaps a few days' pause. It's definitely one of America's handsomest and most historically exciting cities.

A good place to begin seeing Portsmouth is at the John Paul Jones House, where the Portsmouth Historical Society has done a monumental job of preservation. A tour takes about an hour, and sometime during that period you are bound to catch the spirit of those days when sailor John Paul Jones himself stayed here while supervising the fitting-out of the *America*.

The Warner House, a Registered National Historic Landmark, is another place that ought to evoke the pages of history for you. Be sure to get one of the attendants to tell you about the startling stairway murals, and don't be surprised if, upon leaving the house, you halfway expect to see a coach or carriage waiting for you at the curb. Portsmouth's houses sometimes do that to some visitors.

Of utmost importance here is Strawbery Banke, which takes its name from an earlier settlement which was so dubbed by settlers impressed with the strawberry-covered riverbanks. This area may not have any houses as impressive as those you have seen so far. Work on the houses here is going on and will be for some time to come, however. Worried at seeing beautiful old houses being torn down or turned into grubby tenements, and cognizant that what lay here was potentially as brilliant as Williamsburg, anxious citizens managed to wrest control of a large plot of land in the area. They began restoring buildings and moving other noteworthy ones in, such as an impressive home in which Daniel Webster once lived. Picket fences are going up along little lanes, gardens are being planted, and each year Strawbery Banke resembles more the former proud days of Portsmouth. Visitors are already welcome in many houses, and in some they can see artisans working at colonial crafts. Folders at Strawbery Banke and in many places about the city will give you full information.

But this is far from all the city offers. There's the Governor John Langdon Memorial, one of the great Georgian houses of America, built by the first president of the U.S. Senate. George Washington, John Hancock, James Monroe, General Lafayette, and Lous Philippe (who later became King of France) were among noted visitors here. Another great example of Georgian architecture is the Wentworth-Gardner House. Among its succession of owners has been the Metropolitan Museum of Art, which at one time wanted to move it to New York. The carvings and Dutch tiles throughout are memorable.

The Moffatt-Ladd house, built in 1763, once belonged to General William Whipple, a signer of the Declaration of Independence. Throughout is rare wallpaper from the series known as "Bay of Naples," made by Parisian Joseph Bufour about 1815. In the garden is a counting house, an indication of what early 19th-century business offices were like.

By now you may have picked up the brochure on Portsmouth's historic houses and can decide which additional ones you wish to visit. Perhaps the Jackson House? Built about 1664, it is believed the oldest of the period left in this area. It's furnished in the style of the times.

St. John's and the Rockingham

Not in the folder, but worthy of note, are the Old St. John's Church and the *Rockingham Hotel.* The church, which began as a "chappele" in 1639, was destroyed by fire in 1806. Even so, the present church dates from 1808. In it are the Brattle Organ, which was imported from England before 1708 (said to be the oldest pipe organ in America), a copy of the rare Vinegar Bible, and several other highly noteworthy objects. The Rockingham Hotel, its entrances flanked by bronze lions, has been a hotel since 1833, and you can still see the Langdon Room, which is much as it was back in 1785 when it was part of a famous home here.

There are several summer theaters here, and many travelers take the boat trip to the Isles of Shoals. There's a story that in the old days, before ship-to-shore communications, the Isles of Shoals boats used to carry carrier pigeons. Once the boat had left Portsmouth, passengers were asked how many intended to dine at the restaurant at the Isles. The count taken, it was written on a piece of paper, clipped to a pigeon's leg and the bird sent winging east, ahead of the boat.

From Portsmouth take US 4 to Durham, site of the University of New Hampshire. At the Paul Creative Arts Center here you can get information on various places to see on the campus, as well as a program for the Summer Repertory Theatre. Among well-known residents of Durham is Thomas Williams, author of *A High New House,* whose work appears regularly in *The New Yorker* and in *Esquire.*

From Durham take State 108 south to Exeter, home of Phillips Exeter Academy, one of the nation's most famous preparatory schools for boys. Exeter is a pretty, elm-shaded town that belies its amusingly belligerent past, which began as early as 1734. In those days, an agent of the king went about, searching out the likeliest trees for masts for the Royal Navy. No matter on whose property they were, when the King's mark went on, down the trees came, to be shipped to England. Exeter men didn't like this, but instead of sitting around and complaining, a group of them dressed as Indians, went to the local tavern where some of the men who picked out the trees were sleeping, and hustled them out. The agents hurried to the river, only to find their boat had been scuttled. There was nothing to do but trudge the wearying miles back to Portsmouth.

Exeter's War Memorial (Front & Pine Streets) was done by the famous sculptor Daniel Chester French, who was born here. The discerning will come across various works of his in New Hampshire, though he is, of course, most noted for his heroic seated figure of the Great Emancipator in the Lincoln Memorial in Washington. The Garrison House here is furnished in Colonial style and the Lamont Art Gallery at Phillips Exeter frequently has worthwhile art exhibits (open during the school year and from late June to mid-August).

From Exeter take State 111A to State 107, turn right onto 107, and then left (south) when you reach State 102, to Derry. The poet Robert Frost lived here for quite a few years and the state plans to make his home an historic site. Nearby, in East Derry, is the boyhood home of Alan B. Shepard, Jr., our first astronaut in space.

(Before long, if it hasn't happened already, you're almost bound to become confused by township markers in New Hampshire. The names of towns are posted, true, but not at the entrance to the town proper. Marking the actual, legal town line, they may be literally miles from the settlement itself.)

From Derry take State 28 to its intersection with State 111, where you turn left (east toward Salem) to Mystery Hill. It is well named. Archeologists, amateur and professional, have been puzzling over the stone structures here for some 30 years, coming up with a number of theories concerning who built them and why. The theories range from one alleging that a colonial farmer involved in smuggling built them, to one claiming they were erected by a group of monks who left Ireland back in the 10th century because they couldn't stand the harassments of Scandinavian invaders any longer. Still others conjecture the structures are disturbingly like some found at Malta and other Mediterranean sites.

From Mystery Hill take State 111 west to Benson's Wild Animal

Farm. There's always something special going on here as the farm is continually receiving newly-imported animals which they train, condition, and exhibit.

Continue on 111 to Nashua. Primarily an industrial city, Nashua was originally a trading post to which Indians brought fur pelts from the north. Many French-Canadians, Irish, Lithuanians, Polish, and Greeks have settled here over the years.

Taking State 101A west out of Nashua, turn right (north) when you intercept 101. You'll soon come to Amherst (named for Lord Jeffrey Amherst), a lovely little village. President Franklin Pierce married Jane Means Appleton here in 1834, and George W. Kendall, who founded the *New Orleans Picayune,* was born here, as was Horace Greeley, founder of the *New York Tribune.* After taking a look around Amherst, return to State 101 and continue north. Several miles beyond you'll find a marker which tells about Greeley, who made "Go west, young man" such a famous admonition. The house where he was born (several miles from here) is a private residence.

Continuing north on State 101, you'll come to Bedford. Here, at the *Wayfarer Motor Inn* is a fine collection of the original equipment once operated by water power at the famous John Goffe's Mill. This is the mill written about by George Woodbury in his books, *John Goffe's Mill* and *John Goffe's Legacy.*

Manchester's Memorials

Just beyond Bedford you come to Manchester, well worth a stop of several hours. The Currier Gallery of Art, 192 Orange Street, has an outstanding collection of European paintings which includes works by Tintoretto, Corot, Monet, Rouault, and Picasso. Its American paintings run from Copley to contemporary works. The early New England decorative arts are well represented by outstanding furniture, silver, and glass collections. Here, too, is the Manchester Historic Association, where are displayed prints, maps, and other early documents, Indian relics, and old tools. Also here are a memorial to General John Stark, at Stark Park, overlooking the Merrimack River, as well as the home of General Stark. He was one of the leaders of Rogers' Rangers during the French and Indian Wars; some of his exciting adventures were related in Kenneth Roberts' *Northwest Passage.* Stark is perhaps best remembered for his phrase, "Live free or die," which was later adopted as the state's motto.

Once Manchester was a thriving manufacturing town, with its Amoskeag Textile Mills said to be the largest in the world. Strikes, followed by the depression, forced the company to file a bankruptcy petition. Local businessmen, however, managed to scrape together enough money to buy the complex, and began leasing and selling sections to new and smaller companies. Within less than a decade, more than 100 firms were occupying the property, hiring more people than the former, great company. It was New Hampshire's own "Operation Bootstrap."

From Manchester, take State 101 east to 101B, where you then jog left, then turn right on State 107A. Candia here used to be called Charming Fare. Sam Walter Foss lived here, and though few people know his name, almost everyone knows the poem which made him famous, the one that begins, "Let me live in my house by the side of the road . . ." Candia's Fitts Museum has a nice collection of early furniture, as well as military and local historical memorabilia.

State 107A joins 107 at Deerfield. This is the town from which John Simpson set out one June day in 1775 for Bunker Hill, where he is credited with having fired the first shot of the battle. But that didn't prove his only distinction. Returning a major after the Revolution, he went back to farming, never applied for a pension, and was never paid for his services. He explained, "My country is too poor to pay pensions."

Travelers in this area in August and September should check newspapers as there are usually country fairs which they may wish to attend.

Concord, Capital and Coach

Continuing north on State 107, turn left (west) on US 202 to Concord, capital of New Hampshire. In the State House, the military-minded will want to visit the Hall of Flags, with its battle flags of New Hampshire troops from the 18th century onward, and its other items commemorating the state's stalwart sons.

Almost everyone visiting this pretty, orderly little city includes the New Hampshire Historical Society in the itinerary. Its five rooms, furnished in the period from 1680–1720, are lovely, as is the main rotunda with its beautiful Italian marble and its exciting Concord Coach. To anyone who has seen Westerns (is there anyone who hasn't?), the coach will look more than vaguely familiar. Those big stagecoaches, as any Western buff can tell you, were made in Concord, and they wrote a very exciting chapter in America's history.

Concord's First Church of Christ Scientist is particularly noteworthy, as it was erected by Mary Baker Eddy, founder of the Christian Science movement. Mrs. Eddy, who lived for a time in Concord, was born at nearby Bow, New Hampshire.

The New Hampshire League of Arts & Crafts has a fine display (and salesroom) at its headquarters here, and there is also the campus of St. Paul's School, one of the country's most distinguished preparatory schools for boys, to visit.

From Concord, drive east on US 4 to State 106. Driving north on 106, watch for a sign (about six miles north) pointing to Canterbury Center and the Shaker Settlement. Here you'll find a pristine village, built and lived in by one of the last of the Shaker groups. There's also a museum of Shaker inventions and handcrafts, and a lovely view.

Continuing west on this road, turn right briefly onto State 3B, then left, into an unmarked road to Boscawen. For such a small town, this handsome, elm-shaded settlement packs in quite a bit of history. One of its native sons, John Adams Dix, one-time governor of New York and U.S. Secretary of the Treasury, is credited with saying at the beginning of the Civil War, "If anyone attempts to haul down the American flag, shoot him on the spot." William Pitt Fessenden, also born here, was Secretary of the Treasury under Lincoln in 1864–65. And there was John Morrill, who invented the eight-day clock. Boscawen, too, was the site of Daniel Webster's first law office, and just south of here, at Penacook, on a tiny island in the Merrimack River, there is a statue to one of colonial times' most celebrated heroines, Hannah Dustin. Kidnapped in a raid by Indians who killed her week-old baby, she and others were forced on a long march. One night, at this place on the river, she convinced several of her fellow captives they could kill the Indians as they slept. They succeeded, and marched back to Haverhill, Massachusetts, carrying 10 scalps with them.

Driving north on US 3, you'll come to Franklin. Named in honor of Benjamin Franklin, this industrial town was the birthplace of Daniel Webster. (You can visit the Webster family cabin.) Here, too, is the Congregational Church, a restored 1802 building, where Webster used to attend services.

From Franklin take State 11 to Tilton, then 140 to Gilmanton. The name of this town may mean nothing to you, but many people are aware that Grace Metalious, author of *Peyton Place,* lived here. It's a charming, sleepy town, with a lovely little meeting house that was built in 1774. If you ask any localite where the late Grace Metalious lived, he'll direct you to the house, but don't ask for "Peyton Place." The native will just look you in the eye and probably say, "Ain't no such place hereabouts." The fact that Ralph Waldo Emerson attended school here (at Gilmanton Academy) is a more important reason for the town to be placed on a traveler's itinerary.

Leaving Gilmanton, take State 107 to Laconia, where the World Sled Dog Championships are held each year during the last weekend in February. This sport, which is becoming more popular each year, draws more and more visitors to Laconia, as well as to other parts of the state, where races leading up to the Laconia event are held. These preliminary races are held weekends, beginning early in January, in a number of communities throughout the state.

From Laconia, take US 3 north to Lakeport. Here you can take a cruise on Lake Winnipesaukee (71 square miles, 25 miles long). Its many islands, inlets, and shore settlements are intriguing. The Lakes Region Playhouse here is considered first-rate.

From Lakeport, continue on US 3 north to Weirs Beach. There are lovely views from here (if you look on past the commercialism—carnivals, amusement parks, parades, the works). The new (1965) Animal Forest Park is also near here.

At Meredith, north on US 3, is the well-known Meredith Auto Museum, with some 50 vehicles which show the growth of the auto industry. Just above Meredith, State 25 branches off to the right and brings you to Center Harbor. The New Hampshire Music Festival presents concerts here (as well as at Meredith and Wolfeboro), and at the Bryar Patch Farm Norvik Kennels there is an exhibit of Alaskan and Siberian huskies and arctic equipment. Mrs. Jean Bryar is, by the way, women's national champion sled dog driver.

From Center Harbor, continue northeast to Moultonboro, where you turn south on State 109. Here is the Old Country Store, and while some consider it merely a stopping place for tourists, many enjoy pottering around and purchasing from its supply of maple products, bright penny candies, and the contents of the pickle barrel.

Continue south from here on 109, running now along Lake Winnipesaukee's eastern shore to Wolfeboro. There are boat trips on the lake available from Wolfeboro, and the Libby Museum has special arts shows as well as its regular natural history and Indian exhibits. A pretty, lakeside settlement, Wolfeboro is the home of well-known Brewster Academy (chartered 1820).

Continuing south, take State 28 at South Wolfeboro to Alton. This entire area is a summer colony. At Alton, take State 11 south to Farmington, watching for the yellow arrows directing you to the Schuller Museum, three miles west of 11. This museum has a fascinating collection of 14th to 17th-century European and Japanese arms and armor, handsome British heraldic plaques, and a collection of French, Italian, and Spanish palace furniture and tapestries. From here, take the unmarked road north to Union, turning north (left) onto State 16.

In some unaccountable way that happens with highways in New Hampshire, State 16 magically turns itself into State 25 along here.

So continue on 25 to Whittier, where both town and nearby mountain are named for poet John Greenleaf Whittier, who often summered here, penning a number of poems about the region.

Here turn north (right) on State 113. Tamworth, very pretty, is the site of the famous Barnstormers Theatre. Nearby, the dogs that went on many Arctic and Antarctic expeditions were bred and raised. Continuing on 113 you'll come to the Madison Boulder Wayside Area. The boulder is 83 feet long, 37 wide and 23 high; geologists believe it was brought from farther north by a glacier, and some say it is the largest displaced boulder in America.

Ski Country at Conway

Beyond, at Conway, covered bridge fanciers will find two of these structures, and there are two more in the area to which you can be directed. Just above this settlement you'll find North Conway and, all the way along, superb views of the White Mountains. For a really spectacular view, drive out to Cranmore Mountain and take a skimobile ride up 4,895 feet. Mt. Washington, its Tuckerman Ravine, and famous Headwall tower there before you. Famous, too, is the skimobile on which you're riding. Built in 1938, it was a forerunner of the ones used in the booming ski business of today. The late Harvey Dow Gibson, internationally-known financier and philanthropist of New York, who was born in North Conway, foresaw the day when skiing would skyrocket as a sport. The skimobile's success caused North Conway to become an important ski center much sooner than most resorts in America.

Four miles north, at Intervale, take State 16A, where in summer you just might see a barefoot boy in an old straw hat whistling his way along the road, a fishing pole over his shoulder. He might be a good candidate for the TV show *What's My Line?*, as this is his job, the boy having been hired by some local merchants to add a little color to the local scene. Youngsters may enjoy *Story Land* at Glen, where some 20 fairy tales come to life. There are a pumpkin coach to ride in and tame animals to feed, among other attractions.

Continuing on State 16, when you come to Jackson, turn right, crossing Honeymoon Bridge, a latticed, covered structure. Here the Wildcat River tumbles merrily through the town and everyone shops at the *Wildcat Valley Country Store*.

About eight miles north, on 16, you'll find the Glen Ellis Falls and Wildcat Mountain with its Gondola Cable Car (the first such enclosed cars in the U.S.).

From Glen House, the Mount Washington Auto Drive begins. It's an eight-mile trip to the top of the 6,288-foot mountain, and after four miles you pass the timberline. If you're squeamish about this long drive at such altitudes, there are commercial station wagons, with drivers, which will whisk you to the top. The road, which was cut over 100 years ago, was begun as a carriage road, and P. T. Barnum once called this trip "the second greatest show on earth."

By the time you get to the top you'll probably be marveling not only at the superb views, but also at the fact that one Darby Field not only found the White Mountains way back in 1642, but also scaled Mt. Washington at that time. Obviously, during his climb, the winds weren't blowing at anything like the 231-mile velocity recorded in April, 1934.

Although Field is definitely credited with having been the first to climb Mt. Washington, he wasn't, according to historical records, the first to see it. Giovanni Verrazano, for whom the longest suspension bridge in the world was named in New York in 1965, is credited with being the first European to sight the mountain. In 1524, having sailed along the Maine coast, he reported "high mountains within the land." Several other explorers mentioned Mount Washington and other White Mountains, and Gerard Mercator put them on his Great Map in 1569.

Continue on north on State 16 to Berlin, where one of the outstanding sights is a Russian Church with its onion-shaped domes. Just outside the city is the Nansen Ski Jump (west of State 16), said to be the tallest ski jump tower in the country (171½ ft.). It belongs to the Nansen Ski Club, which is the oldest ski club in America, having been founded by Norwegian-Americans in the late 1800's. Norwegians weren't the only ones to come here from abroad in the 19th century, however. Settlers came from other areas of Europe, including the British Isles, France and Canada. Berlin, too, is the home of "Big Bella." A mobile horn with a horrendous hoot, she is used to lead lost people out of the woods.

From Berlin, take State 16 north to Errol. You are now in Christmas tree country. Authorities say there are literally billions of spruce trees in this north country. At Errol bear left (west) on State 26. You might want to take a picnic lunch along in this area. Not only are there three good wayside picnic spots (here at Errol, at Dixville Notch, and near Coleman State Forest Park), but also there aren't many restaurants in this region.

At Dixville Notch you'll probably find more alpine ruggedness than at any other area in New Hampshire. At the pass, the space narrows until there's barely room for the road, while above tower great stone crags and pinnacles, which some liken to the crazy peaks in French Polynesia.

At the farther end of the pass you'll see the huge hotel called *The Balsams* beside pretty Lake Gloriette. Farther west you'll see a road to the right where, just a few hundred feet beyond, is the Colebrook Fish Hatchery, which welcomes visitors.

Fishing, Hunting and Gold-Panning

Colebrook, which somewhat resembles a western frontier town, is one of the North Country centers for fishermen and hunters. These days the latter have an added attraction to look for, at least while out on the prowl, as several wolves have been shot here recently, though it was long believed they were extinct in this area. Beloit, Wisconsin, was settled in 1837 by migrants from here.

If time allows, and you're a history buff, go on north, on State 145, to Pittsburg. This settlement should also interest you if you have a yen to pan for gold. It's done here, at Indian Stream. There are three covered bridges here, too, the ones at Happy Corner and River Road being the northernmost in the state.

For many years following the Revolution, much of this territory was claimed by both Canada and the U.S. Finally the inhabitants grew so annoyed at being the objects of a tug-of-war they formed their own local government and, in 1832, declared themselves the independent Republic of Indian Stream. At the end of three years' time, following a local dispute with Canadian authorities, the New Hampshire Militia moved in, and the republic was dissolved. In 1840 the settlement took the name of Pittsburg, and in 1842 the whole bothersome boundary squabbling was settled when the Webster-Ashburton Treaty gave the region to New Hampshire.

Returning south, on State 3, just beyond Colebrook you'll come to the religious shrine, Our Lady of Grace, a pilgrimage destination for many Catholics. Now, all along 3, you'll be skirting the infant Connecticut River, green farmland nestled along its banks, the hills and mountains of Vermont to your right.

At Groveton you'll see plenty of pulpwood piled up at the Groveton Paper Mill and, nearby, a covered bridge. When it became unsafe for vehicular traffic, instead of taking it down, the state built a new road and bridge, and you can still walk across the covered bridge.

Lancaster is noteworthy for its St. Paul's Episcopal Church and for the house nearby, built in 1859, which has often been called the "House of Seven Gables," though a careful count reveals there are nine gables. Charles Farrar Browne, who wrote under the better-known name of Artemus Ward, spent his apprenticeship years here.

From Lancaster, continue south on 3 a few miles for memorable views from a famous hilltop here. In Mt. Prospect State Park (also called Weeks State Park), a road (turning left) will take you to the top of Mt. Prospect. This 430-acre tract was once the summer estate of John Wingate Weeks who, as a member of Congress, worked successfully to establish the White Mountain National Forest. Following his death his daughter, Katherine Weeks Davidge, and his son, Sinclair Weeks, Secretary of Commerce under President Eisenhower, gave the park to the state.

Returning to State 3, turn left on the unmarked road at the sign for *Mountain View House,* a superb hotel in the luxury-resort tradition. You may dine here if you reserve ahead of time, but even if you don't, you can enjoy their truly magnificent view. You can also enjoy the story of how this inn, which has been owned and operated by the same family for four generations, came into being.

The story started on a dark and stormy night in 1865, when a stagecoach, bound for Montreal, struck a mudhole and tipped over. Soon the two passengers aboard were sloshing off on a dirt road toward a little farmhouse. In time they found themselves so enchanted with the comfort, hospitality, and food they asked to stay for a few days, and catch a later coach. The following summer they wrote, asking to spend several weeks, and then and there William and Mary Jane Dodge decided to take summer boarders. Over the years the farmhouse has been added to, and now the huge complex boasts, among other facilities, a swimming pool and nine-hole golf course. But nothing, of course, has ever changed the dreamlike view of the central Presidential Range.

Returning to 3, just south of Mountain View, rock hounds will find Rock Haven (jewelry is sold here, too). Farther south, at Whitefield, take State 116 to your left (east) to Jefferson. In this vicinity—north and south on intersecting State 2—you'll find *Santa's Village,* a commercial venture, as are the *Yankee Notions Museum* and *Six-Gun City*. Here, too, at Jefferson, is the *Waumbek Inn and Country Club,* which has been a resort haven for the discriminating for over 100 years. It got its start when an itinerant minister liked what he saw, and said so in print, adding the suggestion that someone ought to build a hotel here.

For anyone interested in alpine and hardy rock garden plants there's a highly unusual nursery here. The *Mountain Valley Nursery,* run by Donald J. Lennox, has over 1,000 varieties of these plants. The route you'll follow from Jefferson takes you right near his place, but since he definitely hides his light under a bushel (or a Dennstedtia Punctilobula, or some other alpine plant), it's best to ask directions.

Crawford Notch

From the Waumbek, drive south on State 2 and turn right on State 115 to Meadows (a highly appropriate name), continuing on till you reach State 3 again. Turn left on 3, and again at Twin Mountain, taking US 302 to Crawford Notch. As you travel south, the huge white hotel you see on the left is the *Mount Washington.*

Just south of the *Crawford House* you'll enter Crawford Notch State Park, a region of superb, rugged scenery. South of Silver Cascade and Flume Cascade a sign marks the site of the spine-chilling event which occurred in 1826 and was later recounted by Nathaniel Hawthorne in his *Twice-Told Tales.* It is the story of a great landslide which thundered into this valley just above the house of the Willey family. Hearing the roar of the slide, the family rushed from the house to what they thought was safer ground, but were all crushed beneath the rubble. Would-be rescuers, arriving at the site the next day, were startled to find the house still standing. The slide had been temporarily diverted into two streams by a huge boulder that stood just back of the house, and flowed together again farther on, crushing the Willeys.

Returning north on State 302, if you like winding forest by-ways, take Woodland Road (it's at the right, almost opposite Crawford House), then at Four Corners, turn right to the base station of the Mt. Washington Cog Railroad. As an alternate, you can proceed north to Fabyans and take a right turning on the road indicated to the Cog Railroad. But Woodland Road is much prettier.

Mt. Washington Cog Railroad

Even if you don't have the time, or the courage, or whatever it takes, to make the three-hour round trip on the fabulous Mt. Washington Cog Railroad, drive up to see the little engines and passenger cars at the base station. The story of this engineering feat, the first mountain-climbing cog railway in the world, is full of marvels. And if you didn't take the auto road up Mt. Washington, this is a fine and exciting way to get to the top and see all that glorious scenery.

At the time the railroad was contemplated, scoffers suggested one might just as well attempt to "build a railroad to the moon," but in 1858, a model engine and cog railway was exhibited before the New Hampshire State Legislature which, probably to its own surprise, granted a charter for the project. Work began in April of 1866, and at the end of August the first demonstration was successfully given. After a great deal of engineering ingenuity and back-breaking labor, the track was laid to the top, passenger service was inaugurated on July 4, 1869, and it has continued to the present day.

Arriving at the top, visitors may be surprised to find two TV antennae (one transmits for Jack Paar's WMTW), weather observatory buildings, the hostelry called *Summit House,* and various other structures. The trip takes an hour up, an hour at the top, and an hour descending.

Returning to the main highway (302), turn right to Littleton, continuing from there on State 18 to the Samuel C. Moore Power Station and Dam. The largest hydro-electric station in New England, it has a capacity of 190,000 kilowatts. Visitors are welcome at the site and, during the summer, there is a tour of the power plant.

Returning on 18 to Littleton, take 302 to Bethlehem. Here turn left (south), again taking 18. On this road, west of Mount Agassiz, you'll find another place for a breathtaking view of the White Mountains as well as of Vermont's Green Mountains. Continue south on 18 to Franconia. The imposing white building here is the site of the new (1963) Franconia College, which welcomes visitors to its lovely campus. Robert Frost lived in Franconia for a number of years and, as a summer resort, the region attracted such notables as Washington Irving, Nathaniel Hawthorne, William Cullen Bryant, John Greenleaf Whittier, and Henry Wadsworth Longfellow.

That the area continues to attract many visitors will be quite evident to you as you continue south along 18. At the sign for *Mittersill Inn,* turn right. More than a mere inn, Mittersill is a dream come true for Baron Hubert Pantz. Deeming it wise to leave Austria in the early 1940's, the baron came to the United States, where he had many friends. While becoming a citizen of the U.S., he also did some traveling, including shunpiking, and fell in love with the Bavarian alpine aspects of the Franconia area. Deciding he could not only build an inn here, but also make it the nucleus of a chalet colony, he set to work. In the process he was told by many that what he proposed couldn't be done—chiefly on the premise that it never had been done before.

Today, over 70 privately-owned chalets stand hidden among the trees of the 165 acres that make up this handsome resort. Some of the chalet owners come to Mittersill at all seasons, others only in winter to ski on the 26 miles of trails and slopes here, which culminate in 4,121-foot Cannon Mountain.

Beyond Mittersill State 18 joins 3. Turn right (south) and you are in Franconia Notch State Park, most famous and most extensive of the notch areas in the state. There are many things to do and see here. The Cannon Mountain Aerial Tramway, for instance, operates in summer as well as winter. You ride in an enclosed, 27-passenger cable car to an observation platform at the summit for fantastic views of the surrounding mountains, notches and gorges.

The Old Man of the Mountains

Here you will see the "Old Man of the Mountains" (Hawthorne wrote a story about it, called *The Great Stone Face*). There it is, above a steep precipice that plunges down toward the gorge. Geologists surmise it was formed over 200 million years ago. Farther along at the notch is the remarkable Basin, a granite pothole 20 feet in diameter, at the foot of a waterfall. Experts believe it was eroded in this manner some 25,000 years ago, while a glacier of the last Ice Age was melting. Here, too, is The Flume, a natural chasm 800 feet long. With walls 12 to 20 feet apart, rising 60 to 70 feet above you, it terminates at the 25-foot Avalanche Falls. There are bus rides and footpaths within the notch area and many awesome and handsome sights in addition to the outstanding features mentioned above.

Two miles south of the park, a left turn on an unmarked road will take you to Lincoln, and just east of here, leads to the new (1966) million-dollar ski area at Loon Mountain. It is the project of ex-Governor Sherman Adams.

South from here, on 3, if your bones are weary, you'll be delighted to note numerous, good-looking motels all along both sides of the highway.

At North Woodstock, turn right on State 112 to Lost River Reservation. At the reservation, there are guided tours of glacial caverns, as well as a waterfall, and a garden filled with alpine plants in a natural setting. There is a museum, too, and a good mineral collection. Sponsored by the Society for the Protection of New Hampshire Forests it, like Franconia Notch, is a fine place for a family to visit.

From here return on 112 to the junction with State 118, where you turn right. After 118 joins State 25, continue on south and east to the much-touted Polar Caves, where there are glacial caverns and a maple sugar house. Continue southeast on 25 to 3A, turning right (south) to Bristol (do not follow Rte. 3A straight ahead to Plymouth). Here, you will be skirting Newfound Lake. Fourth largest lake in New Hampshire, it is considered by some the prettiest, with majestic Mt. Cardigan backdropping the area.

At Bristol take State 104 southwest to Danbury, where you turn right on US 4. Here is real rock hound territory, with the Ruggles Mine, oldest mica mine in the U.S. (opened 1803). A two-mile road takes you to the top of the hill known as Isinglass Mountain, with its lovely view. Here are mine tunnels, pits and specimens galore for the picking. Ruggles Mine's exhibit includes many of the 150 minerals that have been found here.

Continue on 4 to Lebanon, where you'll turn right onto State 120 to Hanover, site of Dartmouth College and the history-making Hopkins Center, opened in 1962. Dartmouth's campus is lovely to see and there are the famous Orozco murals at Baker Memorial Library, as well as the largest college library in the U.S. It includes a rare books division and, among its special collections, that of

Vilhjalmur Stefansson (long a familiar campus figure after his retirement from exploring) on Arctic, Antarctic, and permafrost regions.

But these days, it is the Hopkins Center that is Dartmouth's greatest attraction. This handsome complex of art galleries, sculpture gardens, theaters, and concert halls, often has outstanding art and other cultural exhibits, concerts, and shows classic films. In addition, plays are given regularly by the Dartmouth Repertory Theater Company, a group whose work is generally outstanding. You might want to write ahead to Hopkins Center for the summer calendar of events.

From Hanover, State 10 will take you south to West Lebanon and to State 12A south. Watch for the sign for the Augustus Saint-Gaudens Museum. In summer there are special art exhibits here. The house, grounds, and sculptor's studio are lovely; you may be surprised to find how many of the works of this brilliant American sculptor are familiar to you. He is especially noted for his *The Puritan* and for the statue of Lincoln in Chicago's Lincoln Park. Another American of note connected with this area was Salmon P. Chase, who served for a time as Secretary of the Treasury under Lincoln. Mr. Chase, a prominent figure in defending fugitive slaves, was also Chief Justice of the Supreme Court at one time, and, while with the treasury, originated the national banking system. It is probably for this latter reason his picture appears on our $10,000 bills. The other prominent man was the American author Winston Churchill. Though his novels were published in the early 1900's, his *Coniston, The Crisis* and *The Crossing* are still being read.

Returning to 12A, continue south. On your right, the covered bridge (the Windsor-Cornish) which crosses the Connecticut here to Windsor, Vermont, is New Hampshire's longest. Again, if you are a covered bridge fancier you'll want to know that there are five in this immediate area of New Hampshire.

South of here, take State 103 east through Claremont to Newport. The highly-photogenic Congregational Church here was built in 1828 and has a Paul Revere bell. Newport, too, was the site of the Little Red School House, since removed to the Wayside Inn, in Massachusetts. Dedicated to Sarah Josepha Hale, for years the editor of *Godey's Lady's Book* (a famous Philadelphia publication), it commemorates her writing here of *Mary Had a Little Lamb*. Undoubtedly she should be better remembered than she is, for she also persuaded Lincoln to make Thanksgiving a national holiday. Newport is proud, too, of its Clock Museum (a private endeavor). On its tour you'll see a delightful collection of some 400 pieces, dating from the 16th century to the present. There are other noteworthy objects besides clocks, among them the exquisite Mozart music box.

From Newport, take State 11 to New London, a pretty hilltop town. Colby Junior College is here, and it's the current hometown of J. Duane Squires, whose *The Story of New Hampshire* was published in 1964. From New London, return on 11 a mile or so to State 103A, taking this road south to Newbury. Where it joins 103, turn right. You'll find Mt. Sunapee State Park here, and four-passenger gondolas which go to the 2,700 foot summit, where there are a cafeteria and observation platforms. This is another area where New Hampshire was a forerunner in the development of the popularity of skiing.

Just beyond Sunapee State Park, west on 103, take the unmarked road to Goshen, then State 10 south a very short distance to State 31. On 31, drive south to Washington. This is one of New Hampshire's most pristine towns, white and sparkling, and with a 1789 meeting house. In December of 1776 it took its name in honor of George Washington. Although it claims to have been the first town in America to do so, the fact remains that Washington, North Carolina, can claim the honor, having written proof of its name dated October 1, 1776.

Continuing south and east on 31 you'll come to Hillsboro. The homestead of Franklin Pierce, 14th president of the U.S. is here. The Homestead (look for prominent sign) is just off the highway and open to the public during the summer. Daniel Keith, famous theater owner (Radio-Keith-Orpheum), was also from here.

Ocean-Born Mary House

From Hillsboro drive north on State 9 (a left turn coming from the Pierce Homestead) and watch for signs for the Ocean-Born Mary House. Not only is this home furnished with authentic antiques of the early 1800's, but it also has an enchanting story to tell, and explains how Ocean-Born Mary got her rather strange name. The tale includes a swashbuckling pirate who attacked the ship on which Mary's parents were bound for America. Bursting into a cabin, the fierce fellow suddenly softened. There in a bunk, cradled in its mother's arms, lay a newborn baby girl. The swarthy miscreant was so touched, in fact, that he asked if he could name the baby for his dead wife Mary. He then went back on deck, made his men give back all the loot they'd been busily gathering, and, admonishing the ship's crew to wait, rowed off to his own ship. He returned shortly with a length of silk brocade he said he hoped little Mary would wear on her wedding day. Returning to his ship he sailed off. Legend says further that in later years he visited Mary at her home in Henniker, known today as the Ocean-Born Mary House.

Returning to Hillsboro, take US 202 to Antrim and, several miles beyond, turn right on an unmarked road to Hancock. It's a very pretty town with a village green and, beside Norway Pond, the 1820 Congregational Church with its three-tiered steeple. The Paul Revere church bell still calls the congregation to worship. One gets the impression John Hancock, first signer of the Declaration of Independence, for whom the town was named, would be very proud of this village if he could see it today.

From Hancock go east on an unmarked road to Greenfield. Just north of this community is the Crotched Mountain Rehabilitation Center. Many hundreds of people visit each year to see this handsome center for training handicapped children and adults, deaf people, and rehabilitation workers who later go on to other institutions.

From Greenfield continue south on State 31, turning right (west) at Wilton on 101. At Miller State Park, you'll find a road to the summit of Pack Monadnock Mountain, with spectacular views from the 2,280-foot elevation. Returning to 101, continue west. Just before Peterborough, watch for signs, to the left, to Sharon, on 123 (in this area again, New Hampshire road signs, or the lack of them, leave something to be desired). South on this road you'll find the Sharon Art Center. Its exhibitions of arts and crafts make it a favorite with visitors. Howard Shapley, famous, former Harvard astronomer, lives here.

By now you are in what has often been called the "Currier & Ives Corner" of New Hampshire, and some of the towns here will show you why.

South of Sharon, turn left on 124 to New Ipswich. This was the site of the first textile mill in New Hampshire. The Barrett House here (open to the public) is an impressive mansion with outstanding period furnishings.

From New Ipswich, retrace your route and drive north on 124 to Jaffrey. There are over 200 lakes in this, the Monadnock area, and Jaffrey has a prize one with its Woodbound Lake. Jaffrey's Meeting House is especially noteworthy, not only for its antiquity (1774) and Paul Revere bell, but also for its old burying ground, undoubtedly one of the better known in New Hampshire. The Countess Vigo Brandt Erickson, a former Jaffrey girl, so loved this spot that, when she and her infant daughter died, her husband had a memorial built here, where their ashes were placed. Here, too, is the grave of Amos Fortune. At the age of 60 he bought his freedom and came to Jaffrey, where he became known as the best tanner in the area. His gravestone reads: "Sacred to the memory of Amos Fortune, who was born free in Africa. A slave in America, he purchased liberty, professed Christianity, lived reputably and died hopefully Nov. 17,

1801, AEt. 91." At his death Amos left $100 to the church and $233.85 to the town for the public school. Far from forgotten, a weekly forum at the Jaffrey Meeting House (it brings many outstanding speakers to the area) is called the Amos Fortune Forum in his memory. F. Alexander Magoun, Jaffrey resident and ex-M.I.T. professor now teaching at the nearby Franklin Pierce College, numbers among his published works *Amos Fortune's Choice.*

As if all this weren't enough for this small burying ground, Willa Cather, famous author *(My Antonia, O Pioneers!, Death Comes for the Archbishop),* is also buried here. While at the nearby Macdowell Colony one summer, she fell so in love with thc Jaffrey Meeting House and grounds she requested that upon her death her remains be placed here.

Peterborough and the Macdowell Colony

North from Jaffrey, on US 202, is Peterborough. Few other American towns, if any, have harbored, at one time or another, as many well-known people of letters as Peterborough. The main reason for this is undoubtedly the Macdowell Colony just north of the town. After the famous composer Edward Macdowell *(Woodland Sketches, Indian Suite)* died, his wife and friends established this hideaway workshop for writers, artists, and musicians. Among those who came here were Edwin Arlington Robinson, Stephen Vincent Benet (perhaps inspired here to write *The Devil and Daniel Webster),* Hervey Allen *(Anthony Adverse),* William Rose Benet, poet and playwright Padraic Colum, Thorton Wilder, and others. Here Wilder wrote his famous *The Bridge of San Luis Rey,* and perhaps gathered background for his *Our Town,* laid in Grover's Corner, a mythical New Hampshire hamlet.

From Peterborough, continue on State 101, west to Dublin. This town used to be the nucleus of a large summer colony and Mark Twain and Amy Lowell were among those who summered here. Both the well-known *Yankee Magazine* and *Old Farmer's Almanac* are published here.

Just beyond the center of Dublin, take a right turn on an unnumbered road to Harrisville and Nelson. At Harrisville you'll find a virtually unbelievable little mill town, done almost entirely in red brick. Its other-century visage is enhanced by its church and vestry (the latter used in the winter for worship as, smaller in area, it is easier to heat) which dominate the scene on serene Harrisville Pond. Many artists and photographers come here to record the sight.

Other-century, too, is the post office, with its marble steps and blackboard with such local notices as "4 A.K.C. registered Siberian

Husky dogs and sleds for sale. Contact Peter Fisher. Not to be sold separately," and the glad tidings that "Mr. & Mrs. Donald McNamara are parents of a baby girl born on Sept. 25. Congratulations!"

Beyond, at Nelson, a tiny, sleepy town, there's a well-kept monument that reads: "Nelson will cherish in perpetual remembrance the memory of her heroic Sons who fell in the War of Great Rebellion for the Preservation of Liberty, and the Unity of the Republic. 1861–1865." This is where Newton F. Tolman, author of the charming, often funny book, *North of Monadnock,* lives.

Beyond Nelson turn left (south) at State 9, which farther along joins State 10 to Keene. You may want to inquire at the Keene Information Booth about *Steamtown, U.S.A.* Long a favorite with visitors (40 steam locomotives, including Big Boy, largest locomotive ever built, 1½-hr. steam train excursion, etc.), it has been located for a number of years at Walpole, north on State 12. However, due to proposed highway construction, it is said Steamtown will have to move to a new location, hopefully in the same vicinity.

Keene, with the widest paved main street in the world (156 feet), was recently given the "All-America City Award" by *Look Magazine,* so have a look around. John Dickson from here made the first anti-slavery speech in Congress (1835) and Joyce Kilmer wrote his famous poem *Trees* while summering near here at Swanzey. From Keene, continue on 9 to the vicinity of Chesterfield and the Museum of Old Dolls and Toys, a delightful collection—some 300 years old—for all ages.

Returning to Keene on 9, take State 12 south to Fitzwilliam. Here, about mid-July, some 16 acres of rhododendron burst into bloom (a wondrous sight) at Rhododendron State Park. Some say Fitzwilliam is just about the most beautiful old American village extant. The Congregational Church here is outstanding: it has a four-story steeple, each deck surrounded with a carved balustrade.

From Fitzwilliam take State 119 east to Rindge and follow signs to The Cathedral of the Pines, on Cathedral Road, a most remarkable memorial. Begun in 1945, it has been visited by over five million people, many from distant points of the globe. Called an international shrine, The Cathedral, high on a hilltop, has been given stones from all parts of the world, by people of every known faith. Many of these are incorporated in the Altar of the Nations. And although the U.S. Congress unanimously voted recognition of this area as a Memorial for all American war dead, no state or Federal authority has any jurisdiction here, nor has any religious sect, except at the time of conducting services (there is no building or church here, the cathedral being a pine forest).

This National War Memorial was begun by Dr. and Mrs. Douglas Sloane. A plaque at the site states "Cathedral of the Pines, dedicated to Almighty God as a place where all people may worship. In memory of Lt. Sanderson Sloane, killed in action over Germany, Feb. 22, 1944." Every Memorial Day a white rose, sent by each of the governors of the 50 states and the territories of the U.S., is placed on the Altar of the Nations. In 1966 a Memorial Bell Tower was dedicated here, the only memorial in the world to the American women who lost their lives in various wars: nurses, pioneer women, U.S.O. volunteers, factory workers, and Red Cross personnel, among others.

Exploring New Hampshire, one comes to realize there is no one season for the tourist, nor even only two. Summer, it is true, is the popular time, but in New Hampshire summer has scarcely begun to wane when country fairs burst forth, and there are, too, the many apple farms to visit. (A number of museums and other attractions stay open through mid-October.) From late September there is the magnificent fall foliage to see throughout the state. Scarcely has this subsided before the skiing season begins, augmented in January and February with the sled dog races. In March and April, while skiing continues at full steam, it is maple sugar time, with orchards and groves to wander through, sugar houses, redolent with the scent of boiling sap, to visit, and maple festivals and sugaring-off parties to attend. And then it is May and June, and lilac bushes and apple trees burst into bloom. Then it's summer again. And so the cycle goes, and so the traveler comes, often on a second or third trip, to this northern land of pleasant vistas and pleasant people.

AROUND THE STATE

HOTELS AND MOTELS. Families with children, championship skiers and golfers, and sedentary types will all enjoy the more-than-adequate accommodations offered by New Hampshire hostelries, winter and summer. Some of the hotels and lodges can rival the scenery in magnificence; some are very reasonable, with housekeeping facilities. If you can arrange it, plan to stay awhile. Many of the places listed below are resorts, with cheaper rates for a long stay. As a further inducement, day camps are often operated for children and entertainment provided for adults at night.

BETHLEHEM

Reasonable

Perry House. Summer vacation spot in White Mountains. Swimming pool, free golf. Entertainment. TV in motel rooms. Kosher cuisine. Open, June 15 to Oct. 15. Agassiz St. (tel. 869–3322).

Sinclair Hotel. In the shadow of White Mountains' Mt. Agassiz. Largest swimming pool in N.H., 18-hole golf course. Movies, stage shows, sports. Special family American-plan rates. Two supervised day camps. Teen programs. Dietary cuisine. Open summer months. Tel. 869–3311.

Inexpensive

Spinning Wheel Motel. A small place specializing in family housekeeping facilities. New swimming pool, play

area on spacious grounds. Open June 15 to Oct. 15.
On US 302 (tel. 444–2175).

HAMPTON and HAMPTON BEACH

Reasonable

Aqua Rama Motel. A medium-sized place facing the ocean. American and European plans. Dining room. Swimming pool. Season, May 1 to Nov. 13. Open the year round.
On US 1A, 235 Ocean Blvd. N. (tel. 926–2587).

Dalton's Motel. Small pleasant facility in Hampton. Family rate. Lower rates off season. Conveniently located to restaurants, shopping, and beach. Open the year round.
On US 1 (tel. 926–2466).

Donna Jean Motel. Country setting but only a few minutes from beach. Family rates and kitchenettes available. Season, May 30 to Sept. 15. Recreation room and play area.
State 101C off expressway, North Shore (tel. 926–3540).

Harris Sea Ranch Motel. A new medium-sized boardwalk motel in Hampton Beach with large nicely decorated rooms. Family rates and kitchen units available. Restaurant next door. Complimentary continental breakfast. Open mid-May to Sept. Seasonal rates from the end of June to Labor Day.
75 Ocean Blvd. (tel. 926–2100).

Lamie's Motor Inn (The Dunfey Family). Medium-sized motel-hotel combination in Hampton with family rates. New England menus featured in *Colonial Hearth Room*. Excellent food. *Fancy Shoals* cocktail lounge. Complimentary continental breakfast. Lower rates Sept. 28 to May 15. Swimming pool. A well-managed delightful place to sleep and eat.
On US 1, at jct. of 101C (tel. 926–3335).

Spindrift. A medium-sized beach resort with Olympic pool, beach games. Coffee shop. Family and long-stay rates. Well-appointed rooms, some overlooking the Atlantic. Open mid-May to mid-Sept.
Jct. of US 1A and State 101C (tel. 926–3313).

JACKSON

First Class

Eagle Mountain House. A large resort on 400 acres overlooking Wildcat Valley. Seasonal rates from June to mid-Oct. Restaurant. Sports activities include golf, tennis, fishing, swimming pool. Entertainment, dancing, and movies take care of the evenings and rainy days. Families like this older comfortable hotel.
On State 16B (tel. 383–4264).

Wentworth Hall. A large outstanding White Mountains resort with spacious Early American-styled rooms. American plan, with family rates. Gourmet cuisine, cocktail lounge. Swimming pools fed by cascading falls. Two orchestras for evening fun, cinemascope movies, supervised day camp. Tennis courts, 18-hole PGA golf course. Open for summer months to Oct.
On State 16B (tel. 383–4343).

Reasonable

Christmas Farm Inn. A small Colonial inn with attractive rooms. Owner-managed. This delightful place has a good restaurant. Recreation barn, swimming pool, putting green, practice ski slopes. American plan; also dormitory rates. Open Dec. 15 to Oct., closed Nov. 1 to mid-Dec.
Nr. State 16B (tel. 383–4313).

The Hawthorne Inn. Scenic view from gazebo, looking at Mt. Washington. Good food, comfortable rooms with private baths, summer sports, golf and tennis. Ski center on premises. Open summer, fall, and winter.
On State 16A (tel. 383–4213).

Whitney's in Jackson. On the edge of Black Mt. ski area, this medium-sized resort has a wide choice of accommodations: lodge rooms, kitchen units, cottages, and dormitory beds. American plan with seasonal rates from mid-Dec. to mid-April. European plan, if desired, for kitchen units. Dining room. Private swimming and fishing pond. Ski slopes, skating rink, putting green with 18-hole course nearby. Open mid-May to mid-Oct.; mid-Dec. to mid-April.

On State 16B (tel. 383–4291).

KEENE

Reasonable

Motor Inn. Small motel but with family units and rates. Cable TV and radio. Open all year. Near restaurants, shopping.

On State 12 (tel. 352–4138).

Palmer Lodge. Well-situated small facility with restaurant. Scenic setting. Open mid-May to mid-Oct. Seasonal rates from July to Aug.

4 mi. e. of Keene on State 9 (tel. 352–4358).

Pine Grove. New small motel consisting of cottages and some housekeeping units. In-room coffee with restaurant nearby. Bathing, boating, fishing. Open April 10 to Nov. 1.

Lower Main St., s. of Keene (tel. 352–4208).

Valley Green Motel. A medium-sized Superior Motels' affiliate with restaurant. Miniature golf. Pleasant comfortable rooms. Open the year round, with seasonal rates from June to Oct.

379 West St. (tel. 352–7350).

LACONIA

Reasonable

Christmas Island. A medium-sized, year-round Lake Winnipesaukee motel with beaches. Some family units and family rates. Well-appointed rooms, many with scenic view. Complimentary continental breakfast in winter. Restaurant short drive away. Play and picnic areas. Lower rates from Labor Day to June 15. European plan.

Nr. US 3 (tel. 366–4378).

The Lord Hampshire Motel and Cottages. Pleasant small resort facility with housekeeping cottages which are available only in summer. Well-furnished accommodations. Italian-American cuisine in season. Seasonal rates mid-June to Labor Day. Swimming, dock, rental boats and motors. 500-foot lakefront.

Off US 3 (tel. 524–4334).

Margate Motel. Modern brick medium-sized motel. Heated swimming pool, play area, private beach. Complimentary continental breakfast. Restaurant nearby. Open the year round. Lower rates from Labor Day to June 30.

3 mi. n. on US 3 (tel. 524–5210).

Inexpensive

Laconia Tavern Hotel. Special weekend package. Nice dining room, coffee shop, and lounge in this medium-sized hotel. Transportation provided to Belknap Mt. area, 10 minutes away.

667 Main St. (tel. 524–2233).

MANCHESTER

First Class

The Wayfarer Motor Inn (A Dunfey Motor Inn). A medium-sized, very attractive motor hotel with excellent restaurant and country store. Colonial look, complete with waterfall and covered bridge. Seasonal rates from end of May to mid-Sept. Large swimming and children's pools.

Jct. US 3 and Interstate 193 (tel. 622–3766).

Reasonable

The Elms. Several minutes from Manchester Airport. Small, but with recreational activities. Swimming pool, TV and telephone.

On State 3A (tel. 625–6426).

Holiday Inn. Reasonable. This large chain member has family plan (children in parents' room free). In-room coffee, restaurant, coffee shop, cocktail lounge, swimming pool. Meeting facilities.

At Amoskeag Bridge, Everett Tpke. Interchange, Interstate 93 (tel. 669–2660).

Inexpensive

Carpenter Motor Hotel (A Dunfey Hotel). A large downtown hotel which has been well maintained. Wide selection of accommodations and rates; family plan (children in parents' room free). Rooftop restaurant, cocktail lounge. Civic and social meetings held here. Free parking.

323 Franklin St. (tel. 625–5422).

NORTH CONWAY

First Class

Eastern Slope & Motor Lodge. A large, well-known, year-round resort. Elegant accommodations in inn and motel. A few cottages are also available on modified American plan. Other units on American plan during peak season: mid-June to mid-Oct.; mid-Dec. to mid-March. Coffee shop open all day. Restaurant, cocktail lounge. Dancing and entertainment. Recreation program, heated swimming pool, outdoor sports, nearby summer theater. All winter sports, skating rink.

Main St., on US 302 and State 16 (tel. 356–5533).

Reasonable

Birchmont. Medium-sized hotel on scenic hilltop. Informal sports, swimming pool, and tennis court. Family vacations. Family rates. Free parking. American plan. Open June 15 to Oct. 15; Dec. 22 to April 1.

S. Main St., on US 302 and State 16 (tel. 356–2991).

Cross Country. Small motel with year-round comfortable accommodations. Near good restaurant. A delightful lounge with fireplace, a gathering place in the winter. Lower rates from Nov. 1 to July 1.

On US 302 and State 16 (tel. 356–5557).

Edgewood Inn. Pleasant rooms in inn; 2-bedroom cottages and modern motel units. Seasonal rates July to mid-Oct. Family rates. Modified American plan in winter. Swimming pool. Dining service in summer.

On US 302 and State 16 (tel. 356–2622).

Forest Glen Inn. Home-like country inn in beautiful White Mountains setting. Excellent facilities for sports; wading and swimming pool. Nearby golf course, theaters, and ski trails. Open from June 18 to mid-Oct., from Dec. 26 to mid-March.

Rte. 16 So. of North Conway. (tel. 356–5346).

Stonehurst Manor & Motel. Modernized mansion in secluded setting. Medium-sized but with choice of lodge rooms, new motel units, and cottage suites. American plan. Swimming and children's pools, tennis, other games on spacious grounds. Free parking. Open mid-June to mid-Oct.

N. on US 302 and State 16 (tel. 356–2432).

PORTSMOUTH

First Class

Wentworth By-the-Sea Hotel. Large, old, but well-maintained resort with a full round of activities, social director, directors in sports. Heated saltwater. Olympic-sized swimming pool, children's pool, 18-hole course, 27 holes for putting, and 4 championship tennis courts, water skiing. Pier fishing, boat outings. Nightly entertainment, square dancing, bridge, lectures, late movies, clambakes, excellent gardens. Open May thru Oct. American plan. Primarily convention season: May, June, Sept., and Oct., when guests are welcomed at convention rates. Many rooms have a view of the ocean. A few cottages are available. Dining room and snack bar. Complete meeting and convention facilities.

On Newcastle Island, between Little Harbor and the Atlantic, nr. Portsmouth (tel. 436–3100).

Reasonable

Howard Johnson Motor Lodge. Near Pease Air Force Base, University of New Hampshire, naval shipyard, beaches. Medium-sized with family units. Restaurant, cocktail lounge on premises. Oversized, attractive rooms. Swimming pool. Seasonal rates from July to Labor Day.
At Interstate 95 traffic circle (tel. 436–7600).

Meadowbrook Motor Inn. Medium-sized with family rates. Restaurant, cocktail lounge. Spacious grounds with putting green, heated swimming pool, play area. Seasonal rates from June to Sept.
At Interstate 95 traffic circle (tel. 436–2700).

Quality Courts Port City. Moderate-sized motel with nicely furnished large rooms and efficiency units. Seasonal rates from June to Labor Day. Swimming pool. Near restaurants and resorts.
On US 1 Bypass, nr. Jct. Interstate 95, US 4, and State 16 (tel. 436–4379).

Inexpensive

Rockingham Inn. A large downtown hotel amidst historic homes. Recently redecorated but retaining its history such as the *Langdon Room* cocktail lounge. Dining rooms. Family rates and free parking. Meeting facilities. Civic and social activities are concentrated here.
401 State St., on US 1 (tel. 436–4300).

RYE and RYE BEACH

First Class

The Farragut Hotel. Long-established, medium-sized on-the-coast resort with 95-guest capacity. American plan with family rates. Private and connecting rooms. Restaurant, cocktail lounge. Swimming pool, 18-hole golf course. Weekly clambakes. Theater on premises. Convention facilities. Open June to Oct. 1.
Ocean Blvd. w. on State 1A (tel. 964–5566).

Reasonable

The Dunes. New medium-sized modern motel with a view of the ocean. Beach across the street, swimming pool. Restaurant, cocktail lounge. Lower rates from Labor Day to mid-Oct.
2281 Ocean Blvd., n. on State 1A (tel. 964–5520).

Lee's Ocean View Motor Court. Small cottage-styled place with housekeeping facilities. Spacious grounds, lawn games. Open May 1 to Oct. 1.
On State 1A (tel. 436–8672).

Orwood Lodge. Small motel and private cottages. Some kitchen facilities. Sundecks on beach; near restaurants and shops.
Rye Beach. (tel. 436–9782).

South Wind Motor Inn. Small well-furnished motel with Chinese and American dining. In-room coffee. Cocktail lounge. Sat. dinner-dance; Sun. Chinese buffets. Banquet facilities. Seasonal rates from July to Labor Day.
On US 1 (tel. 964–5545).

Inexpensive

Rye Beach Motel. Small place with kitchenette cottages. Quiet and shady area. Restaurant nearby.
Ocean Blvd. (tel. 964–5511).

SUNAPEE

Reasonable

Ben Mere Inn. Largest hotel at Sunapee. American plan and special rates for children. Planned entertainment, water sports, open June 25 to Labor Day.
Main St. (tel. 763–2772).

Dexter's Lodge. A small resort overlooking Lake Sunapee, with swimming pool, tennis court, putting green. Ski tow nearby. Beach on lake. Modified American plan. Restaurant, cocktail

lounge. Open from late May to late Oct., from Dec. 26 to April 1.
Stagecoach Rd. (tel. 763–5571).

Indian Cave Lodge. Lodge on Lake Sunapee, specializing in family accommodations; season from June 25 to mid-Sept.
At Sunapee Harbor (tel. 763–2762).

WEIRS BEACH

Reasonable

Hi-Spot Motor Court. Small place with private beach. Housekeeping cottages. Rooms have showers, hot water, TV, and heat. Open from May 1 to Nov. 1.
Weirs Blvd. (tel. 524–3281).

Lakeside Hotel & Motel. Large family hotel, with cottages and kitchenettes. Private beach at Lake Winnipesaukee. Large recreation room, TV, lounge. Open from Memorial Day to Oct. 15.
Lakeside Ave. (tel. 366–4662).

Lake Winnipesaukee Motel. Large, well-furnished rooms. Restaurant nearby. Year-round operation. Lower rates from Oct. 20 to June 15.
Nr. US 3 (tel. 366–5502).

Ledgecroft Motel & Cottages. Medium-sized famliy-type accommodations, with family units and rates. Some motel units with TV. Beach and play area. Open May 1 to Oct. 15.
On US 3 (tel. 366–4442).

Look-Off Rock Motel & Chalets. Small hillside facility with million-dollar view of lake. Swimming, fishing. Restaurant short drive away. Open May 15 to Oct. 15. Seasonal rates from July 4 to Labor Day.
Off US 3 (tel. 366–4443).

Shangri-La Resort Motel. Complete facilities overlooking Lake Winnipesaukee. Capacity, 300 guests. Restaurant, cocktail lounge. Indoor, outdoor swimming pools. 220 acres of vacationland. Modern well-furnished rooms. Open the year around.
On US 3 (tel. 366–4316).

WOLFEBORO

Reasonable

Allen A. Resort. A square mile on the lake, with scores of cottages. All sports, dude ranching, yacht trips, campfire parties, shows and movies, Fiesta Weeks in late Aug. American plan. Open late June to Labor Day.
On Lake Wentworth (tel. 569–1700).

Lakeview Inn. Small, but rooms have baths; *Liberty Room* for dining.
120 N. Main St. (tel. 569–1335).

Point Breeze. Medium-sized hotel with good location on Lake Wentworth. Bass fishing. American plan. Open June to Sept. 8.
On Lake Wentworth (tel. 569–1330).

ELSEWHERE

ALTON. *Sandy Point Beach.* Reasonable. Lake Winnipesaukee resort opened in recent years. Accommodates 375 in 35-unit motel and 40 kitchenette cottages. Restaurant, 2 bathing beaches. Free boat docks, game room. Shopping center and golf course nearby. Open from May 15 to Oct. 15. On State 11. Tel. 875–8571.

ASHLAND. *Black Horse Motor Court.* Reasonable. Capacity 90 at motel and cottages on Little Squam Lake. Heated pool. Beach and restaurant. Open May 15 to Oct. 15. 3 mi. off Interstate 93. Tel. 968–3959.

BRETTON WOODS. *Mount Washington Hotel & Country Club.* Reasonable. This large, renowned mountain resort has a wide variety of accommodations and rates, including family and long-stay. American plan in season. Restaurant, cocktail lounge, dancing, and entertainment. All-round sports, social facilities, 18-hole PGA course, supervised indoor and outdoor swimming pools, tennis, riding over scenic trails. Children's day camp, teen sports. Open May 30 to mid-Oct. On US 302. Tel. 1000.

CENTER OSSIPEE. *Deer Cove Lodge.* Reasonable. Medium-sized resort hotel with motel, honeymoon and housekeeping cottages, recreation hall, on Ossipee Lake. Extensive outdoor sports, recreational activities. Free transportation to churches. American plan. Open from May 28 to late Sept. Tel. 539–4888.

Tyrolean Motor Inn. Reasonable. Comfortable rooms have TV, phones, individual heat controls. Restaurant and cocktail lounge. Jct. of States 16 and 25. Tel. 539–4536.

CONCORD. *Howard Johnson Motor Lodge.* Reasonable. This medium-sized member of this chain is near N.H. Historical Society. Family rates. Lower rates from mid-Oct. to May. Restaurant on premises. Swimming pool. Rooms are spacious and nicely located. Gulf St., at Everett Tpke., US 3 at Interstate 93. Tel. 224–4011.

New Hampshire Highway Hotel. Reasonable. This large motor hotel is only a few blocks from the State House and downtown area. Colonial atmosphere in four dining rooms; *Grand Ball Room* for large conventions; domed patio for meals. Swimming pool. Two gift shops, art gallery, dress shop, and beauty salon on premises. Open the year round. Jct. of State 9, US 202, US 3, US 4. Tel. 255–6687.

CRAWFORD NOTCH. *Crawford House Hotel & Motor Lodge.* Deluxe. This large White Mountains vacationland offers a wide choice of accommodations in hotel, cottages, and motel. American plan in season. Lower rates before July and after Labor Day. Good restaurant and cocktail lounge. Every outdoor sport available, 9-hole golf course, swimming pool, two lakes, supervised play area. Nighttime is also active with dancing, entertainment, movies. Open from mid-May to mid-Oct. Lives up to its reputation of over 100 years of warm New England hospitality. At entrance to Crawford Notch State Park, US 302. Tel. 846–5511.

DIXVILLE NOTCH. *The Balsams.* Deluxe. This large, topnotch resort in the White Mountains has elegant accommodations and superb continental cuisine. American plan with family rates. Extensive recreational facilities both indoors and outdoors, 18-hole championship golf course, boating, fishing, tennis, swimming pool and beach, dancing, movies, entertainment in the evening. Open mid-June to mid-Sept. Off State 26. Tel. 9010.

DURHAM. *Highland House.* Reasonable. Modern rooms with home atmosphere. Near University of New Hampshire campus. Bennett Rd. Tel. 659–3631.

EXETER. *Exeter Inn.* Reasonable. Colonial setting with comfortable rooms. Family rates and free parking. Excellent dining facilities, cocktail lounge. Guests have use of the academy's tennis courts; golf nearby. 90 Front St., State 111. Tel. 772–5901.

FITZWILLIAM. *Fitzwilliam Inn.* Reasonable. An 18th-century inn with a few delightful rooms available. Excellent food in quaint dining room. Cocktail lounge. Offers both American and European plans. Swimming pool and sauna. Skiing and ice-skating in winter. On State 12 and 119. Tel. 585–6527.

FRANCONIA. *Mittersell Alpine Inn & Chalets* (A Treadway Resort). First class. This medium-sized resort has an Alpine, Austrian motif throughout its lodge, motel, and chalets. Spread over 165 acres in the heart of White Mountain National Forest, it offers every outdoor sport: 9-hole golf course, tennis, riding, skiing, skating, swimming pool. Restaurant, cocktail lounge with dancing. Each chalet accommodates up to 8 persons, has different design, large living room, fireplace, 2 to 4 bedrooms, fully equipped kitchenette, telephones, and private bath. These are usually rented for long stays. Family plan (children in parents' room free). Open late June to mid-Oct. and mid-Dec. to mid-April. On Cannon Mt., off State 18 nr. village of Franconia at top of Franconia Notch. Tel. 823–5511.

GILFORD. *King's Grant Inn & Chalets.* Reasonable. An American-plan, medium resort on 180 beautiful acres at Lake Winnipesaukee. Full round of entertainment and sports. Two-room honeymoon chalets. Private picnic island and 38-foot cruiser. Open May 15 to Oct. 15, Dec. 15 to April 15. Lily Pond Rd., on State 11B. Tel. 293–4431.

Saunders Bay Motel & Cottages. Reasonable. Small family vacation spot, 14 housekeeping cottages. Sandy beach, boats, playgrounds, movies, outdoor cooking. Riding, golf courses, and playhouse nearby. Open May 15 to Oct. 15. On Lake Winnipesaukee. Tel. 293–7871.

GLEN. *Storybook Motor Inn.* Reasonable. White Mountains facility with excellent dining room, cocktail lounge, and swimming pool. Offers both American and European plans. Jct. of US 302 and State 16, next to Story Land. Tel. 383–4323.

HANCOCK. *John Hancock Inn.* Reasonable. Gracious Early American atmosphere in small inn. Offers both American and European plans. Excellent cuisine. *Carriage Lounge.* New ski area. On State 123. Tel. 525–3318.

HANOVER. *Chieftain.* Reasonable. A small Superior Motels, Inc. facility a short distance from Dartmouth College. Family rates and units. Complimentary continental-style breakfast. Restaurant a short drive away. On State 100. Tel. 643–2550.

Hanover Inn and Motor Lodge. Reasonable. A delightful blending of the old and new. The large inn is located across from the Dartmouth campus. The old inn has meeting facilities and most civic and social affairs are held here. Restaurant, cocktail lounge. A complimentary continental breakfast is served. Modern attractive rooms. Both facilities are owned and operated by Dartmouth College and are near the Dartmouth skiway. The inn is on State 10, the motor lodge a short distance away on Lebanon St. Tel. 643–4300 (inn); 643–4400 (motor lodge).

HOOKSETT. *China Dragon Motor Inn.* Reasonable. Distinctive small motel. Large well-furnished rooms in Oriental decor. Chinese dinners in exotic restaurant and *Tikki Lounge.* Complimentary continental breakfast. Diner cards honored. On US 3, 7 mi. n. of Manchester. Tel. 485–9586.

Indian Cliff Motel. Attractive cottages with some kitchen facilities. Restaurant short drive away. Children's play area. On US 3. Tel. 485–9861.

INTERVALE. *Holiday Inn.* Reasonable. Spacious grounds. Excellent accommodations with TV, phones. Floodlit skating, coasting in winter. Ski trips planned. American plan. On State 16A. Tel. 356–9772.

The New England Inn. First class. A small resort with tastefully decorated rooms. Cottages with family rates. Restaurant, cocktail lounge. Modified American plan, except for overnight guests. 4-hole golf course, outdoor games, swimming and children's pools, playground. Exudes the warmth of age. Open June 1 to Nov. 1, mid-Dec. to mid-April. On State 16A. Tel. 356–5541.

JAFFREY. *Woodbound Inn & Lake Cottages.* Reasonable. Monadnock region's popular resort. Rustic atmosphere; restaurant. Focus on sports activities: fishing, tennis, golf, swimming, skiing, skating. Social events. Open from May 29 to mid-Oct., Dec. 26 to mid-March. Woodbound Rd., on Contoocook Lake. Tel. 532–8341.

LINCOLN-NORTH WOODSTOCK. *Beacon Motel.* Reasonable. Small housekeeping units, with TV. Swimming pool. Lower rates from May 1 to July 1 and from Sept. 5 to Nov. 15. Tel. 745–5911.

LITTLETON. *Thayers Hotel.* Inexpensive. Old New England establishment with modern facilities in its 60 rooms. Year-round operation. Dining room. Dancing nightly in *Ox-Bow Cocktail Lounge*. Short distance from Cannon Mt. ski area. Fishing, hunting. Modified American plan available. 136 Main St. Tel. 444–3923.

NASHUA. *Hannah Dustin*. Reasonable. Small, with well-furnished rooms, some connecting units. Seasonal rates from mid-June to mid-Oct. In-room coffee with restaurant next door. Swimming pool and play areas on spacious grounds. On US 3. Tel. 883–3315.

Thunderbird. Reasonable. Medium-sized motel with tastefully decorated rooms. Breakfast served in breakfast room; restaurant across the street. Swimming pool. Lower rates from mid-Oct. to June 1. On US 3. Tel. 882–6995.

NEW LONDON. *New London Inn*. Reasonable. A medium-sized, attractive old inn with charming atmosphere. Near Lake Sunapee ski areas and golf courses. Colby College nearby. Open the year round. Main St., on State 11. Tel. 526–2791.

Sundart Motor Lodge. Reasonable. Small resort motel with wonderful Mt. Sunapee view from terrace and lounge. Swimming pool. Complimentary continental breakfast. Open the year round. Lower rates from Labor Day to May 26. Tel. 763–5592.

NORTH WOODSTOCK. *Red Doors Motel*. Reasonable. New small motel with family rates and units. Seasonal rates from July to Labor Day. Near Franconia Notch and restaurants. N. on US 3. Tel. 745–2267.

PIERCE BRIDGE. *Wayside Inn*. Reasonable. Rural inn with neat rooms. New housekeeping cottages. Excellent meals. Swimming, outdoor sports, 9-hole golf course. No pets. Open mid-June to mid-Oct., Dec. 23 to early April. On US 302. Tel. 869–5734.

PIKE. *Lake Tarleton Club*. Deluxe. A fabulous White Mountains resort with 400 capacity. Extensive beautiful grounds offer 18-hole PGA golf course, 7 tennis courts, boating, water skiing, swimming, sandy beach, riding. Famed cuisine, outdoor dining to music; 2 orchestras, dancing and entertainment. Open mid-June to mid-Sept. On State 25C. Tel. 989–4011.

PLYMOUTH. *Gilcrest Motel*. Reasonable. Well-furnished motel units, nice cottages. TV. Playground, heated swimming pool. Pets allowed. Open May 15 to late Oct. Lower rates off season. 8½ mi. n. on US 3. Tel. 726–2801.

Tobey's Motor Court. Reasonable. Medium-sized facility on pleasant grounds. Some cottages at family rates. Restaurant. Heated swimming pool. Seasonal rates from July to Labor Day. 1 mi. n. on US 3. Tel. 536–2330.

SEABROOK. *Ye Cocke & Kettle Motor Inn*. Reasonable. Well-known landmark with good restaurant and cocktail lounge. Large swimming pool. Short drive to beaches. Seasonal rates from June to Oct. On US 1. Tel. 474–3507.

SHELBURNE. *Town & Country Motor Inn*. Reasonable. A large motel with air-conditioned rooms, TV, telephones. Cocktail lounge and golf course. Seafood and steak cuisine. Tel. 466–9466.

SNOWVILLE. *Snowvillage Lodge*. Reasonable. Small Swiss resort on 1,100-foot elevation with trails and slopes. Free ski lessons and equipment. Modified American plan. Attractive rooms. Open May 1 to Oct. 15, Dec. 15 to Apr. 15. Off State 153, nr. Conway. Tel. 447–2818.

WEST LEBANON. *Sunset Motel*. Reasonable. Hanover, medium-sized, with homey atmosphere near Wilder Lake. TV, phones, & baths in rooms. Free morning coffee. Picnic, playgrounds. On State 10. Tel. 298–8721.

WHITEFIELD. *Mountain View House*. First class. A large, distinguished resort with gracious country house, beautiful gardens. *Sports House,* swimming pool, snack bar. Two tennis courts, 9-hole golf course, 18-hole putting green. Dancing, entertainment. Excellent restaurant, cocktail lounge. American plan; special honeymoon rates. Open end of June to Oct. Mountain View Rd., ½ mi. off US 3. Tel. 837–2511.

Spalding Inn Club. First class. Moderate-sized resort with a few cottage units on spacious grounds. Sports, boating, outdoor games, swimming pool. Social program. Restaurant, bar. Open May 25 to late Oct. Mountain View Rd., 1 mi. off US 3. Tel. 837–2572.

WOODSTOCK. *Jack O'Lantern Motor Resort.* Reasonable. A 400-acre mountain-playground estate with swimming pool, golf course, tennis. Elegant motel rooms with family units and rates available. Modified American plan. *Cabana Club. Continental Room Supper Club,* cocktail lounge. Open May 21 to Oct. 15. On US 3. Tel. 745–6033.

YOUTH HOSTELS. New Hampshire has been a pioneer in youth hosteling. The first unit, chartered in 1935, was one of the original American Youth Hostels in U.S. It is *Cotton's Youth Hostel,* 2 mi. w. of Warren, on Beech Rd., with 20 beds. Most facilities are small. Rates are $1 per day in summer; $1.50 in winter. Year-round hostels are so indicated; others are open in summer only.

Alton, *Green Top Youth Hostel* (30 beds) on State 28. Brookline, *5 B's Campground Youth Hostels* (16), South Main St. Claremont, *Community Center,* for use only by groups with leaders. Franconia, *All Go Hungry Ordinary Youth Hostel* (22), Harvard St., year round. Henniker, *Eleven Acres Youth Hostel* (30), State 9 and US 202, year round. Lebanon, *Barden's Barn* (12), School St. Mt. Sunapee, *Alpenhof Youth Hostel* (30), State 103B, year round. North Conway, *Community Center* (20), in town's center. North Haverhill, *Lime Kilns Youth Hostel* (30), 4 mi. e. of North Haverhill, State 10.

CAMPING OUT. New Hampshire has an excellent system of camping facilities for individual and family purposes; both tent and trailer sites. More than 80 privately-operated camping areas are listed by the *New Hampshire Campground Owners' Assn.* Fifteen areas are in the *White Mountain National Forest;* 10 are in *state parks,* maintained by the New Hampshire Division of Parks; one in the *Gunstock-Belknap Mountains Recreation Area.* All state and federal camping areas are on "first-come, first-served" basis. No advance reservations. All camping areas must be approved by New Hampshire Department of Health. A folder, *Family Camping,* listing campsites, fees, and general information, is sent free by New Hampshire Division of Economic Development, Concord. Details on state campsites available from New Hampshire Division of Parks, Concord; on federal campsites, write Supervisor, White Mountain National Forest, Laconia, N.H. 03246.

TRAILER TIPS. Several private operators of camp grounds in New Hampshire have established in recent years camping areas for tents and for trailer parking. This is an improvement for the trailer vacationists because there are more than 80 privately-owned campgrounds in the state. Trailers are admitted to the public campgrounds of 10 state parks, providing they fit conveniently into the tent sites. No facilities have been set up by the state parks for trailer purposes, according to the New Hampshire Division of Economic Development, which issues free a brochure, *Family Camping.*

Among the trailer sites set up in the past few years are: *Arcadia Tent & Trailer Park,* Lake Winnipesaukee, 5 mi. from Center Harbor, off State 25. Open June 25 to Labor Day. *Camper's World,* 2½ mi. n. of North Woodstock on US 3. Free movies nightly. Open May 1 to Oct. 15. *Ferndale Acres Camping Area,* at Lee, 3 mi. from State 125; 70 trailer sites, 40 with water, electricity, and sewerage; May 1 to Oct. 1. *Lake Sunapee Campgrounds,* 1 mi. from Mt. Sunapee State Park Chairlift and beach, on State 103B. About 100 places. Open from May to Nov. 1. *Monadnock Mt. Recreation Area,* 170 acres near state park at Jaffrey, off State 124; 52 tent and trailer sites. Open May to Oct.

DINING OUT. The clear mountain air in this state can make a traveler hungry enough for two. Fortunately, New Hampshire, though relatively small in area, can provide tasty New England food aplenty. Lobster, steak, turkey, ducklings, and homemade baked goods head most menus.

FRANCONIA

First Class

Horse and Hound Inn. Specializes in sirloin steak, lamb chops, and lobster. Sun. buffet. Dinner from 6:30 to 9 p.m. Children's plates. Dining on terrace.
S. off State 18.

Mittersill Alpine Inn. European dishes are popular in this famous resort with carefully detailed Swiss chalet decor and view of the ski slopes. Try the wiener schnitzel, steak, or lobster pie. Lunch from 12:30 to 2 p.m. Dinner 6:30 to 8 p.m. Dancing on Wed. and Sat.
State 18.

Reasonable

Bonnie Briar Restaurant. This pleasant summer restaurant has an à la carte menu. Lobster is the feature every Fri. Open from 2:30 to 8:30 p.m., Sun. from noon. Children's plates.
State 18.

LACONIA

Reasonable

The Arlberg. You will find topnotch German-American cuisine here. Specialties include schnitzel, frogs' legs, Cornish hen, and sauerbraten. Cocktail Lounge. Open daily to 8:30 p.m., July and Aug. to 9:30 p.m., Sun. from noon to 8:30 p.m. Closed Apr.
E. on State 11A.

Hickory Stick Farm. Country-style roast duckling and beef are featured in the dining rooms of this converted farmhouse. Daily from 5:30 to 9 p.m., Sat. noon to 10 p.m., Sun. and holidays until 9 p.m. Closed Oct. 18 to May 8.
Bean Hill Rd., State 11.

Winnisquam House. Features Italian dishes, steaks, lobster. Home cooking. Dinner 5 to 9:30 p.m. Children's plates. Breakfast and lunch also served.
4½ mi. s. on US 3.

MANCHESTER

Reasonable

Carpenter Motor Hotel Town Tavern. A charming dining room with Old English decor. Roast beef and lobster among the favorites. Glass-enclosed *Top of the Town* lounge provides rooftop view of the city. Dinner 5:30 to 10 p.m., Sun. until 8 p.m. Dancing nightly except Sun.
323 Franklin St.

Wayfarer Motor Inn. A scenic country dining spot, with beef specialties and roast duck. Bar and music. Open daily to 11 p.m.
Jct. US 3 and State 101.

Inexpensive

Tambini's. A family-style establishment featuring Italian-American dishes plus steak and roast beef. Open 11:30 a.m. to 9 p.m. Closed Tues.
19 S. River Rd.

NORTH CONWAY

Reasonable

Eastern Slope Inn. Excellent dining facilities and menus in first-class resort.

Steak and roast beef among top favorites at dinner. Coffee shop open from 7:30 a.m. to midnight, *Red Carpet Room* from 7:30 to 10 p.m. in season. Bar, entertainment and dancing.
On US 302.

The Eating House. A picturesque setting for an excellent menu of seafood specialties as well as steak. Breakfast, lunch, and dinner in summer. Bar and music. Cafeteria service during ski season. Children's plates.
1 mi. off US 302, nr. the Skimobile at Cranmore.

Hoffman House Dining Room. This excellent dining room overlooks majestic scenery. German cuisine, featuring goulash, sauerbraten, and schnitzel. Cocktails and music. Breakfast, lunch, and buffet also served. Closed Apr. and May, Nov. to Dec. 23. Children's plates.
On US 302.

PORTSMOUTH

First Class

Wentworth-by-the-Sea. Overlooking picturesque harbor, serving full-course meals with all the trimmings in large dining hall. Travelers as well as guests at this distinguished resort may enjoy the Friday clambakes on the beach. Wine list. Bar. Open from May 15 to Oct. 15.
On Newcastle Isle.

Reasonable

Fisherman's Pier Restaurant. Seafood is featured as well as steaks and chicken. *Captain's Cabin Lounge* is also in this port o' call. Open daily from 11 a.m. to 11 p.m.
On US 1, at Memorial Bridge.

Valle's Steak House. Popular roadside restaurant with full-course dinners. Lavish portions of prime porterhouse and sirloin steak. Lobster is also featured. Open 7 a.m. to midnight. Cocktails. Children's plates.
Jct. of Interstate 95 and US 1.

Inexpensive

Yoken's "Thar She Blows." At the sign of the big whale, you'll find amusing decorations and a menu that emphasizes seafood. Children like it, too, and you can get special plates. Lunch, dinner until 8 p.m. Closed Mon. and from Dec. 23 to mid-Feb.
3 mi. s. on US 1.

WOLFEBORO

Reasonable

Barn Dining Room. This restaurant in the *Colonial Arms Inn* features a New England menu. Cocktails. Open from late June to Labor Day.
29 Main St., State 109.

General Wolfe Inn. In this old New England inn you can enjoy roast beef or baked stuffed shrimp among a variety of entrées. Children's plates. Bar. Lunch. Dinner 5 to 10 p.m. Closed from mid-Oct. to Apr.
1 mi. s. on State 28.

Wolfeboro Inn. A Colonial atmosphere and regional menu. Baking on the premises. Breakfast, lunch. Dinner from 5:30 to 8:30 p.m. Children's plates.
On State 109.

ELSEWHERE

AMHERST. *Horace Greeley Restaurant.* Reasonable. Seafood and Continental dishes are featured in this attractive spot. Open 7 a.m. to 10 p.m., Sun. to 8 p.m. Cocktails. Closed Mon. and from Jan. 1 to March 1. On State 101.

CONCORD. *Angelo's.* Reasonable. This large, well-known Italian-American restaurant has accommodations for 350 people. Paintings of the Rapallo era add to the decor. Cocktail lounge and bar. Open daily 11 a.m. to 11 p.m. 166 N. Main St., nr. state capitol.

New Hampshire Highway Hotel. Reasonable. New England decor in open-air dining terrace. *Tavern Cock-*

tail Lounge, Coach Dining Room, and coffee shop. Lobster, steak, and chicken are specialties. Children's plates. Nightly entertainment. Jct. US 3 and State 9.

DOVER. *Provincial Room.* Reasonable. This attractive dining room specializes in lobster, roast beef, and baked stuffed shrimp. Children's plates. Open daily 7 a.m. to midnight, Sun. 8 a.m. to 9 p.m. In Sherwood Motor Hotel, on Spaulding Tpke.

DUBLIN. *Dublin Inn.* Reasonable. This charming 1789 inn features a German-American menu. Specialties of the house are sauerbraten, dumplings, pot roast, goulash. Lunch. Dinner from 5 to 9 p.m., Sun. from 1 p.m. State 101.

EXETER. *Exeter Inn Dining Room.* Reasonable. Colonial decor in this well-known inn with New England dinner, featuring seafood and beef. Dinner 6 to 7:30 p.m., Sun. noon to 2:30 p.m. Buffet 5:30 to 7 p.m. Wine list. Outdoor dining in season. Children's plates. 90 Front St., on State 111.

HAMPTON BEACH. *Lamie's Tavern.* Reasonable. A historic inn with New England fare. Seafood dishes are the specialties. *Shoals Lounge* has a waterfall and pool. Open daily from 11 a.m. to 10 p.m. Bar and music. Children's plates. On US 1.

HANOVER. *Hanover Inn.* Reasonable. This charming inn features New England dinners. London broil and cheese soup are favorites. Patio dining during the summer. Children's menu. Breakfast and lunch. State 10, nr. Dartmouth College campus.

HOOKSETT. *China Dragon Restaurant.* First class. Cantonese food is highlighted in the three lovely dining rooms and in the *Tikki Lounge.* French-fried jumbo shrimp is especially recommended. Open from noon to midnight. Entertainment some evenings. US 3, 8 mi. n. of Manchester.

INTERVALE. *Idlewild.* Inexpensive. Hearty New England fare for breakfast. Dinner features roast beef and steak served to 8:30 p.m. Children's menu. State 16.

New England Inn. Reasonable. This delightful New England dining room features filet mignon and codfish cakes. Bar. Breakfast and lunch. Dinners served from 6:30 to 8 p.m. State 16A.

KEENE. *Black Lantern.* Reasonable. New England dishes are featured, including fried chicken and lobster. Open from 11 a.m. to 8:30 p.m., Sun. noon to 7:30 p.m. Closed Mon. and month of Feb. Bar and music. Children's plates. S. on State 12.

LEBANON. *Montshire Restaurant.* Reasonable. Dining for the traveler in modern surroundings. Prime ribs of beef, stuffed lobster are featured. Lunch. Dinner to 11 p.m. On State 10.

MEREDITH. *Hart's Turkey Farm.* Inexpensive. Family-style turkey dinners with home-grown birds. Open from 11:30 a.m. to 9 p.m. Closed from Oct. 27 to June 19. Fish served on Fri. only. Jct. US 3 and State 104.

Wakitatina. Inexpensive. Varied menu and good service. Buffet on Sun. Daily from 8 a.m. to 9 p.m., mid-June to early Oct. Cocktails. On US 3.

NASHUA. *Green Ridge Turkey Farm.* Reasonable. Besides turkey raised on local farm, you will find chops, roast beef, seafood. Children's plates. On US 3, 1/4 mi. from Mass. line.

Olde Coach Inn. Reasonable. Charcoal-broiled steaks, prime ribs of beef, and baked stuffed lobster are specialties. Open from 11:30 a.m. to 10 p.m. Cocktail Lounge. On US 3.

NORTH WOODSTOCK. *Jack O'Lantern.* Reasonable. An attractive resort dining facility specializing in seafood and roast beef. 7:30 a.m. to 10 p.m. Bar and music. Children's plates. Closed mid-Oct. to mid-May. On US 3.

Woodland Restaurant. Reasonable. Home-styled meals including homemade rolls and pastries. Cocktails. Children's plates. Open 7:30 a.m. to 10 p.m. June through mid-Oct. On US 3.

OSSIPEE. *Sunny Villa*. Inexpensive. A long-time favorite with tourists, this spot serves typical New England fare. 9 a.m. to 9 p.m. Bar. Children's plates. Open late May to Nov. 1 and Dec. 27 to Mar. On State 16.

PLYMOUTH. *Open Gate Restaurant*. Reasonable. New England menu features roast beef, stuffed shrimp, and special desserts. Children's plates. Cocktail lounge. Open 8 a.m. to 9 p.m. from late June to mid-Oct. On State 25.

Tobey's. Reasonable. Specializing in New England dishes such as chicken pie, Yankee pot roast, and homemade pastries. Wine list. Children's plates. Breakfast. Open from mid-May to late Oct. On US 3.

RYE. *Saunders Lobster House*. Inexpensive. Features lobster and steak dinners in a charming waterfront setting. Noon to 8 p.m. Closed Mon. and from Labor Day to May 28. Rye Harbor Rd.

South Wind Dining Room. Inexpensive. Chinese delicacies and seafood. Open during summer from 8 a.m. to midnight. Children's plates. Lafayette Rd., West Rye.

SUNAPEE. *The Schweitzers*. Reasonable. Cottage restaurant with Bavarian flavor. Featuring *schnapps, schlagers,* and *schnitzels* in true *gemutlichkeit* style. On State 103, 1 mi. from Mt. Sunapee State Park.

Woodbine Cottage. Reasonable. Specializing in New England fare such as steak and lobster. Homemade pastries and ice cream. Children's plates. Wine list. Closed from Oct. 13 to Apr. 19. Off State 103B at harbor.

WEST LEBANON. *Montshire Restaurant*. Reasonable. This pleasant restaurant with a patio features regional specialties. Wine list. Open from 11 a.m. to 10 p.m., Sun. noon to 10 p.m. On State 10, N. Main St.

WHITEFIELD. *Mountain View House*. First class. Exquisite meals to equal splendor of this famed resort, which is open from late June to mid-Oct. Cocktails and nightly entertainment in the *Caravan Room*. On US 3.

Spalding Inn Club. Reasonable. Gracious dining atmosphere and good food. Open daily for breakfast, lunch, and dinner. Closed late Oct. to late May. Mountain View Rd.

MUSIC. Increased stature in the music culture of the Northeast is being achieved at the new *Hopkins Center* on Dartmouth College campus, Hanover. Since 1963 the *Congregation of the Arts* has starred international composers, conductors, and artists in air-conditioned Spaulding Auditorium where concerts on several nights a week take place at 8:30 p.m. in July and Aug. Adm. $2 for symphony; $1.50 for chamber music. For schedules write Hopkins Center, Hanover.

Symphony and *chamber music* is featured at *New Hampshire Music Festival* (since 1953) during July and Aug. at Meredith, Wolfeboro, Center Harbor. Adm. $1. Details from P.O. Box 146, Laconia. *Annual New Hampshire Drum & Bugle Competition* at Spaulding Field, Rochester, in Aug.

STAGE AND REVUES. Newly organized New Hampshire Theatre Council promotes advancement of theatrical efforts. *Theatre-by-the-Sea,* Portsmouth, presents classical to contemporary plays by resident company; year-round schedule. Wed. thru Sun. at 8:30 p.m. Matinees by request. Adults $2, children $1.25. Children's Theater, Sat. and Sun. afternoons. Year-round student theaters at University of New Hampshire, Durham, and Dartmouth College, Hanover. Eleven playhouses offer summer stock.

SPECIAL INTEREST TOURS. From the southern seacoast shores to the northern slopes dropping into Canada, New Hampshire affords hundreds of miles of exciting auto trips. Some of these motoring adventures are off the main highways into the mountain woodlands, rolling countrysides, and cool valleys. Any section of the state has its special attractions; any region is now traversed over modern highways.

Seventeen Scenic Shunpikes is the title of a brochure being issued by the New Hampshire Division of Economic Development. Here are digest listings of some of the most picturesque and historic routes for happy traveling. There are marked *apple blossom tours* in the Monadnock region after May 15; *mountain laurel trips* are posted after June 15. *Flower tours,* conducted by qualified botanists, are arranged by the *Appalachian Mountain Club,* Pinkham Notch Camp, Gorham, on the Mount Washington and Mount Monroe slopes.

Increasing popularity is noted in the marked *foliage color tours* which cover the length and width of the state beginning around Sept. 25. Colored leaf symbols are used on some routes in the Monadnock, White Mountains, and Dartmouth–Lake Sunapee regions. State agencies provide coloration news reports to the press, radio, and television. This is big news for New Hampshire tourism.

Some historic-minded motorists enjoy leisurely drives to the state's 60 *covered bridges* over streams where there's good fishing. A few of these wood structures are called "kissin' bridges," a designation given them during the horse-and-buggy days. For other relaxing tours, there are *cruises* on various lakes and at the seashore. The best-known cruise is the daily one by the motor vessel *Mount Washington* on Lake Winnipesaukee during the summer. Upwards of 1,500 passengers can be accommodated on the 600-ton vessel.

Free brochures on these tours and cruises are available from the New Hampshire Division of Economic Development, Concord.

HISTORIC SITES. Since its creation in 1955 by the State Legislature, the State Historical Commission has set up markers throughout New Hampshire at designated places of historical significance. The markers are placed with the cooperation of the State Department of Public Works and Highways. The 26 bronze markers are described in a booklet of the State Historical Commission, 71 South Fruit St., Concord, distributed free. They are identified on the *New Hampshire Tourist Map,* obtained free from N. H. Division of Economic Development, State House Annex, Concord.

Following are these designated historic sites: *Amherst,* Birthplace of Horace Greeley; *Canaan,* Canaan St.; *Center Harbor,* Dudley Leavitt; *Center Ossipee,* Capt. Lovewell's War; *Chester,* Early American Clocks; *Charlestown,* Fort at No. 4; *Cornish,* Winston Churchill; *Deerfield,* Major John Simpson; *Durham,* Site of Piscataqua Bridge; *Francestown,* Soapstone; *Franconia,* Stone Iron Furnace; *Gilmanton,* Old Province Road; *Jaffrey,* Hannah Davis, Amos Fortune; *Jefferson,* Thaddeus S. C. Lowe; *Loudon,* Shaker Village; *New Castle,* William and Mary Raids; *New Ipswich,* First Textile Mills; *Newport,* Sarah Josepha Buell Hale; *North Wakefield,* George A. Wentworth; *Northwood,* Lafayette's Tour; *Pinkham's Grant,* First Ascent of Mount Washington; *Pittsburg,* Republic of Indian Stream; *Rye,* Isles of Shoals; *Sandown,* Old Meeting House; *Sharon,* Temple Glass Factory; *Swanzey,* Denman Thompson.

MUSEUMS AND GALLERIES. Three centuries of accomplishment in government, education, industry, and culture are preserved in museums and historic homes. *Strawbery Banke,* multi-million-dollar historic restoration of the old section of Portsmouth when it was the colony's capital, is being done according to an architectural study of 1813. Twenty-seven houses on nine-acre site of old South End (settled 1630) are being restored in nation's first program to convert a slum area into a historic showplace with federal, state, local, and private funds. Ten historic homes in Portsmouth are open for tours from mid-June to mid-Sept.

Exhibits of Americana, dating to late 17th century, are preserved in the *New Hampshire Historical Society's* neoclassic building, near the State Capitol, Concord. Among rare documents is the *Thomson Indenture,* original agreement in 1622 between David Thomson, New Hampshire's first settler, and three English merchants who financed his venture. Open year round, Mon. thru Sat., 9 a.m. to 4 p.m. Adm. free.

Saint-Gaudens, studio and home of famous sculptor, with special exhibitions of paintings, in Cornish, off State 12A. Open May 30 to Oct. 15. Adults 50¢, children under 12 free. *Schuller Medieval Arms & Armor Museum,* 14th- to 17th-century arms and armor, European palace furniture, royal clocks. On Ten Rod Rd., near Farmington, off State 11. Open daily to sundown. Adm. 90¢.

Hopkins Center, Hanover, cultural settings in $7.5-million home of creative and performing arts on Dartmouth College campus. Outdoor Sculpture Court, 4 art galleries, 2 theaters, auditorium, social lounge, student workshops, refreshment lounge, Orozco frescoes at Baker Memorial Library. Guided tours, Sat. and Sun., 2 p.m. College museum open weekdays, 9 to 5 p.m.; Sun., 2 to 5 p.m.; closed Sat. and Sun. during summer vacations. Free admission.

Steamtown, USA, North Walpole, museum of steam railroad engines, steam fire engines, and railroadiana in abandoned roundhouse, across Connecticut River from Bellows Falls, Vt. Rail-fan 26-mile excursion between Bellows Falls, Vt., and Chester, daily in summer, at 11 a.m., 2, and 3 p.m. Extra run on Sun. and holidays. Weekend foliage trips between Labor Day and Nov. 1.

GARDENS. The magnificent gardens of New Hampshire are those that grow with little or no care in the mountain regions. Flowers of many kinds blossom with the coming of spring. Perhaps the most colorful garden in the state is in *Rhododendron State Park,* near Fitzwilliam, where 16 acres of wild rhododendron are in bloom about July 14. Tour parties to this and other flower areas are often organized by naturelore groups, with the state park and the White Mountain gardens as their subjects of admiration and study.

SUMMER SPORTS. Any season is a good reason for sports enthusiasts to participate or to witness their favorite pastimes in New Hampshire. The focus, naturally, is on outdoor games throughout the four seasons. *Fishing, hunting, hiking,* and *boating* are among the lures for thousands of aficionados of these sports who flock into the far-flung regions of the state. Hundreds of miles of streams and an estimated 1,300 lakes and ponds contain many varieties of *fish* from brook trout to yellow perch. Hunters invade the marked *game areas* of state parks, White Mountain National Forest, and abandoned farmlands. The game ranges from cottontail rabbit to wildcat and woodcock. A special season is set aside for hunting deer with bow and arrow. All persons over 16 years of age must have licenses to fish and hunt within the state. Nonresident minors must obtain nonresident hunting licenses but do not require fishing licenses. Listing of the fishing and hunting areas, as well as state regulations, can be obtained free from the New Hampshire Fish and Game Dept., Concord.

No license is needed for *saltwater fishing,* but it is required for oysters, clams, and smelt fishing. Scheduled charter boats are at several seacoast points. Free information is available from the Seacoast Regional Development Assn., Box 807, Portsmouth.

There are about 105 lakes, ponds and rivers marked for nearly 40,000 registered *boats* and *motorboats*. Boating information and fees sent, on request, by the New Hampshire Division of Economic Development, Concord. Facilities and regulations on saltwater boating are provided by the New Hampshire Port Authority, Portsmouth.

About 70 public and private *golf courses* are open from spring to autumn. The majority will accept transient golfers. A brochure listing the courses is available from the New Hampshire Division of Economic Development.

Racing is held during the summer months, with well-known jockeys and horses competing at *Rockingham Park Track,* Rockingham (where state lottery drawings are made), and at *Hinsdale Raceway,* Hinsdale.

For novice and expert *hikers,* there is a network of marked trails, the best being in the White Mountain National Forest. *Climbing Holidays,* a free folder, is issued by the Appalachian Mt. Club, 5 Joy St., Boston, Mass.

Since 1888, New Hampshire has pioneered in the "hut" system by accommodating many thousands of hikers who ascend the high country of the White Mountain ranges. The huts are well-furnished buildings at elevations of from 3,400 to 5,000 ft., sponsored by the Appalachian Mountain Club. Each hut accommodates from 40 to 104 persons. Overnight lodgings are available for hikers. Meals are served family-style, by staffs of high school and college boys. A.M.C. headquarters at the base of Mt. Washington (beginning of the famed Tuckerman Ravine Trail) has accommodations for 100 lodgers and is open year-round. The other huts are open from mid-June to mid-Sept. Information on the hut system may be obtained free from A.M.C. Hut System, Gorham, N.H.

Mineral-hunting. "Granite State" is the synonym attached to New Hampshire. But granite is only one of more than 200 minerals found throughout the state. Rock hounds have a virtual happy mining country. Some mines are posted for mineral collectors. Largest mineral display in the state is at Woodman Institute, Dover. Displays at Dartmouth College Museum, State House Visitors' Center (Concord), and many business places. A State Gem and Mineral Festival is held at Mt. Sunapee State Park, Newbury (Aug.). Special folder from Division of Economic Development, Concord.

Sweepstakes. New Hampshire has the only state-operated sweepstakes program in the United States. Two public drawings are held prior to the Sweepstakes Race at Rockingham Park Race Track, Salem; dates are announced weeks in advance. Tickets of $3 each are sold to adults only at 49 state liquor stores, Rockingham Track and Hinsdale Raceway, Hinsdale, and at the turnpike interchanges at Hooksett and Hampton. No sales are made in the mail, in accordance with U.S. postal regulations. Proceeds of sweepstakes, first run in Sept., 1964, are for educational purposes in school districts. Dates of races at the two parimutuel tracks are listed in the New Hampshire Recreational Calendar of the N.H. Division of Economic Development, Concord.

WINTER SPORTS. Since the 1930's, New Hampshire has developed many of its majestic slopes into first-rate winter resorts. There are now 27 major *ski areas* with a total of 74 cable lifts, or an average of almost three for each resort. Many overhead-type cable lifts are used by skiers and spectators who appreciate panoramic viewing from up high. Skiing and allied sports are held from mid-Dec. to April, some of the events in the highest peaks of the Northeast. The most challenging sector is the *Tuckerman Ravine* in the lea of 6,288-ft. Mt. Washington, where not one rope tow has been installed. It's the only truly Alpine slope west of the Rockies where expert skiers may find good powder from mid-Mar. thru May, and even June. The free *Winter Vacation Guide* of the Division of Economic Development, State House Annex, Concord, lists the resort areas and their activities.

National and international competitors take part in the *Alpine ski meets* during Mar. at Cranmore, Wildcat, and Cannon mts. *Dartmouth College's Winter Carnival* at Hanover in Feb. always draws national attention. Berlin, site of the first ski club in the U.S., is the home of the nation's highest steel *ski jump tower*. About six *sled dog races* are held in Lincoln, Tamworth, Meredith, Pittsfield, and Manchester. The season's climax is the world's sled dog championships at Laconia in late Feb.

RECOMMENDED READING. *Tales of the White Hills,* by Nathaniel Hawthorne; *The Government of New Hampshire,* by Leonard S. Morrison; *Indian Legends of the White Mountains,* by J. S. English; *Mount Washington Reoccupied,* by Robert S. Monohan; *The Devil and Daniel Webster,* by Stephen Vincent Benét.

MAINE

Sculpted by Glaciers, Slashed by the Sea

For many travelers, a trip to Maine is a journey into the past in a very alive present. Aspects of the past, not only of the state's recorded history, but also of unrecorded eras, walk hand in hand across summer's bright and sparkling days. It is like a special gift Maine subtly gives, a gift of a sometimes gentle, sometimes awesome, sense of timelessness.

This gift, which adds immeasurably to the visitor's enjoyment and understanding of this unique state, may appear at any time, anywhere, quietly, unexpectedly. Perhaps it will be interwoven in the soft soughings of an outgoing tide, or perhaps in a pine-needle-carpeted woodland, or at the edge of a briny cove. Suddenly the visitor senses the ages, all mixed together in a marvelous kaleidoscope of present, past and trackless time.

Against a background of lobster boats bobbing on blue waters, of coastal houses, their yards heaped with the ubiquitous piles of firewood and mounds of lobster traps, of men, singly or in groups, mending nets, he may realize these present-day aspects are almost as old as the records of the first settlers. The scent of birchwood may send his mind reeling back to a half-forgotten childhood—and then beyond. Back perhaps a thousand years, or further, when this same scent signalled warmth and refuge to the coastal Indians.

Today's life may encompass the melancholy clangs of a restless bell buoy, the deep-throated admonitions of a fog horn, the raucous cries of saucy gulls, the distant booming of a returning tide. There are the soft sighs of a vagabond breeze in some nearby pines, the staccato crack of a clam or mussel shell just dropped from on high to a rocky ledge by a hungry gull. But, except for the bells and the horns, these things have been here–since when?

And one day, the traveler begins to see the face of Maine, to note how it was carved and scarred by the great glaciers that long, long ago bulldozed their way relentlessly south. Now his mind reaches back still further, for what is now was then.

And so this subtle timelessness becomes an intimate part of one's sense of Maine's being, intricately interwoven with its history, for since days before recorded time, Maine's history has also been the story of nature and man walking down the centuries together.

Maine's Simple Complexity

In a dates-and-places sense one finds Maine's history is both simple and complex. Its simplicity stems from its having gotten an early start (something like 1000 A.D.) and its then getting up a full head of steam by the early 1600's and marching right along in a 1-2-3 fashion.

Its complexity lies in the facts surrounding its status. As an Atlantic state it got a late start, only joining the Union as the State of Maine in 1820. And early in its life it had already become a hodgepodge of land grants, patents, and outright presents from a succession of English kings to a succession of favored subjects. At times, exactly who owned which portions of Maine reads like some of the genealogical tracings in the Bible.

To further complicate Maine's status in the scheme of things, until it became a separate state in 1820, it was first a part of a huge area that was shuffled around from one owner to another. It was once a part of the Massachusetts Bay Colony and, later, a part of the Commonwealth of Massachusetts, as the state of Massachusetts prefers to be called. And so it is sometimes difficult, particularly in major events, to separate the strands of Maine from those of Massachusetts.

But certain characteristics of Maine–things you can see today–go much further back than 1,000 A.D. More than many another area in the world, Maine bears the historical imprint of the last great Glacial Age. It's in her boulder-strewn hillsides and fields, in the presence of her 2,500 lakes and ponds, her five large rivers and her 5,000 small rivers and streams, in her coastline, which geologists label "drowned." As the great glaciers inched relentlessly forward, they gnawed at Maine's coast, working, working at sheer destruction. Instead, they left it one of the prettiest, laciest coastlines on the entire globe. Only Alaska, Chile, and Japan can begin to compare their coasts to its delicate traceries. Virtually no other area can claim that 250 miles of an otherwise straight coastline actually measures over 2,400 miles.

Discovering and Rediscovering Maine

The first person to actually pinpoint Maine in a written report was Giovanni da Verrazano, the same man for whom the world's longest suspension bridge is named. This happened in 1524, when he was out exploring for the French. Earlier, John and Sebastian Cabot had explored the entire New England coast. Their reports are said to have been the basis of England's later claim to this whole area. That's who the Cabots were working for at the time, though they were Italians by birth. John, the father, had been born Giovanni Caboto, in Genoa, and when his son was born in Venice, in 1476, he was probably christened Sebastiano.

The year following Verrazano's visit, the Portuguese Estevan Gomez came over to have a look around. He saw and liked the Penobscot and named it the River of Stags. He was working for the Spanish (nobody in those days ever seemed to explore for his own country).

In 1569, on the Gulf of Mexico, an incident occurred which led to the first Englishmen setting foot in Maine. Sir John Hawkins, miffed at three English sailors, stranded them on the shores of the gulf. Scarcely daunted, the trio set off on foot and walked all the way to Nova Scotia. They all talked about it later, of course, but one of them, David Ingram, wove the better yarns. He embellished and embroidered, and after a time his listeners began to surmise most of his talk was pure fabrication, including his accounts of the mythical city of Norumbega on the Penobscot.

So it wasn't until 11 years later that Sir Humphrey Gilbert sent John Walker out to have a look around. He visited the Penobscot region and went back home. Perhaps he was the taciturn type, or lacked enthusiasm. At any rate, nothing further is known to have happened until 1602, when Bartholomew Gosnold not only stopped on the Maine coast, but also did some trading. When he returned to Falmouth he brought with him furs, cedar, and sassafras. These caused fresh interest in the New World, and Martin Pring was sent out the following year to trade with the Indians. He made a careful exploration of the Maine coast from present-day York to Penobscot Bay and reported good fishing in the area.

Before anyone's interest had time to cool down, Capt. George Waymouth was in Maine waters the following year. James Rosier, chronicler, also obviously interested in sea food, said in his account of the voyage: "And towards night we drew with a small net of twenty fathoms very nigh the shore; we got about thirty very good and great lobsters . . . which I omit not to report, because it sheweth how great a profit fishing would be . . ." But trading with the Indians and lobstering weren't the only things Waymouth did. He also kidnapped five Indians. That just about did it. That the Indians' friends on shore were terribly distressed is obvious. But there was another side to the tale that had far-reaching consequences.

Everyone was fascinated by the Indians in England, but after awhile, when they stopped attracting so much attention, three of them went to live with Sir Ferdinando Gorges, the other two to Sir John Popham's house. Both men soon set about teaching Tahnedo, Amoret, Skicoworos, Maneddo, and Shaffacomoit the English language. Gorges and Popham weren't just being kind, as they wanted to learn as much as they could about the country across the Atlantic.

Meantime, the French had become so interested in the Maine coast that, under the aegis of Henry IV, a group of gentlemen adventurers sailed west. Samuel de Champlain, a member of the expedition, made detailed maps of the coastline and islands and sailed up the Penobscot to the site of present-day Bangor, which he found "most pleasant and agreeable." He also got to know the Indians, and his tact and courtesy is said to have impressed them so favorably that, then and there, were built the foundations of the amicable Indian-French relationship which was to last as long as the colonial French remained in Maine. And this just after England's Capt. Waymouth had pulled his famous snatch act, incurring Indian enmity.

Back in England, what Sir John Popham learned from his Indians inspired him to send out an expedition in 1606. Sailing too far south, they were captured by Spaniards. Sir John, his enthusiasm undiminished, sent out another 100 colonists the following year. On the peninsula south of present-day Bath they built a fort, "trencht and fortified yt with 12 pieces of ordnance, built howses . . ." The early account also notes they built a "pretty Pynnace of about some thirty tonne," which they called the *Virginia.* The Popham colonists probably didn't even consider important the fact they had produced the first ship built by Englishmen in North America, but they had.

Following a severe winter, all but 45 of the colonists returned to England. The ship that took them home returned in the spring with supplies and word for Captain Gilbert, then in command of the small remaining group, that his brother was "newly dead" and had left a rich inheritance. Deciding the fortune was too tempting he, and everyone else, "ymbarged and sett saile for England." Thus the Popham Colony gave up the place it would have shared with

Jamestown, Virginia, of being the first permanent English settlements in the New World.

The first person to give the name of New England to the coastline from Cape Cod to Nova Scotia was Captain John Smith (the same one who brought fame to Pocahontas, or vice versa). John Smith explored the entire area in 1614, sounding "about 25 excellent harbors" on the Maine coast. It was a busy time for Smith and his men, fishing, hunting, exploring, trading for furs, making maps. Still, they found time to plant a garden and, says Smith, it "served us for salads in June and July."

Up North to Down East

Quite possibly it was during this time—maybe earlier—that the puzzling expression "Down East" came into being. Actually, as anyone can tell from looking at a map, the coast of Maine does go east, but at the same time, it trends north, too, or *up*. However, what early mariners knew was that the prevailing winds blew from the southwest, as they do today. Therefore, they most frequently sailed with, or down the wind, as they moved east. Conversely, if the wind had been from the northeast, they would have had to "beat up" the coast. It may, as the king of Siam said, be a "puzzlement" to landlubbers, but to mariners it makes much sense.

Two years after John Smith's extensive visit, Captain Richard Vines, along with 16 other men, settled in at Fortunes Rocks, near Biddeford Pool. Sir Ferdinando Gorges had sent them out especially to learn if they could endure a Maine winter. This was not an idle gesture on Gorges' part. Not only had he talked with his three Indians, he had also had some long conversations with Martin Pring and John Smith following their voyages to Maine.

Vines and his men not only endured the Maine winter, they reported they had had a fine time and went on to marvel at the fact not one of them had suffered a headache all winter long. Actually, Vines was so enamoured of the area he came back with some of his friends about a decade later and settled down for the remainder of his life, thus establishing the first successful settlement on Maine's mainland.

By 1626 the Pilgrims, from Plymouth, had begun coming into Maine. They trapped along the Kennebec and elsewhere, and set up a trading post at Castine. There was an urgency about their operations as their transatlantic trip had been taken on an early version of the go-now, pay-later plan. Once they had settled in at Plymouth, they had to do some scurrying to meet their installments. Their trapping and trading successes annoyed the French: it was the beginning of many years of squabbling between them and the

British over the territory between the Penobscot and St. Croix Rivers. This bickering quickly turned to outright pillage when the Pilgrims set up another trading post to the east, at Machias. The French forthwith swept down and captured it.

About this time the French stronghold in Maine was further strengthened by the appearance of Baron de St. Castin. He was not only a friend of the Indians, he also married one. Settling in at what is now Castine, with the faithful Indian warriors he'd gathered about him, he proceeded to wreak havoc on the English in the area. He continued to do so until the spring of 1688, at which time Sir Edmund Andros, who was then governing much of New England, attacked Castine. This so enraged Castin, he swept down to destroy a number of settlements along the Maine coast. Thus King William's War (2nd Indian war) began. Due to the British wresting of Castine from the French, the influence of the latter in this particular area of Maine rapidly declined. However, four more French and Indian Wars were to follow.

But long before this, in 1675, King Phillip's War, first of those Americans call the French & Indian Wars, began. It raged for three years. By 1690, during King William's War, the French and Indians from Canada had become so destructive only four settlements in Maine continued to be inhabited. Though this war lasted nine years, it was finally ended by a treaty signed near present-day Brunswick, and still the settlers held steadfast.

The third war, which lasted 10 years, left Kittery, Wells, and York the only permanent English settlements in Maine. Those colonists who later filtered back were confronted with the fourth war in 1722, which ended in 1726. In that conflict a singular incident occurred which dealt a telling blow to the morale of the Indians. The English killed the Jesuit missionary Father Sébastien Râle, and the sway he had held over the Kennebec was ended. Father Râle had been one of the most beloved men in early Maine. The French liked him and many of the Abnaki Indians virtually adored him, for he lived among them, followed their ways, learned their language, and ever sought honest dealings for them.

Again, in 1732–33, a concerted effort was made to resettle Maine through offers of free land made by Massachusetts. Things moved along well until the outbreak, in 1744, of still another Indian war, the fifth. During this, King George's War, the colonists captured Louisbourg from the French. It was an outstanding feat, for in those days well-fortified Louisbourg was considered the Gibraltar of the New World. Though this war ended in 1748, the French and Indians were at it again in 1754, waging their sixth war. It was their final one, too, and though it lasted for six long years, the Indians had reached the end of their warrior days in Maine. Only a scattering of them appeared at the peace-making ceremony, faded into the forest, and vanished for good from military records.

But they left a great heritage.

History doesn't tell us when Maine's settlers stopped being Englishmen, Scotsmen, Irish, or French, German, Dutch, or any other of the scattering of peoples who early came to Maine. The end of the Revolutionary War, of course, made them officially Americans. But long before that they had become non-European. Long before, they had taken on many of the skills, knowledge, and lore of the Indians, and, in the doing, been permanently set apart from the British Isles and Europe. An independence, born of the downright need to do for themselves, became theirs. Now almost nothing could dampen the spirit of Maine's people.

Learning from the Indians

From the Indians they had learned to preserve apples, to bank their houses with fir branches against bitter weather, to make maple sap into syrup, and into cakes which they could carry with them. From them, too, they learned all about corn, squash, cranberries, blackberries, blueberries, and the turkey, and how to make and use snowshoes. Our popular backyard barbecues of today are a heritage of what they learned from the Abnaki about cooking food outdoors and keeping it warm.

Under the Indians' tutelage, they learned about clams and lobster, about fishing, hunting, and trapping, and all the attendant lore of the woods. And these things set them apart, made them stand tall. From the Indians, too, they learned how to be invisible in the forest, to live with the hardships nature imposes, to creep silently, to march Indian file, to track.

Maine men were tough, and hard, and quiet. In 1775, many of them joined Benedict Arnold in an almost hopeless trek to the wilderness, up north, to capture Quebec—Lexington, Concord, and Bunker Hill at their backs. The attack failed, but the march didn't: it proved the timbre of the American colonials.

The year 1775 also saw the first naval engagement of the American Revolution, fought off Machias, way Down East. One small boat from here attacked and captured the armed British schooner *Margaretta*. It was an insignificant little incident as big naval conflagrations go, but it is said to have inspired the Revolution's leaders' desire for a navy.

In 1778, the Revolution still going on, a chink began to appear in the armor that bound Maine to Massachusetts. The Continental Congress divided Maine into three electoral districts.

The Revolution over, Down Easters turned some of their efforts toward agitation for separation from Massachusetts. And then along came the Embargo Act, seriously hampering foreign trade, causing a severe depression in maritime-attuned Maine. But it didn't take them long to remember they had a border and a large smuggling operation soon swung into high-gear at Eastport.

Two years later the Embargo Act was lifted, but soon after, the War of 1812 broke out. Having gotten in a lot of practice during the time of the Embargo Act, the Maine and Canadian smugglers were soon at it again.

In 1813 the British brig *Boxer* was poking around off Pemaquid Point. This was probably a mistake. At any rate, the American brig *Enterprise* soon appeared on the scene, peaceful Pemaquid once again reverberated to the sounds of powder explosions, and the *Boxer* surrendered to the Americans. In 1814, the British, anchoring one end of their line at Castine, dug in all the way from there down east to the St. Croix River.

In 1815, a western migration began which built up to such great proportions in Maine and elsewhere that it was called "Ohio Fever." Perhaps the reason in Maine for the mounting exodus fever was the year "eighteen-hundred-and-froze-to-death." The winter was so cold, that's what the year became known as locally.

Then came the memorable year of 1820, the time when this 33,215-square-mile area joined the Union as the State of Maine. It was a busy state then: busy felling and shipping huge quantities of lumber, cutting ice from the Kennebec and other rivers, building ships.

Perhaps a legend of 18 years previous was true—perhaps not. It told about the first ship that Bath built and how, in 1802, when she was ready to sail, her captain didn't know where his port of New Orleans was. True or not, things were noticeably different by the time Maine became a state.

Yankee Clipper Days

Prior to the War of 1812 Maine had built a number of boats and quite a few ships, and as early as 1772 the first ship from the Kennebec had begun sailing back and forth to the West Indies. But it was the war that supplied the impetus to shipbuilding. The Down East people were spoiling for a fight with the British, legitimately and in privateering, but they needed ships to get into that fight. Besides, in 1803, Commodore Edward Preble had shown the mettle of a Maine man on the seas. In that year President Jefferson had chosen this Portland man to head up forces to sweep the Barbary pirates from the seas. So successful was Preble's campaign, the once-dreaded Barbary powers were willing to accept peace on any terms offered. Pope Pius VII was so impressed he said that Preble had "done more for Christianity in a short space of time than the most powerful nations have done in ages."

From then on, shipbuilding grew to such heights that in the 1830's Maine built more tonnage than any other state. In 1848, of the 428 brigs, barks, and ships built in America, Maine produced more than half. Those were exciting days. Most of the ships were owned or part-owned by their captains, and crew members were often friends, relatives, and neighbors. Martinique and Madeira became household words, as did Hong Kong and Jamaica, Calcutta, and Curaçao. In turn, places like Portland, Bangor, Searsport, Wiscasset, and Damariscotta became well-known throughout the world. Kennebec ice became so famous for its high quality that even in London, icemen's wagons were lettered with the words Kennebec Ice—even if it didn't happen to be.

Captains often took their wives along, sometimes on voyages that lasted several years. Maine children were born in Rangoon, Colombo, and Shanghai, and wives bought their own silks and china in the bazaars at Canton and Bombay. Back home, rooms were furnished with *objets d'art,* tables, chests, and rugs from far-flung shores. Life was as big to these State-of-Mainers as the world was wide.

Meantime, back home, in 1839, boundary trouble brewing between Canada and Maine almost burst into war. Suddenly Maine had 10,000 troops in the Aroostook region, President Van Buren was authorized to raise 50,000 troops, and $10 million was appropriated to back up possible future action. Things continued to boil off and on from then until 1842, when the Webster-Ashburton Treaty fixed the northeastern boundary and all parties were sufficiently satisfied.

During the Civil War, 72,945 Maine men fought under the Union flag, and the state contributed $18 million. And though not widely known, the war came right to Maine when a Confederate naval officer and his men, disguised as fishermen, seized the revenue cutter, *Caleb Cushing.* In short order, however, several local boats put out after them, and the Confederates, finding no ammunition aboard, burned the *Caleb Cushing,* went over the side into lifeboats, and were taken prisoners.

After the Civil War, shipbuilding declined and more and more people moved inland. As shipping went down, rail transportation rose, and by 1870 it was well established. With the coming of the railroads Maine's popularity as a summer vacationland began and has, with the exception of war years, grown.

Snow on Independence Day

It might have suffered a set back, though, in 1879. Portland had a freak snowstorm that year, on July 4th. It may have indicated that

Maine weather, too, was asserting its independence, just as it did in late September, in 1965, with temperatures soaring into the 90's.

It is true, even today, that the modern Maine man, town or country, doesn't waste words, and for a good reason. In this day of the ubiquitous transistor, it can be a blessing. The Maine man isn't cold or unfriendly. Chances are he's got one eye on a sudden shift in the wind, a fog bank building on the horizon, a patch of herringbone clouds to the southwest. No, right now, he hasn't got time for idle chatter. Chances are, if you find a talkative Down Easter, you'll soon learn he's actually from Massachusetts, New York, or some place else west of Maine. He may have liked what he saw on a vacation here and settled down in Maine, 15, maybe 20 years ago. Still, by Maine standards, he's an outlander, what the Down Easter distinguishes from the summer visitor by referring to him as "an all-year-around summer visitor." As a local expression goes, "If your cat has her kittens in the oven you don't call them biscuits."

Through it all, the spirit of the early men and women still strides the forests, fields, and shores, perhaps because the Maine of today so obviously derives its heritage from the settlers, those early people who began with nothing. And yet from nothing, they built a fine, fair land and a people of principle, honor, and courage.

PRACTICAL INFORMATION FOR MAINE

MAINE FACTS & FIGURES. There are various theories about the origin of the state's name: that it came from the French province of Mayne; that it refers to the "mainland," to set it apart from the offshore islands; that it simply means "important." The state's nickname is *Pine Tree State. Dirigo* ("I direct") is the state motto. *State of Maine Song* is the state song. The white pine cone and tassel is the state flower; the white pine, the state tree; the chickadee, the state bird.

Augusta is the state capital. The state population is 969,265.

Bordering Canada, the northernmost of the 48 mainland states, and the biggest of the five New England states, Maine is famous for the rugged beauty of its rocky, indented coastline, dotted with hundreds of small islands and dozens of popular beach resorts. Most of the state is covered with forests, mountains, and lakes. The forests and the sea supply a major source of the state's wealth. Maine's skilled fishermen bring in a varied catch, but it is the Maine lobster that has achieved international fame. And the Down East farmer is known for his excellent Maine potatoes, grown in flat and fertile Aroostook County in the north of the state. Maine has cool summers, cold winters.

HOW TO GET AROUND. By car, the 4-lane *Maine Turnpike* leads from the New Hampshire line to Augusta. Highway network includes main roads branching out in 6 directions; also third-class roads in five directions. *Route numbers* are US 201 and 202, State 100, 104, 105, 3, 9, 11, 17, 24, and 27. *Airline Route 9* saves 56 miles of driving between Bangor and Calais. *Blue Star Memorial Highway* (US 1) links Kittery, the southernmost town, to Fort Kent, the most northerly town.

Maine is served by *Greyhound* and *Trailways,* plus an intrastate bus system. *Taxis* are readily available, telephone-radio equipped for faster service. Taxi fare from Portland Airport to downtown is about $1.50 for the 3-mi. ride. *Car rental* is no problem. You can be in the driver's seat at Northeast Airlines Terminals in Augusta or Bangor, at Bar Harbor Airways terminal, Bar Harbor, or just about anywhere in the state.

Augusta Airport is about 2 miles from the business district and provides service to Boston, New York, Washington, D.C., Maritime Provinces. Facilities for private planes. *Commercial airports* also in Portland, Rockland, Lewiston. *Small planes* may land at *Wiscasset Airport* (Boothbay Harbor). *Aerial Enterprises, Inc.,* at Wiscasset Airport has charter flights. *Bar Harbor Airways, Inc.,* Bar Harbor Airport, connects between Portland and Boston; air taxi to New England or Canada; sightseeing flights over Acadia National Park. *Seaplane landings* are possible in East Boothbay, Boothbay Harbor.

Car Ferries. Maine leads all of the New England States in the number of ferries; in Boothbay Harbor alone, there are 40 ferry sailings a day. *Maine State Ferry Service,* Rockland, serves Islesboro, North Haven, Swan's Island, Vinalhaven. Also, there are new car ferries from McKinley to Swan's Island, from Rockland to North Haven, Rockland to Vinalhaven. The *MV Bluenose Ferry* provides passenger-auto service between Bar Harbor and Yarmouth, Nova Scotia.

Cable Car Rides. The double chair lift on *Saddleback Mt.,* new in 1964, offers a spectacular mountaintop view all year round. The *Pleasant Mt.* ski area in Bridgton also features a year-round chair lift.

On Foot. By hiking, the visitor will see much magnificent scenery. *Marked trails* begin at Bethel, Denmark, Eustis, Rumford, Rangeley, Wilton, etc. *Acadia National Park* has hiking trails. The *Appalachian Trail* is the longest of all—all the way to Georgia! *Horses* may be rented to follow the bridle paths in Acadia National Park. Stables are conveniently located in all areas.

Boats. It's as easy to rent a boat as a car in Maine. Up north, much of the boat service is handled by sporting camps. The newest marina is the Lok Marina at Camden. Canoeing is another favorite way of getting around.

Railroads. Maine is serviced by *Boston & Maine* and *Maine Central.* Train trip from New York to Portland takes about 9 hours.

SEASONAL EVENTS. *Fairs.* In the good old summertime, it's a fair estimate that there are at least 26 communities featuring agricultural fairs from the end of July to the middle of Oct. Here, too, you will find gymkhanas—a series of contests, mainly racing. July is a big *festival* month in Maine, beginning with *Strawberry Festivals* in Kennebunkport and Greenville Junction; *Potato Festivals* in Fort Kent, Houlton, and Fort Fairfield—and there's a *Bean Hole Bean Festival* the end of July in So. Paris. A *Folk Dance Festival* in Bridgton swings out the first of the month. Famous festivals are the *Maine Broiler Festival* in Belfast the 2nd week in July; the *Maine Seafoods Festival,* Rockland, first week in Aug.; the *Blueberry Festival,* Union, the end of Aug. August also boasts the Mt. Desert Island *Festival of Chamber Music,* Northeast Harbor.

Fourth of July is *parade* time throughout the state. One of the most colorful parades is scheduled usually June 20—*St. John's Day,* celebrated by Knights Templar Masons for their patron saint. Inquire for time and location. *Races.* Fourth of July is celebrated also with *lobster boat races* at Bass Harbor. Also, there are Fourth of July *pony races* at Vacationland Downs, Yarmouth. Regional *sports car races* are scheduled in summer at Norridgewock. *Sailing races* include the Friendship Sloop Regatta, Friendship, the end of July; Retired Skippers Race, Castine, Aug. 23. *Harness racing* is featured at all agricultural fairs.

Pari-mutuel betting at Scarborough Downs (night *horse racing)* from middle of July to Sept.

Shows. Antique shows are popular with both natives and tourists. Some of the popular ones are the *Annual Antiques Show,* Camden, last week in July; *Annual Kennebunk Antique Fair,* Kennebunk, first week in Aug.; *Open House Antique Show,* Boothbay Harbor, middle of August; *Annual Antiques Show and Sale,* Bath Armory, Bath. *Horse shows* are held from the second week in July through the middle of Oct. in the following towns (inquire for schedule): Windsor *(All Morgan Show),* Springvale, Boothbay Harbor, Belfast, Bangor, Gorham, Fairfield, Skowhegan, Camden, Rangeley, Acton, Hampden, Farmington, Topsham. At least 30 *flower shows* are scheduled from July to Oct. The most popular is the *Maine Rose Show,* Portland, the end of June; also the *Maine State Gladiolus Society Show,* Augusta, the end of Aug. *Deer Isle* has a flower show in the Parish House the end of Aug. There are about 20 garden clubs in the state. An *Annual Art Show* is held in Town Hall, York, from the 3rd week in July to middle of Aug.; an arts, crafts and hobby show is held in Stonington the end of July. Houlton features an art show the 3rd week in July; West Harpswell has an Annual Art Show the 3rd week in Aug. There's a *Sportsmen's Show,* Rockwood, first week in June and *air shows* at Rockland Municipal Airport (end of Aug.) and Millinocket (2nd week in July).

Special Days. Windjammer Days are held the second week in July, Boothbay Harbor. A *Lumberjack Roundup* is held in Ashland the 2nd week in July. *Navy Day,* Oct. 27, means Open House at Naval Air Station, Brunswick. There is usually a *Junior Miss Queen Contest,* Fort Fairfield, third week in July; also a *Miss York Vacationland* contest at the Pavilion in York.

Tournaments. The annual *Tuna Tournament* is held the end of July, Bailey's Island; *Deep Sea Fishing Derby,* Cape Elizabeth, last week in Aug. Summer *golf tournaments* (check for dates and places) include Maine Left-Handers Championship, New England Amateur Championship, Maine Open.

TOURIST INFORMATION SERVICES. Maine distributes many colorful folders and brochures which are a great help to the visitor. Information sources are *Maine Dept. of Economic Development,* State Office Building, Augusta, Maine 04330; *State of Maine Publicity Bureau,* 11 Chapel St., Augusta, Maine; *State Park & Recreation Commission,* State Office Building, Augusta, Maine 04330; *Inland Fisheries and Game Dept.,* State Office Building, Augusta, Maine 04330.

STATE PARKS. Most of the 14 state parks open for the season Apr. 15. Usually the season extends to Nov. and Dec. Except for *Baxter State Park,* no campsite reservations are required—they are on a first-come, first-served basis. All have excellent facilities. Leash required for pets; no pets in Baxter State Park.

Aroostook, Presque Isle. Lifeguards on the beach. *Baxter* (includes Mt. Katahdin). Drive there from Millinocket, Patten, Greenville. Sportsmen's camps are on Nesowadnehunk Lake and Togue Ponds. *Bradbury Mountain,* Pownal. Fun for families—big play area. *Camden Hills,* Camden. Good freshwater and saltwater fishing. Many miles of foot trails. *Cobscook Bay,* near Dennysville, Washington County. Newest state park (formerly part of Moosehorn National Wildlife Refuge).

Lake St. George, State 3, Liberty. Campsites and picnic grounds right on lake shore. Arrive early; very popular. *Lamoine,* East Lamoine. Good for boating and swimming. *Lily Bay,* Greenville. Excellent salmon and trout fishing in Moosehead Lake. Very popular. *Moose Point,* US 1, Searsport. No swimming or camping. Excellent for picnics. *Mount Blue,* Weld. Good swimming in Lake Webb; boat rental; fishing. Center Hill is high picnic area.

Quoddy Head, Lubec. No camping. Beautiful spot for picnics. Tides here greatest in U.S.A.—20 to 28 feet. Easternmost point of land in U.S.A. *Reid,* Georgetown. Very popular for sand beaches and warm saltwater tidal pool. No camping; good picnic grounds. *Sebago Lake,* Naples and Casco. Casco for excellent swimming; Naples for camping, swimming, boating. Songo Lock operated daily for Sebago Lake to Songo River boat trips. One-day wait for campsites. *Two Lights,* Cape Elizabeth. No camping or swimming. Magnificent scenery and good picnic area. Only 9 miles from Portland.

DRINKING LAWS. State stores sell packaged liquor; beer at grocery stores. No Sunday sales. State-owned stores open Mon. through Sat., 9:30 a.m. to 5:30 p.m. Age limit, 21.

Drinks in hotels and restaurants until midnight; to 11:45 p.m. Sat. No liquor on Election Day (polling hours), or before noon May 30.

NATIONAL PARKS. *Acadia National Park* encompasses a tremendous area—more than 30,000 acres—on Mt. Desert Island in Bar Harbor vicinity. Camping and trailer sites, also picnic areas, are plentiful. Picnic grounds and all campgrounds are free. Campfire evenings three times a week. Ranger naturalists are available for seashore walks and cruises around the Park area. There are 100 miles of hiking trails; also a road to the top of Cadillac Mountain with spectacular views all along the route.

Horseback riding is part of the fun. Swimming is doubly enjoyable with a choice of salt or fresh water. Watch the surf crash into a rocky ravine (Thunder Hole) and visit the tide pool at Anemone Cave. On the Atlantic Flyway, birdwatchers will spot everything from a heron to an eagle. Lots of wildlife too—deer, beaver, raccoon, fox.

Two of the free park campgrounds are at Black Woods and Seawall; two-week camping limit, no trailer hookups. Although the park is open all year, camping is allowed from May to Oct. Pets require leash (not permitted on beaches). Check at the Bar Harbor Information Office, Main and Park Sts., or write to Superintendent, Acadia National Park, Bar Harbor.

White Mountain National Forest is partly in Maine, southwest of Bethel. There are free campsites, hiking trails, picnic grounds, tables, fireplaces.

INDIANS. The Maine *Penobscot Indians* belonged to the North American Indian, Algonquian linguistic stock. The Penobscots were the most numerous in the Abnaki Confederacy and lived in the Penobscot Bay area in the 17th century. The Penobscots supported the French and were active in all the frontier wars. The 1749 treaty with the English caused ill-feeling with other tribes of the Abnaki group, who stayed faithful to the French. However, the Penobscots were so helpful to the American patriots during the Revolution that they gained a reservation in Old Town. About 500 Indians live there now. At one time their tribe numbered up to 1,500. Indian crafts are sold on Indian Island near Old Town; their annual festival is in August.

On *Maine Indian Day,* July 25, the Penobscot tribe portrays ancient ceremonies and legends. Two performances are at 2 and 7 p.m., beginning with a parade of canoes down the Penobscot River to a re-created Indian Village. The place is Indian Island, Old Town.

Passamaquoddy tribes live in the townships of Princeton and Perry, where baskets and souvenirs may be purchased.

WHERE TO GO. Motorists may enter the state via *Kittery*, noted for the Lady Pepperrell House, John Paul Jones Memorial Park. *York Village* has the Old Gaol Museum (1653), Wilcox House, Elizabeth Perkins House, Jefferd's Tavern, Old Schoolhouse, Old Burying Ground, and York Golf and Tennis Club. Nubble Light, or Cape Neddick Light, is a landmark. York Beach is an ocean resort. *Kennebunk* has the Brick Store Museum, Wedding Cake House, Kennebunk Beach. *Kennebunkport* is a seaport town with playhouse, Arundel Opera Theatre, Yacht Club, Seashore Trolley Museum.

Ogunquit is noted for the Marginal Way, Ogunquit Art Association, Ogunquit Playhouse. *Old Orchard* is a favorite beach resort. *Prout's Neck* was the home of artist Winslow Homer. *Scarborough* features car races; pari-mutuel horse racing at Scarborough Downs. *Bath* has the Bath Marine Museum; also Bath Golf Club. *Brunswick* is the seat of Bowdoin College, with Museum of Art; Harriet Beecher Stowe House; Brunswick Summer Playhouse. *Freeport* includes an Audubon Society sanctuary; also desert dunes.

Portland has Portland Museum of Art, Observatory, Wadsworth-Longfellow House, Old Tate House, Portland Head Light, Cape Elizabeth Light, Two Lights State Park. *Topsham* has quarries. *Yarmouth* is known for Old Indian Burying Ground.

Boothbay is a resort area with Boothbay Playhouse. Boothbay Harbor is setting for windjammers, regattas, 45 excursion sailings daily; location of Marine Aquarium. *Warren* has Indian mounds, ancient cemeteries, Sandy Shores beach. *Pemaquid Harbor* is site of Pemaquid Point lighthouse. *Damariscotta* is vacation area. *Wiscasset* is picturesque seaport (open-house day Aug.). *Belfast* has Curling Society, center of Maine Broiler industry, Perry's Tropical Nut House. *Camden* has Penobscot Bay cruises; weekly sailing races; new road up to Mt. Battie, Edna St. Vincent Millay Memorial Room.

Friendship is where the seals play. *Islesboro* is resort in Penobscot Bay (square dances Wed. night at Dark Harbor). *Monhegan* is island favored by artists. *North Haven* has excellent beaches. *Rockport* is popular resort; also known for Gen. Henry Knox Mansion (1795). *Vinalhaven* is lobster port. *Rockland* is scene of 3-day Maine Seafoods Festival in Aug., birthplace of poet Edna St. Vincent Millay, site of Farnsworth Homestead. *Gorham* has night harness racing in July. *Union* is famous for Aug. Blueberry Festival. *Bucksport* is site of Jed Prouty Tavern. *Castine* has Retired Skippers Race late Aug. *Searsport* is known for Penobscot Marine Museum.

Bar Harbor is popular summer resort. Also entrance to Acadia National Park, with geological wonders, glacial formations, first view of sunrise in America from Mt. Cadillac. *Seal Harbor* has monument to Champlain. *Isle au Haut* is legendary hiding place of Capt. Kidd's treasure. *Machias* is site of Burnham Tavern (1770). *Jonesport* is fishing village; sardine canneries. *Calais* has Moosehorn Wildlife Sanctuary; also marker for 45th parallel of latitude. *St. Croix Island* is a national monument—Champlain spent winter here. *Eastport* is famous for immense tides; Quoddy Village. *Lubec* is known for 20-ft. tides; Quoddy Head Light, easternmost point in U.S.A. Free bridge to *Campobello Island* in Canada, site of Pres. Franklin D. Roosevelt summer home. *West Pembroke* is known for Reversing Falls and nearby picnic area.

Bangor is birthplace of Paul Bunyan (statue), covered bridge, Cascades Park with 45-foot falls. *Peter Dana Pt.* has Indian reservation. *Kenduskeag* has covered bridge. *Old Town* has large Indian reservation. *Orono* is known for *Maine Stein Song* sung by students of University of Maine. *Andover* is noteworthy for Telstar site on Space Hill (daily tours); covered bridge. *Auburn* has semiprecious stones for rockhounds, Lost Valley Ski Area, Androscoggin Historical Society.

Augusta is state capital; State House (designed by Charles Bulfinch), Blaine

Above: Enclaves of tranquillity, such as Walden Pond, to which Thoreau retreated, can still be found in New England.
(B. D. Laschever)

Overleaf: Vermont is a leader in America's fast-growing sport.
(Stowe News Bur.)

Ski Shop
RENTAL SKIS
SKI REPAIRS
WAXING
STORAGE

Above: Summer vacationers on their way to a Cabbage Island clambake, off Boothbay Harbor, Me.
(Me. Dept. of Econ. Dev.)

Below: Old Ironsides, on view in Boston, never lost a battle.
(Mass. Dept. of Comm.)

Mansion. *Bethel* has Sunday River Skiway, near White Mt. National Forest. *Chesterville* has bird sanctuary. *Fryeburg* is home of Admiral Robert E. Peary. *Gray* has State Game Farm and Fish Hatchery open for visitors. *Lakewood* is popular resort; Lakewood Theatre. *Lewiston* is home of Bates College (tours arranged); Stanton Bird Club Sanctuary welcomes visitors, Mt. David has view of city. *Lynchville* is known for famous signpost with foreign city names—all Maine towns. *New Gloucester* has State Trout Hatchery. *Newry* is known for Screw Auger Falls, Horseshoe Falls, covered bridge. *Norridgewock* is old Indian village; drag races held here. *Poland Spring* is home of famous Poland Spring House resort; also site of Shaker Village; excellent skiing. See State of Maine building from Chicago World's Fair on resort grounds.

Rangeley Lakes Region has chair lifts to Bald Mountain and Saddleback Mt., swimming in Rangeley Lakeside Park, covered bridge at *Wilson's Mills*. Moontide Spring at *Rumford*. Mount Blue State Park has observation tower; excellent skiing. *Sebago-Long Lakes Region* is noteworthy for landlocked salmon, Sebago Lake State Park, Wade Fish Hatchery, vacation area for 150 years. *Naples* and *Casco* are history-filled towns. *South Paris* has Snow Falls and photogenic gorge. *Turner* has Bear Pond Amusement Park. *Waterville* is home of Colby College.

In the North Country, *Brownville Junction* is known as the Grand Canyon of the East. *Caribou* has a State Fish Hatchery open to visitors. *Dover-Foxcroft* has a covered bridge. *Fort Fairfield* contains potato fields galore (Potato Festival last week July). See potato blossoms late July to Aug. *Moosehead Lake* is largest New England lake. *Guilford* has a covered bridge. *Houlton* celebrates with a Potato Festival late July; also has horse-racing track. *Littleton* has a covered bridge; State Fish Hatchery welcomes visitors. *Presque Isle* is famous for potatoes; harness racing July and Aug. Flap-Jack Carnival late July; Aroostook State Park, Echo Lake; skiing on Mars Hill Mt. Free tours at Aroostook Experimental Potato Farm.

WHAT TO DO WITH THE CHILDREN. York Beach, York, includes *Animal Forest Park* with tame animals for petting and feeding. *Amusement Area* includes Enchanted Village, Mother Goose Land, 25 rides, a fun house, miniature golf. Old Orchard Beach area is noted for *Palace Playland*, a new *Animal Fair and Game Farm* across from the Country Club on State 98, and an *aquarium* on Ocean Pier.

Old Sand Farm Park, Desert Road, Freeport, has a *Fun Barn*, burro rides, guided tours in horse-and-buggy, nature trails. Snacks served at Oat Bin.

Trolley Museum in Kennebunkport features open trolley rides plus 70 old trolleys on exhibit. *Boothbay Railway Museum*, State 27 near Boothbay Harbor, offers rides on the narrow-gauge railroad; and there's a picnic area. The *Bath Marine Museum*, 963 Washington St., Bath, opened June 1965 and includes displays for children marked "Please Touch." This includes a ship's bell for ringing. *The Circus Farm*, Fryeburg, has *Punch and Judy* shows; also a picnic area. *Vacationland Downs*, Yarmouth, is open daily to visitors who wish to tour the stables. The *Game Farm and Fish Hatchery, Gray*, are interesting. Open daily from 8 a.m. to 5 p.m. For older children accompanied by parents, a half-day trip may be arranged on lobster boats out of one of the fishing ports.

(The above are all summer activities.)

EXPLORING MAINE

Gazing at a map of the United States a young boy recently remarked: "I like Maine best. It looks like a rabbit's head." Then, apparently still musing over Maine, he added, "The rabbit's wet." And the youngster patiently explained that by noting that the rabbit's neck was wet because the fur was matted together in little points.

It is this wet-neck appearance that accounts for the astounding fact that although Maine's coastline, when measured straight, is only 250 miles long, it is actually, with all its capes and peninsulas, more than 2,400 miles in length. This is the sort of thing which ought to bring delight to the heart of the touring vacationer. The scope Maine offers is virtually endless. There are those who say it would take a whole lifetime to know Maine's coast well. Another lifetime, they aver, could be spent exploring the more than 2,000 islands that lie just offshore. A third lifetime could, of course, be devoted to exploring Maine's hinterlands, that vast mosaic of lakes, ponds, mountains, rivers, and streams.

Actually, exploring Maine is both simpler and more complex than many another state. Its simplicity derives from the long coastline that sweeps down East from the New Hampshire border, hugged generally by venerable Route 1. Traveling in the interior, too, is somewhat simplified, especially in the entire northern half, for here so few roads exist that making route decisions is no problem.

The complexities exist in peninsular Maine, in the vast, drowned, wet-rabbit coastline that turns 250 miles of straight coastline into those 2,400 miles of shore. Which capes, which peninsulas to investigate, does require decisions.

Complexities exist, too, in the southwest quarter of Maine where a number of crisscrossing roads invite the traveler to explore a large number of areas, full of cities, towns, villages, mountains, hills, streams and lakes.

To explore Maine's coast the general rule is to stick to Route 1 and, where time allows, dip right, on to Route 1-A, as it appears off and on.

Although there are roads that lead into Maine from New Hampshire and Canada's Quebec Province, the majority of travelers plunge in just beyond Portsmouth, New Hampshire, on the north shore of the Piscataqua River. At Kittery, at the junction of Route 1 and the Maine Turnpike (Route 95), a handsome, white-clapboard building awaits the traveler. It is the Maine Information Center, which dispenses brochures and information about all areas of Maine, as well as the Maine Vacationland Map.

Leaving the center, take Route 1 north to Route 1-A and the Yorks: York Village, York Harbor, York Beach and Cape Neddick. The Yorks are a little corner of Maine that tourism hasn't garnished with myriad road signs, eating shacks, etc., unlike the area just to colonial atmosphere, was the nation's first city with a charter, and the north. York Village, a charming bit of Maine, brim-ful of colonial atmosphere, was the nation's first city with a charter, and the site of the first sawmill (1672). The Old Gaol, which you may visit, is believed the oldest remaining public building (1653) of the English colonies (there are some beautiful crewel embroidery pieces here). The First Parish Church is the first church built in the colonies after that of Jamestown, Virginia. There are a number of other buildings to visit here: the beautifully furnished Wilcox House, Jefferds' Tavern (1750), the Old School House, and the Elizabeth Perkins House, a Colonial home furnished as it was by its last occupants in the Victorian era.

Just out from the Yorks is Fort McClary, in an area fortified as early as 1715. William Pepperell (the family keeps walking through the pages of Maine's early history) once commanded here, and nearby is the Lady Pepperell House. This was built after the death of William Pepperell, the son of the first-mentioned William and hero of the battle for Louisbourg. The beautifully furnished house is noted for its great fireplaces, its fine woodwork.

Mark Twain Vacationed Here

Driving around the Yorks you're sure to cross Sewall's Bridge, a replica of the original, built in 1761. It was the first pile drawbridge in America, and Major Samuel Sewall had to invent a triphammer pile driver in order to build it. Another Samuel connected with this area is Samuel Clemens, for Mark Twain used to summer at a house near the bridge.

At the foot of Lindsay Street in York Village you'll find the John Hancock Wharf still standing. It was once owned by the signer of the Declaration of Independence who wrote his name so large. The area from here, east to the handsome resort hotel, *Marshall House,* used to be called the Market Place. A stipulation in York's original charter stated that fairs should be held here each year on St. James' Day and St. Paul's Day "forever," and historians believe these were the forerunner of all the state and county fairs which are still so much a part of the American rural scene.

Beyond York Village and York Harbor (where boats will take you cruising and fishing), continuing on Route 1-A, is York Beach, with its Short Sands and Long Sands, both hard-packed and popular beaches. Just past Long Sands, turn right on Nubble Road for Cape

Neddick and a fine view of the Atlantic, the Maine coast to the north, and the offshore Isles of Shoals.

Returning to Route 1-A turn right, following the Shore Road to Ogunquit. Look for signs reading variously Cliff House & Motels and Bald Head. Turn right here for Bald Head Cliff where, on a rough day you can see some fantastic surf and on any day can marvel at the view and the huge rocks whose grain runs the wrong way.

Back on the Shore Road you'll soon come to the well-known Ogunquit Museum of Art, followed in quick succession by a cluster of artists' studios, galleries and shoppes. There's a magnificent white-sand beach here that did a lot to bring Ogunquit its fame, along with such magnets as the Ogunquit Art Center, the Barn Gallery and the Ogunquit Playhouse. Eve Arden, Hans Conreid, Walter Pidgeon, Darin McGavin, and Arlene Francis are among the many stars who have appeared here.

Perkins Cove is here, too, and although some working boats dot the cove, it has become a Bohemian's haven, crowded in summer with artists. Ogunquit's Marginal Way is famous, too—a narrow footpath which winds along the cliffs. Sea gulls soar on high and there are beaches and tidal pools below for the exploring.

Many Maine writers plaintively point out that this is not the "Real Maine," but it has its appealing side and is a busy center each summer.

Just beyond Wells, on Route 1-A, turn right on to Route 9, to visit the Kennebunks, a cluster of settlements of the same genre as Ogunquit. and an area given more to the stay-put summer visitor than the touring vacationer.

You'll find Kennebunkport is a colorful little town, if you can separate your gaze from the traffic and crowds long enough to take a good long look. It was probably a lot quieter when Kenneth Roberts *(Northwest Passage, Lydia Bailey, Oliver Wiswell),* and Booth Tarkington *(Penrod, Seventeen, The Magnificent Ambersons),* used to summer in the area. Kenneth Roberts was born here, too, in the General Storer House, in Kennebunk.

There's another famous summer theater here (Jean Pierre Aumont, Marisa Pavan, Kitty Carlisle and Pat O'Brien were among 1965 headliners), and the Olde Grist Mill. It has been owned and operated by one family for over 200 years, first as a mill, now as a restaurant, so if you're hungry about this time, it's a fine place to try old-fashioned New England dishes.

Now follow Route 9 north to Cape Porpoise, a charming projection of land with fine seascapes, lobster boats and sea gulls. When you get to Cape Porpoise bear right, following the sign "To the

Harbor," which you'll find at the end of the little cape. It got its name from Capt. John Smith, who saw a school of porpoise here.

Now return to Route 9 and then 9-A, 35, and drive up 35 to see the Wedding Cake House. Fancier than it is beautiful, local legend says it was built by a sea captain for his bride, but that before it was finished he was suddenly called to sea. Rather than postpone their wedding indefinitely they married hastily, with no time for a reception. To compensate for this the captain had the house finished off to look like the missed wedding cake.

Returning to Kennebunk on Route 35, look for the Brick Store Museum (117 Main St.). The work of professional and amateur artists and craftsmen is displayed here, as well as articles of early American life.

Ask for directions to Log Cabin Road and drive out to see the Seashore Trolley Museum, world's largest electric railway museum. There are nearly 100 old trolleys here (you can take a ride on one), from France, Germany, Japan, England, Canada and, of course, from U.S. cities. Continue north on the Log Cabin Road to Route 1, where you turn right.

Continue on Route 1 to Old Orchard Beach. It's reputedly one of the longest beaches on the Atlantic. French-Canadians hustle down from the north in droves each summer, and teenagers love the Coney Island, hot-dog, merry-go-round atmosphere. To avoid the beach, continue north on Route 1 and turn right on Route 207 (a small sign indicates the way to Scarboro), and you'll be in Winslow Homer country. This is also William King country, for this is where Maine's first governor, at the time Maine joined the Union, was born. His story of rags to riches was so much a Maine–and an American–story that it was entirely fitting he should have been the first governor. When his father died, William, then seven, went to work in a sawmill. When he was 19, he took his only possessions, two steers (legend says he still didn't own any shoes) and drove them to Bath. From working in a sawmill there, he went on to acquire a mill, then timberland, and in a few years was building his own boats and shipping his own cargo. He rose to great wealth and prestige, and, since all during his rise he continually advocated separate statehood for Maine (apart from Massachusetts), it seems just right that this barefoot lad should have become the State of Maine's first governor.

Scenes that Homer Painted

Just beyond Scarboro the western side of this peninsula is a beautiful stretch of marshland, ever-changing in color and shape as light and shadow play across it. At sunset the reflections are magnificent. Just beyond, at Prout's Neck, near the luxury resort

Black Point Inn, Winslow Homer used to live and paint. The Prout's Neck Bird Sanctuary here was given by Winslow's brother Charles in memory of the great painter whose stature continues to grow as the years pass.

But perhaps even here, like William King who went off to Bath to found his fortune, you'll feel you haven't yet found "your Maine," the Maine where you're going to feel you've really arrived. Many travelers find theirs in different places. Kenneth Roberts in *Trending Into Maine,* claims, for instance—and he pins the opinion not on himself, but on those people who know Maine well—that if you don't know what Maine ought to look like, you still won't "until you've crossed the Kennebec." To some these are fighting words, while others suggest "your Maine" often consists of bits and pieces, picked up here and there (such as at Prout's Neck with its lovely seascapes, its dramatic marshland scenes). Eventually these bits and pieces fit into place to form your personal mosaic that is Maine.

For instance, following Route 77 north from Prout's Neck you'll come to the famed Two Lights Lighthouse at Cape Elizabeth. The shoreline here is awe-inspiring, with the Atlantic pounding relentlessly at a jumble of rocks, ferocious and angry after a storm, a time when many people especially like to visit here. In clear weather there's a fine view of the famous Portland Head Light. Built in 1791, it was ordered constructed by George Washington, and is the oldest lighthouse on the Atlantic seaboard.

Returning on Route 77, turn right into Route 207, then right on Route 1 to Portland. Staying on 1, passing many stalwart old homes and stately elms you will come, just beyond the top of a hill, to a statue of Henry Wadsworth Longfellow. Bear right here (do not turn abruptly right) and you'll be on Congress Street. The Wadsworth-Longfellow House is here, at No. 487.

Portland is probably best known to many as the hometown of Longfellow. Once its greatest fame was as a shipbuilding city and port. It was such a bustling place, in fact, that the British thought it wisest to burn it in 1775, and did. Portland is also famous because it is on Casco Bay, with its Calendar Islands: Ram, Horse, Whaleboat, Turnip, Eagle, Pumpkin Nob, Pound of Tea, etc. They are called the Calendar Islands because someone once said there were 365 in the bay. He has since been disputed and found wanting, but a trip on the bay will take you to a few or many of these islands, during the day, at sunset, by moonlight, on a supper cruise. Boats leave from the Custom House Wharf.

Over 100 years ago Oliver Wendell Holmes wrote of this city, "Portland is getting too prosperous to be attractive. Meant for a fine old town, to ripen like a Cheshire cheese within its wall of ancient rind, burrowed with crooked alleys and mottled with venerable mould, it seems likely to sacrifice its mellow future to a vulgar prosperity." Many people would tend to disagree, some violently, with Dr. Holmes. For those who love to visit old homes there's an itinerary mapped out for you in A Walking Tour of Historic Portand. It lists 39 buildings, and one of the most interesting things about the tour is that it doesn't include the Wadsworth-Longfellow House. This is perhaps unfortunate because the easiest place to pick up a copy of the tour is in the foyer of the Wadsworth-Longfellow House, unless you can find a parking space near the Greater Portland Chamber of Commerce at 143 Free Street. It is unfortunate, too, that there is no parking lot for the Wadsworth-Longfellow House. For travelers must find, in a busy, commercial section, empty curb-side space in order to visit the historic building.

The home of the author of *Tales of a Wayside Inn, The Song of Hiawatha, Evangeline,* and many other favorites, has great charm, from its old-fashioned kitchen, to manuscripts of the author and the lovely garden. At the rear is the Maine Historical Society Museum.

Another interesting house not in the walking tour is the Tate House, 1270 Westbrook St. The man who built it was probably far from the most popular in Portland in the mid-1700's, for he bore the title Mast Agent to the King. In those days the king claimed ownership of all white pines in Maine which measured over 24 inches in diameter. These were used for masts for his sailing ships. It didn't matter whose land a tree was on, along would come the agent and put the "broad arrow of the king" on it, and down it would come, to be shipped off to England. The house where George Tate lived from 1755 to 1800 is furnished in the period of that time.

By taking Route 1 out of Portland, and then turning right onto 88, you'll come to Falmouth Foreside. The town has no real claim to fame, but this little stretch of road has pretty houses and some lovely views south to island-scattered Casco Bay.

At Yarmouth Route 88 again meets Route 1 and you pass through this quiet little village that in the early 1800's built over 300 sailing vessels.

The Desert of Maine

Just before reaching Freeport, a left turn takes you to the famous Desert of Maine. Once prosperous farmland, a small patch of sand appeared here one day in the late 19th century. It has since grown to cover portions of ground within a radius of over six miles. Beneath the push of powerful storms the sands shift, drifting into dunes, covering trees measuring as high as 70 feet, some of which now appear as mere bushes. Geologists and students find much of interest in the many minerals found in the sands, and some experts believe the desert was, or is, a deposit left in a lake crater during or just after the last Ice Age.

But Freeport has other claims to fame in such native sons as the famous Arctic explorer-sailor Commander Donald B. MacMillan, who began his Arctic explorations with the late Admiral Robert E. Peary on the North Pole Expedition of 1908–09. (MacMillan's schooner *Bowdoin,* in which he made so many of the Arctic voyages, is now part of the permanent exhibit at Mystic Seaport, Conn.) One of Mark Twain's first stories (remember he used to summer on the Maine coast) was of Freeport's Captain Josiah A. Mitchell who, after his ship *Hornet* burned, sailed 4,000 miles in 43 days in an open boat with 14 crew and only 10 days' provisions. He sailed, too, into the annals of stalwart men of the sea. Of him Twain once remarked, ". . . I remember him with reverent honor."

Just out of Freeport take the Maine Turnpike to Brunswick, site of famous Bowdoin College. Tours, available throughout the year, take you to the student rooms of Henry Wadsworth Longfellow and of President Franklin Pierce, show you mementos of Nathaniel Hawthorne *(The Scarlet Letter, The House of the Seven Gables),* of Admiral Peary, Donald B. MacMillan—all Bowdoin graduates.

You'll also see the new (1965) college gymnasium, with the statue *The Lineman,* by William Zorach at the entrance. The famed sculptor carved the pink granite figure for the 1932 Olympic Games. Another attraction on the Bowdoin campus is the Brunswick Summer Playhouse.

Brunswick started as a fur-trading post known by the Indian name Pejepscot, and the Pejepscot Historical Society Museum here is rich in regional Americana. The society is also accumulating a growing collection of articles associated with General Joshua L. Chamberlain, Civil War hero who later became President of Bowdoin and Governor of Maine. The Stowe House near here is where Harriet Beecher Stowe was living at the time she wrote the memorable *Uncle Tom's Cabin.* Now also a restaurant, the Stowe House is well-known for its Captain's Corner with ship models and antique charts and maps.

When Bowdoin was founded in the 1790's Maine was still a part of Massachusetts, and the founders chose the name of the state's current governor, James Bowdoin (his grandfather had arrived in Maine in 1687 as Pierre Baudouin, but the governor Anglicized his name). The governor's son, also James, during his tenure as U.S. Minister to Spain and France, had collected some excellent Dutch and Italian masters. These, plus an outstanding group of early American protraits, form the nucleus of the collection at the Walker Art Building, and special shows are arranged each summer.

And now Maine's dramatic peninsulas begin, so take Route 24 south (right turn) several miles east of Brunswick. This is where Robert Peter Tristam Coffin, poet, essayist, novelist, and biographer, spent his boyhood, and drew from this area for *The Lost Paradise*.

This area is also the site of a ghost tale about a murdered pirate who nightly stands guard over some buried treasure. His wails have been heard and his light seen by a number of old-timers in the area. But going there by daylight you'll miss him and see many brilliant views of Casco Bay. A short bridge leads to Orr's Island, where you can still see the little white cottage where Harriet Beecher Stowe summered while working on *Uncle Tom's Cabin*. Out of this stay came another book, *The Pearl of Orr's Island*.

From Orr's Island you cross the famous cob-work bridge to Bailey Island. It's made of great granite blocks laid in a diamond or honeycomb shape held in place by their own weight. The bridge's design allows the heavy tides to flow through freely, and is not harmed by spring ice floes. There used to be another bridge done in the same manner in Scotland, but it is said this was bombed into oblivion during World War II.

Offshore here is Ragged Island where the poetess Edna St. Vincent Millay used to summer.

Bailey Island was originally settled in the 1700's by a trader from southwestern Maine. At that time it was called Newaggin. Later a Deacon Timothy Bailey came over from Massachusetts and claimed it. He forthwith banished all the early settlers and renamed the island Bailey. At the tip of Bailey there are extraordinary views of Casco Bay, the many islands, and the Halfway Rock Light.

Returning to Route 1 turn right for Bath beside the mighty Kennebec. Here is the river Kenneth Roberts says one must reach before finding the true Maine. Its praises have been sung most glowingly by Robert P. T. Coffin in *Kennebec, Cradle of Americans,* in the *Rivers of America* series. Undoubtedly, for those who are fond of New England, or of great rivers, this is a book to be read. Coffin also wrote the novels *Red Sky in the Morning* and *John Dawn*. In 1935 he was awarded the Pulitzer Prize for his book of verse, *Strange Holiness*.

Bath's tradition of the sea can be matched by few communities. It goes way back to 1607. That was when the *Virginia,* first ocean-going trading ship built in America, was launched at the nearby Popham Colony. Since then over 5,000 ships (wood, iron, steel) have been built at Bath, right up to the *USS Belknap* in 1964. J. P. Morgan's famous yacht *Corsair* slipped down the ways here, as did the destroyer *USS O'Bannon* (1942), which became one of the most famous fighters in the South Pacific in World War II. From Bath alone, during World War II, 82 destroyers were launched (in the same time the entire Japanese industry built 63).

The clippers *Governor Robie, M. P. Grace* and *W. R. Grace* were Bath-built, and the town has had many maritime firsts: the *Dirigo,* the first American-built four-masted steel bark; the six-masted schooner *Wyoming,* largest wooden vessel of any type ever to fly the U.S. flag on the seven seas; the all-steel *Thomas W. Lawson,* only seven-masted schooner ever built.

Bath is still a shipbuilding center today, with the Bath Iron Works turning out a number of steel-hulled boats each year, adding to the already impressive sum of over 4,000 ships launched here.

Ice to India

A curiosity to the present-day populace is that one of the chief cargos carried in early days was Kennebec ice. So valued was this river product that ice sellers in America's south proudly announced in big letters on their horse-drawn wagons that they carried Kennebec ice. But it was carried further than the south: to Manila, Calcutta, Shanghai, and many another world port, and fortunes were made on this evanescent merchandise.

A quiet excitement fills the air these days in Bath, for new here (1965) is the Bath Marine Museum, which has a superior collection of prints, paintings, models, charts, ships' furnishings, and gear.

The well-marked route to the museum gives the traveler a fine chance to see this settlement's great elms and venerable sea captains' homes. Bath was built by the men who built and went to the sea in ships.

Emma Eames, remembered by many oldsters as a famous, early 20th century operatic soprano was brought up in Bath. She would have been born here, too, except that at that time her mother was accompanying her father on a world voyage, so Miss Eames was born in Shanghai. Bath neighbors were never surprised to meet each other in Calcutta, Hong Kong, Colombo, or many another port half a world away from home.

Bath's City Park is also worth a visit. Here, in a reflecting pool surrounded by lovely gardens, is the fountain *The Spirit of the Sea,* by sculptor William Zorach.

From Bath take Route 209 south to the site of the Popham Colony, near the site of Fort Baldwin. This first settlement on Maine's coast came about largely through what is known as the first hostile act of the English toward the Indians. That was when Captain Waymouth kidnapped five Indians.

Beyond this site is Popham Beach and Fort Popham, partially constructed in the year 1861. A climb to the top of the fort offers a sparkling view of the sweep of the Kennebec.

Returning now on Route 209, you'll again pass through Phippsburg, near the end of the peninsula. It was named for Sir William Phipps, who captured the important fur-trading post Port Royal for the English during the French and Indian Wars. Sir William was born the twenty-sixth member of his family. Perhaps he was more tripped over than tended. At any rate he took his canoe and set off at age 18. Eventually he was building ships and bending King Charles II's ear about Spanish treasure he'd heard of, sunk near Haiti. Unlike most treasure hunts this one netted over $2 million in gold, silver, and gems, and William was knighted. With all the publicity behind him he kept getting assignments which brought him even more fame. There was the capture of Port Royal and later he was made Royal Governor of Massachusetts, which then included Maine.

Returning to Route 1, you'll cross the Kennebec and come immediately to Route 127. Turn right here, to Five Islands, at the end of the peninsula. The warm scent of pines will almost immediately assail you and at many turns in the road you'll come upon placid little fir-lined coves. Pines and lovely reflections are everywhere, and though you know you're at the coast, there's a backwoods feeling here. At the end of the peninsula is Five Islands. Here the Maine coast begins to get a wild, but not wooly, mien: it's as sharp as the clean, clear air. Here you begin to get an idea of the great tides and currents that affect the Down East coastline. Five Islands is at the mouth of the Sheepscot River, and its long-legged wharf is the center of the peninsula's life. Moored lobster boats bob, aloof, on the sapphire and silver waters, a speedboat hustles over to one of the privately-owned islands nearby, a sleek schooner dips its sails as it rounds submerged rocks coming into the harbor, sea gulls mew and screech their complaints and the scent of woodsmoke drifts about you.

Round-trip, the drive to Five Islands is about 30 miles. For those who love their woodlands and sea beautifully interwoven it's well worth the trip. Returning to Route 1, turn right.

Eagles, cows, pineapples, strawberries, rose-thistle-leek, a ram, a rooster, a heart. These are some of the old buttermold patterns available on wares at a shop in Wiscasset. It's the sort of thing that is just right for Wiscasset, a white, green, and brick-red town of great charm, nestled on a western hillside of the Sheepscot River, a dozen or so miles from the sea. Wiscasset, too, was once a seafaring town and many of its fine old homes were built by seafaring families.

Lafayette visited here in 1825. Earlier Louis Philippe (who later became King of France) and Talleyrand came here when forced to leave France. One can't help wondering if Louis Philippe was aware that a long-ago relative of his may have been the reason for Maine being called Maine. Henrietta Maria, wife of Charles I and daughter of Henry IV of France, was feudal ruler of the French province of Meyne. Some think Maine was so named in her honor.

Where Webster Thundered

Among Wiscasset's many attractions are the Lincoln County Courthouse where Daniel Webster's voice used to thunder and cajole, and the Lincoln County Fire Museum, which contains a collection of some of the country's oldest fire-fighting equipment, including an old hand tub dated 1803. The last of Maine's old-time stagecoaches is here, too. This museum is in the barn of the Nickels-Sortwell House, which is also open to visitors. One of Maine's most beautiful old homes, it was built by a retired shipmaster.

The Old Lincoln County Jail of great granite blocks, took over two years to build. The museum, next door in the jailer's house, includes in its exhibits Two Hundred Years of Maine Arts and Skills, as well as work of contemporary Maine craftsmen: weaving, pottery, toys, silk screen prints, etc.

During the summer there is always a large, lively art show at the Maine Art Gallery, and at the Wiscasset Musical Wonder House you'll find a nostalgic collection of gramaphones, pipe organs, pianos, and many other such items in their original setting.

About the town you'll find the Old Powder House, the Old Customs House, the O'Donnell Blacksmith Shop, where you can see and purchase hand-forged iron work, and the shop where old buttermould pattern products are sold.

Returning to Route 1, as you cross the Sheepscot River you'll see a sight to make any sailor's blood run cold. In the mud at the river's edge are two derelict hulls. These are the *Luther Little* and the *Hesperus,* once proud sea going schooners. Experts say the *Hesperus* is beyond repair, but that the 210-foot, four-masted schooner *Luther Little* (50 years old in 1967), can be saved and renovated.

On the east side of the river turn right onto Route 27 to Fort Edgecomb, Edgecomb, the Boothbays, and Cape Newagen. Fort Edgecomb's blockhouse was built at the time when the English were harassing American shipping, and Wiscasset, with one of the deepest harbors in Maine, was a bustling New England shipping center. Though this type of fortification proved inadequate during the War of 1812 it has been fully restored as an historic site.

Wiscasset can claim the tread of royal feet (Louis Philippe) and North Edgecomb almost had that distinction too. Marie Antoinette would have been the visitor, if one Captain Samuel Clough had been able to carry plans through. But, Marie Antoinette was beheaded before Clough's *Sally* could sail from France with the queen aboard. Just why this North Edgecomb captain had been singled out to whisk her away is tauntingly obscure, but when attempts to free her from prison failed and the guillotine plunged, the captain hastily set sail.

Mrs. Clough, who had been forewarned of the arrival of the royal visitor, found her man had brought home not the royal personage, but trunks containing Marie Antoinette's personal belongings and articles friends had sent along with Clough to comfort her and help her furnish her new dwelling. Many of the articles have disappeared; some are in the Metropolitan Museum in New York.

Capt. Clough must have definitely been a man with a bent for the exotic. Local legend credits him with also having brought the first coon cats into Maine. While some said he brought the cats from China, others insisted they originated in China, yes, but China, Maine, the offspring of a house cat and a renegade raccoon. At least all agree they came from China—one or the other.

Further south on the peninsula are the famous Boothbay Playhouse and the new (1965) Boothbay Railway Museum. Here are old railroad stations, a narrow-gauge railroad ride to take, and many mementos of the steam-railroad era which did so much to build America.

Next come Boothbay and Boothbay Harbor, as famous a settlement as any on the Maine coast. Boothbay Harbor is a busy town in summer and a beautiful sight to see, sprinkled with sleek sailboats, backdropped by burly, long-legged wharfs, pleasant homes, pine-clad peninsulas, and tall, slim church spires. The best way to see all of this scene and the whole vast area here—an intricate network of islands, coves, rivers, harbors, and peninsulas—is by boat. There are a number of cruisers that take passengers on sightseeing trips, as well as a Friendship sloop. There are morning, afternoon, and evening trips and they go to, among other places, Ocean Point, up the Kennebec River to Bath, Five Islands, Sequin Light, Damariscove, Squirrel Island (the site where the movie *Carousel* was filmed) Ovensmouth, Burnt Island Lighthouse. Among other things, you'll see where the famous clergyman Harry Emerson Fosdick and Edwin Arlington Robinson, one of America's greatest poets and several times winner of the Pulitzer Prize, used to summer, and where the sculptor William Zorach still does.

You'll also see Cape Newagen. Boothbay, which was settled in 1630, was originally called Newagen, and the cape and the widely-known and lovely *Newagen Inn* here carry on the name.

During a boat trip a talkative captain may tell you the story of Luther Maddocks' whale. It's a tale, too, of so-called Yankee ingenuity. It seems that one day in 1885 Maddocks, a local fisherman, captured a 60-foot humpback, somehow kept it alive and eventually towed it to Portland, deciding it ought to be in an exhibition being held there at the time. This venture netted him $800, to which he added the $150 a company paid him for the carcass: they wanted the hide and blubber. The company in turn had the carcass towed to sea and sunk. But, gas having formed in it, it rose and floated shoreward, much to the olfactory discomfort of nearby inhabitants. It was again towed out. Several times it floated back. When it came ashore again at Old Orchard Beach a profit-minded resident exhibited it as a sea serpent and hundreds of people came to see it. Still later an inland museum purchased the humpback's bones.

On land, take a trip down to Cape Newagen and the town wharf to see the sea and the tides busily at work. Coming or going from here, stop at the aquarium maintained by the State of Maine Sea and Shore Fisheries. Here are all manner of sea creatures, ugly and handsome, minute, newly-hatched lobsters, and playful seals in an outdoor pool.

From Boothbay Harbor go around east on Route 96 to see the shop of the Andersens, who work wonders in stoneware and porcelain, the *Studio of Ships,* with its paintings by Earle Barlow, the many yards where you can watch men building sailing vessels. Continue around to Ocean Point for further brilliant seascapes.

Now, heading northeast on Route 27, look for a sign pointing to Damariscotta. This is River Road, which forks right off Route 27 and has no route number. Here you'll find *Emerson's,* one of Maine's better-known restaurants, and an especially good gift shop called *The Cables.*

Lovely Homes of Damariscotta

When you reach Damariscotta make certain you take the branch of Route 1 that is marked "Business District." Otherwise you will miss the many enjoyable things this now-quiet town has in store for the discerning. Here, too, is Newcastle. Though the two settlements are separated by the Damariscotta River (long famous for the running of the alewives each spring), they blend together so that the traveler can see the attractions of both in one visit.

Architecturally both have much to offer, in churches and in homes. St. Patrick's for instance, is the oldest Catholic Church between Quebec and New York, being finished in 1808. Some of the Irish settlers, who began arriving in the 1780's, brought along their own architect, who built some impressive houses as well as the church. The Episcopal Church was the first one built in this country by Vaughan, who went on to distinguish himself as builder of the Washington Cathedral.

Many stalwart ships slid down the ways in this area during the 1800's, and their captains came home not only with the wherewithal to build lovely homes, but also with treasures from the earth's four corners. So though Damariscotta may in many ways seem a sleepy town, it had and has a sophistication that can be born only of generations of seafaring folk. An intriguing example of this is the Gilbert E. Gay grocery store on Main Street, a real gourmet's gourmet shop. This same tradition makes it not surprising to find here such an outstanding gift shop as *The Cricket,* with its fine merchandise from many countries. Hundreds of people come to the shop each year to see and purchase from the collection of famous Santons de Provence, the cottage-industry crêche figures from southern France.

Many Damariscotta shops should intrigue the connoisseur: one is famous for handwoven fabrics, another, at nearby Medomak, with its intriguing stained-glass medallions. Look, too, for the work of such local artisans as goldsmith Ernest Thompson, Jr., and John Upton, who has carved his way to fame with his door panels and eagles—after he thought he was retiring here, following an already full life in the advertising business in New York.

Carving is not new to Damariscotta. The visitor can see many handsome doorways in the town, and there are some figureheads and other pieces by the famous early carvers William Southworth and Edbury Hatch on display at the Chapman-Hall House.

Believed Damariscotta's oldest remaining dwelling, the Chapman-Hall House was constructed in 1754, and it's probably one of the few early houses that escaped the torch of Indian raiders. You've been looking at quite a few rather grand houses up to now, so that probably the charm of the early craftsmanship displayed here will add a new dimension of interest, especially as the house somehow manages to have an almost lived-in look.

Ancient Arts and Crafts

Perhaps there's something in the very air in the Damariscotta-Newcastle area that just naturally makes residents creative. Edwin Arlington Robinson was born here at Head Tide. The painter Maurice Day, who designed Disney's Bambi, has a studio here in the Day's ancestral home, built in 1798 by his shipbuilder great-grandfather. Grevis Melville, great nephew of Herman Melville, and a painter, lives here. Elizabeth Coatesworth, who wrote *The White Room, The Noble Doll,* and other popular children's books lives here with her equally well-known nature-writer husband. The artist Eugene Klebe lives in the area and several world-famous concert masters vacation here yearly. Mr. and Mrs. Godfrey carry on the almost-ancient American craft of hooking and braiding rugs (people come to their Colonial Crafts Shop from great distances), and at nearby Sheepscot you'll find the shop of Gordon Davis, well-known for his handwrought pewter.

But no one in this area can, after what happened in the late summer of 1965, claim himself an early visitor. It all has to do with some diggings, which were being carried out by amateur archeologists. Spade and pickaxe in hand they were attempting to unearth an area just to the south at Pemaquid Beach. Old records indicated there had been a substantial trading post here in the mid-1600's. Logic was on their side because at one time clearance was required at Pemaquid Beach for all vessels entering Maine waters between the Kennebec and St. Croix Rivers.

As time went by the amateurs found an old customs house, a tavern, and what was probably a forge. But one day that had started out as innocently as any other, their interest was abruptly diverted, and the 1650's began to look as modern (by comparison) as the present day. One of their group had come across several skeletons. One of these was believed to be that of an Indian, but the other was enough to bring experts flying from all parts of the U.S.A. For the second figure was dressed in armor, and sewn in animal hide. The time of the burials could not, of course, be immediately determined, but archeological experts note the armor indicates the man was a Viking, a fact further suggested by the ancient Norse custom of sewing bodies in animal hide prior to burial. Local authorities believe the Indian and the Viking remains will be kept in the area and not carted off to a distant museum.

To get to this site and all the beauties of the Pemaquid Peninsula, including famous Pemaquid Point Light (1824), turn off Damariscotta's Main Street onto Route 129. At this intersection is the local Information Center.

Christmas Cove, at the tip of the western fork of this peninsula (on Rte. 129), is a lovely unspoiled area. Ambassador Henry Cabot Lodge visits here, as do the Ted Kennedys, and Gene Tunney has a summer home on nearby John's Island. Christmas Cove was named by Captain John Smith, when he anchored here on Christmas Day in 1614. In his report on the area he wrote, "And more than 300 Iles overgrowne with good timber, of divers sorts of wood, which do make so many harbors as requireth a longer time than I had, to be well discovered . . ." Present-day travelers, too, have the same complaint.

From Christmas Cove, heading back north, the first right turn will take you to Route 130 and to Pemaquid Beach and Fort William Henry. This latter is said to be the only site in the U.S.A. that has had a succession of four different forts. The first, built about 1630, fell to the pirate Dixie Bull two years later. The second, erected in 1677, was destroyed by Indians in 1689. Sir William

Phipps built the third (the first one to be called Fort William Henry) in 1692, during King William's War. Four years later it was leveled by Indians under the famous Baron de Castin (more of this gentleman later). In 1729 the fourth fort was built, and it too was destroyed, during the Revolutionary War, by locals who didn't want the British to occupy it. The present fort is, in a sense, the fifth fort, as it is a replica of the fort Phipps built.

A Classic Lighthouse

In sight of the fort is the current excavation site where the purported Viking was found. At present (1966) visitors are welcomed, but if the number of curious becomes too great (as indicated in late summer of '65) other regulations may have to be made.

Returning to Route 130 and continuing south you'll come to one of the most-painted, most-photographed lighthouses in all America —Pemaquid Point. The Atlantic tosses its mane and pounds sonorously at the fascinatingly stratified rocks that form the shore here.

By now, if you haven't already eaten in one, you've certainly noticed lobster pounds—a great Down East institution. The pound usually serves two purposes: it supplies local residents with fresh, live lobster, and also serves boiled lobster. At most pounds, if you're eating there, you pick your own lobster and watch it go into a pot of boiling water. The lobsters are cooked in the open air and most pounds have tables and benches outside where you can eat. (Most also have an indoor dining room for cold or rainy days.) You can, if you wish, merely sit and drool while you wait for your lobster. However, most diners order either New England clam chowder or steamed clams. Now come the bibs, claw-crackers, picks, and melted butter—and the lobster. Some lobster pounds also offer corn-on-the-cob and many have fresh fruit pie on the menu—in late summer it is, of course, the ubiquitous blueberry.

Returning a short distance on Route 130, take a right turn onto Route 32 for a long, slow look at exquisite little New Harbor. You'll note the wharfs here are even longer-legged than any seen to date and, as you proceed further east (and northerly) they'll grow longer and longer, as the height of the tides becomes greater.

Further along on Route 32, past pretty Chamberlain, Hog Island lies off to your right. This is the site of the Audubon Nature Camp in Maine, the first such camp in the U.S.A.

Back at Route 1 turn right for Waldoboro. The earliest settlers here were Germans, who were induced (no one says how) to come here by one General Samuel Waldo, holder of the patent on this area. There are still families here with German names, but most moved on to other Maine communities. Not, however, before leaving this inscription on one of the gravestones in the local cemetery:

"This town was settled in 1748 by Germans who immigrated to this place with the promise and expectation of finding a prosperous city, instead of which they found nothing but wilderness." This may, after all, explain the type of inducement General Waldo used.

Confirmed shunpikers and those interested in American Colonial boats will want to turn right off Route 1 at Route 220 and dip south to the village of Friendship, famous for its Friendship sloop. A charming, natural seaport town, local pride in trim boats is evident, and many people who take fishing vacations try to keep this little treasure out of conversations and correspondence.

Thomaston—Village of Captains

From Friendship take Route 97 back to Route 1 and east to Thomaston, a village of lovely, stately sea captains' homes. All of these, however, are remorselessly upstaged by Montpelier, a reproduction of the magnificent house built here by General Henry Knox. The rebuilding of Montpelier was possible largely through funds given by Cyrus H. K. Curtis who, born in Portland, moved to Philadelphia, where he founded the *Ladies Home Journal* and became head of the Curtis Publishing Co.

General Knox was a commander of artillery during the Revolution, the first Secretary of War of the U.S.A., and was instrumental in the founding of the U.S. Military Academy at West Point. A close friend of George Washington's, legend recounts that it was he who, while a colonel under Washington at Valley Forge, persuaded a disheartened Washington to continue at his post despite the appalling odds.

Imposing Montpelier contains a bookcase of Marie Antoinette's (Knox purchased it after her execution, perhaps from Capt. Clough of N. Edgecomb), a traveling chest given him by the Marquis de Lafayette, many pieces of rare china and family silver and other personal effects of the General and his wife. The kitchen has great charm, and the house is especially noteworthy for its "flying staircase."

When you drive on to Rockland, consider the following side-trip before exploring that community. Take Route 73 from Rockland, then Route 131 to Tenants Harbor, where you'll find the Spouting Horn, where the water is sometimes forced as high as 40 feet into the air. Tenants Harbor and Port Clyde, further south, are primarily fishing villages, through the latter has other claims to fame. This is where the outstanding painters N. C. Wyeth and son Andrew used to summer, it is the area from which Waymouth kidnapped the five Indians, and it is where you can take a boat to some of the nearby islands, including Monhegan. This island, long a haven for artists, was noted by John and Sebastian Cabot way back in 1498, and by Champlain in 1605.

From Port Clyde drive back on Route 73 where you'll find the small, but well-known Old Spalding House at South Thomaston. Here Mrs. Worth Kaufman has gathered a representative collection of work by Maine's outstanding craftsmen. Travelers can either do all their looking here, or, from what they see here, decide which other craft and gift shops and studios they definitely wish to visit in the state.

Further along on Route 73 take the road that branches right to see Owl's Head Light. The proud little lighthouse—it's only 26 feet high—stands 100 feet above the sea on a red-and-yellow streaked headland.

If this little peninsula particularly intrigues you perhaps you'd like to make a note to read Sarah Orne Jewett's *The Country of the Pointed Firs* when you return home. Born in Maine, Miss Jewett was a well-known writer in the late 1800's and her deceptively simple tale of a summer spent here is still being read.

Back in Rockland you'll find it busy with a number of commercial pursuits. So busy in fact it does little to attract the tourist. As a consequence, the traveler will not find it particularly attractive, though he'll probably find himself admiring Rockland's industry.

If you like fishing fleets you'll love the waterfront here, and if you wish to visit a sardine-packing plant a phone call (ask the operator for the local cannery) will get you the information (and permission) you seek. If you're in Rockland any time from late afternoon on a Saturday, during Sunday, or early on any Monday morning during the summer you can see *Victory Chimes* at the public landing. Last of the Atlantic coast three-masted windjammers, and engaged in the enjoyable business of taking passengers on week-long coastal tours, the *Victory Chimes* is the largest passenger-carrying sailing ship under the American flag. If you miss her here, chances are good you'll see her in some harbor further Down East.

Wyeth Paintings on Display

The most impressive attraction in Rockland is the famed William A. Farnsworth Library and Art Museum. Its collection of 19th- and 20th-century paintings, drawings, prints, and sculpture is top-drawer. The museum has the largest collection extant of works by Andrew Wyeth, who is often referred to as "the most successful contemporary American artist." In addition, the museum owns works by N. C. Wyeth (father of Andrew), Winslow Homer, Stephen Etnier, Fitz Hugh Lane, Waldo Peirce, George Inness and others. The museum's purchase of Andrew Wyeth's *Her Room* brought the number of their paintings by this artist to 12, and its purchase price of $65,000 is the highest price yet paid by a museum for the work of a living American artist.

Now heading toward the Camden Hills, which you have begun to see to the northeast, you come to Rockport and Camden. With their pasts and presents so closely interwoven they are virtually twin communities. You can visit Rockport first by turning right off Route 1 at Route 90. However, if you plan to stay awhile in Camden, you can visit Rockport during the course of your Camden browsings. Like the Damariscotta area, Camden-Rockport should not be passed over lightly.

Camden—City of Flowers

The first thing that captures the attention of many first-time visitors to Camden is the pretty flower baskets on the lampposts. A Camden resident saw similar baskets in an English village in 1921 and brought back photos of them. His family, intrigued, had a local blacksmith make similar baskets which have graced the lampposts in the business district ever since. The local garden club sees that they brim with flowers each summer.

Several things will probably attract you to the waterfront. Camden's Information Bureau is at the public landing and from near here there's a captivating view of the waterfalls of the Camden River, whose waters cascade into the harbor after running beneath the main street. Some of the windjammers that sail the Maine coast each summer also tie up and depart from here, and there are boats on which you can cruise to nearby islands.

Mrs. Mary Louise Bok, daughter of the late Cyrus H. K. Curtis (who was largely responsible for the restoration of Montpelier) has been one of Camden's best-known summer residents here for many years. It is she who was responsible for the landscaping of Rockport's waterfront as well as the Vesper Hill Chapel. There's a magnificent view of Penobscot Bay from the chapel. Other regulars are the Procters of Procter & Gamble and newspaperman Hodding Carter. Charles Dana Gibson, famous for his black-and-white renderings of the Gibson Girls used to summer here, and Edna St. Vincent Millay, though born in Rockland, went to school here. It was in Camden, at the Whitehall Inn, that guests were so intrigued with the shy girl and her poetry, they quietly took up a collection that paid her tuition at Barnard College in New York. Later she won a scholarship to Vassar.

Camden's outdoor Garden Theater is a summer setting for many events, and visitors here can attend Bay Chamber Concerts, chamber concerts at the famed Carlos Salzedo Harp Colony, as well as concerts by the Harms Piano Summer Colony given at the Farnsworth Museum in nearby Rockland.

Shoppers will want to visit the *Strawberry Hill Studio,* the *Yarn Shop* (it has original crewel patterns), the studio of the painter Sigafoos, and the *Country Cousin* with its reproductions of classical primitive paintings of ships and people.

The historic Old Conway House, on Conway Road just off Route 1, is an authentically furnished 18th-century farmhouse. Nearby Rockport has a delightful harbor, some crazy, mixed-up gift shops, and boat-building yards. Near the Sail Loft you'll find Andre, the seal, and his wife. They came to visit, apparently decided they liked it, and stayed. Andre has a little routine he usually goes through about seven each evening to the delight of visitors and residents alike.

If you feel you'd like a bit of diversion away from the sea about now, why not duck inland at Rockland, taking Route 17 to Augusta, capital of the State of Maine. During the trip, stop at Halowell. Though more than 30 miles from the sea, Halowell is on the banks of the Kennebec and was once a big shipbuilding center. The Kennebec Valley Art Association, located here at the *Harlow Gallery* (160 Water St.), shows and sells original paintings, ceramics and sculpture, and at the *Sherrymike Pottery* (Pleasant Street) there are stoneware and Maine earthenware with unusual glazes. If there is an antique fancier among you, please note Halowell calls itself the antique center of Maine.

In Augusta ask for directions to Fort Western. Even before the fort was erected, back in 1634, a John Howland and a John Alden were in charge of the trading post here. Alden was later immortalized in Longfellow's *The Courtship of Miles Standish.*

Fort Western, originally built in 1754, was restored in 1921. Some of the barracks rooms are furnished in keeping with early days and there are rooms devoted to military and naval articles, to early spinning and weaving, to a collection of Indian relics. Fort Western is perhaps best known as the place where Benedict Arnold's men regrouped and transferred to bateaux while on their historic, unsuccessful march to Quebec.

The State House was designed by Charles Bulfinch, who succeeded Benjamin Henry Latrobe as architect of our national Capitol.

Leaving Augusta, take Route 3 to Palermo, site of *Dowe's,* a Maine country store. Here they sell Barbados molasses by drawing it from the barrel with a pump. You'll see pickle barrels, bins of cookies, cheese in 40-pound wheels and many other items an old-fashioned country general store carried.

Continuing on Route 3 turn right at Route 173. Now you're in the country where Ben Ames Williams used to summer and on which he based his town of Fraternity, locale of many of his Hardscrabble Farm stories which appeared in the *Saturday Evening Post.*

At Searsmont bear right and take Route 105, which soon makes a left, and you'll be back in Camden. You're back, too, at the sea, which is probably more or less as things should be in Maine. As someone recently pointed out, "Why everyone knows all you need to do is add an 'r' between the 'a' and 'i' in Maine and you have marine."

Again driving east on Route 1, you'll come to the new road (1965) which goes up Mt. Battie. This is the place for a panoramic view of Penobscot Bay, of the islands, and of the peninsulas that lie beyond. If you should be overnighting in the area this view is breathtaking at night, too, a point to keep in mind at many places along the peninsular coasts.

Continuing east on Route 1, you'll come to the *Red Barn,* a pleasant gift shop, and then to Lincolnville Beach. Wheel-thrown stoneware is made at the *Lincolnville Studios* here, and there's an exceptionally attractive gift shop in this old house with its huge fireplace. It's quite fitting that Marvin Garner should have a shop here as, it actually isn't a house, but a general store, or it was for some 200 years. In the old days the creek just beyond the parking area was kept dredged and schooners from Isleboro and Vinalhaven used to tie up while passengers shopped and caught up with the local gossip. Some of the store's records have been kept and it's interesting (and disheartening in our inflationary age) to note that at the time of the Civil War you could have a tooth pulled here for 25 cents. Whiskey was even cheaper, pegged at 12 cents a pint. In other words, for 37 cents you could have a relatively painless extraction, with some whiskey left over for a frigid day. Boats still come and go between Isleboro and Lincolnville Beach, but the boat now runs on schedule, is called the *Governor Muskie,* and carries 24 cars and 125 passengers.

Continuing east, Belfast is the next settlement. Here follow the route marked "Business District" to see some of the many lovely old homes. If time allows, drive through a few of the back streets to see others.

Just out of Camden, on Route 1, the traveler encounters confusing directions at a road junction. Take the eastbound road following signs to Ellsworth and Bucksport.

Museum of the Sea

Searsport once rang with the sounds that go with shipbuilding, and in the Penobscot Marine Museum, in what is locally referred to as the Rogue's Gallery, there are portraits of 284 sea captains, all from Searsport. The museum's exhibitions, in three buildings, include a whaling room, many treasures from the faraway lands where the captains (and often their families, too) visited and traded. There are paintings of famous ships, a collection of ships' half-models, charts and many other mementos of the days of the tall ships.

Taking Route 1 out of Searsport, turn right at Alternate Route 1, then several miles beyond, left onto Route 174. Driving through hill, pine, and meadow country, you come to Fort Knox State Park with the remarkably handsome Fort Knox, built of granite by master craftsmen, and one of the largest of its type in the U.S.A. It was named for the same Gen. Knox who used to live at Montpelier.

Some of the parts of the fort are underground and dark, so if you're a fort fancier and wish to see most of this huge structure rent a flashlight near the park entrance. From the fort there are impressive views of the Penobscot River. The factory on the opposite bank (its hugeness in this semi-wilderness is a surprising feature of the landscape) is the St. Regis Paper Mill.

Continuing on from the fort you again meet Route 1. Crossing the Penobscot River Bridge you are in Bucksport. Turn left just over the bridge if you wish to be disappointed at the sight of the *Jed Prouty Tavern,* or if you're hungry. Some writers, referring to the tavern as a 1798 hostelry, may have misled more than one traveler into believing vestiges of the 18th century remain. None do. But it was a stop on bygone stage runs and William Henry Harrison, Andrew Jackson, John Tyler, Martin Van Buren and Daniel Webster are known to have been guests. If you're hungry, the surroundings are unpretentious, but the dining room food and service fine.

Just beyond Bucksport, on Route 1, there is a left turning, at Route 175, which will take you into a whole wonderland of Maine peninsular life. This area is most often referred to as the East Penobscot Bay Peninsula, but someone recently discovered it was once called the Nasket Peninsula. For brevity's sake the latter is a better name, though in conversation, to be certain you're understood, the longer name is preferable.

Fortunately, for those who seek the untrammeled by-ways, the Nasket Peninsula is, as a whole, not well known. One reason is there is so much to see that few travelers know the whole peninsula (most extensive on the Maine coast). While it's true people have been writing about and talking about it for years, in most cases they have concentrated on one specific area. Mary Ellen Chase *(Mary Peters, A Goodly Fellowship, Jonathan Fisher)* has written often about Blue Hill, which is well known, too, for its Rowantrees Pottery. Castine has long been known for a number of historical reasons as well as for the location of the Maine Maritime Academy.

One of the first places John Steinbeck went in his *Travels with Charley* was to Deer Isle at the south of the peninsula.

When you reach Route 166 on the peninsula follow it to Castine. This calm, peaceful settlement belies its pugnacious past. For almost 200 years it was in dispute between the French and English, then the English and Americans. It was occupied as late as 1815 by the British during an eight-month period in the War of 1812. Almost 100 signs are posted throughout the town, recounting various events which occurred here. Perhaps you can piece together its past from these. At least you'll find reading the signs an amusing pastime.

Fort George is here. No one is certain how early it was built, but there were fortifications on this site about 1626. Then it was razed and rebuilt many times during a period of 200 years. Visitors can see the *State of Maine,* training ship of the Maine Maritime Academy here at the waterfront, the elm-dotted academy campus, and many, too, drive out to Block House Point to see the sun set over the bay.

Route 166 loops the Castine cape, so that you will arrive back on Route 175 (southbound). At the junction of 175-176 take Route 176. At South Brooksville, a tiny settlement, turn right in front of the Methodist Church for a good look at Buck's Harbor, a favorite of yachtsmen. It's one of the deepest along the Maine Coast, with a beauty all its own.

Further south, where 175 forks, bear right. You'll know you are on the correct road because you'll almost immediately see the Corner Store (which isn't on a corner) and just beyond, a little bridge with four, planted flower boxes atop it. This seems to be a Nasket Peninsula touch. One bridge you'll see later on has window boxes the full length of both sides, brimming with bright-red geraniums and white petunias. Many mailboxes, too, are decorated with flowering plants, and at least one is made from an old well handpump.

Authors and Architects

Following signs to Deer Isle and Stonington you'll cross a bridge at Eggemoggin Reach and, just before the town of Deer Isle, you'll come to Centennial House on your left. Here items made by people attending the Haystack Mountain School of Crafts are on display in the Barn Gallery and for sale in the adjacent shop. The school itself is located at Sunshine. It doesn't welcome visitors, but its site brings up the interesting point that on the opposite side of the island there is a settlement called Sunset. Buckminster Fuller, the man who has designed and patented a whole legion of well-known geodesic and tensgrity structures, summers in this area, and Robert McCloskey, writer and illustrator of children's books *(Centerburg Tales, Time of Wonder)* lives on nearby Scott's Island.

There's an abandoned silver mine and a granite quarry on Crotch Island. A quarry at Oceanville got the contract in the summer of 1965 for the granite to be used in the John F. Kennedy Memorial to be built in Washington. Nearby Stonington, in the quarrying business, too, was the source for the granite used in New York's Triborough Bridge. Taking 172-A to Stonington you'll find a unique and magnificent harbor with the town climbing the little hills that border it.

There are all manner of boat trips to take in this area. For instance, there's a mail boat each morning that goes to Isle au Haut, and regular boat trips go there, to visit this portion of Acadia National Park. Other boats go to North Haven, where Anne Morrow Lindbergh *(North to the Orient, Gifts from the Sea)* used to summer and Robert Montgomery currently does.

Altogether Stonington is a quietly busy harbor, and likely as not you'll see one of the windjammers that cruise Down East in the summer months. By bearing right out of Stonington you'll see its lily pond, covered with a galaxy of pink and white blossoms. Backtracking (less than ½ mi.) to 172 you'll come to the miniature village. Complete in detail (and lighted at night) the village, on the lawn of a home, has been the hobby for some years of its owner, who is pleased to have the public visit.

Returning to Eggemoggin Reach, bear right just over the bridge and take 172-175 to a right turn for 175. Coming up the eastern side of this cape-like appendage you'll see sparkling Blue Hill Bay and, beyond, world-famous Mount Desert Isle. Local wags contend Mount Desert "sits on its view," while Nasket Peninsula folk really get to see its great beauty.

E. B. White, one of America's leading essayists, and one of its most respected, lives here. Probably most widely known as a contributor to *The New Yorker,* he is also author of a number of books, including *The Wild Flag, The Second Tree from the Corner, Charlotte's Web,* and *Points of My Compass.*

From a distance you'll have no trouble recognizing Blue Hill. It not only dominates much of the scenery in the northern section of the peninsula–it is also often blue. But in late summer and fall much of it becomes a brilliant soft red. This is when the leaves of the blueberry bushes turn, and it presents a dramatic sight. The highly creative parson Jonathan Fisher lived here and his house can be visited, and the composer Ethelbert Nevin used to live here *(Narcissus, The Rosary).* Kneisel Hall, a summer school for string and ensemble music, now directed by Marianne Kneisel, is in Blue

Hill, and Rowantrees Pottery is too. Here you can see potters working at their wheels, firing the pottery, etc.

Continuing north on Route 172 be on the lookout for Black House, on your left, at the outskirts of Ellsworth. An elegant red-brick mansion of modified Georgian architecture, Black House is fully furnished and a visit gives one more the feeling of having paid a call, than of having visited a museum.

On Route 1, a short distance beyond Ellsworth, take Route 3 (right turn) to Bar Harbor and Acadia National Park. Almost since the day in 1604 when Samuel de Champlain took a look at the paucity of trees on the upper reaches of the hills here and called this Isle des Monts Desert, this area has been known as Mount Desert Island. But in the mid-1800's, when railroads and steamboats became the modes of transportation, vacationers began to come to Bar Harbor. Soon it became known as a colony of spacious summer homes, owned by people noted for their money, philanthropy, and social position. For almost 100 years Bar Harbor was a chic gathering place for the social set. Then, in 1947, the Great Fire reduced literally dozens of estate homes to rubble. Bar Harbor was no longer "the place."

However, many of the sons and daughters of those who once owned the great estates still come to Mount Desert Island, and though they still shop in Bar Harbor, they have their summer homes in a scattering of other communities on the island. The Fords, Nelson and David Rockefeller, Atwater Kent, Jr., Paul Nitze, the Amory S. Carharts, Mrs. R. Stuyvesant Pierpont, and members of the Milliken and Astor families, summer at Asticou, and at Seal and Northeast Harbors.

TV man Garry Moore summers here, the late Rachel Carson, who wrote so beautifully of this area in *The Edge of the Sea* and in *The Sea Around Us,* used to have a retreat here, and Rachel Field *(Time Out of Mind, All This and Heaven, Too)* summers in the Cranberry Isles.

Acadia National Park

These days almost 2,000,000 motorists annually visit the area, but, as most of them will tell you, they're not going to Bar Harbor (though most stay at hostelries there). They're on their way to Mount Desert Island and, more specifically, to Acadia National Park. What beckons strongest here is the vast, timeless beauty of the region. There's a special sparkle here, and a gift from nature that seems to say, "Look! This is the way things used to be, long, long, ago." Somehow it is Maine unmasked—and the face revealed is handsome and awesome.

In the midst of deep beauty, along the more than 200 miles of paved roads here, travelers stop to poke about Anemone Cave, to see Thunder Hole, great ragged cliffs and coves. They see fjord-like Somes Sound (be sure to take Sargeant Drive out of Northeast Harbor for this), marvel at big Jordan Pond, and drive up Mt. Cadillac for virtually unbelievable views from its 1,532-foot summit. They see a hundred ways in which the glaciers, the winds, and the sea have worked here. The visitor who wants to read more about this area, will find a rich literature. Recommended is *The Story of Mount Desert Island,* by Samuel Eliot Morison, author of the *Oxford History of the American People,* a 1965 best-seller. Morison, a familiar figure to fellow-yachtsmen at Northeast Harbor, won the Pulitzer Prize for his biography of Christopher Columbus and for his *John Paul Jones.*

To fully appreciate all that is here it helps to have some factual material at hand. You can get this by writing ahead to either Acadia National Park at Bar Harbor, or the National Park Service, U.S. Dept. of the Interior, Washington, D.C.

While in the area also take one of the numerous cruises from Bar Harbor, visit Southwest Harbor, and the *Bass Harbor Country Store,* an authentic country store of a century ago, at Tremont. See the sea wall that nature has built at Seawall, Bass Harbor Head Lighthouse. The famous Jackson Laboratory is at Bar Harbor too, and if you'll call for information on tours you can visit this world-famous research center. Just over the bridge, headed back toward Route 1, stop at Aqualand with its live sea and land animal displays.

Back on Route 1, turn right for Hancock. The restaurant here called *Le Domaine* is probably one of the few gourmet dining places in Maine. The owners, who are from Les Baux in Southern France, came to Hancock at the beginning of World War II at the urging of M. and Mme. Pierre Monteux, to whom they are related. Hancock, as most music-lovers know, is where the Monteux conductors' school was held for many years. Begun in 1965, the Monteux Memorial Festival will be an annual event.

Further east on Route 1, just beyond Hancock, look for a sign which notes there is a turn-out. There aren't many turn-out signs in Maine, but when there is one, take advantage of the suggestion as it is always worth it. This one, near Sullivan, surely looks out on one of the most magnificent views of coastal America. From here you can see Mount Desert Island, Cadillac Mountain, huge Frenchman's Bay, many pine-pointed islands—the whole panorama is splendid.

Further along the coast (about five miles), be on the lookout for signs for Route 186 and/or Winter Harbor. Here is the Gouldsboro Peninsula. Virtually unknown to travelers, it has a lot, in a very quiet way, to offer. Gordon Barton, who has a shop on Main Street, is a fine woodcarver, and Syd Browne and Sandra James are widely-known artists (they are A.N.A. and Audubon Artists). Miss James (Mrs. Browne) also does objects in kiln glass.

Be certain to take time to see the peaceful, pretty harbor here, and while in Winter Harbor ask for directions to Grindstone Point. There are tidal pools here and beautiful views, out to sea, over to Mark, Ned, Roaring Bull Ledges, and Turtle Islands—and peace aplenty.

Schoodic Point here on the Gouldsboro Peninsula, is an even larger section of the Acadia National Park than that at Mount Desert. Roadsides to the point are lined with pine in this 2,080-acre area and, as elsewhere on the peninsula, the pink granite rocks, caught between blue-blue water and evergreened shore, make for some startling, memorable scenes. Schoodic Point rises to an elevation above a terraced ledge. The surf here is always spectacular; following a storm, it's awesome.

Returning from Schoodic, take Route 186 around to serene Prospect Harbor, then 195 to Corea. Louise Dickinson Rich *(We Took to the Woods)* has brought to the Gouldsboro Peninsula what small fame it has, in a *Reader's Digest* article, and, more recently, in her book *The Peninsula.*

The village of Corea on the peninsula has a simple charm. It's a working harbor, with many trim little lobster boats and long-legged wharfs; but behind the peaceful scene you sense it isn't so simple, that the lobstering and fishing on this stern coast must, at times, take its toll.

Corea has two main paved streets. Each becomes a little dirt road, which peters out at the harbor's edge—dead end. And perhaps you, too, should halt your journey Down East here and turn back west toward Maine's lake and mountain regions.

But if you're the hardy type and want to explore the moor-like potato and blueberry country, plot a course on east, to Harrington, Columbia Falls, Machias, Lubec, Quoddy Head, nation's most easterly point, Eastport, with its 30-foot tides, and perhaps to Campobello. Out here the country becomes more and more rugged, good accommodations and restaurants more and more scattered. But then there's Pembroke, too, where a gold strike was recently made!

North at Calais you'll be in the heart of the St. Croix Valley. Here nature lovers will want to visit the Moosehorn National Wildlife Refuge.

About 100 miles north of here is Houlton, proposed as the northern terminus of the Maine Turnpike. Further north are

Presque Isle, Caribou, Van Buren, and Fort Kent (about 125 miles from Houlton).

The area around Fort Kent remained in dispute for a number of years and almost brought about war with Canada, but finally this piece of boundary between Canada and the U.S.A. was peacefully settled, in 1842, by the Webster-Ashburton Agreement.

From Fort Kent, head south on Route 11 to Millinocket. To the west of you is wild country, some of it not yet thoroughly explored. With the exception of several private roads built in the interests of logging (plus a route which goes to Allagash out of Fort Kent) there are no numbered roads to the west until on past the Canadian border, which at some points lies almost 100 miles west.

But if you don't take the trip north, then, from the Gouldsboro Peninsula take Route 1 back to Ellsworth, then Alternate Route 1 to Bangor. Though an inland city, Bangor, on the Penobscot, was once a bustling shipbuilding center. Fortunes were made in the lumber and ice carried from here and records show that as many as 700 vessels, from bay coasters to full-rigged ships, from 400 to 4,000 tons, were anchored in its harbor at one time. In the Gold Rush of '49 the Bangor-built *Gold Hunter* was the first to carry men bound for the gold fields around the Horn to California.

A trip to the Bangor Historical Museum recalls bygone days, and the 31-foot statue of the legendary Paul Bunyan, near the Municipal Auditorium, suggests a lot about those Maine lumbermen who followed the pioneers west.

Bangor's Salmon Pool (opposite beautiful Grotto Cascade Park with its 45-foot cascade, dramatically lighted at night), is known throughout the world. Here each May and June gamey 10- to 30-pound sea salmon fight their way up over these falls to spawn.

Orono, north of Bangor on Route 2, is the site of the University of Maine's beautiful campus on the Stillwater River. Singer Rudy Vallee, brought up in Maine, long has been identified with the university's Stein Song.

Old Town, just to the north, is seldom mentioned without talk of its most famous product, the canoe. There is an Indian reservation here, too, and many men who do not like working indoors are guides for fishermen and hunters. A number of travelers are disappointed in the reservation on an island in the Penobscot River, possibly partially because it just doesn't resemble their romantic childhood notions of what an Indian village should look like.

Mr. Baxter's Gift—a State Park

From Old Town continue on Route 2 to just beyond Mattawamkeag where you turn left onto Route 157 to Millinocket. This is a large newsprint manufacturing center and the gateway to Mt. Katahdin and Baxter State Park.

From here you'll drive northwest on the Baxter State Park Road, and don't be disturbed when you note that much of this road which skirts the park is marked "private road," on your map. It does belong to the Great Northern Paper Company, but they permit the public access.

Mt. Katahdin, in the park, is the highest in Maine (5,267 ft. above sea level) and one of the three highest points in the U.S.A. east of the Rockies. The mountain marks the northern terminus of the famous Appalachian Trail. The drive in this area is a remarkable woodland journey, skirting numerous ponds and lakes, the Ripogenus Dam, passing rushing mountain streams—the whole area redolent with the scent of pine. Moose, white-tail deer, and bear roam freely here, and lucky travelers often see a few.

Much of the land of Baxter State Park, which covers more than 200,000 acres, was given by Percival P. Baxter, who worked for years to have some portion of this unique region set aside as a park for public use. Time and again legislatures defeated him. Then, in 1930, on his own, he purchased land here which he then deeded to the state "for the benefit of the People of Maine." At last, seeing the light, Maine purchased further lands and added them to the park.

Continuing on the Great Northern Paper Co. road you'll come to Greenville, active center of the Moosehead Lake region. This is big fishing and hunting country, and that's just the air it wears. The lake front is busy with the pontoon planes of local air services which fly people into the area, and out from Greenville to remote sites to canoe, or to fish. U.S. Supreme Court Justice William O. Douglas vacations in this region and reputedly one of the people most avid with rod and reel here is opera star Eileen Farrell. Moosehead Lake is Maine's largest. Over 40 miles long, and in some places 20 miles wide, it has many islands and bays.

Greenville's most famous emporium is *Sanger's,* a sporting goods store. It deserves its fame: it's been in Greenville over 100 years. Recently it has added a large line of skiing merchandise as more and more skiers discover the snows and tows of nearby Squaw Mountain.

Driving northwest from Greenville, on Route 15, you'll pass *Wilson's,* which some call "a Maine woods legend." This simple, famous fishing camp needs no touting. It, too, has been going strong for over 100 years.

Further along on Route 15 is one of the great sights for travelers in this area. Mt. Kineo, a sheer cliff, rises out of the lake to a height of over 1,000 feet. A geological oddity, it is a solid piece of flintstone and Indian tools of this self-same stone are said to have been found as far away as the Midwest.

Almost as famous as the cliff itself is the *Kineo Hotel,* a luxury resort which nestles at the mountain's foot (the first Kineo House opened 'way back in 1844). The hotel is reached only by boat, a pleasant ride on this great lake.

Traveling in this area in August, don't forget to look for Northern Lights. Some pretty fabulous shows will come your way some nights. And all summer another favorite pastime here is bear-watching. So don't be surprised if you are invited to "come along to the garbage dump." It's an invitation to share the fascination of watching grizzlies forage for an evening snack.

If you love wilderness scenery and want to see more than you have so far, Route 15, after nearby Rockwood, peters out into a rather rough, but very pleasant road. It connects with Route 201 some 30 miles beyond. If you turn right on 201 you'll be in Jackman in minutes, and only 16 miles from the Canadian border. Like Greenville, Jackman, too, is a jumping-off place for deep-woods fishing and hunting, and a station on both the Moose River and Attean Lake canoeing routes. It is this and the Moosehead area which Thoreau wrote about in *The Maine Woods.*

Now, turning back south on 201, take Alternate 201 at Solon (bear right) to North Anson, where you take Route 16, to the right. It follows the Bear River; there are placid riverside scenes and ever-changing farmland vistas all along this route.

If the idea of driving on a road principally built for and used by logging trucks doesn't intrigue you, leaving Kineo return to Greenville and take Route 15 south to Abbot Village. Turn right here, onto Route 16. Again, if this two-lane road is not the type you like, though you'll miss some fine scenery and travel a bit out of your way, turn off 16 onto Route 201 at Bingham. At Skowhegan take Route 2 to Farmington, then 4 north to Rangeley. Skowhegan was the birthplace of the famous humorist Artemus Ward and of Daniel Dole, an early missionary to the Hawaiian Islands. He founded a university there and became its president. A son of his became the first governor of the Territory of Hawaii. Skowhegan is also the home of Senator Margaret Chase Smith.

Rangeley—for Fishing and Hunting

Rangeley, in the heart of the Rangeley Lakes region, is the center of a vast fishing, hunting, and more recently, skiing area. But there are sophisticated touches, too: a Finnish sauna bath on the main street, a new lodge-motel and a long-established lodge. Throughout this vast mountain area are the lakes Cupsuptic, Upper and Lower

Richardson, Rangeley, Umbagog, and Mooselookmeguntic. Altogether the Rangeley Lakes region encompasses 450 square miles of mountains, lakes and streams.

While here be certain to read the local paper so you'll catch any special events going on in the area, and if you haven't bought any maple syrup as yet, this is a good place to get it. Most stores carry State of Maine Maple Syrup and if the can has a square blue, white, and red trademark you'll know you're getting the best. These trademarked cans are given only to reputable producers, and the only reason you never see Maine maple syrup outside the state is that it's so much in demand there's never enough left to ship out.

More and more travelers are driving to Rangeley each winter, not only for skiing, but also for the two-day, 30-mile Sled Dog Race held each March. Contestants and teams come from many areas of Maine, upper New York State, Massachusetts, Vermont, New Hampshire, Ontario, and Quebec, and spectators from as far away as New Jersey and Delaware. Leaving Rangeley, you can take Route 4 southbound, but hardy types, and those with a bent for the beautiful, choose 16 on west to the junction where you turn left onto 17. This also is the most direct route to Andover, site of Comsat's Telstar installation.

Route 17 is probably about as miserable a road as any you'll encounter. Therefore you'll probably be surprised to see many other motorists suffering past the potholes with you. But there's a special reason for it: a turnout (on your right side) with a truly exquisite view. Lake Mooselookmeguntic, other lakes, islands, mountains, golden shores, patches of pines, the blue of sky and water, form an unforgettable mosaic in a view that would be hard to beat anywhere on earth.

When you come to Frye turn right onto 120 to Andover and the Telstar Earth Station. Visitors are welcome (well over 500,000 as of 1965). On a one-hour tour you'll see exhibits which explain the communications satellites, and the radome, world's largest air-inflated structure, which houses the 380-ton horn antenna.

From Telstar continue into Andover and turn left onto 5. When you reach Route 2 turn left for about a quarter of a mile, then right on to 232 to Bryant Pond, where you turn left onto 26, southbound.

White Mountain Views

Before you leave Route 2, however, there are several side trips you might want to consider. Staying on 2, eastbound, visit Rumford, for a view of the Penacook Falls (Androscoggin River), called by some the most spectacular falls east of Niagara. You can also take a guided tour through the Oxford Paper Company at Rumford (telephone for permission and particulars).

By going southwest on 2 you'll come to Bethel, location of the well-known preparatory school, Gould Academy. Many handsome homes line Bethel's streets, there are dramatic views of New Hampshire's White Mountains here, and, in the vicinity, caves and waterfalls to visit. Here, too, is the Artist's Bridge. Located on Sunday River just to the north at Newry (turn north on Route 5 at Bethel), it's the most-photographed, most-painted covered bridge in Maine.

But no matter what exploring you do in the Rumford-Bethel area, be certain that when you drive south it is on Route 26, to Trap Corner in West Paris. Here is Perham's *Maine Mineral Store,* the doorstep of which is crossed by over 70,000 visitors annually, who come to see and buy from the mineral and gem collection. Stanley Perham, owner of this unpretentious shop (though its contents are far from ordinary), is a friend of the rockhound and willingly allows collectors to visit and chip away at the five mines he owns in the area. New fame came to Perham's shop with an article in the *Reader's Digest in* April, 1957, even though the shop has been selling engagement rings since 1919. In addition to local minerals and gems (about 300 different ones have been found in this area), there are minerals and gems in the shop from other areas of the U.S.A. and the world.

A few miles south of Trap Corner be on the lookout for a small sign pointing left (east) to Paris Hill (no route number). Paris Hill used to be a main stop on the stagecoach route between Portland and Montreal and it's one of the most sparkling, prettiest towns in New England, with handsome houses and a wide, peaceful village green. Virtually unknown to the present-day traveler, it was once the business center of this area. Though it's lost its prominence, its dignity remains. Hannibal Hamlin, Vice President under Lincoln, was born here and you can see his home.

Back on Route 26 you'll come to Poland Spring. Just off the road you can drive through the grounds of this once-elegant resort. The offices of Jack Parr's TV Station WMTW, which broadcasts from Mt. Washington, N.H. are located on the grounds, as is the actual Poland Spring and the Maine State Building originally built for the Chicago World's Fair (1893) and later reconstructed here.

Continuing on Route 26 to Gray, if pheasants, moose and other creatures interest you, stop at the State of Maine Game Farm. Thousands of pheasants are hatched and bred here for stocking purposes. Visitors are welcome, and in addition to the pheasants there's an informal zoo, with deer, elk, fox, great horned owls, and a number of other woodland creatures to see, as well as a fish hatchery. Continuing south on 26 you will find access roads to the Maine Turnpike, going south to the New Hampshire border. But, if you passed by the Yorks when you headed Down East, why not stop off there now. You'll find it a charming conclusion to your Maine journey.

AROUND THE STATE

HOTELS AND MOTELS. Accommodations in Maine range from the spectacular, yet comfortable, resorts at Bar Harbor and Ogunquit to the plain and simple hotels and motels to be found in the smaller towns. In this listing, big towns come first, in alphabetical order and by price category. Smaller towns follow in alphabetical order.

AUGUSTA

First Class

Holiday Inn. This new, large chain member, 2-level motel has resort atmosphere in the city. Swimming pool. Restaurant, cocktail lounge.
Route 202 (tel. 622–6371).

Reasonable—First Class

Memorial Bridge Motor Court. Here you will find cozy atmosphere. Free coffee. Breakfast only. Pets welcome.
2 Stone St. (tel. 622–6226).

Senator Motel Hotel. The pool and playground here solve the problem of how to keep children happy. Restaurant and cocktail lounge. Pets welcome.
Western Ave. (tel. 622–5804).

Reasonable

Augusta House. This hospitable hotel is conveniently near the sightseeing and shopping area. Beautician and barber. Restaurant, cocktail lounge. Pets welcome.
170 State St. (tel. 623–3821).

BANGOR

Reasonable—First Class

Wedgewood Arms Motor Inn. Beautifully-furnished rooms distinguish this motel. Restaurant, breakfast and lunch. Pets permitted.
480 Main St. (tel. 942–5281).

Reasonable

Bangor House. Here you will find many conveniences from beauty salon to charming restaurant and cocktail lounge. Free parking. Pets permitted.
174 Main St. (tel. 947–7321).

Charter House Queen. You will be treated royally here, even to off-season continental breakfast free. Amusements. Pets permitted.
1476 Hammond St. (tel. 942–4611).

Woodland Terrace. This motel has attractive, secluded setting. Breakfast only. Game area.
On Route 1A (tel. 989–3750).

BAR HARBOR

Deluxe

Wonder View Motor Lodge. This view is wonderful, especially from penthouse restaurant. Swimming pool.
Eden St. (tel. 288–3821).

First Class

Bar Harbor Motor Inn. The ocean view is a great attraction at this 2-level motel. Pool, sports, dancing. Restaurant and cocktail lounge. Seasonal.
Newport Dr. (tel. 288–3351).

Bluenose Motel. Here you will find resort atmosphere. Terraces with ocean view. Rate includes coffee. Summer season.
Eden St. (tel. 288–3733).

Frenchman's Bay Motel. This summer motel has sweeping scenic views. Swimming. Breakfast.
Eden St. (tel. 288–3321).

National Park Motel. This new motel has luxury underfoot in carpeted rooms. Pool. Extended summer season.
Mt. Desert St. (tel. 288–5403).

Rockhurst. Take your choice of modern motel or old-fashioned inn. Includes continental breakfast, pool. Pets permitted. Play area.
Mt. Desert St. (tel. 288–3140).

Sea Breeze Motel. Enjoy basking in the sun and looking at ocean view. Extended summer season.
Route 3 (tel. 288–3565).

BELFAST

First Class

Belfast Motor Inn. With a beautiful view and location on bay, this new motel has become popular quickly. Breakfast only. Family rates. Seasonal prices. Pets permitted. Pool.
Searsport Ave. (tel. 338–2740).

Yankee Clipper Motel. This pleasant place to stay includes the advantage of a beach. Coffee dispenser in each room.
Searsport Ave. (tel. 338–2220).

Reasonable

The Gull Motel. Family fun emphasized here with lawn games and pool. Summer only. Pets permitted.
Searsport Ave. (tel. 338–4030).

BOOTHBAY HARBOR

First Class

Fisherman's Wharf Inn. Park your boat or car at this beautiful waterfront motel. Restaurant and cocktail lounge. Extended summer season.
42 Commercial St. (tel. 633–5090).

Ocean Point Inn. This combination inn and motel is noteworthy for picturesque location at Linekin Bay. Beach sports. Restaurant and cocktail lounge. Extended summer season.
Shore Rd. (tel. 633–4200).

Reasonable–Expensive

Harborfields. This small resort is enjoyable for both relaxation and water sports. Cottages. Reservations important. Restaurant nearby. Summer season.
McKown Pt. Rd. (tel. 633–5082).

Reasonable

Linekin Bay Camp. Families will have fun in this casual resort. Sports from ping-pong to waterskiing. Pool. Many picnic-style meals.
Wall Point (tel. 633–2494).

Ship Ahoy and Far East. This motel features own fishing dock. Room rate includes light breakfast. Lovely harbor view. Family rates. Extended season.
Route 27 (tel. 633–5222).

CAMDEN

Reasonable

Ducktrap Motel. This small motel offers scenic bay view. Near moderately-priced restaurant. Family rates. Extended summer season.
US 1 (tel. 789–2771).

Marion Village. Check in and take a dip in the pool at this pleasant motel. Good family accommodations. Restaurant. Pets welcome.
US 1 (tel. 236–3306).

Portlaw Inn. This small inn is especially suited for families on a budget. Breakfast and dinner. Free parking. Summer season.
Penobscot Ave. (tel. 236–9327).

Whitehall Inn. This well-established resort has a lovely setting. Social director. Home-style food. Summer season.
52 High St. (tel. 236–3391).

ELLSWORTH

Reasonable

Brookside Motel. Pool and playground keep children happy. Dining room and

cocktail lounge. Open year-round.
Route 1 (tel. 667–2543).

Corkum's Motel. Nice idea to have free coffee in the room here. About 20 min. drive to ferry. Well-equipped.
Rte. 1, Bar Harbor Rd. (tel. 667–2858).

Jasper's Motel. Fine for families, as large rooms have all comforts of home. Restaurant and cocktail lounge. Pets welcome.
Rte. 1, High St. (tel. 667–2538).

Toddy Lake Side Court. Only 10 units but pleasant to stay here. Year-round. Restaurant close by.
Rtes. 1 and 3 (tel. 469–2822).

Twilite Motel. Attractive rooms are heated and have TV. Year-round. Popular with sportsmen. Guides arranged. About 15 mi. from Nova Scotia ferry.
Rtes. 1 and 3 (tel. 667–8165).

KENNEBUNKPORT

First Class

The Colony. New motel rooms are the latest attraction at this well-established resort hotel with ocean view. Good food and cocktails. Summer sports facilities. Pool. Night entertainment. Summer only.
Ocean Ave. (tel. 967–3331).

Narragansett by the Sea. Here the emphasis is on daytime water sports on the beach. Night-time entertainment at hotel. Both cookouts and dining room meals. Free parking. Pets welcome.
Beach Ave. (tel. 967–4741).

Shawmut Inn. Right on ocean front, resort life is emphasized here with water sports, swimming pool, and access to golf club. Dining room, cocktails. Family rates. Extended summer season.
Turbot's Creek Rd. (tel. 967–3318).

Reasonable

Seacrest Inn on the Sea. Relax on your terrace and enjoy the ocean view. Family rates. Good restaurant for breakfast, lunch, dinner. Extended summer season.
Ocean Ave. (tel. 967–2125).

NORTHEAST HARBOR

First Class

Asticou Inn. This Treadway Inn offers a beautiful woodland view and traditional hospitality. Cozy rooms. No charge for parking. Good restaurant serves breakfast, lunch, dinner, cocktails. Summer season only.
State 3 (tel. 276–3344).

Harborside Inn. Stroll along soft pine needle paths at this lovely inn near Acadia National Park. Doubly beautiful view—woodland and harbor. Colonial rooms with fireplaces. Open extended summer season only. Excellent restaurant (cocktails also).
Route 198 (tel. 276–3318).

Reasonable

Kimball House. Old-fashioned Yankee hospitality dominates this Treadway Inn. No charge for parking. Pets permitted. Most rooms are heated by fireplaces. Good meals and cocktails. Check about summer dancing schedule. S. Shore Rd. (tel. 76–3331).

OGUNQUIT

First Class

Cliff House and Motel. Here you have the advantage of a superb ocean view plus swimming in the pool. Surfcasting popular. Popular dining room and cocktail lounge. Entertainment.
Bald Head Cliff (tel. 646–5662).

Lookout Hotel. This popular resort has a magnificent view of ocean and gardens. Swimming pool, summer sports, social director. Good food and cocktails. Rates with or without meals. Open summer season only.
Shore Rd. (tel. 646–5501).

Reasonable

Ogunquit Motel. Families will appreciate the three or four beds in the

newer rooms. Just a few minutes from playhouse and center of town. Open all year around. Pleasant restaurant.
US 1 (tel. 646–2471).

Ontio Hotel. This hotel offers summer sports on the premises. Free parking. Restaurant. No charge for continental breakfast.
Israel's Head Rd. (tel. 646–5501).

OLD ORCHARD BEACH

Reasonable

Diplomat Motel. Right on the waterfront, this two-level motel includes sundeck for basking and beach for swimming. Coffee shop for lunch (no charge for continental breakfast). Open May to Oct.
E. Grand Ave. (tel. 934–4621).

Gull Motel. This two-level motel is convenient to beach and waterfront. Rooms with kitchens for families. Neighboring restaurant is open for 3 meals. Open Apr. to Nov.
89 W. Grand Ave. (tel. 934–4321).

La Voie Motel. Good for families, as there's a choice of rooms with or without kitchens. Some rooms have sun decks and glass doors for better viewing.
91 E. Grand Ave. (tel. 934–4151).

Mt. Royal Motel. Nice bright rooms attract tourists here. Access to swimming pool. Open June to Oct. Units heated individually.
30 W. Grand Ave. (tel. 934–2926).

PORTLAND

First Class

Eastland Motor Hotel. Highly-rated, interesting hotel has everything from top (*Top of the East* penthouse lounge) to bottom (*Down East* coffee shop). Complex includes swimming pool, drugstore, beauty and barber shop, variety of 5 restaurants, entertainment. No charge for parking. Pets permitted.
157 High St. (tel. 775–5411).

Holiday Inn. Part of a dependable, attractive chain, this big motel includes a swimming pool, coffee shop, restaurant, and cocktail lounge. Family plan and free cribs.
79 Riverside Ave. (tel. 781–5622).

Portlander Motel. Everything is big about this motel—including rooms and king-size beds. No charge for coffee in rooms. Swimming pool. Lively restaurant and cocktail lounge with dancing. Family plan. Pets permitted.
645 Congress St. (tel. 773–8181).

Reasonable

Lafayette Hotel. This well-established hotel is a popular meeting place for clubs. Restaurant, cocktail lounge. Barber shop and beautician. Free parking. Pets welcome.
638 Congress St. (tel. 773–6441).

RANGELEY LAKES

First Class

Rangely Manor Cottage Colony & Motel. Exciting water-skiing or relaxing sauna bath, two features here. Maine guides for sportsmen. Motel rooms include free light breakfast. Sandwiches at coffee shop. Extended summer season only. Pets welcome.
Manor Rd. (tel. 864–3340).

Saddleback Lake Lodge. Comfortable cottages have good lake view at this beautiful resort. Water sports on beach. Maine guides arranged. Top-rated restaurant (open to public but reservations necessary). Family plan. Summer only.
Route 4 (tel. 864–5501).

Sky and Lake Lodge and Motel. Bask in the sun, take in the quiet surroundings. Swimming pool. Well-known restaurant, cocktail lounge. Family fun emphasized here.
Hunter Cove Rd. (tel. 864–3396).

SACO

First Class

Oak Ledge Motel. Here you will find well-decorated rooms with all the com-

forts. Cocktail lounge especially popular for dancing. Very good restaurant. Pets permitted.
US 1 (tel. 282–1546).

Reasonable

Cascade Lodge & Cabins. Here you will find a choice of accommodations, especially comfortable for families. Pets welcome. Rustic atmosphere. Popular dining room; cocktails served.
Route 1 (tel. 883–4416).

Saco Motel. You won't go hungry here—the motel is close to seven restaurants. Short distance from Old Orchard Beach. Miniature golf on premises. Pets permitted.
US 1 (tel. 284–6952).

SEARSPORT

Reasonable

Hitchin' Post Motel. You may be lucky enough to get one of the rooms with fireplace. Room rate includes coffee. Pets permitted. Restaurant across the way. Open May to Oct.
Routes 1 and 3 (tel. 548–2822).

Lights Motel & Restaurant. This hospitable small motel stays open from Apr. to Dec. Heated units individually controlled. Coffee shop.
US 1 (tel. 548–7626).

Yardarm Motel. Personalized hospitality has made this motel popular. Beautiful view of bay; attractive landscaping. Very good restaurant for breakfast and dinner. Open extended summer season.
US 1 (tel. 548–2404).

SEBAGO LAKE

Reasonable

Dumar Lodge Motel. This friendly motel is open all year around and offers lower prices off-season.
Route 302, Raymond (tel. 655–4572).

Kernan's West Shore Hotel. From a daytime barbecue to a night-time cha-cha, this resort keeps guests entertained. Variety of sports. Beach. Pets welcome. Hearty food in dining room; cocktails served.
Route 114 (tel. 877–2311).

Migis Lodge and Cottages. Learn water-skiing here or watch enthusiasts from cottage porch. Fine beach on Lake Sebago. Active day sports program and night entertainment. Down East dinners.
Route 302, South Casco (tel. 655–4524).

SKOWHEGAN

Reasonable—First Class

Lakewood Motor Lodge. Summer theater fans will like the proximity of the Lakewood Theatre right on the premises. Resort has variety of summer activities. Excellent food. Pets permitted. Open summer only.
Lakewood (tel. 474–3331).

Reasonable

Belmont Motel. Take a refreshing dip in the pool after you check in at this very comfortable motel. Restaurant nearby. Games on premises. Open all year.
US 201 (tel. 474–3735).

Skowhegan Motel. You will like the convenience to Lakewood Summer Theatre. Good restaurant. Over a dozen units for families. Open all year around.
Route 201 (tel. 474–9752).

Somerset Motor Lodge. Good for families. Swimming pool; play area. Own pond for fishing. Nearby restaurant. Open summer only.
422 Madison Ave. (tel. 474–2227).

WATERVILLE

Reasonable

Arnold Motel. You will like this very comfortable brick motel. Relax at the pool. Special rooms for families.

Heated. Coffee shop. Prices lower off-season.
31 Main St. (tel. 453–7318).

Roosevelt Motor Lodge. A New England atmosphere adds to the charm. Open year-round. Seasonal rates. Dining room, cocktail lounge.
110 College Ave. (tel. 873–0151).

Waterville Motor Lodge. Coffee shop; breakfast. Restaurant nearby. Family, seasonal rates. Pets welcome.
Oakland Rd. (tel. 873–0141).

YORK

Deluxe

Marshall House. This well-known resort has everything under the summer sun for vacation enjoyment. Pool, beach. Access to 18-hole golf course. Fishing, boating. Evening entertainment. Delicious meals in dining room, clambakes also. Cocktail lounge. Beautician.
US 1A (tel. 363–2140).

First Class

Anchorage Motor Inn. This new 2-level motel is convenient to York Beach. Pool. Restaurant nearby. Open May to Oct.
Long Sands Rd. (tel. 363–5112).

Inexpensive

Rust's Motel. Picture windows are an attractive feature at this new motel near beach. Family accommodations. Restaurant nearby. Pets welcome.
Route 1A. (tel. 363–9815).

ELSEWHERE

AUBURN. *Auburn Motor Inn.* Reasonable. This new motel has good-sized rooms. Pets welcome. Breakfast only. Seasonal rates. Route 202. Tel. 784–6906.

Holiday Inn. First-class. All the comforts are at this large motel, one of a well-known group dotting the U.S.A. Excellent restaurant and cocktail lounge. Swimming pool. Route 202. Tel. 783–1454.

BATH. *New Meadows Inn.* Reasonable. Here you have your choice of cottage or inn during summer season. Inn only is open year-round. Restaurant. Route 1. Tel. 443–3472.

BETHEL. *Bethel Inn.* Deluxe. This beautiful country estate is bordered by White Mountains. Swimming in pool or Songo Lake. Social director. Sports, golf to canoeing. Entertainment. Extended season. Route 2. Tel. 824–2175.

BOOTHBAY. *Newagen Inn.* First-class. At this resort you will find a little world of summer sports in spectacular setting of ocean and woodland. King-size pool. Lobster cookouts. Entertainment. Cocktail lounge. Route 27. Tel. 633–5242.

Spruce Point Inn. First-class. Beach, fishing and boating. Games. Restaurant. Family vacation spot. On Spruce Pt. Tel. 633–4152.

BRIDGTON. *Christmas Tree Inn.* Reasonable. The name of this casual resort comes from the pine trees and evergreens surrounding Highland Lake. Water sports. Barbecues. Seasonal. Pets permitted. Route 93. Tel. 647–3482.

Richardson's Motel. Reasonable. Here you will find an all-year emphasis on sports, from swimming in summer to skiing on Pleasant Mountain. Hunters may arrange guides. Restaurant and bar. Pets permitted. On Route 302. Tel. 647–5571.

CALAIS. *Heslin's Motel.* Reasonable. This is a good informal family-type place. Play area. River view. Extended summer season. Pets welcome. River Rd. Tel. 454–3762.

Redclyffe. Reasonable. Restaurant open for breakfast, lunch, dinner, cocktails. Pets allowed. US 1. Tel. 454–3270.

CARIBOU. *Hotel Caribou.* Reasonable. Service clubs meet here weekly. Restaurant and cocktail lounge. Family plans. Elevator service. Free parking. Route 1. Tel. 496–3711.

Red Brick Motel. Reasonable. Comfortable accommodations and amusement area attract families. Restaurant nearby. On Route 1. Tel. 492–7001.

CENTER LOVELL. *Quisisana Lodge.* Reasonable. From French crepes suzette to Jewish-style blintzes, the menu offers variety. Sports on beach. Hootnanny evenings. Cottages. Summer only. Tel. 928–2365.

Severance Lodge. First-class. At this pine-bordered resort, take your choice of rooms in the lodges or a secluded cottage by Lake Kezar. Excellent food. Everything from tennis to water-skiing. Entertainment. Extended summer season. Tel. 928–2100.

DEER ISLE. *Goose Cove Lodge.* Reasonable. Water sports. Family rates. Informal, pleasant atmosphere. Tel. 348–2508.

GRAND LAKE STREAM. *Leen's Hook-N-Hunt Lodge.* Reasonable. From rugged sports to sophistication of cocktail get-togethers, this resort has variety. Arrangements for Maine guides. Water-ski on West Grand Lake. Seasonal. Good restaurant. US 1. Tel. 796–5575.

GREENVILLE. *Indian Hill Motel.* Reasonable. Restaurant nearby. Pets welcome. Highway 15. Tel. OX 5–2623.

Squaw Mountain Inn. Reasonable. Once you see the beautiful view of Moosehead Lake, you won't want to watch television. Arrange for canoe trip with guide. Entertainment. Sports. Pets welcome. Highway 15. Tel. OX 5–2515.

JACKMAN. *Attean Lake Camps.* Reasonable. Whether you stay overnight or for the season, you will receive a friendly welcome here. Own cabin cruiser provides transportation from mainland to camps. Rustic family cottages. Water sports. Summer only. Free parking. Pets permitted. Tel. 668–3792.

Sky Lodge Motel. First-class. If you're in a rush to get to this handsome North Woods Inn on Moose River, take a plane. Private landing strip. Guided canoe trips. Pool. Hunting. Restaurant and lounge. Highway 201. Tel. 668–2171.

KENNEBUNK. *Idlease Motor Hotel.* Reasonable–expensive. Family fun is emphasized at this motel. Pool. Play area. Access to beach and boats. Restaurant nearby. Seasonal. On Wells-Kennebunkport Rd. Tel. 985–4460.

Turnpike Motel. Reasonable. Wood-paneled rooms are heated at this small motel open year-round. Restaurant just a few steps away. Convenient location at Exit 3 Maine Turnpike. Tel. 985–4404.

KITTERY. *Charter House Motor Hotel.* First-class. Convenient location is just one advantage here. Two pools, summer sports. Pets welcome. Fine food at *Valle's Steak House* right next door. Route 95. Tel. 439–2000.

LEWISTON. *Holiday Motor Motel.* Reasonable. This neat, friendly motel is open year-round. Light breakfast at coffee shop. Special seasonal rates. 1905 Lisbon St. Tel. 783–2277.

MONHEGAN ISLAND. *Island Inn.* Reasonable. Pleasant, friendly place to stay on this island favored by artists (10 mi. out to sea). Daily boat schedule. American plan. Tel. 372–9681.

NAPLES. *Chute Homestead.* This friendly family resort has lively schedule including water-skiing and square dancing. Meals served indoors and outdoors. Rustic cottages. Summer only. Harrison Rd. Tel. 693–2425.

POLAND SPRING. *Poland Spring Hotel.* Deluxe. This outstanding resort is open year-round with full schedule of seasonal sports. Famous 18-hole golf course. Lifeguards at pools. Water sports at Beach Club. Superb restaurant, piano in cocktail lounge. Nighttime entertainment. Beautician. Tel. 998–4351.

PROUT'S NECK. *Black Point Inn.* Deluxe. Ocean resort fun is only minutes away from Portland at this excellent hotel. Swimming in pool or on beach. Golf and tennis, Prout's Neck Country Club next door. Delicious meals, cocktail lounge. Route 207. Tel. 883–4311.

ROCKLAND. *Samoset Hotel.* First-class. Large summer resort features sports program. Play area for children. Pool. Good ocean view. Restaurant and cocktail lounge, nightly dancing. Special rate plans. Beautician, barber shop. Pets welcome. Tel. 594–8411.

ROCKWOOD. *The Mt. Kineo.* First-class. Getting to this unusual resort is more than half the fun, a short, free launch ride on Moosehead Lake. King-size pool. Maine guides. Recreation from trapshooting to dancing. Restaurant, cocktail lounge. Beautician. Among U.S.A.'s top resorts. Tel. 534–2571.

RUMFORD. *Linnell Motel.* Reasonable. If you are interested in visiting Telstar, this motel is convenient. Open all year around. Heated units. Breakfast served. US 2. Tel. 364–4511.

SEBASCO ESTATES. *Sebasco Lodge & Cottages.* First-class. Fish from the dock, swim in the pool, or water-ski on the bay. A little city in itself with shops and beauty salon. Down East style food in dining room. Supervised program for children. Social evening programs. Summer only. Route 217. Tel. 443–5561.

SOUTHWEST HARBOR. *Harbor View Hotel.* Reasonable. Motel and cottages have good view of the bay. Restaurant nearby. Open May 1 to late Oct. US 1. Tel. 244–3133.

Moorings Motor Sail Inn. Reasonable. Cozy inn has attractive waterfront view. Popular with boat enthusiasts. Restaurant, cocktail lounge. Variety of rates. Free parking. Pets welcome. Shore Rd. Tel. 244–5523.

WINTHROP. *Cobbossee Motel.* Reasonable. Pool, play area. Coffee shop, breakfast. No highway noise. Pets welcome. US 202. Tel. 395–4111.

YARMOUTH. *Down East Village Motel.* First class. From Apr. to Nov. this popular motel welcomes guests. Family rates. Beautiful grounds include pool, play area. Restaurant, cocktail lounge. US 1. Tel. 846–4091.

Homewood Inn. First class. This attractive resort inn is official greeter to clambake cruises. Beach. Dining room, cocktail lounge. Pets welcome. Route 88. Tel. 846–5271.

YOUTH HOSTELS. Young people who wish to tour Maine may rent campsites in the many excellent *state parks.* There are two free park campgrounds at Black Woods and Seawall in *Acadia National Park* (two-week camping limit). Tourist homes throughout the state are inexpensive; listings from local chambers of commerce. Also, contact *YMCA,* Chestnut St., Camden; *Boothbay Region YMCA,* Boothbay, Maine.

FARM VACATIONS AND GUEST RANCHES. Several rural homes in the state welcome tourists; rates, about $50 a week with meals; special prices for children. *Elms Farm,* a 600-acre sheep farm, fishing, horseback-riding, and deer-hunting nearby. Information from the Eckhardts, Route 2, Coopers Mills. *Dearbrook Farm,* a horse ranch, is near lakes and a trout pond. Write to the Skillins, Route 2, Cumberland Center.

TRAILER TIPS. The *legal size* for a trailer in Maine is: length, 55 feet; width, 8 feet, 6 inches; height, 13 feet, 6 inches. 12-foot-wide mobile homes require State Police escort. *Trailer permits* are obtained at the main office of the Maine State Highway Commission, Maintenance Div., State House Annex, Augusta. Office hours: Mon. thru Sat., 8 a.m. to 5 p.m. On the *Maine Turnpike,* legal size without permits is the same. Permits may be obtained at Maine Turnpike Authority, 17 Bishop St., P.O. Box 839, Portland, or at any interchange.

Trailer parks in Old Orchard Beach are: *Paradise Trailer Park,* Adelaide Rd.; *O.O.B. Tent-Trailer Park,* Ocean Park Rd.; *Wagon Wheel Trailer Park,* Saco Ave.; *Wild Acres Trailer Park,* Saco Ave. Other trailer parks include *Androscoggin Camping and Trailer Park* in Wayne, *Stadig Mobile Park* in Wells, and *Christie's Tent & Trailer Park* in Newport.

CAMPING OUT. The Maine Forest Service maintains over 250 free camping areas. *State parks* provide camping facilities from $1 to $2 a day, limit two weeks; longer with supervisor's written permission. Camping time, usually May 1 to Oct. 15. Many parks have Adirondack shelters, $2.50 a day.

Acadia National Park is open all year and occupies almost half of Mt. Desert Island in Bar Harbor vicinity. Park campgrounds are free; trailers permitted. No utility connections. No reservations required. Headquarters: Main and Park sts., Bar Harbor, open 8 a.m. to 6 p.m.

Hermit Island, privately owned, in Bath, has 270 campsites, showers, toilets, fireplaces, drinking water. Open May 30 to Oct. 12. Reservations to P.O., Small Point. *Shore Hills Camping,* privately owned, State 27, Boothbay Harbor, has trailer hookups, 40 campsites. Rent, $2.50 a day; $15 a week. Pets welcome. Reservations: P.O., Boothbay. June 15 to Sept. 15. *Lake Pemaquid Camping,* privately owned, Damariscotta, has 150 campsites; hookups, 52 trailers. May 28 to Oct. 1. Pets welcome. Fee: $2.50; trailers with hookups, $2.75. *Papoose Pond Camping Area,* privately owned, on State 118, Norway, has 150 campsites. Travel trailers. Rate, $3. May 30 to Labor Day. Tel. Harrison 583–4470. *Wild Acres,* privately owned, Saco Ave. (State 5), Old Orchard Beach, has 50 trailer sites; 200 campsites. Pets welcome. Fee, $2; trailers, $2.50. May 15 to Sept. 15. *Libby's Oceanside Camp,* privately owned, US 1A, York Beach, has 40 trailer sites; 80 campsites. May 30 to Sept. 20. Fee, $2.50 a day.

DINING OUT. Once the visitor tastes a Maine lobster, he will never forget that ocean-fresh flavor. Seafood fresh from the sea is a specialty—clams, salmon, trout, and the tender lobsters. Chowders are featured at most restaurants. Reasonably priced seafood tops the list on just about all menus. Lobsters are caught right in the state so there are no surplus charges to raise the cost.

There are several cruises which incorporate a clambake or shore dinner on an island. A real Down East clambake is cooked in seaweed, covered with tarpaulins and rocks. This retains all the flavor of the Maine lobsters and clams. Clambakes and shore dinners begin with a hot cup of chowder, then the steamed lobsters, steamed clams, corn on the cob, Maine potatoes, baked onions. Blueberry cake is dessert (the blueberries are from Maine, of course), followed by hot coffee.

Blueberry and apple pies are also specialties of the Pine Tree State, where the visitor really has a delicious time.

BAR HARBOR

First Class

Harbourside Inn. Lobster any style is a treat at this luxurious resort. Special Sun. buffet. Children's menu. Apricot bread recipe was featured in *Gourmet* magazine. Cocktails. Breakfast, lunch, and dinner.

Harbourside Rd.

Reasonable

Moorings Motor Sail Inn. Waterfront dining is delightful here. Begin dinner with lobster stew and then order the charcoal-grilled steak. Cocktails. Open for summer only, for breakfast, lunch, dinner.

Shore Road.

Testa's. Salads are something special here—herbs are right from the garden. Luscious strawberry and raspberry pies. Shore dinner is most popular. Cocktail lounge. Open from early morning to midnight, summertime only.
53 Main St.

Tripp's. Treat yourself to delicious seafood specialties, then rum cream pie for dessert. Children's menu. Cocktail lounge, entertainment after 9 p.m. Open spring to autumn from late morning to 1 a.m.
45 Main St.

Inexpensive—Reasonable

High Seas. Try this restaurant for dining under glass (room is glass-enclosed). Delicious seafood and charcoal-broiled steak. Open summer only, for breakfast, lunch, snacks, and dinner.
State 3.

Inexpensive

The Fish Net. The seafood is certainly ocean-fresh—the restaurant has its own fish market. Dine in *Nautical Room* or on open deck overlooking the water. Cocktails.
On Municipal Pier.

BOOTHBAY HARBOR

Reasonable

Brown Bros. Delightful ocean-view dining is just one of the attractions here. Seafood specialties include a great shore dinner. Children's menu. Cocktails. No charge for parking. Open for lunch and dinner, summer season only.
Atlantic Ave.

Cabbage Island Clambakes. The boat trip is usually $1., the clambake $4. Enjoy a pleasant cruise and eat your clambake, too. Boats arrive in time for the feast. June 30 through Labor Day. Reservations necessary.
At Passenger Boat Association Pier 5. Tel. 633–1054.

Fisherman's Wharf Inn. Old salts and landlubbers will enjoy watching the yachts sail by from waterfront dining room and observation cocktail lounge. Extra-special shore dinners. Bread, rolls, and pastries baked on premises. Summer season extends into Oct. Open for breakfast, lunch, and dinner.
42 Commercial St.

Indian Island Cruise Clambake. This is a cruise-and-shore-dinner combination (alternate, fried chicken). Boat trip is 50¢, clam or lobster bake about $5. Host Captain Wade's wife bakes the blueberry cake dessert. Reservations necessary. Indian Island Restaurant open from noon to 9 p.m. for those who arrive on own boat.
Pier 5. Boothbay Harbor.

Inexpensive—Reasonable

Thistle Inn. Owned by a Scotsman and his bonnie wife, but no scrimping on portions. Roast beef is excellent. Unique European dishes on menu. Cocktails. Popular all year around. Open for breakfast, lunch, teatime, and dinner. Closed Sun.
53 Oak St.

Inexpensive

Crab & Lobster Wharf. Relax at a picnic table on a deck overlooking the water and enjoy lobster and steamed clams.
On East Side.

BRUNSWICK

Inexpensive—Reasonable

Eagle Hotel Dining Room. Old-fashioned roast stuffed lamb is the specialty here. Delicious rolls and pastries. Children's menu. Cocktails. Breakfast, lunch, dinner.
Brunswick Plaza.

Howard Johnson's. *Fireside Room* distinguishes this well-known restaurant. Lobster especially good here. Open all year around. Breakfast, lunch, dinner.
US 1 and Interstate 95.

Stowe House. You will be dining in the historic Harriet Beecher Stowe resi-

dence where she wrote *Uncle Tom's Cabin*. Very attractive Colonial setting with many antiques. Cocktails. Home-style cooking. Breakfast, lunch, dinner; dinner only, on Sun.
63 Federal St.

DAMARISCOTTA

Reasonable

The Cheechako. This is the Alaskan Indian name for "newcomer." Everything on the menu from sandwiches to picked-out lobster in butter. Open for lunch, teatime, dinner, for summer season only. Closed Mon.
Lewis Pt.

County Fair. Delicious, ocean-fresh seafood is cooked to order here. Motel dining room is known for tempting pies. Open summer season only. Breakfast, lunch, snacks, and dinner.
US 1.

Saltwater Farm Pier. Once you have the lobster dinner here and then have a hankering for it back in Kansas City, Saltwater will mail one to you. Grilled chicken rivals the seafood. Lunch and dinner from the end of May to the last of Oct.
Right on the wharf.

KENNEBUNKPORT

Reasonable

The Colony. This resort dining room has pleasant atmosphere at breakfast, lunch, or dinner. Buffet very popular Sun. night, so reserve ahead. Open summer season only.
Ocean Ave.

Olde Grist Mill. This historic old mill is filled with fascinating antiques. Excellent Maine dishes from chowder to Indian pudding. Children's menu. No cocktails. Extremely popular. Open summer season only, for lunch and dinner. Closed Mon.
Mill Lane.

Shawmut Inn. Enjoy the sea breezes over an alfresco lunch at this resort by the sea. Not even a calorie-watcher is able to resist some of the desserts here. Cocktails. Open from late spring to early autumn, for breakfast, lunch, dinner.
Off Turbot's Creek Rd.

OGUNQUIT

Reasonable—First Class

Dan Sing Fan Tea House. Sorry, there is no Chinese food here, but you won't mind because the continental specialties are superb and the Viennese-style desserts irresistible. Open summer season only for lunch, teatime, and dinner.
Shore Rd.

Poor Richard's Tavern. Richard won't be poor long if he keeps serving his wealth of fine recipes such as the strawberry rum cake. Jolly good British favorites include roast beef and roast leg of lamb. Cocktails. Elegant dining. Extended season from late spring to late November. Dinner only.
Pine Hill Rd.

Reasonable

Barbara Dean's. Although this pretty restaurant has delicious seafood specialties as on the dinner menu, don't forget to try the blueberry pancakes Sun. morning for breakfast. Children's menu. Open summer season for breakfast, lunch, and dinner.
57 Shore Rd.

Whistling Oyster. Delicious luncheons feature lobster salad. Also pleasant to have tea in the afternoon on the deck overlooking the gardens and ocean. No dinners. Open summer season only. Closed Sun.
Perkins Cove.

Inexpensive

Lobster Bar. Take your choice of garden restaurant or dining deck, both overlooking the water on Old Wharf. Specialties include lobsters, steamed

clams, broiled chicken—and beefburgers.
At foot of Beach St.

PORTLAND

Reasonable—First Class

Eastland Motor Hotel. A world of dining is under one roof, topped by the *Top of the East Cocktail Lounge,* glass-walled for panoramic view. Gourmet dining in the *Egyptian Court,* New England fare in the *Tavern Dining Room,* exotic Polynesian dinners in the *Hawaiian Hut.* Breakfast in *Down East Coffee Shop.* Top-brass lunch in Top of the East.
157 High St.

Reasonable

Boone's. You will like the romance of the sea atmosphere combined with candlelight here. Menu has wide variety. Cocktails. Open for lunch and dinner. Closed Sun.
6 Custom House Wharf.

Lafayette Hotel. Pleasant dining room is known for hearty bowls of clam chowder and Maine shore dinners. Cocktails. Open for breakfast, lunch, dinner.
638 Congress St.

Roma Café. Down East lobster and Roman *trattoria* dishes share the spotlight here. Cocktails and a wide variety of wines. Open for lunch and dinner. Closed Sun.
769 Congress St.

Smith Farm. Just a short drive from the city, this country barn restaurant features turkey dinners, home-baked pies topped with homemade ice cream. Lunch and dinner May through Aug. Dinner only during the rest of the year. Closed from mid-Dec. to Feb.
226 Gray Rd. on State 26 and State 100, about a mile from Exit 10 of the Maine Turnpike.

YORK

Reasonable

Burnett's. Right in historic York Village, this pleasant restaurant features seafood and steaks. Breakfast, lunch, dinner. Cocktails.
16 Long Sands Rd.

Jewell Inn. Delicious surprise to find real Southern-fried chicken here. Convenient for the family who visits Fun-Land about a half-mile away.
Ridge Rd.

Spiller's Restaurant. Sea air at York Beach will whet your appetite for the hearty food here and the luscious home-baked cakes. Breakfast, lunch, and dinner. Summer season only.
17 Ocean Ave.

Yorkway Restaurant. This restaurant has both a dining room and a dining terrace. Tasty dressing in the baked lobster. Children's menu. Cocktails. Open for lunch and dinner for an extended summer season to Columbus Day.
US 1.

ELSEWHERE

AUBURN. *Empire Room* (in the Holiday Inn Motel). Reasonable. Here the menu veers from the Colonial Yankee fare by featuring Continental specialties. Cocktails. Children's menu. Lunch, dinner. US 202.

AUGUSTA. *The Senator* (in the Senator Motel). Whether your preference is roast beef or Chinese cuisine, you will find American favorites and exotic specialties on the menu. Children's menu. Breakfast, lunch, dinner. Cocktails. US 202.

BANGOR. *Bangor House.* Reasonable. It's a surprise to find a Mexican motif complete with *Fiesta Room.* Menu is typically New England. Alfresco dining in summer. Cocktail lounge with entertainment. No charge for parking. Breakfast, lunch, dinner. 174 Main St.

Pilot's Grill. Inexpensive. Home-style food is the attraction here. Wide variety is headed by lobster, of course. Cocktails. Children's menu. Breakfast, lunch, dinner. No charge for parking. 1528 Hammond St.

BATH. *New Meadows Inn* (in the New Meadows Motel). Reasonable. Here you can have your art and eat delicious food, too. Paintings displayed. Shore dinner for hearty appetites. Yummy homemade ice cream. Cocktails. Open from early morning to midnight. US 1.

BETHEL. *Bethel Inn.* Reasonable. This beautiful inn emphasizes gracious dining. Famous for lobster. Reservations important Fri. night. Cocktails. Children's menu. Open all summer to Oct. Breakfast, lunch, and dinner. US 2.

BUCKSPORT. *Jed Prouty Tavern.* Reasonable. Historic background is part of the charm of this quaint restaurant, once a stagecoach stop. Own recipe for baked stuffed lobster. Children's menu. Cocktails. Open for breakfast, lunch, dinner. Not open Christmas Day. 52 Main St.

CALAIS. *Redclyffe.* Inexpensive—Reasonable. Picturesque from the outside, cozy on the inside describes this motel dining room. Succulent fried shrimp highlights the varied menu. Breakfast, lunch, dinner. Cocktails. US 1.

DOVER-FOXCROFT. *Blethen House.* Reasonable. Dining room is famous for New England cooking. About 5 mi. from *Sebec Lake* Public Beach. Lovely 40-mile drive to *Lakewood Summer Theatre.* Parking is free. Homelike Colonial atmosphere. Dinner 6 to 8 p.m. Cocktails. Closed Christmas. 37 E. Main St.

EAST EDGECOMB. *Emerson's Smorgasbord.* Inexpensive. Swedish-dollar pancakes are just one value here. Choice of smorgasbord or regular dinners. Nice lunches (try the lobster salad). Everything from homemade soup to nuts. Summer only. Damariscotta-Boothbay River Rd.

ELLSWORTH. *Le Domaine.* Reasonable. The Maine twang is replaced by a French accent here. Should you want to change from chowder to onion soup, this is the place. Open for lunch and dinner. Necessary to reserve ahead. US 1. Tel. 422-3395.

Lobster House. Those hearty Maine shore dinners seem to taste better than ever in this Dutch Colonial restaurant. Rolls and pies baked in their own ovens. Lunch and dinner. Cocktails. Summer only. State 3.

FALMOUTH. *The Galley.* Reasonable. You can choose the lobster you want right from the pool at this waterfront restaurant. Then it's stuffed and broiled to perfection. Children's menu. Breakfast, lunch, snacks, and dinner. Foreside Rd.

HOULTON. *Northland Hotel.* Inexpensive—Reasonable. Maine foods are featured in the dining room whether it's freshly caught salmon or just-picked potatoes. Cocktails. Breakfast, lunch, dinner. 38 Court St.

JACKMAN. *Sky Lodge.* Reasonable. Gorgeous view of Moose River mountain region makes for enjoyable dining in the rustic dining room with fireplace. Hearty, he-man food. Artistic floral decorations on relish and appetizer plates. Open summer to Dec. Breakfast, lunch, dinner. Cocktails. US 201.

KINGFIELD. *Capricorn Lodge.* Reasonable—First class. Who else but a Capricorn would invent Fish-Ke-Bob? Try the cheese-beer soup, too. Home baking. Children's menu. Bourbon Barrel Cocktail Lounge. Sat. night dancing. In keeping with zodiac sign of mountain goat, lodge is in the shadow of Sugarloaf Mt. ski area. Open all year.

KITTERY. *Valle's Steak House.* Reasonable. Bi-weekly lobster specials are very popular. Steak specials, too. Children's menu. Cocktail lounge has entertainment. Breakfast, lunch, dinner. Interstate 95.

Warren's Lobster House. You probably won't find more immense lobster pools anywhere or more orders for delicious charcoal-broiled lobster than here. Scenic river-front dining. Open for lunch and dinner all year around. Cocktails. 9 Water St.

LAKEWOOD. *Lakewood Restaurant.* Reasonable. Delicious meals and cocktails are served. Popular cottage colony, especially with the Lakewood Theatre nearby. US 201.

LEWISTON. *Steckino's.* Reasonable. When in Maine, do as the Romans do and order lobster *scallopini* or chicken *cacciatore* here. Boiled lobster and grilled steaks, too. Children's menu. Lovely *Starlight Room.* Cocktails. Open for lunch and dinner. Closed Sun. 106 Middle St.

NAPLES. *Chute Homestead.* Reasonable. Dining novelties are fun at this popular family resort—everything from breakfast cookouts to a chuck-wagon buffet. Open summer only, for breakfast, lunch, and dinner. Harrison Rd.

OLD ORCHARD. *Ocean Lobster Pound Restaurant.* Reasonable. Fresh seafood and chops are the specialty. Steak is served on a sizzling platter. Country-style atmosphere. Open for breakfast, lunch and dinner. Cocktails. 40 West Grand Ave., across the street from ocean.

RANGELEY LAKE REGION. *Sky and Lake Lodge and Motel.* Reasonable. The *Terrace Room* is attractive for dining. The *Moonshine Room* is a rendezvous for cocktails. Picturesque view. Near ski centers at Saddleback, Bald Mt., and Sugarloaf. Breakfast, lunch, snacks, dinner. Closed for little over a month between April and May, also 3 weeks in Dec. Hunter Cove Rd.

ROCKLAND. *Thorndike Hotel.* Candlelight glows during the Sat. night buffet in the attractive dining room decorated with paintings. Cocktails. Open every day for breakfast, lunch, and dinner (early dinner Sun.). 385 Main St.

Reasonable

ROCKWOOD. *The Birches.* Reasonable. Hearty fare is on the menu at this resort in the heart of hunting, fishing, and camping areas. Everything from thick, juicy steaks to extra-special home-baked apple pie. Open summer season only. Breakfast, lunch, dinner. On Moosehead Lake.

SACO. *Cascade Lodge.* Reasonable. Shore dinners top the menu in this cozy dining room. Also choice of chicken, steak, and daily specials. Delicious pastries. Children's menu. Cocktails. US 1.

SCARBORO. *Carriage House.* Reasonable. Headliners on the menu are a big charcoal-broiled steak and a tender stuffed lobster. The wild blueberry pie is just one of the home-baked special desserts. Cocktails. Open for lunch and dinner. Closed Mon., also Dec. 25. US 1.

SEAL HARBOR. *Jordan Pond House.* Reasonable. If you can take your eyes away for just a moment from the outstanding view of Acadia National Park, notice the big popovers. Rich homemade ice cream for dessert. Open for lunch, teatime, and dinner, summer season only. Mountain Rd.

SEARSPORT. *Kobs Lobster Pound.* Reasonable. Choose your own lobster from the pool. Then dine here picnic-style or take the lobster home. Try the pecan or berry pie for dessert. Open summer only, for lunch and dinner. US 1.

Yardarm. Reasonable. This is the attractive Colonial restaurant of the Yardarm Motel. Beautiful bay view. Varied menu with favorite dessert of lemon pie. Children's menu. Summer season extends to Oct. Open for breakfast and dinner. E. Main St.

SEBAGO LAKE. *Migis Lodge.* Pine-paneled dining room has picture windows overlooking the lake. It's worth rising early for blueberry pancakes and breakfast cookout. A Prime Rib Bazaar is Thurs. dinner special. Open summer season only, for breakfast, lunch, dinner. On Sebago Lake in South Casco. Off US 302. Reasonable.

SKOWHEGAN. *O Sole Mio.* Reasonable. New *Chianti Cocktail Lounge* strikes a happy note here. Variety of Italian dishes from pizza to lasagna. Sandwiches and Maine dishes, too. Open from late morning to early morning. Lakewood Rd.

Village Candle Light. Just as the name implies, this quaint restaurant has Colonial atmosphere. Seafood is the menu headliner. Open for breakfast, lunch, and dinner. Cocktails. 404 Madison Ave.

WATERVILLE. *The Jefferson.* Reasonable. Down East dishes and Far East specialties share the spotlight here —everything from Maine lobster to Chinese egg foo young. Children's menu. Lunch, dinner. Cocktails. 54 College Ave.

WISCASSET. *Dodge Inn.* Reasonable. This is the place for quaint decor, flickering candlelight, river view. Tasty fried shrimp from chef's own recipe. Children's menu. Open for lunch and dinner. Extended season from May to late autumn. Closed Mon. US 1.

YARMOUTH. *Down East Village.* Reasonable. Of course this motel dining room features all the famous Down East seafoods. Breakfast, lunch, dinner. Cocktails. Extended season from late spring to Nov. US 1.

The Fellsmoor. Whether you order a sandwich or hearty shore dinner, the courteous service is the same. Children's menu. Open summer season only, for lunch and dinner. US 1.

BARS. Top bar in Maine is the Rooftop Lounge in the *Eastland Motor Hotel,* 157 High St., Portland, open from morning to midnight. *The Augusta House,* 170 State St., Augusta, has a pleasant lounge, open from 11 a.m. to midnight.

NIGHTCLUBS. There are no New York-type nightclubs in Maine, where the entertainment is usually at resorts for summer guests. *Eastland Motor Hotel,* 157 High St., Portland, has entertainment and dancing in a beautiful, glass-walled penthouse cocktail lounge. Open until midnight. *Bar Harbor Motor Inn,* Newport Dr. at pier, in Bar Harbor, has dancing every night except Sun from 9 p.m. until closing. Old Orchard Beach features dancing at *Ocean Pier Casino, Palace Ballroom,* and at many hotel cocktail lounges in summer.

MUSIC. At the *New England Music Camp* on Lake Messalonskee, near Oakland, students study and perform with well-known musicians. Free concerts presented in the Bowl-in-the-Pines, usually July and Aug., Wed. at 8 p.m., Fri. at 7:30 p.m., Sun. at 3 p.m. Check ahead for schedules. Other summer music camps are *Camp Encore,* Harrison; *Kneisel Hall,* Blue Hill; *Amherst Music Center,* South Casco.

Summer Harp Colony of America concerts are usually at St. Thomas Parish House, Penobscot Bay. This is also the location for the Thurs. evening summer concerts by *Bay Chamber Concert* group.

In Portland, don't miss the free *organ concerts* July and Aug. in City Hall, featuring the famous *Kotzchmar Memorial Organ.* There are also weekly summer *band concerts* at Fort Allen Park. The *Portland Symphony Orchestra* performs on a pre-announced schedule.

Summer *chamber music concerts* are usually featured Sun. in the Bowdoin College Chapel. In Bar Harbor, there are *band concerts* Mon. and Thurs. Check on occasional concerts by the *Acadia Choral Society.* Farmington features summer *band concerts.* This is the birthplace of Lillian Nordica, the operatic singer, and her home is a museum. Bangor presents summer *band concerts* in the parks. Check on performances by the *Bretton Woods Boy Singers.* They have performed in Ocean Park, Old Orchard Beach.

STAGE AND REVUES. These are the top summer theaters: *Boothbay Playhouse,* Wiscasset Rd., Boothbay; *Brunswick Playhouse,* Bowdoin Campus; Brunswick; *Kennebunkport Playhouse,* Old River Rd., Kennebunkport; *Ogunquit Playhouse,* US 1, Ogunquit; *Lakewood Theatre,* Showhegan. Season, June to Labor Day.

TOURS. *By boat. Casco Bay Lines,* Portland, operate all year to Casco Bay Islands, on the new *Abenaki* and the *Rebel.* Lobster and clam bakes, refreshments. The *Bailey Island Cruise* leaves daily and Sun., 10 a.m. and 2 p.m. This is a lectured cruise sailing by the 365 islands of Casco Bay. Trips cost $4 for adults; $3, children. Motels available.

The *Calendar Islands Cruise* leaves daily and Sun. Fare is $3 for adults; $2.25 for children.

A sunset cruise to *Cliff Island* leaves daily and Sun., 5:30 p.m., the year round. The round-trip cruise is 3 hours. Adults $3; children $2.25. A 2-hour *moonlight cruise* leaves daily and Sun. at 9 p.m. (seasonal), sailing through inner Casco Bay to Long Island and return. The fare is about $2 for adults; children $1.20. Plans are being made to include a Down East Maine supper for the same fare.

All the above trips leave from *Custom House Wharf* in *Portland.* Casco Bay Lines information center, tel. 773–8105.

The *Stardust Tour* is on an 85-foot luxury yacht, beginning with bus trip from Monument Square, Portland, at 12:30 p.m. for the two-hour ride to Boothbay Harbor. The bus passes Bath Iron Works, Bowdoin College, Brunswick Naval Base, beautiful old homes of Wiscasset. After lunch in Boothbay Harbor, the *Stardust* sails at 4:30 p.m. along the coast. The trip is 8 hours in all and costs $5.25 (Sun. July 5, 26, Aug. 16). Tel. 774–0351, *Portland Coach Co.*

Boothbay Harbor region offers a grand variety of harbor tours complete with lunch, clambakes, or supper. *The Balmy Days* features cruises to Monhegan: trips to Indian Island for shore dinners. Tel. 633–5131 or 633–4878. For a sunset-twilight harbor tour with brownies and coffee, tel. 633–3474. The *Argo* cruise includes region from Kennebec River to New Harbor, tel. 633–5307. The *Nellie G II* and *Maranbo II* cruise to Squirrel Island. Tel. 633–3244. *The Liekin*'s features the Cabbage Island lobster bake cruise. Tel. 633–5131.

For a week's tour of the Maine coast, *Victory Chimes* (a large windjammer) sails from Rockland every Mon. during summer season. Tel. 326–8856 or write Captain Frederick B. Guild, Castine, Maine. Weekly cost: $135 to $150.

Acadia National Park features *Naturalist Sea Cruises* and *Historical Cruises.* Tel. 288–5741 for the former, 244–3366 for the latter. For *Baker Island Cruise,* tel. 244–3366. Cruises are accompanied by park naturalist.

Sailing vacations are specialties of Capt. Jim Nisbet on two-masted schooners. Free folder from *Maine Windjammer Cruises,* P.O. Box 404F, Camden; also schooner *Mary Day* sails on weekly cruises. Information from *Coastal Cruises,* Sedgwick, Maine. Schooners *Stephen Tabor* and *Adventure* make weekly cruise; write *Yankee Schooner Cruises,* Box 696, Camden, Maine.

Telstar Tour takes nine hours, a tour of 75 miles from Monument Square in Portland to Andover, where one of two satellite earth stations is located (the other is in France). Visitors may walk in the great Radome and see how Telstar functions. On the return there is a stop for lunch at Rumford. The cost is $4.75; dates for the trip are July 12 and Aug. 23. Check with Portland Coach Co. in advance, tel. 774–0351. Portland Coach Co. also schedules an *Apple Blossom Tour*—$2 for the four-hour trip—and an *Autumn Foliage Tour,* $3.75 for the seven-hour trip. Other tours by Portland Coach, from $2 to $4.25, are the *Mountain Tour, Fun Tour, Bailey and Orrs Islands Tour, Belgrade Lake Tour, York County Tour, Bean Hole Bean Festival Tour, Belfast Tour, Pemaquid Point Tour, Fryeburg Fair Tour, China Lake Tour, Rangeley Lake Tour* ($5).

Acadian Bus Tours feature narrated sightseeing trips through Acadia National Park. Tour lasts about 2½ hours. Bus company office is in Bar Harbor.

There is a *City of Portland Tour,* daily and Sun. the year round, by *Gray Line* (motor coach or limousine) in cooperation with *Casco Bay Lines.* All tourist attractions are covered, including the history trail, and the tour may be combined with any boat cruise. Fare, $4 adults; children $3. Tel. 773–8105. *Parker Tours,* and *Greyhound Bus Co.* include State of Maine tours from starting points in other states.

Sightseeing flights are arranged by *Bar Harbor Airways, Inc.,* Bar Harbor Airport, Trenton. Tel. EL 667–2233. The plane flies over Acadia National Park, and Cadillac Mt. *Aerial Enterprises,* Wiscasset Airport, also has scenic flights. Tel. 882–9265.

A 10-day *canoe trip* with guide, paddling down the Allagash River, costs about $15 a day for the guide, $5 for each camper, plus the cost of food, gasoline, canoe, and gear. For a canoe trip through the wilderness, contact *Maine Publicity Bureau,* 11 Chapel St., Augusta, for names of guides.

SPECIAL INTEREST TOURS. *Museums:* Museum-goers and archeologists will enjoy a double feature at *Abbe Museum of Archaeology,* near Sieur de Monts Spring, in Acadia National Park, Bar Harbor region. The area's Stone-Age Indian culture is exhibited. *Islesford Historical Museum,* Little Cranberry Island, is also part of Acadia National Park and worth a visit. Inquire at Park Headquarters for boat schedules. Railroad and trolley-car buffs should visit *Seashore Trolley Museum,* Log Cabin Road, Kennebunkport; and *Boothbay Railway Museum,* State 27, near Boothbay Harbor. Both include rides. Ship enthusiasts will like the *Bath Marine Museum,* 963 Washington St., Bath (just follow the sign of the clipper ship).

Historical Societies: Bangor Historical Society, Union and High Sts., Bangor, is open all year round; free admission. *Pejepscot Historical Society Museum of Regional Americana,* 12 School St., Brunswick, is open summer afternoons. Adults 50 cents; children, 25 cents. *Camden Historical Society,* Washington St., Camden, is free; open summer only on Wed. afternoons. *Maine Historical Society,* 485 Congress St., Portland, is open daily; free admission.

Art: Art colonies and art schools welcome the tourist at *Haystack Mt. School of Crafts,* Deer Isle; *Skowhegan School of Painting and Sculpture,* Skowhegan; *Art Center Workshop,* Kennebunk; *William Fisher Studio,* Kennebunkport; *Roger Deering Studio,* Kennebunkport; *Edward Mayo Studio,* Kennebunkport; art colony on Monhegan Island.

Audubon: Bird-watchers have much to watch in Maine. *Acadia National Park,* Mt. Desert Island, has nature walks scheduled morning and afternoon. Most important observation point: the Atlantic Flyway. Inquire at Information Center, 339 Main St., Bar Harbor. Visit *Moosehorn National Wildlife Refuge,* Charlotte Rd., Calais, daily and Sun., summer only; Deer Isle Area is noted for Russell's Bird Sanctuary (guided tours); Todd Wild Life Sanctuary and Audubon Nature Camp are on Hog Island, boat service available. *Audubon Society Headquarters* is in Portland. Tel. 772–1038.

Photography: For the photographer, there's a wonderland of rugged coast and primeval wilderness. *Acadia National Park* boasts the most beautiful coastal scenery and interesting plant life in the country. *Stonington* is known as the most photogenic of New England's fishing ports. *Camden* is the home of the windjammers. The lighthouse at *Pemaquid Point* is one of the most photographed. The Wedding Cake House in *Kennebunk* is photogenic. *Brownville Junction* is known as the Grand Canyon of the East. The signpost at *Lynchville* is a good subject (includes Paris, Poland, Peru, Mexico, etc.).

INDUSTRIAL TOURS. For a look at the diversity of Maine industry, you may enjoy these tours: Shoes are made at *Charles Cushman Co.,* 209 Court St., Auburn; linens are manufactured at *Pepperrell Manufacturing Co.,* Biddeford; canoes and boats are built at *Old Town Canoe Co.,* Old Town; potatoes grow at the *Aroostook Experimental Farm,* Presque Isle; newsprint is manufactured at *St. Croix Paper Co.,* Woodland.

Arrangements necessary.

HISTORIC SITES. York Village includes *Wilcox House* (1740), *Old Gaol Museum* (1653), *Jefferd's Tavern* (1750), *Old School House* (1745). Summer season only. No charge to visit School House. Buy a combination ticket (adults 75 cents, children 25 cents) to see the old buildings. Also in York Village, the *Elizabeth Perkins House* is noteworthy for antiques. Summer only, daily and Sun. Ticket 30 cents; 10 cents, children.

The *Wadsworth-Longfellow House,* 485 Congress St., Portland, was the home of the famous poet. Summer only. Admission 50 cents, children 30 cents. *Stowe House,* 63 Federal St., Brunswick, is a registered national historic landmark. Here Harriet Beecher Stowe wrote *Uncle Tom's Cabin.* The *Lady Pepperrell House* (1760), on State 103, Kittery, is also a registered national historic landmark, owned by the Society for the Preservation of New England Antiquities. Open daily, summer only. Admission 50 cents, children 25 cents. *John Paul Jones Memorial* (free admission) is also in Kittery.

Burnham Tavern, Machias, dates back to 1770 and retains the original sign. Summer only. Tues. and Wed. afternoons. Admission 50 cents. *Fort O'Brien Memorial* in Machiasport commemorates the wars of 1775 and 1812; free admission.

MUSEUMS AND GALLERIES. Maine is the subject for many an artist's brush which means the visitor will find landscapes galore displayed throughout the state.

Ogunquit is known for the *Museum of Art* open summer season only, free admission. The *Ogunquit Art Center* also features American artists, in summer only. Admission is 50 cents. The *Portland Museum of Art,* 111 High St., Portland, is in a mansion. Admission is free to view a collection of art by Maine artists, and the mansion itself. Closed Mon. and holidays. *Maine Art Gallery,* Warren St., Wiscasset, features sculpture and paintings by Maine artists. Open summer only; no charge. American and European art is exhibited at the *William A. Farnsworth Library and Art Museum,* 19 Elm St., Rockland. The handmade ship models are fascinating. Admission is free.

Bass Harbor Country Store Museum in Bass Harbor opened in 1965 to recapture the old country store with ancient counters, cracker barrels, tea chests, etc. Costumed ladies serve as guides. Open summer only. *Bowdoin College Museum of Art,* in Brunswick, has interesting collections. Admission is free. *Maine Historical Society Museum,* near the Wadsworth-Longfellow House in Portland, features exhibits dating back to Revolutionary days. Admission is free.

GARDENS. *Black House,* on West Main St., Ellsworth, has lovely flower gardens bordered by old-fashioned lilacs. The two-story brick mansion dates back to 1800. Mansion and gardens are open from June to Oct. (closed Mon.); admission 50 cents; children 25 cents. At the end of June, visitors may tour beautiful rose gardens in Portland.

SHOPPING. In *Portland,* the state's largest city, stores are open until 5:30 p.m. daily and Sat., until 9 p.m. Mon. and Thurs. For one-stop shopping in Portland, *A. H. Benoit & Co.* is a family apparel store with branches in Biddeford, Ogunquit, Lewiston, Westbrook, Brunswick. No visit to Maine is complete without moccasins. Portland is the home of

Quoddy, with 200 styles of leather moccasins, at 208 Anderson St.

Some of the *Maine Antique Dealers' Association* stores are *F. O. Bailey Co.,* 72 Free St., Portland; *Getchell's Antiques,* Shore Rd., Falmouth; *Smith's Antique Shop,* 4 South St., Brunswick; *Mrs. Lincoln Cleaves,* 16 Church St., Gorham; *Goldthwaite's Antiques,* Route 302, Naples Village; *Roosevelt Trail Antiques,* Westbrook.

Boothbay Harbor has the state's largest *art supply store* north of Portland: *Bay St. Studio,* behind Brewer's Market. *Art and handicrafts* are featured in the following shops as well as many others throughout the state: *Courjon Studio,* Dover Rd., Boothbay Harbor; *Americana Shops,* US 1, Kittery; *Gray Elf Studio,* Hulls Cove; *Perry's Tropical Nut House,* US 1, Belfast; *The Pottery,* north of Town Hill, Bar Harbor; *Willis and Sons Rock Shop,* 68 Main St., Bar Harbor; Maine's *Massachusetts House Workshop,* US 1, Lincolnville; *Smiling Cow,* Main St., Rockport.

SUMMER SPORTS. For the *fisherman,* this is the only state with 7 rivers where the Atlantic salmon is caught. Maine holds the world record for landlocked salmon, cod, and perch. The Tackle Busters Club has caught record tuna, striped bass, pollock, cod, and mackerel. No license required for saltwater fishing. Open fresh water fishing (lots of trout) is from early spring to end of Sept. Fishing license is about $3.75 for 3 days. The registered Maine guide is $15 a day, plus expenses.

Boating: The *Boothbay Harbor Boatel* has complete facilities. Or you may charter a boat complete with Maine guide on Mooselookmeguntic or Rangeley lakes (lunch prepared over an open fire).

Canoeing is a popular sport in the Rangeley Lake Region. Day-trips may be done on your own but a Maine guide is suggested for 4-day to 2-week trips. Information available from State Dept. of Economic Development, Augusta. Spectators may watch *regattas* during the active boating season from Apr. through Nov. Or they may book *boat-sightseeing-clambake cruises* available mostly in the Boothbay region.

Water Sports: All state parks offer a variety of saltwater and freshwater *swimming.* Seven miles of white sandy beach on the Atlantic attract surf swimmers to Old Orchard Beach. In the Rangeley Lakes Region, *water skiing* is featured. For the spectator, there are *water carnivals* here, *water ski shows,* and *novices* taking lessons.

Horseback Riding: Just about all the state parks have riding trails. There are 100 riding clubs. Visitors are welcome to trot along for the ride. Information about club trips and stables is available from William R. Smith, Editor, Northeast Horseman, Box 47, Hampden Highlands. Spectators may look at horses at all the *horse shows* scheduled from July thru Oct. Or they may attend *horse races* at Lewiston Raceway, Gorham Raceway, Scarborough Downs, Northern Raceway on Presque Isle, Vacationland Downs in Yarmouth.

Golf: Golf courses are open to visitors. *Augusta* has three courses; *Portland* has an 18-hole course at Riverside. *Boothbay Region Country Club* is open early spring thru Nov. *Camden-Rockport-Lincolnville* area has three 9-hole courses and an 18-hole course. *Kebo Valley Club,* Bar Harbor, has an 18-hole course. *Poland Spring House* is famous for its 18-hole course. *Rangeley Lakes Region* has two 18-hole courses, both above 1,600 feet. For the spectator, there are golf tournaments scheduled from June thru Sept.

Archery: The *Rangeley Lakes Region* welcomes visitors to watch or participate at their new 14-target field range, located on a game preserve. Highland Bowmen meet regularly.

Mountain Climbing: This sport reaches the heights in Maine—such lofty challenges as 10 peaks 4,000 feet or higher. The *Appalachian Trail* is the longest in the world, crossing a few thousand miles from Mt. Katahdin to Mt. Oglethorpe in Georgia. Just through Maine, the course is 269 miles. All state parks and forests have marked trails. Climb *Mt. Blue* in Mt. Blue State Park, Weld, for a 3,000-ft.-above-sea-level view. Copies of *Mountain Climbing in Maine* are free from Maine Publicity Bureau, Gateway Circle, Portland.

Hunting: In mid-Oct. the great North Woods is open for deer hunting (bow and arrow only). The southern area is open Nov. 1. The first feeding grounds on the Atlantic Flyway attract duck and geese. Pheasant and woodcock are in the woodlands. Charter duck boats are available. Snowshoe rabbit season is from Oct. 1 thru Feb. Bear and bobcat are game all year round. Moose may be shot with camera only. Registered guides are available. Free information from *Maine Hunting Service,* 900 Gateway Circle, Portland.

WINTER SPORTS. Snowfall begins early and skiing extends thru Easter. There are more than 30 ski areas, many lighted at night. There are winter carnivals at schools and universities. The *Rumford Winter Carnival* includes ski-jumping. Summer resorts in ski areas become winter resorts with *ice-skating, sleigh-riding, ice-fishing, snowshoeing, tobogganing.* Sugarloaf in Kingfield even features *dog-sledding* by moonlight.

All major ski areas have their own direct telephone number. These are some of the *ski areas: Agamenticus,* York; *Bald Mountain,* Bangor; *Bald Mountain,* Oquossoc; *Baker Mountain,* Bingham; *Black Cat Mountain,* Millinocket; *Camden Snow Bowl,* Camden; *Chisholm Park,* Rumford; *Colby College,* Waterville; *Eaton Mountain,* Skowhegan; *Hurricane Slope,* Portland; *Lone Mountain,* Andover; *Lost Valley,* Auburn; *Maggie's Mountain,* Freeport; *Mars Hill,* Mars Hill; *McFarland's Hill,* Bar Harbor; *Mt. Abram,* Locke Mills; *Municipal Slope,* Millinocket; *Nopar Slope,* Norway; *Pal Ski Slope,* Fairfield; *Pleasant Mt.,* Bridgton; *Poland Spring,* Poland Spring; *Powder House,* So. Berwick; *Saddleback Mt.,* Rangeley; *Sky-Hy-Park,* Topsham; *Spruce Mt.,* Chisholm; *Squaw Mt.,* Greenville; *Standpipe Hill,* Guilford; *Sugarloaf Mt.,* Kingfield; *Sunday River,* Bethel; *Sunrise Slope,* Alexander; *Titcomb Slopes,* Farmington. Complete listings are free from Maine Winter Vacations, 900 Gateway Cicle, Portland.

Ice-boating is becoming popular in the *Rangeley Lakes* area. Conditions are best Oct. and Nov. Races are in class competitions. As they roar over the ice the sound is similar to that of jet planes.

RECOMMENDED READING. The following books are recommended for visitors who want to become more acquainted with Maine: *Folklore of Maine,* by Horace Beck; *State o' Maine,* by Louise Dickinson Rich; *Maine and Her People,* by Harold Clifford. In addition, Maine Dept. of Economic Development in Augusta distributes *Facts About Maine.*

RETIREMENT AREAS. Maine's climate is sometimes as rugged as its coastline but that does not deter retiring there. Winters are cold and snowy, summers very pleasant and cool. July and Aug. are the driest months. Rain is distributed fairly evenly during the year. The vast woodlands and ocean-splashed coast are appealing to those who like the great outdoors.

One of the events features the young at heart when the *Annual Retired Skippers' Race* is held in Penobscot Bay the middle of Aug. Competing skippers range in age from 66 to 85 years.

Retirees don't have to figure the cost of clothing if they join the one nudist camp, near Gray (halfway between Portland and Lewiston via the Maine Turnpike).

INDEX

In the Geographical Index, "H" stands for Hotels, *"R" for* Restaurants.

CONNECTICUT

PRACTICAL INFORMATION

GEOGRAPHICAL

HARTFORD

PRACTICAL INFORMATION

GEOGRAPHICAL

RHODE ISLAND

PRACTICAL INFORMATION

GEOGRAPHICAL

MASSACHUSETTS

PRACTICAL INFORMATION

GEOGRAPHICAL

BOSTON

PRACTICAL INFORMATION

GEOGRAPHICAL

CAPE COD

PRACTICAL INFORMATION

GEOGRAPHICAL

VERMONT

PRACTICAL INFORMATION

GEOGRAPHICAL

NEW HAMPSHIRE

PRACTICAL INFORMATION

GEOGRAPHICAL

MAINE

PRACTICAL INFORMATION

GEOGRAPHICAL

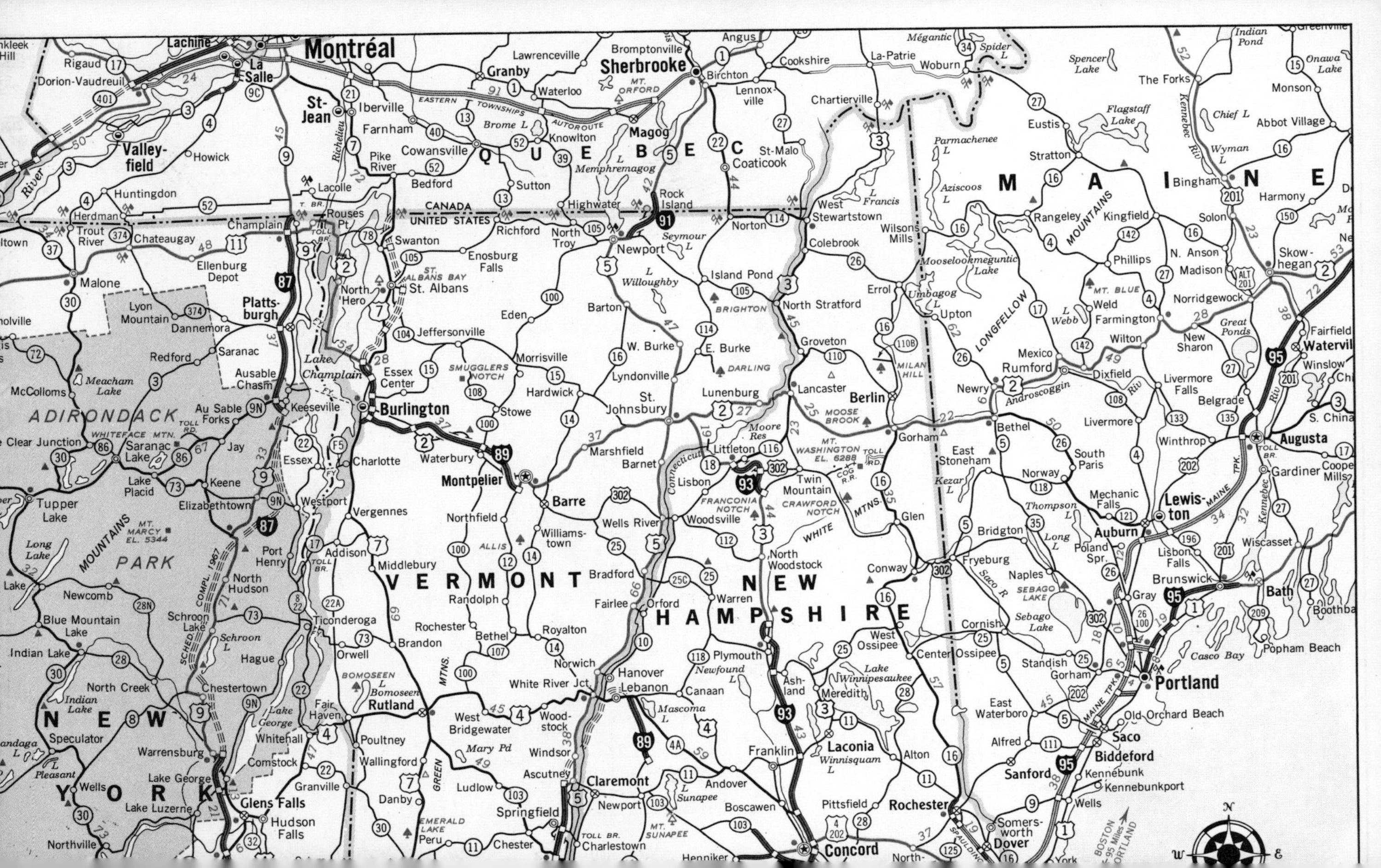

Montréal
Lachine
La Salle
Rigaud
Dorion-Vaudreuil
Valley-field
Howick
Huntingdon
Herdman
Trout River
Chateaugay
Malone
St-Jean
Iberville
Farnham
Pike River
Cowansville
Bedford
Lacolle
Granby
Waterloo
Knowlton
Sutton
Brome L
Magog
Sherbrooke
Mt. Orford
Lawrenceville
Bromptonville
Angus
Birchton
Lennoxville
Cookshire
St-Malo
Coaticook
Chartierville
La-Patrie
Woburn
Mégantic
Spider L
Eastern Townships Autoroute
Q U E B E C
Memphremagog L
Canada
United States
Rouses Pt
Champlain
Richford
North Troy
Highwater
Rock Island
Newport
Seymour L
Norton
West Stewartstown
L Francis
Colebrook
Wilsons Mills
Swanton
St. Albans Bay
St. Albans
Enosburg Falls
North Hero
Plattsburgh
Ellenburg Depot
Lyon Mountain
Dannemora
Saranac
Redford
Ausable Chasm
Keeseville
Lake Champlain
Burlington
Essex Center
Jeffersonville
Smugglers Notch
Stowe
Morrisville
Eden
Hardwick
Barton
L Willoughby
W. Burke
E. Burke
Lyndonville
St. Johnsbury
Brighton
Darling
Island Pond
North Stratford
Groveton
Lancaster
Lunenburg
Berlin
Moose Brook
Errol
Umbagog L
Upton
Milan Hill
Mooselookmeguntic Lake
Aziscoos L
Parmachenee L
Longfellow Mountains
Rangeley
Stratton
Eustis
Spencer Lake
Flagstaff Lake
Kingfield
Phillips
Mt. Blue
Weld
L Webb
Mexico
Rumford
Newry
Androscoggin Riv
Dixfield
Wilton
Farmington
Livermore Falls
Livermore
Belgrade
New Sharon
Great Ponds
Norridgewock
Madison
N. Anson
Solon
Bingham
Wyman L
Chief L
The Forks
Kennebec Riv
Monson
Abbot Village
Onawa Lake
Indian Pond
Harmony
Skowhegan
Fairfield
Waterville
Winslow
S. China
Augusta
Gardiner
Winthrop
Lewiston
Auburn
Mechanic Falls
Poland Spr.
Lisbon Falls
Brunswick
Bath
Wiscasset
Popham Beach
Boothbay
Casco Bay
Portland
Gray
Old Orchard Beach
Saco
Biddeford
Kennebunk
Kennebunkport
Wells
Sanford
Alfred
Gorham
Standish
Sebago Lake
Naples
Bridgton
Fryeburg
Saco R
Thompson L
Long L
Norway
South Paris
Bethel
East Stoneham
Kezar L
Gorham
Maine Tpk.
M A I N E
Boston 95 Miles
Portland
Montpelier
Waterbury
Barre
Williamstown
Northfield
Allis
Marshfield
Barnet
Charlotte
Vergennes
Middlebury
Addison
Essex
Westport
Port Henry
Ticonderoga
Orwell
Brandon
Rochester
Randolph
Bethel
Royalton
Norwich
White River Jct.
Woodstock
Bomoseen L
Rutland
Fair Haven
West Bridgewater
Mary Pd
Green Mtns.
Poultney
Wallingford
Danby
Emerald Lake
Peru
Ludlow
Chester
Springfield
Ascutney
Windsor
V E R M O N T
Wells River
Bradford
Fairlee
Orford
Hanover
Lebanon
Canaan
Mascoma L
Littleton
Lisbon
Woodsville
Franconia Notch
Crawford Notch
Moore Res
Connecticut
Mt. Washington El. 6288
Cog R.R.
Twin Mountain
White Mtns.
Glen
Conway
North Woodstock
Warren
Plymouth
Newfound L
Ashland
Meredith
Lake Winnipesaukee
West Ossipee
Center Ossipee
Cornish
Laconia
Winnisquam L
Franklin
Andover
Sunapee L
Mt. Sunapee
Claremont
Newport
Charlestown
Boscawen
Pittsfield
Concord
Henniker
Alton
Rochester
Somersworth
Dover
East Waterboro
Spaulding
North-
N E W H A M P S H I R E
Adirondack Park Mountains
Whiteface Mtn.
Saranac Lake
Lake Placid
Keene
Jay
Au Sable Forks
Elizabethtown
Mt. Marcy El. 5344
North Hudson
Schroon Lake
Schroon L
Hague
Chestertown
Lake George
Whitehall
Comstock
Granville
Glens Falls
Hudson Falls
Lake George
Lake Luzerne
Warrensburg
North Creek
Indian Lake
Blue Mountain Lake
Newcomb
Long Lake
Tupper Lake
Clear Junction
McColloms
Meacham Lake
Speculator
L Pleasant
Wells
Northville
N E W Y O R K
Sched. Compl. 1967

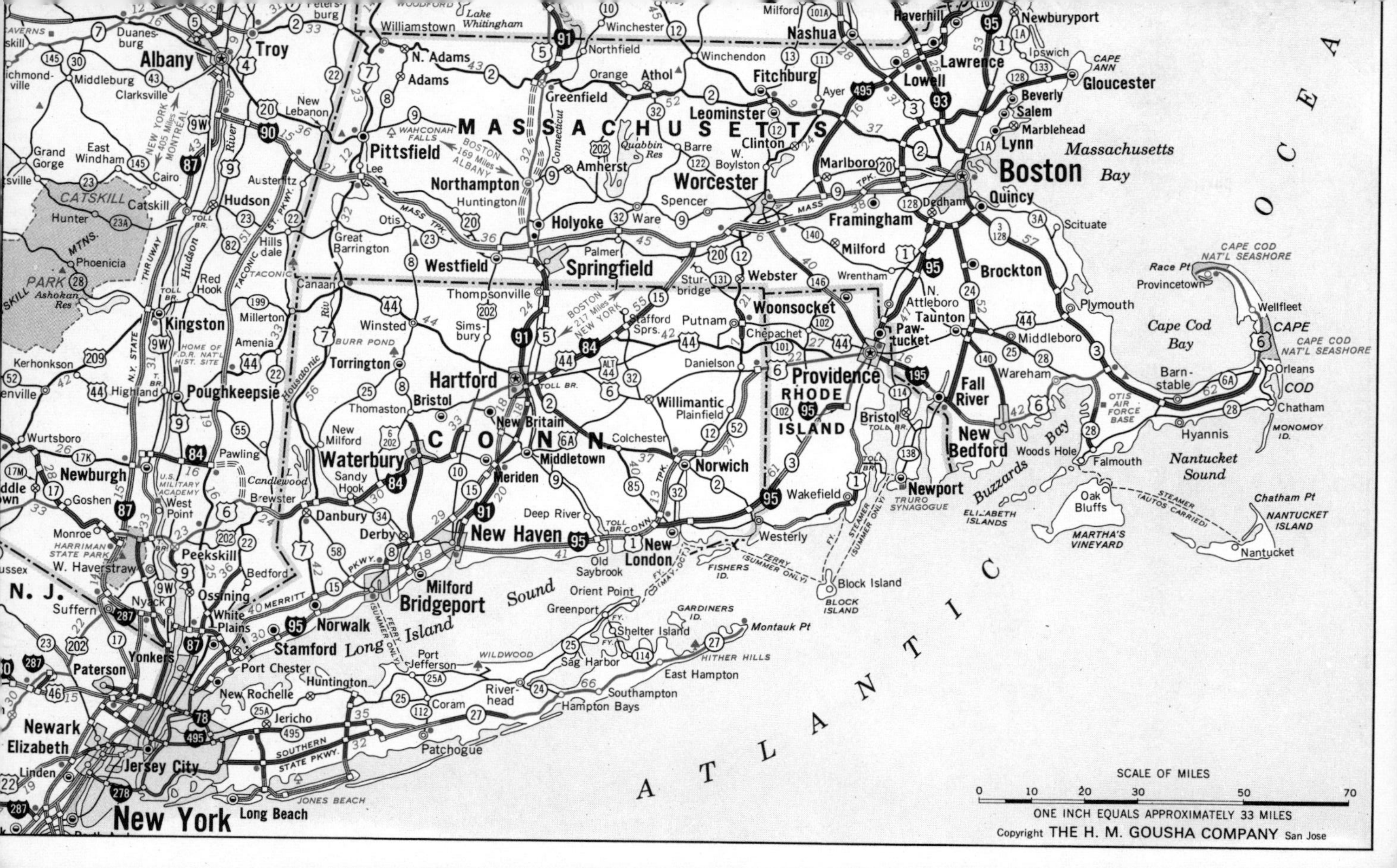

MASSACHUSETTS
CONN.
RHODE ISLAND
N. J.
ATLANTIC OCEAN
Boston
Massachusetts Bay
Cape Cod Bay
Nantucket Sound
Buzzards Bay
Long Island Sound
Albany
Troy
Pittsfield
Northampton
Springfield
Worcester
Holyoke
Westfield
Framingham
Lowell
Lawrence
Haverhill
Newburyport
Gloucester
Lynn
Salem
Beverly
Marblehead
Quincy
Brockton
Plymouth
Provincetown
Wellfleet
Orleans
Chatham
Barnstable
Hyannis
Falmouth
Woods Hole
New Bedford
Fall River
Taunton
Pawtucket
Providence
Woonsocket
Newport
Bristol
Westerly
Wakefield
Block Island
Nantucket
Oak Bluffs
MARTHA'S VINEYARD
NANTUCKET ISLAND
Hartford
New Britain
Waterbury
Meriden
Middletown
New Haven
Bridgeport
Milford
Norwalk
Stamford
Danbury
Norwich
New London
Kingston
Poughkeepsie
Newburgh
Peekskill
Ossining
White Plains
Yonkers
New Rochelle
Paterson
Newark
Elizabeth
Jersey City
New York
Long Beach
Patchogue
Riverhead
Southampton
East Hampton
Montauk Pt
Sag Harbor
Greenport
Orient Point
CAPE COD NAT'L SEASHORE
CATSKILL PARK
HARRIMAN STATE PARK
BOSTON 169 Miles ALBANY
BOSTON 217 Miles NEW YORK
NEW YORK 405 Miles MONTREAL
SCALE OF MILES
0 10 20 30 50 70
ONE INCH EQUALS APPROXIMATELY 33 MILES
Copyright THE H. M. GOUSHA COMPANY San Jose

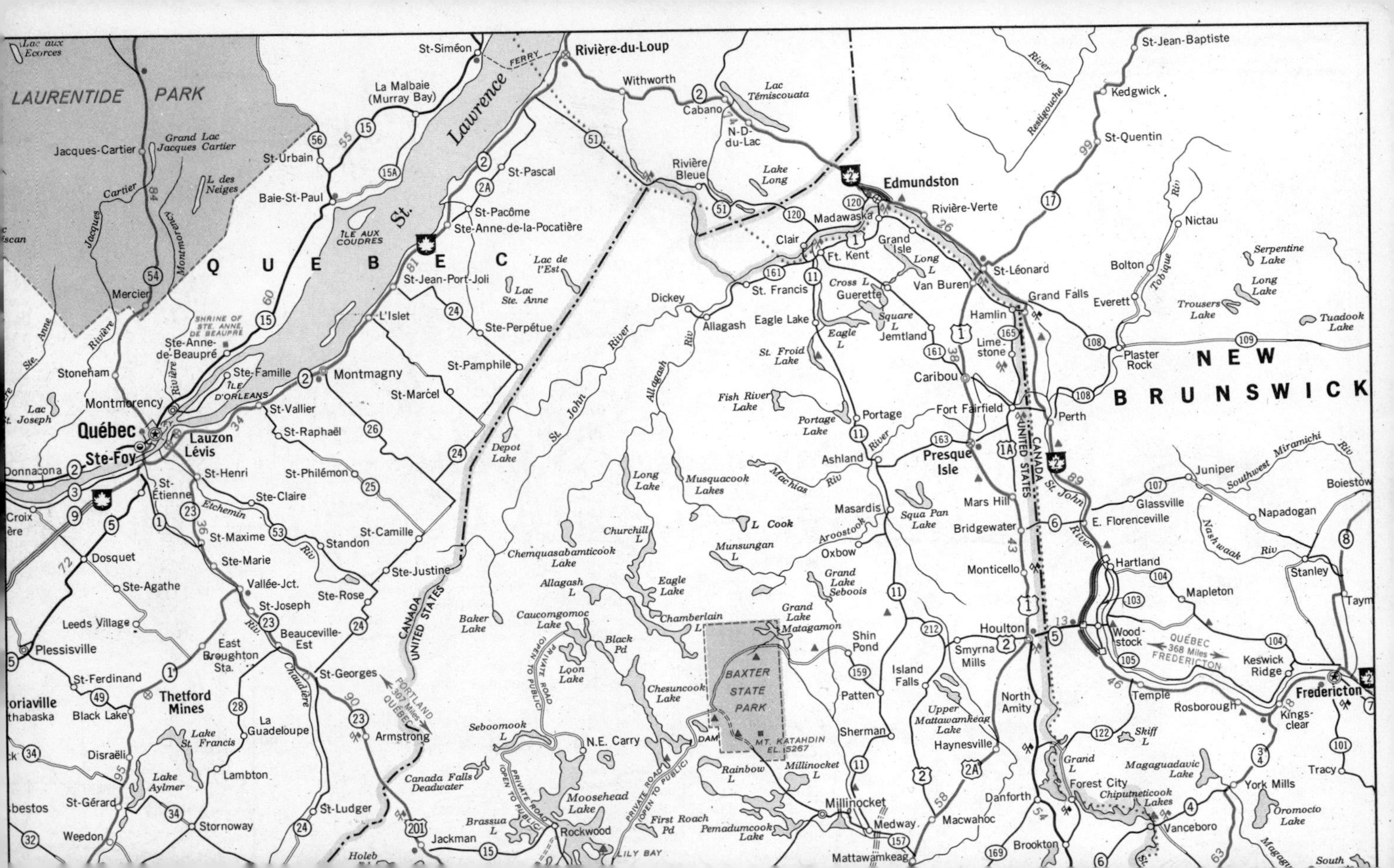

LAURENTIDE PARK
QUEBEC
NEW BRUNSWICK
CANADA
UNITED STATES
St. Lawrence
Lac aux Ecorces
Jacques-Cartier
Grand Lac Jacques Cartier
L des Neiges
Cartier
Jacques
Montmorency
Mercier
St-Urbain
Baie-St-Paul
La Malbaie (Murray Bay)
St-Siméon
FERRY
Rivière-du-Loup
Withworth
Cabano
Lac Témiscouata
N-D-du-Lac
Rivière Bleue
Lake Long
Edmundston
Rivière-Verte
Madawaska
Clair
Ft. Kent
Grand Isle
Long L
St-Léonard
Van Buren
Grand Falls
Hamlin
Limestone
Caribou
Fort Fairfield
Perth
Plaster Rock
Everett
Bolton
Tobique Riv
Nictau
Serpentine Lake
Long Lake
Trousers Lake
Tuadook Lake
Kedgwick
St-Quentin
St-Jean-Baptiste
Restigouche River
Juniper
Southwest Miramichi Riv
Boiestown
Glassville
Napadogan
E. Florenceville
Nashwaak Riv
Stanley
Hartland
Mapleton
Woodstock
QUÉBEC 368 Miles FREDERICTON
Keswick Ridge
Fredericton
Temple
Rosborough
Kingsclear
Skiff L
Magaguadavic Lake
Tracy
York Mills
Oromocto Lake
Grand L
Forest City
Chiputneticook Lakes
Vanceboro
South
St. John River
Presque Isle
Mars Hill
Bridgewater
Monticello
Houlton
Smyrna Mills
North Amity
Island Falls
Upper Mattawamkeag Lake
Haynesville
Danforth
Macwahoc
Brookton
Squa Pan Lake
Masardis
Oxbow
Aroostook
Grand Lake Seboois
Ashland
Portage
Portage Lake
Fish River Lake
St. Froid Lake
Eagle L
Eagle Lake
Square L
Jemtland
Cross L
Guerette
St. Francis
Dickey
Allagash
Allagash Riv
Machias Riv
Musquacook Lakes
L Cook
Munsungan L
Long Lake
Churchill L
Eagle Lake
Chemquasabamticook Lake
Allagash L
Chamberlain L
Grand Lake Matagamon
Shin Pond
Patten
Sherman
BAXTER STATE PARK
MT. KATAHDIN EL. 5267
DAM
Millinocket L
Rainbow L
Millinocket
Medway
Mattawamkeag
Pemadumcook Lake
First Roach Pd
LILY BAY
PRIVATE ROAD (OPEN TO PUBLIC)
Chesuncook Lake
Black Pd
Caucomgomoc Lake
Loon Lake
N.E. Carry
Seboomook L
Moosehead Lake
Rockwood
Brassua L
Jackman
Holeb
Canada Falls Deadwater
Baker Lake
Depot Lake
St. John River
PORTLAND 307 Miles QUÉBEC
Armstrong
St-Georges
St-Ludger
Chaudière
Beauceville-Est
St-Joseph
Vallée-Jct.
Ste-Rose
Ste-Justine
St-Camille
Standon
St-Maxime
Ste-Marie
Etchemin
Ste-Claire
St-Philémon
St-Henri
St-Étienne
St-Raphaël
St-Vallier
Montmagny
St-Marcel
St-Pamphile
Ste-Perpétue
Lac Ste. Anne
Lac de l'Est
L'Islet
St-Jean-Port-Joli
Ste-Anne-de-la-Pocatière
St-Pacôme
St-Pascal
ILE AUX COUDRES
SHRINE OF STE. ANNE DE BEAUPRE
Ste-Anne-de-Beaupré
Ste-Famille
ILE D'ORLEANS
Stoneham
Montmorency
Lac Joseph
Québec
Ste-Foy
Lauzon
Lévis
Donnacona
Dosquet
Ste-Agathe
Leeds Village
Plessisville
East Broughton Sta.
St-Ferdinand
Thetford Mines
Black Lake
La Guadeloupe
Lake St. Francis
Disraëli
Lambton
Lake Aylmer
St-Gérard
Stornoway
Weedon